THE OZARKS

THE OZARKS

Land and Life

SECOND EDITION

MILTON D. RAFFERTY

The University of Arkansas Press

Fayetteville 2001

Copyright © 2001 by The University of Arkansas Press

First edition: Copyright © 1980 by the University of Oklahoma
Press, Norman, Publishing Division of the University.

05   04   03   02   01   5   4   3   2   1

Text design by Ellen Beeler

⊛ The paper used in this publication meets the minimum requirements of the American National Standard for Permanence of Paper
for Printed Library Materials Z39.48-1984.

Frontispiece and title page photographs: Boston Mountains cove
south of Harrison, Arkansas, 1978 (Milton Rafferty Collection,
photograph by the author) and Ozark pioneer couple (Courtesy of
Arkansas History Commission).

Library of Congress Cataloging-in-Publication Data

Rafferty, Milton D., 1932–
    The Ozarks, land and life / Milton D. Rafferty. — 2nd ed.
        p. cm.
Includes bibliographical references and index.
    ISBN 1-55728-714-7
    1. Ozark Mountains Region—History. 2. Ozark Mountains
Region—Description and travel. 3. Ozark Mountains Region—
Social life and customs. 4. Natural history—Ozark Mountains
Region. I. Title.
    F417.O9 R17 2001
    976.7'1—dc21
                                                2001004446

CONTENTS

ILLUSTRATIONS

FIGURES

LIST OF FIGURES

TABLES

PREFACE

When *The Ozarks: Land and Life* was first published in 1980 it was, in at least one sense, a pioneer effort because there had been no treatise on either the geography or history of the Ozark region of Missouri, Arkansas, Oklahoma, and Kansas. It was a study of the geography of the Ozarks, with emphasis on historical development and contemporary conditions of life. Its purpose was to provide an explanation of the land and people at a time when the region was experiencing unprecedented population growth and environmental change.

I wrote the first draft of the book for use in a course, "Land and Life in the Ozarks," taught at Southwest Missouri State University and filmed and telecast by KOZK, Channel 21, the Public Broadcasting System station in Springfield, Missouri. Favorable responses from students and other viewers of the television lectures encouraged me to expand and publish my material. Twenty years have lapsed since the book was first published. The Ozark region has experienced rapid change in almost every sector of human experience during that time. My own inquisitiveness and the encouragement of Dr. James Baker, Southwest Missouri State University executive assistant to the president and director of the SMSU Ozark Studies Institute, and Professor William Cheek, associate dean of the College of Natural and Applied Sciences, led me to revise the book for republication.

Following the model in the first edition, I have chosen to present information that will educate the reader and provide background for understanding the Ozark scene. The selection of material and its organization reflects my professional training and personal interests. Like that of any observer, my view is imperfect and subject to the limitations of personal impressions. However, intimate first-hand acquaintance is, at best, the beginning of thorough understanding. The fascination with the region that began when I first studied the changing economy and landscape in the Springfield vicinity in the 1960s has continued for thirty-five years. One can only hope to meld the little he has learned about the lives of people with material he has observed or found in the record. I hope I have helped to make sense of the historical and geographic aspects of human experience in the Ozarks.

A central theme throughout this book is that of persistence versus change in the relationships of people and land. In large part, it is a story of constant adjustment of the relationships. Different peoples (Indians, French, Americans, European immigrant groups, and present-day immigrants) have in different times opted for contrasting systems of land and resource use and have produced an evolving series of cultural landscapes. Human adjustments have been mainly in terms of natural resources and cultural preferences, as attested by the sites selected for settlement by the pioneers and by the first systems of agriculture that they used. The first wave of pioneers had scarcely put down roots when the Civil War broke out and the Ozarks became a major battlefield and stage for guerrilla warfare in the western campaigns. After the war, far-reaching innovations and adjustments were made when railroads were constructed and people from the northern states entered the region. Commercial agriculture, mining, and forest exploitation progressed rapidly, and, all too frequently, little attention was given to the wise use of natural resources.

In more recent years, several human-induced factors have worked to reshape the economy and geography of the Ozarks. Among the more important are these: development of an integrated and fully serviceable network of roads; depletion of mineral deposits and discovery of new ore bodies; a shift from animal power to mechanical power in agriculture; growth and acceptance of many federal assistance programs in agriculture, commerce, trade, and social services; establishment of electrical utilities and improved communications; improved educational opportunities; construction of a dozen large reservoirs; and development of alternative and part-time employment, particularly in manufacturing services and tourism-recreation businesses.

In the twenty years since the first edition of *The Ozarks* appeared, new and potent forces have worked to reshape the Ozark scene. Some very scenic areas have been

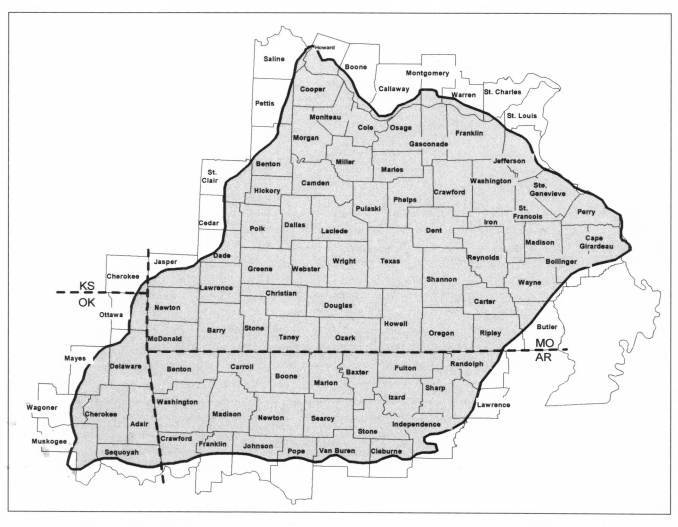

FIGURE 0-1. Counties in the Ozarks region. Adapted from Nevin M. Fenneman, *Physiography of Eastern United States* (New York: McGraw-Hill Book Co., 1938).

remolded as tourist landscapes, brightly lighted entertainment strips, and crowded shopping malls. Springfield, Joplin, Fayetteville-Springdale-Rogers, and other urban areas are robust cities with their own exploding suburbs and satellite towns. Residential subdivisions, hardly discernable from those that surround large cities, crowd the shores of Ozark lakes. The burgeoning resident population and thousands of tourists jam streets and highways, crowd shopping malls and theaters, stressing the environment with their human and material wastes. As streams, forests, and lakes change in character, their inhabitants—fish, fowl, fur bearers, and animals of all sorts—find their habitats change daily. Each day and each year present Ozarkers and their guests with new opportunities, different challenges, fresh issues. The give and take of change has affected each economic sector: farming, lumbering, mining, manufacturing, and tourism. I have tried to bring these elements of change into focus to present a

comprehensive and understandable picture of the Ozarks as the new millennium begins.

The region's future involves unforseeables. One cannot predict reliably from present trends. However, I have attempted to identify patterns that may be established and to point out potential problems that should be of concern to everyone. In the first edition, I closed the book with the statement that the Ozarks is a region whose time has come. The Ozarks had not shared on par with other regions in the great western expansion of population and flourishing economic development during the nineteenth century. While the Ozarks made great strides in economic growth and modernization during national economic expansion following World War I, it was not until the end of World War II, and especially during the 1960s that the region's economy sprang to life. Robust population growth and economic expansion have continued into the twenty-first century. It has brought long sought-after prosperity to some parts of the region, especially southwest Missouri and northwest Arkansas. Other parts of the Ozarks have been affected to a lesser degree. Some towns and counties have had to deal with the new problems that growth bequests, while many others continue to struggle with the old problems: poverty, limited employment opportunities, and poor educational, medical, and social services.

Modern Ozark agriculture has become capital intensive. Animal husbandry—dairying, beef cattle, and poultry farming—appears to have the upper hand, and there are no signs of revival of the old tillage agricultural systems. Corporate farming is growing along with the size of farms. New technology in the form of computers, the Internet, and cellular telephones combined with thousands of innovations in science and medicine have improved communication, medical care, business operations, education, entertainment, and recreation. The new technology continues to stimulate the economy, all the while making life in the Ozarks more comfortable, but less tranquil.

The population continues to grow, and the greatest growth is in the category the U.S. Census Bureau calls "rural non-farm," those who choose to live in the country and commute to their jobs in towns and cities. Rural living in a bucolic Arcadian setting, in houses as comfortable as those found in a city, is one of the great attractions of the Ozarks. Tourism is a growing Ozark industry, and prospects seem good for its continued growth. It is a clean industry compared with many "smoke stack" industries that often bring major environmental worries, but tourism carries its own environmental and economic problems. The work ethic of the people continues to be the region's ace in the hole. The attitude of "self-help" and the belief in "a day's work for a day's pay" are alive and well in the Ozarks, where the rural and small-town lifestyle and family traditions have nourished them. Employers see the Ozarkers' work ethic as an important resource they can count on when seeking out a new industrial plant site.

Provinciality has declined to the point that in larger towns it is all but gone. It has slowly fallen to the advance of education and the founding and growth of a host of developments in cultural enrichment: libraries, museums, live theaters, festivals, historical societies. Newspapers, magazines, radio, and television have no doubt played an important role in broadening Ozarkers' point of view. Along with the growth of a more cosmopolitan outlook have come negative changes in the cultural and social environment. Crime, alcohol abuse, and drug use have become urgent concerns. Citizens must vote on tax levies to construct new court buildings and jails to relieve crowding. The old county "poor farms" closed long ago, so

nowadays, as in communities throughout the United States, Ozark communities struggle to find new ways to deal with the problem of homeless people and the recovery of people who have chosen to "drop out" and become a part of a nonproductive subculture.

Ozarkers are justifiably proud of the natural beauty and recreational opportunities to be found in the region. The preservation of the region's forests, streams, and lakes are of great concern. Population growth places great stress on the environment. Many population-related issues have become commonplace: pollution from overloaded city sewer systems, from septic tank leachate, and leachate from growing solid waste landfills threaten streams and lakes. Proper disposal of agricultural wastes from dairy farms and poultry farms is a concern in some areas. The introduction of chip mills, which have the capacity to devour thousands of acres of forests in short order, is an immediate concern. Recently communities and industries in the western Ozarks have had to drill deeper wells in response to dropping ground-water levels. The large lakes present several thorny management problems—downstream landowners think the lakes should entrap flood waters; the U.S. Army Corps of Engineers places high priority on power generation; owners of boat docks and resorts along with sportsmen and vacationers want more constant lake levels. Many other environmental issues stem from the stances taken by the various users of natural resources—farmers, sportsmen, urbanites, and vacationers. With increasing population and more intensive use of resources, the issues will likely multiply and become even more difficult to resolve.

I wish to acknowledge many people who have given generously of their time in explaining points of difficulty and in helping in many other ways. To Professor Leslie Hewes, my mentor at the University of Nebraska, I owe continuing gratitude for introducing me to the study of the Ozarks and for impressing upon me the fact that research, learning, and teaching are all part of the same process. My former colleagues in the Department of Geography, Geology, and Planning at Southwest Missouri State University have always been ready with helpful advice. The SMSU Ozark Studies Institute provided funding for research assistants, photographs, research materials, and office space with computer access to do the work. Special thanks go to two graduate students in the Department of Geography, Geology, and Planning for their patience and hard work in helping to revise the book. Without the considerable skill and knowledge of Jason White, who produced the maps and helped in other ways, the book could never have been completed. I am also indebted to Deborah Thompson, who helped with library research and many other tasks required in preparing the book for the publisher. Lynn Morrow, archivist in the Missouri State Library in Jefferson City and prolific author of books and articles on the Ozarks, offered suggestions, provided invaluable references, and critiqued chapters 14 and 15. Professor Neal Lopinot, director of the SMSU Center for Archaeological Research, provided references and suggestions for an important section on the Ozarks' prehistory. Dr. Stanley Fagerlin, professor of geology at SMSU, critiqued chapter 2 and offered suggestions for revisions.

The bibliography lists the many authors whose work was crucial to the revision. Also listed are the informants who gave specific insights into the geography and history of the region. Several institutions provided advice and resources through their professional staff. They include the Mullins Library at the University of Arkansas, Fayetteville; the Butler Center for Arkansas Studies at Central Arkansas University, Conway; the John Vaughan Library at Northeast Oklahoma State University, Tahlequah; the Springfield-Greene County Library; the Missouri State Archives; the Western Historical Manuscript Collection, University of Missouri, Columbia; the Curtis Laws Wilson Library at the University of Missouri, Rolla; the St. Louis Public Library; and the Duane Meyer Library at Southwest Missouri State University, Springfield. Professor Byron Stewart, head of government documents in Meyer Library, was especially helpful in obtaining documents and other archival materials, and the professional staff in charge of interlibrary loans was also very helpful in processing many requests for materials. Tami Sutton, secretary in the SMSU Assistants to the President's Office, helped with correspondence and other clerical work.

Federal agencies that provided data and information included the National Forest Service, the United States Army Corps of Engineers, and the National Park Service. State agencies in Missouri, Arkansas, and Oklahoma that provided statistical data and information included the Missouri Department of Conservation, the Missouri Department of Natural Resources, the Missouri Division of Tourism, the Arkansas Game and Fish Commission, the Oklahoma Tourism and Recreation Department, and the Oklahoma Department of Wildlife Conservation. The Arkansas History Commission, the State Historical Society of Missouri, the Oklahoma Historical Society, the Ozark Folk Culture Center, Mountain View, Arkansas, and the Rogers Museum, Rogers, Arkansas, kindly provided photographs. Dr. Deborah Sutton, director of educational technology, Missouri Department of Elementary and Secondary Education, provided recent survey data and information about Missouri's schools. Cheryl M. Seeger, geologist with the Missouri Department of Natural Resources, provided information on current mining operations in the Ozark region. Several companies assisted by providing information, statistical data, and photographs. Special recognition is extended to Dr. Thomas Yanske, senior mine engineer, the Doe Run Company, for publications and current information about mining operations in the New Lead Belt.

I continue to owe a debt of gratitude to the students in my classes in the Geography of the Ozarks whose questions and enthusiasm helped spur me on to further inquiry. Finally, I wish to recognize my wife, Emma Jean, whose help and encouragement went a long way toward seeing the task to completion.

MILTON RAFFERTY
Springfield, Missouri

THE OZARKS: WHAT AND WHERE

As defined by geographers, a region is part of the earth's surface that has one or more elements of homogeneity distributed more or less throughout the area.[1] The Ozarks is one of America's great regions, set apart physically by rugged terrain and sociologically by inhabitants who profess political conservatism, religious fundamentalism and sectarianism, and a strong belief in the values of rural living. This popular image of the Ozarks, though widely accepted, is poorly understood in geographic terms. In a word, the boundaries of the Ozarks are vague to most people and subject to interpretation and disagreement by the experts.

As delimited by geographers, the Ozark Region includes parts of four states: Missouri, Arkansas, Oklahoma, and Kansas (fig. 1-1). We may estimate the total area of the Interior Highlands or Ozark-Ouachita Province, of which the Ozarks is a part, at sixty thousand square miles, an area larger than Arkansas. The Ozarks encompasses about forty thousand square miles, or about two-thirds of the area of the larger physiographic province. A few writers have called the Shawneetown Hills of southern Illinois the "Illinois Ozarks," but most geographers and geologists link them to the limestone low-plateau country that extends through southern Indiana, central Kentucky, and into Tennessee.[2] Since neither Nevin M. Fenneman's *Physiography of the Eastern United States* nor William D. Thornbury's *Regional Geomorphology of the United States* includes the Shawneetown Hills in the Ozarks, I have not included that area in this discussion of the Ozark region.

Major rivers mark the boundaries of the Ozarks in a general way (fig. 1-1). On the east is the Mississippi. Its significance as a boundary is enhanced because it forms also the boundary between Illinois and Missouri. On the north the Ozarks extends just beyond the Missouri River to include a narrow strip of ravines and ridges that etch the north bluffs.

The Black River parallels the southeastern boundary of the Ozarks, collecting runoff from Ozarks streams as it finds its way across the alluvial flatlands to join the White River. The southern boundary follows along the low hills that parallel the north side of the fertile Arkansas River valley. The western boundary is not as well defined. In the southwest the Neosho River (sometimes the Grand River) and its tributary, the Spring River, form a visible boundary. The remainder of the western boundary, from a few miles north of Joplin to Howard County, follows the seam where Pennsylvanian-age rocks (formed 280–320 million years ago) overlap older Mississippian-age rocks. No striking changes in landform features distinguish the Ozarks from territory to the west, but instead there is a gradual transition from forested hills to grassy cuestas and level, cultivated fields.

The unifying geographical criteria of the Ozark region include greater relief and steeper slopes than surrounding areas; surface rocks that are older than those exposed outside the Ozarks; the abundance of dolomite, as opposed to limestone (the two appear similar to the eye, but replacement of calcium in the limestone by magnesium forms dolomite); the prevalence of the flinty, hard rock known as chert as nodules in limestone and dolomite; the abundance of karst features, such as springs, caves, and sinkholes that ground-water action on bedrock produces; the prevalence of average to poor soils except in the stream valleys; the extensive forests of oak, hickory, and pine; and the abundance of high-quality water resources, including moderately swift-flowing streams and large man-made reservoirs. These are the physical traits most remembered by visitors, most widely publicized by the tourist-recreation industry, and most commonly associated with the region by those who have never visited it. Visitors perceive it as a sparsely populated semi-wilderness with superb scenic attractions. This is essentially correct.

The cultural traits that distinguish the Ozarks are more difficult to define, and for the most part they are more argumentative.[3] First, the region is rural.[4] This is the least argumentative and perhaps the most important cultural fact relating to the Ozarks. Rural suggests open country, farming, and contrasts with city life. To some it implies rudeness and lack of polish; to others it signifies idealized simplicity, peacefulness, and apartness from the world. All

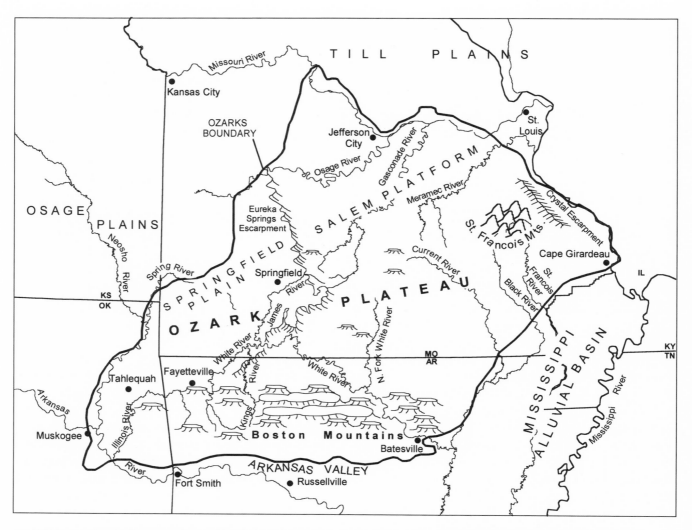

FIGURE 1-1. Ozark physiography and bordering rivers. Adapted from A. K. Lobeck, *Physiographic Diagram of the U.S. 1:3,000,000* (Madison: University of Wisconsin, 1954).

these things may be found to a greater or lesser degree in the Ozarks. Although it is true urban centers—such as Springfield, Joplin, Fayetteville-Springdale-Rogers, and the urban fringes of St. Louis—exert strong cultural influences on the Ozarks in many ways, the general character of day-to-day living in most of the region is rural.

Second, the Ozark heritage springs from the Upper South hill country.[5] The first immigrants, mainly from Tennessee, Kentucky, and nearby parts of the southern Appalachians, occupied the choice lands and established self-sufficient farms. Most were descended from Scotch-Irish stock. Even today most of the Ozark counties are more than 98 percent white, native born. Most are Protestants. Because for many years only a few outsiders entered the area, the economic activities, technologies, values, beliefs, and general way of life became patterned after that of the first immigrants. Settlement geographers recognize this process of cultural imprint as the *Doctrine*

of First Effective Settlement, or first in time, first in importance.[6] The existence of a distinctive Ozark regional character is conjectural, but if it exists, it must reflect the cumulative propensities of the people who gave the culture its decisive early impetus. Their attitudes, beliefs, and material culture reflected the peculiar conditions of life wrought by the limitations and advantages of the region's land and resources.

The Ozarks has been a semi-arrested frontier.[7] This useful notion recognizes the persistence of traditional lifestyles, slowness to accept change, and the presence of a distinctive cultural landscape in which much of the past has persisted. The combined framework of rurality, the Upper South hill country heritage, and semi-arrested frontier supports most of the cultural baggage and popular imagery of the Ozarks: disdain for city life and education, suspicion of outsiders (especially representatives of federal and state agencies), conservative politics (whether Demo-

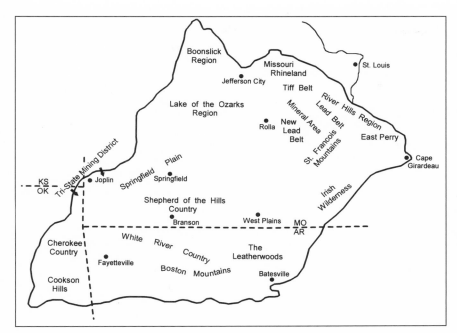

FIGURE 1-2. Vernacular regions of the Ozarks. Adapted from Arthur B. Cozzens, Analyzing and Mapping Natural Landscape Factors of the Ozarks Province. *Transactions of the Academy of Science of St. Louis* (Champaign: University of Illinois Press, 1939); Curtis F. Marbut, "The Physical Features of Missouri," *Missouri Geological Survey* 10 (Jefferson City, Mo.: 1896); and Carl O. Sauer, "The Geography of the Ozark Highland of Missouri," *Geographical Society of Chicago* 7 (Chicago: University of Chicago Press, 1920).

crat or Republican), good-old-boyism, rednecks, clannishness, casual regard for time, reverence for outdoor activities (especially hunting and fishing), independence and closeness to nature, tall tales, fundamental religious beliefs, brush-arbor revivals, river baptisms, and characteristic speech habits. To say that the culture of the Ozarks is changing is a truism, for change is universal. However, the rate of change and the process of change from place to place within the Ozarks has been variable, so that change has been geographically uneven. While much of the past is gone, in some places things have changed very little. The contrived popular imagery never existed. The process of modernization, including the acceptance of new technologies and the adoption of mainstream America's entertainment and recreation patterns and its social standards, has eroded much of the distinctiveness that once characterized the people of the Ozarks.

A third distinctive cultural element is the Ozarker's uncommon sense of place. They think of themselves as Ozarkers, and half jesting, they call nonresidents outsiders. This is apparently a learned trait; outsiders soon begin to think of themselves in the same terms, either as acculturated Ozarkers or as dyed-in-the-wool outsiders. The word *Ozark* appears everywhere and in various forms.[8] Schools, churches, planning agencies, clubs, and businesses carry the name. The *1999–2000 Southwestern Bell Springfield-Branson Area Telephone Directory* gave no fewer than 369 listings with *Ozark* in the title.[9]

The consciousness of place and the liking for naming things is a primitive trait. There are no names without people, and with people there are names. The namer has found rich resources in the Ozarks. Countless ridges, hills, valleys, branches, hollows, coves, caves, springs, creeks, rivers, stores, hamlets, villages, towns, cities, mines, and mills call for names. A variegated topography invites many names. The *Gladden Quadrangle,* 7.5-minute map, which covers a small portion of Shannon County, Missouri, includes no fewer than sixty-two place names for physical features.[10] The Ozarks encompasses many vernacular regions with undefined boundaries (fig. 1-2). Even a single county may include several named subregions recognized by all residents.[11]

High density of place names seems to coincide most often with a cultural background in agriculture.[12] In most European countries—and in many countries outside Europe—the peasant held tenaciously to his land, cultivating his fields, building walls, and bestowing names on them. In a hill district such as the Ozarks a field of corn might have been no larger than a lawn for a private home, and they usually fenced and often named it. Generations of the same family often lived in the same community, so that family history became mingled with the landscape in an uncommon way. Life becomes integrated with the landscape in a natural way that is understood by everyone. Thus in the idealistic sense, the Ozarker is a kind of homespun Lockian who thinks of the landscape as an object that penetrates the mind and alters the person.[13]

The fourth cultural trait of the Ozarks is the relative stability of the social system compared with the fluidity of social relations that is typical of the United States. Things are uncomplicated. Strong and stable kinship relations extend back generations. Social activities focus on schools and churches, and these institutions are dependable and predictable. Ozarkers know who their friends are, and who their enemies are, and know what to do about it. Ego problems or questions about belonging or fitting in do not plague them. The rigors of making a living in a region blessed with only modest resources have built character, or at least the idea is widely accepted, and a kind of kinship or bond forms from a shared experience in an Ozarks understood by all.

The cultural traits described herein are hardly unique to the Ozarks. They are traits found everywhere to a certain extent, but particularly in rural America. In the Ozarks, these traits are accentuated, drawn together, and combined in unique and interesting ways. Isolation has played a part in this, as have physical and cultural barriers to the diffusion of new ideas and the immigration of new people. It is a culture worth studying and a region worth visiting. And most important, the people, in all their varying circumstances of life, are worth knowing.

Like any large region the identifying physical and cultural traits are not the same throughout the Ozarks. Both natural and social scientists find it convenient to subdivide regions to make them more understandable. Likewise, the people who live in the Ozarks have segmented the region to better characterize their particular area and to communicate something about its history or culture. These informal or vernacular regions (fig. 1-2) seldom have distinct boundaries.[14] Nevertheless, we recognize and use them in everyday conversation and in popular writing. Some subregions are large and some are small, encompassing only a part of a county or perhaps only a drainage basin, stream valley, or small "branch." The origins of the names may be based on obvious geographical factors or relationships; for example, the Lake of the Ozarks region, the St. Francois Mountains, the Boston Mountains, the Cookson Hills, the White River Country. Some vernacular regions—the Boonslick Country, the Missouri Rhineland, the Cherokee Country, the Irish Wilderness—are named for a prominent person or a distinctive group of people who settled there, and others—the Lead Belt, Mineral Area, the New Lead Belt, the Tri-State District—were mining districts. The Shepherd of the Hills Country is based on the setting of Harold Bell Wright's book, *The Shepherd of the Hills*.[15] The name—Branson—has become an all-inclusive name, vying with Shepherd of the Hills Country as the name for the tourism region. The Leatherwoods, a rugged area in the middle White River valley roughly bounded by Batesville, Calico Rock, and Mountain View, was named for the hardy shrub that grows so profusely there.[16] The origins for some regional names are obscure; for example, residents and others widely know Douglas County, Missouri, as

"Booger County" for no apparent good reason.[17] Some vernacular regions are small. For example, Taney County, Missouri, residents divide the county into two parts: West Taney, the western part of the county, where tourism has completely changed the economy and landscape, and East Taney, the eastern agricultural part. It is common knowledge that the two areas are worlds apart in economy and attitudes toward change. A similar bifurcation occurs in Perry County, Missouri, where East Perry, an area heavily settled by Lutheran Germans, is distinguished from West Perry, where many Catholic Germans live.[18] Highway 61 roughly marks the boundary between the two areas.

IMAGE AND REALITY

Writers who formed their opinions after only brief visits or cursory reading of popular magazines have written so much about the Ozarks that sorting out what is real is difficult. The Ozarks evoke many images. New visitors arrive with an idea or expectation of what they will see and experience. That image may be formed by viewing television and videotapes or by reading books, popular literature, and travel guides. Advertising by Branson music shows, Bass Pro Shops, Silver Dollar City, and other businesses catering to tourists may help people shape mental pictures of the Ozarks. Sometimes visitors form opinions about the Ozarks by listening to the reports of acquaintances who have traveled to the area. The visitors then depart the Ozarks with the image either confirmed or changed depending upon the experiences during the visit.

A popular image of the Ozarks is that of an idyllic forested Arcadia, a place of transparent lakes, rippling streams, and small towns and farms nestled in picturesque valleys amid hills covered in virescent hues of green, red, and gold. Hunters view the Ozarks as a place where one can be in harmony with nature (whether or not they bag their deer or turkey), while anglers see images of bass, crappie, and trout lurking in quiet lake coves or deep blue pools in rippling streams. Others picture the Ozarks as the last remaining region of pure rural cultural values, a refuge of Jeffersonian democracy, where people cherish their freedom, cling to old ways, resist change, and remain in their home communities among family and friends, clinging to the same schools and churches their parents attended, even when moving away would improve their lot.

Another image is that of a poverty-stricken land. Some view the Ozarks as a land with abandoned mines and mills, depleted soils, decaying villages, and run-down farms, inhabited by shiftless hillbillies. For some people the lack of education and outright ignorance of some

Ozarkers is reflected in their quaint sayings and tendency to say "agin" for "again" and "tin" instead of "ten."[19] Which of these images is correct? Probably none is wholly correct, nor is any totally untrue. The true Ozarks, as if one mold for the variegated pattern of land and people that make up the region would fit, would lie somewhere between these extremes.

It is the latter image that offends Ozarkers.[20] It is the image of hardscrabble farms, tough living conditions, isolation, poverty, and uneducated people with little ambition to change their way of life. Where did this negative image come from? Who first used the name hillbilly to describe the region's residents? The Ozarks, like the southern Appalachians, has long suffered from a negative image. Perhaps it was the apparent sterility of the rugged forested terrain that so perplexed visitors from the fertile farmlands to the north and east and made them wonder how anyone could wrest a decent living from the land. Some negative views of the Ozarks probably originated with the stories northern soldiers wrote or brought back home to their families in Iowa, Illinois, and Wisconsin. Professor William Shea discovered a great wealth of negative comments about the Arkansas Ozarks in soldiers' diaries, letters, reminiscences, and newspaper accounts of the time.[21] John F. Bradbury Jr. used the same methods to illuminate the negative impressions of soldiers who served in the Missouri Ozarks.[22] It is not surprising that the soldiers' experiences living far from home in an unfamiliar area, at risk of being wounded or killed, with daily contact with starving refugees fleeing guerrilla raids, provided plenty of negative material to write home about. Nevertheless, some soldiers mentioned the natural beauty of the region and one, Major William G. Thompson, wrote that he would like to live in Springfield.[23] More than a few northern soldiers did return to the Ozarks to establish homes following the war.

Part of the negative Ozark image may have been transferred from Arkansas, a state that has suffered from an image problem as much as any.[24] The problem began with the days of the first settlement and continues to the present. As recent as August 2000, on NBC Television's *Tonight Show*, Jay Leno made light of Arkansas governor Mike Huckabee and his family moving into a double-wide mobile home while the governor's mansion underwent renovation.[25] Though thinly guised as humor, the snobbery was clear. Some of Arkansas's first "tourists"—Henry Rowe Schoolcraft, George W. Featherstonhaugh, Friederich Gerstaecker—wrote of the rustic lifestyle, wild parties, poverty, and disdain for education. When Featherstonhaugh visited Little Rock in the 1830s, then a town of six hundred, he scoffed about the town having three newspapers.

Had Little Rock been a town in New England, he might have seen it differently. Louis Brister attributes the slow progress of German immigration to Arkansas to the negative descriptions of the state in Traugott Bromme's *Hand- und Reisebuch fuer Auswanderer nach den Vereinigten Staaten von Nord-Amerikic* (1849), a widely popular guide for Germans seeking to relocate in America.[26] Lee A. Dew attributes some of Arkansas's negative image to Thomas W. Jackson's book, *On a Slow Train through Arkansaw.*[27] The book sold for twenty-five cents post paid when they published it in 1903. It was a collection of regional humor including humorous railroad stories and minstrel jokes of the day, many of which cast the residents of Arkansas in a bad light.

Missouri and Oklahoma have had their detractors as well. Oklahoma, particularly when it was Indian territory, was held in low regard. For many years people knew it as a lawless refuge for society's misfits. In the 1940s, Professor Leslie Hewes called attention to the lack of progressiveness and slower economic progress in Indian territory, noting that in most measures of culture and economy the Cherokee country was less progressive than adjacent parts of Missouri and Arkansas.[28]

By 1900, the word "hillbilly" appeared in print when a *New York Journal* reporter defined a "Hill-Billie" (as) ". . . a free and untrammeled white citizen who lives in the hills . . . has no means to speak of, dresses as he can, talks as he pleases, drinks whiskey when he gets it, and fires off his revolver as the fancy takes him."[29] From this point on journalists and travelers applied the term *hillbilly* to the marginal farmers of the southern mountains. With little knowledge of the mountain people, first in the Appalachians and later in the Ozarks, popular journalists attributed the poverty of marginal farmers to laziness and shiftlessness. Outsiders came to believe that poor mountain farmers would rather make "moonshine" whiskey than do hard work to improve their living conditions.[30] They wrote the stories to entertain and to sell newspapers and magazines. Sometimes anecdotal material was added to books to give color and interest, often gratuitously with a full measure of exaggeration and little concern for facts. For example, the otherwise factual *1895 Road and Handbook of the Missouri Division of the League of American Wheelmen* advised the reader that besides poor roads and no bridges in Douglas County, Missouri, "All the cooks are women, chew tobacco and smoke—nothing when you get used to it."[31]

Clearly the Ozarks image as a poor, backward area began early, but it was the attention brought by tourism advertising, movies, and television media that locked the image in the public mind. The tourist industry through its advertising is partly responsible for creating the homespun yokel image to the public. It began with postcards and other tourist gift shop items. Today, the hillbilly comedian is a fundamental part of many Branson country music shows. Perhaps the most agonizing depiction of the hillbilly was Dogpatch, a theme park south of Harrison, Arkansas. The park's theme was based on the hillbilly characters in Al Capp's Dogpatch comic strip. Not many Ozarkers were sorry to see it close.

Television reporters, viewing themselves as pioneers of a new way of looking at the world, focused on the integration problem in Little Rock in 1957.[32] *Time Magazine* depicted Governor Orval Faubus, the man from Greasy Creek in Madison County, who history had assigned to deal with the problem, as a "slightly sophisticated hillbilly."[33] While some writers such as Michael Harrington, *The Other America* (1962), called attention to the plight of the southern mountaineers, including those who had migrated to "hillbilly ghettos" in northern cities, and recommended federal aid to improve their lot, television produced *The Beverly Hillbillies* (1962) and *The Andy Griffith Show.* Both television shows included characters that were honorable and forthright along with characters depicting the stereotypical poor, lazy, ignorant, drunken, moonshining hillbilly. The high point of the negative hillbilly stereotype was James Dickey's best-selling novel of 1970, *Deliverance,* later released as a movie in 1972.[34]

Today the Ozark region is a land of national forests, prosperous farms and ranches, mines and mills, a booming tourist industry, and growing cities. The region hardly resembles the rural agricultural land it was in the early twentieth century. Yet the negative hillbilly image lingers on in the popular mind. As one Ozarker said, "You know, when it comes to name calling we could use a few choice words ourselves for those who don't like our ways . . . words like, arrogant, conceited, contemptuous, egotistical, and condescending."

Ozarkers have more to be concerned about than the region's hillbilly image. More critical issues include the emerging problem of deterioration of the quality of water in the region's lakes, the lowering of water tables, and growing concern for adequate supplies of water for expanding communities. Ozarkers are justifiably proud of the natural beauty and recreation opportunities to be found in the region. The preservation of the region's forests, streams, and lakes are of great concern to them. Population growth places great stress on the environment. Many population-related issues have become commonplace: pollution from overloaded city sewer systems, from septic tank leachate, and leachate from solid waste landfills threaten streams and lakes. Proper disposal of agricultural wastes from dairy farms and poultry farms is a concern in some areas. The new woodchip mills have the capacity to gobble up thousands of acres of forests in short order. For some Ozarkers the mills conjure up memories of barren hills and eroded soils, the legacy of the big timber companies. Recently communities and industries in the western Ozarks have had to drill deeper wells in response to dropping groundwater levels. The large lakes present several knarly management problems—downstream landowners want flood protection, the U.S. Army Corps of Engineers places high priority on power generation, owners of boat docks and resorts along with sportsmen and vacationers want more constant lake levels. Many other environmental issues stem from the stances taken by the various users of natural resources—farmers, urbanites, and tourists. The pressure on the region's natural resources will increase with population growth and expanding tourism.

The work ethic of the people continues to be the region's ace in the hole. The self-help, a day's work for a day's pay attitude is alive and well in the Ozarks, where the rural and small town lifestyle and family tradition has nourished it. Employers see the Ozarkers' work ethic as one input they can count on when they seek out a new industrial plant site. It is this image that needs to be preserved.

TWO

LANDFORMS AND GEOLOGY

The Ozarks has the general shape of a parallelogram. The region is part of the Interior Highlands Province, which includes the tightly folded and faulted Ouachita Mountains (see fig. 1-1). The Interior Highland Province, or Ozark-Ouachita Province, because of the geologic and geomorphic similarities to the Appalachian Highlands, is considered its extension. Geologists think the folded and faulted Appalachian type geology continues under the younger rocks of the Coastal Plain and then surfaces in the Ozark-Ouachita Province before continuing westward under the Coastal Plain.[1] Its major subdivisions are the Boston Mountains in the south, the St. Francois (St. Francis)[2] Mountains in the east, the Springfield Plain in the west, and the Salem Plateau, which incorporates the remainder of the upland surface. The region and its parts are named rather carelessly; established use takes precedence over definitive meanings. Thus, the Ozark Mountains, Ozark Plateau, Ozark Plateaus, Ozark Upland, Ozark Highland, and Ozark Hill Country are some names applied to the region.[3] Because the region is neither high nor truly mountainous and because *upland* has a very general meaning, it is probably the most accurate descriptor. The western tableland of the Ozarks is called the Springfield Plain or the Springfield Plateau. Considering the general elevations, which are only slightly higher than the central Ozarks, and in view of its more gentle terrain, one name seems as suitable as the other.

The bedrock is domed upward elliptically, being highest along the central line running from a point near Ste. Genevieve, beside the Mississippi River, to the Missouri state line near the southwestern corner of Stone County and then into Arkansas. The highest elevations in the region are found in the Boston Mountains of Arkansas, where extensive uplands of more than 2,000 feet elevation crown summits in Madison, Newton, Washington, Franklin, Johnson, and Pope counties. A few summit areas in extreme western Newton County exceed 2,500 feet. For the most part the central Ozarks are lower than the southern and western rim lands, but elevations in the St. Francois Mountains generally exceed 1,600 feet. The highest elevation in Missouri (1,772 feet) is at the summit of Taum Sauk Mountain in Iron County. Elevations reach nearly as high on the western rim lands in western Wright County, Missouri. A summit near the hamlet of Cedar Gap reaches 1,728 feet above sea level.

The variegated landforms and relief are the result of several factors: different resistance to weathering and erosion of any adjoining rock masses, the structure (tilt) of the rock layers, the porosity of the rocks, and the work of streams.[4] For some readers it may be helpful to visualize the Ozarks as a huge layer cake in which someone has eaten the center leaving the margins higher. In-facing cuestas (hills with steep scarp slopes and gentle back slopes) mark layers of resistant rock that weaker rocks underlie.

RIVERS AND STREAMS

The elevation of the country around the foot of the Ozark Upland varies from four hundred to eight hundred feet above sea level, causing streams to flow outward radially. From a northeast-to-southwest line near the center of the dome, the drainage runs northward to the Osage, Gasconade, Meramec, and Missouri rivers and southward to the White, Eleven Point, Current, Black, and St. Francis rivers. Small streams drain the eastern border to the Mississippi River; the north slope of the Boston Mountains is tributary to the White River by way of the Kings, Buffalo, and upper White rivers; the south slope of the Boston Mountains drains to the Arkansas River through the Illinois, Mulberry, Cadron, and Little Red rivers. All of the streams have cut valleys of substantial depth. Toward the heads of the streams that flow northward the valleys are shallow and wide because of the small size of the streams and the great distance they flow before reaching a larger river.[5] The same characteristic holds for the streams flowing southeastward from about the central part of Howell County, Missouri. The streams flowing from the western and southern parts of the Ozarks have cut deep, narrow gorges from their heads. Chert gravel eroded from surrounding bedrock clogs most stream channels.

Gravel bar at Mill Spring on the Black River, Wayne County, Missouri, circa 1918. (Reproduced from Charles L. Dake, "The Sand and Gravel Resources of Missouri," *Missouri Bureau of Geology and Mines*, 2d Series, 15 [1918]: 236.)

Gradients of streams in the interior are for the most part steep, rarely falling below three to five feet per mile, and in some stretches gradients may reach twenty-five feet per mile.[6] Meanders reduce gradients. The great meanders on the Osage River reduce its gradient to less than half that of the White.[7] Steep slopes and steep gradients contribute to damaging and life-threatening flash floods when heavy rains fall. During heavy rains in May 1892, the Big Piney River rose thirty feet from 4:00 P.M. to midnight, and the Current River rose twenty-seven feet in about the same time.[8]

The streams of the Ozarks are distinctive. Though they deeply entrench the plateau surface, they follow meandering courses. This may be due to establishment of the stream courses at a time when they drained a low-lying plain.[9] The entrenchment occurred gradually as diastrophic forces thrust the region upward over geologic time. The belts of hills along major streams have bold limestone bluffs, particularly along the outside bend of meanders. Frequently the processes of weathering and erosion have resulted in cutoff meander loops and the isolation of hills in the center. Geographers know these isolated hills as lost hills because of their detachment from other ridges or uplands.[10] Pine Hill, a lost hill about a mile north of Theodosia, Missouri, formed when the North Fork River cut through a meander loop, leaving Pine Hill separated from surrounding hills by the abandoned river channel. Cote Sans Dessein, another lost hill in the alluvial valley of the Missouri River east of Jefferson City, was isolated by widening and eventual coalescence of the valleys of the Missouri and Maries rivers.

The valleys of the larger Ozark streams, notably the Missouri and the Mississippi, have flat meadow-like floors over which the stream channels meander in winding courses. Meander scars, oxbow lakes, backwater swamps, marshes, and sandbars are typical flood-plain landforms. Such lowland areas, called bottoms or bottomland, were preferred sites of settlement by pioneers. The fevers (malaria) discouraged some from settling in the first bottoms, but the second bottoms were nearly always settled early because of their fertile soils, good drainage, and elevation above flood stages. These sites were likewise the preferred locations for Indian settlements; today they provide rich hunting ground for archaeologists.

Water power is a great resource of the Ozarks. The rainfall, relief, character of rock formations, entrenched stream valleys, and forested slopes provide exceptionally advantageous conditions for construction of dams and reservoirs. The first settlers built water mills on small streams and at larger springs to grind grain and saw logs. Modern dams of comparatively small size may back up water for several miles, providing power for generation of electricity and freshwater-lake recreation. Because little land is in cultivation, the rate of siltation is very slow. Powersite Dam, constructed in Taney County, Missouri, in 1913, was the first of several reservoirs eventually constructed in the Ozarks. Other dams and reservoirs followed in the 1940s, 1950s, and 1960s. The last large impoundment was Truman Lake, completed in 1979.[11] Including the impoundments on the Ozarks' bordering rivers, the region's eighteen lakes cover 534,000 acres and provide 7,350 miles of shoreline for sports and recreation.[12]

KARST FEATURES

Geologists and geographers refer to landscapes characterized by the dissolution of the underlying bedrock as karst landscapes.[13] The limestones and dolomites of the Ozarks are subject to solution by ground water (fig. 2-1). Over millions of years the movement of rainwater through cracks and crevices (joints) in the rocks has caused large amounts of the rock to dissolve, resulting in solution channels, caves, springs, and the development of sinkholes and karst valleys at the surface.

The Ozarks has literally thousands of caves. Some are so large they adapt to commercial tours. A 1985 survey revealed thirty commercial caves in operation.[14] Blanchard Springs Cavern, near Fifty-Six, Arkansas, is probably the most spectacular Ozark cave.[15] It is operated as a tourist attraction by the Ozark National Forest. Fantastic Caverns, near Springfield, features motorized tours. The Springfield Symphony Orchestra has performed in the largest chamber

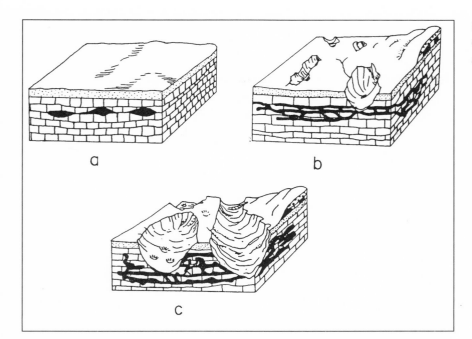

a

b

c

in the cavern several times, and in 1987, the National Council for Geographic Education met there for their annual honors banquet.[16] Other well-known commercial caves include Meramec Caverns, Onondaga Cave, Bridal Cave, and Marvel Cave.

Sinks are very common; literally thousands speckle the uplands. When several large sinks are formed close together, the result is a solution valley. Some of these valleys are very large. The Limestone Valley, a solution lowland stretching for five miles in southern Newton County, Arkansas, cuts into the plateau several hundred feet.[17] Similar karst valleys include nearby Hidden Valley and Walnut Valley, Wiley's Cove in Searcy County, and the Richwoods near Mountain View, Arkansas.[18] Large collapsed cavern systems, such as Grand Gulf[19] near Koshkonong, Missouri, are unusual, but small collapsed caverns, like Devil's Den in Greene County, Missouri, are commonplace. Cone-shaped sinks (dolines) number in the tens of thousands, and many reach depths of eighty feet or more. Natural bridges are also common. Alum Cove Natural Bridge, south of Jasper, Arkansas, is one of the largest, with a span of nearly one hundred feet. Because water moves freely through the limestone, many small surface streams are dry much of the year. Such streams, known as losing streams, lose water through subsurface channels and may have dry stream beds only a few miles downstream from points where water is flowing freely at the surface.[20]

Upland areas, described as prairies by early settlers,[21] are typically karst plains where much of the rolling surface is an expression of sinkhole development. Extensive karst plains

Diamond Cave, Newton County, Arkansas. (Courtesy of Arkansas History Commission.)

are found near Springfield, Lebanon, Mountain Grove, Salem, West Plains, and Perryville in Missouri and near Harrison, Mountain Home, and Springdale in Arkansas.

Perhaps the abundance of sinkholes and caves may account for the many stories of lost treasures. The stories are varied but usually involve gold or silver coins hidden away and then mysteriously lost. Often the stories tell that the person who hid the treasure could not find the secret place when he returned to recover it.

SPRINGS

Except for the igneous rocks in the St. Francois Mountains, parts of the sandstone areas, and a few border areas, most Ozark valleys have springs. No one knows just how many springs are in the Ozarks, but the number surely runs in the tens of thousands. Webster County, Missouri, alone has more than twenty-four hundred springs, "by actual count."[22] The largest springs are in the interior Ozarks. Spring flow data recorded by Jerry D. Vineyard and Gerald L. Feder in *Springs of Missouri* show that the average daily flow of water from the ten largest springs in Missouri amounts to more than a billion gallons.[23] All these springs—Big Spring, Greer Spring, Double Spring, Bennett Spring, Meramec Spring, Blue Spring (Shannon County), Alley Spring, Welch Spring, Blue Spring (Oregon County)—are in the Missouri Ozarks. Big Spring, near Van Buren in Carter County, is the largest, with an average daily flow of 276 million gallons and a maximum recorded flow of 840 million gallons.[24] The large springs in the Ozarks of Arkansas and Oklahoma add substantially to the region's total spring flow volume. For example, Mammoth Spring, the largest spring in Arkansas, flows 9 million gallons hourly or 216 million gallons daily.

Springs were important resources for the Indians and the first French and American settlers. Settlers sought out springs for cabin sites and for water mills. Springs have always been important for water for livestock and wild animals. Salt springs were especially prized. Salt from springs near Ste. Genevieve and in the Boonslick settlements was among the first items of commerce.[25] In the latter part of the nineteenth century, other mineral springs —chalybeate (iron), sulfur, magnesium—became sites for hotels and health resorts. Today the major use of large springs is for recreation and tourism, and many, including their natural sites, have become state and national parks and preserves.

Springs harbor interesting plant and animal life, some of which are rare species restricted to springs and caves. Blind, white organisms such as fish, crayfish, and salamanders and other forms may spend their entire life cycles in the total darkness of water-filled caves that feed springs. Common plants in Ozark springs recorded by J. A. Steyermark include watercress, water milfoil, water starwort, and water weed, and also bryophytes and algae.[26]

The quality of water from Ozarks springs is generally good, but not potable without treatment. Because surface water can easily penetrate the bedrock near springs, the water quality varies depending on the type of land use in the vicinity. Also, following heavy rains, the water becomes more turbid due to the suspended material carried by the higher volume of flow. High concentrations of fecal colliform have been found in many clear, cool Ozark springs.[27] None are safe for drinking water without treatment.

LOCAL RELIEF

As for ruggedness, the central part of the Ozarks is not extremely rugged. The most traveled highway, Interstate 44, traverses the region, following mainly upland divides where relief is very modest. Only in Phelps and Pulaski counties in the rugged land along Roubidoux Creek and the Little Piney and Big Piney rivers does the relief and scenery rise to the expectations of most travelers. The greatest local relief (distance between valley bottoms and ridge tops) and steepest slopes are in the Boston Mountains, the St. Francois Mountains, and in the drainage basins of the White, Current, and Black rivers[28] (fig. 2-2). The greatest relief occurs where resistant strata form escarpments. The most striking relief of all is at the north front, or boundary, of the Boston Mountains, where sandstone beds stand eight hundred to thirteen hundred feet above the limestone plains extending northward.[29] Another sharp topographic break occurs at the Eureka Springs Escarpment, which outlines the headwaters of the White River and extends north of Springfield. Another is the Avon Escarpment at the eastern border of the Farmington (Missouri) Basin. Yet another is the Crystal Escarpment, which runs north to south from a point near Pacific, Missouri, through Ste. Genevieve County and Perry County. The Burlington Escarpment, which parallels the Crystal Escarpment nearer the Mississippi River, is the eastern counterpart of the Eureka Springs Escarpment (see fig. 1-1).[30]

GEOGRAPHIC REGIONS

One can divide the Ozarks into geographic regions to distinguish each area that has internal unity of geographic environment and also contrasts with the surrounding areas. For this purpose geographers take the location of the area, surface features, drainage, soils, minerals, water supply, and

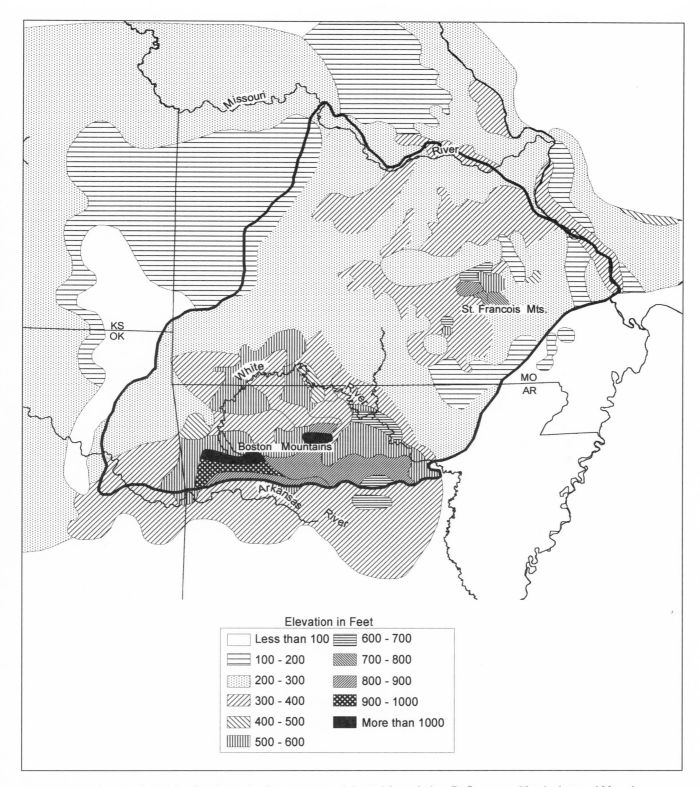

FIGURE 2-2. Local relief in the Ozarks and adjacent areas. Adapted from Arthur B. Cozzens, "Analyzing and Mapping Natural Landscape Factors of the Ozarks Province," *Transactions of the Academy of Science of St. Louis* (Champaign: University of Illinois Press, 1939); with updates from "Forest Inventory and Analysis Data Base Retrieval System," U.S. Department of Agriculture, Forest Service (Starksville, Miss.: SRSFLA, 1999). http://www.srsfia.usfs.msstate.edu/scripts.ew.html (April 17, 2000).

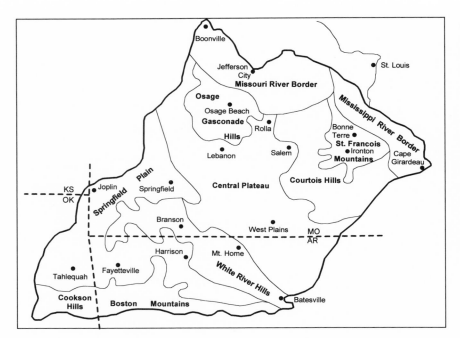

FIGURE 2-3. Geographic regions of the Ozarks. Adapted from James F. Collier, "Geographic Regions of Missouri," *Annals of the Association of American Geographers* 45 (1955), 368–92; Curtis F. Marbut, *The Physical Features of Missouri* (Jefferson City, Mo.: Tribune Printing Co., State Printers and Binders, 1896). Extracted from *Reports of the Missouri Geological Survey* 10 (1896); and Carl O. Sauer, "The Geography of the Ozark Highland of Missouri," *Geographical Society of Chicago* 7 (Chicago: University of Chicago Press, 1920).

vegetation into account. The map of the geographic regions of the Ozarks (fig. 2-3) follows closely the work of Marbut,[31] Sauer,[32] and Collier.[33] To round out the entire Ozarks, I extended Thornbury's boundaries for the Springfield Plain into Oklahoma and Arkansas and included the Boston Mountains.[34]

The Ozarks include only two regions worthy of being called mountains: the St. Francois Mountains in eastern Missouri and the Boston Mountains in northern Arkansas. Three border regions—on the north the Missouri River Border, on the east the Mississippi River Border, and in western Missouri and extreme northern Arkansas, the Springfield Plain—enclose the interior mountains and plateaus. Belts of hills surround the Central Plateau, a less-dissected region in southern Missouri.[35] The Courtois Hills are on the east, the Osage-Gasconade Hills on the northeast, and the White River Hills on the south.

The *Missouri River Border* is a transitional area to the glacial plains of northern Missouri. Included is a narrow band of hills north of the Missouri River. In its course through this region, precipitous rock bluffs confined the river in a two-mile-wide alluvial valley. The river channel, deflected from valley-side to valley-side for eons, is the sculptor of the steep bluffs. The stream bed is constantly shifting, particularly in its valley crossings.[36] Navigation on the Missouri River, though safer than in former times, continues to be hazardous. Farms in the bottoms are flooded frequently. Limestone bluffs, undercut by the river and faceted into pyramidal forms by tributary valleys, are bare of vegetation except for a few hardy cedars (*Juniperus virginiana*) that cling to precarious ledges.

Most of the region is rolling upland suitable for agriculture. The largest and best of the level tracts is the Tipton Upland, a remarkably level upland at the east edge of the Mississippian rocks (fig. 2-4).[37] Soils are much above the average of the Ozarks. In stream valleys, first-bottom soils are fertile but subject to flooding and poor drainage. Second-bottom alluvial soils, which are flood-free and better drained, command higher prices. Upland soils benefit from the presence of a wind-deposited silty loess. Near the Missouri River, where the wind-blown deposits are thickest, farmers know the rich yellow loam as bluff soil.[38]

The *Mississippi River Border* consists of a narrow strip along the Mississippi River. Small streams drain directly to the Mississippi and away from the St. Francois Mountains. The general slope is steeply eastward, from 1,772 feet on Taum Sauk Mountain to 460 feet at Ste. Genevieve. Because the layers of limestones and sandstones tilt steeply to the east, their eroded faces form west-facing escarpments. The most notable of these is the Crystal Escarpment, where soft sandstones have weathered and eroded, leaving the overlying limestones standing in bold relief.

Hilly belts extend away from the streams; the Beckett Hills comprise an extensive hilly belt in the drainage area of the River Aux Vases. The most extensive upland area is the Barrens in Perry County, where large sinkholes are more numerous than in any other section of the Ozarks. In Perry and Cape Girardeau counties many sinks, clogged with loess, form natural ponds. Farmers have relied on the ponds as a source of water for livestock since the first white settlers arrived.

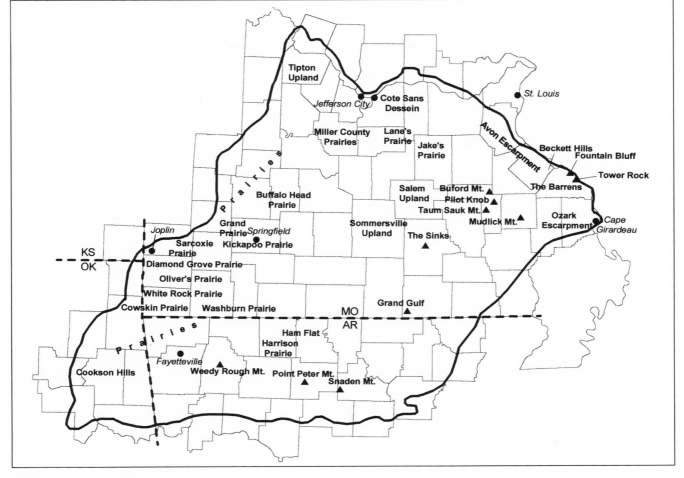

FIGURE 2-4. Major physical features of the Ozarks Adapted from Curtis F. Marbut, *The Physical Features of Missouri* (Jefferson City, Mo.: Tribune Printing Co., State Printers and Binders, 1896). Extracted from *Reports of the Missouri Geological Survey* 10 (1896); and Nevin M. Fenneman, *Physiography of Eastern United States* (New York: McGraw-Hill Book Company, 1938).

The relief is greatest along the west-facing escarpments and where streams descend to the Mississippi River. In many locations the hills overlooking the Mississippi flood plain take on the appearance of bluffs. At Wittenburg, in Perry County, glaciers (Illinoisan age) blocked the main valley, diverting the river to its present narrow channel.[39] Fountain Bluff, cut off from the Ozark Upland, forms a lost hill in the Mississippi Valley. Two miles downstream is Grand Tower, a small, steep-sided limestone island in the river channel.

At Cape Girardeau the Ozark Upland ends abruptly at the Ozark Escarpment, which extends in a southwesterly direction into Arkansas, marking the boundary between the Ozark Upland and the Gulf Coastal Plain Province. Thornbury and others credit the remarkably straight alignment of the escarpment to erosion by the Mississippi River when it occupied a westerly course at the foot of the Ozarks.[40]

The *Springfield Plain* is a gently sloping surface that forms the western border of the Ozarks. The Eureka Springs Escarpment and the rugged hills along the Pomme de Terre and Osage valleys form its eastern boundary. Relief is less and soils are better than in any other large district of the Ozarks. Near the escarpment, relief is as much as five hundred feet. Ages of weathering and erosion produced the picturesque detached hills along the eastern escarpment. The first pioneers often named these hills variously as balds, knobs, mounds, or mountains.[41] Balds and cedar glades are especially common where the chert-free Jefferson City formation crops out along the escarpment. Much of the upland originally was in prairie grass and resembled the plains region in eastern Kansas. Although they have plowed the native bluestem grasses under, in scattered locations the names of the prairies remain to designate local vernacular regions. The larger and better-known uplands in Missouri include Kickapoo Prairie and

Taum Sauk Reservoir on Profitt Mountain near Lesterville, Missouri, 1978. (Milton Rafferty Collection, photograph by the author.)

Grand Prairie (Greene County), Sarcoxie Prairie (Jasper County), Diamond Grove Prairie (Newton County), Washburn Prairie (Barry County), and White Rock Prairie (McDonald County). McDonald County's broad Cowskin Prairie, in the extreme southwest corner of Missouri, was the marshaling site for General Sterling Price's Missouri militia forces before the Battle of Wilson's Creek.[42] In Oklahoma, Jay Prairie in Delaware County is worthy of note. Several large upland prairies are found in the Arkansas portion of the Springfield Plain (fig. 2-4). The larger ones are Ham Flat, Pine Flat, Kings Prairie, the Western Grove uplands in the eastern part of Boone County and the western part of Marion County, Harrison Prairie in Boone County, Berryville Prairie in Carroll County, and the extensive coalescing prairies of Washington and Benton counties.

Though isolated in pioneer days because of its distance from navigable streams, settlers eventually populated the Springfield Plain more heavily than the interior hill districts. Several towns grew up in the rolling prairies. Springfield, which has adopted the title Queen City of the Ozarks, is the largest city in the Ozark region with a population of 142,898 (304,464 in the Springfield MSA) in the federal census estimates for 1998.[43] Washington and

Benton counties in Arkansas also attracted heavy settlement early. Today the cities of Fayetteville, Springdale, Rogers, and Bentonville form the Ozarks' second-ranking urban area.

The *St. Francois Mountains* lie in the eastern Ozarks, but they are geologically and physiographically the center of the region. Their landforms are unlike those in any other district. Sauer likens the knobs of igneous rocks to isolated remnants rising "like irregularly distributed mountain islands above the basins formed by the weak limestones and shales."[44] Weathering and erosion are slowly exhuming the knobs of granite and felsites. These slow but powerful forces etched the relief in the igneous rocks in ancient times and are slowly uncovering their former work by removing the overlying sedimentary rocks. Some mountains, such as Buford Mountain, Bono Mountain, Taum Sauk Mountain, Black Mountain, Mudlick Mountain, and Profitt Mountain, are linear in shape. Others, such as Shepherd Mountain and Pilot Knob, are cone shaped.

Streams have cut deep gorges, called shut-ins, in the resistant igneous rocks.[45] Only the Boston Mountains exceed the area's relief. The St. Francois Mountains include four major limestone basins: Fredericktown, Farmington,

Mineral Point-Potosi, and Richwoods. Minor basins include Belleview (Bellevue) and Arcadia valleys in Iron County and Patterson and Lodi in Wayne County. These basins were among the first permanent settlements in the Ozarks and became prosperous farming communities.

The *Courtois Hills Region* has the steepest average slopes and wildest terrain of any part of the Missouri Ozarks.[46] Although it does not have the greatest relief, it is the most rugged district in Missouri, consisting of a maze of deep, confined valleys and sharp ridges. The ridges, ordinarily forested with oak, are chert covered. Chert (flint), a resistant rock imbedded in softer limestones and dolomites, accumulates at the surface in many sections of the Ozarks. It is especially abundant in the Courtois Hills.

Courtois Creek, in Crawford County, is the region's namesake. The creek is only one of several streams in the district with steep valley walls and chert-clogged channels. "Down in the hills and hollers" applies to this region more than any other section. Tributaries of more than two dozen rivers and large creeks have cut the plateau surface into intricate details. The *Gladden Quadrangle* covers approximately thirty-six square miles along the Current River and includes more than forty hollows.[47] Similar landscapes are found throughout the Courtois Hills, including the strikingly rugged terrain of the Irish Wilderness in Oregon, Carter, and Ripley counties.[48]

Greer Spring, near the Eleven Point River, is only one of the several spectacular springs in this region. Among the best known are Round Spring and Alley Spring near Eminence and Big Spring near Van Buren. Caves, sink-

Granite boulders at Elephant Rocks State Park near Graniteville, Missouri, 1979. (Milton Rafferty Collection, photograph by the author.)

holes, and solution valleys are also quite characteristic of the region. The Sinks and the natural tunnel on Sinking Creek, a tributary of the Current River, are spectacular solution landforms.[49] The Sunklands, three miles south of Akers and thirteen miles north of Summersville in Shannon County, Missouri, is the Ozarks' largest sinkhole or collapse structure, being nearly a mile long.[50]

Until recent years, timber was the main source of income. Revenues from deep lead and zinc deposits discovered around 1960 provide another source of income for one of the poorest districts in the Ozarks. Mining of lead and zinc ores from the New Lead Belt, or Viburnum Trend, provides employment for several hundred workers.

Agriculture possibilities are very limited. Most people live in the valleys, where soils, terrain, and excellent springs provided settlement niches. The best farming conditions are in the south, where the Castor, St. Francis, Black, and Current rivers have wide bottoms. Because it is the largest area of severely dissected country, the Courtois Hills rivals the Boston Mountains of Arkansas in isolation and limited agricultural possibilities. Residents know that the many rocky roads are best traveled in a pickup truck, and even the best surfaced roads wind along ridge tops and descend into valleys on steep grades. Only a few good highways, U.S. 60 for example, traverse the region.

The *White River Hills* lie at and beyond the margin of the Burlington limestone in northern Arkansas and southwest Missouri. Weaker beds underlie the limestone, so that the Burlington forms a high and persistent prominence, the Eureka Springs Escarpment. Though lower in relief, its

Johnson's shut-ins on the Black River near Lesterville, Missouri, 1978. (Milton Rafferty Collection, photograph by the author.)

Cedar glade in the White River Hills. Thin soils and exposed bedrock are typical of glade land, 1979. (Milton Rafferty Collection, photograph by the author.)

forested, which adds to their bold appearance. They often appear on topographic maps as named knobs, balds, or mountains. Large detached outliers, like the Gainesville Monadnock Group in Ozark County, Missouri, are visible for many miles. Names like Bald Jesse, Naked Joe, and Griffith's Knob suggest the character of prominent conical hills.

The hills are nearly as rugged as the Osage-Gasconade Hills and the Courtois Hills, and the scenery is even more attractive. Forested slopes, bold limestone cliffs, and park-like cedar glades combine with lobate ridges and fertile bottomland. Narrow bands of cedars and other hardy trees form natural contour lines on hillsides as they grow along bedrock contact zones where soil and water conditions are better. The region has some of the largest caves in the Ozarks, and streams and springs abound. Several large lakes—Beaver, Table Rock, Taneycomo, Bull Shoals, and Norfolk—occupy most of the middle White River valley. The result is a scene that combines splendor, variety, and charm.

persistence rivals the Boston Mountain Front. Erosion along the escarpment accounts for the long narrow ridges. Outliers, occasionally from one to ten miles across, have become detached from the main body of limestone. These conspicuous limestone buttes are sometimes sparsely

The *Osage-Gasconade Hills Region* includes the ridges and steep tributary valleys along the Osage and Gasconade rivers and their larger tributaries. In no other place in the Ozarks are the large meandering streams so deeply entrenched into the upland. The dam at Bagnell on the

Alum Cove Natural Bridge south of Jasper, Arkansas, 1983. (Milton Rafferty Collection, photograph by the author.)

Boston Mountains cove south of Harrison, Arkansas, 1978. (Milton Rafferty Collection, photograph by the author.)

Osage River formed Lake of the Ozarks in spectacular meander loops. In Pulaski County the Gasconade River has created Moccasin Bend, an eight-mile loop that closes back within a thousand feet of its beginning.

Karst features, notably springs, caves, sinks, and natural bridges, are the hallmarks of the region. Two highly publicized attractions are Hahatonka Spring near Lake of the Ozarks and Stark Caverns near Eldon.

The *Central Plateau* (Salem Plateau) is an open rolling upland.[51] Rugged hill districts surround it on three sides. The plateau and the Springfield Plain have escaped heavy dissection by large streams. However, portions of the plateau, where steams cross the region, show extreme dissection.

Karst features are common throughout the region, including the part that extends into northern Arkansas. Near Mountain View, Missouri, ground water has dissolved huge sinkholes as much as fifty feet deep. As late as the 1950s, miners took iron ores from deposits in deep sinkholes near West Plains and at other locations. Nearly every valley has abundant springs. Many are well known by canoeists and tourists. Among the better known are Blue Spring, Double Spring (Rainbow Spring), and Althea Spring on the North Fork River, and Mammoth Spring in extreme northern Arkansas.[52] Near Koshkonong, Missouri, is Grand Gulf, a large collapsed cavern nearly ninety feet deep and more than one thousand feet long, the centerpiece for one of Missouri's newer state parks.[53]

The best agricultural land is on the uplands, which are extensive in some areas. The first settlers named the larger upland tracts, and many of the names have persisted in the local vernacular. The uplands, called prairies in the early days, commanded respect as agricultural islands in the forested interior Ozarks. The larger tracts are the Salem, Licking, and Sommersville uplands, the Lebanon and West Plains prairies, and the Buffalo Head Prairie in Dallas County, Missouri (fig. 2-4).

The *Boston Mountains* lie in northern Arkansas and northeast Oklahoma. The origin of the name "Boston" is obscure, although it is probably related to the tiny settlement of Boston in southeastern Madison County. The Cookson Hills comprise the westernmost prong of the Boston Mountains in Oklahoma. Schoolcraft called the hilly district at the headwaters of the White River, in western Arkansas, the Pawnee Mountains.[54] The name is no longer used. The northern boundary, the Boston Mountain Front (escarpment), marks a sharp change in topography, rocks, and soils from the country north of it. The boundary is a definite line, easily identified, and traceable on the ground. The southern Boston Mountain boundary is not so sharp and easily recognized, since the change in the character of rocks, soils, and topography is more gradual.

The highest elevations along the Boston Mountain Front are in Newton, Madison, and Searcy counties. The single highest elevation is 2,578 feet[55] in extreme western Newton County, 806 feet higher than Taum Sauk Mountain in the St. Francois Mountains. South of Jasper, in Newton County, Highway 7 climbs 1,321 feet. Following a series of switchbacks the road ascends from Jasper (834 feet) to a scenic overview (2,155 feet above sea level) at the crest of the flat-topped summit.[56] From the summit, one can see the Boat Mountains, a detached outlier of the Boston Mountains, a few miles to the north.[57] Similar outliers occur near Fayetteville and farther west in Oklahoma. The striking feature of the Boston Mountains is a moderately smooth, but hardly flat, plateau surface, which, except in small areas, slopes gently southward.

The sedimentary rock strata in the Ozark dome slope downward in all directions from the St. Francois Mountains in eastern Missouri so the rocks on the margins are younger than the ancient crystalline rocks in the core. Thus, the rocks of the Boston Mountains are among the youngest in the Ozarks. Shales stand first in importance, sandstones second, and limestones third.

Within the Boston Mountains are a few lowland basins. Though unimportant in area, they were once important for the prosperity of the few farmers who were so fortunate as to occupy them. The most important of these are the Richwoods of Stone County, Wiley's Cove of Searcy County, and the Limestone Valley of Newton County (fig. 2-4).[58] Streams enter and leave these valleys through narrow gorges, so both outlets are narrow, deep, and wild canyons. The floor of Limestone Valley is about seven hundred feet above sea level and is smooth and nearly flat. The slopes rise steeply to the upland about two thousand feet above sea level. Solution of limestones formed the valley in part.

The Limestone Valley, like the other isolated valleys, was once well settled, but now it is nearly unpopulated. Brush and scrub timber now choke fields that formerly grew crops of corn and cotton. All that remains of the old town of Limestone are two or three dilapidated store buildings that are slowly falling down. Agriculture has declined over the years because of isolation, poor roads, long distances to markets, and the small amount of level land and fertile soils.

Map makers have named most of the highest summits in the Boston Mountains, often using the names applied by the first pioneers. In Oklahoma, there are several prominent mountains southeast of Tahlequah, including Sugar, Walkingstick, Welch, Muskrat, and Brushy. From west to east in Arkansas some better-known mountain summits are Hale, Anderson, Pine, Grassy, Locust, Meadow, Patrick, Weedy Rough, Moss, Owens, Ricketts, Horn, Point Peter, Greenshaw, Irons, Blue, and Snaden (fig. 2-4). Besides the mountains, many high flats and ridges have names.

GEOLOGY AND MINERAL RESOURCES

Ozark rocks are mainly sedimentary. These rocks were formed by the settling into beds of masses of sediment, mainly of marine origin. Igneous rocks, those formed by solidification of hot mixtures of minerals, are abundant in the St. Francois Mountains. Metamorphic rocks, those transformed from preexisting rocks by heat and pressure, are limited to small outcrops near the igneous rocks in the St. Francois Mountains. Carbonate rocks, limestones, and dolomites, are the most abundant.[59] The bedrock varies in age from Precambrian through the Paleozoic era to include rocks of the Pennsylvanian period (fig. 2-5). The oldest rock formations are the Precambrian age igneous rocks. They cover the surface of about five thousand square miles in the St. Francois Mountains in southeastern Missouri. While these rocks are very old, *they are not the oldest rocks in North America.*[60] The igneous rocks are of two kinds, granites and rhyolite porphyries. One may imagine that ages ago the surface of much of the Ozarks consisted of lava, with molten rock below. The lava probably cooled quickly and formed rhyolite porphyries, a name derived from the texture, in which larger crystals occur in a mass of finer crystals. Streams have cut into the resistant rhyolite, forming many steep-walled shut-ins, such as the Johnson's shut-ins near Lesterville.[61] Porphyries of varying colors form most of the symmetrical knobs or mountains of the St. Francois Mountains.

Beneath the insulating cover of rhyolite porphyry, other molten material solidified slowly to form a coarse-grained granite, such as that occurring in quarries near Graniteville. Missouri granite is composed of pink feldspar and clear, glassy quartz mineral grains. Huge blocks have weathered into spheroid shapes at various locations, notably at Elephant Rocks State Park near Graniteville.

The sedimentary rocks are of two main groups. One is composed of limestone formed while water covered the Ozarks, when it was far from any land area. This limestone underlies nearly all the Ozarks. The other group of rocks, formed when Missouri either was part of a continent or covered by a shallow sea near land, included sandstones, shales, and certain limestones. Rocks of this type are found mainly in the Boston Mountains.

Geologists also classify rocks of the earth's surface according to age. Rocks from three of the four major time spans (eras)—Cenozoic, Mesozoic, Paleozoic, and Precambrian (Proterozoic and Archean)—outcrop in the Ozarks, along with eight or nine of the subdivisions or geologic periods (fig. 2-5).[62] If geologic forces had deposited these rock units at any single place, they would form a column thirty-five hundred feet high from the top

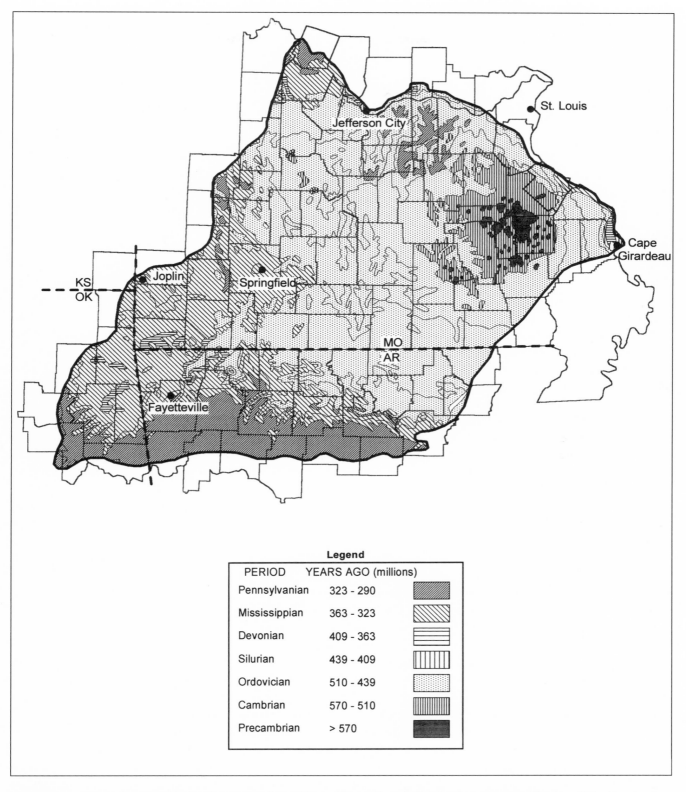

FIGURE 2-5. Geologic age of bedrock. Adapted from Missouri Department of Natural Resources, Division of Geology and Land Survey. Downloadable GIS Data. Rolla, Mo.: DGLS, 1993, http://www.dnr.state.mo.us/dgls/geoserv/gdamhp.html (May 3, 2000); Brian W. Harland et al., *A Geologic Time Scale* (New York: Cambridge University Press, 1990).

Unconformable contact between Precambrian rhyolites and stratified Cambrian sedimentary rocks, Taum Sauk Power Station near Lesterville, Missouri, 1977. (Milton Rafferty Collection, photograph by the author.)

of the granites and felsites. The thickness of the igneous rocks is unknown. The rocks do not underlie the whole region, but by upfolding of beds or through downcutting by streams they rise to the surface at one place or another. The oldest rocks, which appear in the St. Francois Mountains in Iron, Reynolds, and Madison counties, form the center of the Ozark Dome and form the foundation for the rock beds that underlie large parts of Missouri, Kansas, Arkansas, Illinois, and Iowa. In the Forest City basin in northwestern Missouri, the Precambrian igneous rocks exposed in the St. Francois Mountains lie buried beneath thirty-seven hundred feet of Paleozoic sediments.[63]

For mapping purposes, geologists divide rocks into groups, each group usually including more than one kind of rock or more than one formation. On the geologic map (fig. 2-5) the darkest shading depicts the Precambrian age granites, felsites, and rhyolites. They are found in southeastern and southern Missouri, with the main outcrops in the St. Francois Mountains and smaller exposures in Shannon County, where the Current River cuts deeply into the overlying sedimentary rock layers. A long period later, an ocean invaded the valleys and rose high on the rounded igneous-rock hills. The sandstones and conglomerates of the Cambrian-age La Motte formation formed from cemented gravel and boulders accumulated on the low surfaces. Clay mud, washed far out into the quiet arms of the ancient sea, compacted to become shale as we see it today. The Lamotte Formation, so named because of its occurrence at the old Mine La Motte in Madison County, Missouri, is from two hundred to three hundred feet in thickness, but in a few places reaches nearly five

hundred feet.[64] Gradually the land sank beneath the sea, and the calcium and magnesium that went in solution to the ocean became limestone and dolomite (calcium-magnesium limestone) in the clear-water portion of the ocean. The latter rocks formed when the Ozarks was part of a shallow marine shelf extending from New York to Mexico. The sea covered a large area including most of Missouri and Arkansas except the igneous knobs (today's St. Francois Mountains) which were high enough to be out of the water during sea encroachment.[65] The Bonneterre dolomite, a gray and coarsely crystalline variety, lays in thick beds. It is comparatively free of flint and decomposes readily to a fertile and easily tilled red clay soil. The Bonneterre dolomite holds the remains of many forms of life, including fossil brachiopods, trilobites, and a few snails.[66] Imbedded in the Bonneterre formation are huge deposits of disseminated lead (with zinc, and small amounts of copper, and silver). The lead-zinc ores were mined for more than two hundred fifty years in the Old Lead Belt in St. Francois and Madison counties. They also make up the chief ore bodies in the New Lead Belt of western Iron and northern Reynolds counties.

Barite (barium sulfate, $BaSO_4$, locally called tiff) is formed by weathering of portions of the Cambrian dolomites. Deposits of barite become concentrated in the residual soil above the limestones. The Tiff District of northeastern Washington County was until recently one of the major barite mining districts in the United States. Although mining companies now use machinery to mine and wash the barite, the earlier hand mining by tiff diggers received wide publicity in writings about the district.

The top of the Cambrian rocks is the Eminence formation, a sandy dolomite imbedded with large quantities of chert. Large chert masses, probably formed by algae, occur in the Eminence and sometimes appear in road cuts.[67] The Eminence formation is the host rock for many large caves and springs that draw visitors to the interior Ozarks. Big Spring, near Van Buren, Missouri, the Ozarks' largest spring, is in the Eminence formation.

The second period of the Paleozoic Era, the Ordovician, began with the advance of seas over the Ozarks. They laid down deposits of dolomite up to five hundred feet thick; then the seas retreated from most of the state. Weathering and erosion cut many narrow valleys in the emerging surface. Sand formed thick deposits in these valleys as the seas readvanced, and over much of the eastern Ozarks sand covered the uplands and the valleys. These loose and friable sands formed the St. Peter sandstone, an easily quarried, widely exploited glass sand.[68]

After the St. Peter sandstone formed, the seas advanced again and laid down dolomite (Gasconade formation), thin fossil-rich limestone (Kimmswick formation), shale, sandstone, and dolomite (Roubidoux formation), and, finally, thick deposits of dolomite (Jefferson City formation) across most of the region. The Jefferson City formation's dolomite rocks are the thickly bedded soft, white noncrystalline "cotton rock" and the heavily bedded, crystalline gray dolomite called "spotted rock." Both "cotton rock" and "spotted rock" dolomites appear in old stone buildings in the German communities on the northern Ozark border.[69] Modern quarries extract stone for aggregate and building material from both dolomites.

During Silurian time the seas covered only the extremities of the Ozarks, in the southeast, northeast, and northwest. Limestones and shales accumulated to a thickness of less than one hundred feet. In the early part of the Devonian Period, seas advanced over a small area near Grand Tower, Ste. Genevieve County, and in late Devonian time, a narrow bay extended westward about a hundred miles from the mouth of the Missouri River and along the northeastern Ozark border.

After erosion in late Devonian time, seas of the Mississippian Period advancing from the east and south covered the region. Thick deposits of limestone formed, notably the St. Louis, Keokuk, and Burlington formations. These rock layers now form a partial ring around the Ozark region from Perry County to the extreme southwest. Mississippian rocks have been very important for the Ozarks economy because it is this system that contained the great deposits of lead and zinc ore of the Tri-State Lead-Zinc Mining District and the North Arkansas Lead-Zinc Mining District. Huge quarries operate in the Mississippian limestones, particularly those in the Burlington formation. Some large underground quarries house commercial storage, refrigerated coolers, and manufacturing space. The Springfield Underground, Inc. (Griesemer), quarry in the Burlington-Keokuk formation at Springfield has forty acres of developed underground space, including cold-storage rooms. At Carthage, thirty or forty acres quarried from the Warsaw formation have been converted to general warehouse use, offices, and a large tennis court. A third site at Neosho contains about thirty to forty acres of office and warehouse space developed in a quarry in the Burlington-Keokuk.[70]

The end of Mississippian time was the final chapter of Ozark marine history. The later stratified rocks of the Ozarks formed from land material. The first formation was a series of sand and clay beds, called the Cherokee shales. The beds probably formed around an Ozark island. Thick beds of Pennsylvanian-age sandstones and shales are found in the Boston Mountains.

In Pennsylvanian time, fireclays filled ancient sinkholes along the northern Ozark border. In many localities during the same period, iron ores became concentrated in sinkholes. After the seas withdrew from the Ozarks late in Mississippian time, the entire region was land. The rock record leaves no evidence that Triassic or Jurassic seas covered any part of the Ozarks, and not until late Cretaceous time did the Gulf of Mexico extend as far north as the mouth of the Ohio River.

Geologic evidence shows that crustal forces uplifted the Ozarks in Tertiary time (65 million years ago) following a long period of erosion to a subdued surface. Since the large Tertiary uplift, others followed, producing additional

Griesemer Quarry and underground storage in the Burlington limestone at Springfield, Missouri, 1976. (Milton Rafferty Collection, photograph by the author.)

erosion of the surface. The exact cause is uncertain, but geologists think gradual adjustments of a similar nature result from imbalances in the earth's crust.

The last major event in the geologic history of the Ozarks was the advance of three glaciers. They affected only the northern and eastern margins of the region. Along the Missouri River, which was the approximate southern boundary of the ice, and in a narrow belt extending down the Mississippi River, are deposits of porous, brownish clay loam. Meltwaters laid this material, loess, in river valleys before winds carried it onto nearby bluffs. It forms the basis of the most fertile body of upland soil in the region.

The Ozarks lie within the part of North America that is generally free of serious earthquakes, but on December 16, 1811, a quake of very high intensity occurred in the New Madrid region of southeast Missouri. Other severe quakes and minor shocks followed for several months. Jared Brooks, a Louisville engineer and surveyor, counted a total of 1,874 shocks between December 16 and March 8, eight of which he classed as violent, ten as very severe, and thirty-five as moderate but alarming, and the rest as just perceptible.[71] No deaths are known to have resulted because the area was only sparsely settled, but if a similar quake were to occur today, the loss of life, and property would almost certainly be great. Nearby cities—St. Louis, Memphis, Evansville, Louisville, Cape Girardeau, and other cities—have a total population estimated at approximately 12 million. A. C. Johnson calculated that if another quake of equal strength to those in 1811–1812 were to strike in the year A.D. 2000, it would kill more than three thousand persons. Estimates of property damage in Memphis alone exceed $1.3 billion.[72]

The severe quakes of 1811–1812 opened great fissures in the ground and formed craterlets and mounds of sand. During the quakes, much of New Madrid fell in the river, and the effects of the quake were felt over an area that reached as far as New Orleans, Charleston, Savannah, Baltimore, Pittsburgh, Washington, D.C., Richmond, and in the Great Lakes region and Quebec.[73] The largest surface manifestation of the New Madrid earthquake was the dropping of a basin that filled with water to form Reelfoot Lake in western Tennessee a short distance east of the Mississippi River. The lake is sixty to seventy miles long, three to twenty miles wide, and in some places fifty to one hundred feet deep. The tremors nearly completely submerged the forest trees in the area. Smaller shocks that occur occasionally show that further deep adjustments in the earth's crust have continued to take place northward toward St. Louis. Minor regional shocks, discernible as far away as Springfield, occurred in 1967 and 1975.[74]

Earthquakes are the tremors or vibrations that arise from fracturing of rocks within the earth. Other causes of quakes are of so little consequence that they need not be mentioned. Stresses develop near the earth's surface, or at some depths, until they exceed the strength of the rocks, which then fail or break. Movement may be vertical or horizontal or both. The fracture in the rock strata is technically called a fault. The great New Madrid earthquakes of 1811–1812 probably resulted from slippage along one or more of three deeply buried faults in the region.[75] Recent studies by the Missouri Division of Geology and Land Survey and the United States Geological Survey have revealed several new, previously unknown faults near the New Madrid fault zone. This new evidence shows that faulting has been an ongoing process to relieve crustal stresses since about seventy-five thousand years ago.[76]

At some point, another large earthquake or series of earthquakes like those of 1811–1812 likely will occur again. While scientists cannot accurately predict the precise date of the onset of an earthquake, magnitude and frequency studies show that large earthquakes in the New Madrid region can be expected to recur every six to seven hundred years.[77] Nevertheless, in December 1989 Iben Browning, a "self-taught climatologist," predicted that an earthquake would occur in the New Madrid area on December 3, 1990. While seismologists did not take his prediction seriously, the news media grasped onto the prediction and during the following year they published many stories on past earthquakes and the potential damage from a future earthquake. Large crowds of visitors, including many television and newspaper reporters were in New Madrid on December 3, 1990, but nothing happened.[78]

A CONTROVERSIAL GEOLOGICAL PROBLEM

There are six interesting geologic features that outcrop in the Ozarks that geologists call cryptoexplosive structures.[79] These isolated structures appear to occur linearly along the same latitude, approximately 37˚40' N. Each is named after a nearby location; the Weaubleau disturbance in St. Clair County, the Decaturville dome in southern Camden County, the Hazelgreen volcanics on the Pulaski-Laclede county line, the Crooked Creek structure in southern Crawford County, the Furnace Creek volcanics in Washington County, and the Avon structure in Ste. Genevieve County. The upper Cambrian rocks in the Avon structure show signs of shattered igneous material, probably caused by explosions. The Furnace Creek structure contains a funnel-shaped crater filled with material resembling rock debris ejected from explosive volcanoes. In the Crooked

Creek structure, the Ordovician age Jefferson City formation shows evidence of faulting most likely connected with volcanic activity. Volcanic ash and other volcanic detritus are found in the Hazelgreen structure.

Because of the east-west alignment of these structures, some observers have speculated that meteorite impacts may have created them. An interesting fact is that sometimes meteorites enter the earth's atmosphere almost simultaneously from the same orbit and, if large enough, crash to the earth's surface and form large craters of up-warped shattered-rock structures (explosive structures).

Since these unusual Ozark structures formed at different times, the meteor impact theory is not a likely explanation for all of them. However, after a detailed study of the Decaturville dome using core drill samples, detailed mapping, and intensive study of the rocks, the geologists T. W. Offield and H. A. Pohn concluded that a meteor or comet impact formed the structure.[80] Nevertheless, the structure has been studied by many geologist over many years and variously described as cryptovolcanic or of impact origin.[81]

THREE

WEATHER AND CLIMATE

The first white settlers from Tennessee and Kentucky found few unfamiliar climate conditions in their new homeland. Since the Ozark region lies at the same latitude as Kentucky and Tennessee, the temperatures are similar. Its more westward position in the continent of North America makes the Ozarks less humid and more subject to droughts.

The Ozarks' mid-continent location in the middle latitudes influences both the day-to-day fluctuations in temperature, precipitation, and humidity that determine weather conditions and the long-term averages and extremes of these elements that comprise the region's climate. The altitudes and relief are not sufficient to affect, to any significant degree, the climate of the region.

The northern two-thirds of the Ozarks has a Humid Continental climate; in the Boston Mountains and a portion of southern Missouri the climate is Humid Subtropical.[1] These climate boundaries are arbitrary and are convenient only for identifying broad climate types. In fact, the climate of the Ozarks is so variable that a person who has lived in the region only a year cannot make a true estimate of the kind of weather to expected during the next twelve months.[2] One may say that concerning the seasons: the experience of one summer, or of one winter, will not give a correct idea of general summer or of general winter conditions. The same may be said for any month of the year.

WINDS AND STORMS

The winds are largely cyclonic and the weather is quite variable.[3] The Ozarks are too far south for their temperatures to be affected for long periods by the strong winter high-pressure cells of the north-central states, but occasionally a strong high-pressure cell or two from high latitude will bring prolonged and bitter cold temperatures. The extreme cold temperatures, reaching -10°F to -15°F, that occurred in January and February 1977, were unusual for their severity and duration. Rivers and ponds were frozen over with thick sheets of ice and some communities were without water when their main water lines were frozen. Lesser lows and highs from the Great Plains region move across the Ozarks regularly.

The wind of maximum frequency is southerly or southeasterly. There is a slight increase in the frequency of northerly winds with increases in latitude, and northerly winds are more frequent throughout the region in the winter months. Summer winds are more noticeable during the day than at night; winter winds are as common at night as during the day. At Springfield the mean velocity is 10.4 miles per hour, being highest in March (12.4 mph) and lowest in August (7.4 mph).[4] In midsummer a brisk continuous wind from the southwest for a few days is likely to become a hot wind, and much damage to growing crops may result. During late summer and early fall, over a period of several weeks, wind is light, the sun seems as hot as in midsummer, and the sky takes on a hazy, purplish color, especially in the late afternoon; this is the renowned Indian summer of the Ozarks, the time of storing away crops for winter, gathering nuts and apples, and greeting tourists, who come in large numbers to enjoy the Ozarks' finest season. In winter the winds often change direction quickly; cold, brisk winds may blow from the north for several days, sometime accompanied by fine, dry snow. At other times during the winter the brisk wind of the day quiets down at the approach of sunset, and the night is calm.

Tornadoes are of annual occurrence in the region, although the likelihood of visitations for any single locality is very slight. Most of these storms invade the Ozarks from Oklahoma and Kansas, and the western border is most subject to them. Between January 1, 1993, and September 30, 1999, Missouri, Arkansas, and Oklahoma suffered 116 deaths and 1,332 injuries from tornadoes.[5] Between 1883 and 1995, twenty-eight tornadoes hit Springfield resulting in 13 deaths.[6] Powerful twisters have struck nearby on at least six occasions: 1880, 1883, 1915, 1972, 1983, and 1988. The first destroyed the town of Marshfield and resulted in the death of nearly 100 persons.[7] The storm of December 14, 1971, caused heavy damage in Republic and destroyed several airplanes and severely damaged buildings at Springfield Municipal Airport.[8] Although tornadoes are most frequently in the period from April 1 to June 30, they occur in all months. The storm that hit Springfield's airport came in mid-December 1971.

Tornado forecasting and storm warning systems have done much to reduce the number of deaths and injuries. The violent tornado that struck Neosho in April 23, 1975, just before 8:00 P.M. caused three deaths, twenty-two injured, and severe property damage amounting to eight to ten million dollars in residential areas and in a shopping center.[9] Because of advance warning, the number of casualties and injuries was small, considering the violence of the storm and the congested areas that were hit.

The average temperature of the Ozark Upland is 55°F, which is also the average for the city of Springfield. The coldest month of the year is January. This does not neces-

sarily mean that the temperature during January is always lower than it is during the other winter months, but an average January has a few more cold days than either an average December or an average February.[10] January is also the month in which the temperature contrasts among various parts of the Ozarks is greatest, amounting to a maximum of twelve degrees between the extreme north and south. Only four degrees' difference between the north and south occurs in April, and in the three summer months almost none (fig. 3-1).

Winter in the Ozarks usually sets in about the latter part of December and continues through January and February, with occasional cold outbursts in early March. Each of the winter months has twenty-five to thirty days when the temperature during the warmest part of the day is at 32°F or above and only one to three days when the temperature drops below zero. About three cold waves a season sweep over the region, the average length of each

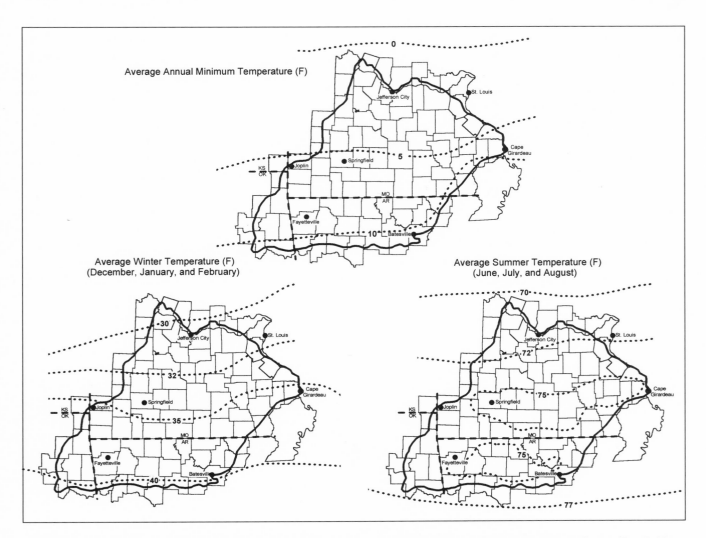

FIGURE 3-1. Temperature averages. Adapted from Stephen Sargent Visher, *Climatic Atlas of the United States* (Cambridge: Harvard University Press, 1954).

being about three days, but prolonged cold periods, such as those of January and February of 1977 and 1978, may occur. The mean daily range in temperature (the day's maximum minus the day's minimum) throughout the year is 18.2 degrees; in winter 16.8 degrees, in spring 19.0 degrees, in summer 18.3 degrees, and in autumn 18.8 degrees.

Extreme temperatures of 100 degrees or above are normal during an Ozarks summer. For the region as a whole, extremely high temperatures are likely to occur on one or two days in late June, three to five days during each month of July and August, and perhaps a day or two in early September.

HUMIDITY AND PRECIPITATION

The average relative humidity at Springfield is 73 percent; 77 during the winter months, 75 in summer, and 70 in spring. The average number of clear days per year is 150, partly cloudy 127, and cloudy 88. August, September, and October have the largest number of clear days; those with the most cloudy days are December and January, each with 11. May has an average of 12 rainy days, whereas October has only 7. In the eastern part of the Ozarks and on the south flank of the Boston Mountains, the humidity is moderately higher than at Springfield. On the whole the region is one of abundant sunshine. The maximum frequency of rains in spring, and of sunny weather in late summer, is favorable for production of a variety of crops.

Most precipitation falls as rain (fig. 3-2). The average totals range from 36 inches on the northern Missouri River border to more than 50 inches near the Arkansas River. Annual amounts at representative stations: Jefferson City 36 inches, Springfield 41, Poplar Bluff 48, Eureka Springs 49, Fayetteville 45, Harrison 43, Marshall 50, Muskogee 42.

The average annual snowfall at Springfield is only 15.9 inches, or about 3.5 percent of the total precipitation and less than half the snowfall at Chicago or New York. Snow that falls is quite variable. Stations on the northern border have received no snow in January in some years, while very heavy snows of 20 or more inches are not infrequent. Even in December heavy snowfall may occur. Springfield received a record 14-inch snowfall December 13, 2000.[11] Snowfall can be heavy in the Boston Mountains, but averages are modest: Fayetteville 10 inches, Harrison 12, Muskogee 6, and Ozark 6. On the northern border, snow may remain on the ground a week or perhaps two, but in the Arkansas Ozarks it usually melts in a day or two. Nevertheless, because state and county highway crews are sometimes poorly equipped to handle heavy snow, roads may at times be difficult to travel. Schools in the region usually allow two to five snow-days in their schedules to make up for days when roads are impassable. Even after snow and ice has been cleared from major highways, many schools in the hilly districts may remain closed for several days because school busses cannot travel on steep-graded secondary roads where north-facing slopes and timber retard melting.

The latitudinal position of the Ozarks favors sleet storms and freezing rain. Freezing rain causes considerable damage to trees and electrical and telephone wires and makes travel extremely hazardous for a day or two. In November 1848, the western Ozarks experienced a big sleet that was extraordinarily destructive. In December 1972, a heavy freezing rain in the same section brought down power lines and left farms and communities without electricity for several days.[12] Dairies were unable to milk until National Guard units brought in portable generators to power the electric milking machines. Another severe ice storm hit the western Ozarks on Christmas 1987.[13] The freezing rain commenced in the morning, and by noon so many power lines were down that many Christmas turkeys went uncooked. This storm wreaked havoc on trees and power lines and caused communities and farmers to call on assistance from the National Guard. Many communities were without power for several days, and streets and roads were nearly impassable. Another severe ice storm hit northern Arkansas in late December 2000. Farmers in Searcy County lost an estimated twelve hundred cattle, and one dairyman alone lost thirty-three head of prime dairy heifers.[14] Hail is most frequent in the western Ozarks, but the region as a whole normally experiences fifteen to twenty damaging hailstorms in the period May to September.

GENERAL WEATHER VARIATIONS

Ozarks weather is very changeable throughout the year, but more so during winter than any other season. The dry season usually sets in about late June or early July and lasts forty to sixty days. During this period, widespread rains of more than one inch are not common, and the greater part of the rainfall comes in showers. Summer rainfall can vary widely. The year 2000 had unusually variable weather. It started with mild temperatures in January and February, then a dry spring and a very dry June, followed by one of the wettest July's on record, followed in turn by a record dry August, when no measurable precipitation fell during the entire month at Springfield. The year ended with record-setting low monthly temperatures for November and December and a record-setting snowfall on December 14.

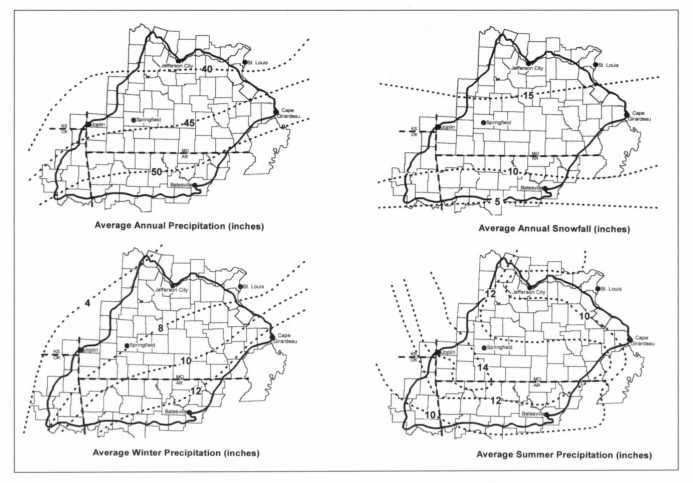

FIGURE 3-2. Precipitation averages. Adapted from Stephen Sargent Visher, *Climatic Atlas of the United States* (Cambridge: Harvard University Press, 1954).

More damage results from droughts than losses from excessive rain and flooding. Droughts cover a larger area and are prolonged, they affect both uplands and river bottomland, they cause permanent injury to field crops, and they affect farm and village alike by depleting water supplies.[15] Reservoirs are lowered and springs stop flowing. In the Ozarks, severe droughts have occurred in 1881, 1911, 1913, 1914, 1934, 1935, 1936, 1955, 1956, 1975, 1976, 1999, and 2000. Eugene M. Poirot, who pioneered many conservation practices on his farm near Golden City, Missouri, tells in his book, *Our Margin of Life,* of the devastation wrought by the drought of 1934:

That summer the breath of the prairie was hot, the soil cracked open and the grass turned brown and died. Wild cherry leaves became a deadly poison. One morning, five cows on their way along the pasture fence, stopped and took a bite of these leaves from a broken limb. In that unguarded moment they began a death march of only a hundred yards, at the end of which all

of them fell in a circle not more than forty feet in diameter. Conditions were so dry that a fire destroyed 160 acres of crops and burned up a two-mile hedge of Osage orange trees (to the ground). Another blaze measured a perimeter of thirteen miles after it was extinguished.[16]

The drought in 1975 persisted through the fall and winter months, and reservoir levels dropped to record lows. Many boat docks and marinas on Lake of the Ozarks, Table Rock Lake, and other Ozark lakes were stranded high and dry. Water levels on Beaver Lake dropped to expose the foundations, stone bridges, and amphitheater of Monte Ne, the popular resort constructed by the eccentric but nationally known William "Coin" Harvey.[17] People flocked to the site to take their first look at the well-known resort, covered by water when Beaver Dam was completed in the early 1960s. Also in 1975, many small communities and farms without reliable water supplies had to haul water as ground-water levels dropped and wells went dry. The drought of 1999 began in July after heavy rains in June and continued through the fall and winter. By March 2000 the tinder-dry conditions and strong winds caused many fires in the Lake of the Ozarks area. Although firefighters from St. Louis and other areas fought vigorously, eighteen homes went up in flames and thousands of acres of forest and woodland burned.[18]

Heavy downpours are often associated with squall lines, fronts, and isolated thunderstorms. Because of steep slopes, runoff is rapid, and flash floods are frequent. Such floods are of short duration but are destructive of property and farmland. On July 1, 1973, nineteen inches of rain fell southwest of Springfield and sent torrents of water down small valleys that a few hours before had been without even a sign of flowing water. Chert gravel, washed from hillsides, covered acres of bottomland along the Finley River. Some roads in Stone County were closed for days by deposits of gravel that in some places reached the second strand of wire on fences.[19] Washed-out bridges disrupted travel for several weeks.

On May 7, 1961, an even more disastrous flash flood swept through Harrison, Arkansas, and destroyed four-fifths of the business district.[20] A wall of water roared down normally placid Crooked Creek and swept over the levee a block south and east of the courthouse square at approximately 3:30 A.M. The flash flood built up over a span of twelve hours after eleven inches of rain had fallen, with the heaviest amount in the early morning hours. The damage exceeded $5.4 million as 80 percent of the business district was under as much as twelve feet of water.[21] It was not the first flood in Harrison. A year after the 1961 flood a U.S. Army Corps of Engineers study reported that water from Crooked Creek and Dry Jordan Creek had flooded the town in 1908, 1915, 1927, 1928, 1933, 1938, 1943, 1945, 1956, and 1957.[22]

Heavy rains often fall unexpectedly and cause severe property damage. A heavy five- to seven-inch rain in the early morning hours of July 12, 2000, caused flood waters to raise four to six feet deep in low-lying Springfield homes. The flood water drove more than one hundred people from their homes. The estimated damage was more than two million dollars.[23] A mobile home park in the Jordan Creek flood plain was hit hardest, but relief agencies estimated that more than half of the damage occurred on the upland where houses occupied sinkhole areas.

Temperature ranges are extreme at times. The highest temperature ever recorded in the Missouri Ozarks was 116°F at Marble Hill in 1901; the absolute high in the Arkansas Ozarks was 120°F at Ozark. Absolute minimum temperatures are hardly mild; both Fayetteville and Marshall in Arkansas have recorded -24°F. Springfield has recorded an absolute range of 135 degrees, with such anomalous temperatures as 74°F in January and 33°F in October and April.

MICROCLIMATE

Within the Ozarks, temperatures will vary widely with the orientation of slope, nature of surface materials, relief, and presence of water. South and west-facing slopes receive the greatest amount of sunlight and are subjected to higher rates of evaporation. Ferns, most mosses, and most wildflowers do not appear on south-facing slopes. Here also are the purest stands of oaks, hickory, and red cedar. North-facing slopes generally have much more undergrowth. In winter, perhaps the most noticeable effect of temperature differences within a small area is the duration of snow and icicles on the north-facing slopes. The latter, often several feet long as they hang from cliffs, may not melt completely for many days after daytime temperatures have reached the fifties.

Air drainage creates the most readily observed temperature differences in summer. Nights are notable for the cool breeze that drains down the slopes, beginning an hour or so before sunset. The effects of daytime temperature variations are most easily felt in flying over the Ozarks in a light plane, which air currents easily affect.

Early-morning radiation fog is common in the valleys in the hill and mountain districts because of the drainage of cool air into the valleys overnight.[24] The fog, which usually dissipates by midmorning as temperatures climb in the valleys, can be very heavy at times. While making his celebrated Ozark tour in 1818–1819, Henry Rowe Schoolcraft reported that heavy fog along the North Fork of the White River prevented them from traveling until the fog lifted.[25] Heavy fogs often hover over the large water bodies, such as Lake of the Ozarks, Beaver Lake, Pomme de Terre, Table Rock, and Bull Shoals. A bluish haze is characteristic in panoramic views in the hill districts, even in fair weather.

Shade and cool spring water moderate hot summer temperatures. Many early resorts were built close to large springs or caverns. At Welch's Cave and Spring on the Current River, Dr. C. H. Diehl constructed a rest home at the entrance to the cave in 1916 and benefited from the natural air conditioning. Pipes brought cool air from the cave to patients' rooms.[26]

The average length of the growing season for the Ozarks as a whole is nearly six months. The likelihood of unseasonable frost depends much more on topographic location than on latitude. Northern Arkansas and extreme southern Missouri have more than two hundred frost-free days, enough to allow cotton to mature. Cotton was once an important crop in the fertile bottomland soils along the White River and other larger streams of the southern Ozarks, but crops were sometimes lost due to early frosts. As a rule, frosts occur in the valleys several weeks earlier in fall and later in spring than they do on the uplands, especially in the larger valleys in the hill regions. The margins of the uplands have the best air drainage and are least subject to frosts.

The Ozarks has a humid climate free from severe drought in most years. It is well moderated, of the continental type, pleasant and healthful, and well suited to a large variety of crops.

WEATHER LORE

Being concerned about weather conditions is natural for agricultural people. Before scientific forecasting was available, farmers had to depend upon their own observations. Some of them, through long experience in observing the weather, became extraordinarily skilled in making short-range predictions of rain and frost. For long-term forecasts, people depended on *The Farmer's Almanac,* folklore, and weather signs.[27] They believed certain people possessed the ability to predict weather, and many Ozarkers still take amateur weather predictions very seriously. For more than twenty years, until December 1977, the Springfield newspaper published a periodic forecast by John Ward, a local weather prophet.[28]

Vance Randolph, noted folklorist and authority on Ozark folk culture, compiled the most comprehensive list of weather signs.[29] Many, if not most, of the weather signs and superstitions collected by Randolph were not unique to the Ozarks but were widely popular in rural America. A few of the signs have some basis in actual atmospheric changes or changes in organisms that are broadly predictive of weather trends. Many others have no apparent connection to weather.

A few of the popular Ozark weather signs serve to illustrate their general character. A strong wind in tall, dry grass is a sign of rain before nightfall. A cat's sneeze, a wolf's howl, the cock's crow, and livestock (of any type) turning their backs to the wind are sure signs of rain. Many people believe that wild animals become more active before a storm. Other signs popular in the Ozarks and familiar to most readers include the groundhog, rainbow, fog, rings around the moon, early budding of trees, and the croaking of frogs.

Many weather superstitions have a humorous character. The dried blood of a murdered man will supposedly liquefy when heavy rain is approaching.[30] One may assume that this forecast method can be used only infrequently. The number of fogs in August is supposedly predictive of the same number of snows in winter. Every 100-degree day in July predicts a 20-below-zero day the following January. Long-range folk forecasters hold that the weather conditions for the first twelve days of January are predictive of the weather for the next twelve months.[31] When extrapolated to the ridiculous, a dry January 4 produces a dry April and snowfall on January 8 results in August snow flurries.

FOUR

INDIANS OF THE OZARKS

Information about the native Indians of the Ozarks is largely available in archaeological reports and the journals of explorers and traders. Written history provides only a bare sketch of the Osage, Missouri, and Caddo Indians, who lived in and along the margins of the Ozarks. More has been written about the transient Indians who settled temporarily in the Ozarks before moving further west. The Cherokees, who settled permanently in Indian Territory (Oklahoma), have been the focus for many books and articles. Some of the earliest descriptions of the native people of the Ozarks relate to the historic voyage of Jacques Marquette and Louis Joliet down the Mississippi River in 1673.[1] Much that can be learned through archaeology was left unwritten between 1673 and 1830, and thousands of years of unwritten history preceded that period.

The Indians of the Ozarks were not seriously studied until the government had moved them to reservations, and by that time customs, habits, and possessions had been altered considerably through contact with people of European background. Even while in the Ozarks the native inhabitants were undergoing cultural change as they adapted to metal tools, firearms, trade items, and new religious beliefs. In the meantime, smallpox, measles, plague, diphtheria, trachoma, whooping cough, and influenza decimated the native populations. Having been isolated for more than ten thousand years, Native Americans had no genetic defenses against such epidemic diseases. By the time of frequent European contact and description, the numbers of Indians in the Ozarks were mere vestiges of what they were throughout most of prehistory.

Archaeologists are carefully reconstructing the prehistory of the Ozarks using research conducted by several institutions, but many areas have not been adequately examined by trained specialists.[2] Research on Ozarks prehistory has been directed toward the establishment of a general cultural chronology or sequence. The thousands of known campsites, villages, burial grounds, inhabited caves, small mounds, and rock art sites represent only a small fraction of the archaeological resources in the area. Most sites remain unknown to the professional archaeological community interested in preserving and learning about the prehistoric past. Nevertheless, many excavations at shelters, mounds, and open-air sites have produced much useful information for archaeologists to use in interpreting the region's prehistory.[3]

A relatively detailed discussion of the prehistoric cultural sequence for the Missouri Ozarks may be found in a two-volume set written by Carl H. Chapman.[4] Michael J. O'Brien and W. Raymond Wood have written a more recent treatment of the prehistoric Indians of Missouri, although the coverage of the Ozarks is spotty.[5] Two regional journals, the *Missouri Archaeologist* and the *Arkansas Archaeologist,* often contain articles about the prehistory of the region. Times extending back into prehistory have been described for both Missouri and Arkansas.[6] The stages and their approximate duration are shown in Table 4-1.

The *Paleoindian stage* extends through the period from about 9,500 to 8,000 B.C. Recent evidence from south-central Chile has lead archaeologists to abandon the long-held belief that the Paleoindians were the first immigrants to the New World. However, it does appear that the Paleoindians (often called the Clovis Culture) were the first people in the New World to produce highly specialized and well-crafted stone tools. Their settlements tend to be on uplands, especially along river bluffs, or on high terraces in major river valleys, and in close proximity to

TABLE 4-1. STAGES IN EARLY MISSOURI AND ARKANSAS INDIAN OCCUPANCY

Stages	Duration	Attributes
Historic Period	A.D. 1,700–A.D. 1,835	European Contact
Mississippian Period	A.D. 900–A.D. 1,700	Village Farmer
Woodland Period	1,000 B.C.–A.D. 900	Prairie-Forest Potter
Archaic Period	8,000 B.C.–1,000 B.C.	Forager
Paleoindians	12,000 B.C.–8,000 B.C.	Hunter-Forager

sources of high-quality chert (flint) used to fashion their tools.[7]

Archaeologists have pieced together enough evidence to provide some insight into Paleoindian economy and culture, although the Early Paleoindian record for the Ozarks is poor. Evidence from Mastodon State Park near Kimmswick, Missouri, suggests that the early Clovis hunting and gathering groups inhabited the Ozarks at least 11,500 radiocarbon years ago. Now-extinct forms of mammals, such as the mastodon and mammoth, ground sloth, giant beaver, short-faced bear, and saber-toothed cat, roamed at least parts of the Ozarks. Some of these large faunal species perhaps furnished part of the diet for the first Indians to penetrate the region.[8] However, archaeologists now think the Paleoindian diets included a diverse array of smaller mammals, amphibians, reptiles, birds, mussels and fish, besides greens, fleshy fruits, seeds, and underground parts of plants.

The distribution of Paleoindian sites in Missouri suggests these early hunters were exploiting resources that were more abundant along the Missouri and Mississippi river valleys. Elsewhere in the Ozarks, little has been found or reported that pertains to the first half of the Paleoindian period. Nevertheless, the paucity of Early Paleoindian sites in the Ozarks may reflect inadequate archaeological investigations and the related fact that most of the rugged Ozarks are either forested or in pasture, thereby limiting surface visibility and artifact collecting activities.[9] Chapman has proposed, based on the distribution of fluted points in Missouri, that Paleoindian groups first entered the Ozark region from the Mississippi valley by following the White River and its tributaries.[10]

The Paleoindian period culminated with the *Dalton Culture* (circa 8,500 to 8,000 B.C.), which flourished in the Ozarks and portions of adjoining regions in Missouri, Arkansas, Illinois, Kansas, and Oklahoma. Archaeologists regard the abundance and widespread distribution of Dalton tools, compared to earlier tools, as a reflection of substantial population growth.[11] Petroglyphs and pictographs provide considerable evidence of the lifestyle, economy, and spiritual interests of the people of the late Paleoindian period.[12]

By Dalton Culture times, glaciers had retreated well to the north, marking the end of the Pleistocene epoch; many large faunal species had become extinct; and the climate had moderated and modern vegetation became dominant. Several social and technological changes are evident, suggesting that Late Paleoindian Dalton populations were well adapted to the new environmental conditions. During this period, the size of Dalton hunting-gathering groups apparently increased, they began to use seasonal villages or campsites repeatedly, and they established trade networks.

The *Archaic stage* (8,000 to 1,000 B.C.) is traditionally divided into three periods: the Early Archaic (8,000 to 5,000 B.C.), the Middle Archaic (5,000 to 3,000 B.C.), and the Late Archaic (3,000 to 1,000 B.C.).[13] Regional population increased substantially; territories diminished even further; and the inhabitants used a wider range of resources. Ground-stone tools (for example, the full-grooved ax) are evident during Archaic times, along with a greater diversity of chipped-stone tools. They mostly fashioned the stone weapons and tools from native cherts, which occur abundantly throughout the Ozarks, and resources appear to have been obtained on an increasingly localized basis. Several types of notched points and other artifacts including manos, grinding stones, scrapers, and various other chipped tools dating from Archaic times occur commonly throughout the Ozarks.[14] The nature of domestic dwellings for most of the Archaic stage is unknown, but Archaic peoples often frequented caves or natural rock overhangs. Major open-air villages and campsites were typically situated on high terraces or hilltops near springs and permanent streams, although they commonly used flood plains of large stream valleys also for village sites.[15]

A great amount of change occurred during the approximately seven thousand years comprising the Archaic stage. This span of time is marked by the Hypothermal Interval, a warming and drying trend that peaked during Middle Archaic times, or about 4,000–3,000 B.C. in the Ozarks. Owing to the increased aridity that attended warmer and drier conditions, Middle Archaic groups became concentrated in the flood plains of Ozark valleys where water was still available and where food resources were more readily obtained during the drier climatic conditions. After about 3,000 B.C., increased precipitation and cooling occurred, and the widespread distribution of Late Archaic sites suggests substantial population growth. The various groups responded by localizing their subsistence activities, reducing territory sizes, and by starting to independently domesticate a suite of plants native to the Ozarks and the Eastern Woodlands. In fact, some of the best evidence for a separate center of plant domestication in eastern North America derives from sites in the Ozarks.[16]

The *Woodland stage* (1,000 B.C. to A.D. 900) is also traditionally divided into three periods: the Early Woodland (1,000 to 300 B.C.), the Middle Woodland (300 B.C. to A.D. 400), and the Late Woodland (A.D. 400 to 900). The use of pottery and the construction of burial mounds are often viewed as hallmarks of the Woodland stage, but evidence from Missouri and elsewhere demonstrates that such developments also had their seeds in the Late Archaic period. The commonplace construction of burial mounds and the everyday use of ceramic vessels is evident for the first time during the Woodland stage, but the break between Late Archaic and Early Woodland times in the Ozarks is a somewhat arbitrary one. Clearly, great continuity between these two periods of prehistory in the Ozarks is evident, and the changes in material culture are more obvious elsewhere than in the more isolated Ozark valleys.

Early Woodland pottery was crude and fragile, and many peoples in the Ozarks seemed to have been little concerned with this new technology. Instead, they continued their more mobile settlement-subsistence strategies and used more transportable basketry and bags. Usually the Woodland Indians made pottery from clay that often contained small particles of sand, igneous rock, limestone, and crushed shards, which they added to act as temper. Technological attributes of pottery improved throughout the Woodland stage, and the use and diversity of ceramic vessels likewise increased during this time in the Ozarks. The practice of constructing low mounds for burial of the dead began on a large scale during the Woodland stage, but particularly during the Middle Woodland period. Pipes and evidence for ceremonial smoking became more common in the region, and the earliest evidence for the use of tobacco in the Midwest and Midsouth currently dates to the Middle Woodland period.

Archaeologists think the bow and arrow was in use by at least Late Woodland times, or about A.D. 400–600. The bow and arrow increased the effectiveness of hunting and ambush and warfare. The accompanying increased use of and refinements in pottery expanded the Indians' ability to cook and store food, allowing for an increased sedentary lifestyle. At the same time, they tended small gardens and perhaps even fields of native plants, such as chenopod, maygrass, knotweed, little barley, sunflower, and marshelder, to supplement food that they hunted and gathered.

Substantial Middle and Late Woodland villages and burial sites have been discovered along the eastern and northern margins of the Ozarks. Nevertheless, the Ozarks appear to have been peripheral to major Middle Woodland developments referred to as Hopewell. The centers of the Hopewell Culture were in Ohio and Illinois (lower Illinois River valley and adjacent portions of the Mississippi Valley), where prehistoric burial sites consist of large circular mounds that contain elaborate trade goods. Hopewell sites in these areas suggest extensive trading, involving such exotic commodities as obsidian (volcanic

glass) from the Yellowstone; mica, quartz crystals, aventurine, and chlorite from the southern Appalachians; marine shells from the Florida Gulf Coast; and galena (lead) from northwestern Illinois or from the St. Francois Mountains area of the Ozarks.[17] Research at Hopewell sites along the Missouri River has suggested that the sites in this area were possibly colonies established along trade routes.[18]

Evidence of Hopewell influence in the interior of the Ozarks is meager and mainly confined to artifacts reflecting very limited trade, sporadic intrusions by Hopewell groups, or intermittent borrowing of technology between isolated Middle Woodland groups in the interior Ozarks and larger Hopewell villages along the Missouri and Mississippi rivers. Archaeologists think the Hopewell communities along the margins of the Ozarks declined along with the general deterioration of major Hopewell centers east of the Mississippi River. Isolated resident populations probably lived in the interior Ozarks during this period, but their material cultures have not been fully defined, at least based on ceramics.

After the Hopewell Culture languished, the subsequent Late Woodland inhabitants of the Ozarks maintained their self-sufficient social and subsistence institutions. There is good evidence that populations grew dramatically during the Late Woodland period in the Ozarks. Late Woodland sites are virtually ubiquitous.

After the six to seven hundred years of the Late Woodland period, two other outside cultures had an influence on the Indians of the Ozarks. These include the Mississippian and Caddoan cultures. The Mississippian Culture developed in what is now the southeastern United States and was present throughout the Mississippi Valley after about A.D. 1,000 to 1,100. These people were mostly maize agriculturalists and lived in permanent villages. Houses were permanent structures, rectangular or square, often with thatched roofs and walls of wattle and daub. In the fertile Mississippi Valley, large, flat-topped earthen mounds were built for ceremonial purposes and elite houses. These pyramids were sometimes tiered and had large buildings on top, with ramps or stairways leading to them. These Indians produced varied ceramic vessels and sometimes molded elaborate effigies of animals and human beings on their containers. Extensive trade was conducted, including that with Gulf Coast peoples for marine shells.

Caddoan Culture developed along the southwestern flanks of the Ozarks. Caddoan peoples were mainly centered in the Arkansas and Red River valleys, but they did expand for a time well into northwest Arkansas and southwest Missouri. While the development of Caddoan Culture occurred somewhat independently from Mississippian Culture, they came to share similar characteristics in social and political organization, settlement, subsistence, and treatment of the dead. Caddoans constructed earthen platform mounds for civic-ceremonial structures in important communities, and they were traders, maize agriculturalists, and ceramic artisans.

The Ozarks were mostly peripheral to these two mainstreams of late prehistoric development, although the eastern and southwestern margins of the Ozarks were significantly modified. The St. Francois Mountains also were very important in the Mississippian world, since they supplied basalt, galena, and other desired materials.

Some investigators speculate that the interior Ozarks was occupied by more isolated groups who were largely oblivious to these grand developments along the Ozarks periphery. Remains of massive ceremonial mounds like those at the Lilbourn site in southeast Missouri are absent, and evidence for Mississippian and Caddoan presence in the central Ozarks is sparse. They have offered several theories to explain the paucity of Mississippian materials in most of the Ozarks. These include the difficulty of travel, low population density, scarcity of suitable land for extensive maize agriculture, the presence of change-resistant peoples, longstanding hostilities between groups living along a largely unpopulated buffer zone (most of the Ozarks), and a lack of interest among the Mississippian and Caddoan peoples for contact with groups living in the interior of the Ozarks.

The process of unearthing the artifacts that allow archaeologists to reconstruct the prehistoric past is slow and painstaking. Archaeologists have given many sites cursory examinations, but have examined comparatively few intensively. The task of examining known sites, not to mention the sites that have yet to be discovered, is enormous. For example, in the valley of Flat Creek in Barry County, Missouri, investigators mapped more than one hundred and thirty village and campsites about fifty years ago.[19] None of these sites has ever been carefully studied and reported. When one considers the hundreds of river and stream valleys, stream terraces, and advantageously located uplands that have known Indian habitation sites, or the potential for them, the size of the task of unearthing and studying Ozarks prehistory is apparent. Agriculture, road building, man-made lakes, and other forms of construction have rendered thousands of Indian habitation sites useless for archaeological study. This is particularly true of those on fertile bottomlands. Some of the most intensively studied areas are on lands owned by the federal and state government. For example, the Big Eddy Site, in the Sac River flood plain below Stockton Dam in Cedar County, has had intensive study by the Southwest Missouri State University Center for Archaeological Research with support from the U.S. Army Corps of Engineers.[20]

THE HISTORIC PERIOD

The final period of Indian occupation in the Ozarks was marked by the appearance of groups that were present during European contact. The larger native tribes include the Osage, Illinois, Caddo, and Quapaw. The Osage occupied most of the interior and western Ozarks; the Illinois lived along the Mississippi River Border; the Caddos hunted in the Arkansas and southwest Missouri portion of the Ozarks, and the Quapaws occupied only a small section of the southeastern hills. All these tribes were dependent upon both hunting and agriculture for their food. Although their villages were permanent, much of their time was spent on extended hunts.

The Osage styled themselves as *Wa-ca-ce,* meaning "people," which was corrupted, modified, and then changed by various French interpreters into "Ouchage," "Autrechaha," "Zages," "Huzzaus," and other forms, all of which the Americans mispronounced.[21] The realm of the Osage was from "the Great Bend of the Missouri south to the waters of the Arkansas and east toward the Mississippi," a region they had used as a hunting ground for several centuries before the arrival of the Europeans.[22] Their principal village was on the upper reaches of the Osage River about seventy-five miles south of Fort Osage (fig. 4-1). A smaller village of Great Osage was on the Neosho River not far from three villages of the Little Osage people.[23]

The first reporters described the Osage as tall, not many being of less than six feet in height, "of fine figure," athletic, agile, robust, with broad shoulders, and with strength and endurance that enabled them to walk as much as sixty miles in a single day.[24] They were reported to be intelligent, quiet, and reserved, and although they drank they were not given to drunkenness.[25] Their relationship with neighboring Indians generally was not good, and while they got along well with the French traders, their relationship with the Americans was often troubled. While on hunting trips, they frequently raided frontier cabins taking food, weapons, and livestock. The American settlers in remote areas stayed on guard and avoided going on hunts when they knew the Osage to be in the vicinity.[26] Even after selling their tribal lands in the Ozarks to the United States, the Osage continued to claim hunting rights. They also objected to the removal of Kickapoos, Cherokees, and other eastern tribes into the land they had sold, and they often had conflicts with the newcomers when they encountered them on hunting trips in the area.

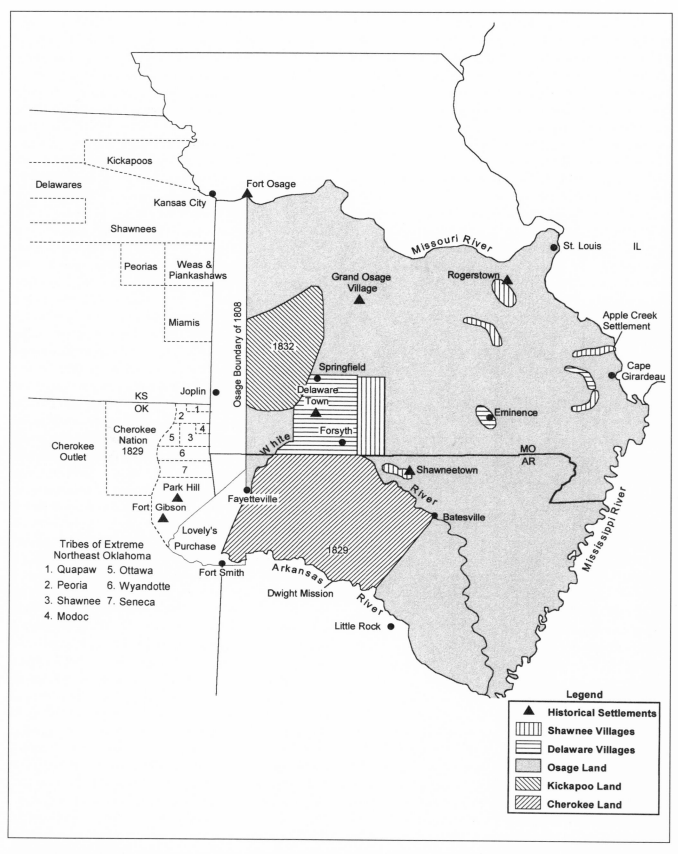

FIGURE 4-1. Ozark Indian lands and areas of removal. Adapted from Charles O. Paullin, *Atlas of the Historical Geography of the U.S.* (Washington, D.C.: Carnegie Institute of Washington, 1932).

The Osage were primarily hunters, but they raised annually small crops of corn, beans, and pumpkins, cultivated entirely with a hoe, with planting in April. In May they started their summer hunts that lasted until August, when they returned to their villages to harvest their crops, left unhoed all summer. Following a harvest feast, they cached (buried) the remainder of the food, before they set out again on their fall hunt, which lasted until about Christmas. Through the winter they remained in their villages, living off their *caches,* except for brief hunting trips when the weather was favorable.

The Osage, Caddo, and Quapaw produced good pottery vessels and tools that were well made and decorated. By 1700, trade was well established with the French; consequently, the Indian cultures began to change. The Indians found that some European goods were superior, and the old arts fell into disuse. The horse brought rapid change; it allowed the Osages to hunt on the plains west of the Ozarks.

The story of the Indians' displacement from their homelands in North America is a most tragic epic. The government made treaties containing terms never met, and some documents were never considered seriously by the whites. Congress often knew little of the Indians' circumstances. Some agents and military officers who administered the terms of the treaties were able and did good work, but nearly as often they were corrupt or inexperienced and incompetent. Often the leaders of the tribes were themselves corrupt, so that bribery and personal favors to prominent Indian families became an accepted way of doing business. By the time the Cherokees reached the Ozarks, intermarriage had become so common that many of their chiefs had more white ancestors than Indian.[27] All of this caused an undue and unnecessary amount of suffering and hardship for the Indians in the inevitable transfer of lands and the melding of cultures.

So it was, then, that the Ozarks first became part of the western dumping grounds for tribes dispossessed in the East; then, as white settlers entered the region, they again dispossessed and crowded these Indian peoples into smaller and smaller land reserves farther west. They immediately conflicted with the Indian peoples who inhibited these western lands.

Even before the Ozarks came into the possession of the United States in 1804 after the Louisiana Purchase of 1803, several groups of eastern Indians had moved into the region. Anticipating that the Americans would soon hem them in on all sides, Shawnees, Delawares, and other Algonquian-speaking peoples of the southern Great Lakes region first emigrated to the lower Missouri River country in the 1780s.[28] Louis Houck, drawing on reports by Nuttall, Morse, Flint, Harvey, and Brackenridge, recorded many settlements by Indians from east of the Mississippi.[29] Serene, a chieftain of the Kickapoos, led a small group, probably fewer than four hundred souls, to land west of St. Louis. The Spaniards were receptive to Indian immigration, believing that the presence of a friendly Indian population would help them to retain possession of their land west of Mississippian River.[30] By 1784 they had settled Shawnees and Delawares on land grants in what is now southeast Missouri and northeast Arkansas. In 1785 a group of Cherokees who were dissatisfied with the Treaty of Hopewell immigrated to the vicinity of the St. Francis and White rivers in northeast Arkansas.

In 1794, in a further effort to protect the settlements from the Osage and to strengthen the west bank of the Mississippi against the Americans, the Spanish authorities encouraged Shawnees and Delawares to settle above Cape Girardeau in an area between the Mississippi and Whitewater rivers, bounded on the north and south by Cinque Hommes Creek and Flora Creek.[31] A band of Shawnees—including a few Americans, some Delawares and Miamis—led by their chief, Jimmy Rogers, an American who had been captured as a child and raised among the Indians, settled on a branch of the Meramec in western Jefferson County, near the present town of Union. This settlement was known as Rogerstown.[32] Among the Shawnees, who lived in two villages on Apple Creek in northern Cape Girardeau County, was Peter Cornstalk, an articulate defender of Indian interests, and a sister and other members of Tecumseh's family. The Indians in the Apple Creek villages lived in log houses built in the French style with logs placed vertically in trenches.[33] Delawares occupied villages on nearby Indian Creek and Shawnee Creek.

Shawnees and Delawares from the settlements near the west bank of the Mississippi gradually moved farther west, successively establishing villages on the Whitewater River, then on Castor River, and in the Mississippi lowlands. The Delawares later established villages on the White River, near Forsyth, on James River in Christian County, and on Wilson's Creek, in Greene County. Other Shawnee and Delaware villages were on the Meramec and Current rivers, and on the headwaters of the Gasconade, and other points in the interior.[34] Schoolcraft reported two Delaware villages and a Shawnee settlement on Huzzah Creek in 1818.[35] Another band of Indians, probably Delawares or Shawnees, had a village near Pilot Knob in Iron County. Additional Delaware and Shawnee villages were found on the Meramec and Current rivers and on the headwaters of the Gasconade and other points in the interior. Small bands of other eastern tribes also settled in the Ozarks, including a village of Piankashaws on the St. Francis River, a village of Peorias on the Current River, and another near Ste. Geneviève.[36]

These remnants of Delaware, Shawnee and related tribes, and small numbers of southern tribes, each left their imprint on the region's history just as the Ozarks became a part of their history. After the Louisiana Purchase many Indians who migrated to the Ozarks came as wards of the federal government and received cash annuities that they spent for trade goods provided by a few white traders. Successful traders, such as the Lorimers, the Menard-Valle interests, and the Chouteaus, became skillful in their diplomacy to monopolize the Indian trade and become wealthy.

One very successful trader among the Delawares who had established a trading post along the James River in southwest Missouri was William Gillis.[37] Following adoption into the Delaware tribe in 1818 at Kaskaskia, Illinois, Gillis and merchant friends in Kaskaskia, Ste. Geneviève, and St. Louis entered the mobile Indian trading markets with Delawares and associated migrant groups, namely, Shawnee, Peoria, Piankashaw, Wea, Creek, and Kickapoo. In 1822, Gillis established a trading post near the mouth of the Finley River and near the Delaware villages where about twenty-five hundred Delawares were concentrated by the mid-1820s.[38] With the help of his right-hand man, Joseph Philibert, he transported trading goods from Ste. Geneviève through the Ozarks to the trading post. In spite of efforts by John Campbell, the local Indian agent, to control unfair trading and illegal sale of alcohol, Gillis, along with other traders and settlers, managed by legal and illicit methods to acquire much of the Delaware annual government stipend. American settlers near the Delaware villages established stills and sold whiskey to the Indians.[39] When the Delawares ceded their land back to the government at the Council Camp Treaty on James Fork in September 1829, and the Castor Hill Treaty in St. Louis, the federal government awarded $12,000 to pay their debts. When the Delawares moved to a new tract of land near the mouth of the Kansas River during 1829–1831, Gillis followed and established another trading post.[40]

The Osage Indians gave up their claims to most of the Ozark Plateau in their first treaty with the federal government in November 1808. The document was drawn up at Fort Osage, situated on a bluff overlooking the Missouri River about twenty miles east of the present site of Kansas City. The Osage gave up their land between the Missouri River and the Arkansas River lying east of a line running due south from Fort Osage to the Arkansas River (fig. 4-1).

The War of 1812 was a time of bitter conflict between American frontier settlers and Indian tribes. The Indians entered the conflict thinking they would profit from the defeat of the Americans. After the war, renewed emphasis was placed on Indian removal. Under the terms of the Treaty of Edwardsville and the Treaty of Fort Harrison, both of which were signed in 1819, they granted the Indiana and Illinois Kickapoo tribes land in southwest Missouri and a stipend of money (fig. 4-1) in exchange for their land east of the Mississippi River.

In 1821 and 1822 the government gave a band of twenty-one hundred Delawares, already twice removed from their homeland in the Middle Atlantic states, land along the James River on land now encompassed by Christian, Stone, and Barry counties (fig. 4-1). Although the location was to be temporary, some Delawares and a few Shawnees from southeast Missouri joined the main body of Kickapoos in the James River country. The Kickapoos and Shawnees ranged widely in the Ozarks and had hunting camps as far east as Jefferson County and on the Current and Gasconade rivers.[41]

Most counties in southwest Missouri and northwest Arkansas have accounts of Shawnee and Delaware villages within their boundaries. The sheer number of reports would lead one to think that many of them were seasonal hunting camps. Ingenthron[42] noted several Shawnee settlements, including Shawnee Town, near present-day Yellville, Arkansas; Crooked Creek Camp, near what is now Harrison, Arkansas; Gaither Cove Camp, at the eastern foot of Gaither Mountain in Boone County; Long Creek Camp, near the present town of Alpena; and a camp on Short Creek in Marion County. The Delawares had several dwellings on Long Creek in what is now Carroll County, Arkansas, besides their main villages between the White and Osage rivers. Reportedly, a large village of about five hundred inhabitants was found within the present boundaries of Springfield.[43]

By the 1820s the Ozarks had become a kind of refuge for fragments of the eastern Indian tribes buffeted about for several years. Probably, to some of these people the rugged isolation of the Ozarks provided a welcome relief from the harassed and vagabond life they had been leading. In 1819 a group of about sixty Peorias was living at the mouth of Bull Creek. A few miles east, a village of Miamis was at the mouth of Swan Creek, and a band of Piankashaws had settled on Cowskin Creek near the present town of Ava, Missouri. Peorias and Piankashaws reportedly lived near the present site of Forsyth, Missouri, on the White River, and a small band of Wea Indians lived near the spot where Beaver Creek flows into the White River. By the mid-1820s about eight thousand Algonquins and six thousand Cherokees inhabited southwest Missouri and northwest Arkansas.[44]

Cherokees were among the first eastern Indians to move across the Mississippi. A few had moved into the vicinity of the Missouri lead mines even before the Revolutionary War. In 1775 the Spanish governor Luis de Unzagay Amezaga received news that Cherokees had driven the miners away from Mine La Motte.[45] The first Cherokees to enter Arkansas, a band led by Chief Bowl, settled south of the Arkansas River in 1794.[46] Another band fled to the swamps of the St. Francis River in 1795 after participating in a massacre at Mussel Shoals on the Tennessee River in 1794.[47] In later years, others who wished to escape the white man's encroachment on Cherokee territory in the East, augmented these bands. By 1807, about ninety Cherokees were living near Bear Creek Springs six miles north of Harrison, Arkansas.[48] The Spanish did not object to the Cherokee settlements, accepting them as they did the Delaware and Shawnee villages as useful buffers to the Americans across the Mississippi.

By 1800, the practice of encroachment on Indian lands was well established. The Cherokees had already given up Kentucky by the time of the American Revolution, and they ceded four counties in South Carolina during the war to placate the Americans who were embittered by the raids of the Chickamauga Cherokee band.[49] There was intense political pressure to seize Indian lands in the East to provide new land for American settlers. Indian removal also fit the thinking of Thomas Jefferson and his regime regarding the Indians. Jefferson hoped that education would be the tool that would weld the "noble savages" into the new brotherhood of civilized men, which was the United States. He also thought that the quicker the Indians gave up their land, the sooner they would drop their old ways and become civilized.[50] The government soon perfected techniques that became common practice in dealing with the Indians: subversion of the tribal political systems, inauguration of private land ownership, including failing to expel whites who settled on Indian lands, use of government trading stores to encourage indebtedness, and outright bribery of tribal chiefs.[51]

Among the Cherokees there was considerable difference of opinion regarding relocation, although most surely would have preferred to have been left alone to live in their Appalachian homeland. By 1801 the Upper Cherokees in eastern Kentucky and North Carolina had adopted much of the American culture. They lived in "white" houses, practiced American agriculture and crafts, and were rapidly adapting to coexistence with the whites. Resistance to change was strongest among the Lower Cherokees in South Carolina, Georgia, and Alabama, and it was this group that began to clamor for wholesale emigration to escape the nocuous American influence.[52]

In 1808, some so-called Western Cherokees in Arkansas petitioned President Thomas Jefferson for land elsewhere, so that they might move from the swamps. Jefferson encouraged them to move west and to select lands on the Arkansas and White rivers, "the higher up the better, as they will be longer unapproached by our settlements."[53] It was an opportune time. The Osage had just ceded their Arkansas and Missouri lands to the federal government at the Treaty of Fort Osage that same year. The Lower Cherokees, pleased with Jefferson's support of emigration, sent exploration parties under Chief Talontuskee to examine the Arkansas land. Following a favorable report, emigration began, and between 1809 and 1811 more than two thousand Cherokee had settled along the Arkansas and White rivers.[54] The settlements along the White River were so numerous that when President Jefferson appointed Major Jacob Wolf as Indian agent to the Arkansas Cherokees in 1809, he built his house at Norfork on the White River rather than on the Arkansas River.[55] These Cherokee groups were joined in 1812 by the St. Francis Cherokees who fled the lowlands following the devastating New Madrid earthquakes. No treaties had been signed to grant the land to the Cherokees, so in fact, these groups were "squatters" with no legal rights to the land.

Because the United States and many Indian tribes became embroiled in the Creek Wars for several years, further progress on emigration was delayed. Though the Eastern Cherokees fought with the Americans against the Creeks, their efforts had no beneficial effects on their land tenure. During this time the Western Cherokees became embroiled in their own war with the Osage. Finally, in 1817, at a conference called by General Jackson at Calhoun on the Hiwasse River, they gave the Eastern Cherokee a choice. They would cede all Cherokee lands to the United States in exchange for land in the Arkansas Ozarks. The Cherokee could either resettle in Arkansas or stay in the East, accept United States citizenship, and receive one section of land.

On July 8, 1817, the United States and the Cherokee Nation signed a treaty granting a large tract in northern Arkansas to the Cherokees (fig. 4-1). Only a few chiefs signed the treaty, the majority preferring to remain in the East and trust that Congress and the president would protect them. When the Senate and the president accepted the treaty as binding, government officials began preparations for massive emigration. Amid turmoil among the Cherokees, legal battles, and logistical planning for the removal and survey of the land in Arkansas, an estimated thirty-five hundred to six thousand Cherokees immigrated to the Arkansas Ozarks during 1817 and 1818.[56]

There were two crucial problems with the treaty. One problem stemmed from the fact that many Cherokees had settled south of the Arkansas River outside the treaty lands between the Arkansas and White rivers. Most of the Cherokees south of the Arkansas protested the exchange of their farms for land in the rugged Ozarks. The government decided this issue in 1819 when the secretary of war John C. Calhoun declared that the terms of the treaty should stand and the settlers south of the river should move north into treaty lands.[57] Since the Cherokees requested land surveys to prove ownership of their new lands north of the river, the moves were still not completed by 1822.[58] Since about twelve hundred Cherokees lived south of the Arkansas River, it is likely that some never moved. The second problem stemmed from the treaty's stipulation that the Cherokees were to receive an equal amount of land in Arkansas as they had held in the East, acre for acre. Because the government had no way to know how many Cherokees were going to abide by the treaty and emigrate, it could give no quantitative land measure. Instead, officials decided to survey an eastern line between the Arkansas and the White rivers, and then later, when they had assessed the eastern lands, the western boundary of the Arkansas lands would be drawn to enclose the same amount.

On April 14, 1819, William Rector, surveyor general for the territory, reported that the surveys of the eastern boundary and the specified townships east of the White River were completed.[59] A line extending northeastward from the mouth of Point Remove Creek near the present city of Morrilton to the White River near Batesville was the eastern boundary. The survey of the eastern townships did not mesh with the eastern Cherokee boundary, and the topographic maps of the Batesville area still show the Cherokee boundary as a diagonal line cutting across the U.S. Land Survey.[60] The western boundary, undecided until 1825, began at a point ten miles upstream from Fort Smith, extending northeastward parallel to the eastern boundary to the White River. The Arkansas and White rivers were the southern and northern boundaries, respectively. No record was kept of the exact number of Cherokee Indians who made a new home in this grant. At the time the chiefs and government officials signed the treaty, between two and three thousand Cherokees were already in Arkansas, and another three thousand probably had immigrated by 1819.[61]

The Lovely Purchase (fig. 4-1) was a fleeting part of the complicated treaties negotiated to extinguish Osage land claims and to provide land for the displaced Cherokees. In 1816, Major William L. Lovely, official agent to the Cherokees, negotiated to purchase land in northwest Arkansas and northeast Oklahoma from the Osage Indians and transfer it to the Cherokees. Difficulties delayed the transfer until 1818. Only a few Cherokees settled in the Lovely Purchase. The tract was made part of a county (Lovely County) by the territorial legislature of Arkansas in 1827. About a year later the federal government gave the Cherokees permanent tribal lands in Oklahoma in exchange for all their Arkansas lands, including the Lovely Purchase. In the same year, the Arkansas legislature formed Washington County and Lovely County ceased to exist.[62]

Discontent among white settlers was directed toward the Cherokees living on the land awarded the Indians in 1817. When Schoolcraft and Pettibone passed down the White River in 1818, they stopped and spent a night at the home of Mrs. John Lafferty, the widow of one of the first settlers above Batesville.[63] Schoolcraft found Mrs. Lafferty very much excited, as were all her neighbors on that side (the right bank) of the river. She and others had improved farms upon which they had lived several years but which, under the treaty with the Cherokees, they were to be forced to relinquish. Mrs. Lafferty and her sons were arranging then to move across the river to another farm on Lafferty Creek (now in Izard County) that had belonged to her husband. She died there in 1832.[64]

The uncertainty of the situation led some displaced settlers to sell their preemption rights rather than establish a new homestead on the east side of the White River. Robert Bean, land speculator and donor of the land at Poke Bayou that would become Batesville, purchased many preemption rights from settlers along the White River.

The precise location of the Cherokee settlements on the White River is uncertain. They were in two main locations—on Spring Creek off the Buffalo River and at the mouth of the North Fork (today's Norfork).[65] Chief Peter Cornstalk lived at the Spring Creek settlements. He married a beautiful white woman, the daughter of pioneer Bob Adams, at Norfork in Jacob Wolf's house.[66]

Because of agitation by white residents and others who wanted to extinguish Indian claims in Arkansas Territory, negotiations were entered and the Cherokee Nation ceded to the United States all the land obtained in 1817. In return the Western Cherokees received land in Indian Territory (now eastern Oklahoma). More than three thousand moved from Arkansas to lands in Indian Territory (northeast Oklahoma) between 1828 and 1830.[67] Eventually most of the Cherokees in Arkansas moved there, joined by an almost steady stream from the Eastern Cherokee Nation during the next decade. Some Cherokees on upper White River stayed longer. In the mid-1830s many of them still lived on their improved claims, having intermarried with the white settlers, and more than a few descendants of these mixed marriages still live in the region.

The Cherokees who moved to Indian Territory were joined in 1839 by the main body of Eastern Cherokees, who were driven from their homes and marched along the Trail of Tears across the Ozark Plateau. Because the Cherokee Nation remains an important aspect of Ozark cultural geography, its story will be elaborated later as one of the permanent immigrant groups.

Conditions were hard for the potpourri of Algonquin peoples scattered about the Ozarks. By the mid-1820s, wildlife, a principal part of the Indians' livelihood, was becoming scarce; armed with the white man's weapons, the Indians were becoming quite destructive to it. Many tribes had become accustomed to a government dole and had become, essentially, wards of the state. Frequently, people depict Indian life sentimentally as a kind of carefree existence in which a simple, untroubled people live in harmony with nature. This letter, written by William Anderson, principal chief of the Delawares, to General William Clark, tells of their pathetic condition:

Last Summer a number of our people died just for the want of something to live on. We have got a country where we do not find all as stated to us when we was [sic] asked to swap lands with you and we do not get as much as promised us at the treaty of St. Mary's neither. Father we did not think that big man would tell us things that was [sic] not true. We have found that a poor hilly stony country and the worst of all no game to be found on it to live on. Last summer our corn looked very well until a heavy rain came on for 3 or 4 days and raised the waters so high that we could just see the tops of our corn in some of the fields and it destroyed the greatest part of our corn, pumpkins, and beans and great many more of my people coming on and we had to divide our stock with them . . .[68]

Over seven years—between 1825 and 1832—the government negotiated treaties with the several tribes in southwest Missouri for their removal from the newly created state into what is now Kansas. General Clark, whom most of the Indians respected, aided in working out treaties that cleared the Ozark region in Missouri and Arkansas for settlement by whites.

The final phase of Indian settlement in the Ozarks occurred in what is now Oklahoma. Before the Civil War, the government had removed bands of Senecas, Seneca-Shawnees, and Quapaws from Ohio to the northeast corner of Indian Territory between the Neosho River and the Missouri state line. In 1867, officials completed negotiations to make room in this area for several small bands of Indians from Kansas. Kaskaskias, Miamis, Peorias, Weas, and Piankashaws settled on the land vacated by readjustment of the Seneca-Shawnees. The Ottawas occupied a small reservation on the border of Missouri, and the Wyandottes occupied twenty thousand acres ceded by the Senecas (fig. 4-1).

THE CULTURAL LANDSCAPE

Except for the Cherokees and the other small bands of eastern tribes that settled in Oklahoma, the Indians had little permanent impact on the landscape. The Cherokees, the Shawnees, the Delawares, and other tribes that had been in contact with the whites for a generation or more lived in cabins much like the white settlers built. The Osages, hereditary landlords of most of the Ozarks, still lived at a primitive cultural level when they were removed to lands father west. They lived in a hunting-gathering-farming economy, with heavy emphasis on hunting. In April or May they planted their crops near the villages and, leaving them unfenced and sometimes unattended, took off on hunting excursions that sometimes lasted up to three months. In late summer they returned so that the women could harvest, dry, and store crops of beans, corn, pumpkin, and squash. An autumn hunt lasted into early winter. Furs, wild game, nuts, and wild fruits were brought back to the villages. Winter was a time to feast—until food supplies were exhausted—and to make preparations for the spring hunt for beaver and bear. At other times the Osages participated in trading and periodic warring expeditions.

Their settlements consisted of round or oblong huts built of poles forming a bow or arch and meeting at the apex. Over this framework, buffalo hides, reeds, cattails, and other thatch materials were interwoven to provide a weatherproof shelter. The shelters built at hunting camps were much more crude. Schoolcraft described those he saw on Swan Creek in 1818 as "inverted birds' nests" made of slender poles and interwoven branches and thatch, apparently somewhat in the fashion of the modern-day brush arbor used in the Ozarks for outdoor church services in the summer months.[69]

Compared with the American settlers, however, the Osages did not modify the physical landscape greatly. Their greatest landscape impact stemmed from their practice of burning the vegetation to drive wild game and to clear land around their villages. The cultural landscape they built was simple, consisting of a few huts and clearings that were quickly obliterated by forces of weather and encroaching vegetation. The eastern tribes that settled temporarily in Missouri and Arkansas possessed many of the white man's tools and implements, but their residence was of such short duration they left few imprints on the land other than depleting the population of wildlife.

The Cherokees, however, one of the so-called Five Civilized Tribes, possessed not only the white man's tools and implements but also his culture, including religion; the desire to provide for education; a system of tribal government; improved and systematic planting, cultivation, and harvesting of crops; and construction of substantial dwellings and laying out of towns. The Cherokees were great builders by Indian standards, and they developed a cultural landscape much like that of the white settlers and their descendants. However, their mode of occupation of the land created differences in landscape, some of which one could still see as late as the 1940s.[70]

FIVE

SETTLEMENT: THE FIRST PHASES

The settlement of the Ozarks progressed in three phases.[1] The first phase was the Old Ozarks Frontier, which progressed from the eastern border to the lead and iron mines in the eastern interior and finally overspread the whole region, though thinly by 1850. The first white settlers were French Creoles who established small settlements on the banks of the Mississippi River. A few Americans arrived before the Louisiana Purchase of 1803, but most came later. By 1840 the residue of the Cherokee nation had come over the Trail of Tears to the western Ozarks beyond the new states of Missouri and Arkansas. The exceptional characteristic of the Old Ozarks Frontier was that, except for the German border settlements close to the Missouri and Mississippi rivers, a few mining districts, and a few trade centers, it did not pass away.

The second settlement phase was part of the post–Civil War national development that historians call the New South.[2] It was a time of rapid railroad construction and the spread of the elements of modernity that always followed the rails. The New South Ozarks developed as corridors cutting through and eventually surrounding the Old Ozarks Frontier. The railroad brought commercial agriculture, corporate mining and lumbering, prosperity, energy, money, and urbanization.[3] The new Ozark immigrants were progressive, liberal, capitalistic, educated, and bourgeois in culture. This second-sequent occupancy, superimposed on the Old Ozarks Frontier and powered by the steam locomotive, influenced the back country for half a century or more, resulting in a variegated pattern of economic linkages, cultural landscapes, and ways of life. The railroads cut swaths of modernity and economic vitality through the hill country. Elsewhere the traditional economy and lifestyle remained only moderately changed.

The third phase of occupancy began with the events connected with World War I and has continued to the present. World War I "sent shock waves along the railroad corridors and into much of the region: the draft, high agricultural prices, borrowing to bring more marginal land into production, soldiers' pay sent home, new war-stimulated extractive industries."[4] Three more times (during World War II, the Korean War, and the Vietnam War) such shock waves washed over the Ozarks, each time reaching farther onto ridge tops and back into isolated valleys, now carried by the new power generated in the internal-combustion engine. In the early 1930s the New Deal agencies "discovered" Ozarks poverty, a problem that had plagued the region from the days of the first settlements. Through political propaganda the Ozarks' hillbilly stereotype received even more nationwide notoriety. Ozarkers received relief "commodities" and discovered such new foods as grapefruit and oranges, and for the first time for man.y, they learned that they were poor by comparison. The federal government became the Ozarks' largest landholder, employer, builder, preserver, destroyer, political power, social servant, and dependent. During the 1930s, the Works Progress Administration, the Civilian Conservation Corps, and a host of social agencies provided work, training, education, and sustenance. They established the national parks and national forests during the same decade. The army bases at Fort Leonard Wood, Fort Chaffee, and Camp Crowder came later, as did the Corps of Engineers and its dozen reservoirs. From the 1960s to the beginning of the twenty-first century, the Ozarks has experienced unprecedented population and economic growth. The rapid growth that began in the 1960s introduced the cosmopolitan Ozarks, marked by new people, new ideas, urban lifestyles, savoir faire in economic and political life, tourism and second-home development, skyrocketing land prices, new immigrants from foreign shores, along with a steady stream of retirees and other immigrants from nearby midwestern and southern states. All these changes are part of cosmopolitan Ozarks history.[5]

All three archetypal national histories persist in the Ozarks. They are manifested in human attitudes, beliefs, and daily activities. The careful observer of the Ozark landscape may discover them also in relict buildings, abandoned farms, and traditional technologies.

PRIMARY PHASE—THE FRENCH

The peculiar development of the Ozarks is due in large part to its location at the funnel opening of the Ohio-Mississippi river immigration route. The Ohio Valley served as a great collector of people who had moved westward progressively from the Tidewater to the Piedmont and through the Appalachian Mountains to the uplands of Kentucky and Tennessee and the fertile glaciated plains north of the Ohio River. The Ozarks was a rugged bastion deflecting the main flow of population to the bordering river routes via the Mississippi, Missouri, and Arkansas. People who moved along the river borders were of variegated origin, drawn from large sections of the East, yet for decades the Ozarks remained a backwater area along the mainstream of westward settlement and economic development.

The present territory of the Ozarks was originally part of the French province of Louisiana, but before cession of the western bank of the Mississippi to Spain in 1762, it was almost unexplored and unoccupied. Nevertheless, the French were the first immigrant group to explore and settle in the region. They entered the Mississippi Valley from their settlements on the Great Lakes. In their quest for furs and minerals, the French systematically explored the rivers of the interior lowlands of the United States. The Mississippi was the main link between the major French settlements on the Great Lakes and in lower Louisiana. The eastern Ozarks was strategically located in the midsection of their vast domain, where the great east-west navigable rivers, the Ohio and Missouri, entered the Mississippi. It is not surprising that the French early established settlements along this strategic section of the Mississippi that linked the great interior rivers: the Upper Mississippi, the Wisconsin, the Illinois, the Missouri, the Ohio, and the Arkansas. Many expeditions followed the voyage of Marquette and Joliet, who, in 1673, traveled from Quebec through the Great Lakes and down the Mississippi to the mouth of the Arkansas River.[6] By 1699 the French had established a permanent settlement at Kaskaskia, on the Illinois side of the Mississippi across from Ste. Genevieve, as a mission to the village of Kaskaskia Indians.[7] Soon after that, Cahokia and Fort Chartres were constructed on the fertile Illinois bottom (fig. 5-1). Reports of Scottish financier John Law's plans for the Mississippi Company focused France's attention on the Mississippi Valley in the years 1717–1720.[8] Though the plans did not materialize, the French soon followed with trading and mining ventures.[9] Settlements were in familiar sequence: missionary, followed in order by fur trader, soldier, and farmer. The French, familiar with frontier conditions in Canada, eked out a living by combining fur trading, boating, and a casual form of agriculture. Because of fertile soils and favorable growing conditions, a surplus of grain was available to ship to New Orleans in exchange for manufactured goods.

Probably through their contacts with the Indians, the French soon were apprised of mineral wealth in the hill country to the west. The lead deposits on the Meramec were known as early as 1700, and in 1702, Pierre Le Moyne d'Iberville asked for patents to work the mines.[10] Salt springs on Saline Creek below Ste. Genevieve were known even before Kaskaskia was settled. It was the salt springs, lead ore, and fertile bottomland that attracted permanent settlement to the west bank of the Mississippi. Father Gabriel Marest, of Kaskaskia, reported in 1712 that the residents of Kaskaskia worked and utilized the salt springs.[11] The French also quarried fine blocks of limestone near Ste. Genevieve for the construction of Fort Chartres near Kaskaskia. In 1704, Governor Jean-Baptiste Le Moyne de Bienville reported that Frenchmen were settled west of the river. Thus the first official documentation of white settlement in the Ozarks was made three-quarters of a century before the American republic was born.

Stories of huge stores of silver and gold seized by the Spaniards in Peru and Mexico prodded the French to explore the interior Ozarks. The apparent abundance of lead, which often occurs with silver, inflamed the French with the hope that they would find a bonanza. As might be expected, dishonest prospectors falsely reported discoveries of silver, and unsuspecting investors were quick to underwrite prospecting and mining ventures. In 1717 the Company of the West gained control of Louisiana, and by 1719 it had established exploratory mining on the Meramec. Failing to find silver, the master smelter apparently salted the mine with a few ounces of the precious metal.[12] Thus, by these spurious reports, they established the legend of silver mines in the folklore of the region, and the legend never died out entirely.

The first large-scale effort to explore and exploit minerals was the expedition of Sieur Philip Francois Renault, who in 1720 entered the lead diggings in Washington and St. Francois counties "with two hundred artificers and miners provided with tools" and, reportedly, with slaves for working the mines.[13] The expedition uncovered rich deposits of lead at the confluence of the Big and Meramec rivers, and Renault obtained rights to the site in 1723. It was the first land grant of record in Upper Louisiana.[14]

Renault's party, after exhaustive explorations, discovered several rich deposits of lead, but precious metals were not found. In 1723, French miners opened Mine La Motte a few miles north of present Fredericktown. The mines at

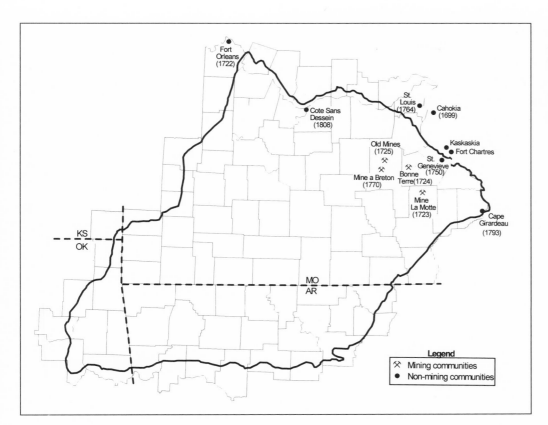

FIGURE 5-1. French settlements. Adapted from Milton D. Rafferty, *Historical Atlas of Missouri* (Norman: University of Oklahoma Press, 1981)

Forge à Renault were opened in 1724–25 and work at Old Mines north of Potosi started about 1725 (fig. 5-1).[15]

As mining operations gradually expanded, the French established permanent residences on the west bank of the Mississippi River. They established the first settlement on the flood plain in the Big Field below the present site of Ste. Genevieve and across the river from Kaskaskia (fig. 5-1). The date of earliest settlement in old Ste. Genevieve is uncertain. Houck placed the date at about 1830.[16] Professor Carl Ekberg, in his exhaustive study of colonial Ste. Genevieve, places the date at about 1750.[17] After 1763, when the lands east of the river were deeded to Protestant England, many French families moved to Ste. Genevieve to be under a Catholic government. By 1773, the population of Ste. Genevieve and vicinity was estimated at 691, nearly a hundred more than the St. Louis area at the time.[18] Indian raids and George Rogers Clark's capture of Kaskaskia brought on additional immigration to the Mississippi's west bank during the American Revolution.

The site of Ste. Genevieve was subjected to flooding, and in 1785, later known as the year of the great flood (*l'annee des grandes eaux*), floodwaters virtually destroyed the town.[19] Residents of the old town and many residents of Kaskaskia on the Illinois side moved to the new town founded at the bottom of a hill to the north. Then, in 1787, the new government of the United States established the Northwest Ordinance, which prohibited slavery in the Northwest Territory, and this prompted several wealthy slave owners to move to Ste. Genevieve. At the close of the eighteenth century, near the end of the French period, the French population lived primarily in Ste. Genevieve and New Bourbon, a town about a mile downriver, and in scattered temporary settlements at Mine à Breton (sometimes Mine à Burton, now Potosi), Old Mines, Mine La Motte, and St. Michaels (Fredericktown) (fig. 5-1).

Most of the Frenchmen were engaged in one of four occupations: salt making, mining, farming, trading. Salt was made by evaporating weak brine from springs on Saline Creek below Ste. Genevieve. The salt not only supplied the needs of the French settlements, but it was also an important item of commerce. The digging and smelting of lead in the area now included in Washington, St. Francois, and Madison counties were done in the fall after the crops were in and lasted until the onset of winter. This was the time when the pits were driest. The miners dug the galena ore entirely from residual clays with wooden shovels. Then they heaped it on piles of burning logs and melted it down. At first they molded the lead into the shape of a collar and draped it across a horse's neck for transportation to the Mississippi River; later, two-wheeled carts were used to transport lead to the wharf at Ste. Genevieve.[20] Farming was done in the Big Field and in upland Grand Park. Wheat and corn were staple crops in the Big Field, and in spite of the constant threat of flooding and a somewhat casual approach to cultivation, enough wheat was grown to supply local needs and to ship surpluses to New Orleans. They divided the fertile bottomland Big Field into long narrow lots in the French custom and distributed them to the heads of households. Grand Park was a communal pasture for livestock. Trade in furs, grain, and salt provided a livelihood for many settlers. Besides the settlement at Ste. Genevieve, the French established small ones, consisting of only a few families, at Cape Girardeau and on the Meramec.

By 1700 the French had pursued the fur trade into the Missouri Valley. They built Fort Orleans near Brunswick in 1722 to control nearby Indians. Since the fur traders frequently moved about, often living with the Indians, only a few permanent settlements were established. St. Charles and a small village at the mouth of La Charette Creek in Warren County were the only Missouri River settlements at the time of the Lewis and Clark Expedition in 1804. The villages were a collection of poor cabins and huts. Unlike the French at Ste. Genevieve, the voyagers of the Missouri River frequently intermarried with the Indians.

The founding of St. Louis was a milestone in the settlement of the Mississippi Valley. The first house in St. Louis was built by Pierre Liquest of the firm of Maxent, Laclede, and Company, merchants of New Orleans, who held a license for the fur trade on the Missouri River.[21] After a winter at Fort Chartres, Laclede established his trading post at St. Louis in February 1764. The location, near the mouths of the Missouri and the Illinois rivers, was ideal for control of the fur trade of the Upper Mississippi basin, and the site, a natural landing on a limestone outcrop on the first high ground south of the mouth of the Missouri, was free of flooding and malaria. St. Louis was strategically located to serve as an entrepôt for the products of the Ozark region.

French explorers and traders penetrated the southern reaches of the Ozarks very early. In 1673, nearly a century before the founding of St. Louis, Marquette and Joliet, with only two canoes and five boatmen, reached the mouth of the Arkansas River. Almost ten years later, in 1682, Robert Cavelier de La Salle visited the village of the Quapaws in Arcansa—the land of the downstream folk. In 1686, La Salle's faithful lieutenant, Henri de Tonty, on an expedition to look for his missing leader, established Arkansas Post some fifteen miles west of the Mississippi near the confluence of the White and the Arkansas rivers.[22] The main thrust of French interest, however, was concentrated on the branching Mississippi, Ohio, and Missouri river systems.

In 1765 an English garrison arrived at Fort Chartres,

and the exodus of the French from the east bottomlands on the Mississippi began. In three years St. Louis was a thriving town of more than five hundred inhabitants, already rivaling Ste. Genevieve as the largest settlement in the Mississippi Valley north of New Orleans.

After Spain took formal possession in 1770, that portion of Louisiana north of the Arkansas River was known as the Illinois country and was ruled by a succession of Spanish lieutenant governors at St. Louis. The governors, however, identified themselves with the province; French remained the official language, even of official documents, and the transfer of allegiance brought no break in the continuity of the history of the district.[23] The Spanish lieutenant governor was an absolute ruler receiving orders only from New Orleans; he controlled the troops and the militia, acted as chief justice under a code that did not recognize trial by jury, and was unrestrained by any popular assembly.

At the time of the Louisiana Purchase, the population of the district was more than six thousand. A steady and healthy growth in immigrants had built it up, at first Frenchmen from Canada, Kaskaskia, or New Orleans, reinforced after 1790 by Americans from Kentucky. The Spanish government had assigned commandants, subordinate to the governor of St. Louis, at New Madrid, Ste. Genevieve, New Bourbon, St. Charles, and St. Andrews. The towns were strung out down the Mississippi from the mouth of the Missouri. New Madrid and Cape Girardeau contained many Kentuckians, but most of the newcomers settled on detached farms along the creeks between St. Louis and Ste. Genevieve and around St. Charles. The settlement, French in culture but governed by Spaniards, was made up largely of Americans.

The economy was mostly agricultural, but as always rank and wealth distinguished various groups.[24] The wealthier men were merchants who sent the products of the colony to New Orleans or Montreal and sold manufactured goods to traders. Some wealthy merchants owned slaves and a few free Negroes inhabited the settlements. The younger men spent their winter with professional trappers on the upper Missouri or Mississippi rivers collecting furs, a staple export. Furs, lead, salt, and wheat were carried downriver; in the long and tedious return voyage against the current, the boats were laden with a few articles of luxury for the colonists, such as sugar, spices, and manufactured goods. Artisans were few and barely competent, so that nearly all tools, except the rudest, were imported. Even the spinning wheel was a rarity among the French, and butter was a delicacy. The Americans were more enterprising, but they had only slight influence on their neighbors.

The intellectual life was not of a striking character. The French did not arrange for education, and illiteracy was prevalent.[25] The few books in the settlements were mainly in the libraries of the priests. Religion was Roman Catholic by law, but officials did not molest Protestant Americans since they worshiped quietly. Since the governor ruled by decree, political life, town meetings, and elections were absent. Taxation was light, land was freely granted for nominal fees, and on the whole the Spanish governors were lenient and tolerant. There was rude abundance, a gentle, easygoing people, and a general absence of unrest. Early travelers commented on the contrasts between the French and the Americans. The French were characterized by having an aversion to labor, preferring the wandering life of trappers and traders, which the Americans attributed to an inherent inferiority of the French.[26]

The French controlled the great interior plains and low plateaus of the United States for nearly a century and a half, but they left almost no landscape imprint—and precious little to remember. As one geographer has said, the French were like Kilroy; and, like the imaginary omnipresent World War II soldier who wrote "Kilroy was here" on trucks, buildings, and latrine walls around the world, people know the French presence in the Ozarks mainly through place names and, except for the eighteen-century houses at Ste. Genevieve and a few French families in Washington County, Missouri, little else.[27]

PRIMARY PHASE—THE AMERICAN

The Louisiana Purchase was consequent to westward expansion of population and colonization in America. Four main routes from the Atlantic led to the Ohio River. All followed river valleys as lines of least resistance (fig. 5-2). The Iroquois Indians barred the northern and easiest passage—via the Mohawk River valley, later followed by the Erie Canal and now by the New York Turnpike—until about 1800. So the earlier pioneers crossed Pennsylvania to Pittsburgh or followed the Potomac or the Yadkin rivers into the Shenandoah Valley and crossed the ridges of the Appalachians through several passes, of which Cumberland Gap was the most popular. In any case the settlers planned to reach the Ohio, or the Tennessee, or the Cumberland. The wanderings of Daniel Boone in eastern Kentucky in 1769–1771 mark the beginning of migration.[28] Constantly increasing streams of settlers followed him from the back country of Virginia and the Carolinas. They were quite different from the planters of Tidewater plantations. In their veins was a liberal infusion of Scottish and Irish blood. They were restless, adventurous, enter-

Mountaineer in coonskin cap and homespun jacket. (Courtesy of Arkansas History Commission.)

prising, and brave to a fault, the ideal people to win the first struggle with the wilderness.

Probably, the first American settlement in trans-Mississippi territory was Colonel George Morgan's colony at New Madrid in 1788.[29] Because Spain feared British attack on her far-flung empire, Spanish officials welcomed American immigrants and offered attractive land grants. The Americans, accustomed to loose government on the frontier, were willing to transfer their allegiance to the Spanish king in return for large, gratuitous tracts. Because French traders boasted widely of the lead mines and fertile soils and because the prairie regions to the north were considered less suitable for agriculture, American settlers who moved down the Ohio River were quick to take up lands along the eastern Ozark border. Slave owners settled in the Missouri River bottoms, where they found the soils and climate suited to hemp and tobacco. Settlers sought the cheaper trans-Mississippi lands because they could acquire them in smaller tracts. Also, the titles were more secure than in Kentucky, where titles were often contested.

From 1796 to 1803 the Spaniards were overwhelmed with petitions for land grants. The Spanish grants, as they still call them, form a mosaic of irregular tracts, some in

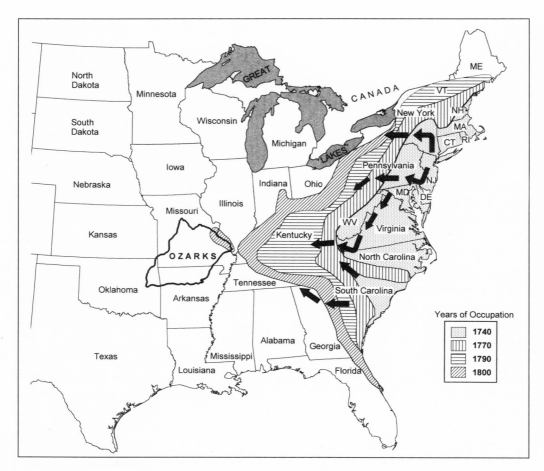

FIGURE 5-2. The settlement frontier and migration routes. Adapted from Henry Gannett, *Statistical Atlas of the United States, Based Upon Results of the Eleventh Census* (Washington, D.C.: U.S. Government Printing Office, 1898); and Russel L. Gerlach, *Immigrants in the Ozarks: A Study in Ethnic Geography* (Columbia: University of Missouri Press, 1976).

the mineral areas, but mainly in the Fredericktown soils, the Hagerstown loess, and the alluvial soils (fig. 5-3). Settlers occupied the better lands of the Mississippi and Missouri river borders and the St. Francois Mountains first. Speculators claimed large tracts in Arkansas, but settlement was sparse.

Many Spanish grants were fraudulent and were subjected to title investigations for many decades. The 1815 law that allowed settlers to relocate lands damaged or lost in the New Madrid earthquakes of 1811–1812 introduced many contested titles in the Missouri Valley, especially in the Boonslick area (Howard County).[30] Perhaps even more rapid settlement would have occurred if land titles had been more secure and the price of land ($1.25 per acre) had been lower.

The first immigrants were southerners, mainly of Scotch-Irish descent and of the yeoman farmer type, mainly poor, nonslaveholders. Most were from Tennessee, North Carolina, Virginia, Pennsylvania, and Kentucky. Most probably were of the restless frontier type cut in the mold of Daniel Boone and Kit Carson. A wealthier group, slave owners from the South, occupied the better river bottoms, where slaves cleared timber and planted fields for hemp, tobacco, and corn. A third type was the townsper-

son, who usually had some capital to invest in commerce or in manufacture of commodities needed on the frontier. Very often, members of this group became the leaders of communities and the organizers and initiators of things modern and progressive.

THE GEOGRAPHY OF EARLY AMERICAN SETTLEMENTS

The progression of settlement was, largely, as detached farms or small hamlets, along rivers and creeks. Uplands were usually settled later because of their generally poorer soils and problems in obtaining water. Very soon there was an inhabited strip along the Mississippi and inland to the lead mines. Another strip of settlement followed the Missouri River.

One of the first American settlements was at Cape Girardeau. Farmers cleared land on a creek south of the present site of the city in 1795, on bottomland along nearby Hubble Creek in 1797, and on the Whitewater River in 1796 (fig. 5-4).[31] By 1799 settlers began to occupy the upland soils, and these, derived from weathered limestones (Hagerstown soils), were well suited to corn and wheat, the staple pioneer crops. Mill sites were plentiful, soils were fertile, and settlements were linked to the outside world via the Mississippi River. Settlement progressed rapidly, and by 1821 the county had a population of 7,852.

Cape Girardeau, the river port and first established town in Cape Girardeau County, had three hundred inhabitants by 1811.[32] However, fraudulent land claims and uncertain land titles retarded its growth, and soon a newly founded town, Jackson, eclipsed the growth of Cape Girardeau. Jackson was in the midst of a fertile upland soil district. Jackson is still the county seat, though Cape Girardeau, after challenges to land titles were cleared, became the county's largest city.

Settlement throughout the eastern border progressed along with that in the Cape Girardeau district and in the same sequence; settlers selected well-drained bottomland first, but fertile upland soils were entered nearly at the same time. In Perry County, Pennsylvanians entered the Bois Brule Bottoms of the Mississippi in 1787, and other Americans occupied the bottoms along Brazeau and Apple creeks in 1797. A large group of Kentuckians entered the upland prairie of Perry County from 1801 to 1803.[33] Perryville, founded in 1822, became the primary settlement of the Barrens, a large upland prairie, and St. Mary's became the chief port for the district and for Mine La Motte.

Americans settled at Ste. Genevieve primarily to engage in business and commerce, particularly that connected with the lead mines to the west. However, even larger numbers of Americans went to the lead district in St. Francois and Washington counties. Moses Austin, an entrepreneur and metallurgist, obtained a Spanish grant for a square league of land at Mine à Breton (Potosi) in 1798, and in 1799 the Austin party established a settlement in a district where miners had discovered lead even earlier.[34] Families who accompanied Austin settled near the mines and on fertile farmlands in the Belleview Valley. Prospectors made several new discoveries of lead in St. Francois County at Mine à Joe (Desloge), Mine à Lanye, Mine à Maneto, and Mine à la Plate. These mines, all on the Big River, were the beginning of what was to become the fabulous Old Lead Belt, which produced lead and zinc ores until 1973. Many other mines were opened in Washington County. In 1819, Schoolcraft listed forty-five, of which twenty-five were close to Potosi.[35]

Only a few sections of the granite-rock St. Francois region were suitable for agriculture, and these were discovered and settled by 1810. The reputation of the soils in the limestone basins became widely known, and settlers occupied both the Belleview Valley and Murphy's (Farmington) by 1798.[36] The Arcadia Valley, St. Michael's (Fredericktown), and other pockets of alluvial and lime-

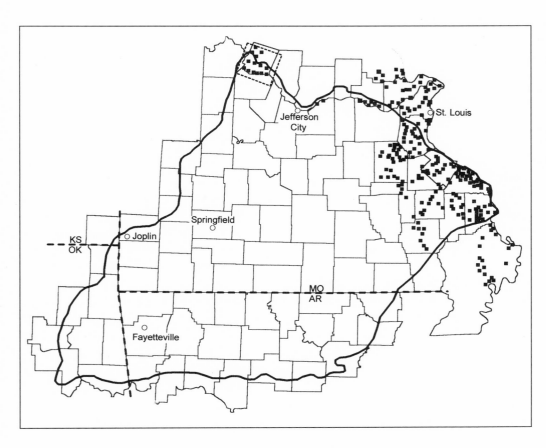

FIGURE 5-3. Spanish land grants in the Ozarks. Adapted from Russel L. Gerlach, *Immigrants in the Ozarks: A Study in Ethnic Geography* (Columbia: University of Missouri Press, 1976).

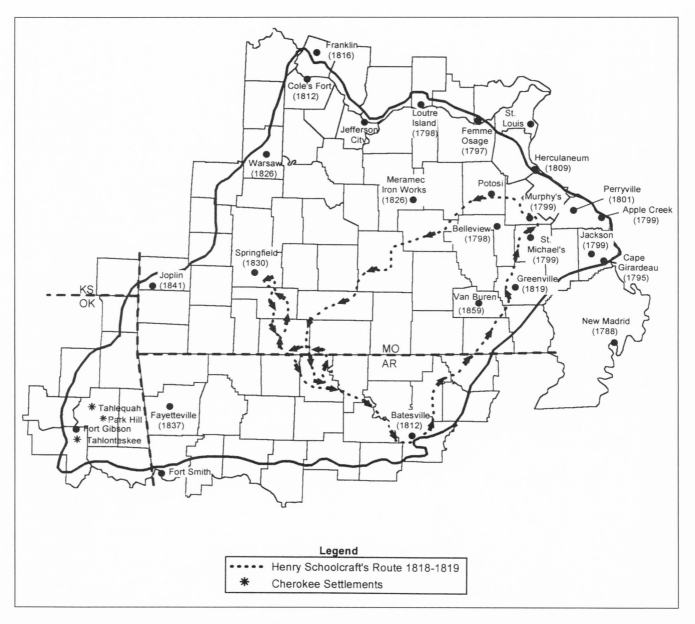

FIGURE 5-4. American settlements. Adapted from Milton D. Rafferty, *Historical Atlas of Missouri* (Norman: University of Oklahoma Press, 1981).

stone soils were settled at about the same time. Farms were widely scattered farther north on the Meramec and on Plattin and Joachim creeks.

An examination of topographic maps shows that settlers claimed the better soils and mineral lands with Spanish grants before the Louisiana Purchase. The Spanish grants spread across the Missouri Ozark counties of Cape Girardeau, Perry, Ste. Genevieve, St. Francois, Washington, Madison, and Jefferson.[37] These grants, usually rectangular but only occasionally oriented in cardinal directions, were especially numerous near Jackson, Perryville, Ste. Genevieve, Farmington (Murphy's), Potosi (Mine à Breton),

Fredericktown (St. Michael's), Greenville, and along the Joachim and Plattin valleys in Jefferson County (fig. 5-3).

The Missouri River was on the main route to the west and was nearly as accessible as the Ozarks' Mississippi River Border. This is born out by the fact that Americans had established several settlements before 1800. Kentuckians, notably Daniel Boone and his followers, settled in St. Charles County and southern Warren County only a few miles above the mouth of the Missouri. In 1797, Boone moved to the bottoms of Femme Osage Creek in Warren County, and settlements soon followed on Toque, La Charette, and Lost creeks.[38] Apparently they preferred the tributary valleys. The small valleys offered fertile soils and good springs and provided easy access to the Missouri River. They were also safe from the Missouri's devastating floods. The Loutre Island settlement (1798) in Montgomery County was established in the Missouri flood plain but on a higher tract of alluvium that remained dry during floods.

The Boonslick country in Cooper and Howard counties was settled first in 1810, although Boone reportedly boiled salt at the springs as early as 1807.[39] The region extended on both sides of the Missouri from the mouth of the Osage to the western Indian boundary. The well-respected Boone family name attracted early immigrants to the Boonslick, but it was the deep loess soils, good water, sufficient timber, and the salt springs that sustained the region's reputation, which spread quickly.[40] The earliest settlements were at Heath's Creek Salt Springs on the Lamine River in Cooper County and at New Franklin in Howard County. Although immigrants of diverse circumstances and origins came to the Boonslick country, the region was especially attractive to southern slave owners.

Boonville (Cole's Fort) was established in 1812 on the south bank of the Missouri River where it makes a rectangular bend to the north. In 1816 the town of Franklin was laid out, near the present site of New Franklin, across the river from Boonville. Franklin profited from the land office established there, while Boonville was a harbor and trading town for the western Ozarks.[41] Many other towns soon sprang up between Boonslick and the Loutre Island settlement. Bottomland could be purchased at one to five dollars an acre, and the influx of immigrants encouraged entrepreneurs to establish towns at strategic locations. Gasconade was founded at the mouth of the river of the same name as one of the proposed sites for the state capital. At the mouth of the Osage River, town promoters sold lots for Osage City; Newport occupied a similar position at the mouth of Boeuf Creek. The bustling examples of Pittsburgh, Cincinnati, and St. Louis inflamed nearly every settler with visions of wealth and business. Several towns (Pinckney, Thorntonsburg, Missouriton, Roche au Pierce, and Columbia) were set up on the flood plain at landings.[42] Malaria and floods took their toll, and only the bluff towns, Boonville and Jefferson City, survived to prosper.

Settlements along the Ozarks' southern river route progressed much slower. In 1804, Thomas Jefferson dispatched William Dunbar and Dr. George Hunter, both natives of Natchez, Mississippi, to explore the Red and Ouachita rivers and look for some hot springs that—as reported by the Indians—lay in the mountains near the headwaters of the Ouachita. The journal of the Dunbar-Hunter trip reveals that the region through which the travelers passed was practically uninhabited.[43] In 1806, Lieutenant James B. Wilkinson of the Zebulon M. Pike Expedition descended the Arkansas River from the Great Plains to the Mississippi in two canoes, but all he had to record concerned the topography, the forest, and the great herds of buffalo, deer, and other wild animals.[44] Thomas Nuttall, an Englishman trained in botany, geology, and geography, traveled down the Ohio and Mississippi rivers and ascended the Arkansas to a point a short distance beyond Fort Smith in 1819 and 1820.[45] He described New Madrid as a dying French hamlet after the great earthquakes of 1811 and 1812, Arkansas Post was a settlement of thirty or forty houses scattered along almost three miles, and widely scattered settlements clung to the riverbank as far upriver as the garrison at Fort Smith. A spot where the Southwest trail from St. Louis crossed the Arkansas was known as "Mr. Hogans, or the settlement of the Little Rock." Cadron, a few miles from Interstate 40 west of Conway, was the third of the earliest settlements in the Arkansas Valley. By the time of Nuttall's visit, Arkansas lands had caught the attention of speculators, notably William Russell of St. Louis, who had claimed large Spanish grants and became the dean of large-scale speculators.[46]

Settlement of the Springfield Plain lagged behind that of the eastern and northern Ozark borders. Its few navigable streams, the Osage, White, and Neosho, were far from the main routes of commerce, sometimes dangerous and only seasonally navigable. The rugged hills of the interior discouraged overland travel, and the vast mineral wealth of the Joplin area was not discovered until later.

The earliest white settlement of record was at Delaware Town, eight miles southwest of Springfield, in Christian County, Missouri, where Wilson's Creek joins the James River. A party of twenty-four settlers, led by John P. Pettijohn, loaded their possessions in a keelboat and followed a circuitous route from their homes on the Muskingum River in Ohio: down the Ohio, south on the Mississippi, then up the Arkansas and White rivers. After stopping for two years near the mouth of the North Fork, Pettijohn and other members of the party continued up the White and James rivers to the mouth of Wilson's Creek in 1822.[47] Pettijohn claimed a tract of land on the upper Finley River that included a large spring (Patterson Spring), but sold it to John Patterson that same year. The first settlers lost their new properties within a few months when their claims were invalidated because a band of five hundred Delaware Indians had arrived to occupy their newly granted reservation on the James River.[48] In spite of the uncertainty of land titles, the region (southwest

Missouri) had already gained an excellent reputation for game and was known in Tennessee as the Country of the Six Bulls (corrupted from *boils,* or springs). It was from Tennessee that most of the early immigrants came.

The Osage River had become a navigation route by 1830, and Warsaw became a major jumping-off place for immigrants and, later, for wagoners and traders. In spring and fall, keelboats could reach Osceola. Nevertheless, Warsaw was the main port on the river and second in importance only to Springfield among towns in southwest Missouri. Overland roads leading into the Ozarks left the Missouri River at Boonville and Jefferson City.

Other overland routes from the Mississippi River crossed the interior Ozarks via upland divides. The most important was the ridge trail from St. Louis by way of Rolla, Lebanon, Marshfield, Springfield, Mount Vernon, Neosho, Bentonville, and Fayetteville, a route later followed closely by the Frisco (St. Louis-San Francisco Railroad), U.S. Highway 66, and most recently by Interstate 44. A branch of this road, beginning at Ste. Genevieve and passing through Caledonia and Steelville, joined the main trail near St. James.

The pioneers were preponderantly from Tennessee, followed by Kentucky, because of easier access from these states. They were, largely, of the same type as those who settled the Mississippi and Missouri river borders, but they were mountain people who owned few slaves. They followed the usual practice in selecting sites for homes; the first to enter the region chose bottomlands near springs and close to timber. They settled the fertile upland prairies next, and succeeding immigrants settled less choice tracts.

The settlement of Springfield was typical. John Polk Campbell, a Tennessean, visited the site in 1829, found good soils in the Kickapoo Prairie and in the small bottoms along Jordan Creek (a tributary of Wilson's Creek) and abundant good water issuing from springs along the creek bank. He returned the following year with his family and brother-in-law, Joseph Miller. They built a cabin close by a sinkhole spring, or "natural well," under the north-facing valley slope.[49] Not only was Campbell the first settler in Springfield, but he was also the first real-estate promoter and developer, building, with the help of Miller's slaves, "no less than thirteen cabins in one year, turning himself and family out of one of them after another, that some newly arrived family should have shelter."[50]

Isolation and poverty of resources in the interior Ozarks were the principle reasons for the slow progress of settlement there. As noted earlier, by 1810 settlement had penetrated nearly every fertile valley in the St. Francois Mountains to the margins of the Courtois Hills. This region of scanty resources served as a barrier that deflected immigration north and south. Only after the border regions of the Ozarks were well settled did immigration begin to fill in the interior.

In much of the interior the valleys were narrow and offered fewer possibilities for agriculture. Therefore, settlement was slow in the Courtois and Osage-Gasconade hills and longest delayed in the wilderness on the Arkansas-Missouri border and the Boston Mountains. Many who came were unable or unwilling to meet the competition of life in more progressive regions.[51] Except for minerals and timber, the central Ozarks offered few prizes for the ambitious. Being cut off from the rest of the state, people developed slight interest in outside affairs. Only in more recent years, as schools have improved and radio and television have become nearly universal, have residents grown interested in the history and culture of the region.

The vanguard pioneers established scattered settlements in the interior in the 1820s. Small sawmill settlements, undoubtedly temporary, were mentioned by Schoolcraft on the upper Gasconade in 1818. Gunpowder makers took saltpeter from caves in the same area at about the same time. In 1825, Samuel Massey opened the Maramec ore bank and in 1829 the Maramec Iron Works. By 1835 fifty families lived in the settlement. Later, iron makers built other furnaces in Crawford and Dent counties.

From 1817 to 1825, land bounties granted to soldiers of the Revolutionary War and the War of 1812 stimulated population growth in the Ozarks. Surveyors began charting the preemption lands in 1819, ushering in an era of speculation with the Preemption Act of 1820. However, because of the availability of superior lands in other districts, these laws had little influence on land purchases in the interior Ozarks.

Agricultural settlement went first to the larger and more accessible valleys and then to progressively smaller and more isolated streams. Schoolcraft reported rapid settlement was underway in the valleys of the Spring, Eleven Point, Current, and St. Francis rivers when, in 1819, he followed the Southwest Trail north from Poke Bayou (Batesville).[52] By 1825 there were settlements in Wayne County on the St. Francis River, in Ripley County on the Current River, in Oregon County on the Eleven Point River, and along the Osage, Gasconade, and Meramec rivers on the north slope of the Ozark Dome.

In Arkansas, settlement progressed in the established manner: from the larger river valleys to smaller tributaries and finally to upland prairies or, in the Boston Mountains, to benches and upland flats. Missourian John Reed settled Batesville about 1812.[53] He built a house at the mouth of Poke Bayou, where a fork of the Southwest Trail crossed the White River. A ferry was put into use there as early as

1818, and a land office was established about the same time. Major Jacob Wolf established a trading post at the mouth of the North Fork of the White River in 1810 when he became the agent for the Arkansas Cherokees.[54] Shortly afterward, Jacob Mooney of McMinnville, Tennessee, established a community at Wildcat Shoals in Baxter County. Settlement spread up to the White River and its tributaries so that by 1818, when Schoolcraft visited the White River country, settlers had built cabins at the mouth of Beaver Creek in Taney County, Missouri.[55]

The Osage Indians relinquished most of their land north of the Arkansas River, including nearly all of the Boston Mountains in the Treaty of Fort Clark (Fort Osage) on November 10, 1808. This area was then legally open to white settlers, but because of the abundance of land in more accessible areas, few took advantage of the opportunity to acquire tracts in the Boston Mountains. Between 1817 and 1828, the government gave Cherokee Indians land in northern Arkansas in exchange for their property in the East. Since only a few whites were living in the Boston Mountains, this had little effect on settlement.

The first Americans in the Boston Mountains came by way of the Arkansas River and its larger tributaries: the White, Neosho, Illinois, and Little Red rivers. Eight families from North Carolina set up housekeeping on the south side of the Arkansas River at Crystal Hill in 1806. This settlement was so isolated that when Major George Gibson of the U.S. Army stopped there in 1815, he learned that the people had not heard of the War of 1812. Kentuckians immigrated to the vicinity of Batesville about 1812. The Oil Trough (Trove) Bottoms on the White River below Batesville were regarded as prime land, and the fertility of the soils reportedly rivaled that of the soils in the American Bottoms on the Mississippi River below St. Louis.[56]

Data on the early residents of Newton County, Arkansas, show that the initial settlement of the county was fairly complete by 1860. Settlers had taken most of the good land in the previous three decades following the Cherokee Treaty of 1828. They purchased most of the best land in tracts of forty acres for $1.25 per acre. Only a few settlers claimed land under military warrant. Very little good land was left at the time Congress passed the Homestead Act in 1862. The leading states of birth of heads of families in the county were Tennessee with 126, North Carolina 48, Kentucky 21, and South Carolina 13.[57] Between 1851 and 1860 Newton County received 111 new arrivals, of which 39 were from Missouri and 32 were from Tennessee.[58] Missouri and Tennessee continued to provide half the arrivals in the Arkansas Ozarks as late as 1880.[59]

Settlers considered the minimum price of $1.25 an acre for public lands too high for uplands in the interior.[60] The Graduation Act of 1854 stimulated land entries, however, and by 1858, 1,890,000 acres of Missouri Ozark land had sold, of which 1,140,304 brought 12.5 cents per acre and 227,940,000 acres brought 25 cents an acre.[61] Speculators purchased much of the land, so the increase in population was not proportionate to the amount of land sold. Geographic factors were very important in the disposal of the public domain. Settlers took the best lands first, of course, and by 1867 only 1,800,000 of Missouri's 41,000,000 acres remained unclaimed.[62] All of the land granted to the University of Missouri under the Morrill Act of 1862 was in the Ozarks. What remained north of the Missouri River had by that time been picked over so much that only small tracts remained.

The region suffered heavily during the Civil War because the settlements were weak and isolated and the wild, broken hills afforded protection for lawless bands. Many counties on the Missouri-Arkansas boundary suffered substantial decreases in population during these troubled years.

Professor Harbert L. Clendenen, in his study of the southern Courtois Hills, has shown that kinship strongly shaped the morphology of settlement in the interior districts.[63] The Chilton family of Shannon and Carter counties in the southern Courtois Hills of Missouri serves as an example. Thomas Boggs Chilton, the son of a Welsh immigrant, was born in Maryland in 1782 and eventually immigrated to eastern Tennessee, where he married. In 1816 he moved his family from Rhea County to New Madrid in southeast Missouri. Two years later the family moved to the mouth of Henpeck Creek on the Current River in what later became Carter County. Later, Thomas C. Chilton, a cousin, moved from Knox County, Tennessee, to a point on the Current River two miles below the Jacks Fork. A year later, in 1837, his brother, Truman Chilton, joined him, having immigrated from Boone County, Tennessee. From the same county in 1814 came Thomas T. Chilton, son of Truman Chilton, to settle near the original site of Eminence on the Jacks Fork. Many other Chiltons immigrated to the southern Courtois Hills, mainly from counties on the upper Tennessee River.[64]

Regarding site selection and manner of placing fields and houses, the Chilton farmsteads, on slip-off slopes on the Jacks Fork below the mouth of Storys Creek, on the Current River below Blair Creek, and near the mouth of Big Shawnee Creek, are no different from those of contemporary and later immigrants.[65] Very often an entire creek valley or hollow would be taken up by an extended family. Surname sequences in the manuscript census of Reynolds County affirm that kinship was important in the settlement process. The surname of heads of households in one sequence reads: Satterfield, Martin, Parker, Parker, Asher, Satterfield, Parker, Bay, Satterfield, Robinnet, Asher. Another series of family names from the Shannon County manuscript census for a tributary valley reveals this was commonplace: Crabtree, Crabtree, Lewis, Summers, Summers, Summers, Summers, Lewis, McDonald, Lewis.[66]

THE CHEROKEES

The history of the settlement of the Oklahoma Ozarks is largely the story of the removal of the Cherokees from the southern Appalachians to the southwestern Ozarks. It was part of a larger story of Indian removal as the Five Civilized Tribes—Cherokees, Chickasaws, Choctaws, Creeks, Seminoles—moved from their ancestral homes in the southern Appalachian uplands to make room for white

John Ross, principal chief of the Cherokees at the time of removal to Oklahoma. (Courtesy of Oklahoma Historical Society.)

settlers. The vanguard of these tribes, six or seven thousand Choctaws and Chickasaws from northern Mississippi and West Tennessee, moved up the Arkansas Valley in 1832 to settle south of the Arkansas in what is now Oklahoma.[67] These Indians had been stricken with cholera and had to be driven almost like sheep.

The real tragedy, however, involved the removal of the Eastern Cherokees, who occupied a large area in southeast Tennessee, Alabama, western North Carolina, and northwest Georgia. By the 1820s, most Cherokees were living on separate farms rather than in villages as they had in 1776 when they reportedly lived mainly in towns and villages.[68] They numbered more than 16,500 by official count in 1835. Many of them lived as prosperous farmers in houses that often had two stories and were well furnished. They were in the happy possession not only of devoted missionaries but a written language, with books and journals printed in it since 1828. In 1829 the Cherokees owned some 22,000 cattle, 1,300 slaves, 2,000 spinning wheels, 700 looms, 31 gristmills, 10 sawmills, 8 cotton gins, and 18 schools.[69] They had never recognized as full members of their tribe the three thousand Cherokees who went west to Arkansas in 1818, under the terms of Andrew Jackson's 1817 treaty. They had foreseen, rigidly, that the early removal was but part of a deep-laid government plan to force all Indians from the country.

The discovery of gold near Dahlonega, Georgia, brought on a rapid series of events that led to Cherokee removal. The state of Georgia now declared, despite the Cherokee Treaty of 1817, that it had the right to seize all Cherokee lands and property.[70] Since no Cherokee was accepted as a witness in court, this was the beginning of the end. A huge rift appeared in the Cherokee's ranks as the force of armed mobs drove them from their homes. One faction favored selling the tribes' Georgia lands to the state and moving to Indian Territory, where the Arkansas Cherokees had preceded them by 1828. This was the compromise group led by John Ridge, the best orator in the tribe, and Elias Boudinot, said to be the most learned and intelligent of the Cherokees. John Ross, who lived where Chattanooga stands today, opposed the removal plan.[71] He insisted that the Cherokee's lands, for which the United States was ready to pay five million dollars, were worth at least twenty million.[72] All this was in keeping with Ross's character; he was only one-eighth Indian, the son of a Scottish trader and a quarter-blood Cherokee woman.

Through an emissary who was not at all averse to bribery, the government induced about five hundred members of the tribe to assemble, and on December 29, 1835, they signed a treaty in which they sold all their lands for the sum originally proposed and agreed to go

Rose cottage, home of Chief John Ross, at Park Hill near Tahlequah, Oklahoma. (Courtesy of Oklahoma Historical Society.)

west. The first group to leave consisted of about 600 comfortably fixed members of the Treaty Party. Major Ridge, father of John Ridge and the most politically powerful of the treaty signers, departed March 3, 1837, with his family, eighteen slaves, and 466 other Cherokees, half of them children. They traveled by flatboat down the Tennessee River from Ross's Landing to the Mississippi and then traveled up the Arkansas River to Fort Smith, arriving there on March 27. Dr. John S. Young, who took charge of the movement, ordered about 150 bushels of cornmeal, 78 barrels of flour, and 12,000 pounds of bacon stowed on the boats to feed the travelers along the way.[73] The second party of approximately 365 Cherokees departed the Cherokee Agency near Calhoun, Tennessee, on October 14, 1837, and took the overland route through Kentucky, Illinois, and Missouri. They reached their western destination around December 30 of that year, "saddened by sickness and the deaths of fifteen of their number—eleven of whom were children."[74]

The Ridge Party arrived in time to see the bottomlands bright with redbud blossoms that ranged in color from pink to purple. Dogwood bloomed in gleaming white among the oaks, which, in late bud, were just taking on a greenish hue. Ridge settled at the mouth of Honey Creek, which rises in Arkansas, flows for a brief stretch through the corner of Missouri, and turns in Oklahoma at Southwest City before it flows into the Neosho, or Grand

River. Ridge put his slaves to work, bought stock and farming equipment, and soon had the beginnings of a splendid farm.

The movement of the Ridge Party contrasts sharply with that of the main body of Cherokees, under the supervision of John Ross, over the Trail of Tears.[75] The name for the trek was applied to the tragic removal of all the Five Civilized Tribes, but the generic terminology for the trek—*nuna dat suhn' yi*—"the trail where they cried," came from the Cherokee language.[76] When the fifteen thousand remaining Cherokees refused to leave their homes, the government called in the U.S. Army, and in the winter of 1837 and 1838 federal troops rounded up all but a few hundred, who had retreated into the inaccessible fastness of the Great Smokies, and put them into what they would today call concentration camps along the Tennessee River.[77] By this time even John Ross realized that nothing further could be done and agreed to depart, if it could be done without further interference by the army. The Cherokees were unable to leave until the end of the very hot, very dry summer of 1838. They were to be conducted to their new lands in thirteen parties of about a thousand each. They left in wagons, or on horseback, or on foot, taking a winding route by way of Nashville, across western Kentucky and through Illinois to cross the Mississippi at Cape Girardeau. There they took several routes across northern Arkansas and southern Missouri to

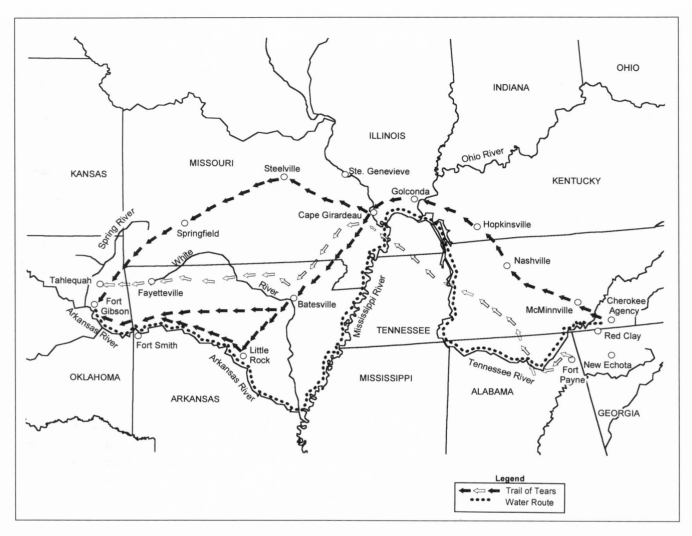

FIGURE 5-5. Cherokee migration routes and the Trail of Tears, 1838–1839. Adapted from "Map of the Trail of Tears." Danny Farrow and Rose City Net, 2000, Cape Girardeau, Missouri, http://www.rosecity.net/tears/trail/map.html (February 12, 2000).

their destination in northeast Oklahoma. The main trail crossed the Mississippi River at Cape Girardeau, Missouri, then threaded its way through Jackson, Farmington, Potosi, Rolla, and Lebanon to Springfield, where they often purchased supplies; then the trail continued southwest through Aurora, Monett, and present-day Southwest City.[78] Some of the people entered Cherokee country via Rogers, Springdale, Fayetteville, and Prairie Grove, Arkansas. This was the Trail of Tears, witnessed by a few white travelers who marveled at the Indians stoicism and discipline (fig. 5-5). The journey by an estimated eighteen thousand Cherokees cost about four thousand lives in all and was not completed until March 1839.[79] Along the way the Cherokees buried several renowned old chiefs, innumerable infants, and Ross's own Cherokee wife, Quatie, who sickened and died aboard the steamboat that carried her and her husband. They buried her at Little Rock.

When they arrived in Indian Territory, members of the Treaty Party accepted the government of the Western Cherokees as their own.[80] The Cherokees still had no written constitution and only a few written laws. Twice a year the Old Settlers met in council at Tahlonteskee, their capital, where in a small council house, they elected their chief and other national officers. The coming of the Ross faction, later known as Late Immigrants (or Late Arrivals), created an integration problem. Under their persuasion the capital was moved to Tahlequah in 1839, and since they outnumbered the Old Settlers and the Treaty Party by more than two to one, their leaders soon gained control of the government. On June 22, 1839, three parties of the Late Immigrants, bent on revenge on leaders of the Treaty Party, murdered John Ridge, Elias Boudinot, and Major Ridge. This led to reprisals and counter reprisals, factional and family feuds, and bitter political struggles among the Cherokees for decades.[81]

The Trail of Tears, a painting by E. James. (Courtesy of Oklahoma Historical Society.)

The migration of the Cherokees to the Oklahoma Ozarks was part of the final chapter of the primary phase of immigration. The settlement of the Ozarks, which had begun with the eighteenth-century French settlements, was complete by 1850. Density maps (fig. 5-6) show that the population moved inward from the region's major rivers: the Mississippi, the Missouri, and the Arkansas. The areas in St. Francois and Washington counties in Missouri were settled early, as were the more favorable agricultural lands. The heaviest early settlement occurred in the more accessible places; this was particularly true of areas near the land offices at St. Louis, Frankfort, and Springfield in Missouri and around Batesville and Fayetteville in Arkansas. It is probably not too much to say that settlement followed the surveyor's chain and compass. Some early surveyors became wealthy by purchasing the best lands for resale to speculators.[82] As surveyors charted new lands and information concerning them became available, settlers were encouraged to spread outward from the heavily populated sections into the remote interior.

CHARACTER OF THE IMMIGRANTS

It has been noted that most of the American immigrants were of Scotch-Irish stock. They were experienced frontier people; independent, resourceful, strong, familiar with frontier inconveniences, possessed of an amazing knowledge of ways to wrest a living from the forest, and accustomed to facing the hardships of arduous travel or starvation or the dangers of Indian raids. The Scotch-Irish were known as Ulstermen, Presbyterian Irish, or, before 1812, when the first large groups of Irish Catholics began

to arrive in America, simply the Irish. After large numbers of Irish Catholics arrived, it was necessary to distinguish between the two groups, so the immigrants from northern Ireland were known as Scottish-Irish.[83]

Better people to subdue a frontier could not have been recruited. They were descended from Lowland Scots who immigrated to Ulster Plantation in northern Ireland in the early years of the seventeenth century at the time when the first Virginia plantations were being established. The Scots

Murrell Mansion at Park Hill near Tahlequah, Oklahoma, was built by George Murrell, white trader and supporter of John Ross. Many of the house's furnishings were imported from France. (Courtesy of Oklahoma Historical Society.)

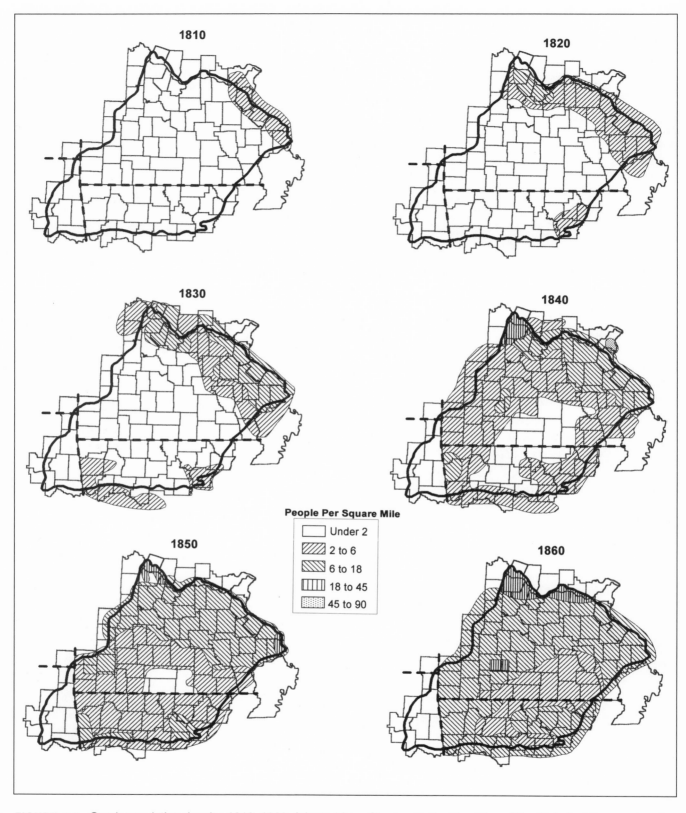

FIGURE 5-6. Ozark population density, 1810–1860. Adapted from Charles O. Paullin, *Atlas of the Historical Geography of the U.S.* (Washington, D.C.: Carnegie Institute of Washington, 1932).

who flocked into Ulster carried with them long experience in dealing with predatory Celtic clans in north Scotland. The Lowlanders were accustomed to regarding the clans as raiders, pillagers, cattle thieves, and murderers. Hardened by perpetual contact with barbarism, the Lowland Scots had no scruples about making merciless reprisals. The people were hard; the law was hard.

At the time the Scots immigrated to Ulster, Ireland was a wilderness of forests, bogs, and peat barrens inhabited by Irish clans whom the Scots called the Irishes. The Scots settled in towns, around castles, and made use of a small amount of adjacent land; the Irish stayed in the back country. The guerrilla war that ensued between these two hardy groups has continued to the present, with only brief times of relative peace between major conflicts. A proverb read, "The Irish will never be tamed while the leaves are on the trees," meaning that winter was the only season in which they could pursue them in the woods.[84] A hostile population surrounded the settlers, with almost daily risks from raiders and in almost constant alarm of a general uprising. Long familiarity with the raiding Highland Scots enabled the Scotch-Irish to cope with the Irishes, who wandered with their cattle all the summer in the hill country and all the winter in the woods. The Scotch-Irish held their ground, throve, and spread, gradually giving Ulster a Scottish character.

A people accustomed to pacification of wild Irish clans and inured to the hardship of the Irish wilderness were natural-born frontier persons, and so they were when they emigrated to North America. From Nova Scotia to the West Indies, the Scotch-Irish were among the frontier vanguard. They became the chief frontier settlers of Maine, New Hampshire, and Massachusetts; in the South they moved from the Tidewater settlements into the Piedmont; and from their main base in Pennsylvania and Maryland they crowded into the western counties of Pennsylvania along Braddock's Road and along the major river routes. They engulfed the Quaker settlements and crowded south down the Great Valley into western Virginia and eastern Tennessee. Following the trail cut by Daniel Boone via the Cumberland Gap, the Scotch-Irish entered middle Tennessee and the Bluegrass region of Kentucky. A flood of Scotch-Irish descended on the new states in trans-Appalachia as additional routes through the Appalachian Mountains were perfected.

The Scotch-Irish attained wide acclaim as Indian fighters; accusations that they were cruel to the Indians go back to the beginnings of Scotch-Irish settlement. The Scotch-Irish settlers were descended from a people familiar with hostile neighbors, and they were accustomed to rendering cruel punishment in kind. When scalps were taken by

Fort Gibson military garrison in the Oklahoma Ozarks. Among its distinguished visitors and officers were Robert E. Lee, Jefferson Davis, Sam Houston, Zachary Taylor, George Catlin, and Washington Irving. (Courtesy of Oklahoma Historical Society.)

Indians, the frontiersman would retaliate by taking Indian scalps; in Massachusetts a bounty of one hundred pounds sterling was placed on scalps.[85] During the Indian Wars, the trans-Appalachian region became a no man's land beset by general guerrilla warfare. The Scotch-Irish, by historic tradition and temperament, were suited to the conflict.

Gerlach's study of the Scotch-Irish in the Ozarks shows that they found the rugged hill districts to fit their lifestyle.[86] They tended to settle in the shut-in valleys in the St. Francois Mountains, in the Courtois Hills region along the tributaries of the Black, Current, Eleven Point, and Meramec rivers, in the rugged country in the Osage-Gasconade hills, in the wilds of the White River Hills, and in the remote Boston Mountains. Scotch-Irish settlers also spread throughout the Ozarks, but the rugged hill districts became their core areas (fig. 2-3).

Much of the information concerning the Scotch-Irish immigrants to the Ozarks comes from family diaries and a few early histories. The detailed reports found in the manuscript census are an additional source. Lynn Morrow's study of the manuscript census of 1870 for Richwoods Township in Miller County, Missouri, provides an over-

Ozark pioneer couple. (Courtesy of Arkansas History Commission.)

view of the population at the end of the primary phase of settlement.[87] Demographically, the Ozarks frontier had many similarities with today's third-world countries. There were 2,283 people in the township, most of them under forty years of age. In fact, only one person in eight (12.5 percent) was over the age of forty, and 63 percent of the population was twenty years old or younger. Only two octogenarians lived in the township. Three-fourths of the population was literate, but among the people more than thirty years of age the illiteracy rate increased to more than 30 percent. The average household had 5.3 persons, but the household ranged in size from one person to thirteen. Three-fourths of the residents had migrated from Tennessee and Kentucky or from other parts of Missouri, but nineteen states provided immigrants. There were very few foreign immigrants: three from England, one from Ireland, and one from Russia.

Most of the people were farmers. The occupation breakdown yields 199 farmers, 17 farm laborers, 15 domestic servants, 12 widow ladies, 11 housekeepers, 6 teachers, 3 blacksmiths, 3 physicians, 2 dry-goods merchants, 2 store workers, 2 sawyers, and 1 each of the following: shoemaker, harness maker, retired farmer, miller, and minister of the Gospel. There was little wealth aside from the land; more than 30 percent of the population listed between six hundred and one thousand dollars as the value of their estate, and only seven residents had land holdings assessed at more than two thousand dollars. As for personal property, the largest number of people had between three and four hundred dollars' worth, so that the average settler was worth perhaps one thousand dollars to fifteen hundred dollars in real and personal property.

At the close of the primary phase of immigration, then, the Ozarks was inhabited by a hardy breed of Scotch-Irish immigrants who were engaged mainly in subsistence farming. Among them were a few artificers, professional persons, and preachers. They were poor but nearly self-sufficient and skilled at living under isolated conditions.

NEGRO POPULATION

The Negro population of the Ozarks has never been large, but the largest number of Negroes entered the region during the primary phase of settlement. In fact, the French in the eighteenth century brought Negroes to the Ozarks as slaves. Probably Jesuit missionaries were the first owners of black slaves in the Illinois country.[88] The missionaries used the slaves primarily as agricultural laborers and domestic servants. Philip Renault purchased slaves in Santo Domingo in 1719 to provide laborers for the mines to be opened in the eastern Ozarks.[89] The French at Ste. Genevieve owned slaves to do the rugged work connected with tilling fields and digging lead in the mining districts. The 1773 census of Ste. Genevieve reported 404 whites and 287 slaves.[90] In 1819, Nuttall expressed surprise that a small French settlement at Arkansas Post in the Arkansas Valley was not self-sufficient in foodstuffs, since the residents owned slaves.[91]

The American settlers brought their slaves with them, so the Negro population of the Ozarks, in nearly every section, was contemporary with the first white settlements. The wealthier planters who possessed slaves also could afford the most fertile and most accessible lands; consequently slaves were not numerous in the interior sections of the Ozarks. The largest numbers were found in the border districts, the Missouri Valley, the mineral area in St. Francois and Washington counties, and in the Arkansas Valley. By 1860, when the Negro population reached its zenith, Negroes accounted for slightly more than 10 percent of the population in these counties. Only a few interior areas were fertile enough or sufficiently well settled to attract slave owners.[92] The most notable areas were in Greene County, Missouri, and in Washington and Benton counties in Arkansas. Then, too, the Cherokees who settled the Oklahoma Ozarks owned several hundred slaves.

A few white slave owners settled in the mountain counties with the first wave of settlement. Usually these settlers could afford to own only a few slaves, often only one or two. A few free blacks lived in the Ozarks, and most counties with slaves also reported free blacks. A few free blacks migrated to the Ozarks with the first wave of white settlers, where, dressed in homespun clothing, deerskin moccasins, and coonskin hats and possessing firearms, they lived the same lifestyle as their white counterparts. Silas Claiborne Turnbo, a nineteenth-century chronicler of frontier life in the Arkansas and Missouri Ozarks, reported that David Hall, a "colored man," from North Carolina, settled in 1819 on the White River seven miles below the mouth of the Little North Fork.[93] Hall, a large burly man, was a mulatto and his wife, Sarah, was "near white." They lived in a log cabin, and Hall made a living for his family by selling deer hides and making whiskey in the first still to appear in that country.[94] Hall's brothers also settled nearby so that in all six Hall families were living along the White River. Other free blacks listed in the Marion County tax books before the Civil War included Henly Black, Rachel Bowman, Clarissa Burns, John Dickson, John Turner, Peter Calder, Charles Moore, Charles Madewell, Solomon Madewell, Goodman Madewell, James Madewell, Willis Johnson, and Frances Nesbet.[95] In Little North Fork Township, where David Hall and his sons lived, blacks accounted for one-third of the population. The township included 178 whites, 19 slaves, and 80 free black people.[96]

Many free blacks in Arkansas left when the General Assembly passed a law providing that no free Negro or mulatto could immigrate to the state after March 1, 1843.[97] Still more blacks left when the Arkansas General Assembly in 1859 passed a law titled, "An Act to Remove the Free Negroes and Mulattoes from the State."[98] Although the law was never enforced, and was repealed in 1863, many free blacks left the state in fear of being sold into slavery. In 1840 the free black population was concentrated in Marion County with a total of 129 of the total of 162 free blacks in northern Arkansas. The Marion County free black population fell from 129 to 18 between 1840 and 1850. By 1860, the number of free black persons in the county dwindled to 8, all of them with a surname of Madewell.[99] On the other hand, for reasons not readily apparent, the free black population in Washington County, Arkansas, increased from 14 to 47 between 1840 and 1850.[100]

Black population decreased dramatically in the Ozarks between 1860 and 1870, the decade of the Civil War. Some counties with several hundred black people lost more than half of them. In Washington County, Arkansas, the black population declined from 1,540 to 674, but the black population of Greene County, Missouri, increased from 1,677 to 2,156 during the same time span.[101] Racial tensions brought on by the war may have caused the out-migration, or it may have been the lack of economic opportunity in counties where rural population accounted for more than 90 percent of the total.[102] The safety provided by the Union garrison in Springfield may have attracted blacks from war-torn rural areas, just as it attracted whites.

Some older blacks remained rooted to their places of birth and home places. This was especially true where

Union forces offered protection in some of the larger towns. Springfield's black population increased through the latter decades of the nineteenth century as emancipated blacks sought out new places to settle outside the old slavery heartland in the South. The black exodus spread mainly into the North, the border states, but some black communities were founded as far west as Nicodemus, Kansas, and even to Logan County near the Colorado border.[103] The Freedmen's Bureau established a post in Springfield to help resettle and provide education and assistance for the many black immigrants of Greene County and surrounding counties.[104] The black colony near Hartville in Wright County, Missouri, was established during the black exodus of the 1870s. Gradually the settlement died away, but descendants of the Wright County black colony still own land in the area and continue to maintain two black cemeteries.[105]

Discerning slaveholders' feelings toward their bondsmen is difficult. Gordon Morgan, in his study, *Black Hillbillies in the Arkansas Ozarks,* speculates that many blacks were personal slaves and the social relationship between the slaves and their owners may have been so close that neither preferred to break it when the white pioneers ventured into the Arkansas highlands. This relationship may have accounted for the lower incidence of runaways in Arkansas's northern counties though there was little law enforcement there.[106] Wills, tax records, and other documents, however, showed that Negroes were considered as property.[107] From a physical standpoint, slaves probably received reasonably good treatment. The family of George Washington Carver, the noted botanist, were slaves on a farm close to Diamond, Missouri. Apparently, the owners treated them relatively well.[108]

Slave owners who hired out their slaves used hiring contracts that stipulated how the renter was to maintain the slaves. Samuel Massey, superintendent of the Maramec Iron Works near present-day St. James, Missouri, regularly leased or owned fifteen to twenty-five slaves from 1828 until the Civil War. They were assigned the heaviest and dirtiest work connected with digging and hauling the ore. Most of the hired Negroes at the ironworks belonged to masters living in counties bordering the Missouri River. The standard price was $100 per year and maintenance for good unskilled hands, $120 and up for skilled hands, and $25 to $50 for women and young people who worked as domestic servants in the boardinghouse.[109] The contracts protected both sides with legal provisions. If a slave ran away or died, the ironworks paid only for the time worked. The owner could collect damages if a slave were injured or died because of neglect or cruelty.

Occasionally, probably rarely, slave owners treated slaves almost like members of the family. Jacob Mooney, one of the first settlers in Baxter County, Arkansas, brought in several "Lungeons," presumably the mixed blood people—Negro, Cherokee, and white—known as Melungeons in the southern Appalachians.[110] Mooney was ostracized for living with these "foreigners." Reportedly, he permitted his men to marry Quapaw women who lived in the area.[111] His neighbors never forgave his actions; after he and his men had died and the cemetery was fenced, Mooney's grave and the graves of the mixed bloods who lived with him were left outside.

Some racial intermixing was accepted in rural areas. Gordon Morgan tells of an interview with a seventy-nine-year-old mountain mulatto woman who told him that her father was a white man whose parents died when he was very young. He lived with a black family and shared the experiences of black life. When he was old enough to get married and start his own family, he married a slave woman and raised eleven children by her in a mountain community. This couple and their family lived without molestation, encountering only the problem of mountain poverty common to most of the people in the northwestern Arkansas area.[112]

The New South phase in Ozarks history was a time of declining Negro population. The withdrawal of the Federal troops after the war signaled the return to southern home rule and reenactment of the policies of legal, social, and economic mistreatment of black people.[113] Slavery had been abolished; possessing no land or property, and faced with little opportunity for employment, many Negroes moved to cities in the North. The living conditions for blacks in the Ozarks were the same as throughout the South, except there were fewer social ties to cause them to remain in their home areas. In the rural areas the decline in Negro population occurred mainly as slow attrition; as young Negroes moved away, and as their grandparents died, many Ozark counties became pure white. Morgan, in his study of black hill people, notes that towns that formerly had black residents, but through emigration had become all white, gradually became opposed to blacks and other nonwhite people.[114] The blacks called these places "Gray Towns."[115]

There were troubled times for Negroes after the Civil War. One lynching occurred in Springfield in 1859 before the war, and others followed in 1871 and 1906. All were for alleged rapes. The 1906 lynching of three young Negroes took place in the public square and received publicity throughout the Ozarks. The *Springfield Republican* carried seven-column headings on its front page:

THREE NEGROES LYNCHED BY MAD MOB—INFURIATED MOB OF WHITES TAKE AN ALLEGED MURDERER AND THE ASSAILANTS OF A BOLIVAR GIRL FROM THE COUNTY JAIL AND STRING THEM UP TO THE ELECTRIC LIGHT TOWER IN THE PUBLIC SQUARE—JAIL DOORS ARE BATTERED DOWN WITH HEAVY TIMBERS AND THE PLEADING BLACKS ARE HALF CARRIED, HALF DRAGGED TO THE SCENE OF EXECUTION—WHEN LIFE IS EXTINCT THE MOB IN ITS THIRST FOR VENGEANCE APPLIES THE TORCH—HOWLING, SURGING MASS OF HUMANITY CROWDS THE PUBLIC SQUARE AND APPLAUDS THE LYNCHERS[116]

After this ghastly event there was a great deal of anti-Negro sympathy in the rural counties, which probably contributed to some Negro migration.

Between 1860 and 1930, the Negro population in the Ozarks declined from an estimated 62,000 persons to 31,000.[117] In 1930, six Ozarks counties had no Negroes, and in most of the remaining interior sections, most counties had no more than 10. Growing to adulthood without seeing a Negro was possible for young whites, and octogenarians may have seen black people on only one or two occasions. Fifty years ago Negroes faced considerable discrimination in eating establishments, movie theaters, and other public and private gatherings. In the 1920s a few towns sported signs at their city limits: "Nigger, don't let the sun set on your heels here." Few racial problems occurred, however, because Negroes had no reason to stop off in such towns.

Despite scattered racist actions and the general lack of wide social interaction, some blacks stayed in the Ozarks. Most blacks who can trace their roots to antebellum times lived in the larger towns where opportunities for employment on the railroad and in other industries and services have been better. The larger towns also offered more opportunity for interaction with other blacks. Still, some black people clung to their homeplaces in small rural communities for many years, bonded to their families, churches, and friends. In the Cane Hill-Lincoln-Summers vicinity of Washington County, Arkansas, there was considerable cooperation between the blacks and whites, especially when disasters such as tornadoes and fires struck a family. Members of the community, both black and white, would combine their energies to cut logs and raise houses and barns for the family that had suffered. When it came to helping blacks in getting back on their feet after a disaster, discrimination did not enter the picture. Also, considerable social interaction occurred during casual visits, talking, and joking and engaging in camaraderie.[118]

Most of the black hill families generally stressed family stability. Morgan found that older citizens remembered very few separations of husbands and wives, and divorces were very rare.[119] Families were familiar with each other, and the qualities of young people who might serve as spouse prospects were well understood by community members. The marital and family stability was consistent with the fundamentalistic beliefs of the black hill folk.[120]

The current distribution of black population in the Ozarks is not unlike the pattern established during primary immigration; the border counties have the largest numbers, and only very few blacks live in the interior rural counties. Only five counties—Cole and Boone in Missouri, Faulkner and Conway in Arkansas, and Muskogee in Oklahoma—had more than 2,500 blacks in 1970. These counties are on the margins of the Ozarks. The largest black populations in the interior counties were found in Greene County (Springfield) and in Pulaski County, which included the soldiers at Fort Leonard Wood. The total black population of the Ozarks in 1970 was estimated at 26,758, of whom 19,938, or 75 percent, were in the border counties.

The distribution of black population changed very little between 1960 and 1998, the most recent year for which census data are available. The Negro population is still concentrated in the larger cities, particularly the cities in the border counties. However, the black population has experienced steady increases. For example, between 1960 and 1998, the black population of Greene County, Missouri, grew from 2,358 to 4,884 for a 107 percent increase. Pulaski County's black population grew from 2,772 to 5,557, while the black population of Fayetteville, Arkansas, increased from 466 to 2,414, a gain of 418 percent.[121] The number of blacks in all five of the border counties with larger black populations also increased. For the region as a whole, the black population increased from 21,262 in 1960 to 48,825 in 1998, an increase of 129 percent. The same factors that account for the recent vigorous general growth in Ozark population contribute to the growth of black population.

The present black population of the Ozarks has almost no connection with traditional rural Ozark culture. While some families can trace their Ozarks roots back to the nineteenth century, and a few into the pre–Civil War slavery days, their family heritage of rural customs and farm life have vanished.[122] Too many generations of urban living have passed, and now like many of their white urban neighbors, modern Ozark blacks know little of rural life other than what they have learned in school and from the print and broadcast media.

For contemporary blacks, living in the Ozarks is probably not much different from the lives of blacks living in small cities throughout the Midwest. While blacks no longer have to cope with school segregation, and they have breached many social barriers, they still face considerable subtle discrimination. Many progressive blacks have moved up economically and socially, but others still have minimal skills and hold low-paying jobs. Discrimination in housing, despite federal and state laws forbidding it, presents a problem, and many blacks live in old established mixed black and white neighborhoods. Perhaps some prefer to reside in the older neighborhoods where long-established family and neighbor relationships are strong, but others cannot afford to pay the rent or purchase a house in newer neighborhoods. Overall, the whites and blacks of the Ozarks get along rather well, compared with racial problems in some of America's larger cities.

SIX

SETTLEMENT: THE LATER STAGES

As mentioned previously, the earliest settlements in Missouri were along the Mississippi, Missouri, and Arkansas rivers, and until the later half of the nineteenth century these rivers and their tributaries were the main avenues for immigration. The American population of the Ozarks was largely from the states lying immediately to the east, from the upper South and lower Middle West; it has been noted that many were of Scotch-Irish descent. The rank of states according to origin of immigrants to Missouri in 1860: Kentucky (99,814), Tennessee (73,954), Virginia (53,957), Ohio (35,389), Indiana (30,463), and Illinois (30,138).[1] The Cherokees who lived in the Ozark portion of Indian Territory had immigrated from eastern Tennessee, western North Carolina, and northern Georgia. The cheaper Ozarks land especially attracted the mountain man from middle and east Tennessee. Manuscript census records show that the settlers in Shannon, Dent, and Carter counties between 1820 and 1860 originated in Tennessee (284), Illinois (171), Kentucky (63), Arkansas (54), Indiana (48), Alabama (38), Virginia (11), and North Carolina (4).[2] The settlers in the Arkansas Ozarks were little different from their counterparts in Missouri. Records for Newton County, Arkansas, in the Boston Mountains show a preponderance of settlers from Tennessee. The leading states of origin in 1850 were Tennessee (126), North Carolina (48), Kentucky (21), South Carolina (13), Alabama (9), Virginia (9), and Missouri (8).[3]

After the Civil War, and with resumption of peaceful conditions, a new era of railroad construction began, and this stimulated immigration (fig. 6-1). The railroads provided improved connections with the states north of the Ohio River, and by 1890 the lower Middle West had replaced the upper South as the leading source of immigrants to Missouri. Illinois (135,585) was the top supplier, followed by Kentucky (99,985), Ohio (84,907), Indiana (70,563), and Tennessee (67,591).[4] By about 1910 many Ozarks counties had reached their maximum population density (fig. 6-2). A number of counties declined in population for many years, and some have only recently surpassed the levels of a century ago.

The background of many immigrants to the Ozarks in the post–Civil War era differed from that of the pioneer people. They were the carriers of the New South culture: government officials; entrepreneurs; veterans of the Civil War; capitalists interested in mining, lumbering, railroad building, and town founding; land speculators; resort builders; and venturers of assorted types who would take hold of almost any project that promised rewards. Compared with the primary immigrants from the southern uplands, the newcomers were urbane, educated, and progressive. Some lingered only a while before seeking more promising opportunities elsewhere; most found a permanent place in Ozark society. Whether they stayed briefly or permanently, however, all of them helped to shape the culture of the Ozarks in the areas where they settled.

FOREIGN BLOOD

Among the post–Civil War immigrants were foreign people, some of whom still carried their own European customs and traditions. In fact, some foreign groups were among the first settlers, and the story of foreign immigration to the Ozarks goes back a generation before the Civil War, when many Germans settled in the hills bordering the Missouri and Mississippi rivers. Gerlach found that the culture of the several immigrant groups persisted to varying degrees, depending on their numbers and the strength of their traditions.[5] The foreign groups helped shape the geographic patterns of language, religion, education, and land use in the areas in which they settled.

Germans were the only major non–English speaking group in the Ozarks. The Polish and Bohemian settlements of Franklin and Gasconade counties and the Italians at Tontitown and Rosati were nearly negligible by comparison. The larger part of the Germans located in the Missouri and Mississippi River border regions in compact settlements (fig. 6-3).

The earliest Germans were the so-called Whitewater Dutch (Deutsche), who settled in Bollinger County.[6] These colonists from North Carolina, not being in contact

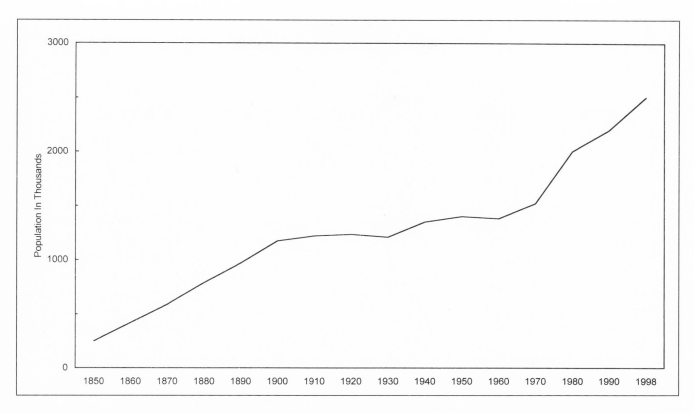

FIGURE 6-1. Population trends in the Ozarks, 1850–1998. Prepared with data from U.S. Department of Commerce, U.S. Census Bureau, *U.S. Censuses 1850 thru 1990* (Washington, D.C.: Government Printing Office, 1853, 1862, 1872, 1882, 1895, 1901, 1913, 1922, 1932, 1943, 1956, 1963, 1973, 1982, 1992); with updates from "National Population Estimates," U.S. Department of Commerce, U.S. Census Bureau, (Washington, D.C.: Laura K. Yax and the Population Division, 2000). http://www.census.gov/population/www/estimates/popest.html (April 15, 2000).

with other German groups, gradually dropped their use of the German language.

Between 1830 and 1850, many Germans immigrated to the northern and eastern Ozarks. They were primarily of four types: educated men of the *Jungdeutschland* movement, whom a reactionary government had suppressed; romanticists, who wished to escape a convention-ridden society, religious separatists, who sought to escape the repression of an established church, and ordinary people, who sought to improve their economic situation.[7]

A book by Gottfried Duden, *Berict uber eine Rise nach den westlichen Staaten Nordamerika,* was circulated widely in Germany, and because of its glowing description of the region along the Missouri River, many Germans were influenced to move to the lower Missouri Valley.[8] By the end of 1832, at least thirty-three German families had settled on the Missouri and twenty in the old Boone settlement on Femme Osage Creek.[9] Dutzow was founded in 1834 in Warren County by the Emigration Society of Giessen.[10] Washington was settled by an emigration society from Berlin,[11] and in 1838 the largest colony settled at Hermann.[12] Hermann was settled by an emigration society

in Philadelphia. On the Mississippi River Border, Germans settled in Cape Girardeau County in 1833, and in 1835 or 1836 a Swiss colony was established at Dutchtown.[13]

Catholic Germans settled at Westphalia in Osage County in 1833.[14] Several other Catholic settlements grew up nearby at Taos in Cole County and at Richfountain, Loose Creek, Lustown, and Frankenstein in Cole County. Other German Catholics settled at Ste. Genevieve, New Offenburg, and Zell in Ste. Genevieve County.[15] In a short time German-speaking people outnumbered other groups in both Ste. Genevieve and the county. In 1839, Protestant separatists settled at Wittenburg, Altenburg, and Frohna; it was this group that nurtured the Lutheran Church-Missouri Synod.[16]

Several factors attracted German settlement. Besides the frontier location, the geographic bases of German settlement were the region's accessibility from Europe by way of New Orleans and the Mississippi River, the low cost of land, and the similarity of soil, climate, and vegetation to conditions in the homeland. The Germans were successful farmers, especially with the loess soils on the uplands; these lands were cheaper, and many immigrants had

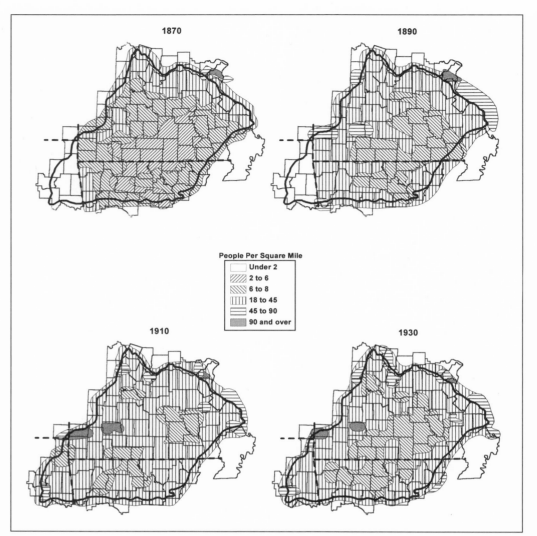

FIGURE 6-2. Density of population in the Ozarks, 1870, 1890, 1910, and 1930. Adapted from Charles O. Paullin, *Atlas of the Historical Geography of the U.S.* (Washington, D.C.: Carnegie Institute of Washington, 1932).

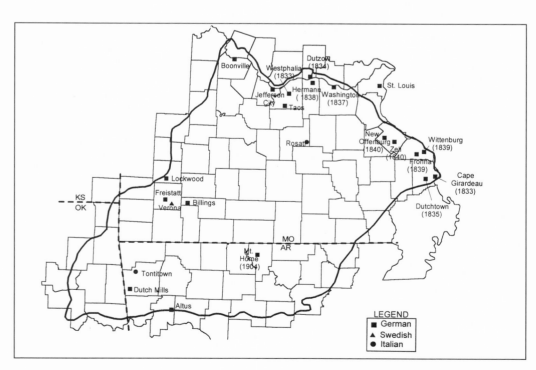

FIGURE 6-3. Foreign settlements. Adapted from Russel L. Gerlach, *Immigrants in the Ozarks: A Study in Ethnic Geography* (Columbia: University of Missouri Press, 1976)

worked similar soils in Germany. Gradually the German settlements expanded from poor land to better land. The immigrants were clannish and many did not speak English, so they settled amid the older German communities. As they accumulated wealth, they bought out their American neighbors; many of the latter reportedly sold out because they did not want to live among the Germans.[17] Furthermore, the Americans had become great buyers and sellers of all kinds of property, and land, which they could obtain free or at little cost farther west, was but another commodity to be bartered or sold. By 1859 the German settlements of Washington and Hermann had become important towns; Jefferson City was half-German, Boonville one-fourth.[18] The Census of 1870 showed that people of German birth or parentage accounted for more than 20 percent of the population in Osage, Franklin, and St. Louis counties.[19] These counties, along with the city of St. Louis, made up the so-called Missouri Rhineland. German-born made up 10 percent of the population in Cole, Jefferson, Ste. Genevieve, Perry, and Cape Girardeau counties.[20]

The German settlement of the eastern and northern borders of the Ozarks was part of a larger settlement picture as Germans occupied lands along the interior waterways of the United States.[21] Many counties bordering the Ohio River and the upper Mississippi River and their tributaries received large numbers of German immigrants, and Milwaukee, Cincinnati, and St. Louis became important centers for German culture. By 1900, south St. Louis had become widely known as a German community. Even now the city is known for its fine German restaurants and for the traditional music and customs that have been preserved to some degree. Although the Germans of south St. Louis have dispersed widely in the metropolitan area, the *Greater St. Louis Telephone Directory, 2000/2001* lists twenty-eight pages of names beginning *Sch,* an indication of the importance of Germans in the population of St. Louis.[22]

The pattern of ethnic settlements in the Ozarks is related to physical conditions and transportation routes (fig. 6-3). The influence of navigable rivers and railroads on the location of settlements is apparent. Few Germans settled in the less accessible parts of southern Missouri, northern Arkansas, and northeastern Oklahoma.

The larger of the scattered German settlements in Missouri, outside the northern and eastern Ozark borders, include Freistatt in Lawrence County, Lockwood in Dade County, and the settlements in Greene and Christian counties.[23] The larger towns along the railroads in southwest Missouri, notably Springfield, Monett, and Pierce City, attracted many Germans. The railroads, particularly

Bollinger Mill and covered bridge on the Whitewater River, Cape Girardeau County, Missouri, 1975. Surrounding farms are operated by descendants of Germans who immigrated in the 1790s. (Milton Rafferty Collection, photograph by the author.

the Atlantic and Pacific (Frisco), had acquired large federal land grants and were anxious to attract settlers. Some railroads sent executives directly to Germany as recruiters trying to dispose of land and to promote growth and prosperity for their lines.[24] Likewise, the Scottish-owned Missouri Land and Livestock Company, which owned more than 350,000 acres in southwest Missouri, advertised extensively in Europe.[25]

Although the railroads did not succeed in attracting the variety or number of foreign-born people to the Ozarks that they did in the upper Middle West and Great Plains, there were, nevertheless, several different groups. French Waldenses settled south of Monett, German Catholics settled mainly in the larger towns, a Swedish colony was set up at Verona, a small colony of Polish settlers located at Pulaskifield in Barry County, and Moravian settlements were founded in Laclede, Dade, and Ripley counties and in scattered locations in southeast Missouri.[26] Italians established colonies at Tontitown in Washington County, Arkansas, and at Rosati in Phelps County, Missouri, in 1900 after an earlier attempt to settle in the cotton country of the Mississippi bottoms in Arkansas.[27] These immigrants were more successful in the Ozarks where they established vineyards and orchards. In southeast Missouri a small Hungarian group settled near Poplar Bluff, and small colonies of Poles, Yugoslavs, and Germans settled in nearby counties.[28]

Until Oklahoma attained statehood in 1907, the conditions of tribal land tenure were not conducive to the

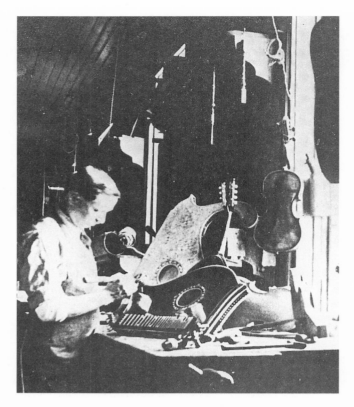

George Hesse working on a zither, circa 1912. (Courtesy of the State Historical Society of Missouri.)

settlement of foreign-born groups. For agricultural people interested in establishing homes, clear title was essential, and because Oklahoma land titles were always in doubt, many immigrants were discouraged from settling in Indian Territory. Until the last years of the Cherokee Nation, Cherokee controlled immigration, backed up by the United States Army, caused the Cherokee Ozarks to lag behind the Arkansas and Missouri Ozarks in population.[29] The Arkansas Ozarks attracted a few more Germans, but because of the remoteness, far from other German groups, their number was small and the imprint of their culture was never very strong. In the 1830s a small German settlement led by the Hermann family founded Dutch Mills (formerly Hermannsburg), in Washington County, Arkansas.[30] It flourished for a time and had a post office in 1855, but most of the families moved because of the unsettled conditions during the Civil War.

After the war, when railroads built into northwest Arkansas, the larger towns—Fayetteville, Rogers, Bentonville—attracted a few German immigrants. One of the most distinctive groups was the German-speaking Swiss who settled near Altus, Arkansas, on the extreme southern flank of the Boston Mountains. They arrived in the 1880s and immediately planted their vines and religion in Ozark soil.[31] Both the vineyards and the Roman Catholic church

have thrived; today several vineyards and commercial wineries near Altus attract visitors from a wide area. The largest of these, Wiederkehr Wine Cellars, produces wines of national reputation. Overlooking Altus from the Boston Mountain foothills is the massive stone church built by parishioners.

Germans also settled between Mountain Home and Norfork in 1904. The first three families were those of Gustav Keller, E. Hauerkin, and O. Hermann, and by 1910 about thirty families lived in the settlement, known locally as the German colony.[32] The "colony" never grew as large as Gustav Keller had hoped, but a few German families still live in the area.

JEWS

Small numbers of Jews were among the second-phase Ozark immigrants. Since the major cities on the Atlantic seaboard have been home to most of America's Jews throughout our nation's history, it is surprising how many Jewish people found their way to the remote Ozarks. Though not a large group in numbers, they were, because of their strong propensity to establish businesses, important in the economic history of the region. These immigrants settled mainly in the larger towns. They were a diverse group including those who immigrated from England and western Europe and later groups who came from eastern Europe and Russia. Many early settlers had adopted various American customs by the time they arrived. The Jews who first settled in Missouri and Arkansas were from Germany and had followed the great migration of Germans to the Mississippi Valley. They espoused Reform Judaism, which was an acculturated form of worship including organ music, choirs, Sunday schools, and sermons in English.[33] Later arrivals from eastern Europe practiced Orthodox, or Traditional, Judaism. They were city dwellers who usually had to adjust some of their religious practices if they settled in smaller towns. A few were well educated; most had business skills and soon became leaders in the development of commerce in their home towns. Many post–World War II Jewish immigrants to the Ozarks were educators and managers. These new immigrants arrived just as the older German and eastern European stock was dying out. Their arrival breathed new life into Jewish communities that had begun to stagnate.

St. Louis was the major Jewish center in Missouri, as it is today, and through the years St. Louis Jews provided assistance for small Jewish groups in smaller cities in Missouri. In a much smaller way, Little Rock was the chief Jewish community in Arkansas. By the 1850s Jewish businessmen were active in twenty-six Arkansas counties, mainly in the central, southern, and eastern parts of the state. Very few Jews, except a small settlement at Batesville and another near the southwest border at Ft. Smith, had settled in the Ozarks. Ninety-nine percent of Arkansas's Jews were from the German states, and almost 100 percent were engaged in business, especially dry goods (44 percent), groceries (19 percent), and general stock (18 percent).[34] By 1860 two hundred Jewish merchants lived in Arkansas and more than seventy served the Confederacy during the Civil War.[35]

Simon Adler led in the establishment of a small Jewish settlement at Batesville. He settled there in the 1850s and opened a mercantile store and a bank. Adler brought relatives and young Jewish workers in to help him with running stores at Batesville, Clarendon, Evening Shade, and Newport. As often happened with other Jewish merchants, Adler helped his community culturally and economically and through charity. In the second story of his business building he constructed an opera hall, which people called the "Daisy of the Town." The hall was the host to grand Christmas balls, dramatic productions, and concerts that benefited the Methodist church.[36]

Some Jews who settled in the Ozarks began their careers as peddlers. These foot merchants brought goods and news to isolated families and country communities. One of these foot merchants who worked in the hills of the southeastern Ozarks in the 1870s was Isaac Less. He established a store in Walnut Ridge, Arkansas, in 1875 and by 1990 he was one of the largest landowners in Lawrence County with more than nine thousand acres.[37]

By the 1870s several Jewish families were living in Ft. Smith, Arkansas, just beyond the Ozark border. Isaac Cohn, a friend of Judge Isaac Parker (the Hanging Judge), had business dealings with leaders in the Indian Territory. Iser Hiram Nakdimen, a Russian Jew, immigrated to Ft. Smith in 1894 after several years working as a peddler in the Chicago area. He opened an overall store in Ft. Smith, then became a banker and eventually opened sixteen banks in Oklahoma and four in Arkansas.[38] By 1950 the Jewish community of Fort Smith supported a temple, a B'nai B'rith lodge, and the United Hebrew Congregation's Sunday School had five trained teachers.

Fayetteville, sixty miles north across the Boston Mountains, was a true Ozarks town, and only a few Jews had settled there over the years. Most were businesspeople, but a few worked at the University of Arkansas. The beginning of rapid industrialization in northwest Arkansas in the 1960s, which included companies such as Hudson Foods, Tyson's, Wal-Mart, Jones Truck Lines, Daisy Corporation, and others, created the need for new workers and professional managers. Among the new immigrants were Jewish families who settled in Fayetteville, Rogers, Springdale, Bentonville, and Bella Vista. The growing enrollment and professional staff at the University of Arkansas also contributed to the increase in Jewish settlement. By the mid-1980s the thirty-odd families holding membership in Temple Shalom in Fayetteville included fifteen who had earned a Ph.D.[39]

The pattern of Jewish settlement in the Missouri Ozarks was much the same as in Arkansas. Because most Jews were engaged in business, they settled in towns, especially growing towns where the prospects for success would be most likely. Springfield and Joplin attracted the largest numbers. During the last three decades of the nineteenth century Joplin was the focus of the expanding Tri-State Lead-Zinc District and a thriving business town. Springfield was a railroad hub, wholesaling center, and a growing agri-manufacturing town. The Jewish population of Joplin consisted of shopkeepers, businesspeople, and executives and managers in the mines, some with ties to St. Louis. Joplin's Jewish community grew slowly, but finally in 1916 they built a synagogue. It served Joplin and scattered Jewish families in southwest Missouri and southeast Kansas.

Little is known about early Jewish settlers in Sprinfield, but a small community of German Jews had moved to Springfield by 1880. In 1893, after immigrant Jews from Eastern Europe increased the size of the Jewish community, the German Jews of Springfield organized a synagogue, Temple Israel.[40] Additional Jews settled during prosperous times—the 1920s, World War II, and especially during the current population and economic boom that began in the 1960s. During the post–World War II period, Springfield's Jewish population was augmented by professionals, physicians, college professors, lawyers, and managers. At the turn of the twenty-first century, Springfield had the largest Jewish community in the Ozarks, nearly three hundred people.[41] Joplin's Jewish congregation, which had about two hundred members during World War II but had declined to about one-fourth that number, had increased again to about eighty or ninety, including members from the surrounding area.[42] Fayetteville's Jewish congregation had about one hundred and fifty members. The congregations at Fort Smith, Arkansas, and Muskogee, Oklahoma, both just beyond the Ozarks border, were less than a hundred each.

In general the Jewish community has encountered relatively few incidents of discrimination or anti-Semitic sympathy. While nationally known anti-Semites like Gerald L. K. Smith[43] and Gordon Winrod[44] settled in the Ozarks in their waning years, they had very little influence on the region's people. However, in the predawn hours of

February 6, 2001, two vandals painted swastikas on about fifty tombstones in the Jewish cemetery in Springfield.[45] The incident, thought to have been promulgated by white supremacy "skinheads," did not reflect any widespread anti-Jewish sympathy.

AMISH AND MENNONITES

The Amish and Mennonites who have immigrated to the Ozarks since about 1954 make up another distinctive group. Their nineteenth-century lifestyle and tight-knit group behavior warrant their inclusion as a separate group. For almost three hundred years, the Amish in America have successfully maintained the religious beliefs that dictate their style of living. Their history provides insight into their values and beliefs. Emerging as a separate movement during the Protestant Reformation in Europe in the sixteenth century, a group led by Menno Simmons thought that the Catholic church was not being reformed sufficiently. As Anabaptists, or re-Baptists, those who believed in baptizing after infancy, they were subject to condemnation and execution.[46] The history of persecution later became a symbol of the commitment and sacrifice of Menno Simmons's followers, the Mennonites, and for centuries after strengthened their belief in separateness from the mainstream of society. In 1693, a group led by Jacob Amman broke away from the Mennonites to form a separate group. The separation stemmed from a disagreement regarding the *Meidung*, or shunning of excommunicated members. The followers of Amman, known as the Amish or Old Order Amish, believed that they should strictly observe the Meidung.[47]

Unsuccessful attempts to establish Amish settlements in Missouri occurred between 1850 and 1870. The settlements in the Ozark counties of Hickory and Cedar failed, as did those in Johnson, Vernon, Cass, Henry, and Boone counties. The reasons for their failure have been related to the quality of the land they selected, their rejection of modernization, or internal issues within the various groups.[48] Gerlach identified sixteen separate groups of Amish and Mennonites in the Missouri Ozarks.[49] These groups, all settled since 1954, represented nine different affiliations with a total population of 230 families. The settlements extend from Carter County in the southeast to Webster, Morgan, and Moniteau counties in the north. Currently, the largest clusters are in Webster County, where enterprising real estate agents have made it their business to help with the resettlement of Amish groups, mainly from states east of the Mississippi River.

The 1968 settlement of the Webster County Old Order Amish is typical.[50] First, they purchased existing farms through a local real estate agent. Then all electrical wiring and telephone connections were taken out of the houses, and hand pumps and windmills were installed. Once settled, the Amish often remodeled the old houses to make them larger, or they demolished the houses and constructed new houses to accommodate the large families.

Like many Amish groups across the United States, the Ozarks Amish take off-the-farm employment to supplement their earnings and to keep all members of the family productive. Most Amish families prefer to have the whole family working at home, but many have taken jobs as housekeepers, babysitters, and laborers doing carpentry, demolition, and farm-related duties. Buggy shops provide income for some families. In the early 1990s, the Rueban Y. Schwarz buggy shop on Highway C near Seymour was building more than fifty buggies a year, 80 percent of which went outside the area to places as far away as Japan.[51] Some Amish families make and sell faceless Amish dolls, jars of home-canned preserves, and carpentry shop products such as furniture and wooden novelties.[52] The potential for expansion of tourist-related home manufacturing seems good considering the growing tourism industry and expanding urbanization.

Amish farming practices are similar to those of their non-Amish neighbors. The emphasis is on livestock farming.[53] Many are engaged in dairying and raising poultry under contract with large producers. Because they do not use modern agricultural machinery, and they try to be as self-sufficient as possible by raising gardens and keeping dairy stock, poultry, swine, and horses, their system of farming represents a throwback to the late-nineteenth-century general farm. The Amish readily accept modern practices, such as the use of commercial fertilizers, but to reduce costs they continue to apply barnyard manure and use crop rotation.

Ozarkers have accepted the new Amish immigrants just as they have other new immigrants for the past two hundred years. The Amish are important customers for businesses in nearby Ozark towns, and when they can arrange for transportation they make trips to Springfield and other larger towns to shop. Businesspeople have installed hitching rails for horses in Seymour's shopping areas to better serve Amish customers. The Amish are also good customers at farm auctions where they purchase oil lamps, hand tools, hand grinders, and other tools and farm machinery of times past.

Amish builders, who began as barn and fence construction contractors, have earned a good reputation as house builders. Competing contractors and other workers sometimes complain when the Amish accept lower wages.

However, the greatest debate among Webster County residents has focused on the safety problems created by Amish buggies, especially on four-lane U.S. 60 near Diggins and Seymour. In the fall of 1988, two petitions signed by 550 non-Amish residents in Webster County resulted in hearings on the problem. Coincident with the Webster County debate resulting from the petitions, the Missouri Legislature passed a law on August 15, 1988, requiring horse-drawn vehicles to have two flashing lights, one on the left and one on the rear at least six feet above ground. No regulations resulted from the petitions, but the highway department put up warning signs along the major highways, where horse-drawn vehicles travel most frequently. When a truck-buggy accident on a farm-to-market road resulted in the death of an Amish woman in January 2000, it pointed out the fact that they had clearly not solved the problem of mixed slow and fast vehicles.[54] Various proposals were put forward following the accident, including widening the roads to add a buggy lane. After consideration, Webster County officials rejected road widening as too expensive. When a second pickup-buggy accident on August 15, 2000, caused the death of a twenty-year-old Amish man on the same stretch of road, another round of debate occurred.[55] Thus far, officials have taken no action on suggestions for posting speed limits along stretches of roads carrying buggy traffic.

CHARACTER OF THE SECOND-PHASE IMMIGRANTS

The carriers of the New South culture in the Ozarks were a mixed lot. The New South image consisted not only of the works of individuals but also the widespread influence of institutions, notably the agencies of state and national government, schools, and churches, and the pervasive effects, sometimes dominance, of the new corporate immigrants: the lumber companies, the mining companies, and the railroads. The role of corporations and institutions in shaping the Ozarks scene is discussed elsewhere; three examples of individuals from the New South will serve to illustrate representative types.

Jonathan Fairbanks, a graduate of the New Ipswich Academy in Massachusetts, moved to Springfield, Missouri, in 1866 after holding teaching positions in Massachusetts and Ohio and venturing into an ill-fated partnership to manufacture steam engines.[56] He was encouraged to go to Missouri and enter partnership with John C. Wilbur, an old friend from Ohio. The two men operated a sawmill and planing business, with mills at Strafford and Carthage, and a retail outlet in Springfield. Fairbanks immediately became active in civic affairs, serv-

ing as city council member, mayor, and board member of the newly founded (1867) public schools. In 1873, because of the financial panic, Fairbanks's business failed and he was forced to sell his home and real estate holdings. Disheartened, he planned to leave Springfield and return to Ohio, but a school board member, who had recognized Fairbanks's educational training and aptitude, persuaded him to serve as superintendent of the Springfield schools.

Fairbanks filled that post continuously (except 1877) until 1912. He was a capable teacher with outstanding administrative ability, a man adept and sensitive in dealing with the Negro population, particularly when the expansion of Drury College required condemnation of the colored school. During his tenure the faculty in the Springfield schools increased from a "handful of teachers" with county certificates to a "corps of over one hundred," most of whom were graduates of state normal schools.

Fairbanks's experience in politics was useful in dealing with financial matters. Under his direction the city constructed nineteen schools, and Springfield High School, the pride of the city, was considered one of the best in Missouri. Fairbanks has been called "Mr. Springfield Public Schools," an appropriate recognition of his contribution to the development of one of the significant institutions of the New South Ozarks.[57]

Another New South immigrant from the North, Dr. Charles Bunyan Parsons, was to play an important role in the development of lead mining in the eastern Ozarks of Missouri.[58] His work and ingenuity aided in devising methods to extract ore. He was a dentist, but after practicing in Michigan, he served as a captain in the Union Army, resigning in 1863 because of bad health. In 1867, persuaded by his doctors that he must get into some calling where he could be outdoors more than his dental practice would allow, he assumed responsibilities as resident manager of the St. Joseph Lead Company's Ozark operation.

The company, incorporated in New York in 1864, had acquired, from Anthony La Grave, 946 acres of land around the present town of Bonne Terre. When Dr. Parsons arrived in 1867, the works consisted of a small crushing mill, three small furnaces, and a few hand-operated jigs. Miners gathered ore by hand from so-called openings, which were no more than shallow pits, and from a few inclined drifts leading to bedrock.

Dr. Parsons had read a magazine article about a new invention, the diamond drill, that would cut deep and bring up samples of the rock through which it had passed. He brought such a drill to the Ozark lead district, where its uses were the first step toward progressive modernization. Over the years, miners discovered large areas of good ore as diamond drills continued to reveal the character of the rock and the minerals imbedded therein.

The discovery of new ore bodies and the increase in production led to improved smelting processes and new means of separating ore from waste rock. Skilled metallurgists from Germany were employed, and the St. Joseph Lead Company extended its holdings near Bonne Terre, Leadwood, and Doe Run. During the 1890s, many mining companies were organized in St. Francois County; they merged with the larger companies and later became part of the St. Joseph operations. Among the new ones were Desloge Consolidated Lead Company, Flat River Lead Company, National Lead Company, Doe Run Lead Company, Central Lead Company, Federal Lead Company, and Theodore Lead Company. Between 1867 and 1910, under Dr. Parsons's management, St. Joseph Lead Company grew from an uncertain operation producing a little more than seventeen thousand dollars worth of salable goods annually to an entity that distributed nearly two million dollars in dividends, invested a like amount in improvements, and was responsible for creating a thriving community of five thousand persons.

A third example will serve to round out the characterization of the New South immigrants. Powell Clayton, born in Pennsylvania, went to Kansas in his youth and there acquired considerable knowledge of the violent political movements that attended the birth of that divided state.[59] As an officer in a Kansas regiment, he served in Arkansas in 1862–1863 and showed himself to have much courage and resourcefulness as a commander; his defense of Pine Bluff, by means of cotton-bale barricades, against a violent Confederate attack in 1863 was well known. In 1865, like many other northern men, he married a southern woman and, with cotton selling at record prices, soon became a wealthy planter.

His entry into politics came with Reconstruction. He was an able speaker, capable of coherent and forceful argument, and was especially adept at backing his opponent into an untenable or ridiculous position. It was for this reason that the Arkansas Republicans, led by such men as Logan H. Roots, builder of a large carpetbag fortune, and other shrewdly unscrupulous men chose him as candidate for governor. He was elected in 1868 at the age of thirty-five, and four years later, at thirty-nine, he was elected to the U.S. Senate.

In 1871, Clayton persuaded the legislature to pass an act establishing a state university. True to its traditions, Fayetteville, a booming New South Ozarks town, voted bonds to build the University of Arkansas, which enrolled its first students in 1872. Apart from the state university, the Clayton administration set up public school systems throughout Arkansas. Institutes for the blind and the deaf were established, and other institutions offering education for a nominal fee sprang up. They also established a flourishing small college serving many of the brightest boys of the Ozark region at Quitman in Van Buren County.

After completing his Senate term in 1877, Clayton moved from Little Rock to the new-rising watering place of Eureka Springs, a stagecoach journey of some eighty-four miles through a wild and remote part of the Ozarks. He arrived at Eureka Springs with visions of grandeur: the area should be developed as a nationally known health resort. In short order he had persuaded several men of considerable wealth to associate themselves with his effort. He was the prime mover in encouraging the Frisco to build the Missouri and Arkansas Railroad from Seligman to Beaver.[60] The Eureka Springs Railway, with financing largely by Logan Roots and other close associates of Powell Clayton, built south from Beaver to Eureka Springs. The locomotive used on the first run in September 1883, was appropriately, the *Powell Clayton*. By securing a railroad for Eureka Springs, Clayton hoped to support his heavy investments in real estate. His most notable was the widely known Crescent Hotel, a massive resort structure equipped with a grand ballroom overlooking the spring basins below.[61] This elegant hotel, still in operation but showing its age, is a salient reminder of the New South era in Ozark history.

While heavily involved in real estate ventures, Clayton remained active in Republican politics as a speaker and power broker. In 1897, Powell Clayton became the ambassador to Mexico, a position he held until 1905.[62]

SEQUENT OCCUPANCY: THE THIRD PHASE

The beginning of the cosmopolitan phase of Ozark immigration is contemporary with the automobile age and has continued through the spate of technological advances and governmental and institutional changes of the past half century. These Ozark immigrants are even more difficult to characterize than those of the New South era. They are mainly of three types: returnees, escapists, and opportunity seekers. The returnee is a familiar type.[63] In this group are people who once lived in the Ozarks, moved away, but, for one reason or another, returned. Some came back in the 1930s when depression hard times hit the automobile plants in Detroit, the steel mills in Chicago, and the packing houses in Kansas City.[64] The returnees came to weather the depression among friends and family, where familiar patterns of subsistence living could be supplemented by cash income from "working out" in a "green mill" or canning factory, or by "catching on" with a harvest crew headed north across the plains, or, perhaps, by picking peaches "on the western slope," or working in whatever manner they could to make a dollar.[65]

More recently, returnees are coming back to the Ozarks, usually in their later years (but not always), to retire or to prepare to retire.[66] Many, if not most, have met with some success in the outside world. They are returning not of necessity but of free choice; they are seeking out familiar surroundings, old friends, and they hope to find—and sometimes do—the stable social relations and slower pace of life that they have remembered.[67] Some have good reason to return; they have inherited property, a family business or a farm. Others, depending on their circumstances, settle in a comfortable house overlooking a golf course at Bella Vista, or they may purchase a five-acre "farmette" and contemporary bungalow overlooking one of the large lakes, while others may live in a mobile home on a country road conveniently close to friends and relatives.

A second cosmopolitan immigrant type is the escapist. The civil-rights movement of the 1950s and 1960s, followed by the environmental movement of the 1960s and 1970s focused the nation's attention on the ills of city life: traffic congestion, crowds, racial strife, crime, routine and colorless jobs, and the problems of air and water pollution. The city's glitter and mystique had been tarnished; for many city dwellers the good life was to be found someplace else. The backflow of population from the inner cities of large metropolitan centers to the suburbs and medium-size cities grew steadily, spurred by newspaper headlines calling attention to the fact that people were fleeing the major cities. In St. Louis, on the Ozarks border, the population of the central city declined from 750,026 in 1960 to 339,316 in 1998, a loss of 410,710.[68] Escapists are a mixed lot. A few dyed-in-the-wool escapists, mainly those who came during the unsettled 1960s, rejected twentieth-century city life, preferring to live a back-to-the-land communal lifestyle. Most escapists were simply people who had tired of the fast-paced city life with all of its apparent negative aspects during that time span.

Included among the opportunity seekers are people from all walks of life who are seeking employment in the robust and growing economy of some sections of the Ozarks. Growth begets growth. As more people immigrate to the area, and more of the native residents find employment in the local area, the growing population must be serviced by more teachers, doctors, lawyers, accountants, barbers, beauticians, and store sales clerks. An expanding housing market and nearly every other sector of the economy create more jobs, thereby stimulating more immigration. An expanding tourism and recreation industry stimulates additional demand for seasonal and full-time employees.

NEW ETHNIC DIVERSITY

During the latter half of the nineteenth century, the number of immigrants to the United States from Europe declined while immigration from Latin America and the Far East increased. This same pattern of immigration is reflected in the Ozarks where immigrants from Mexico, China, and Vietnam are part of the current Ozark population expansion. These new immigrants are truly among the opportunity seekers, for not only are they seeking economic opportunity and a better standard of living they are also becoming acculturated Americans. The Hispanics, mainly immigrants from Mexico, have become an important part of the population mix in southwest Missouri and northwest Arkansas. Those with skills have found employment in service positions and construction. Many others work in the poultry processing plants, food service, and various unskilled jobs. Because most of the poultry plants and other jobs are found in towns and cities, the new immigrants are mainly urban dwellers.

Most of the Hispanic immigration has occurred since 1980. The greatest increases in Hispanic population have occurred in Benton and Washington counties in northwest Arkansas, where large poultry processing plants provided employment (fig. 6-4). Benton County's Hispanic population increased from 716 to 4,403 between 1980 and 1998 while Washington County experienced an increase from 794 to 4,393 in the same period.[69] Other counties in the Arkansas Ozarks with important increases in Hispanic population include Baxter, Boone, Carroll, and Crawford. In Missouri, Greene County's Hispanic population increased from 1,282 to 2,677 in the 1980–1998 time span. Other Missouri Ozarks counties with important increases included Jasper (Joplin), Newton, and Pulaski. In Oklahoma the Hispanic population increased fourfold in Cherokee County, growing from 176 to 724. The Hispanic population in each of the remaining sparsely populated Oklahoma Ozarks counties amounted to a few hundred in 1998. Even so, these numbers represented increases ranging from 169 percent to 400 percent. In the ninety-three-county Ozark area, Hispanic population rose from 14,270 to 24,856 between 1980 and 1998, an increase of 74 percent. While many counties experienced some increase in Hispanic population, the greatest increases were in the larger towns in southwest Missouri and northwest Arkansas.

Because many new immigrants and their children have poor English skills, an extra burden is placed on schools

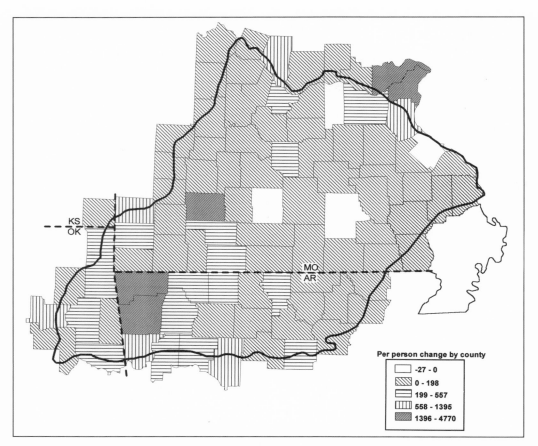

FIGURE 6-4. Change in Hispanic population, by county, from 1980–1998. Prepared with data from "National Population Estimates," U.S. Department of Commerce, U.S. Census Bureau (Washington, D.C.: Laura K. Yax and the Population Division, 2000). http://www.census.gov/population/www/estimates/popest.html (April 15, 2000).

Per person change by county
- -27 - 0
- 0 - 198
- 199 - 557
- 558 - 1395
- 1396 - 4770

where they have settled. New churches have been founded to offer services in Spanish. Also, the heads of household in many Hispanic families have low-paying jobs and need assistance from local, state, and federal social agencies.

The Asian immigrant population is heterogeneous, but most are Vietnam refugees or emigrants from China. When the United States completed its evacuation program in South Vietnam as the Saigon government surrendered to the Communists in April 1975, thousands of "boat people" fled the country in boats and even makeshift rafts. Many refugees were picked up by United States ships patrolling near Vietnam and delivered to refugee camps. There they assigned them American sponsors who agreed to help them start new lives in the United States. Fort Chaffee, near Fort Smith, Arkansas, became a processing center for Vietnamese refugees, and groups in several larger Ozark towns sponsored relocation of the refugees. The Springfield Council of Churches, for example, helped with the settlement of many Vietnamese refugees in Springfield. The Marian Association, working for the Catholic church in Carthage and Joplin, helped settle hundreds of families in the tri-state area. Many Vietnamese families stayed in the Ozarks, but others moved on, usually to larger cities where more opportunities and larger Vietnamese colonies existed. Nevertheless, strong

bonds to the Marian Association and to the Ozarks persists even among those who did not choose to stay. In 1977 they held the first annual Marian Celebration, a reunion of Vietnamese from throughout the United States, in Carthage, Missouri. Twenty-three years later, in August 2000, more than fifty thousand Vietnamese crowded into Carthage for the annual Marian Celebration.[70] Organizers of the celebration prepared steaming kettles of "pho"—a Vietnamese concoction of carrots, potatoes, onions, beef, and ginger—and thousands of hamburgers and hot dogs for the Vietnamese visitors.[71]

The Vietnamese, like the Hispanics, are urban dwellers. Their culture or capital resources hardly equipped them to attempt to establish farms. Most live in Springfield, Joplin, Fayetteville, and other larger cities. Between 1980 and 1998 the Asian population of Greene County tripled, increasing from 796 to 2,386.[72] Other Missouri counties with growing Asian populations include Jasper and Newton (Joplin), Jefferson, Phelps, and Pulaski (fig. 6-5). The Fayetteville and Fort Smith urbanized areas are the main centers for Asian settlement in the Arkansas Ozarks.

The new immigrants from the Far East have found work in a wide range of occupations, including both low-skill and high-skill jobs. Like many groups who immigrated to America before them, they initially

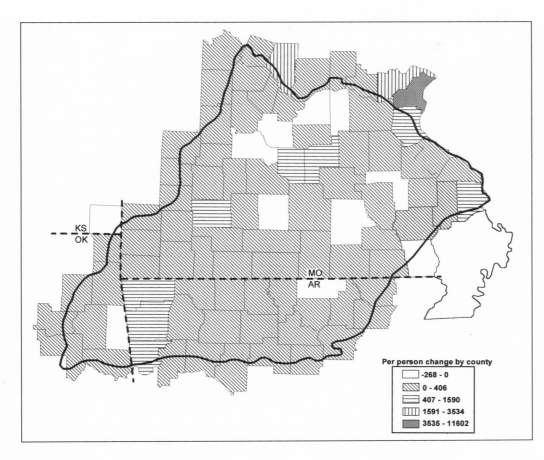

FIGURE 6-5. Change in Asian population, by county, from 1980–1998. Prepared with data from "National Population Estimates," United States Department of Commerce, U.S. Census Bureau (Washington, D.C.: Laura K. Yax and the Population Division, 2000). http://www.census.gov/population/www/estimates/popest.html (April 15, 2000).

Per person change by county
- -268 - 0
- 0 - 406
- 407 - 1590
- 1591 - 3534
- 3535 - 11602

accepted whatever jobs they could, stocking groceries and hiring themselves out as housekeepers. The unemployment level of those who immigrated in 1980, once very high because of the language barrier, had been reduced to 14 percent by 1983.[73] Most quickly advanced to better-paying jobs. Second-generation immigrants have been better able to take advantage of educational opportunities that may allow them to move upward economically. Many immigrants from the Orient have established diverse businesses. A large number own or work in Oriental restaurants. Springfield, widely known in the Ozarks as a city with many Oriental restaurants, offers a variety of Oriental foods. Many Vietnamese restaurant owners learned the business while working in the popular restaurants owned by the Leong family, who were themselves immigrants from China. By 1990 Springfield had more than fifty oriental restaurants.[74] Much of the success of the Oriental restaurants is said to be based on a popular dish, cashew chicken, that piqued the native Ozarker's appetite for deep-fried battered chicken. By the turn of the twenty-first century Oriental restaurants were widespread in the larger towns throughout the western Ozarks. The *Southwestern Bell Springfield-Branson Telephone Directory, 2000/2001,* listed sixty-one oriental restaurants.[75]

THE CHANGING GEOGRAPHY OF POPULATION

Beginning in the mid-1960s there were unexpected population shifts in several regions of the United States. The Ozarks, along with the forested land in Wisconsin, northern Michigan, and Minnesota and the recreation-retirement states of the South and Southwest, have experienced rapid increases in population. Between 1960 and 1998, while the nation's population grew 50 percent, the Ozark region grew 81 percent (fig. 6-1).[76] It appears that many people have moved out of central cities, most of them to the suburbs, but many have chosen to move to sparsely populated regions. Eight of the ten largest central cities in the United States have decreased in population since 1970.[77] The biggest rates of nonmetropolitan growth have occurred in retirement counties, such as those in the Sunbelt, in the forested Ozark-Ouachita and Upper Great Lakes regions, in counties next to metropolitan areas, and in counties with larger cities that can support good healthcare facilities and colleges and universities.

In the Ozarks, beginning in the 1960s, the greatest rates of in-migration occurred in the lake districts and in the counties with larger towns. The growth rates have continued unabatedly so that by 1998 thirteen counties had doubled in population and six others were more than three times the size they were in 1960.[78]

Almost as striking are the population changes shown by 1998 U.S. Bureau of the Census estimates for counties in the entire Ozark region (fig. 6-1). In the thirty-eight-year period from 1960 to 1998 the population of the Ozarks increased to 2,506,511 from an estimated 1,385,726. The total increase of 1,120,785 amounted to 81 percent. More than half the increase was due to net migration; the remainder was due to excess births over deaths (fig. 6-6). During the 1960 to 1998 period, only four of the ninety-three counties in the Ozark region experienced a net decline in population. Pulaski County, Missouri, the only losing county wholly within the Ozarks, experienced a substantial decline (8,060) in population due to a reduction in the number of military personnel and their dependents at Ford Leonard Wood.[79] In the late 1990s, when the chemical warfare school moved to the fort, Pulaski County's population decline was reduced. Two border counties in Missouri, Howard (369 net decline) and Saline (244 net decline), suffered small declines in population. One Arkansas county, Searcy, experienced a small net decline (363 people) in the 1960 to 1998 period. None of the Ozark counties in Oklahoma or Kansas suf-

fered declines. However, the "back to the land" surge had waned by 1980, and population growth became more concentrated in economically favored areas during the 1980s and 1990s. The out-migration in several sparsely populated counties in the interior caused them to return to a pattern of population decline. Between 1980 and 1998 ten Ozark counties lost population while eighty-three counties grew. The losing counties were as follows: Missouri, seven counties (Dent, Howard, Iron, Oregon, Pulaski, Reynolds, Saline); Arkansas, two counties (Lawrence, Searcy); Oklahoma, one county (Ottawa). These counties, except Pulaski County, Missouri, are strongly rural in character, and Pulaski County, as we have seen, is subject to the economic vicissitudes that accompany cutbacks or expansions at Fort Leonard Wood.

There have been three important trends in population distribution since 1910. The first is farm-to-city migration. This movement may be slowing, and, as was noted earlier, in some areas it has been reversed. Detailed study of the census reports shows that in the Springfield vicinity the movement continued strongly for many years. Graphs (fig. 6-7) provide visual comparisons of the population trends of Springfield, Greene County, seven outlying counties, and the composite population of the eight coun-

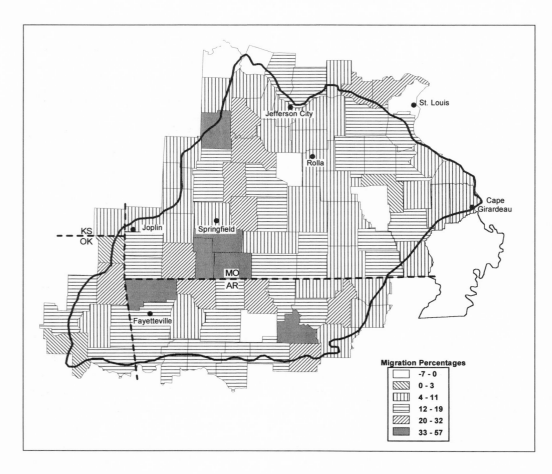

FIGURE 6-6. Percent net migration, 1990–2000. Prepared with data from "National Population Estimates," United States Department of Commerce, U.S. Census Bureau (Washington, D.C.: Laura K. Yax and the Population Division, 2000). http://www.census.gov/population/www/estimates/popest.html (April 15, 2000).

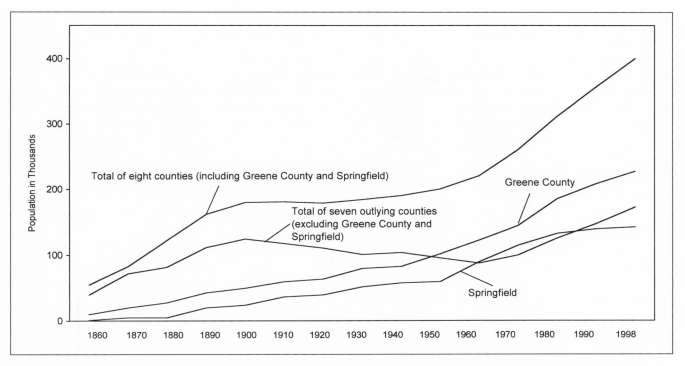

FIGURE 6-7. Population trends in the Springfield vicinity. Prepared with data from *U.S. Censuses 1860 thru 1990.* U.S. Department of Commerce, U.S. Bureau of the Census (Washington, D.C.: U.S. Government Printing Office, 1862, 1872, 1882, 1895, 1901, 1913, 1922, 1932, 1943, 1956, 1963, 1973, 1982, 1992); with updates from "National Population Estimates," U.S. Department of Commerce, U.S. Census Bureau (Washington, D.C.: Laura K. Yax and the Population Division, 2000). http://www.census.gov/ population/www/estimates/popest.html (April 15, 2000).

ties. The composite population has increased each decade since 1860, except between 1910 and 1920, when the region's population declined slightly. Greene County has shown a steady increase because of and parallel to the growth of Springfield, but some growth was at the expense of the outlying counties. The seven outlying counties had marked increases in population during the settlement phase before 1900, but since then, until about 1960, these counties declined in population. Since 1960 the outlying counties near Springfield have shown strong population and economic growth. The Springfield vicinity is a microcosm of the Ozark region: growth in the region as a whole, but major redistribution of the population, resulting in a less dispersed rural population and increasing importance for growth centers.

The Missouri Ozarks' most rapidly growing urban counties since 1960 include Greene (79 percent) and Christian (296 percent). Their growth reflects the brisk growth of Springfield, Ozark, Republic, and Nixa, as well as rapid rural increases. Christian County's 296 percent growth rate was second only to St. Charles County's 414 percent (St. Louis suburban county) among Missouri's 114 counties over the thirty-eight-year span. Other Missouri growth center counties include Cole (70 percent),

home to Missouri's capital city; Phelps (Rolla); Cape Girardeau; and Newton (Joplin and Neosho). In northwest Arkansas, Benton and Washington counties had large population increases (269 percent and 148 percent) resulting from the growth of Fayetteville, Springdale, Rogers, and Bentonville. The Standard Metropolitan Area, formed by Benton and Washington counties, is now second in size only to the Springfield SMA. Benton County, which shares the urban growth of Springdale, Bentonville, Rogers, Siloam Springs, and Bella Vista and the rapid growth of subdivision and houses around Beaver Lake, was the fastest growing Ozark county in Arkansas for the period 1960 to 1998.

Muskogee, Oklahoma, and Fort Smith, Arkansas, are additional regional growth centers on the southwest Ozark border. Like Springfield and Fayetteville, these cities are experiencing strong growth. Many smaller towns within a fifty-mile radius (commuting distance) of the larger cities are also increasing in population. Much of the population growth is occurring as suburban sprawl in the open country so that the minor civil divisions (townships) closest to the larger growth centers experience the greatest growth in population.

Professor Kathleen Morrison's comparative study of five

rural counties in south-central Missouri provides evidence that smaller cities of a few thousand population may serve as second-order growth centers.[80] These smaller growth centers provide employment, shopping, and services for a few bordering counties. Thus, the economy and population growth of West Plains and Howell County are more robust than surrounding counties, but at the same time residents of the surrounding counties derive economic and social benefits from West Plains in the form of jobs, hospital care, higher education, and other services. Other sec-

ond-order growth centers in Missouri include Poplar Bluff, Farmington, Park Hills (Flat River), Lebanon, and Neosho; in Arkansas, Batesville, Mountain Home, and Harrison are small growth centers, and Tahlequah is another second-order growth center in the Oklahoma Ozarks.

The second major population trend is the growth of small towns and rural subdivisions near the large lakes (fig. 6-8). This is most striking close to Lake of the Ozarks, Table Rock Lake, Lake Taneycomo, Bull Shoals Lake, Lake Norfork, Greers Ferry Lake, Beaver Lake, and Lake

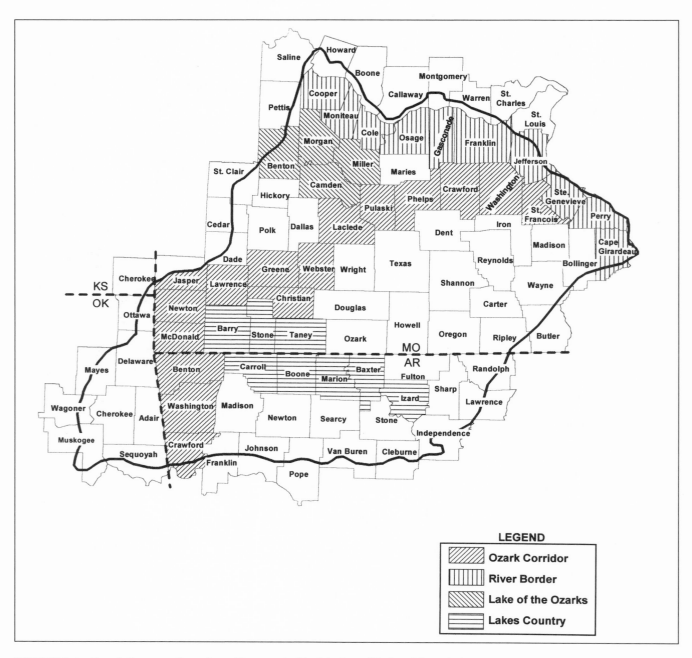

FIGURE 6-8. Population growth regions. Prepared with data from "National Population Estimates," U.S. Department of Commerce, U.S. Census Bureau (Washington, D.C.: Laura K. Yax and the Population Division, 2000). http://www.census.gov/population/www/estimates/popest.html (April 15, 2000).

of the Cherokees (Grand Lake). Growth in these areas has paralleled the rapid growth on the fringes of large cities. Land developers and builders have built hundreds of subdivisions and more than twenty incorporated towns. Just as the era of railroad building spawned a boom in town building, the Ozarks' eleven thousand miles of lakeshore have sired a host of retirement and recreation towns. Some of these new towns have grown to be among the largest towns in a given county (fig. 6-9).[81] The new towns in the Arkansas Ozarks include Cherokee Village, Fairfield Bay, Horseshoe Bend Estates, Diamond City, Lakeview, Holiday Island, Bull Shoals, Norfork Lake Estates, Lost Bridge Village, Briarcliff-by-the-Lake, Ozark Acres, Gaither Mountain Estates, and Bella Vista Village.[82] In Missouri, Kimberling City, Branson West, Camdenton, Osage Beach, and Lake Ozark are towns founded on or near lake shores, while Langley and Tia Juana are lakeside "new towns" in the Oklahoma Ozarks. Some new communities include large tracts; Bella Vista encompasses more than forty-five square miles.

Examination of U.S. Census Bureau population statistics shows the demographic impact of rapid land subdivision and new town building. The White River lake counties experiencing rapid rates of growth between 1960 and 1998 included Taney (237 percent), and Stone (227 percent) in Missouri, and five counties in Arkansas: Baxter (226 percent), Marion (94 percent), Boone (97 percent), Carroll (99 percent), Izard (93 percent) (fig. 6-6). Three Lake of the Ozark counties—Camden (272 percent), Morgan (94 percent), and Benton (95 percent)—also grew rapidly. Two Lake of the Cherokees counties—Delaware (158 percent) and Cherokee (120 percent)—are among Oklahoma's fastest growing counties.

Geographically, the population is strung out along the lake shores where roads penetrate the uplands between inlets. Of necessity, because the lake shores are usually steep, the dwellings occupy the uplands. Houses crowd the water's edge on the lakes built by private power companies—Lake Taneycomo and Lake of the Ozarks—but "set back" rules prevent the building of water's edge houses on the U.S. Army Corps of Engineers lakes. Retired people occupy many of the lake area homes; some are residents who have moved from nearby farms and towns, but more are from outside the region.

The third trend is toward redistribution of population along lines of transportation, which occurs on two geo-

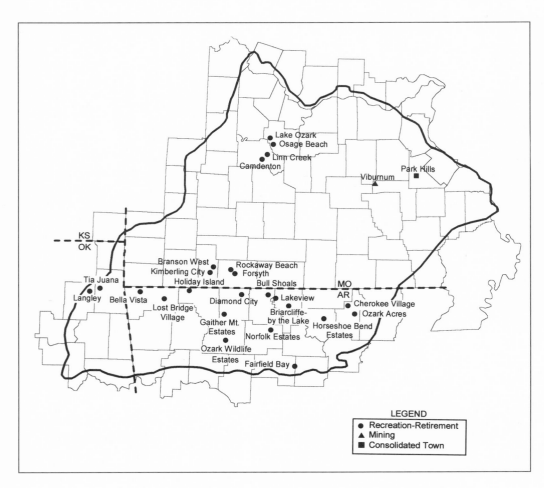

FIGURE 6-9. Post-railroad construction era new towns, 1925–2000. Adapted from H. B. Stroud, "Problems Associated with the Regulation of Recreational Land Development in Arkansas," *Arkansas Journal of Geography* 1 (1985): 15; and Milton D. Rafferty, *The Ozarks Outdoors: A Guidebook for Fishermen, Hunters, and Tourists* (Norman: University of Oklahoma Press, 1980).

graphical scales. The first is the major transportation corridor, such as Interstate 44 (including the BNSF railroad beside it), which attracts industry and commerce to the towns along it. The second is the state highway or farm-to-market road, which provides easier access to non-farm jobs. The net result of the latter situation has been to depopulate large areas that have poor roads and to concentrate population along the improved roads. Maps showing habitation in the hill districts reveal many places in which several contiguous survey sections of 640 acres have no habitation at all.[83] These "empty areas" of the Ozarks are restricted to very rugged districts and especially to the national forests.

Two major corridors of counties contain approximately 55 percent of the Ozarks' population (fig. 6-8). The ten river border counties account for 17 percent of the Ozarks' total. Although they have grown faster than most interior Ozark counties, the River Border counties are a distant second to the fast-growing sixteen counties in the Inter-

state 44–U.S. 71 corridor, which account for 39 percent of the region's total population. These two corridors comprising twenty-six counties account for more than half (56 percent) of the population increase in the ninety-three-county Ozark region from 1960 to 1998.[84]

CASE STUDIES OF POPULATION RELOCATION

To understand better the details and consequences of rural population shifts, let us examine two areas in detail. Maps of the two locations, quite unlike in physical conditions, afford insights into significant population redistributions.[85] The map of Buck Prairie Township in Lawrence County, Missouri, in 1879 shows that farmsteads were scattered and were much less oriented toward roads than in 1968 (fig. 6-10 and 6-11). Apparently the controlling factor in location of a farmstead in this rolling upland was the property boundary of the farm. The 1968 map of the

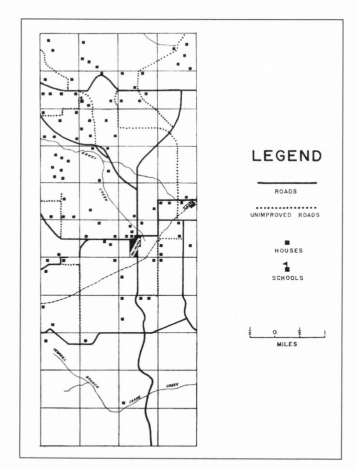

FIGURE 6-10. Settlement in Buck Prairie Township, Lawrence County, Missouri, 1879. Adapted from Milton D. Rafferty, "Population and Settlement Changes in Two Ozark Localities," *Rural Sociology* 38 (Spring 1973): 46–56.

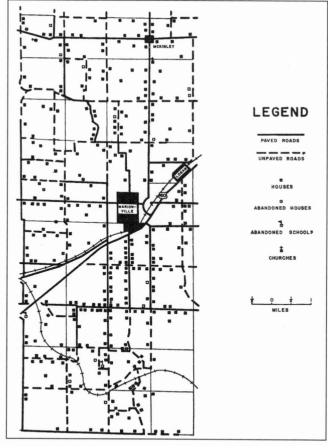

FIGURE 6-11. Settlement in Buck Prairie Township, Lawrence County, Missouri, 1969. Adapted from Milton D. Rafferty, "Population and Settlement Changes in Two Ozark Localities," *Rural Sociology* 38 (Spring 1973): 46–56.

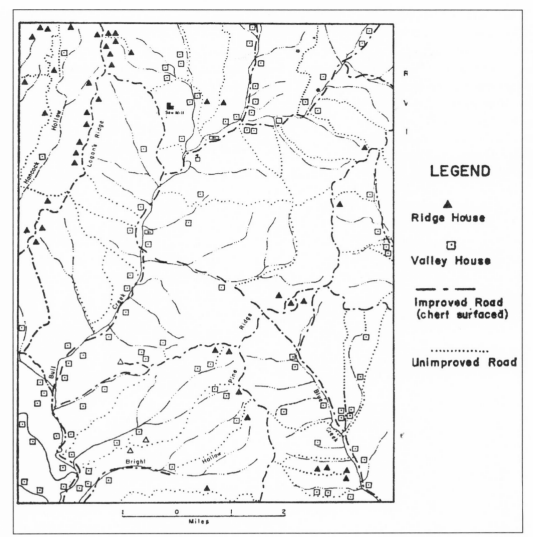

FIGURE 6-12.
Settlement in Linn Township, Christian County, Missouri, 1912 Adapted from Milton D. Rafferty, "Population and Settlement Changes in Two Ozark Localities," *Rural Sociology* 38 (Spring 1973): 46–56.

LEGEND

▲ **Ridge House**

▫ **Valley House**

— · — **Improved Road (chert surfaced)**

············· **Unimproved Road**

township shows a much denser pattern of settlement, but people had abandoned many farms and houses. More farmsteads had become oriented toward roads, probably a long-term process that occurred as some farmers abandoned farms and others built new farmsteads. Gradually, those farmsteads at some distance from the improved roads were abandoned to avoid the trouble and expense of maintaining private lanes.

Even more marked changes have occurred in the settlement pattern in rugged Linn Township in Christian County over the past half century. A map compiled from the Christian County Plat Book of 1912 shows that of 131 houses in Linn Township, 89 were in stream valleys and only 42 were on ridge tops (fig. 6-12). In 1968 the situation was nearly reversed (fig. 6-13). Of 99 occupied houses, only 21 were in valleys and 78 were on ridges. Most of those in valleys were on the better-quality county roads.

At the first appraisal, it appears that the population of Linn Township has moved uphill to gain easier access to the better public roads that follow the ridge tops. However, interviews with residents suggest that the population inversion that has occurred since 1912 is complicated and is the result of several factors. Some people abandoned the valley farms when they decided to quit farming. No alternate economic activity was available to attract new people to the isolated valleys, where roads are often poor and subject to flooding during rainy periods.

The decrease in valley occupancy did not contribute to the increase in the ridge-top settlement; that is, the people who abandoned valley farms usually did not resettle on the ridges near the roads but instead left Linn Township. The people who lived in the houses scattered along the ridge roads and logging trails in 1911 were, for the most part, not farmers. Settlement was sparse, except on Logan's Ridge.

The houses on the ridges in 1911 can be credited mainly to the growth and decline of the logging industry. With the completion of a railroad spur to Chadwick in

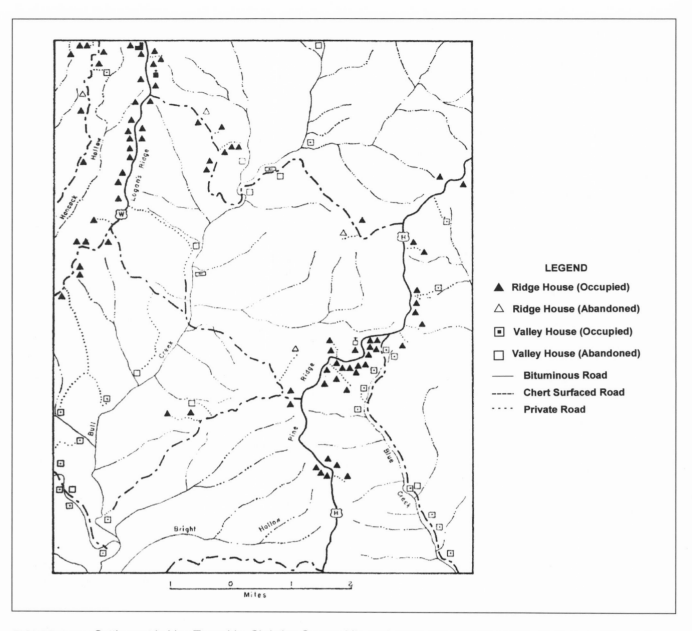

FIGURE 6-13. Settlement in Linn Township, Christian County, Missouri, 1968. Adapted from Milton D. Rafferty, "Population and Settlement Changes in Two Ozark Localities," *Rural Sociology* 38 (Spring 1973): 46–56.

1882, the forests were rapidly exploited. By 1920, lumbermen had cut most of the better-quality timber, and they sold large timber tracts off in small acreages. Many former sawmill workers stayed on, eking out a living from part-time logging employment and production from the small acreage they had acquired. The former logging trails, which followed the cleared ridge tops, attracted settlement in the form of cabins or small houses. Improved well-drilling technology undoubtedly was important for the increase in ridge-top settlement, since early ridge-top homes used sometimes unreliable water supplies from cisterns. Unemployed timber workers established small ridge-

top farms when they discovered that strawberries and tomatoes could be grown profitably there.

Interviews with knowledgeable, longtime residents of Linn Township in 1968 provided insight into the character of the people of Linn Township, their occupations, their attitudes, and possible explanations for the persistence of ridge settlement. The male residents of the township could be classified as farmers, part-time farmers, and nonfarmers. According to a retired farmer who assisted the author with the survey of the township, there were thirty-two nonfarmers, forty-five part-time farmers, and nine full-time farmers.[86] Part-time farming was the largest category, accounting for 52 percent of the employed males. Those classed as part-time farmers usually cultivate a garden and keep a few cattle from time to time but support themselves mainly by Social Security, welfare, or regular or periodic off-farm employment of one or more members of the family.

Many farmers in the marginal lands of the Ozark and Appalachian highlands have always looked to off-farm employment, either permanently or seasonally, to bolster family incomes. In the largest group are those who have chosen off-farm employment as a means to better living. A second group is comprised of former full-time farmers who choose to continue living on their farms after retirement. A third group includes those who either have returned to the area after a long absence or have chosen to move there because of low-cost land and low-cost retirement living. One resident of Logan's Ridge established residence in the 1930s to "weather" the depression, returned to his home in Detroit to work in the 1940s, and finally returned to the Ozarks in the late 1950s to spend his retirement years.[87] Movement of people alternately between city jobs and rural living among family and friends was common in many other parts of the Ozarks. Sometimes whole families moved back and forth between the Ozarks and midwestern industrial cities, and even to jobs as far away as the Pacific Northwest.[88]

Most of the people in Linn Township, like those throughout the Ozarks, have strong family and social ties in the local community. All are white, and most are descended from old-stock Americans who migrated to Missouri before 1900. In conversation, one detects their preference for their nearly classless, individual-oriented, slow-paced life to the only visible alternatives. Similar attitudes have been noted in other sections of the Ozarks. Although Linn Township declined in population between 1940 and 1970, that trend has been reversed. Since about 1970, newcomers have built several new houses and placed mobile homes on small acreages near Christian Center on Logan's Ridge and a few other locations.[89] Most of the new residents commute to jobs in Springfield, Ozark, or Branson. These residences, occupied by new people, are on ridge tops close to all-weather roads. The new residents generally do not have close family or community ties in Linn Township, although some are native Ozarkers. The inducements to settle in the township are the comparatively cheap land, compared to land closer to Springfield, Ozark, or Branson, and the attractive rural setting along the Eureka Springs escarpment overlooking national forest land that will likely never be settled. Improved black-top roads bring the scenic ridges along the Eureka Springs escarpment within the commuter zone for employment in the growing cities in Greene, Christian, and Taney counties.

The population redistributions that have occurred in Linn Township are strikingly different from those that Professor Kersten described for an area of similar topography and relief in the interior Ozarks. Kersten found that ridge-top settlement in Dent County declined markedly after the forests were depleted.[90] Settlement in the Courtois Hills was more permanent in the valleys. A more recent study of settlement patterns in the interior Ozarks revealed that long-distance commuting could help stabilize out-migration. Residents of Reynolds County traveled one hundred fifty miles to St. Louis to work during the week and returned to their families and strong community ties on weekends.[91] Such long-distance commuting has been shown to be important in holding population in the coal fields of Pennsylvania. The persistence and moderate growth of ridge settlement in the rough hill country southeast of Springfield probably is due to the greater opportunity of residents to combine part-time farming with off-farm employment. This requires both reliable roads and nonfarm employment opportunities, conditions that do not always prevail in the interior Ozarks.

SEVEN

THE CIVIL WAR AND ITS CONSEQUENCES

"May you live in interesting times," goes an old Chinese proverb. Millions of Americans were destined to live in the "interesting times" between 1861 and 1865 when the American Civil War was fought. The entire nation became embroiled in the horrific struggle for survival that followed the attempt at succession from the union and the scourge that followed. For four years and more, hundreds of thousands of men, women, and children, nearly all of them residents of the upper South, suffered great hardships in an enormous no man's land that stretched from Kansas and the Indian Territory through Missouri, Arkansas, Kentucky, and Tennessee to Virginia and the Sea Islands.

Several factors account for the development of the Civil War in Missouri and Arkansas.[1] Fear of a high Republican tariff or of northern-elected Republican administration policies were of some importance for the plantation owners in the Arkansas, Missouri, and Mississippi valleys, but probably not for most inhabitants of the Ozarks. Since the war was national in scope, all states had to take a stand. Although some states, including Missouri and Kentucky, tried to remain neutral, it was not possible. At least for Missourians and Arkansans, concern over states' rights was more important than the fear for the continuance of the institution of slavery. Following the Republican platform of 1860, President Lincoln himself in his inaugural address had declared that he would not disturb slavery where it already existed.[2]

Concern for the institution of slavery in the Ozarks was limited. Because physical conditions were not suited to the development of large plantations of cotton, hemp, or tobacco—nor was there adequate transportation to support these commercial enterprises—most residents of the Ozarks were not slaveholders, and as we have seen, there was only a small number of slaves in the entire Ozark Plateau. Most of the slaves were brought to the counties bordering the Mississippi, Missouri, and Arkansas rivers where plantation owners had settled. Also, by 1854 there were nearly fifty thousand slaves worth about $25,000,000 in western Missouri in the counties bordering Kansas.[3]

Slave owners had also settled in east central Missouri, in an area later known as Little Dixie. These counties were north of the Missouri River and mainly outside the Ozarks.

Nevertheless, slaveholders and slaves were in several interior counties, and both Missouri and Arkansas had become addicted to the evil habit. Even the Cherokees, who moved to what is today the Oklahoma Ozarks, who themselves the whites unfairly treated, were slaveholders.[4] Principal Chief John Ross could speak eloquently in the defense of Cherokee rights and use slaves to work his property at Park Hill. Most of the American Indians had long practiced making slaves of their war prisoners, but white traders were chiefly responsible for introducing the purchase and sale of Negro slaves to the Cherokees.[5]

There were great incongruities, even hypocrisy, among the political leaders of the times. Missouri senator Thomas Hart Benton was a slave owner throughout his life, but he recognized slavery as an evil and would not be a part of the extension of the practice.[6] Others who owned no slaves at all defended slavery with their votes and sympathies, and in many cases they later had to defend it with their lives. Owners of large plantations and many slaves often raised and helped support military units for the Confederacy. Often the most ardent supporters of succession, including slave owners, somehow managed to avoid military service, although ultimately they could not escape the horrendous impact of the war itself.[7]

Although Ozarkers owned few slaves and had little sympathy for slavery, they could not avoid being drawn into the conflict. In the 1850s, remoteness and isolation buffered Ozark people from the struggle over slavery in bleeding Kansas, and they were not involved in the abolitionist activity that flared in states east of the Mississippi River. Political leaders tried in both Missouri and Arkansas to steer a neutral course before the South fired on Fort Sumter on April 12, 1861, and they continued these efforts even after the conflict had begun. Men such as Sterling Price, former governor of Missouri, were willing to compromise to the end.[8] Price was to play a major role in the war as a Confederate general.

Many Ozarkers had strong Union empathy. The influx of Germans and a new wave of people from the northern states in the years immediately preceding the war resulted in a large population that was hostile to slavery. St. Louis was a strong Union city because of the large number of Germans and Irish. Northern leaders knew that many residents of Springfield, Rolla, Poplar Bluff, Cape Girardeau, and the other larger towns in the Missouri Ozarks had strong Union sentiments. Residents of Fayetteville and Batesville and the upland Ozark counties in Arkansas, if not pro-Union, were antisecessionist. However when they took the vote in the Arkansas convention to consider secession, only five of the seventy delegates had the temerity to vote no. Isaac Murphy,[9] a tough old frontiersman from the Missouri border, and four others from the Ozarks Upland were the only dissidents.[10] Later, after the Union Army captured Little Rock in 1863, Union officials appointed Murphy provisional governor of Arkansas.

Among the Five Civilized Tribes in the Indian Territory, secession was largely a matter of latitude. Wedged in a corner between strong pro-slavery populations in southwest Arkansas and northern Texas, the Choctaws had little chance to assert any choice in the matter. The Creeks, Chickasaws, and Seminoles were in a similar position but with less direct pressure from southern interests. The Cherokees were strongly divided on the issue. Their principal chief, John Ross, wanted neither Union nor Confederation alliances; he sought neutrality and peace.[11] Yet the tribe allied itself with the South, and the warriors fought for the Confederacy—or shifted their allegiance from one side to the other, trying to anticipate the outcome.

The defeat of Union forces at Wilson's Creek near Springfield on August 10, 1861, brought a surge of Confederate sentiment so strong to the Cherokee Nation that John Ross was no longer able to maintain his neutral position. Surrounded by armed Cherokees who were eager to fight for the Confederacy, he felt obliged to sign a treaty of alliance with the South.[12] The Battle of Pea Ridge (Arkansas), fought between March 6 and March 8, 1862, caused a sharp reversal of Cherokee opinion. Cherokee recruitment into Union service became very brisk, and many soldiers who enlisted were veterans of Confederate regiments. Nevertheless, Ross would not disown the Confederate alliance. Throughout the war, the Ross Party (Late Immigrants) and the Ridge Party (Treaty Party) maintained separate fighting forces, although both supported the Confederacy. The Cherokee National Council, a legislative body, raised John Drew's regiment of Cherokee Mounted Rifles as the Cherokee government's defense force. This regiment, which favored the Ross Party, also served as a counterbalance against Stand Watie's battalion of Ridge Party supporters.[13]

THE CONFLICT

Although the rugged terrain of the Ozarks seemed to dictate a marginal role in military affairs, the region's geography was such that the opposing armies fought some of the more important battles of the western campaign within its border. Among the responsible geographic factors for this was, first, the fact that the rugged interior prevented movement of large armies through the region between the core population areas in the Missouri and Arkansas river valleys. Thus the armies were forced to go around the western end of the Ozarks, where moving men and equipment was easier and where foraging and raiding farms and settlements could sustain the troops. Second, the armies quickly recruited a trained cadre of officers from the garrisons stationed in Kansas and Indian Territory. Although many officers, both northern and southern, had been classmates at West Point or had fought as comrades in the Mexican War, those with the most recent battle experience came from the frontier. Third, Missouri was truly a border state in both geography and sentiment, and both the Confederates and the Federals expected military victories to win the state. Fourth, both the Arkansas and Missouri rivers were considered strategic routes to the West. Fifth, both sides coveted the allegiance of the Indians who lived west of the Missouri and Arkansas borders. Sixth, the rugged Ozarks interior was well suited to guerrilla warfare, not only by raiding parties from Federal and Confederate military units, but also by quasi-military groups, such as William Quantrill's Confederate Raiders and Jim Lane's Kansas marauders.[14]

More often than not, both Confederate and Union troops were ill clad and poorly equipped. Many units had no uniforms and only squirrel rifles, if they had weapons at all. At first the number of volunteers exceeded the supply of weapons. Sterling Price recruited many new troops in Missouri after his victories at Wilson's Creek and Lexington, but two-thirds of his men were unarmed, and reports of an approaching Union force scared many away.[15] Colonel Thomas L. Snead, Governor Jackson's aide-de-camp who served as General Price's chief of ordnance of the army, gave an appalling account of the conditions in Price's camp. He said,

> Of the 7,000 or 8,000 men that he [Price] had, only a few had been organized into regiments. Several thousand had no arms of any kind. The rest were for the most part armed with the shotguns and rifles which they had brought from their homes.[16]

They had no tents, no ammunition for their seven pieces of artillery, and no funds to purchase food and supplies.

General Price had appointed Colonel Snead to serve as chief of ordnance though Snead had told the general that he "did not know the difference between a howitzer and a siege-gun, and had never seen a musket cartridge."[17] To overcome their shortages, they improvised. They even fashioned wooden bullet molds from the logs of trees cut in the nearby forest and used them to make quantities of buckshot and musket balls.[18]

Beans, cornmeal, and coffee were staples for both armies. Soldiers took garden vegetables, fruits, and meat animals from farmers, at times leaving the civilian population with little or nothing to eat. Civilians who were fortunate enough to be paid for confiscated supplies with the Union vouchers sometimes received payment, but those given the Confederates' Missouri scrip received nothing. Short-term enlistments of ninety days and a strong propensity for soldiers to desert after a major battle made it difficult for generals to know the strength of their own forces, let alone those of the enemy. When General Lyon hastened to engage the Confederate forces at the Battle of Wilson's Creek, fully half his men were three-month volunteers whose terms of enlistment had nearly expired.[19]

In proportion to their populations, Missouri and Arkansas provided more men than any other states in the nation. Missouri, with a white population of 1,182,012, had 109,000 Union soldiers, and 30,000 were in the Confederate army.[20] Together, these troops made up more than 60 percent of the men eligible for military service. The Arkansas History Commission has listed 58,000 Confederate soldiers, and another 4,000 served in the Union army (another 2,000 blacks served in the Union army)—an astounding number for a state with a white population of only 324,335 in 1860.[21] Truly, there were few pacifists or shirkers among the frontiersmen.

Nevertheless, neither the Confederate nor the Federal governments considered the military activities west of the Mississippi of vital significance. After the Battle of Wilson's Creek, the officer corps of the opposing forces considered the conflict west of the Mississippi a sideshow. The residents of the Ozarks would not have agreed, for them the war continued in a nearly unbroken chain of skirmishes and raids interspersed with major battles. These formal or quasi-formal military actions were punctuated by a never-ceasing, ever-increasingly bitter and bloody internecine guerrilla war.

The war came quickly to the Ozarks (fig. 7-1). A last-minute conference at the Planter's House in St. Louis, which was an attempt to avert war in Missouri, took place on June 11, 1861. Congressman Blair and General Nathaniel Lyon[22] presented the Union arguments while Governor Claiborne Jackson[23] and General Sterling Price represented the secessionists. The conference ended abruptly when General Lyon shouted:

Rather than concede to the State of Missouri for one single instant the right to dictate to my government in any matter however important, I would see you, and you, and you, and you, and you and every man, woman and child in the State, dead and buried.[24]

Lyon was a vigorous commander and in a matter of hours following the Planter's House conference he began moving against Price. He occupied Jefferson City on June 15 and two days later landed two thousand men near Boonville. His forces routed the State Militia at Boonville and sent it and its commanders, Governor Claiborne Jackson and Colonel John Sappington Marmaduke, fleeing to the south. Price then abandoned the defense of Lexington and fled toward Arkansas. On July 5, near Carthage, a Union detachment under Colonel Franz Sigel, a veteran of the German Revolutionary War of 1848, intercepted Jackson's forces, but quickly retreated.[25] Sigel's force of one thousand men, mainly Germans from St. Louis, retreated in the face of a Confederate force of four thousand. This minor victory greatly bolstered morale in the successionist camp.[26] Following the engagement at Carthage, General Price again assumed command of the state guard and established his headquarters at Cowskin Prairie in the extreme southwest corner of Missouri. Confederate general Benjamin McCulloch, commander of an army from Arkansas, established his headquarters just a few miles south at Maysville, Arkansas.[27]

The Federal forces were the clear winners of the first round of the war in Missouri. The Federal government quickly established garrisons at St. Louis, Rolla, Boonville, Hermann, and Jefferson City in the summer of 1861. They now controlled the wealthy northern and central areas, all the principal towns including the capital, and the Missouri River and the railroads. The pro-Confederates, on the other hand, lost their main source of recruits, the state treasury, and their main area of sympathetic supporters.[28]

It was a different story in Arkansas. Governor Henry Massie Rector rejected the Federal call for troops and then dispatched Colonel Salon Borland with four companies of volunteer state militia and a four-gun battery to seize the Federal arsenal at Fort Smith. At about the same time the army commissary supplies at Pine Bluff, and the ordnance stores at Napoleon, including seventy thousand rounds of carbine and pistol cartridges, were captured by state militia forces.[29] With control of the Arkansas Valley accomplished, Rector and other pro-Confederacy leaders turned their attention to preparing for the convention where the

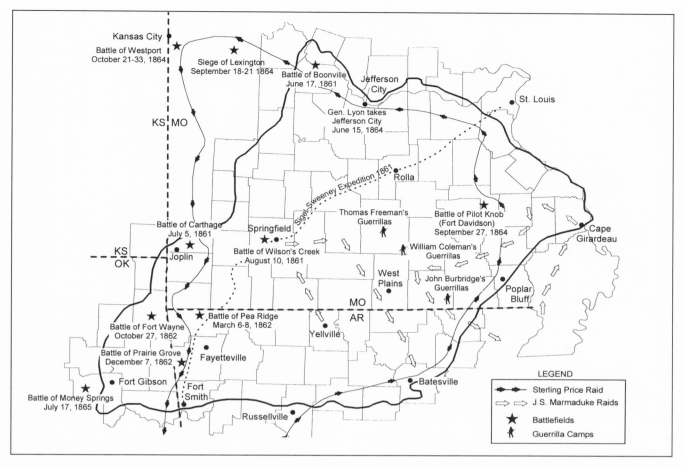

FIGURE 7-1. The Civil War in the Ozarks. Adapted from Robert Flanders, *Civil War in the Ozarks* (Map) (Springfield: Center for Ozarks Studies, Southwest Missouri State University, 1992).

representatives would decide the question of Arkansas's relation to the federal government. The final vote at the convention was sixty-nine to one in favor of secession, and Arkansas formally left the Union on May 6. Isaac Murphy of Madison County in the Ozark Mountains cast the sole dissenting vote when he arose and stated:

> I have cast my vote after mature reflection, and have duly considered the consequences, and I can not conscientiously change it. I therefore vote "no."[30]

By the last week in July, Sterling Price considered his army ready for war. It consisted mainly of inexperienced volunteers with a sprinkling of older men who had served in Mexico, or with the Border Raiders in Kansas, or in the Indian campaigns in the Great Plains. On July 25 Price's army left Cowskin Prairie in southwestern McDonald County and made a three-day march eastward across the Ozarks to Cassville. McCulloch joined Price at Cassville on July 29 with an army of 5,700, consisting of a brigade of Confederate troops from Louisiana and Texas, and a

"division" of Arkansas militia commanded by Brigadier General N. Bart Pearce.[31] Before agreeing to commit his Arkansas army in an attack on Union forces McCulloch insisted that Price turn over full command of the operation to him.

Since General Lyon had moved his soldiers to Springfield to join Sigel's in mid-July, the stage was set for a battle. Upon arriving he found that the more than ten thousand Confederate soldiers and state militiamen in southwest Missouri under General Benjamin McCulloch outnumbered his four thousand men.[32] Lyon decided to make a surprise attack, believing he would either win or weaken the enemy forces so that they could not follow his retreat. Lyon's troops moved into position around the Confederates camped on Wilson's Creek about twelve miles southwest of Springfield, and at dawn on August 10, 1861, the Federal forces struck.

The Battle of Wilson's Creek (Oak Hills) raged for six hours.[33] The heaviest fighting took place on Bloody Hill, where both Union and Confederate forces made only short advances before being driven back. Sigel's German

General Lyon's charge at Battle of Wilson's Creek, an engraving by F. O. C. Darley and H. B. Hall. (Courtesy of the State Historical Society of Missouri.)

battalion, which separated from the main Union army to attack the Confederates from the rear, was soundly beaten, allowing the Confederates to concentrate on Lyon's forces. Finally, with the full force of McCulloch's army pressing ahead and with ammunition running short, the Union army retreated toward Springfield. General Nicholas Bartlett Pearce said afterward, "We watched the retreating enemy through our field glasses, and we were glad to see him go."[34] Raw northern and southern farm boys had slugged it out, hour after hour, inflicting casualties that veterans were not supposed to withstand. The ferocity of the battle was captured by an Arkansas soldier when he said, it was "a might mean-fowt fight."[35] Casualties reached 2,330: 1,235 Union soldiers, including General Lyon, and 1,095 Confederates.[36] In one battle, Wilson's Creek, the overall percentage of casualties among those engaged surpassed the percentage of casualties in any battle east of the Mississippi.[37] The Greene County Courthouse was filled with wounded, and so many wounded soldiers were cared for in private houses throughout the town that one observer noted that "Springfield is a vast hospital."[38] The Federal troops limped back to Springfield, then retreated toward the railhead at Rolla. Technically, the Confederates were the winners, but because they suffered severe losses, they could not take advantage of the situation.[39] The battle generated renewed spirit among southern sympathizers, however, for they believed that "Old Pap" Price and his Missouri troops had upheld the fighting ability that Missourians had traditionally assigned to themselves.

It was reported after the Battle of Wilson's Creek that some Union troops were found scalped on the battlefield.

The prime suspects were Captain Joel Mayes's company of Cherokees, who were part of Stand Watie's battalion.[40] The Cherokees returned to their Nation when General McCulloch started enforcing strict military discipline in camp.

After occupying Springfield, Price led the state militia northwest to "clear out" some Kansas jayhawkers under Jim Lane, United States senator and part-time general, who were marauding in the Missouri counties east of Fort Scott, Kansas. There, on Drywood Creek on the Kansas-Missouri boundary east of Fort Scott, Price's force skirmished with about five hundred jayhawkers amid prairie grass higher than a man's head, "with neither side inflicting any particular damage on the other."[41] After the badly outnumbered jayhawkers retreated, the state militia advanced to Lexington, where, after a three-day siege, Price's forces captured a Union Irish brigade of three thousand men and substantial quantities of military supplies. At the Battle of Lexington, Price displayed both personal daring in battle and clever military strategy by employing water-soaked hemp bales as barriers for his men in their advance.[42]

Fearing that Union forces might cut him off from the main Confederate force in Arkansas, Price retreated into southwest Missouri, where, after a while, he recaptured Springfield and held it during the winter of 1861–62. There, they built log huts and went into winter quarters. Price spent much of his time writing letters to the Confederate leadership requesting reinforcement and defending his desire to pursue the war more aggressively by reestablishing himself in the Missouri Valley. Simultaneously, General McCulloch and his aide, Colonel McIntosh, defended their conservative position, pointed out the recklessness of Price's proposals, and criticized Price for failing to insist on discipline and good military conduct in his command. They also mentioned Price's fondness for drinking and the widespread use of rotgut among the troops.[43] The winter sojourn in Springfield was the last time Confederate forces controlled any part of Missouri for a protracted period.

Placed in command of Federal forces at Rolla, Brigadier General Samuel R. Curtis marched an army of 10,000 men to Springfield in February 1862, forcing Price to retreat into northwest Arkansas. After their retreat into Arkansas in 1862, Price's Missouri militia became part of General Ben McCulloch's Confederate army; under the command of Mississippi-born general Earl Van Dorn, a West Point graduate.[44] The combined forces reached 24,000 men. Another 1,000 Indians from the Five Civilized Tribes were added before the engagement with 10,500 Union troops, under the command of General Curtis, around Elk Horn Tavern at Pea Ridge, Arkansas. The battle lasted three days, March 6–8, 1862. After heavy losses on both sides and despite General Price's reluctance to halt the fighting, the southern army withdrew.

It was a great victory for the Union. The Confederate force lost much of its effectiveness when three key leaders —General McCulloch, General McIntosh, and Colonel Rives—were killed in action. The casualties of the battle, or rather battles, for they fought three distinct engagements, were very heavy. As near as can be determined, in the Federal army 203 men were killed, 980 were wounded, and 201 were missing. For the Confederates, an estimated 800 to 1,000 were killed or wounded and between 200 and 300 were captured.[45] The Confederate thrust through the western Ozarks toward the Missouri heartland was blunted at Wilson's Creek, but at Pea Ridge, Confederate hopes to bring Missouri under their control were smashed.

Four months later, on July 3, 1862, Colonel William Weer led a force of six thousand Union whites and Indians against the Confederate Cherokees under Colonel Stand Watie and a larger force of white Confederate soldiers under Colonel J. J. Clarkson.[46] The battle, fought at Locust Grove in Indian Territory (Oklahoma), resulted in a rout of the Confederate forces. Men who escaped went to Tahlequah, where their story of Clarkson's defeat gave a powerful impulse to Union recruiting of Cherokees. Weer's Union troops advanced to Tahlequah, where they arrested and removed Cherokee chief John Ross to Fort Scott (Kansas). From there officials sent Chief Ross to Washington and finally they permitted him to remain in Philadelphia for the duration of the war.[47]

In December 1862, General Thomas Hindman, the newly appointed commander of Confederate forces in Arkansas, mounted the last major southern advance into the western Ozarks.[48] On December 7, 1862, Hindman's forces met a Union army under General James G. Blunt at Prairie Grove, Arkansas, a conflict that had extensive consequences for the entire Southwest.[49] After units commanded by Marmaduke and Shelby successfully routed General Herron's Union cavalry, Hindman inexplicably took a defensive position.[50] An artillery battle followed with the Union long-range rifled guns getting the better of it. When Blunt's forces joined with Herron's late in mid-afternoon the Union line became more secure. After heavy

Last Hour of the Battle of Pea Ridge. (Courtesy of the State Historical Society of Missouri.)

Stand Watie, prominent Cherokee, member of the Ridge faction (Treaty Party), and Confederate general. (Courtesy of Oklahoma Historical Society.)

fighting all day, the two armies, still locked in a desperate struggle, ended the conflict only when darkness came. Both commanders claimed victory, but after nightfall the Confederate infantry began a withdrawal toward Van Buren. At noon on December 28, 1862, Blunt's cavalry swept into Van Buren with the infantry close behind. After a short artillery duel, Hindman ordered his army east toward Clarksville, and Blunt began his march back across the Boston Mountains, having found it impossible to subsist an army around Van Buren.[51]

After 1862 the Confederates could not mount a major military campaign in the Ozarks, except General Price's foray into Missouri in 1864. Most of the many engagements—135 in Missouri alone in 1863—consisted of Confederate recruiting operations or hit-and-run bushwhacking raids by Confederate guerrillas. Union garrisons at Springfield, Rolla, Pilot Knob (Fort Davidson), Batesville, Fayetteville, and Fort Gibson were fortified outposts in a vast region open to raiding parties. In particular, the Arkansas cavalry and the Missouri cavalry, under the command of daredevils J. S. Marmaduke and Jo Shelby, were intensely active. Marmaduke's mounted force fairly rode around Curtis's army of occupation at Batesville, cutting off his line of communications through Missouri for

ten days on one occasion, capturing wagons and supplies, and intercepting his telegraphic correspondence with his supervisors in Missouri.

The official records of the War of the Rebellion lists 573 battles, skirmishes, actions, burnings, and encounters in Missouri between 1861 and 1865.[52] No part of the Ozark region escaped the depredations of both sides, and nearly every county lists some event connected with the war as part of its history. Actions and skirmishes took place not only near the garrison towns, such as Batesville, Fort Gibson, Springfield, Boonville, and Cape Girardeau, but in quite remote locations, including Forsyth, Mountain Grove, West Plains, Doniphan, Warsaw, Eminence, Salem, Linn Creek, Humansville, and Hartville. However, the great battleground of the Ozarks was in southwest Missouri and northwest Arkansas. Springfield fell to the Confederates twice, and units fought skirmishes near Neosho on nine different occasions: March 1862, May 1862, August 1862, September 1862, March 1863, October 1863, November 1863, June 1864, November 1864. Fayetteville fell alternately under Confederate and Union control four times.

The Confederates' last major military effort was Price's raid in the fall of 1864. Aware that Union commanders had moved many troops to the eastern battlefields, Price moved his men north from the western Confederate heartland south of the Arkansas River. In his five-week foray into Missouri, Price aided the Confederacy by forcing the Union high command to recall some six thousand men from the Georgia campaign.

Although Price was anxious to begin the Missouri campaign, he waited so they could gather sufficient wagons and supplies, rest troops and horses, and be sure that the corn crop in Missouri was ripe enough to provide food and forage.[53] Suffering from several recent personal disappointments, he was anxious to make his mark. The Confederate high command had not recognized or advanced him in rank after what he considered a "brilliant campaign" at the Battle of Jenkins' Ferry, and then, even more galling, he saw Marmaduke advanced to the rank of major general over his objections.[54] He thought that Missouri was ready for a general uprising and wrote to General Kirby Smith, commander of the Confederate trans-Mississippi forces, claiming that large guerrilla parties were operating, and the "Confederate flag floats over nearly all the principal towns of North Missouri."[55]

With orders in hand, Price crossed the Arkansas River at Dardanelle on September 7, 1864. He divided his army's three divisions headed by Marmaduke, Fagan, and Shelby. Price's army of twelve thousand men entered Missouri in Ripley County with the intention of raiding

St. Louis. The Confederates captured the garrison town of Patterson on September 22, burning all the government stores and the fort.[56]

On September 27, 1864, at the Pilot Knob railhead, Price encountered a force of one thousand two hundred federal troops under General Thomas Ewing. Shelby, the junior officer present, favored bypassing Fort Davidson, arguing that the Union infantry offered no threat to a mounted force.[57] Marmaduke and Fagan, on the other hand, urged that the Pilot Knob garrison be disposed of before advancing on to St. Louis. Price decided to follow Marmaduke and Fagan's advice. Price at first planned to bombard the garrison into submission with artillery placed atop Shepherd Mountain. Just as he was about to give the necessary orders, a group of local citizens came to him, pleading that he should not shell the fort because the Federals were holding several southern adherents, including old men and boys. The Union commander, General Thomas Ewing, a veteran of the Kansas border war, staunchly refused to surrender. His entire command consisted of about 1,050 troops, about half of which had never before seen active service, about 100 volunteer citizens from Pilot Knob and the vicinity, and a small company of Negro volunteers. Southern guns began firing at 3:00 P.M. and simultaneously the divisions of Marmaduke and Fagan poured off the mountain sides and across the open valley. Firing from behind earthworks at Fort Davidson, the Union troops inflicted more than 1,500 casualties on the advancing troops.[58] Union losses were very light, about 200 killed, wounded, and missing. At nightfall the Union garrison slipped through the Confederate lines toward St. Louis after setting a slow fuse to blow up the powder magazine at the fort.

After losing some of his best cavalrymen at Fort Davidson, Price abandoned the plan to attack St. Louis. He marched north, then swung west toward Jefferson City. His troops fanned out across the countryside, burning bridges, destroying stores, capturing militia units by the score, disrupting communications, "exchanging" tired horses for fresh ones, and "liberating" dozens of small towns—De Soto, Pacific, St. Clair, Washington, Mount Sterling, Linn, Moreau—until he reached Jefferson City. Concluding that it was too well defended, he continued west. They fought major skirmishes at Glasgow and at Lexington, and Jo Shelby's cavalry units, who had become proficient in burning railroad bridges and tearing up long sections of the Pacific Railroad, made many raids. The captured men had the choice of joining the Confederates or promising not to join Union forces. Most chose the latter.[59]

Confederate guerrilla bands, encouraged by Price's advance into Missouri, became more active. These bands were made up of pro-southern Missourians who did not wish to serve in Price's or any other army, preferring to fight the Yankees "on their own hook" as guerrillas under the leadership of such men as Quantrill, William "Bloody Bill" Anderson, George Todd, John Thrailkill, Clif Holtzclaw, C. Calhoun "Coon" Thornton, and Dick Yaeger. These hard-riding and hard-fighting freebooters ravaged the Kansas-Missouri border region throughout the war. From their ranks came such postwar outlaws as Frank and Jesse James and Cole Younger. Bloody Bill Anderson and his gang rode into Price's camp near Boonville fresh from wiping out 150 Union militia at Centralia. Anderson's men had decorated their horses' bridles with the massacre victims' scalps. Price refused to talk to Anderson until he ordered his men to remove the scalps.[60]

As the Union defensive units grew and became organized, Price's situation became precarious. The daring raid became a retreat. As Price's forces moved westward from Lexington, they fought the final crucial battle of the campaign at Westport, October 21–23, in what is today part of Kansas City. It was a decisive victory for the Union forces commanded by General Curtis, and when Price ordered his troops to move south, they abandoned supplies and burned their wagons in their haste to regain refuge in Arkansas.[61] The 1,434-mile raid ended in defeat.

GUERRILLA WAR

The war brought out the best in some men, but it also revealed the worst in others. Men who might otherwise have led normal lives were prompted to pillage and rob. Foraging troops and raiding guerrillas drove many people from their homes. Guerrilla warfare was not new to the region. It predated the Civil War. Along the Kansas-Missouri border guerrilla units carried out bloody raids for nearly ten years before the Federals fired on Fort Sumter.[62] The Kansas guerrillas raiding in Missouri were called jayhawkers and their pro-slavery counterparts who wreaked havoc in Kansas were called bushwhackers.[63] The name jayhawker was applied initially to General James Lane and the men of his Kansas brigade, who achieved notoriety for their savage burning and plundering in Missouri.[64] Their counterpart, the Missouri "bushwhacker," was no less a robber, a thief, a rogue, and an assassin. Some of these bands of freebooters claimed allegiance to either the United States or the Confederacy and confined their depredations mainly to the civilian sympathizers and uniformed personnel of the opposite side. These groups could legitimately claim to be "guerrillas," although the Confederates preferred to use the term *partisan rangers* for those irregulars of southern sentiment.[65]

The historian Daniel Sutherland has suggested that in Arkansas they fought the true Civil War outside the formal military units and traditional battlefields as ambushes and midnight raids, with civilians treated as combatants and neighbors turned predators. It was

> not a war within a war, as some historians have suggested, not even a second war, but *the* war. Traditional set-piece battles did unfold at places like Pea Ridge and Prairie Grove, but most of the fighting, most of the terror and suffering in wartime Arkansas, came from irregular warfare, and it devastated the land and people.[66]

In Arkansas the northern two tiers of counties—the Ozark counties—particularly were dominated and overrun for most of the war by thieves and freebooters. These outlaws called themselves—as the situation demanded—Confederates or Federals. When they raided and robbed the families of Confederates they claimed to be Federals, but when they robbed families with Union sentiments they became Confederates.[67] The Confederate authorities actively encouraged the formation of guerrilla units and so must bear part of the blame for some of these bands getting out of hand and turning outlaw. Following the Confederate defeat at Pea Ridge, General Thomas Hindman, commander of the trans-Mississippi district, published an order on June 17, 1862, calling upon all citizens not subject to conscription to organize themselves into "Independent Companies," for more effective annoyance of the enemy.[68]

The Federals and freebooting jayhawkers inflicted harsh punishment upon known or suspected Confederate guerrillas and bushwhackers and their families. This in turn caused many Confederate soldiers to desert from the army and become bushwhackers to get revenge because the Federal guerrillas had burned their homes or mistreated or murdered their relatives.[69] On the other hand, southern guerrillas or bushwhackers, who were sometimes neighbors, preyed upon the many Union sympathizers in northern Arkansas. Because the history of the war in Arkansas was, until recently, written mainly by men of substance and education who supported the Confederacy, they wrote it from the Confederate point of view, with little mention of the more than eight thousand white Arkansans who volunteered for service with the Union army.[70] These white southern Unionists were the unknown soldiers of the Civil War.

Professor Kenneth C. Barnes has illuminated the precarious position of a northern Arkansas family with Union sympathies.[71] The men of the Williams clan, headed by Thomas Jefferson (Jeff) Williams, was very typical of the Union sympathizers in the backwoods Ozarks. In the 1840s, the Williams clan moved from Franklin County, Tennessee, to the hill country of southern Van Buren and northern Conway counties. The clan, consisting of Jeff's four sons, three sons-in-law, two brothers, four nephews, and a brother-in-law, did not oppose slavery, but they were staunch Unionists and when their neighbors joined or were conscripted into the Confederate militia and army units, the Williams clan fled to Batesville to join the Union army. Like many Confederate and Union guerrillas, they managed to stay in southern Missouri and northern Arkansas where they could maintain communication with their families. A bitter enemy of the clan was Colonel Allen R. Witt, the leader of a band of Confederate guerrillas from Conway and Van Buren counties. On the night of February 12, 1865, in the final months of conflict, the rebels managed to catch Williams at his log house near Center Ridge and kill him with a volley of buckshot. Family stories suggest that the Rebels beat the Williams women before they left. Both the Williams descendants and the descendants of the Rebels tell the story of the vengeance taken by the Williams clan. Leroy Williams, Jeff's eldest son, tracked the scattered band down, shooting one man in a cabin where he had sought refuge, then he killed three more as they watered their horses in a creek, and while the trail was still hot came upon the men again in camp and killed four more. Family tradition holds that Leroy Williams alone killed as many as sixteen members of the Rebel band that killed his father.[72] Terrorism and murder by Confederates and Federals alike were answered in kind. Bitter family feuds born during the Civil War lasted for generations.

Arson became a frequently used tool of warfare for military units and guerrillas from both sides. Both sides torched dozens of towns and thousands of cabins. Because water mills were centers for grinding of corn, wheat, and barley, and for sawing timber, planing wood, ginning cotton, carding wool, and weaving cloth, they were prizes for both Confederate and Union military units and guerrilla bands. When General McCulloch retreated after the Battle of Pea Ridge, Confederate soldiers burned about half of the fifteen to eighteen mills in Washington County, Arkansas, to keep them out of Federal hands.[73] McCulloch's men applied the same "scorched earth" policy to Fayetteville, where several homes, businesses, and the Female Academy fell to their torches.[74]

Murders were commonplace. William Baxter of Fayetteville, a Union sympathizer and president of Arkansas College, described how in June 1861 guerrilla bands under Confederate colonels John Coffee and James S. Rains brought prisoners to Fayetteville. They had taken these men, who had committed no crimes, from their homes. Baxter described how about midnight, without the least form of trial, four prisoners were marched southward out of town about a mile and shot.[75]

Guerrilla warfare in Missouri was fought just as bitterly. Throughout the war large guerrilla bands roamed the Missouri-Kansas border, the Missouri valley and the northern counties where southerners had settled. Here the more prosperous farms and towns could support larger guerrilla bands. Some guerrilla bands, led by dynamic leaders like "Bloody Bill" Anderson and Quantrill, numbered more than a thousand at times. William Quantrill's guerrillas, which included the likes of Frank and Jesse James, raided all along the western Missouri border. One of his most successful raids was the ambush of a Union column under General Blunt near Baxter Springs, Kansas, in October 1863.[76] Quantrill's quasi-military unit often worked closely with regular Confederate units and were involved in the battles of Wilson's Creek and Pea Ridge.

Smaller guerrilla bands roamed the Ozarks (fig. 7-1). Thomas Freeman's Confederate guerrillas used Texas and Shannon counties as their base for raids on farms and towns over a wide area of the interior Ozarks. When Union forces at Rolla and Fort Davidson (Pilot Knob) responded with search-and-destroy missions they produced little positive results because by the time they could respond, the guerrillas had escaped through the rugged hill country. Sam Hildebrand's Confederate guerrillas were the scourge of the lead belt counties. Based in St. Francois, Madison, and Washington counties, they raided over much of the eastern Ozarks. Two bands of pro-southern guerrillas roamed the southeastern Ozarks between the Union garrisons at Cape Girardeau and Batesville. Timothy Reeves's guerrillas were active in the lower Current River country along the Missouri-Arkansas boundary. John Burbridges's guerrillas roamed the hills along the Eleven Point River in Oregon County, Missouri, and adjacent counties in Arkansas. Alfred Cook's pro-Confederate band rode the hills along the Missouri-Arkansas border in the White River hills of Ozark County, Missouri, and in Marion and Baxter counties, Arkansas.

Some men who may have led uneventful lives in peaceful times were led into banditry by the war. Alfred "Alf" Bolin, whose sympathy appeared to be with the South, commanded no special notice in Christian County before the war. During the war he led a small band of ruffians who operated along the state boundary in Taney County, Missouri, and in Boone County, Arkansas. Bolin's haunt was the wagon road that wound from Little Rock to Springfield. Legend holds that his men would swoop down on a helpless freighter or small band of federal troops from the bluffs that became known as the "Murder Rocks" along the Missouri-Arkansas boundary.[77] As noted earlier, Jeff Williams commanded a band of Union sympathizers on the southern Ozarks border until they fled to Batesville to join the Union army, hoping they would find more safety there than in the backcountry.[78] Guerrilla activity was so fierce that by the end of 1864 ten counties along the Missouri-Arkansas border had been pillaged and torched so severely that much of the population had fled.

Margaret Gilmore Kelso never forgot the terror of bushwhacker raids on her father's Greene County farm. Margaret's father was a staunch Union man and member of the "Home Guard." The "Secesh" frequently raided the family though the farm was close to the Union garrison at Springfield. She describes one such occurrence:

I remember one time when father was away, there was a forage train of I don't know how many wagons. They took all the corn we had in the crib and all the hay we had. They also went to the smoke house and filled one wagon box of meat. The foragemaster paid mother with Confederate money. It was perfectly worthless, he knew, but he put up a good show of being honest.[79]

The raiders at the Gilmore farm apparently were local people who did not belong to either army. When they knew the women would be alone, they carried out raiding parties. Mrs. Kelso recalled that "they had their lookouts and their get-together signals and we could hear their whistles and horns when they were planning a raid. They usually disguised themselves and dressed in Union uniforms."[80] On one occasion when young Margaret Gilmore and her brother went to warn a neighbor about a party of bushwhackers, she watched from a hiding place as the band turned into a relative's farm:

At the corner, they took another road and went to Aunt Lucinda Gilmore's home and robbed her. She was alone. Uncle John had not been dead very long, and she kept his clothes in a little side room. They were taking his clothing, his hat, and his gun. She clung to his gun and begged them to let her keep her husband's things. They knocked her down and kicked her, breaking her ribs, and beat her over the head with the butt of the gun.

When Aunt Lucinda heard the bushwhackers had been to our place, she came over to see us. I can see her yet, as she sat there in the chimney corner, crying and telling us how they had abused her, and how bruised and battered she was. How black her face was! It was as black as flesh can be. She died a few days after she visited me, from the terrible beating they had given her.[81]

By the end of the war, much of Missouri and Arkansas had been thoroughly devastated. The war had been fought mainly in the border states, and the rural areas had borne the brunt of the war. St. Louis, Kansas City, and a few other cities had escaped the direct effects of the war, but few communities in the Ozarks had not experienced the ravages of a military or guerrilla raiding party. Invading armies and raiding parties visited and revisited some areas. Armies following the Wire Road between Springfield and Fayetteville, had, through their pillaging and raiding, created a "burn zone" in which two-thirds of all structures had been burned in a swath several miles wide on either side (fig. 7-1). Many interior counties had been virtually depopulated and the "safe" garrison towns, like Springfield, Fayetteville, Batesville, and Rolla, experienced such an influx of refugees that they increased in population.[82]

Great hardship and shortages, even the threat of starvation, were immediate concerns when the war broke out. William Baxter, Fayetteville's outspoken Unionist, wrote,

> . . . all at once we awoke to the fact that we were in the Confederacy, within the Southern lines. The mails stopped, newspapers ceased to be seen, men began to look at the resources of the country, and soon the fact stared every man in the face, that for nearly every necessity, and all the luxuries of life, we had hitherto been dependent on the now hated North. Hardware, schoolbooks, stationery, dry-goods, medicines, implements of agriculture, groceries, carpets, hats, shoes, pins, needles, matches, almanacs, nay everything, one might say, were now foreign articles. . . . In the new zeal for independence, the nature and extent of former dependence had been entirely overlooked, and the effect, when it first flashed on many minds, was to produce blank astonishment.[83]

For a time some things could be purchased at "fabulous prices" but after both the Confederate and Union armies passed through Fayetteville, there was nothing left to purchase. In the rural areas, where there were few luxuries to begin with, the people dealt with fending off starvation.

Professor Carl H. Moneyhon compiled compelling evidence of material losses at the end of the war in Arkansas. Tax records revealed that in 1865, as compared to 1860, Arkansas had lost half of its horses and 39 percent of its mules. Both horses and mules were essential to the restoration of agriculture. Cattle were down 43 percent, from 24,407 to 14,221. Personal property, including furniture, carriages, and jewelry, declined by a half to two-thirds, not to mention the total property loss of slaves due to emancipation.[84] It is reasonable to assume the losses were similar or worse in all other war-devastated parts of the Ozarks.

Throughout the war, the hills were a dangerous no man's land between Union and Confederate power. Unlike the western border of Missouri, depopulated by decree under the Union army's Order No. 11, the interior of the Ozark upland emptied gradually because of four years of military action and nearly complete destruction of the region's modest resources.[85] The refugees fled to the only places that provided a chance of safety, the military garrison towns, namely, Cape Girardeau, Pilot Knob, Sedalia, Jefferson City, Springfield, and Rolla, and in Arkansas, Fayetteville, Lewisburg (near Morrilton), and Batesville. There they relied on the charity of the local population or pled for food and necessities from the Union army. Margaret Gilmore Kelso was a young person during the war, but she recalled that many families from Arkansas moved into her neighborhood on Clear Creek in Greene County, Missouri. These people had lost everything they had:

> We called them refugees. Father gave them work, let them have corn and wheat for bread, cows to milk and a team to plow with. They were all honest and industrious, hard working people. Some of them stayed on after the war was over. Some of them went back to Arkansas and rebuilt their homes on their own land.[86]

Because of the great influx of refugees from Arkansas, transients probably outnumbered native residents for much of the war at Springfield.[87] Springfield and Rolla became the primary relief centers in the interior Ozarks.[88] Refugees who could afford it traveled to Rolla where they boarded the train for points east. Because of the increasingly destitute condition of the refugees, some Union army commanders doled out military rations to them. Many ordinary requests for rations went unfilled, and the commanders who requested rations for refugees were seldom successful. The refugees depended on the "buckwheat cake philanthropy, of a hard and somewhat frigid world for a sickly existence upon sheet-iron crackers and pork of the highest rank."[89] Many refugees accompanied the Union army when they retreated to Rolla following the Battle of Wilson's Creek. Marmaduke's raid on Springfield and other southern advances in early 1862 inspired more civilians to move toward the army lines. Many refugees accompanied General John C. Fremont to Rolla when he was ordered to give up his command. The battles at Pea Ridge and Prairie Grove produced additional waves of refugees.[90] The refugee problem continued until the war ended.

RECONSTRUCTION AND REDRAWING THE POLITICAL MAP

The Civil War had several important effects on the land and people of the Ozarks, and these lasted for several years. The broad national issues, such as slavery and the right of states to disregard federal laws, had been settled by the war. The western frontier states, including the Ozarks, participated in Reconstruction. Railroad building soon reached a furious pace, and economic development took the form of new farms, new manufacturing plants, new commercial and banking enterprises, and mineral and timber exploitation. Immigration to the Ozarks increased rapidly, and this time more of the immigrants came from the North. Many leaders in the economic resurgence were former Union officers who had served in the Ozark campaigns.

Forces outside the region shaped the political destiny of the Ozarks. The core political areas of both Missouri and Arkansas lie in the valleys of the two great rivers that flow through the two states. During the entire span of white occupation of the Ozarks, the region has contributed comparatively few elected state officials. On the other hand, the Missouri and Arkansas valleys are in the mainstream of the state politics. The three major contributors of state and national political leaders are Greene County, Missouri, which included the Ozarks' largest city, Springfield; Washington County, Arkansas, which includes Fayetteville, site of the state university; Tahlequah, Oklahoma, the capital of the Cherokee Nation. Jefferson City and Little Rock lie on Ozark borders but are politically aligned with the core areas of Missouri and Arkansas, respectively.

To say that Ozarkers were apolitical after the Civil War would be an overstatement, but no doubt isolation and lack of a developed economy were factors in the comparatively lesser role Ozarks people played in the rapidly changing political situations of Missouri and Arkansas. In both states they required a loyalty oath of voters; they compelled the individual to swear he had never given aid or sympathy to the Confederate movement. This effectively disenfranchised at least a third of the otherwise eligible voters. Voters elected Radical Republican governments in both Arkansas and Missouri, but the Cherokee Nation regained the Oklahoma Ozarks under the supervision of the federal government. The Democrats regained control of the legislature and governorship in Missouri by 1870 and in Arkansas by 1874. Both states have been firmly in the Democratic column ever since, except for the terms of Republican governors Powell Clayton, Elisha Baxter, Winthrop Rockefeller, Frank White, and Mike Huckabee in Arkansas and Republican governors Herbert

S. Hadley, Arthur M. Hyde, Forest C. Donnell, Sam A. Baker, Henry S. Caulfield, Christopher S. Bond, and John Ashcroft in Missouri. By 1876, Democrats had recaptured most of the elected offices in the county governments. However, over the past thirty years the Republican Party has gained strength in both states.

The transition period brought on by the Civil War was not yet over. At the county level, economic and social changes crippled Democratic ambitions; the Civil War had left the Ozarks ravaged and ruined. The Panic of 1873 brought on a depression, and the grasshopper plague of 1874 destroyed most of the crops. Most of the counties were heavily in debt as they borrowed to finance railroads, to build new courthouses to replace those destroyed in the war, and to undertake other types of public improvements. Many people blamed the Democrats, who were in power when the counties made the debts, for the high taxes required to pay them off. Taney County, Missouri, owed $44,000 in 1874, an extremely large debt for that time, and it was not liquidated until the 1930s.[91]

The great amount of social unrest in the western Ozarks was another factor in the defeat of the Democrats and the rise of Republicanism in the mid-1880s. Crime and violence, which had become common during the war, continued. A certain class of citizens had grown accustomed to a shiftless way of life and held little regard for laws and the property of their neighbors. The region was still not fully settled, and isolation was a magnet for transient outlaws. Bands of marauders, led by such men as Jesse James and Cole Younger, robbed and plundered two decades after the Civil War, and the Republicans used outlawry as an issue to weaken the Democratic Party.

People formed vigilance committees to combat lawlessness and to oppose further increases in county debts. The vigilance groups were not of the same ilk as the Ku Klux Klan, but their central purpose—establishing order—was not altogether out of line with the Klan's goals. It was a time when law and order at any cost were gaining popularity and growing in strength throughout the South.

Vigilance committees were not new to the Ozarks. In the 1840s people in Benton County, Missouri, formed an organization known as the Slickers, to "slick," with hickory switches, all suspected lawbreakers. Another group, known as the Enforcers, was active in Greene County, Missouri. During the war, nearly every county had a home guard, which took on the job of guarding bridges and railroads and providing some measure of civil control. A secret political order, the Union League, flourished in Greene County during the war for the avowed purpose of "aiding and abetting by all honorable means of the Federal government in its efforts to put down the rebellion."[92]

Unfortunately they allowed these purposes to deteriorate to the worst uses, and the order was frequently used for the gratification of private revenges in the name of loyalty.

Following the war, lawlessness continued. Even when officials arrested and indicted men, and brought them to trial, it seemed an impossibility to convict them. Under these circumstances a group of Greene County citizens formed a vigilance band, the Honest Man's League, which became known as the Regulators. This group helped the sheriff in arresting men accused of various minor crimes, but also seized several men and hung them without trial. On or about June 1, 1866, the Regulators rode into Springfield in strength. About two hundred and eighty horsemen formed a hollow square in the public square in front of the courthouse where a local minister who was an active member addressed them. Following the meeting, the group rode south into Christian County where they arrested a Greene County fugitive, a man named James Edwards, tried him for theft, found him guilty, and hung him to a large oak tree at the side of the road.[93] The Regulators struck terror into the hearts of the thieving element, "and very quickly rendered Greene County . . . free from depredations."[94] When the worst forms of lawlessness declined, the group disbanded.

One of the largest and most influential of the vigilance committees was the group of Taney County, Missouri, residents who watched the proceedings of county government and assisted law-enforcement officials in the pursuit, capture, and conviction of criminals. People called them the Bald Knobbers because they sometimes held their meetings on isolated, treeless hills.[95] Citizens of nearby Christian County organized another Bald Knobber band in the 1880s when the railroad and sawmill town of Chadwick developed a lawless character.

After a few men allegedly were murdered by the Bald Knobbers and others severely intimidated, another group of citizens organized to combat the activities of the Bald Knobbers. Known as the Anti-Bald Knobbers, they were mostly Confederate Democrats. The Bald Knobbers membership originally was composed of Unionists, Confederates, Democrats, and Republicans, but as time passed, some degree of polarization toward Republicanism developed.

In his account of Taney County politics, Elmo Ingenthron describes how the transfer of allegiance from the Democratic Party to the Republican Party occurred:

The Bald Knobbers won the election of 1886, and the Republican Party which they dominated has won the majority of county offices in the elections ever since. For several years following the political victories of the mid-1880's, the two principal political parties in the country were the Bald Knobber-Republican and Anti-Bald Knobber-Democrats.[96]

When members of the Bald Knobbers raided an innocent family in Christian County and killed two men, the public discredited the group both locally and nationally. Officials arrested more than a dozen Bald Knobbers, and on May 10, 1889, three of the convicted men were hanged at Ozark, Missouri.[97] Whether or not the vigilance groups helped to shape the future of politics in the Ozarks is conjectural, but surely the Republican counties of southwest Missouri and northwest Arkansas suffered severely during the war and its aftermath.

CONTEMPORARY POLITICS

The political map of the Ozarks has not changed much since the 1880s. Southwest Missouri has the reputation of being solid Republican country, and the main strength of Republicans in Arkansas always has been in the northwestern counties. This part of the Ozarks had many pro-Union sympathizers during the Civil War, and it suffered greatly through the devastation wrought by marching armies and by guerrillas and bushwhackers. It was here too that vigilantism was strongest. Residents of the eastern interior Ozarks, which experienced less bloodshed and civil strife, are strongly Democrat, although equally conservative in their ideology as the rural Republicans. The northern and eastern Ozarks border counties, where there is a large German population, often vote Republican in state and national elections.[98] The counties of the eastern Mineral Area lean toward the Democratic ticket.

Over the years, in both political parties, a system of earning political clout has been practiced in Ozark counties much as it has in many rural counties of the United States. This system can be described as good-old-boy politics. A birthright in a pioneer family is helpful in being elected to a local political office. However, performance of certain ritualistic activities usually is expected before one is selected to run for sheriff, county commissioner, county clerk, or another office. Those who are successful in gaining the approval of the dominant party have usually performed various chores and possess various attributes that make them qualify as trustworthy for elected office. For instance, this would include being on hand to help with preparations for political picnics or gatherings; helping to get out the vote on election day by driving seniors or the infirm to the voting places in one's personal car; being a good hand at most things one undertakes; and for male candidates, having a strong liking for manly sports, especially hunting and fishing; being good at telling an off-color joke in proper surroundings; being good at social conversation with women, but not to the extent of being a lady's man; having a good sense of humor; and being willing to help with family emergencies, such as serious illness or death, that strike one's neighbors. In the counties that vote solid Republican or Democrat, election to an office is usually assured when a "good old boy" gains the nomination of the dominant party. Successful tenure in a county office is sometimes the steppingstone to a state or national political office.

Loyalty to political parties, often passed down from parents to children, can be very strong. Dewey Short, longtime Seventh District representative from southwest Missouri to the United States Congress, was known as an eloquent orator and a fervent Republican.[99] Congressman Short was born at Galena, Missouri, graduated from Marionville College, attended Baker University, earned a bachelors of Divinity from Boston College, and attended Harvard Law School. After short stints before the bar, teaching college, and in the pulpit, he was elected to the U.S. House of Representatives in November 1928. Short's speaking abilities earned him the title, "Orator of the Ozarks." During the 1928 campaign he spoke on "Republicanism and Americanism" at the Lincoln Day Banquet in Springfield where he expressed his strong Republican sentiments this way:

Republicanism is Americanism. It is part of my religion and if I can convert any democrat, I will have served God as well as my country. . . . (We), with unflinching courage and unswerving loyalty, will march together under the united, inspiring and intrepid banner of Republicanism to victory next November.[100]

Short served through much of the New Deal era, maintaining steadfast, but unsuccessful, opposition to many of the depression-era proposals of President Franklin Roosevelt and what he called the "professorial nincompoops" in Roosevelt's New Deal "Brain Trust," and the Democrat-led congress.[101] Conservative Seventh District voters elected him in 1928, and then reelected him in 1934, and in subsequent elections until he left the United States House of Representatives in 1956. He left the Congress just three years before the dedication of the Table Rock Dam, a project he had fought hard for in Washington, D.C.

There are signs, mainly in the counties that have experienced considered growth, that the old system is dying out. In counties with large populations, such as Greene, Cole, Jasper, Jefferson, Cape Girardeau, and St. Francois

in Missouri and Benton, Washington and Independence in Arkansas, the elected county officials may be responsible for budgets running into millions of dollars. As recently as the August 2000 primary election, a widely popular Republican sheriff of Greene County, Missouri, who had held the office for twenty years, lost a hard-fought election to a younger Republican candidate with considerable law-enforcement experience with the highway patrol.[102] Increasingly, voters are coming to recognize that an officeholder should possess more qualifications than being a good old boy. Moreover, as more new people move into the region, one's birthright in a long-line Ozark family becomes less important in gaining political office. Another factor in the weakening of partisan politics is the growing importance of "personality politics" in which a popular candidate, backed by strong financial support, can sweep into office behind heavy media advertising no matter party affiliation.[103]

THE QUESTION OF GUNS AND LAWLESSNESS

Frontier areas, mining camps, and lumber camps have always had a certain propensity for rowdiness and lawlessness. The Ozarks has had its share of violence and crime, and the historical geography of the region may have been a factor. The terrain is rough, and even now still difficult to traverse in remote areas. Heavy forest cover, deep valleys, secretive caves, and remote houses and abandoned buildings provided hiding places for criminals on the run. The western border experienced ten years of depredation by Kansas border ruffians. The Oklahoma Ozarks, then Indian Territory, suffered from internecine murders and outlawry committed in the name of revenge among the warring factions of the Cherokee nation. Then followed nearly five years of Civil War in which Confederate and Union armies, clashing in large battles, whipsawed the southwestern Ozarks. Throughout the war the entire countryside suffered countless guerrilla raids of unspeakable savageness. Desperate people formed home guard units to try to provide protection from these marauding quasi-military bands. Following the war lawlessness was so severe that they formed vigilance groups to deal out on-the-spot punishment. When the legal process seemed too slow, or people feared that it might fail altogether, they resorted to lynchings. Two large mining districts developed in the region, and the western border remained Indian Territory and became a refuge for gangs of outlaws, such as the notorious band led by Tom Starr, a Cherokee descended from a family among those who signed the treaty of removal.

Before the emergence of effective interstate law enforcement, which the creation of the Federal Bureau of Investigation facilitated, state boundaries were effective protection for lawbreakers. Four states meet in the rugged forested hills of the southwestern Ozarks: Kansas, Missouri, Oklahoma, and Arkansas. Hundreds of caves and thousands of abandoned farmhouses and barns provide hiding places. Thus the Ozarks, particularly the southwest, possessed many things that attracted the likes of the James gang, the Daltons, the Younger brothers, the Starrs, and, in the twentieth century, John Dillinger, Bonnie and Clyde, and Alvin Karpis, not to mention hundreds of lesser criminal luminaries.[104] This section, more than any other, became the robbers' roost of the Ozark region.

Even now there is sufficient lawlessness to alarm most people. The legacy of moonshining—whiskey stills, bathtub gin, bootleg beer—seems tame compared with the modern drug problems and the burglaries, robberies, and other criminal acts associated with their manufacture and use.[105] Unfortunately, the Ozarks has gained a reputation as a refuge for producers of marijuana and methamphetamine. The production of marijuana on private land and on hidden patches in the national forests has been a persistent problem over the past thirty-five years. While no accurate assessment of the volume of production can be made, it has been estimated that marijuana is the leading crop in several Ozark counties.

Cocaine and crack cocaine are "big city" drugs, said to be mainly imported from St. Louis, Chicago, and Kansas City, but dealers market both in the Ozarks. In recent years, methamphetamine has become the scourge of the Ozarks. In some ways, the manufacture and sale of "meth" resembles the manufacture of moonshine or white lightning whiskey. Drug makers produce various forms of meth from anhydrous ammonia, batteries, and household chemicals, products all readily available or easily stolen. They produce the meth in city warehouses and dwellings, in farmhouses and barns, and sometimes in mobile labs set up in automobiles and vans.[106] The materials are dangerous, potentially harmful to the manufacturers and to law-enforcement officers and nearby residents. Special skill and training is required for the arrest and conviction of the criminal manufacturers and marketers of the illicit material.

Illicit drugs appear ubiquitous. They appear in nearly every city, town, and hamlet in the Ozarks. Many residents blame the widespread distribution of the drug lifestyle on the myriad television "drug operas" and movies depicting use and commerce of meth, cocaine, crack, and marijuana. Mobility and the breakdown of isolation have made drugs easy to obtain. Residents of small Ozark towns, some who have moved there to find a safer place to raise their children, are often surprised to read newspaper and television reports of drug arrests in their own community.

There is no denying that the problem is severe and that people are concerned about it. A simple library search of news stories related to drug crimes for the period June 4, 1971, to September 1, 2000, in the *Springfield News-Leader* revealed 400 accounts dealing with marijuana and 170 stories dealing with cocaine. In a period of less than twelve years, between November 8, 1988, and September 1, 2000, the same newspaper printed 448 stories dealing with methamphetamines (meth) from a thirty-county area in southwest Missouri and north-central Arkansas.[107]

Like most parts of the United States, sadly, criminal justice with all of its supporting components—courts, prosecuting and defense attorneys, bail bond companies, probation officers, jails, halfway houses, with all the abetting logistical personnel—has become big business in the Ozarks. Many counties have had to increase tax levies to increase funding for courtrooms, jails, and personnel. Presently, Greene County, Missouri, is building a large addition to its jail after recently constructing a new courts building. In nearby Christian County, a new jail is rising on the square across the street from the courthouse in Ozark, the county seat.

Some elements of frontier attitudes toward crime and the use of firearms persist. People living in rural areas of the United States usually own guns and know how to use them. Many adolescents—boys and girls—can shoot rifles and shotguns. After all, hunting is an important form of recreation. Often, schools dismiss during deer seasons so that teachers and students alike may take up positions in the forest.

There is a more subtle, deeper reason rural people cling to their guns. They are in exposed positions, often out of sight of neighbors; sometimes county law officers are an hour or more away by automobile. When a fugitive on a killing spree killed a Polk County resident at his home in January 2000 and later broke into another house seeking food and guns, residents over a wide area locked their doors and kept a close watch. One resident of Bearcreek exclaimed to a reporter, "I never slept a lot last night. And we had the gun handy."[108] The woods and hills still provide cover for those who are fleeing from the law. When the culprit is a local, someone who knows the land and landscape as well or better than the searching officers, the hunt may go on for days or even weeks. Rural people, recognizing the challenges law officers face, feel they must be prepared to protect themselves. The home guard idea of individual protection is still strong in the Ozarks.

EIGHT

TRANSPORTATION, TECHNOLOGY, AND CULTURAL TRANSFORMATION

The story of transportation, communication, and provision of electrical and fuel energy to the Ozarks is a story of cultural transformation. Surely the Ozarks' progression from an isolated backwoods area to a growing mixed economy of manufacturing, retailing, services, and tourism is based in large part on effective transportation and communication and the power and energy resources to keep the system running.

One can hardly imagine the isolation of the early settlements in the Ozarks, situated almost in the center of the continent, surrounded by warlike Indians. A trip by land from the interior meant a journey for as much as two hundred miles on foot or horseback along Indian trails and war paths, across unbridged streams, often flowing out of their banks. At the end of a hard day's travel, the voyager had to find a dry spot to camp and dry wood to build a fire to cook rabbit, squirrel, turkey, or whatever game he might have been lucky enough to have killed during the day's journey. It is little wonder that rivers were the preferred means of travel.

In the days of first white settlement the Mississippi, Missouri, and Arkansas rivers and their tributaries were the arteries that carried the Indian canoes, flat-bottoms, and keelboats bringing raw products and needed supplies to trade centers and settlements. Before steamboats arrived on the western rivers, keelboats were the workhorse commercial carriers.[1] Keelboats were large, heavy-timbered crafts with rounded bottoms, ranging in size from forty to seventy-five feet long and from eight to twelve feet wide. The heavy four-inch-thick keel down the center of the boat was strong enough to withstand scraping over sandbars and bumping into snags along the trip. Most keelboats had a covered cargo box where crew members could find shelter during heavy downpours. They also equipped all keelboats with a cordelle (rope) fastened to the bow with which they could pull the vessel upstream when the current was too strong for oars or poles.[2] Some pioneers traveled to the Ozarks by flatboat, a craft favored by fron-

tier families because they more easily constructed it than the keelboat. These simple, shallow-draft craft, sometimes called "broadhorns," varied in size from twenty to sixty feet long and from ten to twenty feet wide.[3] They were unweildy craft, difficult to pole upstream, but their draft of one to two and one-half feet allowed them to travel farther upstream. Flatboats carried cargoes downstream long after steam navigation became common, and because they were cheap to build, they helped reduce the price of downstream haulage.

The first steamboat on the Mississippi River was the *New Orleans.* It set out from Pittsburgh on the Ohio River in September 1811, and after difficulty passing the rapids at Cincinnati, and further delays due to the New Madrid earthquakes, it finally reached New Orleans, January 12, 1812.[4] The first steamboat to travel up the Mississippi from the mouth of the Ohio, the *Zebulon M. Pike,* traveled from Louisville, Kentucky, to St. Louis in 1817, pushing upstream at the impressive rate of three miles per hour. Two years later a specially designed shallow-draft steamer, the *Independence,* moved up the Missouri River to Franklin. In spite of navigation problems and the danger of explosions, steamboats replaced keelboats and flatboats, which required pulling, poling, or paddling. Steamboats were faster and larger and could carry heavier and bulkier cargoes. They could give passengers rooms, board, fashionable furnishings, and entertainment. Very soon steamboat lines established regular packet service at several Mississippi and Missouri river towns that served as ports for the northern and eastern Ozarks. The usual ports of call on the Mississippi River were Cape Girardeau, Ste. Genevieve, and St. Louis; on the Missouri the main ports serving the Ozarks were St. Charles, Washington, Hermann, Jefferson City, Boonville, and Glasgow.[5]

Steamboats could navigate only a few of the largest streams that drained from the interior of the Ozark Upland. Small steamboats pushed up the Gasconade and the Osage, but with difficulty because of frequent low

Riverfront at Cape Girardeau. (Courtesy of State Historical Society of Missouri.)

water and many snags. The first use of steamboats on the Osage was in 1837, but even earlier rafts, canoes, and keelboats had plied the river to trade with the Osage Indians. Lewis and Clark encountered small rafts loaded with furs and pelts from the Osage River when they moved up the Missouri on their celebrated expedition. In July 1837, the *North St. Louis,* reportedly the first steamboat on the Osage, steamed upstream about thirty miles before running aground when the river fell rapidly. During the spring rise in 1838, the *Adventure* managed to travel one hundred and sixty miles upstream with little difficulty. Benjamin B. Bryan put the *Osage Packet,* the first packet boat, in service in 1840. During the 1840s, river trade was well established with several shallow-draft steamboats operating on the river, including the *Maid of Osage* (built at Osage City), the *James H. Lucas,* the *Wave,* and the *Alliance.*[6] The owners raised the latter two boats after they sank and put them back in service. The 147-ton *Osage,* a sidewheeler that traveled efficiently in shallow water, ran on the Osage for several years. It later ran on the White River and the Little Red River after the Pacific Railroad captured the Osage River trade.[7] Although the Osage River was notorious for widely fluctuating water levels, shallow-draft steamboats landed at Warsaw regularly during the fall and spring months and could reach Osceola when conditions were especially favorable. On the high

floodwaters of 1844, the diminutive *James H. Lucas* ascended the river as far as Harmony Mission in Bates County, beyond the western boundary of the Ozarks.[8] By 1860, sixteen steamboats were carrying "salt, groceries, nails, iron and such products upstream, and apples, dried beef, barley, beans, cattle, chickens, butter, flour, hemp, lard, tallow and other things downstream."[9]

Massey and James, owners of the Maramec Iron Works, persisted in trying to improve navigation on the Meramec and Gasconade rivers. Except during rises, the Meramec was too shallow and had too many fallen trees in the channel to permit even a keelboat to pass the full 172 miles from the Mississippi to the ironworks. Nevertheless, heavy items, such as large forge hammers and anvils, were transported part of the way up the Meramec.[10] In 1835 and 1836, Massey and James petitioned the Missouri General Assembly for state aid in opening the Gasconade River to steamboats. They proposed to clear the Gasconade of all logs and snags obstructing navigation, to construct wing dams to channel the water, and to keep the river clear for a two-year period in return for a charter to collect tolls on the tonnage of all steamboats. The assembly turned down the offer, but Massey and James removed the snags and logs without state aid. They wasted the effort because steamboats still could not reach the ironworks landing at Paydown. The *Iowa,* the *Howard,* the *Dart,* and the

Captain attempted to ascend the river, but low water turned them back.[11] Other attempts to reach the ironworks' shipping point at Paydown also failed. In 1849, flatboats successfully transported iron blooms from Paydown to the Missouri River, where they were loaded on steamboats. Overland drayage from Maramec to Hermann averaged between two and four dollars per ton more than shipping from Paydown.[12]

Because railroads began competing with steamboats on the Missouri River and its Ozark tributaries by the 1850s, steamboat commerce did not last as long on the Osage and Gasconade rivers compared with the White River. The struggle between the steamboat and the railroad on the Missouri River began with the completion of the Hannibal and St. Joseph Railroad in 1859. Competition increased with the completion of the Missouri Pacific from St. Louis to Kansas City in 1866.[13] The Missouri Pacific line to Kansas City captured much of the commerce from the trade hinterland of the Osage and Gasconade rivers.

Although steamboat navigation on the Arkansas River was not as well developed as that on the Mississippi and Missouri, riverboats were important for the early settlement and commerce of the Arkansas River valley and the southern Ozarks. Some Cherokees who moved to their new lands in Indian Territory during the 1830s traveled by way of the Arkansas River.[14] Nevertheless, in the early 1840s only two or three steamboats a month reached Little Rock via a channel frequently described as "four feet deep and falling."

As steamboating developed, small boats were built that could travel short distances into the Ozarks on the Black and Current rivers. The little thirty-three-ton *Malta* ran in the Black River from Pocahontas, Arkansas, to Poplar Bluff, Missouri, and as far up the Current River as it could go, usually to Doniphan.[15] Small boats also could navigate the Little Red River to Searcy, Arkansas.[16]

The White River was the only stream flowing from the interior Ozarks large enough to become an important artery of commerce for steamboats. Most of the navigation was done during high water. W. M. Wolf brought the first steamboat up to Wolf House in Baxter County, Arkansas, probably in the late 1830s or early 1840s. Before the steamboats came—and during the dry seasons—keelboats were poled upriver and floated downstream, carrying up to fifty bales of cotton.

In 1876, boats stopped at forty-five landings between Batesville, Arkansas, and the northernmost landing at Forsyth, Missouri.[17] Beginning at the south and running north the larger shipping points were at Chastain, Norfork, Bomer's, Shipp's, Buford, Buffalo, Buffalo City, Mooney's Landing, Wildcat Shoals, and at McBee's Landing

two miles up and across the river from Cotter. McBee's Landing was in Marion County and served as a shipping point for Flippin and Yellville. No steamboat was successful in passing Elbow Shoals just above Dubuque (near today's Diamond City) until the *Yohogony*, piloted by D. H. Hardy, passed through the shoals and reached Forsyth in June 1852.[18] The steamboat *Ray* reached the mouth of the James River in 1859, the farthest point ever reached on the White River by a steamboat.[19] In 1876, the *Batesville,* piloted by Edwin T. B. Warner, also reached the mouth of the James River to equal the feat of the *Ray.* These were the only steamboats to make the hazardous trip through dangerous waters.

Steamboat builders designed shallow-draft boats to run the rocky shoals and chutes of the White River. Most of them weighed fifty to two hundred tons and could carry seventy-five to five hundred bales of cotton. Several boats held mail contracts including the *Jesse Lazear* and the *Monongahela Belle,* which carried mail from Batesville to Buffalo and Buffalo City. Steamboats provided the fastest and easiest mode of travel. The trip from Batesville to McBee's Landing, a distance of one hundred miles, took twenty-four hours, the return trip twelve hours. The boats' wood-fired steam boilers were fueled with pine knots and split wood. Woodyards were at all landings and at some points between.

The Civil War made river commerce and travel dangerous. While Union troops and gunboats quickly drove the Confederates from the rivers in the northern and eastern Ozarks, guerrillas continued to plague federal boats. The Confederates hoped to control the rivers from the banks. From heavy forest cover snipers fired on the boats with little danger of capture or retribution. It was not until September 1863 that Union forces gained full control of the White River, and even then those steamboats that continued to traverse the White River during the war were in constant danger of attacks by Confederate guerrillas.[20]

Showboats that played regularly to crowds at the Mississippi, Missouri, and Arkansas river towns sometimes traveled up the White River. Their arrival was always a time of great excitement, and throngs of people gathered at the landings. The first black men many children saw were deckhands on the boats.

The federal government spent considerable sums of money in the late 1800s to keep the river channels open. In 1870 the U.S. Army Corps of Engineers survey boat *City of Forsyth* studied the White and Black rivers. It reported 2,019 snags and two wrecks hazardous to navigation. Lead and zinc mine owners along the Buffalo River made many petitions to the U.S. Army Corps of Engineers to make the stream navigable for small steamboats to provide easier transportation of the ore from the mountainous area. After Captain Will T. Warner successfully piloted the *Dauntless* up the Buffalo to Rush, Arkansas, to deliver mine machinery in May 1896, the demand for navigation improvements increased. Following a survey by the U.S. Army Corps of Engineers, it was determined that navigation was possible only by constructing five locks and dams costing $750,000, a cost too high for the amount of expected commerce.[21]

In 1900, steamboats started bringing a new cargo upriver: supplies, equipment, and materials for railroad building. Ironically, the steamboats helped themselves out of business. The railroad constructed the bridge at Cotter, Arkansas, so that it could swing aside to allow passage of steamboats. The bridge turntable opened only once: in 1913 when the steamer *G. W. Huff* came up the White for a load of staves. Its coming created quite a stir along the river because by that time trains provided faster, more economical, reliable, efficient service. Timber boats like the *G. W. Huff* continued to operate on the river hauling logs, staves, and sawed lumber from sawmills. Between July 1908 and May 1910, the *G. W. Huff* made 187 trips in the upper White River, running 3,616 miles and carrying 13,682 tons of freight, the equivalent of 547 freight carloads.[22] The last steamboat to operate regularly, the *Ozark Queen,* made her final scheduled upper White River run from McBee's Landing to Batesville in June 1903.[23]

For a time, boats operated on the White and Black rivers in the freshwater-mussel industry, just as they did on the Cumberland, Tennessee, and other rivers in the uplands east of the Mississippi. Dr. J. H. Meyers of Black Rock on the Black River is credited with starting the "pearling boom." In 1897 he found a fourteen-grain, fine-luster, pinkish-colored pearl that generated a stampede of pearl hunters into the rivers. When some pearls brought five dollars to fifty dollars each, rumors soon spread of pearls bringing even higher prices. One writer described the search on the White River as follows:

> I have seen as many as 500 men, women, and children of all sizes and colors on one bar, indiscriminately mingled, wading in as they could reach bottom, some opening, others gathering shells. The wealthiest bankers, lawyers, merchants, doctors, etc., their wives and children, wading in with the poorest darkies, all laughing, singing, working day after day, the summer through.[24]

Large spherical pearls of desired color and luster were in demand for jewelry, but most shells went to button factories. Most regional button factories were downstream in Arkansas, but portable button extractors on flatboats oper-

ated on the upper White River. It took about forty bushels of mussel shells to make a bushel of buttons, so blank buttons sawed out at upstream locations went downstream to the factories for drilling and finishing.

Twenty-nine species of mussels reportedly inhabited the White River, but the most common types were *Actinonaias carinata, Lampsilis ventricosa,* and *Pleurobema cordatum coccineum.*[25] The industry was seasonal and did not interfere with farm activities. It lasted about thirty-five years, from about 1900 to the mid-1930s. The mussel boats were among the last steam-powered boats to use the White River for commerce.

Downriver flatboat commerce continued well past the turn of the century on the White River. Flatboats built at river landings kept moving cotton, crossties, grain, and cedar logs to markets in Arkansas and other downriver ports. Several small rafts of crossties and cedar logs linked with poles formed a snake raft. These unwieldy craft were hazards for steamboats, and it was no easy task to halt the forward movement of a raft composed of as many as fifteen hundred logs or ties.

Nearly every permanently flowing stream in the Ozarks once floated crossties. Normally they cut the ties in winter and stacked them alongside a stream to await the spring rise. Then they were floated downstream to shipping points on railroads. Most of the time, they floated them in rafts, but sometimes they simply pushed them into the current to float downstream.

Interestingly enough, laws governing the use of streams for navigation during the logging era protect the popular sports of canoeing and float fishing on Ozark streams today. In a landmark case, Elder v. Delcour, the Missouri Supreme Court declared that all Missouri streams are open to canoeing and fishing because they are navigable waters by warrant of their use to float crossties.[26] Arkansas, Oklahoma, and Kansas also allow use of streams for recreational purposes.

Today the Mississippi River and its connecting systems of waterways comprise an expanding 22,000-mile navigation network. The Mississippi has an improved 9-foot channel throughout its course in Missouri; below St. Louis there are no locks or dams. The river is open to navigation from St. Louis to New Orleans twelve months a year and from early March to mid-December on the upper portion. Navigation to Chicago via the Illinois River is open the full year. Navigation of the Missouri River's 7.5-foot channel is normally from late March to the end of November. The Arkansas River and its northern tributaries, the Grand and Verdigris rivers, are navigable to the Port of Catoosa, a few miles east of Tulsa. This remarkable series of dams and locks, patterned after those on the Tennessee River, was the special project of Oklahoma senator Robert S. Kerr, who worked untiringly year after year to secure the necessary votes in Congress to finance the project.

About ten common-carriers barge lines serve the Ozarks' border. St. Louis is the largest river port, with two public docks and thirty-seven private docks. The other major Mississippi port serving the Ozarks is Cape Girardeau, which has twelve private docks and a shipyard. On the Arkansas-Verdigris the main ports are Catoosa (Tulsa), Muskogee, Fort Smith, and Little Rock.[27]

Water moves commodities and products most cheaply, eliminating the element of speed from transportation needs. The coal and steel industries in particular have profited from cheap water transportation. Petroleum products and agricultural chemicals move upstream, while wheat, corn, and soybeans from the hinterlands move downstream toward foreign markets. A. L. Story, owner of Wolf Island Farms in Missouri's rich southeastern delta country, summed up the importance of cheap water transportation this way, "Farmers in the Missouri Bootheel can ship a bushel of soybeans to New Orleans cheaper than they can mail a letter. Having access to cheap Mississippi barge transportation gives farmers in the Mid-South region a competitive edge."[28] Unfortunately, the Ozark region is not a market for large cargoes of bulky commodities, nor are the products produced in the region the types that require water transportation. Such transportation, once essential for Ozarks commerce, is now part of the past and is not likely to regain its former significance.

RAILROADS

The development of a railroad network shaped much of the economic and cultural geography of the Ozarks (fig. 8-1). They constructed railroads to tap mineral and timber resources and to supply and haul products from farms. During the period just before the Civil War, the people of the United States were railroad-minded; they thought and acted in terms of railroads. Politics, legislation, newspapers, public meetings, industry, and invention served this new means of transportation.

On February 13, 1859, the Hannibal and St. Joseph Railroad was completed, the first across Missouri; unfinished lines of other railroads radiated from St. Louis.[29] By February 1, 1861, the Pacific Railroad of Missouri reached Sedalia.[30] Its financiers hoped that by running rails from St. Louis to Kansas City the federal government would select St. Louis as the eastern terminus of the contemplated transcontinental railroad. The Southwest Branch of the Pacific Railroad of Missouri, running from the main line at Pacific, reached Rolla on January 1, 1861. The

Civil War interrupted plans to extend it southwestward by way of Springfield to reach the rich mineral resources of Jasper County and to open that area to settlement.[31] The St. Louis and Iron Mountain, planned from St. Louis to southeast Missouri to serve the lead and iron industries of St. Francois, Iron, and Madison counties, was finished as far as Pilot Knob on April 2, 1858. From Mineral Point, on the main line, a branch line extended to Potosi. Following the Civil War the St. Louis and Iron Mountain built farther south through the eastern Ozark pineries. The Kansas City, Fort Scott, and Memphis, which built southeastward from Springfield to Memphis between 1881 and 1883, was crucial for the exploitation of timber and mineral resources in the interior Ozarks. Two later railroads, the Missouri Pacific White River line, and the Missouri and North Arkansas Railroad served the lumber mills, mines, and farms of the southern Ozarks.

Despite the objections of many Cherokee leaders, who opposed railroads because they feared forfeiture of Indian lands to the railroads, several lines were built into the Cherokee Ozarks.[32] The most important lines were the Atlantic and Pacific Railroad (Frisco), the Missouri, Kansas, and Texas Railway Company (Katy), the Kansas City, Pittsburg and Gulf Railroad (Kansas City Southern), and the Muskogee, Oklahoma and Western Railroad (Ozark and Cherokee Central Railway, later Frisco). From these main lines, many branch lines reached into timber tracts and the lead districts.

In the early years, railroads were passing from the hands of the practical mechanics into the hands of investors. The mechanics knew how to build steam locomotives that could chug along rails of wood or scrap iron. They had proved that the newfangled steam cars could move freight and passengers faster and cheaper than stagecoaches or canal barges. Railroads could also reach into the arid lands of the west, and into rugged areas like the Ozarks.

Railroad building, however, required huge outlays of capital. Track laying alone cost twenty thousand dollars to fifty thousand dollars per mile, and they needed millions for rolling stock, yards, and stations. National, state, and local governments offered aid generously to private undertakings. The United States granted more than three million acres of land, and Missouri authorized an issue of state bonds, backed by mortgages, upon several railroads to the aggregate sum of twenty-four million dollars. Municipal, county, and township governments likewise indebted themselves. The national financial crises of 1861 caused suspension of interest payments by all railroads operating in the Ozarks. Bondholders dropped the question of foreclosure until the Civil War was over, but in the years immediately after the war, all of the railroads went bankrupt.

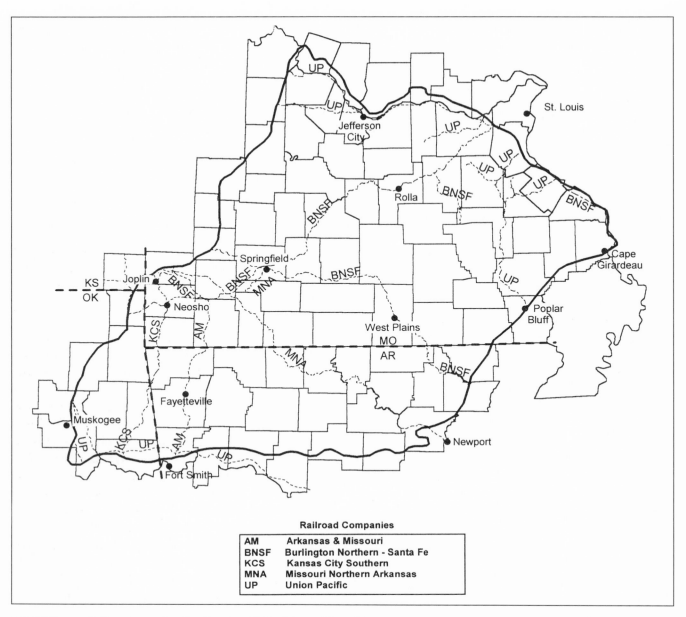

FIGURE 8-1. Railroads serving the Ozarks, 2000. Adapted from Milton D. Rafferty, *Historical Atlas of Missouri* (Norman: Univeristy of Oklahoma Press, 1982), plate 64; Jefferson City Department of Transportation, *Missouri Rail Freight Carriers.* (Jefferson City: Graphics Section, 1999); Oklahoma City Department of Transportation, *Oklahoma Railroad Map* (Oklahoma City: Office of Rails Programs, 1998); Little Rock Department of Transportation, *Railroad Map of Arkansas* (Little Rock, Ark.: Planning and Research Division, 1999); Topeka Department of Transportation, *Official Kansas State Railroad Map* (Topeka, Kans.: Utilities Division, Engineering Section, 1998).

When the West found it did not have the capital and talent to build transcontinental railroads, eastern financiers, among them Commodore Vanderbilt, Daniel Drew, Jim Fisk, and Jay Gould, launched profitable and checkered railroad-building careers. The process was simple. First, select a name, such as the Kansas City, Clinton and Springfield; the St. Louis, Salem and Little Rock; or the Arkansas and Oklahoma Railroad. Second, print a bond issue and map of the proposed route. Next, persuade the state legislature to issue a charter, then distribute part of the bond issue to legislators or other influential citizens. Now, get a land grant of alternate sections along the route. Next, collect subsidies and bribes from counties and towns that might or might not get the railroad. Look over mining lands in your section and establish town companies and real-estate brokerages. When settlers arrive, sell them land and supplies and haul out their products at inflated prices. It was a grand plan and it worked.

Many Ozark towns—Monett, Chadwick, Purdy, and Rogers, to name a few—were born as railheads and were named for railroad men. Other towns that had subscribed funds to construct a railroad saw the tracks pass without entering the towns. Springfield and Lebanon, Missouri, are in the latter category.[33]

Even less fortunate have been those Ozark towns and counties that raised funds but never got a railroad. About 1900, Dallas County, Missouri, owed bondholders more than the value of all property, real and personal, in the county. In 1869, the county court subscribed $235,000 in bonds to the Laclede and Fort Scott Railroad Company, which was to build a line from Lebanon through Buffalo, the county seat, to Fort Scott, Kansas. They never built the road. In 1879 the county offered to pay the debt, which by then amounted to $244,755, for twenty cents on the dollar, but the creditors refused. The case eventually reached the Missouri Supreme Court, which supported the bondholders, but Dallas County judges were successful in avoiding process servers for decades. In 1899 the bondholders offered to settle the debt that by then totaled $1,407,000, for $250,000, but Dallas County refused. Finally, in 1920, bondholders agreed to accept $300,000 in new bonds, which the county retired on July 1, 1940, seventy-one years after the lenders issued the initial bonds.[34] Early in the railroad boom, Laclede County issued $100,000 worth of bonds to build the Laclede and Fort Scott Railroad. The railroad built roadbed but never laid tracks. The county finally paid off the bonds in 1894.

St. Clair County, Missouri, has the distinction of being in rebellion against the federal government for some thirty years. The county issued bonds in 1870 to the Tebo and Neosho Railroad, which was to run from Clinton through Osceola, the county seat, to Memphis. After selling construction bonds to trusting purchasers and making a few surveys, the promoters disappeared. When St. Clair countians refused to pay for merchandise not received, the bondholders secured a judgment in federal court in 1875, the county court (commission) being ordered to pay the claims. After being cited for contempt, the county court still refused to pay. Federal marshals went to St. Clair County repeatedly to arrest the county judges (commissioners), but they could never be found.

Hiding out became the county court's first order of business. Reportedly, for a time, candidates for the court campaigned and were elected principally upon their commitment and ability to evade pursuit. They held court sessions in isolated cabins, and citizens watched strangers in Osceola carefully lest they be U.S. marshals in disguise. Eventually, the county liquidated the debt by compromise and by the death of most of the interested parties.

About the turn of the century, investors recognized that they could not operate all of the railroads at a profit. The sheer complexity of management and transfer of goods worked toward consolidation of the many short lines. Since 1910 there has been substantial reduction of railroad mileage in the Ozarks (fig. 8-2).[35] The abandoned railroads are of three types: lines that ran parallel to others and competed for traffic; short spur lines built to serve a major town; and short lines built by mining and lumber companies to exploit raw materials. Railroads built to mines and sawmill towns usually shut down when the mineral or timber ran out.

Recounting the complete history of railroad construction and abandonment in the Ozarks would be a useful project that would require a volume or more. Nevertheless, a brief survey of most of the lines abandoned between 1910 and 1975 will serve to illustrate the essential patterns of railroad development and decline.

Railroad abandonment was very rapid during two periods: from the 1930s through the early 1940s and from the late 1950s to 1975.[36] These periods correspond to the Great Depression and to the two decades following the Korean conflict. The 1976 Railroad Revitalization and Regulatory Reform Act started a third round of railroad abandonment that is still in process. By the 1930s most of the rail mileage, constructed by several dozen companies, had been consolidated into five major lines: the St. Louis-San Francisco (Frisco); the Chicago, Rock Island & Pacific; the Missouri Pacific; the Kansas City Southern; and the Missouri-Kansas-Texas (Katy).

The Kansas City, Clinton and Springfield, which ran from Raymore (north of Harrisonville) through Harrisonville, Clinton, Lowry City, and Fair Play to Ash Grove and later to Springfield in 1886, was the longest line abandoned in southern Missouri. When the St. Louis and San Francisco Railway acquired the line, they already owned a line between Springfield and Kansas City. They shortly abandoned the Kansas City, Clinton and Springfield starting with the stretch from Lowry City to Harlan Junction, in 1926. By the mid 1930s the entire line had been shut down except a few miles of track from Ash Grove to Phoenix in Greene County, where a large limestone quarry operated until 1943. When the quarry shut down the railroad also ceased operations.[37] Under the aegis of Ozark Greenways, the stretch of the abandoned right-of-way between Springfield and Bolivar has become the Frisco Highline Trail. Ozark Greenways, Incorporated, a not-for-profit group, preserves green space by building linear parks for hiking, bicycling, and horseback riding.[38]

Because of curtailed production in the lead-zinc mines, the Frisco abandoned three spur lines in the Tri-State

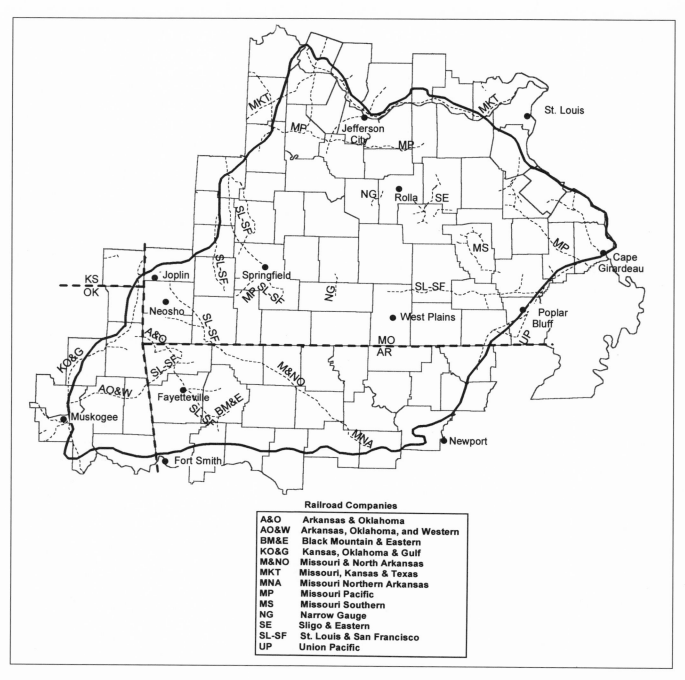

FIGURE 8-2. Abandoned railroads, 1900–2000. Adapted from Milton D. Rafferty, *Historical Atlas of Missouri* (Norman: Univeristy of Oklahoma Press, 1982), plate 63; *Missouri Rail Freight Carriers* (Jefferson City: Jefferson City Department of Transportation, 1999); *Oklahoma Railroad Map* (Oklahoma City: Department of Transportation, 1998); *Railroad Map of Arkansas* (Little Rock, Ark.: Department of Transportation, 1999); *Official Kansas State Railroad Map* (Topeka, Kans.: Department of Transportation, 1998).

Mining District in 1934. In 1939, Frisco abandoned forty-one miles of track connecting Bentonville, Arkansas, with Grove, Oklahoma, via Southwest City, Missouri. Constructed between 1899 and 1900 by the Arkansas and Oklahoma Railroad Company to tap the timber in the Cherokee Ozarks, the line lost money when the virgin

timber ran out. Frisco bought the line in the early 1900s to expand their rail network.

Frisco abandoned two other lines in southwest Missouri. The first, built in 1883 by the Springfield and Southern Railway Company and in 1885 added to the Frisco system, ran from Ozark to Chadwick. It hauled farm produce and railroad ties and lumber from the sawmills at Chadwick and Sparta. After all the timber had been cut, the Chadwick Flyer hauled very little, so in 1934 Frisco closed the line at Ozark.[39] Business was so poor by that time that the engineer reportedly stopped the train so the crew could pick blackberries and shoot quail.[40]

The other abandoned Frisco line ran from South Greenfield in Dade County to Mount Vernon in Lawrence County. The Greenfield and Northern Railroad laid rails to Mount Vernon in 1891, and then extended them to Aurora in 1892. Frisco bought the line during its expansion phase and sold it when revenues no longer turned profits. They abandoned the short spur running from South Greenfield to Mount Vernon in 1950.

Missouri Pacific's abandoned lines in the northern Ozarks include the Warsaw Branch, connecting Warsaw with the main line at Sedalia (abandoned 1946); the line from Boonville through Tipton to Versailles, built by the Boonville, St. Louis and Southern Railway Company (abandoned in 1936); the ten miles of track from Bagnell Dam to Eldon (abandoned 1953), and the remaining 34 miles from Eldon to Jefferson City (abandoned in 1963).

In southwest Missouri, the Missouri Pacific abandoned the spur line connecting Springfield with Crane on the White River line. The spur, first owned by the St. Louis, Iron Mountain and Southern, ran through Battlefield and Clever to Crane. The last train ran in 1970.[41] A part of the abandoned right-of-way, the section from Springfield to Wilson's Creek Battlefield National Park, is under development by Ozark Greenways as South Creek-Wilson's Creek Greenway, a hiking and bicycling trail.

In the southwest quarter of Missouri are three abandoned lines classified as small roads by the Missouri Public Service Commission. The longest of these was the electric trolley line of the Joplin-Pittsburg Railway Company, which abandoned its trackage in 1954. It had provided passenger service in the Tri-State District and in the coal fields of southeast Kansas. The other two roads were the Cassville and Exeter and the narrow-gauge Kansas City, Ozarks and Southern, built from Ava to connect with the Springfield-Memphis line of the Frisco at Mansfield. Track for the Cassville and Exeter was laid in 1896, the other line in 1910. Both suffered from accidents and financial difficulties.

The narrow-gauge line from Ava to Mansfield shut down in 1935 after its primary source of revenue, railroad ties, dwindled. The Cassville and Exeter finally ceased operations in 1956, but for many years preceding its abandonment the little shortline railroad operated intermittently. Two years before it shut down, a Missouri Public Service Commission report had this to say about its condition:

It is also of interest to note that the Cassville and Exeter Railway Company, with a total of 4.7 miles of track is back in operation. This is one of the nation's shortest inter-city railroads. In one of our previous reports we pointed out that the line had been forced to quit operating because of washouts on its tracks and mechanical failure of its motive power. However, some of the businesses in Cassville and Exeter became interested in the line, perhaps out of sentiment.[42]

In the eastern Ozarks, the St. Louis, Salem and Little Rock built south in 1873 from Frisco's main line, passing through Cuba to Salem. Track laying toward Little Rock ceased at Salem because of high construction costs and the Panic of 1873. Several branches from this line served the iron industry; tracks ran to one or more of the sink-fill mines or extended into timber tracts to haul wood for charcoal to fuel the furnaces. One of the first branch lines was the seven-mile spur built in 1877 by the Cherry Valley Railroad Company to serve the Cherry Valley iron mines. Other spurs ran from Howes to Plank Mines, Bangert to Condray, and Bangert to De Camp in Phelps County. Still another spur ran from Goltra in Crawford County to the Sligo Iron Furnace in Dent County. Demand for fuel for the Sligo Iron Furnace required repeated extension of the spur from Bangert to De Camp, first to Winkler in 1877 by the Dent and Phelps Railroad Company, then to Smith in 1900 by the Frisco, and finally to De Camp in 1905.

The Sligo Furnace Railroad Company laid track from Goltra to the furnace in 1880; this line became part of the Frisco system sometime before 1910. The Sligo and Eastern Railroad extended the spur to Dillard but shut it down in 1930, a decade after the furnace closed.[43] The iron mines and furnaces in Phelps, Crawford, and Dent counties (Steelville Iron District) were unable to compete with large eastern iron and steel mills. By 1934, following the closure of the mines and furnaces, all branch lines from the railroad from Cuba to Salem ceased to operate.

Southeast of the sink-fill iron district, in Reynolds County, lumber interests built the most extensive logging railroad in Missouri between 1886 and 1910. This line, commonly known as the Missouri Southern Railroad, commenced at Leeper in Wayne County, where it joined the St. Louis and Iron Mountain Railroad.[44] The Mill Spring, Current River and Barnesville Railroad Company built a twelve-mile narrow-gauge track from Leeper to Penn in 1886. The next year, the Mill Spring, Current River, and Barnesville changed its name to Missouri Southern, apparently contrary to Missouri statutes governing corporations.

By 1896 the railroad had reached Barnesville (now Ellington) in central Reynolds County. After expanding to standard gauge in 1907, the track reached the end of the line at Bunker in northwest Reynolds County. By that time spurs branched to Reynolds County lumber camps at Phelps, Gruber, Farris, and Lyons. Later the line's longest spur meandered from Hobart to Himont and then to Brushy in Shannon County. By 1920, when the good timber was gone, they removed all the spur tracks in Reynolds County, leaving only the main line from Leeper to Buner and the spur into Shannon County. Abandonment of the Shannon County branch followed in 1940. In 1941 they shut down the main line. Thus in little more than half a century the Hydra-like Missouri Southern lived out its life cycle, sprawling across Wayne, Reynolds, and Shannon counties, its many heads being mines and lumber camps where men with picks and shovels dug iron and others with axes and saws chewed into virgin pine and oak-hickory forests.

St. Francois is another Ozark county with many miles of abandoned trackage; the railroads came to haul the lead being mined there. The Mississippi River and Bonne Terre Railroad constructed branch lines in St. Francois County in the mid-1890s while building its main line northeast from Bonne Terre. Its main purpose was to haul lead ore to the St. Joseph Lead Company's smelter at Herculaneum on the Mississippi River. The line made connections there with a railroad running south out of St. Louis. The railroad took up twenty-two miles of track—from Bonne Terre to Howe in Jefferson County—five years before the last mine in the Old Lead Belt closed in 1973.[45] The Mississippi River and Bonne Terre Railroad (now the Missouri-Illinois Railroad Company) abandoned ten miles of track—from Turpin to Derby—in 1941. Most other spurs had closed before 1930.

One of the longest stretches of track abandoned by the Missouri Pacific ceased operations in 1973 when the Interstate Commerce Commission authorized closing the line from Bismarck in western St. Francois County to Whitewater in Cape Girardeau County.[46] Another abandonment in the Old Lead Belt was trackage belonging to the St. Francois County Railroad Company. This small company operated between Hurryville, Farmington, and DeLassus, making a run of about ten miles in central St. Francois County, until its abandonment in 1957.

Some of the most ambitious railroad ventures attempted in the Ozarks were those that penetrated the rugged country in northern Arkansas. Here the hill folk were "introduced to the cold, hard facts of the financial world: you may build a railroad through the Ozarks, but it is a very different story when you try to operate trains over it *on a profit*.[47]

The Missouri and North Arkansas Railroad was one of these ambitious ventures. Built in segments, it eventually connected Joplin, Missouri, with Helena, Arkansas, on the Mississippi River.[48] From Joplin to Seligman, the route was easy, but southward it traversed the wild White River Hills. It then climbed the Boston Mountain Front at Leslie, and followed the Little Red River southeast through the Boston Mountains. Branch lines connected to Eureka Springs and Berryville. The Williams Cooperage Company's extensive tramway connected at Leslie.[49]

The railroad began in 1883 as a short line to serve the resort town of Eureka Springs and was officially completed for 368 miles between Joplin and Helena in 1909. It never prospered, although for a time the trains hauled large quantities of crossties and lumber shipped by various firms, such as Doniphan Lumber Company and H. D. Williams Cooperage Company. Agricultural surpluses were always limited, but towns like Berryville, Harrison, Pindall, Marshall, Leslie, Edgemont, and Heber Springs were points of shipment for cotton, grain, and lumber products.[50] Several large lumber mills grew up along the railroad: Great Western Mill Company, Geyhauser and Galhousen, Pekin Stave Manufacturing Company, and H. D. Williams Cooperage Company in Leslie; C. H. Smith Tie Company, Western Tie and Timber Company, W. R. Lee Wagon Hub Mill, Humphries and Bucklow Lumber Company, Gerwich and Waller Lumber Company, Goblebe Lumber Company in Shirley. A violent strike crippled the Missouri and North Arkansas in the 1920s. It never fully recovered. Declining shipments from lumber mills and farms forced the company to abandon segments of the line. In 1962, they closed the shops and offices in Harrison and ripped up the rails to sell as scrap.

In northwest Arkansas, they built several rail lines to connect with the Frisco when it built south to Fayetteville in 1882. The Arkansas and Oklahoma Railroad, previously mentioned, connected Bentonville, Arkansas, with Grove, Oklahoma. The Monte Ne Railroad, a short line, built east to transport vacationers to Coin Harvey's resort at Monte Ne (near Rogers).[51] The resort, built between 1900 and 1905, consisted of cottages and a hotel overlooking a lake. Special Frisco trains from Springfield, Joplin, and Fort Smith connected with the Monte Ne Railroad at Lowell. Although for a while large crowds visited the resort, the Monte Ne railroad—and eventually the resort—were financial failures.

The Rogers and Southwestern (later the Arkansas, Oklahoma and Western), linked Rogers on the Frisco with Siloam Springs on the Kansas City, Pittsburg and Gulf (Kansas City Southern). Construction of the line, which passed through the small communities of Hazelwood,

Logging train on the St. Paul branch of the Frisco. (Courtesy of Arkansas History Commission.)

Hoover, and Springtown, began in 1904. The Arkansas, Oklahoma and Western took over the Monte Ne Railroad franchise for a time. Plans to extend it eastward failed in 1914 when the entire system went bankrupt.[52]

In 1886 a group of financiers interested in the timber of Washington and Madison counties obtained a charter to build a railroad up the West Fork of White River to St. Paul. The company, incorporated as the Fayetteville and Little Rock Railroad, laid track to Pettigrew in 1897.[53] In 1915 the Black Mountain & Eastern Railroad extended railroad service across the Black Mountains from Combs in the White River valley to Cass on the Mulberry River.[54] Winding through the Black Mountains, a train had to travel about twenty miles to make the twelve miles from Combs to Cass. The difficulties encountered in building the line and running trains loaded with lumber were many:

> To span the deep gulches reaching up the sides of the rugged mountain slopes, several wood trestles were constructed. Of the timber-bent type, they were more than 125 feet high. The bents were formed on the ground, then tilted to vertical position and secured. There is a report that the grade was so steep at the end of the road that a locomotive couldn't negotiate it with a train of logs, so the individual cars were snaked, one at a time, up the track by ox team to the crest of the grade.[55]

When good timber ran out, the railroad to Combs shut down in 1926. In 1937, the last train from Pettigrew made its run to Fayetteville, leaving behind a string of nearly abandoned lumber towns.

Railroad abandonment probably has not run its full course in the Ozarks. During the past half century railroads built only two important lines: the Frisco spur, extending from the Salem branch to serve the new lead mines in western Iron and Reynolds counties in Missouri, and the Missouri Pacific spur from the Pea Ridge iron mine to the main line in Washington County, Missouri. Just when it seemed that with the revitalized economy and population growth they might save most of the remaining railroads, the 1976 Railroad Revitalization and Regulatory Reform Act put forth a federal policy allowing railroads to free themselves from unprofitable branch lines and no longer subsidize them with profits from their main lines.[56] Like most areas of the country, the Ozark states stepped in with subsidies to save railroads deemed critical to their continued economic vitality. Privately owned railroad companies formed to operate these critical lines (fig. 8-1). The lines, subsidized with federal funds and state matching funds under the provisions of the 1976 Railroad Revitalization and Regulatory Reform Act, provide crucial transportation service to many small communities.[57] In order for these connector railroads to survive, they will have to generate sufficient business to underwrite a major part of the cost of doing business. Some businesspersons foresee a day when grain terminals, sawmills, other transportation-sensitive industries will be concentrated along rivers and main line railroads. Farmers and other producers will truck their produce to the major terminals, bypassing the small terminals.[58]

Passenger rail service in the Ozarks is very limited. Amtrak serves only five border cities: Washington, Hermann, Jefferson City, Sedalia, and Poplar Bluff. Ridership, the number of passengers arriving and departing, is low. In fiscal year 1994, Jefferson City led the Ozark AmTrak stations with 39,865 riders boarding or departing; Washington had only 12.[59] The proposed $4.1 billion Midwest Regional Rail System, a largely federally funded nine-state passenger rail improvement program will not greatly impact the Ozarks. The plans call for maintenance of passenger rail (Amtrak) connections between Kansas City and St. Louis with feeder bus lines serving Springfield, Branson, and Joplin.[60]

Freight is the chief business of Ozark railroads. It consists mainly of farm and food products, lumber and wood products, stone and refractory products, and metallic ores. Grain and feed come to the Ozarks to support the dairy and poultry industries; coal and petroleum products come to thermal electric plants and to bulk gasoline and propane depots. In 1998 the Burlington Northern-Santa Fe shut down the line from Springfield to Memphis to lay new heavy-gauge track that would handle anticipated increased haulage of Wyoming coal to the export docks at Mobile, Alabama. Like the unit trains of coal, much of the freight moves as "through traffic" between major cities outside the Ozarks. Several railroads serving the Ozarks get a substantial part of their revenue from so-called piggyback service (trailer transport) and the shipment of new automobiles.[61]

Until recently, the abandoned railroad right of ways, after removal of ties and track for salvage, have reverted to the private owners from whom they were originally taken. However, the rising interest in outdoor recreation, especially hiking and biking, has created a need for safe trails where hikers and bikers will not have to compete with vehicles. Interest in resurfacing abandoned railroad grades to convert them to hiking and biking trails has grown. Two successful hiking and bicycle trails, the Katy Trail[62] and the Frisco Highline Trail[63] serve as examples. The Katy Trail occupies the abandoned roadbed of the Missouri, Kansas and Texas Railroad (Katy) between St. Charles and Sedalia and includes the Katy Trail State Park. The Frisco Highline Trail occupies the roadbed of the abandoned Frisco line between Springfield and Bolivar.

EARLY ROADS

The first routes of overland travel in the Ozarks were the trails followed by the Indians in hunting, warfare, and trading. Some of these early traces may have followed the trails followed by buffalo and other animals.[64] Later, travelers followed roads hacked through the country between Ste. Genevieve and the lead mines. Most early improved roads were military roads or post roads. The chief purposes

of the military roads were to transport troops and munitions to the western frontier. The purpose of the post roads was to provide for mail delivery.[65] The Spanish government, between 1776 and 1799, laid out the Kings Highway to link the Mississippi trading posts at New Madrid, Cape Girardeau, and Ste. Genevieve with St. Louis.[66] This road, which followed an old Indian trace, had several branches that led to small settlements on both sides of the Mississippi River. In 1808, the Missouri territorial legislature authorized the first public territorial road from St. Louis to New Madrid, through Ste. Genevieve and Cape Girardeau, following the route of the King's Highway or El Camino Real.[67] The modern federal Highway 61 closely follows the old road.

The first roads evolved from trails. They received names according to the places to which they led; roads leading from Springfield included the Old Wire Road or Fayetteville Road, the Boonville Road, the Ridge Road or St. Louis Road, and the Forsyth Road.[68] The Boonville Road, also called the Bolivar Road because it passed through Bolivar on the way to Boonville, led north from the public square. Several streets in Springfield were once parts of these old roads and have retained their names. The same is true of streets in towns throughout the Ozarks.

The best-known route across the Ozarks was the Osage trail that led to St. Louis. The route followed the upland or great ridge separating the drainage basins of the Missouri and Arkansas rivers. Indians followed it to the trading post at St. Louis, as did many immigrants to the western Ozarks. It had various names: Osage Trace, the Southwest Trail, the Springfield Road, and, later, when a telegraph line followed alongside it, the Telegraph Road or Old Wire Road.[69] Freighters, including many farmers, spent a large part of the year hauling deer skins, peltry, medicinal roots and herbs, and other frontier products to St. Louis two hundred and forty miles to the northeast, and returning to Springfield laden with supplies.[70] After passing through Springfield, the road turned south toward Fayetteville and Fort Smith and another branch road continued west through Joplin and then southwest as the Texas Road.[71] In the early years when it was a trail, travelers followed alternate routes and branches from the main route. One route led west from Ste. Genevieve through Caledonia and Steelville to join the Ridge Road near present-day St. James. The northern route of the Cherokee Trail of Tears followed this route after crossing the Mississippi at Cape Girardeau (fig. 4-1). Joseph Phillibert, chief clerk, friend, and confident of trader William Gilliss, transported goods from Ste. Genevieve over the same route. After crossing Roubidoux Creek at modern Waynesville, however, he traveled up the Gasconade to Osage

Fork and then to Pleasant Prairie or modern Marshfield. From Pleasant Prairie he followed the upper James River valley across Kickapoo Prairie at the site of modern Springfield, and then to the trading post at the mouth of the Finley River and near the Kickapoo villages.[72] Years later freighters followed an alternate route west from Rolla by turning south following the Big Piney River to Cabool and then west along the approximate route of U.S. 60 to Springfield.

Because the Ridge Road followed the great water divide that separated the drainage basins of most of the larger streams draining the Ozarks, the terrain was less rugged. It was the route selected by the Atlantic and Pacific Railroad to lay track from St. Louis to Springfield and Joplin. With fewer large streams to bridge, it was the least costly route. U.S. Highway 66 also followed the ridge route through Sullivan, Rolla, Lebanon, Springfield, and Joplin. Today, it is the route followed by Interstate 44. Other early Ozark roads included the Iron Road,[73] which linked the Maramec Iron Works with the Missouri River port at Hermann, and the Ste. Genevieve, Iron Mountain, and Pilot Knob Plank Road, over which they hauled iron from Pilot Knob to Ste. Genevieve.[74] Investors who constructed the latter road in 1853 anticipated a drop in the cost of hauling a wagon load of iron from Iron Mountain to Ste. Genevieve from $18.72 to $16.00.[75] Plank roads, chiefly established in northern Missouri between 1850 and 1860, were particularly unsatisfactory because of the cost of upkeep. Gravel and macadam roads were the most lasting and most profitable toll roads.[76]

The iron furnaces had an important influence on road building in the Missouri Ozarks. Before the opening of the iron furnaces, the roads of that area were few and generally poorly adapted to the transportation of heavy loads. Maramec Iron Works, with all its industrial promise, provided incentive for public improvements in roads leading to the plant from all directions. Between 1839 and 1855, at least nine acts passed by the Missouri state legislature, six of them in 1841, approved roads to connect Maramec with neighboring towns and transportation routes. These acts provided for the construction or improvement of state roads from Maramec to Jefferson City, Hermann, St. Louis, Springfield, and to Ste. Genevieve by way of Caledonia and Farmington.[77] They also authorized a road from Maramec to the tiny community of Lick (Licking) in Shannon County, where it connected with the state road leading from Jefferson City to Batesville, Arkansas.[78]

By 1816 travelers followed a well-marked trail to the Boonslick country. It paralleled the Missouri River following the ridge on the north side, connecting most settlements along the Missouri before veering away from the river. West of St. Charles the trail passed Cottleville, Pittman's, Naylor's store, Pondfort, Pauldingville, Hickory Grove, Warrenton, Camp Branch, Jones, Danville, Williamsburgh, passing seven miles north of Fulton, an equal distance north of Columbia, then through Thrall's Prairie, to Franklin, and finally to Boonslick.[79] When Fulton and Columbia became county seats after statehood, the road passed through both towns. Since much of the trade was soon directed toward Santa Fe, the trail extended west through Marshall, Malta Bend, Grand Pass, and Fort Osage to Independence.

In Arkansas, the earliest roads connected Little Rock and other settlements farther west in Arkansas with Memphis. Arkansas's first road connected Little Rock and Arkansas Post, the old French settlement near the mouth of the Arkansas River. Major John H. Pyeatt, an army officer from Georgia who had settled at Crystal Hill in what is now Pulaski County, enlisted the help of his neighbors in opening the road in 1807.[80] It followed the north bank of the Arkansas River for fifty miles and then followed an Indian trail directly to Arkansas Post. Probably the first road in the Arkansas Ozarks was the road from Fort Smith to Fayetteville and then on north to Springfield, Missouri.

The Natchitoches Trace was another trail that later became a road. It led south from St. Louis to the lead mines and then on to Poke Bayou (Batesville). Many immigrants followed this trail that extended on south from Batesville, to Little Rock, through Washington, Arkansas, and eventually to Natchitoches, Texas. It followed an old Indian trace known at various times as the Natchitoches Trace, the Texas Trail, and the Military Road.[81] Many Scotch-Irish and German immigrants who settled the central Texas hill country traveled this route.[82] Adventurers and early chroniclers of the Ozark frontier, including Featherstonhaugh, Schoolcraft, and Gerstaeker traveled the trail and described the land and people along the way.[83] When Featherstonhaugh traveled along part of this road in 1834 he noted that they knew it as a dangerous route because outlaws who lived along the trail "under the pretense of entertaining travelers . . . often murdered them if they had anything to be plundered of."[84]

Other trails branched from the Natchitoches Trace. At Batesville it connected to a trace through the swamps from Memphis. Travel was slow. The trees were "razed close to the ground," a statement that implies that the trail blazers had not removed all stumps. There were no bridges and only a few ferries. Travel along roads from St. Louis to Little Rock must have been an adventure for even the hardiest souls:

Along the Missouri border particularly, it was infested with gangs of desperadoes, living in abandoned cabins off the main route or moving about the country in order to lure any travellers who carried money, towards a woodland ambush in some secluded spot. Taverns were few; and the traveller, if he did not wish to camp out at night—a procedure which was always under risks as to the weather and was sometimes perilous besides because of wild animals, particularly panthers—had to endure an unvarying diet of fried pork, corn dodgers, and bad coffee (sometimes made of parched corn or acorns) sweetened with molasses, or "long sweetening." He had to also endure a table service so scanty that knives and forks were given nicknames; and usually he had to sleep in a single room with several other tenants, oftentimes in the same bed with another guest.[85]

As late as 1836 the journey to Little Rock still entailed weeks of discomfort on board a steamboat or an even more hazardous drive along a primitive wilderness road.

They built many early roads as post roads to ensure the delivery of mail and to maintain communications with St. Louis, which had a central post office in 1805. As early as 1810, post roads connected St. Louis with Ste. Genevieve, Mine à Breton, and St. Charles. Another post road ran from Kaskaskia, Illinois, to Ste. Genevieve, thence, by way of the old Kings Highway, to Cape Girardeau and New Madrid. Later, post roads led from Ste. Genevieve through Potosi to Union in Franklin County and from Potosi to Belleview and Murphy's (Farmington).

By 1819, Missouri boasted at least fifteen mail routes with deliveries once a week or once every two weeks. However, a list of post routes established in Missouri in 1819 published by the *Missouri Gazette* for May 5 of that year included no regularly scheduled routes in the Ozarks. During the 1840s and 1850s settlements demanded more mail facilities and better post roads. In 1850, George R. Smith, the founder of Sedalia, had a contract with the U.S. government for operating passenger and mail coaches over 483 miles of the Missouri Stage Lines.

The first mail-carrying stagecoach between Independence and Santa Fe began its trip to the far southwest on July 1, 1850, over the Santa Fe Trail. The trail was first marked by Pedro Vial in 1792–1793 and by William Becknell in 1821–1822.[86] The establishment of the Butterfield Overland Mail in 1858 was the culmination of more than a decade of struggle toward regular communication with the Pacific Coast. The demand for rapid communication between East and West led to the

Ozarks stagecoach, 1905. (Courtesy of Arkansas History Commission.)

development of the Pony Express, and on April 3, 1860, the first westbound rider left St. Joseph, the end-of-trail connection with the East, for Sacramento, California. In the Ozarks stagecoach routes connected most of the larger towns shortly after the Civil War.

Toll roads became something of a mania about mid-century and forty-nine companies received charters in Missouri to construct plank roads. All but one planned to connect some point in the state with the Missouri or Mississippi rivers. Because of limited state and federal support for road construction, toll roads continued to be built to connect large interior towns with the closest town with a railroad. Some of these connecting roads persisted until the 1930s.

The first wagon roads were very crude. Workers simply removed the timber so that the axle of a wagon would clear the stumps; improvement was left to travel. The soil was quickly worn away, exposing the underlying chert, which formed natural macadam. Bridges were of little concern before the automobile became common. Lawrence County, Missouri, had no bridges in 1875, nor were they considered essential, "the streams being shallow and the fords solid."[87] Dade County got its first bridge in 1892, but only after twenty years of agitation and assurances that the old ford on Sac River would be left intact, "thus giving the traveler an opportunity to water his horses."[88] At key places wooden bridges spanned the larger streams, such as the White, Current, Osage, Gasconade, and Meramec rivers. High steel-trestle bridges replaced the old wooden bridges when they washed out.

Roads were very poor until automobile travel created a strong demand for their improvement. When Eureka Springs, Arkansas, developed as a health spa in the 1880s, visitors found few roads leading to the town, the main ones being a wagon track to Springfield, Missouri, that required a three-day trip, and a military road from Fayetteville to Jacksonport, on the White River on the eastern edge of the mountains, and a fifty-five-mile overland journey from the railhead at Pierce City, Missouri.[89]

Late nineteenth century roads were more like trails than true roads, so that only hardy business travelers and local residents traveled them. While Ozark roads surely rivaled the poorest in the nation, roads all across the United States suffered from lack of planning and maintenance. The nineteenth century was for the road a time of contraction of purposes to very local use.[90] Long-distance travel was less expensive and far more comfortable by rail or water. This was before the Ford Model T brought on the demand for better roads and before state highway commissions received mandates to construct and maintain roads that would support automobile travel.

County road between Linn Creek and Lebanon, Missouri, circa 1907. (Reproduced from Ernest R. Buckley, "Public Roads, Their Improvements and Maintenance," *Missouri Bureau of Geology and Mines,* 2d Series, 5 [1907]: 99.)

The territorial legislatures of Louisiana and of Missouri and Arkansas established the principle of local supervision and financing of public roads. The basis for the establishment of road districts, for the appointment of road overseers and commissioners, for settlement of right-of-way damages, and for distribution of funds for roads among the counties or territorial districts was according to the length of the road in each area. The principle of local road supervision became, in turn, the guiding policy of the newly formed states. Roads were built and maintained by the ancient vestige of feudalism, the corvée, and most citizens looked upon the few days each year of mandated road work as a nuisance. Consequently, roads received very little attention and were considered adequate if river fords were passable and gully washouts were kept filled to allow passage of wagons and buggies. Nevertheless, to put the late-nineteenth-century road-poor Ozarks in perspective, we need to consider that they laid the nation's first Portland cement pavements around the courthouse in Bellefontaine, Ohio, in 1891, the same year that they laid the nation's first brick pavement on a rural road on the Worcester Pike in Cayahoga County outside Cleveland.[91]

Maintenance of secondary roads was usually under the direction of a paid township or special road-district overseer. Theoretically, each male citizen was obligated to spend two days a year helping the supervisor in working the roads or one day a year with a team of horses or mules. Often the unskilled workers made only temporary repairs to the almost impassable parts of the road. The most commonly used implement for improvement consisted of two logs or sawed oak timbers hooked up in a tandem.

Crossing the Meramac River at Sand Ford below Meramac Caverns. (Courtesy of State Historical Society of Missouri.)

This device, known as a split-log drag, smoothed ruts, but did little else.

During the bicycle rage in the latter part of the nineteenth century, organized tour groups explored the Ozarks. Intrepid bikers relied on the *Road and Handbook of the Missouri Division of the League of American Wheelmen* (published in 1895) for information about road conditions in the interior counties. The information for Shannon County, Missouri, places the county and describes the extent and condition of roads:

Shannon. In southern part, near boundary, south of Dent. Roads scarce. The County Surveyor kindly reports: Eminence northeast to Centerville, 40 miles, rough, hilly, dirt road. Eminence west to Houston, 40 miles, rough, hilly, dirt road, no bridges, via Alley, 5 miles; Somerville [*sic*] 18 miles. Riverside south to Somerville [*sic*], 20 miles. Eminence east to Russel, 13 miles. Low Wossie [*sic*] to Birchtree [*sic*], via Winona, dirt road, 18 miles. Eminence southwest to West Plains, dirt road, 50 miles; via Birchtree [*sic*], 15 miles. Eminence to Van Buren, southeast, dirt road, 25 miles. Eminence north to Salem, 40 miles; via Roundspring, 11 miles. Birchtree east to Van Buren, 30 miles. Birchtree [*sic*] west to Mountain View, 13 miles. Eminence northwest to Riverside, 25 miles, and north to Salem, 18 miles more; via Jadwin, 7 miles.

Hotels: Eminence, J. A. Jadwin and J. M. Boyd. Birchtree [*sic*], Cook, DePriest and Mahan. Winona, Lewis R. Pettitt, each $1 per day.[92]

Rural free delivery began in Missouri on October 15, 1896, when three experimental routes started deliveries at Cairo in Randolph County. It is a matter of speculation just why Cairo, a small village of two hundred inhabitants in northern Missouri, was one of forty-four communities selected as centers for experimental routes. Cairo probably received this distinction through the efforts of Uriel S. Hall of Randolph County, who was then a member of the House Committee on Post Office and Post Roads. Rural free delivery, immediately popular, expanded to six other Missouri communities in 1899. By 1901, forty-seven more communities, thirty-five north of the Missouri River and twelve south, had been added.

The development of rural free delivery was coincident with the development of automobiles. The good-roads movement received impetus from the Post Office Department requirement that new mail routes follow roads passable in all seasons of the year. After the introduction of parcel post in 1912, rural free delivery naturally entered upon a period of expansion that further coincided with the growing popularity of the automobile. During the next two decades, the nation's and the Ozarks' first highway system became a reality.

The Auto Club of Missouri championed good roads along with automobile safety, licensing of drivers, registration of automobile titles, and many other improvements related to automobile travel. The club began as the Auto Club of St. Louis in 1902 and, after affiliating with the Automobile Club of America, spearheaded the union of several auto clubs to form the Auto Club of Missouri. In 1916 the club headed a movement to pass a $3 million road bond issue and in 1917 supported the Hawes Act, creating the Missouri State Highway Department.[93] Following the creation of the Missouri State Highway Department in 1917, the legislature passed the Centennial Road Act in 1921, which included provisions for a network of roads connecting county seats.[94] The highway department immediately began to build a system of primary highways, supported by a $60 million bond issue. In 1928, Missouri voters passed Proposition No. 3 that provided an additional $75 million worth of bonds for construction of graveled but well-engineered farm-to-market roads through sections not reached by primary roads.[95] Road legislation was passed soon after this in Arkansas and in the new state of Oklahoma.

The first bituminous-surface highways appeared in the late 1920s, and in 1927 the first stretch of bituminous-surface road in the Ozarks commenced a few miles west of Springfield (table 8-1). Bituminous surfacing of county roads began about 1950. In southwest Missouri the Greene County Court (Commission) is credited with working out a system of priorities so that bituminous surfacing could begin; many Ozark counties now use the

Wagon and team on a dirt road, circa 1907. Split-log road drag is on the wagon. (Reproduced from Ernest R. Buckley, "Public Roads, Their Improvements and Maintenance," *Missouri Bureau of Geology and Mines,* 2d Series, 5 [1907]: 87.)

same system.[96] They charge landowners whose property fronts on the roads a fee (per linear foot) for bituminous surfacing; after construction, the county bears all cost for repair and maintenance.

Bituminous surfacing of roads has progressed very rapidly. The U.S. Census of Agricultural statistics show that in only ten years, 1940 to 1950, the percentage of farms on dirt or unimproved roads declined from 51 to 39. By 1970, approximately 800 of the 1,200 miles of Greene County's roads were hard-surfaced. Thirty years later, they had surfaced all 1,400 miles of county roads in Greene County with concrete or asphalt.[97] In some rural Ozark counties where special road districts still exist, progress has been slower, but improvement of gravel roads has progressed steadily.

In much of the Ozarks the residual chert makes the care of roads lacking bituminous surfacing simple. After the overlying soil is bladed aside, the chert quickly becomes packed, forming a surface that permits all-weather travel. However, such surfaces are usually rough, and the sharp chert causes tires to wear badly.[98] In more remote areas, roads receive little care, and where there are no ditches alongside them, the roads serve as drains for gullied hillsides, often exposing outcrops of bedrock that make the road nearly impassable. Reduced speeds of thirty to forty miles per hour are necessary in some areas to preserve the vehicle and to reduce the risk of rock-cut tires.

Water gaps, places where county road crews scoop out the gravel in stream beds and pour concrete slabs, span

TABLE 8-1. DATES OF CONSTRUCTION OF HIGHWAYS IN THE VICINITY OF SPRINGFIELD, MISSOURI

Highway	Original Construction	Reconstruction
160 West	1927–34	
160 South	1934–45	1967–68
13 North	1936–38	1960
65 North	1925–32	1968
65 South	1922–32	1961–65
60 West	1931–35	1942–66
60 East	1934–35	1967–69
66 West	1926–28	1962
66 East	1923–25	1952
I-44 West	1962–64	
I-44 East	1958–68	

SOURCE: Missouri Department of Transportation, Springfield District Office, 1979.

Low-water bridge on the James River, 1975. This type of bridge is common in the Ozarks. (Milton Rafferty Collection, photograph by the author.)

many small streams. Gravel fords are less common, but are still found in the remote hill districts. Low-water bridges, often simple concrete slabs covering metal culverts, are typical crossings for the headwaters of larger streams. These low structures, safe during normal stream flow, can be very dangerous when floodwaters rise over them after heavy rains. Throughout the region state and county bridge crews replace dozens of low-water bridges with new flood-safe bridges each year in the continuing effort to reduce driving hazards. Despite warning signs and media publicity, the Ozarks suffer several drownings each year when turbulent floods sweep vehicles from these picturesque crossings. The following is a short notice from the Springfield newspaper:

2-YEAR-OLD GIRL DROWNS AFTER TRUCK SWEPT AWAY

A 2-year-old Howell County girl drowned Wednesday after the pickup truck driven by her mother was swept off a rain-swollen low-water crossing six miles east of Willow Springs, the Missouri Highway Patrol said. . . . The child was the first of two in Missouri to drown Thursday after vehicles were swept off low-water crossings.

A Farmington man was killed early Thursday when the car he was driving was swept from a low-water bridge in St. Francois County.[99]

The guidelines for construction of the Ozarks' new federal highways pay more attention to safety than to the advantages of landforms. High concrete bridges span streams well above any water rise ever recorded. These roads cross valleys by long, easy grades made possible by cutting and filling. Vertical cuts of as much as eighty feet in bedded limestone, alternating with valley fills of almost equal height, make the new U.S. Highway 65 north of Branson one of the Ozarks' most easily traveled and picturesque drives.

The overall pattern of roads in the Ozarks is a blend of a radial network, which is descended from the earliest trails through the country, and a rectangular road pattern, which derives from the federal land survey. As mentioned previously, the main highways follow closely the earliest routes of travel.

The main roads often follow the crests of ridges, but this is particularly true in the rougher regions. Although they may be very sinuous, the ridge roads never flood, and they maintain a remarkable evenness of grade. In the breaks along escarpments, stream divides are sometimes so narrow that the roads occupy the entire crest. At other places the surface broadens out so that the farms and fields expand away to the horizon.

Farm-to-market roads vary greatly in geographic pattern. In the Springfield Plain, and other level areas, the rectangular pattern is prevalent with important breaks in the grid occurring in the rough tracts along the major streams. Even in southwest Missouri, where sinkholes are sometimes large, the rectangular pattern is little affected by sinkholes. Roads frequently cross large sinkholes, some of which temporarily hold water. Occasionally, water may block the road for days or weeks at a time. Rarely, usually after heavy rains, sinkholes have collapsed creating serious traffic hazards when the roadbed breaks and falls in.[100]

The rugged areas have the poorest roads. In the hilly districts the rectangular road pattern gives away to a sparse

Steel-trestle bridge on the Finley River at Riverdale, Christian County Missouri, 1975. (Milton Rafferty Collection, photograph by the author.)

pattern of roads that alternately follow the crests of ridges or stream valleys, the former case being the more common. Private roads frequently branch off to farmsteads hid away at considerable distance from public roads. Many side roads are wretched trails, better traveled in a truck than in a car. They sometimes lead to small abandoned houses and assorted sheds in varying states of dilapidation.

Improved highways brought bus service to the Ozarks. By the 1940s nearly every town with a population of a thousand had scheduled bus service. Bus depots, like train depots, became social centers where people gathered to see who was arriving or departing. Small bus lines connected a series of towns with one of the larger transportation hubs. The first small bus lines, often founded by local people, had only one or two buses. Some small lines grew and prospered for a time. Floyd W. Jones, born on a Laclede County farm, started the first bus line between Lebanon and Springfield with money saved during military service in World War I. By reinvesting, adding buses and routes, and establishing new bus lines, Jones ran buses in seven states during the bustling years of World War II.[101] Greyhound Bus Line and Continental Bus Line came to dominate U.S. 66 (I-44) and other major highways while smaller bus lines like Sunnyland Stages served as collector lines connecting smaller towns with St. Louis, Springfield, Jefferson City, Rolla, Cape Girardeau, and Fayetteville. Buses continued to be important through World War II, when people could not purchase new automobiles and the federal government rationed gasoline and tires. Following the war, the number of personal automobiles increased rapidly and travel by commercial buses decreased. Bus travel reached its peak about 1950 and has steadily declined so that now commercial bus lines serve only the larger towns. Presently, Greyhound Bus Line serves only the large towns along I-44, I-55, and a few other federal highways.

AIR TRAVEL

Air travel is very important to the people of the Ozarks, as it is throughout the world. The development of aviation in the twentieth century is truly amazing when one remembers that Orville Wright became the first man ever to fly in an airplane at Kitty Hawk, North Carolina, December 17, 1903. As late as the 1940s the passage of an aircraft overhead brought rural people out of their houses for a look, and when a barnstorming pilot chanced to land in a cow pasture close to a town, the event was sure to attract a curious crowd. By the 1920s air mail transport was opened to private companies by the Kelly Act, and by 1934 Springfield boasted service by TransWorld Airlines with connections to St. Louis and Tulsa. During the 1920s and 1930s,

First commercial bus service to Doniphan, Missouri. (Courtesy of the State Historical Society of Missouri.

when manufacturers built larger and better aircraft, cities built and expanded airports to attract scheduled air service. The Douglas DC-3, first put in service by American Airlines in 1936, was so efficient that it lowered seat-mile operating costs by 33 to 50 percent.[102]

For a time the Ozarks had its very own airline—Ozark Airlines. It was conceived during the summer of 1943 on the Finley River farm of Floyd W. Jones, who then was selling his bus line interests and was looking for new opportunities for investment. Laddie Hamilton, a bus line executive, and Barak T. Mattingly, a St. Louis lawyer, convinced Jones that he should finance the airline.[103] On January 10, 1945, Ozark Airlines started flying its two Beachcraft Staggerwings, small five-seat cabin biplanes, based at Springfield. Within a year the airline closed because it could not earn sufficient revenues with routes restricted to Missouri. After buying out Parks Airline (an affiliate of Parks Airline College) and obtaining permits to fly new interstate routes, Ozark Airlines began again in 1950 with more operating capital and four Douglas DC-3 airliners. The headquarters moved to St. Louis then. By the time Jones died in 1968, Ozark Airlines served sixty cities in twelve states, operated a fleet of thirty-four planes, and employed more than two thousand people.[104] In 1982, amid a flurry of airline mergers, Ozark Airlines sold out to TransWorld Airlines (TWA) and became a part of the TransWorld Express system of connector airlines.

NEWSPAPERS

In the nineteenth century, the founding of a new town produced a new newspaper within a year. Newspaper reading was a great American pastime. Like those of today, early newspapers reflected the attitudes of the period, the politics, the habits, and the hopes of the settlers. George W. Featherstonhaugh described in his dry, humorous style the penchant for newspaper reading in Little Rock in the late 1830s:

Americans of a certain class, to whatever distant point they go, carry the passion for newspaper reading with them, as if it were the grand end of education . . . How could a town of 800 inhabitants in England support a newspaper printed in the place? Where would its useful or instructive matter come from? Why, from those quarters which have already supplied it to those alone who want it. If such a town had a newspaper it could not be supported, and therefore it remains without one. But in Little Rock, with population of 600 people, there are no less than three cheap newspapers which are not read but devoured by everybody.[105]

The number of newspapers is surprising, even when one realizes that many of them lasted only a few years or sometimes only long enough to print a few issues. Nearly every county had a dozen or more at one time or another. For example, newspapers of record in Webster County, Missouri, include the *Marshfield Mail*, the *Sentinel*, the *Radical*, the *Marshfield Democrat*, the *Marshfield Chronicle*, the *Webster County News*, the *Webster County Record*, the

Fordland Journal, the *Enterprise*, the *Flashlight*, the *Herald*, the *Seymour Citizen*, the *Fordland Times*, the *Rogersville Star*, the *Rogersville Reporter*, the *Rogersville Record*, the *Marshfield Herald*, and the *Niangua Tribune*.[106]

Overall the early newspapers were different from their modern counterparts in several respects. The front page, unlike those of today's large dailies, featured advertisements. Poetry was popular, and they published many poems to commemorate notable events, to comment on politics, and to express the poets' sentiments or convictions. Because of the lack of rapid communication, news published in Ozark papers was often very stale. Surprisingly, the early newspapers carried much national and international news and a few vague accounts of local happenings. This was partly because editors were prone to reprint entire editorials or stories from other newspapers. Another explanation for so much national coverage is that before the days of broadcast media, newspapers were the principal means of obtaining national and regional news.

Gradually, as better transportation became available, a few dailies extended their circulation in the Ozarks. The *Springfield News-Leader*, the *St. Louis Post-Dispatch*, the *Jefferson City News Tribune*, the *Kansas City Star*, the *Tulsa World-Tribune*, the *Arkansas Democrat-Gazette* (Little Rock and Fayetteville) are important regional dailies of the present time.

Local newspapers, many of them weeklies, continue to be popular (fig. 8-3). Usually only one, two, or at most

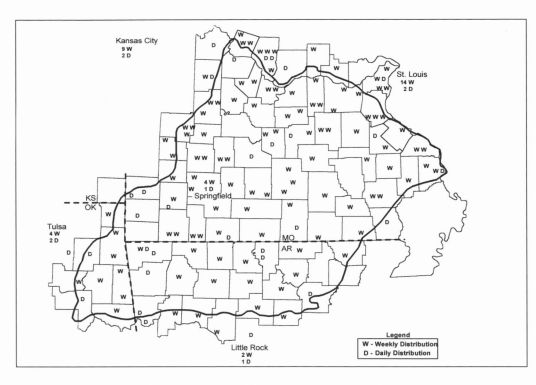

FIGURE 8-3. Daily and weekly newspapers, 1998. Prepared with data from Carolyn A. Fischer, *Gale Directory of Publications and Broadcast Media.* (Detroit: Gale Press, 1998).

three, are in a given county. Often the most widely read newspaper is in the county seat, where publication of public notices brings in revenues. Frequently, local papers are consolidations of several small newspapers once printed in the county, and the old names are carried on the front page. Sometimes the old newspapers may have their own mastheads and news printed on one interior page. One such consolidation is the *Crawford Mirror,* which represents a merger of the *Crawford Mirror,* the *Steelville Ledger,* and the *Cuba News and Review.* In economic parlance, the local newspapers, by consolidating, are responding to the necessities of economies of scale: larger circulation reduces costs. The Ozark farmer understands the problem well, but he would more likely phrase it: "Get big, or get out."

The local newspapers carry mainly regional, state, and national news that has a direct bearing on area economy and life. Because of the many columns of rural neighborhood news, the hometown weeklies circulate outside the Ozarks among subscribers who want to keep up with the Ozarks happenings.

Stories from the Marshall, Arkansas, *Mountain Wave* from 1972 to 1976 illustrate the character of the news reported in a local Ozark newspaper. There was a report of a mortgage burning by a church; several reports of local elections; store remodelings; openings of new businesses; Marshall's first radio station; improvements in physical facilities at several schools; a report on the new teen-age craze, Foosball; a feature article on the back-to-the-land people who settled in Searcy County; several pictures of deer, wild turkey, and fish taken by area sportsmen; several reports on the annual strawberry festival (though strawberry farming died out many years ago); countless accounts of visiting relatives and friends; the events of a canoe race, including a picture of "Wrong-way" Molder, who paddled upstream; several reports of high school alumni banquets; a story on Searcy County matriarchs; a report on a good citizen who experienced a revelation from God; stories on oversize pumpkins, cucumbers, and tomatoes grown by area residents; a story on ribbon-cutting ceremonies for a new road to Snowball, Arkansas; reports on serious car accidents; and, of course, photographs of area beauty-pageant winners.[107]

In recent years drug busts and crime take up more printed lines than in former times. Beginning in the 1960s reports of marijuana arrests for growers and dealers appeared, followed in the 1970s and 1980s by reports of arrests for making and selling crack cocaine, and in the 1980s and 1990s by a steady stream of reports of arrests for the manufacture of methamphetamine or "meth."

THE TELEPHONE AND ELECTRONIC COMMUNICATION

The telephone, a novel instrument that gained an immediate following because of its practical utility and its entertainment value, spread rapidly through the Ozarks in the 1890s. At first, communities called telephone meetings and organized neighborhood telephone companies. Members paid a small fee of five to twenty dollars and donated several days' work and a number of poles. Attaching the wire to fence posts along the way reduced costs. Sometimes at annual and special meetings disputes over rules, dues, and maintenance brought heated debates. A local history reported that final decisions at the Cuba, Missouri, telephone cooperative sometimes followed "a fist fight."[108]

Following the establishment of small neighborhood networks, customers began to express a desire to talk to people on other community lines. To accomplish this, an "exchange" with connecting lines and switches linked the system with other networks. At the outset, exchanges sometimes occupied someone's parlor or extra bedroom. The "exchange" in Cuba, Missouri, was moved to six different locations. In time, larger telephone companies with more elaborate switching equipment absorbed the small companies. For a time during the depression years of the 1930s, small companies went out of business because people felt they could no longer afford the luxury of a telephone. During the 1940s, improvement and consolidation of services continued, but party lines of three to six families were the rule. Most people on the community lines knew their neighbor's rings and would "ring up" a proper sequence of shorts and longs. To call on a different community line or to make a long-distance call, one had to go through the central switchboard operator. As telephone companies consolidated, multiparty lines gradually phased out, but even in the mid-1960s a few two-party lines were still in use in Springfield.[109] Some regional telephone companies continue to operate in the Ozarks, but they connect with the Bell System. Most can handle direct long-distance dialing and computerized billing.

Federal deregulation of the telephone industry gave birth to several large telephone companies providing lower-cost long-distance rates. The improvement of communications technology has been continuous since the development of the telephone. The invention of inexpensive cellular telephones has made instant communication possible from almost anywhere in the Ozarks. Except in the most remote and sparsely settled hill districts, farmers working in their fields, construction workers on the job,

loggers in remote forests, deer hunters on their stands, and vacationers driving their boats can reach the world with their cell telephones.[110] The use of FAX communication for business and personal communication is as common as in any other rural area of the United States.

Personal computers, commonplace in the Ozarks for more than a generation, provide cheap and convenient communication with the outside world through e-mail and the Internet. They are ubiquitous in the Ozark business world. Computers are commonplace in Ozark schools, and students in the smallest communities have access to computers in schools and libraries, if not in their homes. Instruction in the use of computers is part of the curriculum in nearly all secondary schools and many elementary schools in the region. As in the remainder of the United States many older people do not use computers, cell phones, or FAX communication, nor do they want to use them. However, many older people and nearly all younger people have accepted the new communication systems just as they have accepted most other aspects of American culture, both positive and negative. Clearly, except by choice, no person in the Ozarks is truly remote or isolated as for communication.

RADIO AND TELEVISION

The first radio to broadcast regularly in the Ozarks was WEW at St. Louis University. Formerly known as 9YK,

the station went on the air in April 1921, experimentally, broadcasting weather reports. By 1940 radio stations were in nearly all the larger towns on the Ozarks' border and a few in interior Ozark towns. Arkansas stations included KLRA, KARK, KGHI, Little Rock; KFPW, Fort Smith; KBTM, Jonesboro; and KUOA, Siloam Springs. KWTO in Springfield, one of the pioneer Ozark radio stations, gained national attention in the 1950s by broadcasting country music and Red Foley's "Ozark Jubilee." By the 1960s and 1970s, radio stations had become common throughout the Ozarks, so much so that most communities of five or six thousand residents can boast at least one (fig. 8-4). Live programs, often using local people with musical talent, was commonplace on many pioneer stations.

Professor Edgar McKinney illuminated the important role radio played in breaking down the barrier of remoteness and isolation on Ozark farms during the 1920s, 1930s, and 1940s.[111] During the 1950s, 1960s, and later, television served the same purposes. Local radio and television personalities—May Kennedy McCord, Porter Wagoner, Slim Wilson and the Tall Timber Trio, Speedy Haworth, Uncle Carl Haden and the Haden Family, Lonnie Robertson, the Mathews Brothers (The Jordanaires), Doc Martin, Bob White, Zed Tennis, George Rhodes, the Goodwill Family, and others—became familiar household names and were regarded almost as members of the family. Some performers used the products they sold. Their

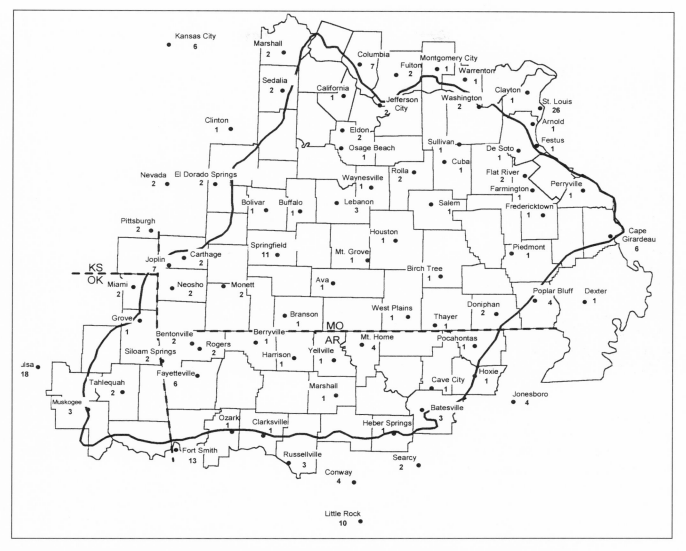

FIGURE 8-4. Radio stations, 1998. Prepared with data from Carolyn A. Fischer, *Gale Directory of Publications and Broadcast Media* (Detroit, Mich.: Gale Press, 1998).

genuineness helped them sell farm implements, new cars, home appliances, and products such as "Sunway vitamins, New Purena, Dr. LeGear's veterinary products, Cardui for women, Waite's Green Mountain Cough Sirup, and Perfex Super Cleaner."[112]

KWTO in Springfield led in the production of shows with local Ozark talent. The station's owner, Ralph Foster, pioneered the notion of broadcasts at sites remote from the station. Many performers achieved local and regional star status and were in high demand for personal appearances. A few—Porter Wagoner, Chet Atkins, Red Foley—moved on and achieved a national reputation. Rural residents listened to radio weather reports and farm market news on battery radios well before electricity became available. Farmers and other rural residents derived beneficial information that made their lives easier and more productive.

After World War II, in the 1950s, television broadcasts began from the larger border towns: St. Louis, Kansas City, Memphis, Little Rock, Tulsa. Reception was poor at first, and television sets were an oddity. Stores that marketed them could be assured of a large crowd of viewers simply by placing a set in the store window and tuning it to the station with the least-fuzzy picture. During the past generation television has become ubiquitous in Ozark homes, and several television broadcasting stations serve the region (fig. 8-5).

The first television broadcast that penetrated beyond the margins of the Ozarks originated at KTTS-TV in Springfield on March 14, 1953.[113] KY-3TV in Springfield inaugurated local live color broadcasts in 1966. At the outset the new television stations produced and broadcast their own shows, and again, musical shows by local

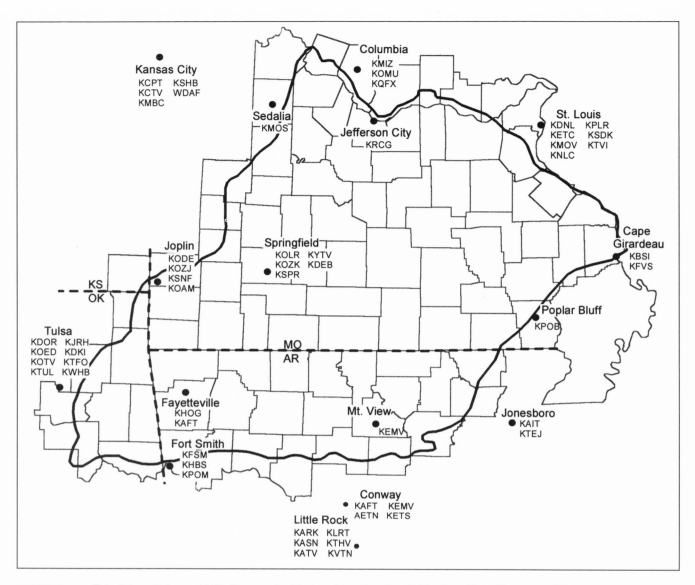

FIGURE 8-5. Television stations, 1998. Prepared with data from Carolyn A. Fischer, *Gale Directory of Publications and Broadcast Media* (Detroit, Mich.: Gale Press, 1998).

performers led the way. In the 1950s Springfield achieved national attention when KYTV broadcast Red Foley's "Ozark Jubilee" from the Jewel Theater on Commercial Street. Guest performers included the likes of Lloyd "Cowboy" Copas, Harold "Hawkshaw" Hawkins, Patsy Cline, Rod Brasfield, Minnie Pearl, Carl Smith, Rex Allen, Tex Ritter, Snooky Lanson, and Jimmy Wakely.[114]

As throughout the United States, the sale of television sets was brisk during the 1950s; in Springfield the number of homes with televisions increased from 3 percent in 1953 to 95 percent in 1959.[115] Technological advances and the construction of tall towers for improved broadcast coverage have improved the reception from most of the major stations serving the Ozarks. Cable television and satellite disks have greatly increased the reception quality

and variety of programs in the more remote sections of the region.

ELECTRICITY, PETROLEUM, AND NATURAL GAS

It is surprising that the history of basic utilities has received so little attention by researchers and writers. They have improved our lifestyle and made possible many innovations in industry, business, and commerce. Electrical power enabled the industrialization of the Ozark economy and is fundamental in making Ozark life comfortable and attractive to tourists and new immigrants. It is not too much to say that without electricity, the great population boom of the last half of the twentieth century would not have happened. Electricity powers the pumps that lift water into our houses. It also provides refrigeration for the preservation of food, air conditioning to make hot summers comfortable, and power for the forced-air heating systems that keep houses warm in winter. It provides power and lights for thousands of recreational vehicles, trailers, and campgrounds around the region's many lakes, in addition to the dozens of gadgets and convenience items found in every home. Rural living in the Ozarks was not always so attractive.

Electricity came first to Ozark cities. Gas lights, which they had installed in Springfield shortly after the Civil War, became obsolete in 1883. In that year, for the first time, electric lights illuminated businesses and homes. The Springfield Street Railway had built a power plant to generate electricity for the railway, and surplus power went to some business and residential customers.[116] Fayetteville got its first electric power plant in the same year, and the Fort Smith Light and Traction Company supplied electricity for streetcars, businesses, and residences in Fort Smith.[117] Because electrical power was a boon to the economic development of cities, many small power companies opened for business in the late nineteenth and early twentieth centuries to generate power for the larger towns. The large capital investments required to build generating plants and distribution lines soon forced the small power companies to merge or to sell out to larger regional power companies. For example, electric service along much of Arkansas's western border came under the control of Southwestern Gas and Electric Company, predecessor of the Southwestern Electric Power Company. This company spread north in 1927, taking over the Southwest Power Company operations in Benton, Carroll, Franklin, Logan, Scott, Sebastian, and Washington counties.[118] In a similar way, other Ozark municipal power companies and small regional electric companies were taken over by large regional companies, including the Oklahoma Gas and Electric Company, Cities Service Company, Arkansas Power and Light Company (AP&L), Show-Me Power Corporation, Ozark Water and Power Company, Empire Electric Company, and Union Electric Company. These companies commanded large markets that brought in sufficient revenue to build large thermal electric plants and even dams with hydroelectric stations.[119] A few cities owned their own electric generating plants. Springfield got a generating plant when it purchased the trolley system. The city's continuing growth provided an expanding market that enabled the Springfield City Utility Company to build power generation stations and to remain independent.

The lights came on much later in the rural Ozarks. Three-fourths of the Ozarks population in 1930 was rural, residing in the countryside or in towns under 2,500. Less than 3 percent of Arkansas's 5,121 farms used electricity in 1930, and the situation on the farms of the other Ozark states was much the same.[120] By the 1890s small gasoline-powered generators manufactured by Delco, Kohler, Fairbanks-Morse, and GencoLight provided electricity for lights and electric motors, but only a few small-town businesspeople and a handful of farmers could afford to own them.

Sometimes small towns purchased power from local industries. Residents of towns fortunate enough to have an industry that had installed a generator to power their equipment could sometimes purchase surplus electricity from the company. This was true in some mining and lumber mill towns. When the Missouri Lumber and Mining Company installed a generator at Grandin to power the mills in 1900, they also provided electricity for the hotel, hospital, barbershop, and other company-owned public buildings, but they did not provide power for the workers' houses.[121]

The process leading to reliable electric service for Mountain Home, Arkansas, is typical of many Ozark communities. It began in 1914 when Dillon Underhill installed an electric generator to power his flour mill.[122] The following year Underhill with two other investors formed the Mountain Home Electric Company to furnish electricity to the town. Shutdowns were frequent and by 1922 the electric plant was shut down. In the same year, with a new owner and manager, Wyatt Wolf, the plant reopened with a 37.5 horsepower engine and a 50-watt generator. The franchise with the city called for power from early dusk to 11:00 P.M. with service through the day on a special "ironing day." After incorporating the company as North Arkansas Power and Light, Wolf closed the power plant and purchased electrical power from Arkansas Power and Light Company. In 1927 he sold his company to Arkansas Power and Light, a regional power supplier.

Many communities struggled to obtain electricity. Voters in Ava, Missouri, approved electrical franchises for private producers in 1905 and 1913, but both companies failed. On August 25, 1913, J. W. Pettit and Company obtained a franchise and built a dam and hydroelectric plant on Bryant Creek to supply Ava with power.[123] They later sold the plant to the Missouri Electric Power Company. Still later Missouri Electric sold out to Show-Me Power Corporation and finally, in 1953, the city of Ava purchased the electrical power distribution system and purchased their power from a regional supplier.

The major power companies, while developing their basic transmission and distribution grids, were cautious about expanding into sparsely settled regions where construction costs were high and the market potential was small. Industry leaders thought that most farmers could not afford electricity even if it were available. The companies were not willing to extend service into remote districts unless the residents would agree to pay higher utility rates than those charged to urban customers. Most Ozark farmers were not willing to pay higher rates, and even after the rates dropped, some families went without electricity. Even today, a few isolated rural dwellings do not have electricity.

The great catalyst for bringing electricity to rural America and the Ozarks was the creation of the federal Rural Electrification Administration (REA) in 1935, followed by the founding of rural electric cooperatives. The REA provided loans for construction of power transmission and distribution lines and guaranteed preferred rates for rural customers. When the REA granted the First Electric Cooperative a $190,000 loan on May 14, 1937, it became Arkansas's first rural electric cooperative.[124] The formation of electric cooperatives went rapidly throughout the Ozarks through the 1930s, 1940s, and 1950s. Nearly all the cooperatives achieved their mandated goal to provide service or "area coverage" in their assigned area. For example, the Webster Electric Cooperative in Marshfield, Missouri, founded September 18, 1945, had by 1955 built 949,628 miles of electric line to provide service to 3,067 customers, which covered about 95 percent of their assigned area.[125]

When rural electric cooperatives were first founded, many farmers thought they could not afford the expense of installing wiring and the cost of monthly utility bills. Some cooperatives allowed rural customers to help with pole and line installation to reduce the cost of hooking up. Most people wanted electricity because word of what could be done with it traveled fast. If electricity was not the most important single factor in improving rural lifestyles, it was surely near the top. Farm wives could do their laundry and ironing with electrical appliances while listening to music or soap operas on a nearby radio. With electricity, they could pipe water to the house under pressure and they could install modern plumbing fixtures in the bathroom and kitchen. They could pipe water to the barn for livestock and to the milk shed for cleaning. Electrically heated incubators and brooders improved the hatch of chickens, and electrically powered drills and saws replaced hand tools. Farmers who could afford an electric welder could not only repair their own machinery, but also were in high demand for welding jobs on neighboring farms. When service improved and efficient electric furnaces came on the market, all-electric homes became popular.[126]

The Ozarks are well served by electrical power now. The entrenched channels of Ozark streams provide nearly ideal conditions for development of dams and reservoirs to generate hydroelectric power. They can build large lakes at lower cost, and because of their forested slopes the lakes are not subjected to heavy siltation by eroded soils. The production from the hydroelectric plants at dams of the U.S. Army Corps of Engineers lakes have added to the power resources of the region. Large deposits of coal, combined with reliable water supplies, both in the Ozarks and along the Mississippi, Missouri, and Arkansas rivers, make development of thermal electric power less costly than in many other parts of the United States. In recent years power rates have increased because federal and state antipollution regulations have forced power companies to substitute coal from Wyoming and other western states for the cheaper sulfur-rich Western Interior coal fields of Missouri, Kansas, and Arkansas.

A well-integrated electric-power grid blankets the region. Trunk lines supply the major urban centers, while smaller lines, many of them built by rural electric cooperatives under the Rural Electrification Administration, serve small towns and farms. The coverage is so complete that power companies now compete with each other for authorization to extend power lines into the suburbs and the growing subdivisions around the large lakes.

The history of the electrical power industry in the Ozarks and throughout the United States records a constant pattern of growing efficiency in delivery systems and equipment. We have seen ever larger power plants, and continuing consolidation of power producers and distribution companies. Union Electric Company, the builder of Bagnell Dam, was renamed AmerenUE when it became a part of St. Louis-based Ameren Corporation.[127] AmerenUE provides electrical power to 1.8 million customers in Illinois and Missouri, including much of the eastern and northern Ozarks. The Empire District Electric Company, another investor-owned pioneering electric utility company headquartered in Joplin, Missouri, provides electric service in a 10,000-square-mile area covering parts of southwest Missouri, southeast Kansas, and northeast Oklahoma. These companies and other electric utility companies and cooperatives are preparing for deregulation of the electric power industry. The recently enacted federal and state deregulation enabling legislation, which will begin to take effect in 2001 or 2002 will, if it follows the pattern of deregulated railroads and airlines, result in additional mergers and other adjustments in the industry.[128]

The power shortages that hit California in January 2001 were alarming to people throughout the United States, including the Ozarks. The effects of "brownouts" and total power failures were devastating to California's economy. The Ozark economy is no less dependent on electricity, and many Ozarkers view the move toward deregulation of the electrical power industry with concern.

The Ozarks is strategically located near the oil and natural-gas fields of the southern Great Plains and the Gulf Coast. Imported crude and refined products from ports on the Gulf of Mexico travel by pipelines to regional distributors serving the Ozarks. Pipelines also transport crude and refined petroleum products from oil fields as far away as Canada's Prairie provinces to refineries near St. Louis. Trunk pipelines carrying oil and natural gas from the Great Plains traverse central and northern Missouri on their way to the industrial states in the Northeast. Feeder pipelines from these trunks branch out to serve towns and cities along the way. Similarly, the main natural-gas and oil pipelines from the Gulf Coast fields pass up the Mississippi Valley to the Northeast. Nevertheless, the Ozark region is conspicuous by the absence of gas pipelines.[129] Only the borders are well served by natural gas. The interior districts rely upon liquid petroleum gas (LP gas or propane), electricity, or wood for heating purposes. The shortages of propane during the "hard" winter of 2000–2001 were of great concern to rural Ozark residents.

The availability of natural gas is extremely important for the development of certain types of industries. It is likely that reliable supplies of fuel will continue to be important in locating manufacturing plants. Probably the most reliable fuel supplies will be from large supply lines tapping underground salt-dome storage structures in Texas and Louisiana, which are supplied by imported crude oil. Existing refineries and pipelines probably will process and distribute the products. As for energy availability, there is little likelihood that large energy-consumptive manufacturing plants will locate in the energy-poor interior Ozarks. The border areas, however, have better prospects.

The question of whether or not there will be a continuing supply of energy is a worldwide problem; it is no less a problem in the Ozarks than any place else. The Ozarks economy and lifestyle, except in a few remote locations, have become geared to cheap and abundant fuel, particularly gasoline, which permits long-distance commuting to off-farm employment. Higher gasoline prices undoubtedly will influence the development of manufacturing, second-home and retirement home development, rural real-estate values, and the tourist-recreation industry. When the first edition of this book was in preparation in the late 1970s, following an oil embargo by the Organization of Petroleum Exporting Countries (OPEC) and worldwide gasoline shortages, long lines at gasoline stations and sharply increasing prices caused considerable alarm. People were concerned for the future of the Ozarks' economy, particularly the tourism industry. As a stopgap measure, Branson businessmen banded together to purchase and sell gasoline at rock-bottom prices, to make gasoline available at affordable prices. Unfortunately, they developed no comprehensive plans for a long-term energy crisis at the local level at that time. The gasoline crisis seemed to go away, even if the price of gasoline stabilized at higher levels. Now, as the second edition of *The Ozarks* goes to press, another nationwide gasoline crisis has occurred. This time the shortage stemmed from refinery problems. Higher international crude oil prices contributed to price increases from near the $1.00 per gallon level in November 1999 to $1.75 in May 2001. The uncertainty of the situation, and the possibility that gasoline prices may increase even more, is of great concern to all businesses and services that have large fleets of vehicles on the road. Tourists, until now, seem to accept the higher travel expense as part of the price of their vacation, but those Ozarkers who must sometimes commute fifty or sixty miles to low-paying jobs are greatly concerned.[130]

NINE

MINING: ITS GEOGRAPHY AND HISTORY

The Ozarks is one of the major mining districts of the United States. Besides major deposits of lead, zinc, iron ore, and barite, the region produces fireclay, limestone, granite, and tripoli. Lead and zinc ores are found in close association. Historically, there have been four main lead-zinc belts in the Ozarks: the Lead Belt (in a larger district called the Mineral Area) in St. Francois and Washington counties; the Tri-State Mining District of Missouri, Kansas, and Oklahoma; the Central Lead-Zinc District, which consisted of smaller and more scattered mines in Camden, Maries, Morgan, and Miller counties; and the North Arkansas Lead-Zinc District, primarily in Marion, Benton, and Newton counties (fig. 9-1).

By far, the most important mining districts were the Tri-State and the Mineral Area. The Tri-State Lead-Zinc District extended over an area of approximately 1,188 square miles, embracing Jasper and Newton counties in Missouri, Cherokee County in Kansas, and Ottawa County in Oklahoma. We know the mining area by a variety of names: the Southwest District of Missouri, the Joplin District, the Tri-State Lead-Zinc District, and the Missouri-Kansas-Oklahoma District. *Tri-State Mining District* has become the commonly used name, although *Joplin District* is not a misnomer, since all mining camps in the three-state area became subsidiary to Joplin.

In the Mineral Area, no one town assumed the dominance of Joplin in banking, merchandising, transportation, ore smelting, and the manufacture and supply of mining equipment. This district included the lead-zinc ores of Washington, St. Francois, and Madison counties; the barite ore of Washington County; and the iron deposits of Iron and St. Francois counties. Various names have been applied to the Mineral Area and its parts. The lead mining areas were known as the *Lead Belt, Flat River District,* and later, after the lead discoveries of the 1960s in western Iron and Reynolds counties, the old lead-zinc mining area became known as the *Old Lead Belt.* Miners applied the name *Tiff Belt* to the Washington County barite mines, while they once called the iron mines of northeast Iron County and western St. Francois County the *Iron Mountain District.*

Smaller deposits of lead and zinc once were mined around the Mineral Area and over extensive areas in southwest Missouri and northern Arkansas. Miners worked shallow lead mines in Crawford and Jefferson counties in the eastern Ozarks. They worked sizable lead-zinc deposits near Aurora, and in Greene County at Ash Grove, Brookline, Pickerel Creek, and at the Pearson Creek mines near Springfield. Small mining companies worked shallow lead and zinc deposits from time to time in many Ozark counties, but the deposits were too small and remote for smelting operations to be of lasting importance. Mines have operated at one time or another in almost every county in the western and southern Ozarks.

EARLY DEVELOPMENT OF THE LEAD BELT

Since the first French entered upper Louisiana, people have recognized the eastern Ozarks as a mining region of a diversified nature. Whether the first tales of mineral wealth were complete figments of the imagination or whether the French actually discovered minerals, we do not know, but by 1700 indisputable accounts of mineral discoveries began to trickle out. While traveling along the Meramec River in October 1700, Father Gravier reported:

> On the 10th day after proceeding a league, we discovered the river Miaramigoua (Meramec), where the very rich lead mine is situated twelve or thirteen leagues from its mouth. The ore from this mine yields three-fourths metal.[1]

The implication that the mine already was in use in 1700 is obvious.

From that moment on, the area was known as a mining region. Prospecting for lead ore (galena) was easy because the deposits were very shallow and sometimes outcropped at the surface. In 1717 the ill-fated Company of the West sent an expedition to explore the Ozarks and work the mines in particular for silver and in 1719, Sieur de Lochon

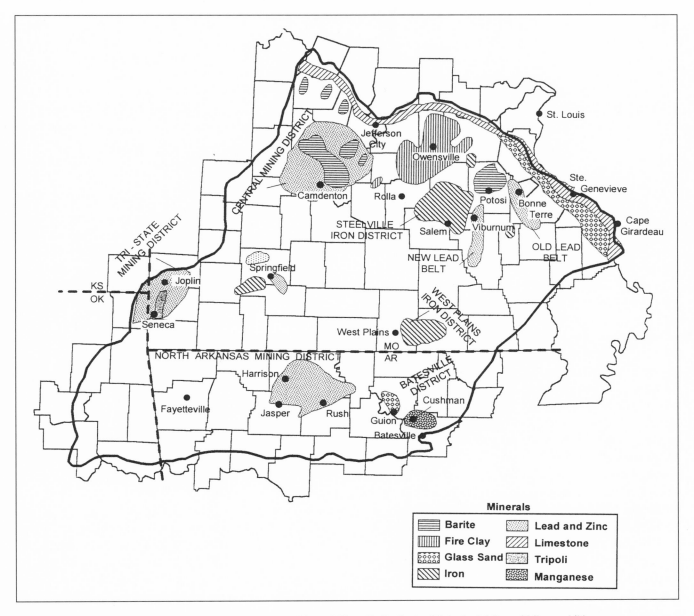

FIGURE 9-1. Mineral districts of the Ozarks. Adapted from Milton D. Rafferty, *Historical Atlas of Missouri* (Norman: Univeristy of Oklahoma Press, 1982), plates 78–87; with updates from William Spier, "A Social History of Manganese Mining in the Batesville District of Independence County," *Arkansas Historical Quarterly* 36 (Summer 1977): 130–57; Dwight Pitcaithley, "Zinc and Lead Mining along the Buffalo River," *Arkansas Historical Quarterly* 37 (Winter 1978): 293–305.

"raised quite a quantity of ore" from a spot on the Meramec River. They obtained some silver, perhaps salted (placed there for discovery), along with forty pounds of lead.[2] As a result, constantly recurring rumors of silver mines became a part of the tradition of the area.

Discoveries and mining ventures followed apace. In 1712 Anthony Crozat received a patent for various privileges in Louisiana, including the proprietorship of all mines and minerals. By 1719, organized mining got underway when Philip Renault (Renaut) had arrived with two hundred artificers and miners and some slaves.[3] By 1720, he had begun operation on the Meramec, and in 1723, according to some, his agent, La Motte, discovered the famous Mine La Motte near present-day Fredericktown.[4] In the same year Renault received a grant for the site at the junction of the Big and Meramec rivers. It is the earliest land grant in upper Louisiana of which any record has been found. The mines at Fourche á Renault were opened in 1724–1725, and the Old Mines tract was opened in 1725–1726.

The discoveries and mining ventures in upper Louisiana soon were reflected in maps of the region, thereby implanting even more firmly the idea that here was a great metalliferous region. Homan's map[5] of 1720 designated the eastern Ozarks as *Regio Mettallorium,* and in 1753, Du Pratz[6] shows *Mine de Plomb, Mine de Meramec d'Argent,* and *Mine de la Mothe d' Argent* as defined aspects of the landscape. Houck and other writers mention many other old maps.[7] All of them show the presence of minerals in the St. Francois region.

At the same time, and subsequently, other changes were taking place. The establishment of Ste. Genevieve around 1750 succeeded the first mining camps.[8] Other early French towns near the mines included Mine La Motte in 1763 and St. Michaels (Fredericktown) in 1798. Mine à Breton (Burton) was discovered in 1773 or 1775. It was discovered by Francois Azor, alias Breton, who found galena (lead ore) lying on the ground while hunting in the area.[9] Other dates for the discovery of Mine à Breton are 1747,[10] 1763,[11] and 1779.[12] When word of Breton's discovery became known, workers from the older mining centers of Mine La Motte, Mine à Renault, and Old Mines abandoned their diggings at those localities and rushed to the new bonanza.[13]

At first, the French carried out mining as an adjunct to agriculture or other activities. The habitation at the mines was seasonal; workers journeyed there after they harvested their crops in September or October and stayed until the mines became too wet to work or the weather became too cold in December or January. Most of the mining was done around Mine La Motte, Mine à Breton, and Old Mines. The men of Ste. Genevieve and New Bourbon engaged in mining or dealt in lead as tradesmen; Ste. Genevieve was known as the lead entrepôt of the St. Francois region.

Besides the appearance of permanent settlements, the actual mining of lead produced little change in the landscape other than that resulting from the appearance of new diggings, more furnaces, a larger area of land stripped of trees for fuel, and better-marked trails. The principal landscape features were the diggings and the furnaces. The diggings were similar to the more recent gopher diggings for tiff (barite); they were nothing more than shallow holes with earth piled up about their edges, resembling a prairie-dog colony. Such individual diggings may be found today, many within a few feet of each other, each being abandoned when it became too deep for easy operation or when the lead gave out. Wrote visitor John Bradbury:

> The workmen employed have no other implements than a pick axe and a wooden shovel and when at work appear as if employed in making tan pits rather than in mining. When they come to the rock, or to such depth that is no longer convenient to throw the dirt out of the hole, they quit, and perhaps commence a new digging, as they term it, within a few feet of that which they previously abandoned.[14]

The miners carried out prospecting haphazardly, but it was well known that most of the ore (galena) came from the Bonneterre dolomite and the residual clays above it. They systematically prospected the dark red Fredericktown soils, which form weathered Bonneterre clays. Bradbury explains the process:

> When the diggings become less productive than usual, they make trials on different parts of their lands, to discover where the ore is more abundant, that the diggers may be induced to remain with them. These trials consist in nothing more than digging a hole in some part of the woods, to the depth of three or four feet, and judging by the quantity of ore what degree of success may be expected.
>
> A little before I visited Rich Woods Mines, the property of Monsieur Lebaume . . . he had made forty trials, by simply digging holes, not more than four feet deep, in places remote from each other on his land.[15]

The impact of American immigration to the mining districts at the turn of the nineteenth century was revealed not only by the settlement of new villages but also by the effects on the older French settlements. The French element and the French atmosphere of Mine à Breton, Old Mines, and Mine La Motte were almost overwhelmed by the Americans. In 1789, Moses Austin received a grant for a square league of land at Mine à Breton, and in 1797 he sent his nephew Elias Bates and several skilled workers to Mine à Breton to build a sawmill and cut lumber for houses and mine buildings.[16] Austin's settlement formed a nucleus for the Americans who came to that section, and by 1804 the place had twenty-six families. When more Americans were attracted to the mines, the settlement of Mine à Breton became the town of Potosi. When Henry Schoolcraft visited Potosi in 1818, he described the town as a place with "70 buildings, exclusive of a courthouse, a jail, an academy, a post-office, one saw, and two grist mills, and a number of temporary buildings necessary in the smelting of lead."[17] The increase in prospecting that resulted from American immigration led to the discovery of several mines. The Mine à Joe (Desloge), Mine à Lanye, Mine à Maneto, and Mine à la Plate (all on the Big River) were opened between 1795 and 1801 and became the foundation of St. Francois County. Because the miners were an unruly class, people in Washington and St. Francois counties organized county governments at an early date to provide for sheriffs, courts, and jails.

Many other mines were opened in the Mineral Area, and Moses Austin—who introduced reverberatory smelters at Potosi and Herculaneum and was engaged in nearly all phases of the lead trade, including banking—complained that even more Americans would have been attracted to the area had it not been for the fact that when a good-paying mine was discovered one of the French residents would produce an old French or Spanish land grant of uncertain origin to claim title to the property.[18] In spite of the sometimes uncertain titles to land, prospecting and development of mine property proceeded so that at the outbreak of the Civil War most of the shallow lead ores were known.

LARGE-SCALE MINING IN THE OLD LEAD BELT

The modern era of mining in the Lead Belt dawned as the district attracted outside capital. The development of most of the lead-producing companies corresponds closely with that of the St. Joseph Lead Company, reorganized later as the St. Joe Mineral Corporation, and since 1986 the Doe Run Company.[19] It organized under the New York "Act to authorize the formation of corporations for manufacturing, mining, mechanical and chemical purposes" on March 25, 1864, with a capital stock of one million dollars, all of which the company issued to Lyman W. Gilbert of New York in payment for a 946-acre tract of mining land in St. Francois County (now in the city of Bonne Terre), Missouri.[20] Anthony La Grave of St. Louis had owned the land. La Grave had for many years been interested in mining in that neighborhood and had produced considerable quantities of lead by using the crude smelting process of that and earlier times. His tract and some adjoining lands were known as the La Grave Mines. La Grave got them through U.S. grants and through Spanish grants confirmed by the United States in 1834.

The St. Joseph Lead Company, a small eastern firm that represented one of the New South elements that were to bring irrevocable change to the Ozarks, had a most troubled beginning. The annual report of the trustee on June 13, 1865, summed up the year's business by stating that there had been "many serious and unlooked for drawbacks to rapid and successful operations during the year," such as "an immense drouth in July preventing the washing of minerals"; then, in early autumn, "a raid by the Confederate General Price's army, breaking up the company's operations and preventing the return of workmen for nearly two months"; then, "an usually severe winter";

and lastly, "the heavy floods of the spring which destroyed railroads and highways, and prevented transportation for several weeks."[21]

Shortly after assuming the company presidency on September 25, 1865, J. Wyman Jones appointed a new resident superintendent and employed several Cornish miners. These experienced hard-rock miners proved their worth in uncovering sheets of galena and blasting them into blocks that they could carry to a crude mill, where they were broken into smaller pieces with a hammer. They then ran the ore through a set of Cornish rolls to pulverize it before it went to the hand-operated jigs. A jig consisted of a long pole lying across a large log or wooden horse with a sieve suspended from one end, filled with crushed ore and supplied with water, and a man astride the other end. The miners operated this teeter-totter arrangement in sharp up-and-down movements so that the heavy lead particles would settle to the bottom.

The reverberatory or reflecting furnace introduced by Moses Austin at Mine à Breton and Herculaneum replaced the crude stone furnaces used by the French miners. French miners soon found it more profitable to abandon their inefficient furnaces and sell their ore to Austin.[22] The reverberatory furnaces were old-fashioned stone ovens, sloping to the front with a large firebox for wood beneath on one side. They threw the cleaned mineral into them. Through the combined action of heat and air, and by means of continuous stirring, after several hours metallic lead commenced running down the inclined hearth of the furnace into an iron pot. From there workers ladled it into iron molds. A single furnace manned by six men could turn out thirty-two pigs of seventy-two pounds each in twenty-four hours.

In 1867, St. Joseph Lead Company employed Dr. C. B. Parsons as superintendent, and in 1869 the company purchased its first diamond drill.[23] Parsons was a capable manager, and under his leadership the company prospered and eventually became the chief producing company in the Lead Belt. The diamond drill, which revolutionized exploration for lead and is used even today, consists of a rotating hollow pipe equipped with diamond-cutting edges that cut out a core of rock several hundred feet long. Thus by boring many holes it may be determined whether mineral ores are of sufficient quality and quantity to warrant sinking a production shaft. In 1869 the St. Joseph Lead Company sank its first exploratory shaft in the disseminated[24] lead deposits of the Bonneterre dolomite.[25] From 1869 on, mining below the surface continued and the miners went wherever the lodes led them. Eventually it became clear that there was significant mineralization in the Lamotte sandstone and the entire Bonneterre dolomite;

St. Joseph Lead Co. concentrator and smelter at Bonne Terre, Missouri, circa 1900. (Courtesy of State Historical Society of Missouri.)

ore was found in the Lamotte down to one hundred feet below the contact with the Bonneterre and throughout the four-hundred-foot thick Bonneterre.[26] Workers hewed out vast cathedral-like drifts and laid tracks for transporting ore to the foot of the hoisting shafts. In the early days, mules were used to haul ore underground, and most of the handling was done with the pick and shovel. Steam engines powered the hoists and mill machinery. When electrical power became available, mining and ore processing required fewer workers.

Rapid expansion of operations followed the discovery of ore deposits with the diamond drill. By 1874 the company had sunk five shafts and had expanded the mill, machinery, and furnaces; houses and shops had been built; horses, mules, tramways, drills, and pumps had been added; and they had purchased about one thousand acres of new land. Because the company depended on wood for fuel, it was necessary to own a large quantity of timberland to prevent higher costs. In 1879, St. Joe hired Gus Sitz, a skilled German metallurgist, and he directed the introduction of the process of roasting ores before smelting them.[27] In 1880 they expanded the mill and laid a narrow-gauge railroad to Summit on the Iron Mountain Railroad. The Summit Railway was a joint project of the St. Joseph Lead Company and the Desloge Consolidated Lead Company. Before 1880 these companies had hauled supplies and pig lead to and from three different points on the Iron Mountain Railroad. During spring and fall the roads became impassable because of heavy, sticky mud. In fact, they changed the shipping stations from time to time with the hope of finding routes with shallower ruts.

Industrial growth and expansion were continuous. A modern mill was built after the old one burned in 1853, increasing the efficiency of extraction processes. St. Joseph Lead Company purchased additional land from time to time, and in 1886 they purchased the property of the Desloge Consolidated Lead Company, consisting of 3,218 acres of land and a complete lead plant. Between 1887 and 1890, St. Joseph constructed the Mississippi River and Bonne Terre Railway to Riverside on the Mississippi River just above Crystal City. The line was then extended southward through the mineral rich Flat River country to intersect the Iron Mountain north of Farmington.

Construction of the new railroad opened the way for removing the smelting furnaces to the Mississippi River, where water and sand were abundant and where coke, coal, and fluxes could be obtained at much lower prices. The company acquired Herculaneum, a former smelting town but entirely abandoned by that time, as the site for its new smelter. Besides a complete and modern smelter, built in 1892, St. Joseph Lead Company constructed houses, a store, and a laboratory in the style of company towns of that era. The smelter at Herculaneum, subsequently improved and enlarged several times, continues to serve as the smelter for Doe Run Mining Company mines in the New Lead Belt. In 1911 St. Joe adopted the selective-flotation (oil flotation) process for separating lead and zinc ores, and in later years new ore milling techniques permitted production increases despite exhaustion of the richer lead reserves.[28]

At the turn of the century the St. Joseph Lead Company employed approximately eight hundred workers, owned about thirteen thousand acres of land, and operated twelve farms under the management of William Hobbs.[29] Over thirty years, the Lead Belt had progressed from very shallow and widely timbered shafts, from which ores were hoisted by bucket and windlass, to modern steam cable hoists that brought ore to the surface from depths of four to five hundred feet. By that time the industry had become firmly based upon the great disseminated galena deposits in the lower half of the Bonneterre dolomite. The formation of late Cambrian age has a thickness of nearly four hundred feet. Geologists believe that solutions that entered the Booneterre dolomite through fracture zones, and then spread laterally along selective permeable horizons within the formations, accomplished the mineralization. The resulting ore bodies are horizontal and vary from a few inches to several feet thick.

The steadily growing St. Joseph Lead Company eventually absorbed most of its competitors. In 1886 the Penn Diggings shaft was sunk. Its lead made it possible not only to pay for the new mill but also to finance the new railroad. Other land acquisitions near present-day Leadwood—such as McKee Diggings, the T. W. Hunt tract, the Hoffman tract, and the Jake Day tract—all proved to contain rich deposits of lead. Shortly after the Hunt tract was purchased, and operations were underway in a good ore body by 1900, houses were built for employees and the town of Huntington was born. St. Joe purchased the Hoffman tract and sunk a shaft in 1901. Again they brought in carpenters and built employee houses, along with a company store. They named the settlement Owl Creek when the post office was established in 1901, but in 1902 the name was changed to Leadwood.

The St. Joseph venture in St. Francois County attracted considerable attention throughout the area. Just north of the company's property in Bonne Terre was a tract originally granted to Jean Baptiste Pratte, an old Spanish grant designated as U.S. Survey No. 3099. The Desloge family of Potosi purchased the land, and mining operations began in 1874 under the name of the Missouri Lead and Smelting Company. They changed the corporate name to Desloge Consolidated Lead Company in 1876.[30] The firm operated three shafts and a large mill until a disastrous fire destroyed the mill in 1886. Rather than rebuild, Desloge sold out to St. Joseph. In the same year, J. Wyman Jones and other St. Joseph trustees formed the Doe Run Lead Company, which St. Joseph Lead Company subsequently absorbed.[31]

During the early 1890s, St. Francois County saw many new mining companies form. They merged with larger companies and later became a part of St. Joseph operations. Among the newly formed companies were Desloge

Desloge Consolidated Lead Company concentrating plant and smelter, St. Francois County, Missouri, 1907. (Reproduced from Ernest R. Buckley, "Geology at the Disseminated Lead Deposits of Washington and St. Francois Counties," *Missouri Bureau of Geology and Mines*, 2d Series, 9 [1908]: 796.)

Consolidated Lead Company, Flat River Lead Company, National Lead Company, Doe Run Lead Company, and Theodore Lead Company. By the mid-1930s, St. Joe had absorbed all of the competing operations; National Lead Company was the last company purchased.[32]

As the larger companies developed deep mines and large mills, the landscape imprint of mining became substantial. Head (shaft) houses, concentrators, new and different furnaces, large sediment basins, and huge chat (waste rock) piles filled the landscape from a given vantage point.[33] Three railroads eventually purchased the smaller roads that served the district: the Missouri Pacific, the Missouri-Illinois, and the St. Louis-San Francisco. Improved highways linked the several towns of the Lead Belt with St. Louis and other cities and towns along the Mississippi River border. The core of the Lead Belt, involving the towns of Bonne Terre, Flat River, Leadwood, Elvins, and Desloge, became an urbanized district of nearly a dozen small towns with a total population of more than thirty thousand persons. Flat River, Elvins, Rivermines, Leadington, Cantwell, Esther, Desloge, Bonne Terre, and Leadwood blend almost indiscernibly. Fredericktown, near the site of the Doe Run mines, and Mine La Motte are nearby in northern Madison County. Because many towns are small they have had trouble maintaining adequate community services. In an attempt to resolve some of these difficulties four separate communities—Flat River, Esther, Elvins, Rivermines—merged January 1, 1994, to form the new town of Park Hills.[34] Following the formal passage of the Park Hills government and tax package the city worked on unifying the fire departments, law enforcement, libraries, and community services. The four-city consolidation has brought a rebirth of optimism and community pride, and since it had never been done before, it is an example for other small towns with similar situations.

By 1960 the St. Joseph Lead Company controlled 90 percent of the area's lead production. They had abandoned several nonpaying shafts and focused operations on a few that were producing richer ores. These included the Federal Mine at Flat River and mines at Leadwood, Bonne Terre, and Indian Creek (Washington County). In September 1961, the huge Boone Terre Mine was closed because of declining production resulting from leaner ores. In 1973 the last of the producing operations in the Lead Belt, the Federal Mine and its mills at Flat River (now Park Hills), were closed.[35] By this time the development of Indian Creek Mine in Washington County and the even more important Viburnum Mine in western Iron County had become focal points of investment and mining development.

THE TIFF BELT

Barite, or tiff, is a comparatively soft, white to gray mineral. The properties of softness, chemical inertness, and high density (weight) make it valuable for many purposes. About 90 percent goes into oil-drilling operations to hold fluid pressure; the remaining 10 percent goes into filler in paint, ink, paper, textile, and asbestos products.

The Tiff District covers about seventy-five square miles in northeast Washington County and southern Franklin County, Missouri. Early on, this region became a French pocket and remains so to some extent today. The story of the French in the area around Old Mines, Fertile, Cannon Mines, Belle Fontaine, Shibboleth, Mineral Point, and Potosi has been one of both exploitation and retention of old ways of living.[36] It would be difficult to learn the extent to which the Creoles of Missouri were exploited.[37] Friction arose from misunderstandings between the two groups of people and from the fact that American settlers considered the French to be lazy, weak-willed, and generally inferior.[38]

Almost immediately after the Louisiana Purchase was consummated, a few progressive Americans began to accumulate land close to Old Mines. It has been noted that Moses Austin laid claim to a large tract of land on which he founded the town of Potosi. Another man, John Smith T, settled at Shibboleth, one of the central Creole settlements. He was a colorful and well-educated individual who had legally affixed the letter *T* to his name to distinguish himself from other John Smiths and to show that he was from Tennessee.[39] By various deceptions and through persistence in finding floating Spanish claims, he gained control of a large amount of land that was being lived on and worked by Creole families. Thus he became wealthy but gained the ill will of many people in the area. When Henry Schoolcraft came to visit in 1818, he referred to Shibboleth as "the feudal seat of John Smith T."[40] These men, and those who came after them as large landowners, gained control of productive lead deposits. They also controlled the region's commerce and sometimes operated large farms.

Living by their old traditions and with their old language and religion, the French Creoles mined lead and sold it to the landowners, who kept royalties for themselves. The Creoles earned barely enough to purchase necessities from the stores, which belonged to the landowners. This mode of life was harsh; the Creoles living rent-free on the land, but impoverished and working for the landowners.

Until the 1850s, lead was the main product of the area. The miners and landowners knew, however, that the district had vast deposits of barium sulfate, also called barite (baryte), heavy spar, or tiff. The first records of tiff buying and selling are dated 1857.[41] As the mining of tiff replaced lead mining as the major industry of the area, the established relationship between landowner and tenant-miner persisted. Today the larger frame houses and huge barns built by American landowners stand in sharp contrast to the log cabins (some constructed as late as the 1950s) and other small houses of the French families.

Shortly after 1900, when petroleum workers discovered that barite made excellent drilling mud to maintain pressure in oil and gas wells, mining companies began buying as much land as they could obtain. Nevertheless, until the 1930s they had introduced no mechanized mining because the cheap-labor force was large. Remaining as they did, illiterate and culturally isolated, the Creoles had virtually no outside assistance toward improving their standards. Washington County became one of the most economically depressed areas in Missouri. In 1939, Henry B. Lieberman, writing for *Ken* magazine, described the living conditions among the Creole tiff mining families living in the Old Mines community:

Hundreds of families are now living as many as eight and ten in one of the one, two and three-room shacks—bundles of log slabs, some without floors, all without gas, electricity and sanitation facilities of any kind, pasted up with oiled newspapers to keep out the wind and rain. In these huts furnished with crude pine beds, nail keg chairs and huge wood-burning stoves which serve for cooking and heating, the average Creole family lives on a steady diet of fried dough-bread, beans and potatoes. A few of the miners have truck gardens, and the diet of the Creoles is also varied occasionally with squirrels and quail shot in the woods.[42]

The retention of old traditions and ways of life were striking to Professor Joseph Carriere when he visited Old Mines in the 1930s:

The reader will understand readily my emotion when, in Old Mines, Missouri, I came into contact with an isolated group, practically unknown to the outside world, among whom the language and some of the traditions and customs of the old French administration district of Illinois have survived until the present generation . . . Scattered all along the countryside I found six hundred French-speaking families living in this community.[43]

Strong community ties prevented some families from seeking employment outside the mining area. When the Forest Service purchased land in Washington County near Palmer to help farmers move to better farmland, they met with resistance. Though the relocation sites were no more than five or ten miles from Palmer, some families resisted the move because of emotional ties to the home place and the community cemetery.[44] Even today, people in some families are reluctant to leave the local community, preferring instead to drive long distances in order to find employment.

In early days the Creoles and many American farmers found it possible to supplement their income with small-scale barite mining. Many French who lived near Old Mines eked out a living digging tiff after the mines closed. The common method of obtaining it is to dig the barite-bearing clay from surface excavations. The material is then placed in a device known as a log washer, which separates the clay and barite by knocking and rolling the material about. The barite freed from the clay is collected, and the clay is allowed to collect in a tailings pond. By the 1960s the independent operator had been forced out of business by a few larger and more efficient operators.

The mechanization of mining, which began fifty years ago, has greatly increased the number of people who look to the city for employment. Today all mining is done with diesel shovels that work in the ore zone, which lies at the contact of the Eminence and Potosi formations. They dig the barite from the clay residuum and some upper levels of bedrock. The shovels load tiff-bearing earth into heavy-duty ore trucks, which haul it to the washer. At the washer, conveyors load cleaned tiff into trucks that haul it to a mill to be ground into powder. Small dams, built with waste rock and gravel, provide a place to put silty waste mud pumped from the washer. Larger dams are built near some washers to form lakes for water supply; other plants pump water directly from creeks. Viewed from the air, the Tiff District, with its shallow pits—some of them overgrown with scrub timber and used as community dumps —its sediment ponds, and its many hauling trails, appears blasted, forlorn, and desolate.

Since 1925, when drilling mud became widely used, annual production of barite in Missouri rarely dipped below one hundred thousand tons, and production often exceeded three hundred thousand tons after 1950. Nearly all of it came from the Washington County Tiff Belt. In 1969 ten companies operated in the Tiff Belt, and two small companies mined in Benton County in the Central Mining District.[45] Twenty-five to thirty washing plants operated in Washington County then. The estimated total employment in all facets of the barite industry was about six hundred.

Production of barite started to decline rapidly in 1985 due to competition from mines in Nevada and from overseas operations, especially the low-cost barite shipped from China. By 1999, one company operated the two remaining small mines in Washington County.[46]

THE IRON MOUNTAIN DISTRICT

Ironworking in the Ozarks began with Ashebran's furnace, built near Ironton in 1815 or 1816.[47] The Springfield Furnace was built on Furnace Creek north of Caledonia in 1823 and reportedly cast cannonballs for the Black Hawk war of 1832.[48] From then until now, iron has exerted a strong influence on Ozark geography and history. Unlike most other products of the frontier, wrought iron could bear the cost of transportation to St. Louis, Cincinnati, and Pittsburgh by virtue of its high value. Therefore, it became a principal commodity shipped to the cities in exchange for manufactured goods. Farmers disposed of their produce in the ironworks settlements, and during off seasons they obtained employment as woodcutters, charcoal burners, and teamsters. Thus, the ironworks furthered the settlement of lands within trading distance. From the late 1830s until the start of the railroad era in the 1860s, many roads were built or improved, primarily to connect the ironworks with their markets. Sections of the Old Iron Road between Maramec Iron Works (in Phelps County) and Hermann correspond to present-day Missouri Highway 19.[49] Likewise, sections of Missouri Highway 32 follow the Old Plank Road, built in 1853, from the mines at Ironton and Pilot Knob to Ste. Genevieve. The Iron Mountain Railroad ran from St. Louis through Iron Mountain, Missouri, and was designed, at least in part, to help the development of iron-working in that area. Correspondingly, the Southwest Branch of the Pacific Railroad, now the Burlington Northern-Santa Fe, served the Maramec and Moselle ironworks.

The early ironworks of the Ozarks were in remote hilly districts. Because of the cost of hauling, choosing furnace sites that afforded iron ore, limestone for flux, water power, and timber for charcoal making within a radius of a few miles was necessary. Therefore, companies founded their ironworks near ore and fuel, with little regard for the advantages or disadvantages of marketing the product. In the parlance of modern-day economic geographers, these early charcoal iron furnaces were raw-material–oriented instead of market-oriented.[50]

Ashebran's ironworks, which was small and primitive, was near the entrance to Stout's Shut-in in Iron County, where a waterwheel provided the power for the air blast and hammer. Springfield Furnace, on Furnace Creek about six miles south of Potosi, opened in 1823.[51] Like most of the early ironworks, it was a plantation or a nearly self-contained community.[52] Ore at the Ashebran and Springfield furnaces consisted of hematites mined from the igneous rocks in the St. Francois Mountains.[53]

Investors became interested in Iron Mountain in 1836, mining began in 1844, and they put the first furnace on blast in 1846. Reports of ore so pure that blacksmiths could melt it down in their forges without treatment led to the wildest kind of enthusiasm. Plans were drawn for Missouri City, a utopian community with many parks and large public buildings where they would finance education, hospital care, and other social services with profits from the mines.[54] Investors were promised $108 annually for every $100 invested. In 1846 mining promoters declared that Iron Mountain and Pilot Knob contained enough ore to supply the world for a century.

Development of the ore bodies, which were less rich than the first wild reports claimed, was substantial after the completion of the Plank Road[55] to Ste. Genevieve and especially when the Iron Mountain Railroad reached the mines in 1858.[56] After the Civil War, iron companies built several new furnaces at the mines and at Carondolet near St. Louis. In 1869, when the Iron Mountain Company began operating, they produced more than 300,000 tons of iron ore each year and nearly one thousand men worked at the mines.[57] In the 1890s hydraulic mining, much like the mining operations in the California gold fields, began at Iron Mountain. The *Road and Hand-Book*

of the Missouri Division of the League of American Wheelmen, 1896 included the hydraulic mining operations at Iron Mountain as one sight to see.[58] Pilot Knob had a parallel, although less-spectacular history, with the greatest production taking place between 1850 and 1890. Of Missouri's output up to 1870, Iron Mountain had produced more than 90 percent. Two flourishing towns—Iron Mountain and Pilot Knob—grew up near the mines. The railroad diverted commerce from Ste. Genevieve to St. Louis, and by 1875 the cost of producing charcoal from timber near the mines had led to the construction of additional furnaces in St. Louis, where they could supply them easily with Illinois coal.

When the huge iron ore deposits in Minnesota's Mesabi Range entered the market in the 1880s, the Missouri mines faced severe competition. The richer Iron Mountain ores supported mining nearly continuously until 1960, but the Pilot Knob mine could not compete as well. There were, however, intermittent attempts to revive iron mining at Pilot Knob, including more sustained production during World War I and World War II when demand and prices were high. Aeromagnetic surveys in the 1940s led to the discovery of large subsurface magnetite-hematite deposits—Pea Ridge, Bourbon, Kratz Spring, Camels Hump, a deep ore body below the old mines at Pilot Knob, and an iron-copper deposit at Boss.[59] To date, only the Pea Ridge and Pilot Knob deposits have been mined.

THE TRI-STATE LEAD-ZINC DISTRICT

The development and decline of the Tri-State Lead-Zinc District occupied much less time than the mining cycle in the Old Lead Belt. Henry Schoolcraft when he visited the Indian diggings on Pearson Creek near the present site of Springfield wrote the first record of lead in the western Ozarks in January 1819.[60] There is some evidence that shallow lead deposits in Jasper County were mined by Indians at about the same time.[61] Miners worked small mines in Greene and Webster counties in the early 1840s and near Joplin in 1848. The initial lead discovery at Granby in Newton County was in 1849, and in 1854 they discovered large deposits in the Granby field. By 1857, miners had built hundreds of cabins and dug scores of shafts. Before the Civil War Granby lead was hauled by wagon to Boonville on the Missouri, to Linn Creek on the Osage, and to Fort Smith on the Arkansas for shipment to outside markets. Also, from 1860, when the Atlantic and Pacific Railroad reached Rolla, until 1870, when the track reached the Granby mines, mule teams pulling heavy ore wagons hauled lead to the railhead at Rolla.

There is no universally accepted explanation for the

WE-TAK-ER Mine, showing hand jig and picking shed, Granby, Missouri, area, circa 1905. (Reproduced from Ernest R. Buckley and H. A. Buehler, "The Geology of the Granby Area," *Missouri Bureau of Geology and Mines,* 2d Series, 4 [1905]: ix.)

origin of the lead and zinc ores of the Tri-State Mining District. Several eminent geologists have studied the problem of how minerals moved through the parent limestones and then concentrated to form valuable ores. One view holds that the ores were concentrated into rich deposits by cold meteoric water, which include descending ground waters and ascending artesian waters.[62] Another view is that the lodes were deposited by ascending hot water and gases from deep molten masses of rock material. Regardless of the theory accepted, the deposits formed in vertical fractures and horizontal solution channels or runs. The greatest concentrations of rich ores extend from Spring River in Missouri through Cherokee County, Kansas, to the Neosho (Grand) River in Oklahoma (fig. 9-1). In the early years, they carried mining out in the manner similar to practices established in the Mineral Area. Professional miners from the Lead Belt are known to have immigrated to the mines of southwest Missouri by 1849.[63] They were joined by local farmers. Most of the districts were regarded as "poor man's camps" because the ores were shallow and could be dug with little else besides a pick, shovel, and a bucket and windlass for hoisting ore.

Miners frequently encountered zinc ore (sphalerite) with lead, often at deeper levels, but because they knew little of its value, they cast it aside. They threw huge quantities of sphalerite onto debris piles. Citizens of Granby

used the accumulated zinc to construct a stockade for protecting the women and children against Civil War raids.[64] After the war, miners removed the mineral from the stockade walls and marketed it at three dollars a ton.

In the early days each camp had its own smelter. Kennett and Blow were at Granby, Mosely at Neosho, and the Hacklerode Company smelted for the Turkey Creek mines.[65] Marketing Joplin's lead posed a difficult problem in prerailroad days. The common method of transporting it to market was to haul pigs by wagon to Spring River and Cowskin Creek, load them onto flatboats, then float them to the Grand River in Indian Territory, from there to the Arkansas, and finally to New Orleans via the Mississippi. Between 1860 and 1870, when Rolla was the closest railroad shipping point, ore wagons sometimes made the arduous trip to the railhead.

The Atlantic and Pacific Railroad's arrival at Joplin in 1870 coincided with the discovery of superb mineral deposits in that district. In 1870 there was not a house in Joplin, but by 1874 it had become a city of three thousand people, one-third of them miners, and thirteen lead furnaces. Rich lead deposits caused the settlement of Oronogo, Webb City, and Carterville in quick succession. By 1872 a process for treatment of zinc blende had been discovered, and almost immediately zinc production became more important than lead.[66] Two more mining districts developed when they discovered zinc and lead in

General view of the concentrating and smelting plant of the Granby Mining and Smelting Company, Granby, Missouri, circa 1905. (Reproduced from Ernest R. Buckley and H. A. Buehler, "The Geology of the Granby Area," *Missouri Bureau of Geology and Mines,* 2d Series, 4 [1905]: 111.)

1866 at Aurora and new mines opened on Pearson Creek at Springfield.

Not only was the geology of the Tri-State District a controlling factor in mining and milling methods and land use, it also exerted much influence in the founding, growth, and longevity of mining camps and towns. The miners needed places to buy equipment, food, and clothing. The nearby towns also provided various types of entertainment and a place to live. Limited means of transportation required them to live near the workings, which in turn produced a large number of mining camps. If the ore bodies were large, the camp became a town; if deposits ran out quickly, the camp folded and the merchants moved on.

Gibson divided the Tri-State camps and towns into four stages of urbanization.[67] First came the mining camp, usually short-lived if the ore deposits in the vicinity were limited. In the second stage, the mining town miners still lived in the area and worked its deposits. Soon the economy of the town became more diversified because it had to supply the smaller outlying camps. In the third stage, workers lived in the larger towns and commuted to the mines by electric trolley. The fourth stage was a time of long-distance commuting, first by trolley and later by automobile. In this stage, when 90 percent of the mining was in the Picher, Oklahoma, field, some miners lived in Picher or Cardin, but many resided in Miami, Commerce, Galena, and Joplin. Many camps failed to pass the first test, so that today only about thirty urban centers from the original array of camps remain.

At one time or another, there were eighty-one camps in the Tri-State District:

In southwest Missouri these included Lehigh, Wentworth, Pierce City, Carthage, Neosho, Grand Falls, Dayton, Scotland, Leadville Hollow, Chitwood, Carl Junction, Thurman, Webb City, Carterville, Oronogo (Minersville), Smithfield, Waco, Thoms Station, Four Corners, Blende City, Duenweg, Prosperity, Porto Rico, Fidelity, Diamond, Murphysburg, Joplin, Blytheville, Stephens Diggings, Sherwood Diggings, Cox Diggings, Pinkard Mines, Leadville Mines, Carney Diggings, Tanyard Hollow, Taylor Diggings, Belleville, Jackson Diggings, Central City, Saginaw, Swindle Hill, Parr Hill, Lone Elm, Moon Range Diggings, Spring City, Racine, Seneca, Alba, Lawton, Granby, Bell Center, Central City, Asbury, Burch City, Klondike, Georgia City, Stark City and Cave Springs. Southeast Kansas produced Galena, Badger, Peacock, Empire City, Crestline, Baxter Springs, and Treece. In northeast Oklahoma were Tar River Camp, Picher, Commerce (Hattonville), Douthat, St. Louis, Hockerville, Quapaw, Cardin, Lincolnville, Peoria, and Century.[68]

The origin of their names is conjectural. Geographical and mineralogical factors were important, as with Grand Falls, Blende City, and Galena. Many settlements were named after prominent individuals: Picher, after the mining family responsible for its development; Joplin, after the Reverend Harris Joplin; Webb City, for the owner of the land where the mineral was found. Other names sprang from the whimsy and imagination of the miners; such are typical of all mining camps. A few of the more productive mines were Poor Boy's Big Run, Klondike, Bonnie Belle, Elta May, Betsy Jan, Mary Gibson, Sunflower, What Cheer, Mahutaska, and Never Sweat.

Although basic operations in the early years of the Tri-State Mining District were not dissimilar from those in the Lead Belt, there were important differences. The nature of the ore deposits and long-established mining practices mitigated against the large-scale development typical of the eastern Ozarks. Hired labor was seldom used before 1885, but two-man operations were very common. The major mining tools were a double-pointed pick, a square scoop shovel for loading the ore can, and a round-pointed shovel for digging. The windlass, equipped with rope and bucket, was operated by a hand crank. Animal and steam power were used as the deeper mines were worked by larger companies.

As in the Old Lead Belt and other Ozark lead-zinc mining districts, the principal underground operations used the room-and-pillar method, whereby columns of bedrock were left undisturbed to support the roof. In this way they eliminated the need for mine timbers. In some places, they developed large open-pit mines, notably the Oronogo Circle Mine, noted for the production of some thirty million dollars worth of lead and zinc.

Because of the scattered nature of the deposits, centralized milling did not develop until late. By 1905 there had evolved a definite system that became recognized nationally as the Joplin Mill Practice. The cost of building a Joplin mill was low, and when a deposit exhausted, workers could dismantle and move the mill to a new location. They poured concrete foundations at the new mine, and the mill was set up again.

The scattered deposits led to land-leasing companies that paid royalties to independent miners according to the amount of ore they produced. Royalty payment to the landowners ranged from 5 to 5.9 percent, depending on the cost of mining, whether the area was in a proven field, whether expenses were shared, and other related factors. The landowner usually surveyed his tracts into lots of about an acre each and leased them on the basis of one miner to an acre. Gradually, the best mineral lands became consolidated under a few mining and royalty companies. Among the larger ones were Granby Mining and Smelting Company, which held large tracts of Atlantic and Pacific Railroad land under a lease; Thompson and Graves Mining Company; Thurman Company; Chapman and Riggins Land and Smelting Company; Jasper Lead and Mining Company; Picher Lead Company; and Moffett and Sergeant Mining Company.[69] The leasing-and-royalties system became so well established in the Joplin area that as mines in Missouri closed and new mines in Kansas and Oklahoma opened, it was used in these areas as well.

Foreign capital was attracted to the Tri-State District in the 1890s when English and Swedish investors purchased mining property near Joplin.[70] Even earlier, in 1882, the stage had been set for the concentration of lead smelting in the hands of a single firm, Picher Lead Company. Through a series of consolidations and transactions, this firm secured the exclusive use in the United States of the process for converting lead fumes into white lead. From 1886 on, Picher Lead Company controlled most of the smelting in the Tri-State District.

Charcoal was the chief fuel until the 1880s, when coal from the nearby Kansas fields succeeded it. After 1900, they imported natural gas into the district for lead smelting. In fact, because natural gas was so effective in the smelting of zinc blende (sphalerite), most of the Tri-State zinc ores were smelted on the fringe of the district in the Kansas, Oklahoma, and Arkansas natural-gas fields.[71]

From 1930 to 1955, most of the mining was in the Kansas and Oklahoma fields, but Joplin continued to be the leading supply and financial center and smelting had been concentrated in the hands of the Eagle Picher Mining and Smelting Company.[72] Wildcat shafts were practically unknown. The company explored ore bodies systematically by core drilling, and they estimated the tonnage of concentrates beforehand. In the 1950s the Eagle Picher West Side Mine near Treece, Kansas, operated at the 428-foot level in a huge gallery, with a 125-foot ceiling, containing a tool and welding shop and a vehicle maintenance center.

In the final years of the Tri-State District in the 1950s and early 1960s, serious labor problems and prolonged strikes interrupted production. After the war years' flurry of activity brought on by high prices for lead and zinc, mining settled into established patterns. Three-fourths of the production was by the large operators. Gougers, usually an association of four to six miners, leased mined-out and abandoned properties and worked small pockets of ore, which they sold to Eagle Picher. A few small mining

companies opened new mines in shallow grounds in the tradition of the poor man's camp.[73] Finally, in 1976 when Eagle Picher closed its facilities, mining in the Tri-State District ceased.

The impact of mining in shaping the cultural landscape hardly can be assessed in its entirety. More than thirty permanent settlements persisted from the eighty-plus mining camps once established. A large network of railroads, including switching yards and sidings, was established by three major lines: the Missouri Pacific, the St. Louis-San Francisco (Frisco), and the Missouri-Kansas-Texas (Katy). One of the largest interurban railways in the United States, the Southwest Missouri Electrical Trolley, connected Tri-State towns from Carthage, Webb City, and Carterville in the north to Miami and Picher in the southwest. This system also carried passengers to Pittsburg, Galena, and Columbus in Kansas. An extensive network of modern roads connected a chaparral of mines and towns. U.S. Highway 66, a major east-west highway, connected the mining district with St. Louis, Chicago, and the West Coast, while U.S. Highway 71 provided a link to Kansas City and the Gulf states.[74]

A major development was electrification of the mines and mills. In 1890 the Southwestern Power Company built a hydroelectric station at Grand Falls on Shoal Creek, the first power plant in the Tri-State. Other nearby generating plants soon produced power, including the Lowell plant on the Spring River near Galena and the Riverton, Kansas, thermal plant two miles upstream. In 1913 the Ozark Power and Water Company completed Powersite Dam and its hydroelectric plant on the White River in Taney County partly to produce additional power for the Tri-State mines. In 1922, the Lowell, Riverton, Grand Falls, and White River power plants were combined into the Empire Electric Power Company, with headquarters in Joplin.[75] Powersite Dam formed Lake Taneycomo, and because it was the first of the large Ozark lakes, it is a landmark in the development of the Ozarks region. In 1931, Union Electric Power followed Empire's lead and constructed huge Bagnell Dam on the Osage River to supply the mines in the Old Lead Belt and for the St. Louis area.

Because of the power required by the mines, smelters, and mills, natural-gas service and electric utilities were available in Tri-State towns long before other sections of the Ozarks were reached. City water mains and sewage facilities were often installed as adjuncts to mining operations.

On the negative side, the Tri-State landscape remains pockmarked by shallow diggings, gaping water-filled open pits, and a few large chat piles, some nearly three hundred feet high, formed by waste rock from milling operations. The former mining areas, strewn with abandoned automobile bodies, castaway refrigerators, and other household dump material create a forlorn and blasted landscape, a constant reminder that mineral resources are, after all, limited and nonrenewable.

OTHER HISTORICAL LEAD-ZINC DISTRICTS

Lead and zinc mining became widely scattered throughout southwest Missouri and northern Arkansas. Most of the mines were small, the ore bodies being neither as rich nor as large as those in the better-known mining districts. The mines east of Aurora in Lawrence County comprised one of the larger mining areas outside the Tri-State Mining District. Even farther east, in Greene County, the Ash Grove District, the Brookline mines and the Pierson Creek District three miles east of Springfield were also important producers. Henry Schoolcraft and Levi Pettibone dug lead at the mouth of Pierson Creek in early January 1819.[76] Joseph Washington McClurg (later a Missouri governor) opened commercial mining there in 1851, making it one of the first commercial mining operations in the western Ozarks.[77] The Pierson Creek Lead-Zinc Mining District produced ore from about a dozen mines from about 1880 until the low prices during the 1930s forced the last mines to close.[78]

The Central Mining District, centering on Morgan, Miller, and Camden counties but including much of the Osage-Gasconade Hills, was never as important as the Lead Belt or the Tri-State District. The mines were smaller and more scattered, and consequently they were not consolidated and mechanized. By 1910 the district was essentially defunct, although some mining continued as late as World War II, when lead and zinc prices were high.

Lead and zinc mining in the North Arkansas Mining District was very similar to that of the Central District. Featherstonhaugh reported a lead mine on the Strawberry River in 1836, but no commercial mining took place in the region until the 1850s when they constructed several reduction plants near Lead Hill in Boone County.[79] In 1858 David D. Owen, Arkansas state geologist, confirmed the existence of large amounts of lead in the Buffalo River region.[80] During the Civil War the increased demand for lead for munitions stimulated activity in the area. The Cave Creek deposits especially were worked by Confederate forces during that conflict, but it was not until the 1870s that mining companies introduced larger-scale commercial lead mining into the Buffalo River basin.[81]

The first development of commercial lead mining in northern Arkansas occurred in Sharp County near Calamine in 1857 and later in 1871. In the 1880s, John Wolfer, an early prospector along the Buffalo River, and

several of his associates discovered a large deposit of zinc on Rush Creek in southern Marion County. George W. Chase from Fayetteville eventually purchased Wolfer's claim and organized the Morning Star Mining Company in 1891. The Morning Star Mine eventually became one of the largest producers of zinc in Arkansas.[82] While the Rush Creek area was the focal point of the Buffalo River zinc mining, small companies established other operations along Water and Tomahawk creeks in northern Searcy County and near the headwaters of the river near Ponca and Boxley.

Poor and unreliable transportation constantly plagued lead and zinc mining in the North Arkansas District. In the early days some ore concentrates were shipped out on flatboats on the White River, but the river never provided reliable shipping. When the Missouri and North Arkansas Railroad built through the area in the early 1900s mining operations expanded. The mines in Newton and Searcy counties had to haul the ore by means of wagons over the tortuous mountain roads to the nearest railhead. Shipping points for lead and zinc concentrates on the railroad included Harrison, Pindall, St. Joe, and Gilbert. Gilbert was the main shipping point for the rich Rush Creek mining area and reportedly wagons sometimes lined up two abreast for three-fourths of a mile waiting to be unloaded at the railhead when the mines were very active.[83] Ores were also shipped out over the St. Louis & Iron Mountain Railroad (Missouri Pacific) from Bergman and Cotter.

The large mines near Rush accounted for about half of northern Arkansas's production of zinc. The deposits in the other northern Arkansas mining areas were small and scattered. Mining and milling operations were never consolidated and developed to a degree anything like that of the two major lead-zinc mining districts in the Missouri Ozarks. Mining was especially concentrated in Marion County, although scattered lead and zinc mines occurred in several surrounding counties in north-central Arkansas. At one time or another, there were more than fifty mines to the north and southeast of Yellville. Seven different zinc mines operated near Monkey Run in Baxter County. The Gold Standard mine had the largest work force among the Monkey Run mines.[84] Ore was hauled by wagon from Monkey Run to the rail siding at Cotter. Several mines operated near the mouth of the Buffalo River and the town of Rush. As in other districts, the mines had colorful names: Cook, Last Chance, Columbia, Morning Star, Red Cloud, Full Moon, Sam Peel, Lone Pilgrim, Tomahawk. The last mining in the region was done in the Rush Creek area in Marion County from 1959 to 1962. Today the town of Rush, a cluster of a dozen or so weather-beaten vacant houses and sheds, resembles a western ghost town.

THE NEW LEAD BELT

Beginning in the mid-1950s extensive exploration and rapid development of mines began in the New Lead Belt in Reynolds and western Iron counties. The ore, primarily lead with some zinc, copper, and silver, lies in flat beds some 500 to 1,000 feet beneath the surface, primarily in the Bonneterre dolomite. In some areas the ore bodies are 130 feet thick and 2,000 feet wide.[85] Geologists believe the ores were deposited in and near a buried offshore algal reef in the Bonneterre formation.[86] The ore body meanders more than forty miles from southwestern Washington County through western Iron County, across the northern half of Reynolds County, to a few miles north of Ellington.

Indian Creek, situated about thirty-five miles northwest of Bonne Terre, was the first major ore body discovered outside the Old Lead Belt. This mine, operated by St. Joe Mineral Corporation, produced some 4.5 million tons of ore in its first nine years of operation, 1954 to 1963.[87] Two concrete-lined circular shafts provided access to the mine to remove ore and to bring in men, machinery, and tools. The mine and modern 2,500-ton mill is a prototype of St. Joe's Viburnum, Fletcher, and Brushy Creek operations. Cominco, Amax, and Ozark Lead Company built similar mining and milling facilities in the New Lead Belt.

Primary mining is by the room-and-pillar method, with twenty-five-foot supporting pillars at intervals of about thirty-five feet. The mines, opened in the 1960s use diesel-powered drill jumbos and rubber-tired trucks to haul to underground crushers. Underground repair and maintenance shops eliminate the need to bring large equipment to the surface for repairs. After primary crushing, they hoist the ore to the surface, where lead and zinc concentrates are separated from the powdered ore by flotation, a seemingly unlikely operation by which tiny lead and zinc particles attach to bubbles and float off the rock waste. The lead concentrates are trucked or railed to smelters at Glover or Herculaneum. The zinc concentrates go to St. Louis or Europe to be smelted. A third smelter at Buick no longer accepts ores, but it continues to operate as a secondary recovery smelter. Batteries and other salvaged lead material received at the Buick smelter are melted down and remolded as lead pigs.

ECONOMIC EFFECTS OF THE NEW LEAD BELT

The economic effects of mining today are substantial. Except for management and technical personnel, the mines employ people who commute from farms and surrounding towns. They have helped to stop the population decline that has been so characteristic of interior Ozark counties. Census data show that the population of Reynolds County, Missouri, declined from 8,923 in 1930 to 5,161 in 1960, but with the development of mining during the 1960s, the population rose to 6,106 by 1970. By 1999 Iron County's population stood at 10,936 after having peaked at 11,084 in 1980.[88] The population fluctuations in recent years are due partly to the rise and fall of lead prices and the corresponding level of activity in the mines.

Income from mining has affected the regional economy. By 1969 lead and zinc valued at $51,058,000 had replaced livestock raising as the leading industry in Reynolds County. At that time, farmers who turned to the lead mines earned as much as $12,000 per year, nearly twice their former income in many instances. A report by the Missouri Division of Geology and Land Survey in 2000 noted that wages earned in the metals mining industry are, on average, almost $5.00 per hour higher than many other sectors of Missouri's economy. For example, the average hourly wage for metals mining production in 1996 was $16.30, while those for other production industries were lower: industrial minerals, $11.20; forestry, $9.40; sawmills, $8.10; and recreation, $7.20.[89] Employment in Doe Run's mining and milling operations fluctuated over the past ten years from a low of 357 employees in 1992 to a high of 642 in 1996.[90] In 1976 the New Lead Belt produced 504,095 tons of lead worth $252,892,000.[91] Zinc, copper, and silver amounted to more than $75,000,000. Over the past twenty years, lead and zinc production has varied considerably following the rise and fall of prices for the refined materials. In 1995 the New Lead Belt produced 319,000 tons of lead

Hoist house and mill buildings at the Amax Homestake Lead Mine in the New Lead Belt, Iron County, Missouri, 1979. (Milton Rafferty Collection, photograph by the author.)

valued at $267 million and 46,000 tons of zinc valued at $49,100,000. Copper output amounted to $26 million, and silver amounted to $6,970,000.[92]

A unique geographic feature of the New Lead Belt is the new town of Viburnum. Planned by Bartholomew Associates of St. Louis for St. Joe Mineral Corporation, the former crossroads settlement, consisting of a general store and a house or two, had blossomed into a modern town of 600 residents by 1979. It had a shopping center, four or five new churches, the Viburnum Inn, a new consolidated school, an airfield, and a new office and research building belonging to the Missouri Division of St. Joe Mineral Corporation. In 1979 an air-pollution conference at the Viburnum Country Club drew meteorologists, geologists, mining engineers, and air-pollution consultants from such distant places as San Francisco and Colorado. Viburnum, formerly served by a logging railroad taken out in the 1920s, now has a new railroad, this time a heavy-gauge system built by the Frisco (BNSF) to haul lead concentrates and pigs. The lead mines brought modernity to the remote Courtois Hills, and it provided tax revenues never before imagined. Remarked a mining executive during the booming 1970s: "The county court of Iron County spends most of its time figuring how to spend tax money from the mines."[93] Declining lead and zinc production has reduced tax revenues from the high levels around 1980, and the population of the "new town" of Viburnum stood at 761 in 1999.[94] The future of Viburnum is bound closely to the economic vacillations of the New Lead Belt. Because of Viburnum's small size and remote location, it will surely test the mettle of town leaders to attract and hold new businesses when the mines close.

Economic conditions in the New Lead Belt have already changed considerably over the past twenty years. Mines formerly operated by various companies, including the St. Joe Mineral Company, Cominco, and Asarco, have been consolidated under the ownership of the Doe Run Company through a series of buyouts and ownership changes. Now all the mines along the Viburnum Trend are owned and operated by Doe Run. There are currently eight operating mines, six mills, two smelters, and one recycling center owned by Doe Run in Missouri. The company produces lead as its primary product along with byproducts of zinc, copper, and cobalt. Two mines opened since 1980, the Casteel Mine by the Old St. Joe Minerals Corporation in 1983 and West Fork by Asarco in 1985. Some older mines in the district have produced for nearly forty years, and the ores are becoming lean. The estimated lives of the mines range from ten to fifteen years depending upon metal prices.[95] Mine No. 27, which opened at Viburnum in 1960, closed in 1978.

The most important development in the last decade of the twentieth century was the introduction of pillar extraction.[96] This secondary mining strategy began in the Buick Mine in 1991. By the end of the century six of the eight mines extracted pillars as part of their total production. Some pillar extraction utilizes cemented backfill. This fortified backfill provides support for the back and support around pillars to give them added strength. The ore from some supporting pillars in the mines has enabled the company to continue production in the older mines. In 1999, Doe Run estimated that secondary mining of pillars amounted to 14 percent of the tonnage, 25 percent of the metal, and 60 percent of the cash flow.[97] Besides leaner ores and declining production, unstable and declining prices for both lead and zinc have plagued the industry for several years. The unstable prices stem from the expanding use of substitute materials in manufacturing processes and from increasing competition from foreign producers of lead and zinc.

THE SINK-FILL IRON DISTRICTS

Sink-fill iron deposits were widespread in the interior Ozarks. These deposits, mainly hematites and limonites, were deposited in buried sinkholes by waters percolating down from overlying rock strata.[98] Companies mined the ores at various times from near Poplar Bluff to West Plains and west of Springfield.[99] A second charcoal-iron smelting district grew up around sink-fill deposits in Phelps, Crawford, and Dent counties in Missouri (fig. 9-1). Apparently, the first bloomery was founded in 1819 or 1820 at Thickety Creek in Crawford County and operated until about 1830. The Maramec Iron Works, or Massey's, was the next to be founded. Thomas James and Samuel Massey of Ohio established the ironworks at Meramec Spring, about six miles southeast of St. James, in 1827. The site offered the advantages of good hematite ore, water power from Meramec Spring, limestone for use as a flux, and an adequate supply of hardwood timber for charcoal. The remote location was not a serious disadvantage at first because the demand for iron was local. The James family financed and constructed a second furnace at Moselle in Franklin County, Missouri, in 1846.

James and Massey organized the Maramec Iron Works as an iron plantation similar to those of eighteenth-century Pennsylvania. All lands, buildings, and equipment belonged to the partners, and the establishment had many characteristics of a feudal manor. Operation of the plant required about one hundred men, of whom about seventy-five were married and lived near the furnace. Men employed as woodcutters and charcoal burners often lived at

Cherry Valley Mine No. 2., Crawford County, Missouri, circa 1912. A filled-sink iron deposit. (Reproduced from G. W. Crane, "The Iron Ores of Missouri," *Missouri Bureau of Geology and Mines,* 2d Series, 10 [1912]: 1.)

some distance from the smelters. Before the Civil War, they leased slaves from plantation owners in the Missouri River valley to do the heavy work.

Workers made charcoal by the old method of piling oak and hickory cordwood on a level piece of ground forty to fifty feet in diameter, covering this with earth, and allowing the wood to char in a low-oxygen environment. They cut wood in the winter and set the crude ovens burning during the summer and fall. Approximately 500 acres of timber were cleared each year to supply the charcoal required for the ironworks. The Maramec Iron Works owned approximately ten thousand acres, which made it nearly self-sufficient in timber resources. Unlike the furnace at Pilot Knob and Iron Mountain, which employed a permanent force of choppers, the Maramec Iron Works employed area farmers as woodcutters in their slack season, thereby reducing the cost of wood by twenty cents per cord.[100]

The practice of cutting all timber (clear cutting) subjected charcoal iron producers, and lead smelters as well, to charges of exploiting the country's natural resources. Many people mistakenly blame the end of Ozark iron smelting on destruction of the forests that provided fuel. In fact, however, the ironworks never experienced a shortage of timber for charring. Unlike a sawmill, the ironworks required a heavy plant investment and could not easily move its equipment. Thus, it was in their best interest to preserve the forests, and they were among the earliest leaders in forest protection. It was self-interest that prompted Samuel Massey, superintendent of the Maramec Iron Works, to ask the Missouri governor John Miller to punish the Indians for firing the woods near the ironworks.[101] Fires near an iron or a lead smelter could easily destroy the fuel supply for the coming year.

Workers and slaves dug hematite from a sinkhole west of the ironworks and hauled it to the furnace in wagons. Water from Meramec Spring provided power to the smelter and the several forges on the property and power to operate the huge trip-hammer that pounded out impurities from the iron. The settlement included a store and a collection of miners' cabins on a ridge, overlooking the Meramec River valley, known as String Town.

They sold iron in various forms. Bars, blooms, and pigs were shipped to St. Louis by way of the Old Iron Road to Hermann or on the Springfield Road to the Gasconade River. Kettles, ovens, stoves, cannonballs, and railroad equipment could stand the charge of direct shipment to St. Louis by wagon. The company's stores, which had exclusive rights to market Maramec iron, operated at St. Louis, Hermann, Jefferson City, Boonville, Brunswick, Independence, Warsaw, Lebanon, and Springfield. As noted earlier, the company attempted to use the Meramec, Gasconade, and Osage rivers to ship iron, but they were largely unsuccessful. Hermann and St. Louis were the chief ports through which Meramec iron found its way to markets as far east as Pittsburgh.

The closing of the Maramec Iron Works in 1876 resulted from the financial problems of William James rather than depletion of the iron or timber resources.[102] The shutdown resulted from the Panic of 1873, coupled with James's heavy investment in a new furnace, the Ozark Iron Works, on an 8,000-acre tract on the Atlantic and

Ore washer at the Orchard Mine in Carter County, Missouri, circa 1912. (Reproduced from G. W. Crane, "The Iron Ores of Missouri," *Missouri Bureau of Geology and Mines,* 2d Series, 10 [1912]: 82.)

Pacific Railroad near the point where it crossed the Little Piney River ten miles west of Rolla. Although the Maramec furnace produced 4,500 tons of iron during 1875, they sold none of it because the price of cold-blast iron would not cover the cost of production.

Often, small manufacturing concerns fail because they do not keep up with advancing technology. The fact that some charcoal furnaces continued production fifty years after the closing of the Maramec Iron Works shows that technological change alone cannot explain the failure of individual ironworks. Even William James's bankrupt Ozark Iron Works operated under receivership until 1890. The Sligo Iron Furnace, a large charcoal ironworks in eastern Dent County, was not constructed until 1880, and it operated successfully until 1921.[103]

The Ozark furnaces built between 1870 and 1881 suffered from competition with low-cost coke and coal furnaces in St. Louis. Nevertheless, iron manufacturers built several furnaces during that time and even later: the Scotia Furnace (1870) about a mile and a half northeast of Scotia in Crawford County; the Reedsville Furnace (1871) about five miles west of Sullivan; the Hamilton Furnace on Hamilton Creek in Washington County; the Osage Ironworks (1873 or 1874) four miles north of Barnumton in Camden County; the Midland Furnace (1874) about one mile north of Steelville; and the Nova Scotia Furnace at Salem in Dent County. During the years 1916 to 1919, Mid-Continent Iron Company built two hot-blast charcoal furnaces at Midco and Brandsville.[104] These plants produced alcohol and other distilled wood products for the war effort. The Brandsville plant was abandoned before it was fully completed.[105]

Sink-fill iron deposits, on which the early iron furnaces in Franklin, Phelps, and Dent counties were based, occur widely in the interior Ozarks. Small mining companies operated at one time or another in Crawford, Franklin, Gasconade, Maries, Miller, Phelps, Dent, Texas, Howell, Reynolds, Carter, Oregon, and Ripley counties. Most of the ore mined far from the smelters was shipped to smelters in the East. Iron mines operated near Poplar Bluff and West Plains as recently as the 1950s.

In the 1960s the Ozarks again became a producer of iron ore, but not for local smelters. Hanna Mining Company, which took over operations at Pilot Knob after a series of ownership changes, opened new hematite deposits nearly nine hundred feet beneath the base of Pilot Knob. Previously, they had mined the ore in an open pit atop the mountain and through a shaft sunk in the west slope. When the new mine opened in the 1960s Hanna milled the ore at the mine and shipped it in pellet form. At about the same time, a second major ore deposit was discovered south of Sullivan by means of magnetic measurements, followed by core drilling. The mine, not far from the old Maramec Iron Works, was operated by Meramec Mining Company, a joint venture of Bethlehem Steel Company and St. Joe Mineral Corporation.[106] There is no geological relationship between the ores that they mined for the old Maramec furnace and the ores at Pea Ridge. The new mine opened in 1963. It is in magnetite ore imbedded in igneous rocks approximately nine hundred feet beneath the surface. The ore is hoisted to the surface, milled, roasted in pellets, and shipped to various places. In 1978, the rising costs (as much as five million dollars per year) of

Charcoal ovens of the Sligo Iron Furnace in Dent County, Missouri, circa 1912. (Reproduced from G. W. Crane, "The Iron Ores of Missouri," *Missouri Bureau of Geology and Mines,* 2d Series, 10 [1912]: 3.)

Sligo Iron Furnace at Sligo in Dent County, Missouri, circa 1912. (Reproduced from G. W. Crane, "The Iron Ores of Missouri," *Missouri Bureau of Geology and Mines,* 2d Series, 10 [1912]: 3.)

pumping water from the mine, coupled with low iron prices caused in part by foreign competition, caused the Pea Ridge Mine to close. The same economic pressures forced Hanna Mining Company to close the Pilot Knob mine in 1980. The Pea Ridge Iron Ore Company reopened the Pea Ridge iron mine in 1987. For more than ten years Pea Ridge has been the only iron producer in the Ozarks. It is the only producing shaft iron mine in the United States. Through 1996, the Pea Ridge company had produced about 51.5 million tons of iron from the mine.[107] While its output has placed Missouri as the third- or fourth-leading iron producer in the United States, the production from the Pea Ridge mine is small when compared with the production in the Mesabi Range of Minnesota.[108] Pea Ridge magnetite is currently used for high-power magnets and coal desulfurization. The potential for discovery of magnetite-hematite deposits throughout southeast Missouri is high, but because there are large known deposits, which are presently uneconomic to exploit, and iron prices are likely to remain low, it is unlikely that any further exploration or development will occur soon.[109]

OTHER OZARK MINING OPERATIONS

Mines near Seneca and Tiff City in Newton County, Missouri, produce tripoli, a porous, decomposed siliceous rock. When first mined there, in 1869, it went to textile manufacturers for scouring lint. It later proved to be an excellent filter for city water systems. In 1919 the Barnsdall Tripoli Company purchased the Seneca deposits and

began to market tripoli as an admixture in concrete. Tripoli, known as tiff (not to be confused with barite), is a soft, friable, porous silica of the chalcedony variety.

The terms *silica* and *glass sand* are applied to sand and sandstone having chemical and physical properties useful for many industrial purposes. The prime requisite is that the sand is essentially pure. Its greatest use is in the glass industry. They mine glass sand in the Ozarks in two widely separated districts. The largest production comes from the St. Peter sandstone along the Mississippi River Border.[110] It was first mined in large quantities when the Pittsburgh Plate Glass Company plant was founded at Crystal City in 1874. The sandstone is soft and easily quarried, and most of it comes from Jefferson and Ste. Genevieve counties.

There are hundreds of millions of tons of glass sand in thirteen northern Arkansas counties, primarily along the White and Buffalo rivers. However, present exploitation is limited to Izard County, where only two firms are mining the sand. The largest producer, Unimin Corporation is at Guion, a hamlet of seventy people. Unimin, an international corporation, claims to be the largest producer of silica sand in North America.[111]

In the early 1880s manganese mines were opened in Independence County, Arkansas, northwest of Batesville. Manganese in pebbles and boulders could be dug from shallow deposits in a soft sandstone. Reportedly, miners discovered some manganese boulders as large as cotton bales.[112] The manganese deposits in the Batesville District, sometimes called the Northeast District, were mostly in northwest Independence County, but partly in Sharp, Izard, and Stone counties. In 1881 the Keystone Mining Company of New York and Pennsylvania began buying rights to mineral deposits around Cushman, Pfeiffer, and Sandtown. However, operations remained small and were similar to the system used in the Tiff Belt in Washington County, Missouri. In 1889, Keystone, the district's largest operator with a total capital investment of $1,215,000, paid $33,191 to ninety-six employees.[113]

From the early years of the twentieth century to the 1930s, Walter H. Denison, who took over the Keystone Mining Company's holdings in the late nineteenth century, was the biggest operator in the manganese district.[114] Denison prospected and opened several of the most productive mines in the district. The one with the most colorful name was the Woodpecker Hollow Mine two miles south of Lafferty.[115] The mining carried out on a contract basis, by which Denison provided the tools and the mining property and purchased the ore that contract miners produced, did not yield large profits for the miners. Because the rewards were low, the mining was often seasonal, and workers drifted in and out of the nearby communities. Local farmers also worked in the mines as seasonal contract workers sometimes using their work animals, slip scoops, wagons, and hand tools. The landowner-worker relationship was similar to that in the old French barite mining district in Washington County, Missouri.

In the early years teamsters hauled the ore to Batesville by wagon for shipment, but when the Missouri Pacific built the White River line, they extended a branch line into the mining district at Pfeiffer and Cushman.[116] The peak production year was 1917 when war-stimulated industries created a high demand for manganese. The mines were closed during the depression years in the 1930s but were opened during World War II and operated until the mid-1950s. Reportedly, when manganese ore prices were high in the 1940s, one man came to the area with a bulldozer and took out fifty thousand dollars' worth in two weeks.[117]

They quarry granite at Graniteville in Iron County, Missouri, near Elephant Rocks. B. Gratz Brown, governor of Missouri from 1870 to 1872, and Thomas A. Allen, founder of the St. Louis and Iron Mountain Railroad, opened the first quarries in 1868.[118] The stone, marketed under the trade name *Missouri Red Granite*, became a popular building and paving material. It was used extensively for construction in St. Louis, and the waterfront docks there and at Cape Girardeau were paved with Missouri Red. Only one quarry is operating now, and they restrict production primarily to cemetery monuments. As the quarries closed, the population of Graniteville declined from 600 in 1940 to 140 in 1970 to 30 in 1998.[119]

Limestone and dolomite are abundant in the Ozarks. One of Missouri's first industries was the manufacture of lime from stone quarried from several formations bordering the Mississippi and Missouri rivers and, in southwest Missouri, close to Springfield. The Burlington and Kimmswick formations have been the most productive rock units because of the absence of clays and shales and their overall purity.[120] Before 1860 they manufactured the lime in the rudest manner: they heaped logs and burned the blocks of limestone thrown on them until the limestone separated into lime and carbon dioxide.[121] Later they burned the lime in small kilns, a few of which are still standing in various states of dilapidation. Two of the larger companies operating at the beginning of the twenty-first century were among the earliest processors of lime: the Ash Grove Lime and Cement Company at Springfield and the Mississippi Lime Company at Ste. Genevieve.

At present, limestone and dolomite quarries are mainly near the major population centers, where they produce building stone, lime, and cement. The largest quarries are in a belt paralleling the Mississippi River, in counties bordering the Missouri River, and in several counties in southwest Missouri and northwest Arkansas.[122]

Some limestones and dolomites have outstanding qualities of beauty and strength. Among the better-known building stones are those from Carthage, Missouri; the Beaver quarries (no longer operating) at Beaver, Arkansas, from which they constructed many large buildings in Eureka Springs; and the so-called black-marble limestones quarried at Batesville, Arkansas, which went into the construction of many public buildings in the Arkansas Valley, including the state capitol. The fine-grained limestone quarried at Carthage Marble Company near Carthage, Missouri, is often polished to high luster and sold as marble.

Global Stone-St. Clair, Inc., operates a large limestone quarry at Marble City, Oklahoma, in the Cookson Hills north of Sallisaw. The quarry produces chemical stone and chat rock for fill and ballast. Around the turn of the twentieth century, when the Marble City quarries produced a high-quality stone for decorative uses, the town boasted a bank, a lumberyard, a livery, and several other businesses. Today Marble City is very nearly a ghost town with crumbling buildings and vacant lots. Drain General Merchandise, an old general store turned latter-day "quick-stop," sells a small line of groceries, hardware, and oil and gasoline. It is the sole remaining "downtown" business.[123]

Mining of clay for structural brick, refractory products, and other uses began early and has remained important. In all of the German towns along the Missouri River, the availability of suitable clays stimulated brick making. Well before German settlement, Americans had established brick making in the larger towns. Sometimes itinerant brick makers set up temporary production on the sites of rural construction. Brick makers worked in St. Charles and Boonville before 1820 and in Jefferson City before 1826. The first brick house in Washington dates from 1824 and in Hermann around 1838.[124]

The discovery of high-quality refractory clay deposits in sinkholes around 1865 brought brick production to Maries, Phelps, Gasconade, and Franklin counties in Missouri. This area, known as the Southern Missouri Fire Clay District, continues as the nation's largest fire clay producer.[125] The beginning of the structural brick industry on a commercial scale in Missouri dates from about 1811 in St. Louis. As settlement spread westward into the Ozarks the structural brick industry followed. Clay suitable for brick making was nearly ubiquitous and the first brickyards used simple hand methods to manufacture the brick. Brick makers scooped clay into soak-pits and allowed it to soak a day or two before they dumped it out on a table for the hand molder.

Many early courthouses were constructed of brick, reflecting a pioneer desire for more permanent and fireproof material.[126] The authorization for the Ozarks' first stone and brick courthouse was in Washington County, Missouri, in 1814.[127] The advertisement for construction bids stipulated that the builder could dig the clay for the brick on the bank of a creek no more than three-quarters of a mile from the building site in Potosi. Brick makers produced bricks from local clays in Washington County, Arkansas, by the 1830s. The Methodist manse at Cane Hill, Arkansas, which still stands on the main road through the town, was built using locally manufactured bricks in the early 1830s.[128] Because so many wooden buildings burned during the Civil War, many people built brick buildings following the war.

Van Ravensway's study of the architecture of Missouri's German settlements revealed that they built many brick buildings after about 1850.[129] They used brick to construct houses, stores, mills, churches, public buildings, and buildings associated with the wine industry and also such minor buildings as smokehouses, privies, and sheds. The number of brick makers in Cooper, Gasconade, Franklin, and St. Charles counties increased from fourteen to fifty-seven between 1850 and 1860, and three-fourths were of German descent.[130]

Many brickyards produced for a very limited market, and when this demand or market declined or disappeared, the brickyards were closed. An example of the decline of small brickyards occurred in Springfield. In 1890, Springfield had five brickyards, all except one being hand-operated units. By 1908 only one of these remained in operation, and it continued production for only a limited time.[131] The number of brickyards in Missouri declined from 277 in 1889 to 14 in 1948.[132] The highly mechanized brick manufacturers in large cities have replaced the small brickyard making products for a restricted locality. It is likely that the tendency for producers to adopt improved machinery and to speed the production process will continue. The local brickyard lives only in memories of the historic past.

One of the earliest mining operations in the Ozarks was the digging of saltpeter from caves for the manufacture of gunpowder. Because gunpowder was necessary for frontiersmen, trappers, and hunters and for protection from Indian attacks, it was in great demand. It was less cumbersome and more marketable than lead ore, especially in wartime. Gunpowder, an explosive mixture, was not difficult to manufacture. It consists of from 70 to 80 percent saltpeter, with 10 to 15 percent of each of the other ingredients—charcoal and sulfur. Gunpowder manufacturers mixed the nitrate (potassium nitrate—KNO_3,

also called *niter*) leached from bat guano with charcoal and sulfur, two products readily available in the lead-mining districts. The process was so simple that they could produce crude gunpowder from guano taken from the many caves on the frontier.

Manufacture of gunpowder clearly began shortly after settlement. It is probable that when Renault and La Motte opened the lead mines in the eastern Ozarks and produced sulfur as a byproduct, they also began to manufacture their own gunpowder.[133] Henry Schoolcraft reported in 1818 that mines operated in several saltpeter caves and a gunpowder works supplied black gunpowder to the lead-mining district in the eastern Ozarks.[134]

Colonel William Ashley as early as 1814 established a saltpeter mining operation at Saltpeter Cave (Ashley Cave) to supply his gunpowder works at Mine Shibboleth.[135] While on one of his frequent hunting forays into the interior Ozarks, Ashley stumbled across a large deposit of saltpeter at Ashley Cave when his horse sank into soil made spongy by potassium nitrate washed from the mouth of the cave. Having recently commanded a ranger unit, which ran critically short of gunpowder while driving Winnebago, Sac, and Renard war parties out of northern Missouri, Ashley immediately recognized the potential value of the large nitrate deposit.

After taking on a partner, Lionel Browne, Ashley began production at the cave in late winter 1814. Their employees purified the saltpeter at Ashley Cave then carted it over crude paths to Shibboleth where they mixed it with charcoal and sulfur to produce gunpowder. Over the next thirty months their factory increased production to an average three thousand pounds of gunpowder a month and annual sales of $20,000.[136] Gunpowder manufacture was risky, not only because of the volatility of the finished product, but also because of the instability of the raw saltpeter. Three times during the period Ashley worked the deposits at Ashley Cave the unstable saltpeter exploded. The explosions killed workers on at least one occasion. In 1818, after one of their wagons carrying gunpowder from their new gunpowder works in Potosi to St. Louis exploded, killing two men, Ashley and Browne abandoned the business.[137]

There are many reports on the manufacture of saltpeter. William Clark Breckenridge reported on several early saltpeter works, including mining at a cave on Clear Creek about four miles southeast of Danville in Montgomery County (1814); a cave near Rocheport operated by Joseph Jolly (1812); and several caves along the Gasconade River.[138] James McDonald, of Bonhomme, and his two sons mined saltpeter from the Gasconade River caves as early as 1810.[139] Another well-known saltpeter cave five miles west of Waynesville was operated by three partners about 1816 to 1818.[140]

During the Civil War, caves with large saltpeter deposits were highly prized. This was especially true for the Confederacy, which viewed the Arkansas niter deposits as a valuable war resource, and beginning in the summer of 1862, expended work force and funds to develop these resources. Early north Arkansas settlers knew about saltpeter deposits and worked them before the Civil War to make gunpowder. David D. Owen, in his 1857–1860 geological survey, reported significant niter deposits in Independence, Marion, and Newton counties, including large deposits in Marion County's Bean Cave.[141] Shortly after the war began, contractors carried out saltpeter mining operating through the Confederate Nitre and Mining Bureau.[142] The refined saltpeter was first shipped down the White and Mississippi rivers to the armory at New Orleans, but later, after New Orleans fell to Union forces, it was hauled overland to the armory at Arkadelphia.

Mining operations were always tenuous because many residents of northern Arkansas were Union sympathizers and were willing to supply information about mining activity to Union military units stationed in southern Missouri. After repeated raids by Union army units from West Plains, Springfield, and Ozark, Missouri, the Confederate army took over the mining operations. It became a cat-and-mouse situation; as saltpeter production began anew following a raid, another raid would follow. Among the targets of General S. R. Curtis's April 1862 drive across northern Arkansas after a victory at Pea Ridge were the saltpeter mines near Yellville and Talbert's Ferry.[143] Even so, on August 1, 1862, mining and cleaning operations were underway at sixteen government caves, with a force of 272 white laborers and 115 slaves, and there were other private works in operation selling to the government.[144] The Boxley caves on the upper Buffalo River in Newton County, Bean's Cave in Marion County, and the John Miller niter cave on Lafferty Creek were among the more productive saltpeter caves.

Because of repeated raids and problems with transporting the niter to distant gunpowder works, the Confederacy could not rely on a steady supply of saltpeter. While Confederate guerrillas in north Arkansas continued to visit the saltpeter caves to replenish their supply of gunpowder after Union forces drove the Confederate army south of the Arkansas River, the mines were not significant in the South's overall war effort.[145]

The Ozarks is poor in fuel minerals. Small heavy oil deposits occur in western Missouri and oil and gas deposits still produce in the Arkansas River Valley, but both areas are beyond the boundaries of the Ozarks.

There are also deposits of bituminous coal in the Arkansas valley, and a few thin-bedded deposits extend into the Boston Mountains. Frederick F. Simonds's 1891 report on the geology of Washington County, Arkansas, suggests that coal mining was of some importance in the early development of the county.[146] Local people dug coal as early as the 1840s at Brown's (later Robinson's) coal bank (mine) near West Fork. Later, in the 1880s and 1890s, they mined it at Lemon's bank, a few miles east of present Lake Fayetteville. It was in this deposit that geologists found fossil insects.[147] They also mined coal at Male's coal bank, east of West Fork, for a time. This coal bank had plant fossils, including *Calamites,* a tree that grew to fifty feet in height in an ancient Pennsylvanian age forest.[148] The best-grade coal, known locally as "Peacock coal," came from a mine in southern Washington County in the Blackburn Creek area.

They used the coal locally for stoves, steam heating, and blacksmithing. Unfortunately, the coal beds were thin, only about eight to ten inches thick, and were inadequate for large commercial mining or industrial uses. Most of the active mining had ceased by the early 1900s, but according to Robert G. Winn, a Washington County historian, they mined some coal "until about the time of World War II."[149] It was mined mainly by landowners who "hauled it in wagonloads or at times carried it in gunny sacks for their own use or sold small quantities locally."[150]

MINERAL LEGENDS

Legends of rich deposits of precious metals and of lost mines, mainly gold and silver, are part of Ozark folklore. They passed down the stories from the earliest European settlers to the present generation. Perhaps people who are poor and who remain poor through several generations have a fascination for wealth that comes easily and quickly from hidden sources beneath impoverished rock-rubble soils. The Ozarks clearly has great mineral wealth, and investors made fortunes when they formed large mining combines. However, this wealth is founded on the base metals (lead, zinc, and iron) and not on the precious metals, such as gold, silver, and platinum. Ozarks geology does not portend the discovery of great riches in the latter metals, nor is it to be found in the new wealth producers: petroleum and coal. Modern prospecting for mineral deposits is scientific business, and there is no active search for precious metals in the Ozarks at this time. Yet this was not always the case; local histories and folklore are replete with attempts to discover and mine silver and gold.

A few examples of mineral folklore will acquaint the reader with the nature and repetitiveness of the stories. This one, from a history of Baxter County, Arkansas, is told with minor variations in several parts of the Ozarks:

Looking back, it seems strange that a student of our county's history could so easily forget that it was the lure of precious metals that brought the first Europeans to our region. De Soto's men camped for a while on the banks of White River at the mouth of Bruce Creek in 1555 and prospected in the surrounding hills.

The slag piles from their crude mining operations are mute testimony of their visit here. Evidently they did not find their gold and silver, although the legend of a lost Spanish silver mine guarded by the skeleton in Conquistador's armor still persists. Not many years ago, a stranger appeared in the Monkey Run community, discreetly asking several boys if they could guide him to a certain cave in the Bruce Creek Hills, and the almost forgotten legend was revived.[151]

It is doubtful that De Soto's men ever penetrated Arkansas as far as Baxter County, and as for the slag heaps, they are more likely the product of a more recent venture, when lead and zinc smelting was common in north Arkansas after the Civil War.[152]

Another common Ozark lost-mine story focuses on an eccentric or recluse who discovered a silver or gold mine but used the ore only when in need of ready cash. He never divulged the whereabouts of the mine:

There is a legend of a lost silver mine on either Hightower (now Carson) or Lithia Creek. Some versions say a lost lead mine, but I prefer the shinier story. The story goes that a Mr. Hightower used silver bullets in his pistol and hunting rifle. Whenever his supply would run low, he would disappear, and in a few days would be back home with a new supply of silver bullets. He promised his sons that he would reveal the location of his secret mine to them before he died, but, alack, Mr. Hightower died with his boots on, accidently killed by a silver bullet from his own pistol. For many years his sons and neighbors hunted in vain for his secret vein of silver. As with all legends, this story is based on facts. And if the silver bullets were fact, then this man was the original "Lone Ranger."[153]

Then there is the more factual folklore of a persistent breed of prospectors with entrepreneurial talents and few scruples. One of the more interesting stories concerns the Splitlog Silver Mining Company:

In 1887, a group of men posing as mining promoters interested Matthias Splitlog in financing a McDonald County gold and silver mining venture. Splitlog was a Wyandotte Indian who had made a fortune in Kansas City real estate, although unable to read and write. "Pay dirt" was reportedly found some four miles northwest of Anderson, Missouri. With Splitlog's financial backing events moved fast. The Splitlog Silver Mining Company was organized, the city of Splitlog laid out, and a daily stage line begun to Neosho. Assay reports claiming heavy deposits of gold and silver threw the countryside into a fever of mining excitement. Roads were reportedly lined with white-topped wagons labeled "bound for Splitlog." A railroad company was capitalized at $3,000,000, and Splitlog was made the treasurer of the construction company. He drove the first spike —a silver one—with appropriate flourish, "after music by the Indian band from the territory."[154]

This mining venture flourished only until it became clear that there were no ores. When Splitlog's lode of cash petered out, the mining boom and railroad venture collapsed. The promoters fled in time to escape punishment, but they ruined Splitlog. The railroad became part of the Kansas City Southern's holdings.

While in full bloom, the Splitlog venture caused heavy mineralization in formerly barren limestones and dolomites in adjacent parts of northern Arkansas. Several prospectors from Benton County claimed that they had discovered these deposits, but only a few ventured their own money to establish mines. The amazing good fortune and skill of Arkansas prospectors reported in local newspapers are recorded in a history of Benton County:

The biggest interest in mining came in 1887. At this time they were working the Split Log [sic] mine northwest of Bentonville in Indian Territory [actually the mine was in Missouri]. The stories of the great wealth to come must have got to the people for every week's newspaper would carry a new article on someone who had found some rich ore while digging a well, or just laying on top of the ground in their back 40.

The following news articles show how they were all year.

"Mr. James Nees, who was digging a well in the northwest part of Bentonville last week, found some of the richest specimens of Jack or zinc ore we have ever seen. It would go for 90 percent zinc."

"Col. Albert Peel of Avoca came by with a fine specimen of copper ore. He said there were strangers in his area locating mineral claims on Government land. . . ."

"The Bentonville Mining Co. [formed in 1887 with a capital stock of $1,000] struck ore in their mine on Pea Ridge that indicated exceeding richness. It is a mineral of some kind, as it melts readily, and has the appearance of silver. Specimens have been sent out to different points and a report of its value is daily expected."[155]

Because galena (lead ore) has lustrous cleavage surfaces and melts at low temperatures, unskilled prospectors and landowners often mistook it for silver.

One of the more colorful Ozark mining stories concerns the Kruse Gold Mine near Rogers, Arkansas. W. H. Kruse established the mine after experiencing a vision. The mining venture began auspiciously on January 27, 1903. That day some fifty people in Rogers received telegrams from W. H. Kruse of Chicago, saying, "Ten million dollars for all the people of Rogers." No one knew what it meant, but most were interested. It seems that sometime around 1900, W. H. Kruse, a successful businessman in Le Sueur, Minnesota, began having visions, which he would write down on paper with his eyes closed. In one of those visions, Kruse received instructions about a gold mine on his father's farm in Arkansas. He was told that under the roots of an old wild apple tree he would find a gold mine so rich that he could reconstruct the economy of the world after the ravages of the great war that was coming.

Not satisfied when members of his family in Arkansas could not find the tree, Kruse journeyed to Benton County and, after some looking, found a wild apple tree. He dug at its roots and found loose and crumbly "ore," which assayers said contained only the faintest traces of gold. Not satisfied with the assayer's tests, Kruse conducted his own and found the ore to contain $425 worth of gold per ton. The improved assay reports led to digging in 1905. Workers built a rustic one-hundred-foot tower of logs and boards and a shaft was sunk a few feet. However, the tower was blown over in a high wind a few months later and never rebuilt. They resumed work from time to time, but never recovered "pay dirt."[156]

They tell the story of a lost silver mine in Shannon County, Missouri, in several versions. If we are to believe them, at least two people spent their lives searching for the mine. Dr. Abijah Tyrell, who bought the site near the Sinks on Sinking Creek, spent his last days searching for the mine, and his son Frank spent a lifetime hunting for it. The story goes like this:

In 1873, Dr. Tyrell of St. Louis treated an injured man who related a story about a lost silver mine and claimed he knew where it was. Dr. Tyrell immediately bought nine hundred acres surrounding the Sinks and organized a min-

ing company. He moved to the sinks and with him came his ten-year-old son, Frank. Frank studied at the Missouri School of Mines in Rolla. Despite the failure of organized searches and an expensive shaft sunk into the hillside and despite scoffing of unbelievers, Frank Tyrell hunted for the silver mine off and on all his life. He believed, and said his studies supported his belief, that the granite porphyry of the sinks contained sulfite of silver. Frank Tyrell died in 1955 at the age of ninety.[157] Sometimes similar characters and incidents appear in the tale of the Old Slater Copper Mine, located southeast of Eminence.

A persistent silver mine legend in southwest Missouri centers on the Yocum silver dollar and a lost silver mine. This legend crops up periodically in different versions. It is kept alive by the tourism industry, which has marketed the legend and replicas of the Yocum dollar at various times.[158] The Yocum dollar was purportedly a personally minted solid silver coin containing more silver than the United States dollar. There persists about as many legends of the Yocum dollar as there are branches of the Yocums (spelled variously as Joachim, Yoachum, Yoakum, Yochum, or Yokum) scattered about the eastern and southern Ozarks. The most commonly related story is that four Yocum brothers migrated to upper James River country just after the War of 1812, or about the time the Delaware Indians were moved to that same area. Some of them worked a silver mine on the White River between where the Kings and James rivers run into it. Within the isolated area much trading was done by barter, but there was still a need for hard money. Solomon Yocum took some silver from the mine, melted it down, and made the dollars. Yocum dollars were used as trade money for several years.[159]

A thorough examination of the Yocum dollar legend by Lynn Morrow and Dan Saults resulted in a more likely account of the coin's origin.[160] The four Yocum brothers did settle in southwest Missouri and northern Arkansas where they became respected farmers, mill operators, and merchants. By 1822, William Gillis operated three trading posts in the area owned by Colonel Pierre Menard of Ste. Genevieve. Menard held the trading concession with the newly arrived Delaware Indians. Americans, including the Yocums settled on the Indian lands, but were supposed to pay rents. Officials expelled the Yocums from the Delaware lands in 1822, along with other "outlaw characters" who refused to pay rent to the Delawares and, worse, for selling alcohol. Solomon Yocum and his brothers left the reservation, but set up whiskey and brandy stills just south of the reservation at the mouth of the Finley River. Since no silver mine has ever been found, nor have the prospects ever been good for silver in the area, a more likely origin of the Yocum dollar is that they coined it to mask the accumulation of federal specie (silver coins) gained from the sale of alcohol to the Delawares.[161] In effect, it was the Ozarks' first money-laundering scheme.

There are many more stories of lost mines and rich mineral strikes, but these will serve to illustrate their nature. It is certain that legends of mineral wealth are firmly entrenched in local folklore. One county history noted that no fewer than seven valuable minerals could be discovered in the subsurface bedrock:

We know it's here and where it's at . . . lead, zinc, marble, rich soil, field stones. And probably, silver, gold, oil, and platinum . . . though we don't know exactly where. But isn't it comforting knowledge? These metals are here, for the future use and economy—if we need them.[162]

Perhaps it would be appropriate to mention that the Ozarks' large lead mines produce silver each day. Silver often occurs in close association with lead, and they have produced silver in the Ozarks for many decades as a byproduct of lead production. However, they have never mined it for its value alone. Trace amounts of silver are separated from the lead ores mined in the New Lead Belt in the smelting process and sold to help pay the cost of refining. They obtain small amounts of copper, gold, and other minerals in the same way. Even so, the mineral areas of the Ozarks are not rich in silver or other precious metals.

With all the spurious claims of gold and silver, the Ozarks can claim one true story of silver mining. A small silver mining operation was attempted in 1877 at the Silver Mines shut-ins on the St. Francis River west of Fredericktown, Missouri. In that year the Einstein Silver Mining Company drove the first tunnels and shafts, on the west side of the river, into lead ore that contained a comparatively high content of silver.[163] Two years later they constructed a dam across the St. Francis River and installed a turbine wheel to provide power for the milling operations. Then they built a smelting furnace, installed machinery for hoisting the ore and a crusher, and constructed other buildings. A townsite was laid out on a hill about one-half mile southwest of the mine. It included a post office, a school, a blacksmith shop, and several stores. At the height of the mining activity the miners and their families made up a village reportedly with a population of eight to nine hundred. Today the miners and their town are gone and the townsite is unrecognizable. Operation of the mine ceased after a few years, after production of fifty tons of lead and three thousand ounces of silver. Traces of gold were found. The mine was reopened in 1916 to mine tungsten, but it was closed within a few months. In 1927 there was another attempt to mine tungsten, but it also failed. When the need for critical metals was high during World War II, they opened the mine again briefly. Though they recovered small amounts of tungsten, the mine closed permanently in 1946, when the need for the critically needed war material ended with the end of the war.[164] The U.S. Forest Service, who now owns the property, uses it as a recreation and camping area.

TEN

OZARK AGRICULTURE: PATTERNS OF TRIAL AND ERROR

For the pioneers who settled the Ozarks, the single most important factor in the economic development of the region was the quality of soil resources. Today, after more than a century and a half of agricultural settlement, the well-being and prosperity of the people are dependent on the continued use of the soil, although perhaps less so than in former times. Nevertheless, of the three groups of renewable natural resources—soils, plants, animals—used by man through the ages, soils are perhaps the least understood by the average person. The primary reason for this is that vegetation covers soils, and to examine a soil therefore requires special effort. The significance of the various soil features, such as color, depth, texture, structure, and tilth, is understood by few.[1]

Soil is complex. It is composed of weathered rock material, decayed and partly decayed organic matter (humus), air, and water in various conditions. The soils of the Ozarks are diverse in physical properties and fertility. The variations result from the several factors that effect soil formation, including the parent, or geological, material from which the soils were derived, climate, topography, drainage, natural vegetation, and the length of time the soils have weathered.[2] Physical features that give diversity to Ozark soils include color, texture, topsoil depth, subsoil, subsoil pans, underlying material, and tilth (ease of tillage or cultivation).[3] Each is significant in identifying soils and interpreting their fertility levels. Soil profiles—the succession of layers, or horizons, in the soil—reflect the diversity of Ozark soils. The chief parent materials of Ozark soils are limestone and dolomitic limestone, shales, loess, and alluvial deposits. Sandstone and granite are of minor importance.

The decay of rock formations formed most of the soil in the Ozarks (fig. 10-1). On upland flats and gentle slopes, soils weathered from the underlying rocks, and rock formation contacts commonly correspond with sharp difference in soils. On steep slopes, more resistant beds of rocks, particularly the cherty limestones and dolomites, dominate the soils and also the topography. Because of their resistance, the cherty limestones form the summit elevations; accordingly their weathered products mantle the lower slopes, where less-resistant rocks outcrop. This, coupled with their extensive distribution, makes the soils derived from cherty limestones by far the most extensive type in the Ozarks.

In cherty soil, the residual chert (flint) is the most conspicuous feature. It is present in the topsoil, the subsoil, at the surface, or in all of these positions.[4] In some localities farmers built fences with chert that they took from the fields.

In some places the soils are free of chert and are quite fertile. Those of the Springfield Plain and the upland prairies and flats in the interior are generally the best of the upland soils derived from limestones and dolomites. The first settlers recognized that basin soils were fertile soils; some better-known soils of this type are in the Belleview, Arcadia, Farmington, and Fredericktown basins of the St. Francois Mountains.[5] The coves, or pocket valleys, in the Boston Mountains, such as the Richwoods, Wiley's Cove, and the Limestone Valley, were considered garden spots in former times.[6] Farmers later abandoned these small isolated valleys because of the limited amount of fertile land and their distance from suitable markets.

On the northern and eastern borders of the Ozarks are deep and fertile soils derived from wind-deposited loess. The fine loess particles, first deposited in the valleys of rivers flowing out of the glaciers, were picked up and carried by wind onto the adjacent uplands. Because the loess accumulated in deposits several tens of feet thick along the Missouri and Mississippi rivers, they became known as bluff soils.[7] These are undoubtedly the most fertile of all upland soils in the Ozarks; their long history of cultivation is testimony to this and their natural resistance to erosion. In sharp contrast are the thin, droughty soils of the glade lands in the White River basin. These soils, and those derived from the resistant felsites and granites in the

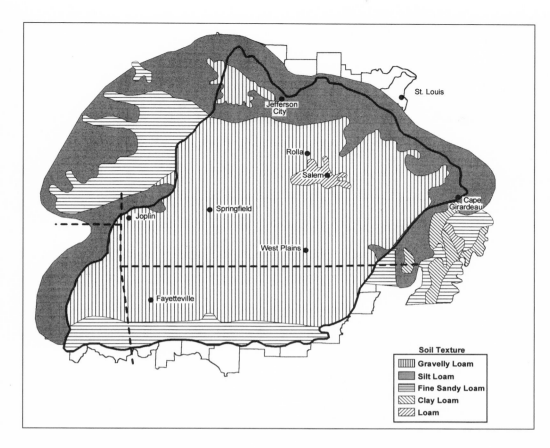

FIGURE 10-1. Soil texture of the Ozarks. Adapted from Curtis F. Marbut, *Soil Reconnaissance of the Ozark Region of Missouri and Arkansas. Field Operations of the Bureau of Soils, 1911* (Washington D.C.: Bureau of Soils, U.S. Department of Agriculture, 1914.)

St. Francois region, are largely useless for purposes of cultivation.

Bottomland soils always have been the most sought after. They are well distributed throughout the Ozarks; even the most rugged hill districts of the Gasconade and Eminence dolomites contain many spacious valleys. The first settlers sought out alluvial land on the lower courses of creeks flowing into larger rivers; it is usually very rich, heavy alluvium and is less subjected to flooding. Land like this was the first selected for settlement.[8]

The natural vegetation of the Ozarks has been an important agricultural resource (fig. 10-2). Surveyors' reports and accounts of early settlers agree that the amount of forested land is greater today than it was when the region was first settled. Apparently, the distribution of prairie and woodland was much the same as right now; that is, grasses grew on the undissected plateau, and forests occupied the hilly regions.

Forests covered three-fourths of the Ozarks in its primeval condition. The other quarter was tall-grass prairie, with big and little bluestem especially prominent. Farmers have plowed and converted most of the prairie land to agricultural uses. Most of the forested land is privately owned, and the average holding is small. There are some large private holdings, but they represent only a small part of the total forest land. The Mark Twain and Ozark national forests occupy approximately 20 percent of the forested area.

The reports of pioneers and the field notes of the men who made the first land surveys show that many uplands supported only stunted timber. Hard, cemented frangipani layers under level upland tracts may have retarded penetration of tree roots and caused slower growth. Many forested tracts had a park-like appearance, and young trees and brush were not as widespread as they are now.

Although small prairies such as the Barrens in Perry County were common in the eastern Ozarks, the western part was about 50 percent park-like grassland. The Springfield Plain had especially luxuriant bluestem grasses that were reported to have grown as high as a man on horseback (fig. 10-3).[9] In Greene County, surveyors' notes and maps showed a land divided about equally between prairie and woodland; the prairies occupied uplands and timber grew on valley floors and slopes.

The practice used by Indians and other hunters, of burning prairies to drive buffalo, deer, and elk, probably helped to retard tree growth in uplands. The fires killed sprouts and seedlings and the grassland profited at the expense of the forests. According to old settlers many prairies grew over with timber after the Civil War. They still call many wooded hills *balds,* a singularly inappropriate name today. It is a relic of the early days when it had

real meaning. Several bald hills described by Schoolcraft during his 1818–1819 Ozark tour are now fully wooded to the top.[10] Steyermark has suggested that soil factors may have been at least as important as fire in limiting tree growth on the uplands in some locations.[11] Settlers continued the practice of burning for many years to provide grazing for their stock. With settlement and fencing, the forest began to claim burned-over tracts. Some farmers reduced or stopped burning because of the risk of burning wood fencing, which tended to accelerate the spread of scrub woodland.[12] Farmers and ranchers still practice maintenance of pastures with fires, though "brush hogging" of persimmon sprouts, scrub cedar, and other "increasers" is the more common method of holding down growth of undesirable plants.[13]

Small grassy areas occur on hilltops where there is a deficiency of soil and ground water. These areas, which typically contain interspersed red cedar (juniper), prickly pear cactus, and scrub oak, are called *glades* when they occur on hillsides or cover large areas. Cedar trees that line fence rows near the glades give every appearance that they were planted by industrious farmers, but were more likely seeded by birds that fed on juniper seeds and then stopped for a rest on nearby fences.

Although they occur most widely in the White River Hills, there are glade lands along the Gasconade, Niangua, and other north-flowing streams where the Jefferson City dolomite outcrops. Thin soil and southern exposures account for the dry conditions and the peculiar vegetation association. Glades also occur near the St. Francois Mountains where the Potosi formation provides similar conditions.

The Ozarks is one if the northernmost regions for the southern pine forest. Extensive stands of shortleaf pine (*Pinus echinata*) were found in early years on the Piney Fork of the Gasconade River and in Ozark, Douglas, Texas, Shannon, Reynolds, Carter, and Washington counties in Missouri. Such forests also were found in the White River country of Missouri and northern Arkansas. In the Boston Mountains, pine forests were found in the eastern part and on the south slope in the central section.

Aerial view of a portion of Perry County, Missouri, 1978. This area of fertile loess soils is populated heavily by people of German ancestry. (Milton Rafferty Collection, photograph by the author.)

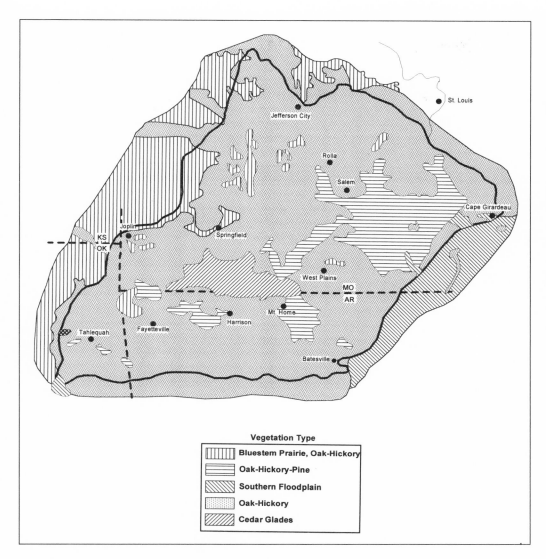

FIGURE 10-2.
Generalized natural vegetation of the Ozarks. Adapted from Julian A. Steyermark, *Vegetational History of the Ozark Forest* University of Missouri Studies no. 31 (Columbia: University of Missouri Press, 1959); with updates from "Forest Inventory and Analysis Data Base Retrieval System," U.S. Department of Agriculture, Forest Service (Starksville, Miss.: SRSFLA, 1999), ttp://www.srsfia.usfs.mss tate.edu/scripts.ew.html (April 17, 2000).

Vegetation Type

	Bluestem Prairie, Oak-Hickory
	Oak-Hickory-Pine
	Southern Floodplain
	Oak-Hickory
	Cedar Glades

Among the hardwoods there is sharp contrast between upland and lowland types. The upland forests consist almost exclusively of oaks, generally 90 percent or more of the total timber. White oak, post oak, black oak, and blackjack are the main varieties. On the ridges, black oak and white oak are common; on the hillsides, post oak and blackjack do well. Chinquapin oak, like the softwood cedar, is a bluff tree. Hickory and walnut do well on better upland soils.

In the valleys, because of better soil and water conditions, there is a greater variety of species and individual trees grow much larger. Sycamore occupies stream-bank locations, often forming canopies that nearly cover small streams. Cottonwood, maple, black walnut, butternut, hackberry, tulip, and burr oak were most abundant originally. In the southeastern Ozarks, bordering the Mississippi embayment, cypress, gum, and birch are present.

The understory has great variety. Flowering redbuds and dogwoods are harbingers of spring. In the summer, berry pickers take to bushy areas to pick blackberries, currants, dewberries, and huckleberries. The heavy stands of wild cane in the bottomlands of the streams of the southern Ozarks reported by Schoolcraft in 1818–1819 fell to the plow when they laid out farms on the richer river-bottom soils.[14]

In the western Ozarks the Osage Orange, also known as bois d'arc and hedge apple, has become widespread in pastures and fence rows. It is hardy, thorny, and resistant to drought. Posts made from the bois d'arc are nearly indestructible. In early days, Osage orange seeds were shipped from east Texas, Arkansas, and western Missouri to Kansas and what is now Oklahoma, where farmers planted them for thorny fences in the treeless plains. About one thousand hedge apples would produce a bushel of seeds that brought as much as twenty-five dollars in the 1870s.[15]

Settlers modified the prairies even more than the forests. They plowed most of them, consisting of bluestem and other tall grasses, when agriculture became more

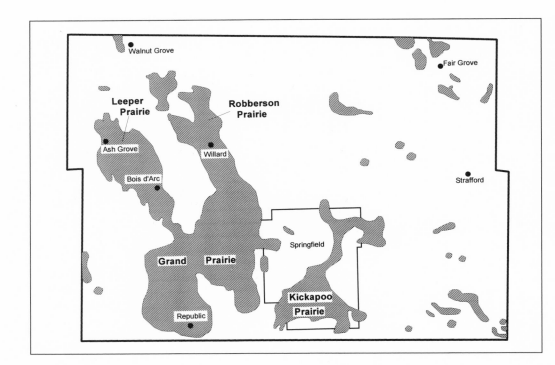

FIGURE 10-3.
Distribution of natural prairies in Greene County, Missouri. Prepared from "Plats and Field Notes," U.S. Department of the Interior, General Land Office, 1893. A true and liberal exemplification of the official plats surveyed between 1835 and 1840.

intensive. In the Ozarks, bluestems gave way to Kentucky bluegrass, which now grows wild wherever soil conditions are good. Most pastures presently are of highly mixed varieties of grass including lespedeza, clover, orchard grass, and fescue. It is winter-hardy fescue, which dominates 70 percent of the pasture land, that has revitalized the range-cattle industry.[16] The practice of clearing land of trees and scrub by bulldozers or by aerial application of herbicides is a controversial issue. Critics maintain the practice converts the Ozarks into a "fescue desert." Aerial spraying with herbicides reached its peak in the 1970s and is no longer used extensively.

TRIAL AND ERROR

The Ozarks lies in the General Farming and Forest Region of the United States.[17] Because of rugged physical conditions, limited accessibility, and difficulty of marketing, agriculture has been marginal, and farmers have tried many experiments. Although several agricultural systems have been used, it is apparent to even the casual observer that there have been great strides toward standardization and the elimination of many specialty crops.

The new settler in the Ozarks had several options in obtaining land. As a squatter, he could choose a likely plot of unsold government land and live on it in the expectation of buying it later. Or he could claim the land and purchase it at auction for a minimum sum of $1.25 per acre. The sale price, depending on the location of the land, was frequently two or three times the minimum. A third way to obtain land was through acquisition of New Madrid certificates, issued by the federal government after the earthquakes of 1811 and 1812.[18] The certificates, intended to assist persons whose land had been ruined in the cataclysm, were sometimes issued fraudulently and totaled more than five times the number of heads of families in the earthquake region. Many were used in the settlement of Howard County on the northern Ozark border. A fourth way to secure land was to purchase property, at prices that ranged from eight to twenty dollars an acre, that had already been claimed and improved.

PIONEER AGRICULTURE

The first settlers from east of the Mississippi occupied the leveler lands and better soils. Most of the agriculture was for subsistence, although some surpluses were shipped from the more accessible settlements. The fertile basins in the St. Francois Mountains produced surpluses for the workers in the nearby lead and iron mines. Nevertheless, commercial agriculture in the pioneer stage developed slowly, partly because the markets were not easily accessible and partly because the first settlers were as much woodsmen as cultivators. In forested areas the cultivation of crops was supplemented by hunting, trapping, fishing, and the gathering of honey, berries, nuts, fruits, and greens from the forest.

Compared with the hardships of pioneer life on the plains, the life of the Ozark pioneer must have been comparatively easy. They could build a log house in a few days.

An unlimited supply of game and fish was close at hand; pigeon, wild turkey, and deer were plentiful. An abundance of mast and prairies of bluestem grass provided for the cattle and hogs, so it was unnecessary to cultivate more than a few acres of basic crops. Statistics for the very early years are not available. As for the number of livestock, a farmer's own account would have been an approximation, for most of it ran loose on the open range. They killed hogs in particular for meat according to need, with no accounting expected. Gradually, livestock came to be marked, usually with a cut in the ear, to denote ownership.

Corn, a staple for man and beast, became the most important crop grown by the first settlers. Early farm produce for eight counties in the Springfield area is shown in Table 10-1. Because of the isolated area and the primarily subsistence economy, nearly all the pioneer farms produced some wheat, tobacco, flax, hemp, and cotton for domestic use. The women spun wool or cotton for clothing. As late as 1868, farmers as far north as Lawrence County, Missouri, grew sixty-six bales of cotton.[19] Cotton was also the principal commodity shipped overland to Springfield, Missouri, from Eureka Springs, Arkansas, in the White River Valley in the late 1800s.[20] While cotton was the principal cash crop of the Arkansas Ozarks by 1880, farmers in the counties of Madison, Carroll, Boone, and Newton produced only 231 bales of cotton in 1870 and only 1,018 bales in 1910.[21]

Unlike the French, the American frontiersman did not live in a community but set up a farm of his own in an isolated place. Using well-established practices, he promptly killed the trees on approximately five-acre plots by girdling, or removing a ring of bark. Since the dead

Sorghum-molasses mill and cooker, Stone County, Missouri, 1975. (Milton Rafferty Collection, photograph by the author.)

trees dropped their foliage, the sun could reach the earth and the field could produce crops the first year. In the second year they cut the trees, rooted out the stumps, and removed the underbrush.

Fields were broken with a bull-tongue plow the single blade of which was preceded by a sharp steel prong, or colter, which either cut the roots or caused the plow to jump over them. It was very suitable for use in rough land and for opening new fields. In the first year farmers yoked their strongest oxen to the plow, but in later years horses and mules could pull it. Harrowing leveled the land; sometimes they simply dragged heavy brush over it. After harrowing, they laid the land out in square with a bull-tongue plow and hand dropped corn in at the intersections. Then they covered the seed either with a hoe or by dragging a rock or log down the rows.[22]

Corn was the favorite crop. It could be fed to stock, sold, or turned into whiskey in a still. The shucks were useful material for chair bottoms, horse collars, mats, brooms, or mattress stuffing. Cobs were used for fuel, tobacco pipes, or dolls for the little children in the family. They raised wheat for white bread and biscuits. Garden crops, consisting of the vegetables most popular today, except tomatoes, were important in adding variety to the diet.[23] Cotton and flax were raised for the home production of cloth; maple sugar and honey served as the main source of sweetening. Sorghums for molasses were introduced later.

Wealthier farmers established hemp and tobacco farms before the Civil War in the Missouri River valley.[24] They brought in many slaves to cultivate these commercial crops. Hill farmers grew small plots of both hemp and

Cultivating with a double shovel in the Missouri Ozarks, 1969. (Milton Rafferty Collection, photograph by the author.)

TABLE 10-1. CROPS AND LIVESTOCK IN THE EIGHT-COUNTY AREA, 1850

Crops		Livestock	
Wheat (bushels)	115,383	Horses	12,688
Rye (bushels)	1,144	Asses and mules	2,651
Indian corn (bushels)	2,126,089	Milk cows	11,352
Oats (bushels)	633,721	Working oxen	9,457
Barley (bushels)	231	Other cattle	29,436
Buckwheat (bushels)	122	Sheep	45,401
Flax (bushels)	45,257	Swine	78,163
Tobacco (hands)	78,614		
Wool (pounds)	88,976		
Hemp (tons)	125		
Maple sugar (pounds)	1,075		
Beeswax and honey (pounds)	166,362		

SOURCE: U.S. Department of Interior, *The Seventh Census of the United States: 1850* (Washington, D.C., 1853), 625, 682.

tobacco, but mainly for local needs. Before the age of wire cables, hemp ropes were much in demand and a rope walk was operating in St. Louis by 1809.[25] The crops were well established in Kentucky and Tennessee, and settlers from these states planted large fields of hemp in the Missouri River bottoms near Lexington, Rocheport, and Glasgow. Tobacco could be grown in commercial quantities along the Missouri River, where transportation costs were lower. Tobacco was also grown in the interior Ozark counties, but much of it was used locally. Cotton, the chief commercial crop of the Arkansas River valley, was farmed commercially in the lower White River valley, where there was reliable river transportation. Farmers in the upper White River valley and the larger tributaries also grew cotton, but they had to ship it out over rough wagon trails to Springfield, Fayetteville, or to towns in the Arkansas valley.[26]

GENERAL FARMING

General farming began about 1870 in the better farming areas, notably the river border areas and Springfield Plain. By that time these areas had become well settled and the native grass, which had been an important factor in the early agriculture of the western Ozarks, began to disappear. Before this, it had been the custom to burn over the prairies and woodlands each spring. This practice was abandoned as the country became more heavily settled and fenced. A thick growth of underbrush, which had been kept down by annual fires, sprang up in the open fields and choked out the grass. At the same time, settlement and cultivation began to reduce the acreage of the natural range to a marked degree.

Another aspect of general farming, comparatively cheap railroad transportation, became important after 1870. Before that time the only feasible commercial agricultural product was livestock, which they could drive north or south to markets on the major rivers. Railroad transportation meant that farmers could produce wheat, corn, and other grains, and also livestock, for market.

The transition from subsistence and livestock farming to general farming occurred quickly, as indicated by the rapid adoption of improved machinery for cultivation. In 1868, for example, the firm of McGregor and Murray in Springfield sold more than seven hundred turning plows.[27]

The shift toward general farming occurred most rapidly in the areas that were settled early because of the smoother topography, better soils, and better transportation facilities. Grain growing proved profitable, especially on the red soils of the Springfield Plain, the Fredericktown soils of the Arcadia, Belleview, Farmington, and Fredericktown basins, and on the loess soils of the northern and eastern Ozark borders. In the interior Ozarks, residents practiced general farming in the valleys, where conditions were favorable, but in hill country the farms continued to be of the subsistence or livestock types. Some interior districts did not develop general farming practices until the turn of the century. As late as the 1930s the farms in the headwater valleys in Reynolds County, Missouri, were noticeably less progressive than those of the lower valleys.[28] In 1911, Marbut notes, in the Richwoods Basin near Mountain View, Arkansas, "there was no possibility of any form of specialized farming that would require frequent and rapid marketing of products. The basin lies too far from a shipping point when both distance and character of road are considered."[29]

Farmers could derive little cash from hill country farms, except for the sale of a bale or two of cotton or a few "hands" of tobacco from the better river-bottom farms. Occasionally they drove cattle to markets in the Missouri and Arkansas valleys. John Q. Wolf, in *Life in the Leatherwoods*, described his uncle's subsistence farm in the hills of Izard County, Arkansas.[30] William T. Swan, according to Wolf, generally raised corn, oats, millet, clover, cow peas, cotton, tobacco, and wheat, besides maintaining a fruit orchard of more than a hundred trees, a strawberry patch, a row of raspberry bushes, and a dozen beehives. Their vegetable garden produced cabbages, lettuce, turnips,

General farm scene including varied crops, orchards, and livestock. (Courtesy of State Historical Society of Missouri.)

potatoes, and beets for the table. A herd of less than ten cows provided milk, cream, and butter and occasionally surpluses that he could sell. Chickens were kept for their eggs and meat. Foraging razorback hogs and cattle supplied the family with pork and beef.

By 1900, general farming dominated the agricultural system in the Springfield Plain and the Missouri and Mississippi borders. They regarded it as a desirable and secure form of agriculture, as attested by an observer's remarks:

> Greene County is especially blessed in not being a region where the farmer has to place his reliance almost wholly on any one particular crop. He can choose for his specialty, if he so wills, almost any standard crop of the temperate zone. Or he can have crops of any and all grains, fruits, and vegetables. Thus, with more than one string to his bow, he can feel sure that if disaster befalls one or two of his crops, the others will hold him safe from harm.[31]

General farming and its diversity of crops and livestock led to smaller farms, especially in the fertile valleys of the larger rivers and in areas near Springfield, Fayetteville, Springdale, Cape Girardeau, Perryville, Hermann, and in the Arcadia, Belleview, and Farmington valleys in the St. Francois Mountains. A 1915 county history stated that "small farms and diversity of crops" well could be adopted

as the motto of Greene County. Another commentary noted the extent to which this subdivision of land had progressed by 1915.

> Take a late map of the county, which shows the names of each land owner, and the size of his holdings, and you will be surprised to see how far this subdividing of land has already gone. In one government township, taken haphazardly from the map. I find one hundred and forty-four farms. Of these, ninety-six, exactly two thirds of all, are tracts of eighty acres or less. Fifty-one are forty acre tracts.[32]

Of course, there were a few large farms then and individuals and lumber companies held some very large timber tracts, but the tendency toward smaller farm units is evident. As farmers used the land more intensively, land values increased.

Between 1890 and 1900 the number of farms in the eight-county area around Springfield increased from 13,540 to 23,311, an addition of nearly 10,000 farms.[33] For the next twenty years the number remained stable, but a marked decline occurred after World War II. This pattern of development is typical of the better agricultural lands in the Ozarks. In recent years, the number of farms has again increased in some sections of the Ozarks as farmers sell their farms and subdivide the acreage to sell to speculators or to people seeking a rural acreage to live on or to hold for recreational use. The U.S. Census often classifies these small acreages as part-time farms, but the land, usually, is no longer used for agriculture.

As in pioneer days, the chief field crops throughout the Ozarks were corn and wheat. Corn, used primarily as livestock feed, always exceeded other grains in acreage. The soil of the river bottoms and the upland prairies were regarded as emphatically corn land. Wheat was the standard cash crop, although unusual weather conditions, chinch bugs, or Hessian flies sometimes caused reduced yields. Oats, barley, feed sorghum, and forage crops provided livestock feed.

Ozark farmers raised cattle and hogs, along with horses and mules, widely, but sheep were not as popular as in earlier years, when they supplied wool for homespun clothing. The general farmer usually kept two types of cattle: those raised for meat and those raised for milking purposes. In the cream-can stage of dairying, the general farmer could obtain a profit from a few dairy cows, and by

stall-feeding a few head of beef stock, he could add to his income. Hogs formerly ran free, but farmers now penned their hogs, fattened them for market, and sold them profitably. Milk goats and Angora goats were introduced in part because their habit of eating brush helped in maintaining pastures. The huge Scottish-owned Missouri Land and Livestock Company, based at Neosho, Missouri, successfully used goats to manage its experimental farm, Sandyford Ranche. This company purchased goats in Texas and sold them to farmers in the western Ozarks.[34] "Goating down" pastures and cutting sprouts with a heavy hoe became established practices that persisted until the large tractor-powered rotary "brush hogs" became common in the 1950s. Even now, though not of major importance, goats are more numerous in Ozark counties than in surrounding areas. (fig. 10-4).

There was considered improvement in production methods during the general-farming era. Smaller farms called for more care, more intensive cultivation of cropland, and improved animal husbandry. Higher land prices

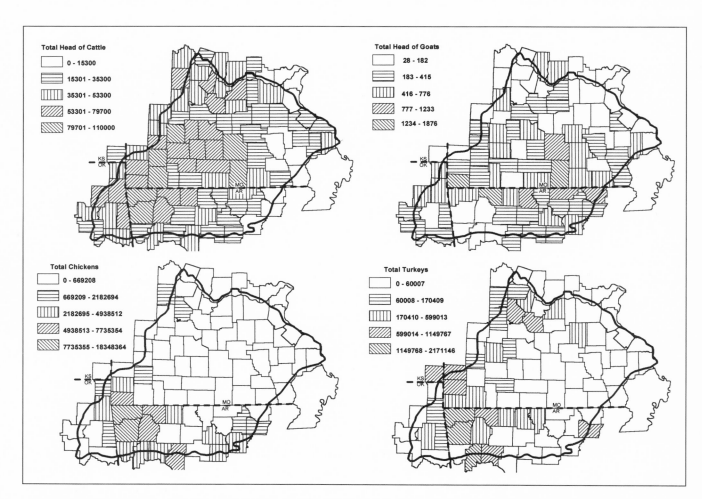

FIGURE 10-4. Distribution of cattle, goat, chicken, and turkey production. Prepared with data from U.S. Department of Agriculture, *1997 Census of Agriculture.* (Washington, D.C.: Government Printing Office, 1997).

and smaller farmsteads required larger yields in crops and livestock.

During the pioneer stage of agriculture, when land was plentiful and cheap, maintaining fertility received little attention. It is reported that farmers would tear down log stables and move them to new locations when the accumulation of manure made it impossible to use the stable.[35] Moving the stables was easier than moving the manure. With the adoption of more intensive land use, farmers hauled manure to fields and spread it as fertilizer.

Not all parts of the Ozarks participated in the progress that followed the Civil War and the construction of railroads. Some sections, notably the Courtois Hills and Osage-Gasconade Hills in Missouri and a vast area extending southward through the White River Hills and into the Boston Mountains, lingered on in the pioneer subsistence phase of agriculture. In Indian Territory (Oklahoma), the unorganized political situation held up progress.[36] Full-blood Cherokees of the Keetoowah Society retreated to the flinty hillsides and valleys in eastern Oklahoma, where they sought to keep alive ancient tribal traditions and by this method shut out reality.[37] Another large nonprogressive group consisted of poor whites, commonly renters, who came to the area during the period of Cherokee government as laborers or renters on Indian land. Thus, many elements of progress associated with the New South era failed to penetrate the Cherokee Ozarks. In the accessible and progressive sections of the Ozarks, the period 1870–1910 saw widespread adoption of scientific farming methods encouraged by colleges of agriculture at universities and by other organizations, such as the Grange, the Agricultural Wheel, and the Farmers' Alliance.

By 1900, general farming began to give way to specialized agricultural production, although it remained the principal type of farming for many years. The general farm (fig. 10-5) retained its position of leadership in the Springfield vicinity until the 1940s, when the dairy farm became the leading type. From 1930 to 1964 the general farm fell from first place to fourth in number of farms. The decline from 11,172 in 1930 to 420 in 1964 meant the statistical loss of 10,742 general farms, a pattern that extended throughout most of the Ozarks and much of the United States as specialized agriculture became necessary.[38]

Several factors contributed to the decline of general farming. Specialty farming, introduced in the 1890s, attracted some farmers from general farming to the production of apples, peaches, strawberries, or tomatoes. Shortly after 1900, even more farmers turned to dairying. More recently, many general farmers switched to livestock, often with part-time employment in nonfarm jobs. However, the overriding forces contributing to the decline

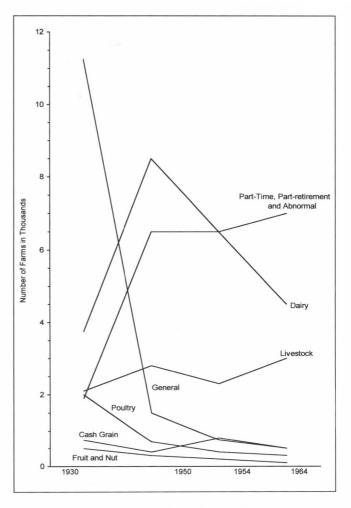

FIGURE 10-5. Types of farms in the Springfield vicinity. Prepared with data from U.S. Department of Commerce, U.S. Bureau of the Census. *Census of Agriculture: 1930, 1950, 1954, 1964* (Washington, D.C.: U.S. Government Printing Office, 1932, 1952, 1956, 1967).

of general farming have been improvements in transportation and in the organization and integration of the marketing of agricultural products throughout the United States. Increasing area specialization and the economies of scale of production have made general farming largely uncompetitive.[39]

The decrease in wheat and corn acreage proved the decline of general farming, which were, for the most part, products of general farms. Data from the U.S. Census of Agriculture illustrate that in the entire Ozark region corn and wheat acreage had declined substantially by 1940, and by 1964 acreages had declined to insignificant levels except in the eastern and northern borders. By 1990 these two traditional staple crops had all but vanished except for the loess soil belt bordering the Mississippi and Missouri rivers and in the far western Ozark border counties

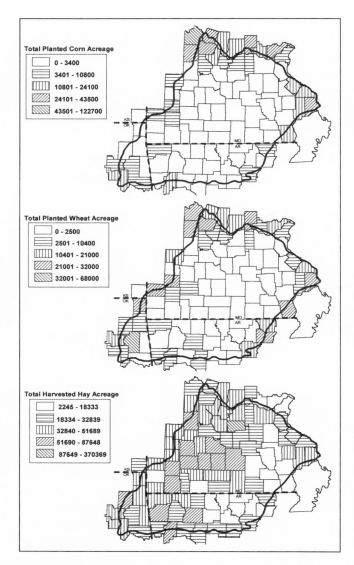

FIGURE 10-6. Distribution of corn, wheat, and hay production. Prepared with data from U.S. Department of Agriculture, *1997 Census of Agriculture* (Washington, D.C.: U.S. Government Printing Office, 1997).

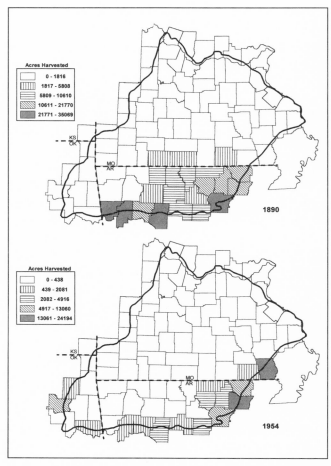

FIGURE 10-7. Acres of cotton harvested in 1890 and 1954. Prepared with data from U.S. Department of Commerce, U.S. Census Bureau, *United States Census of Agriculture: 1954* 1: Parts 10, 23, 25 (Washington, D.C.: U.S. Government Printing Office, 1955); U.S. Department of Interior, Census Office, *Report on the Statistics of Agriculture in the United States at the Eleventh Census: 1890* (Washington, D.C.: U.S. Government Printing Office, 1895).

(fig. 10-6). Cotton, the traditional cash crop in the southern Ozarks counties, also declined during the same time span (fig. 10-7).

TRANSFORMATION OF AGRICULTURE

The building of railroads in the period 1870 to 1910 was important in the transformation of agriculture. Likewise, the continuing growth of road mileage and improvement of roads after about 1920 played a major role in extending commercial agriculture into the more remote sections of the Ozarks. Affordable rapid transportation for grain, fruit, dairy products, and livestock and poultry was the

key to the transition from subsistence to commercial agriculture. Steamboats, even those that penetrated the Ozarks regularly on the White and Osage rivers were unreliable because navigation was not possible during frequent periods of low water, and they could never serve a vast isolated interior. Many other factors helped with this transition. Professor Brooks Blevins, in two separate studies of rural Arkansas, identified several factors that contributed to the modernization of agriculture in the Arkansas Ozarks.[40] Professor Edgar McKinney, in his study of the cultural transformation of the southern Missouri Ozarks, also shed new light on the complex process of agricultural modernization.[41] Not only did the railroads provide employment in shipping, clerical work, and track repair but the industries that grew up in the larger railroad towns provided off-farm employment also and began the long process of transition from full-time farming to part-time farming that continues even today.

The impact of railroads on agriculture was felt almost immediately. Railroads provided one-day delivery of milk and cream to St. Louis and other markets thereby helping to stimulate dairying. For example, northern Arkansas counties sold 140,000 gallons of milk in 1910 compared to only 850 gallons thirty years earlier.[42] Grain, strawberries, apples, peaches, hogs, cattle, and other farm products could reach markets that were nearly impossible to reach before railroads were built.

We have already discussed the impact of improved roads and improved automobiles on agriculture. The internal combustion engine had great utility for farmers. Tractors powered by gasoline and distillate were smaller and much less expensive than the giant steam-powered tractors that preceded them. Ozark farmers where quick to recognize the usefulness of tractors, although many could not afford them. Nevertheless, in 1917, when Henry Ford introduced the Fordson, a small, light, mass-produced tractor for about $750, the transition from horses and mules to tractors was set in motion. Other farm implement manufacturing companies—International Harvester, John Deere, Massey-Harris, Case, Minneapolis-Moline, Oliver—soon offered small tractors suited to the smaller Ozark farms. The McCormick-Deering Farmall series became very popular, especially the smaller F-15, F-20, and the later H and C models. By 1940, one in four American farms had at least one tractor. However, a survey of ninety-three typical farms in the southeastern Ozarks revealed only one tractor in use in 1939.[43] Nine out of ten northern Arkansas farmers were still using animal power as late as 1945.[44]

While the Rural Electrification Administration was important in bringing electrical power to farms and in farm modernization, other developments in the 1930s and 1940s contributed as well to the process of agricultural transition, experimentation, and change. Cooperative extension agents in all Ozark states provided scientific information on improved breeds of livestock, better strains of crops, and a great wealth of technical information on feeds, agricultural chemicals, and conservation methods. Improved farm credit, the spread of feeder cattle auction barns, and the expansion of refrigerated trucking of poultry products induced many farmers to abandon row-cropping for raising poultry and livestock.[45] The transition began in the 1930s and then exploded after World War II.

There was a great surge in agricultural technology following World War II. The federal government had diverted much of the industrial prowess of the United States to the production of things necessary for the war effort. At the end of the war when defense contracts expired, companies were searching for new markets. The new technology and inventions created during the war came to bear on the civilian economy, including agriculture. A new flood of tractors appeared on the market to meet pent-up demand. Radio, television, and newspapers carried advertising for a large line of tractors equipped with improved hydraulics for farm equipment. Professor Blevins described the rapid displacement of animal power in Izard County, Arkansas, following the war this way:

Aging gray mules brushed flies with their tails alongside rusty heaps of horse-drawn equipment in quiet barn lots as automobiles hurried by on hard-surfaced roads carrying drivers to the supermarket or to work in town. The entire county of Izard served as home to only 416 horses and mules in 1974, a decrease of ninety percent from only thirty years earlier.[46]

The improved line of post–World War II equipment included much more than tractors. It included improved trucks, better adapted for hauling livestock and equipped with hydraulic lifts to dump grain. Self-propelled combines harvested grain without the time-consuming labor of binding and putting the bundles in shocks. The list of new and innovative equipment goes on to include corn pickers, cotton pickers, ensilage cutters, feed grinders, elevators to transport grain into new galvanized metal bins and hay bales into haylofts or stacks, electric milkers, farm refrigeration units for dairy products, and a wide range of improved haying equipment including hydraulic-equipped mowers, side-delivery rakes, and improved string- and wire-tie balers. The constant upgrading of equipment continues today, always to improve efficiency and reduce labor and fuel costs. Today, when the chief crop of the Ozarks is hay, large round bales have replaced the smaller square and round bales. The huge round bales, now handled mechanically with a tractor or pickup equipped with a bale spike, greatly reduce hand labor in storing and feeding hay. In recent years the long tandem wheel trailer pulled by a three-quarter or one-ton pickup has replaced the standard farm truck equipped with a grain box and stock racks. The trailers, of various designs, are adapted for hauling grain, livestock, or equipment.

FRUIT GROWING

As general farming began to decline in the Ozarks, fruit farms and other specialized farms increased in importance.

From the earliest time to the present, apples and peaches have been the most popular and most successfully grown fruits. Apples were grown so widely in small household orchards that the Ozarks became known as the Land of the Big Red Apple even before the coming of the railroads and the development of commercial orchards.[47] The Knous, Huntsman's Favorite, and Ben Davis apples became popular in the early orchards. In the early years, most of the peaches were seedling or Indian peaches, the kind that come up where peach pits are dropped. Seedling peaches grew in fence rows, in roadside ditches, among apple trees, and around the back doors of farmhouses where farm wives had discarded the pits. Seedling peaches may still be found today around abandoned farmsteads. Though they vary greatly in size and taste, and are almost never cared for, they are sometimes picked and eaten in season.

Railroad officials encouraged fruit growing. During the 1880s and 1890s, farmers planted thousands of trees, mainly along railways in the western part of Missouri and in northwest Arkansas. In Missouri, large orchards were set out in 1892 near Seymour in the southern part of Webster County. The orchards planted by Ira Sherwin Hazeltine, founder of the Hazeltine orchards, some 1,600 acres and tens of thousands of apple trees, stretched along both east and west sides of the Hazeltine Road five miles west of the Springfield public square.[48] It was an unusually large orchard operation, but only one of many orchards that brought Greene County's acreage of fruit trees to a peak of 540,000 in 1900. Howell County also was an early center for commercial orchards. Pomona, named for the ancient Greek goddess of fruits, was founded as a peach plantation community near the rail lines a few miles north of West Plains. In northwest Arkansas, orchard plantings were heavy in Benton and Washington counties, especially along the St. Louis–San Francisco Railroad. The Cherokee boundary effectively kept out new fruit growers. Because the Cherokee Nation owned the land in common until allotment (which took place in the period 1902–1910) and whites could not buy it, most of the inhabitants of the area were unresponsive to the development taking place to the east. Thus, a cultural fault line began to appear at the Oklahoma boundary.[49]

A major stimulus to fruit growing came in 1899 when the Missouri General Assembly established a State Fruit Experiment Station at Mountain Grove. Then in 1901, there was an apple season that produced an extra-good crop. Because of drought, crops generally failed that year and farmers found the small household orchards an important source of income. Interest in apple culture increased, and farmers expanded their orchard acreage. By 1905, orchards of 500 to as much as 2,000 and 3,000 trees, two and three years old, became common. Plantings were numerous near Seymour in Webster County, close to Springfield and Republic in Greene County, and around Marionville in Lawrence County in Missouri, and near Springdale, Rogers, Farmington, and Prairie Grove in northwest Arkansas. Orchards were so extensive near Lincoln, Arkansas, that it came to be known as "Apple Town." About twenty years later, in 1932, within a radius of six miles of Marionville, Missouri, there were 2,500 acres in commercial apple orchards capable of producing 100,000 barrels of apples.[50] In Greene County, orchards of 40 to 100 acres were common, and some larger ones of 200 to 400 acres occupied the favorable growing sites.

The period of important fruit acreage and production was between 1910 and 1940. Although large orchards were set out before 1910, most of the trees did not reach bearing age until after that time. The peak year was the season of 1919, when from Springdale in Washington County, Arkansas, fruit growers shipped more than one thousand railway carloads of apples and apple products. Benton and Washington counties harvested more than five million bushels of apples that year.[51] By 1940, most of the orchards had fallen into disuse or had been cleared and the land converted to other uses. In that year, the fruit orchard acreage in Greene County, Missouri, had tumbled to only 100,000, or less than one-fifth the acreage in 1899.[52]

During the apple era, much of the Missouri crop went by rail to St. Louis and points east. The bulk of the Arkansas apples were sold in Oklahoma, Texas, Louisiana, and Mississippi.[53] Growers' associations and other fruit wholesalers built apple barns at railroad sidings, where they sorted and graded fruit before shipment. Many large fruit farms operated cider presses. December was the prime month for selling and shipping apples, and growers sold most of the crop by April to ensure good quality. Commercial evaporators produced dried applies and peaches on a large scale, thereby saving year-end surpluses, just as pioneer families had saved their surpluses by sun-drying them on the roof of a shed.

Fruit growers formed associations or cooperatives to deal with the problems of marketing and securing labor to harvest the crop. A large production of apples in southwest Missouri around Marionville and Logan in 1914 and 1915 glutted the fruit market at picking time, resulting in low prices and losses for the growers. Faced with this condition, they organized a stock company and built a large cold-storage building on the Frisco Railroad at Marionville. Eventually the Ozark Fruit Growers' Association marketed a large part of the production from the orchards of southwest Missouri and northwest Arkansas. Privately owned cold-storage plants also purchased and marketed apples. The McIlroy family operated a large cold-storage facility on West Avenue in Fayetteville, and there were other cold storage plants at Fort Smith, Rogers, Bentonville, and Siloam Springs.[54]

Fruit growing declined further in the early 1930s, a time of important geographic and economic adjustment in fruit growing throughout the United States.[55] Increasing commercialization, mechanization, organization, and technology demanded greater specialization if growers wanted to maintain their individual shares of an increasing discriminating competitive market. Gradually, the kitchen orchards and small farm orchards disappeared from the U.S. landscape, and fruit growing became concentrated in scattered specialized locations. It declined in the Ozarks because of growers' reluctance or inability to adjust and remain competitive.

Through the developmental years, as the number of apple trees in the Ozarks increased, the orchards became infested with various diseases and insects. Diseases given in the order in which they occurred during the growing season were scab, fireblight, cedar rust, and bitter rot. As the years passed, apple diseases did not increase in severity, but insect pests did. The most devastating insect was the codling moth, or apple worm. At first growers controlled the moths by repeated treatments of lead arsenate or a mixture of lime, sulfur, and water, but gradually the sprays became ineffective.[56]

Other factors contributed to the decline of apple growing.[57] A depressed economy during the 1930s curtailed the market, and drought caused failure of the fruit crop in 1934 and 1936. Although the war years of the 1940s stimulated a stronger demand for apples, orchardists faced higher labor costs and outright labor shortages during the harvesting season. During the 1930s and 1940s fruit acreage gradually diminished; farmers planted fewer trees, and other crops replaced the aged and less-productive trees. In the outskirts of Springfield, orchards were cleared to make room for new houses as the city experienced unprecedented growth during the 1940s and 1950s. Orchards in Washington and Benton counties in Arkansas also fell to suburban subdivisions. By the end of the severe drought that persisted for several years during the 1950s, most of the large orchards had disappeared. Similar decline in acreage occurred throughout the Ozarks.

Apple growing had a modest revival in northwest Arkansas and southwest Missouri during the 1960s and 1970s with both semi-dwarf and standard trees. The once-dominant Ben Davis was replaced by such quality apples as the Jonathan and the Red and Golden Delicious.[58] New organic pesticides, which deteriorated naturally, readily controlled the codling moth. Now only a few commercial

fruit growers remain. The largest orchards are in areas that were formerly important for production of fruit, notably in southwest Missouri near Marionville, Seymour, and Cassville; in Cooper County where loess soils provide exceptionally good growing conditions; and in Arkansas near Bentonville, Rogers, Springdale, Prairie Grove, Lincoln, and Fayetteville. Among the largest apple growers are Rogers Orchards at Prairie Grove, Arkansas, and Vollenweider and Sons with orchards at Seymour, Exeter, and Lexington, Missouri. In the mid-1950s Vollenweider reportedly produced 125,000 bushels of apples on nine hundred acres of orchard land.[59]

Several factors have contributed to the persistence of fruit growing in these locations.[60] First, orcharding reached its greatest development there during the 1920s; Marionville had adopted the title *Apple Capital of Missouri* by that time and Springdale claimed the same title for Arkansas. Since there was larger fruit acreage to begin with, more of it has persisted to the present. Second, the Orchard Growers' Vinegar Company established a vinegar plant at Marionville in 1924, and plants were built at Rogers and Springdale, Arkansas, about the same time.[61] Apple growers could sell low-quality apples to the vinegar plants during period of drought or heavy insect infestation. In this way, growers near the plants received income from their orchards, but producers in other areas became discouraged and converted orchard land to other uses. Third, the large cold-storage plants built between 1910 and 1930 continued to handle apples until they converted them to store poultry and meat beginning with the war years. The apple-storage plants offered growers improved marketing over that of other growers during the depression years of the 1930s. Fourth, growers could sell apples and peaches to canneries, which were expanding operations in Springdale. Fifth, a tradition of fruit growing became better established in the old growing areas. Knowledge concerning the care of trees and the handling and marketing of fruits has lasted over the years; most of the present-day fruit growers are old hands or are descendants of early growers. A few roadside fruit stands still operate during the harvest season.

TRUCK FARMING

In southwest Missouri and northwest Arkansas, raising tomatoes for canning purposes began around 1900 and expanded very rapidly. For several reasons, tomatoes were well suited to the time and setting.[62] First, they could be grown on very rough and rocky hillside farms. Second, the whole family could help in setting plants, tending them, and picking the crop. Third, tomatoes hauled to the nearest cannery brought in badly needed cash at a time when many farmers suffered reduced income because of the decline of the timber industry. Fourth, women and children found employment in the canning season to bolster family income.

The raising of tomatoes and truck crops rarely became the sole farming operation, but fields of one to three acres of tomatoes became common on farms near the canneries. Canneries purchased most of the tomatoes from farmers within a radius of eight or ten miles. Near Springfield and Marionville and in northwest Arkansas, they were grown on fruit orchards to help defray the cost of cultivation and care of the orchard until trees reached bearing age.

Tomato farming required little investment other than labor, and the profits were substantial at times. In 1905, upland tomatoes in Webster County, Missouri, yielded an average of seventy-two bushels per acre for a gross return of $16.39 per acre.[63] Consequently, they were grown widely, even on small upland subsistence farms in the rougher parts of southwest Missouri and northwest Arkansas.

Commercial canning continues to be important in northwest Arkansas, although the number of plants has declined since the 1950s. In 1950 the number of plants in the Ozark Canners' Association in northwest Arkansas counties looked like this: Benton, 13; Boone, 6; Carroll, 7; Washington, 21; Madison, 20.[64] Springdale became the chief canning center as the plants there enlarged and diversified. The leading processed items were green beans, greens (spinach, turnip, poke), and tomatoes. Other products canned in Springdale at the height of the canning era were strawberries; various other berry crops, such as blackberries, boysenberries, and youngberries; and apples, grapes, and potatoes. In recent years the trend has been toward fewer but larger canneries that process a wide range of products. By trucking in produce from other growing areas, canneries can operate year round.

Apparently, many early Ozark canneries were no more than family enterprises that operated only when prices were high.[65] Any favorable combination of supply and demand brought a marked increase in shade-tree canneries. Normally, they sold the produce of these small ventures to larger canneries in a nearby town. Wild blackberries, beans, and a few other vegetables were packed, but the main product was tomatoes. The small canneries fit into an economic niche created by time and place, taking advantage of the availability of cheap surpluses from the farms and the lack of rigorous competition from other producing areas.

Economic forces and adverse climate factors brought the decline of tomato farming.[66] Droughts of the 1930s and blight in the wet years caused crops to fail and can-

neries to close. World War II caused a labor shortage, probably the most culpable factor in many closings. Stoop labor was almost impossible to hire when workers could obtain better-paying and less-demanding employment in nearby cities.[67] Thus, surplus farm laborers, the main supporter of tomato farming and the cannery industry, drifted away to find better jobs. Even so, farmers in other parts of the southern Ozarks experimented with truck farming during and after World War II. In Marion County, Arkansas, tomatoes replaced cotton as the chief crop during the war, but production had withered by the end of the decade.[68] The Atkins Pickle Company began buying Van Buren County cucumbers before 1950, and the Brown and Miller Pickling Company opened a buying station for cucumbers at Cave Springs.[69]

The products of small canneries could not match the quality and prices of larger plants in more favored growing areas. By 1955, tomato farming and the canneries it supported had all but disappeared from the landscape. Now, only a few small commercial patches of tomatoes are planted near Springdale, Arkansas; the city's canning industry depends mainly on produce shipped in from the Arkansas Valley and even more distant truck-farming areas. One or two truck farms—such as Jones Farm near Springfield—still operate near the larger towns, but most of the produce for local farmers' markets comes from garden plots.

Strawberry growing on a commercial scale developed in the late 1890s in two Ozark localities: southwest Missouri and the lower south slope of the Boston Mountains near Van Buren, Arkansas. By the 1920s, it had spread through southwestern Missouri and northwestern Arkansas and into eastern Oklahoma.

Strawberry cultivation flourished for the same reason that tomato farming became important.[70] Strawberries grew well on the chert-choked soils of the hillsides; in fact, the stone covering in cherty soils provided an excellent mulch, holding frost in the ground in spring so that the plants did not bloom too early and providing a dry surface on which the berries could ripen free of mildew. Tomato growers preferred freshly cleared land because of the greater humus content. The care and harvesting of strawberries consumed much labor, a surplus commodity on the small Ozarks farms of the early 1900s. Furthermore, strawberry farming required little in the way of land and capital outlay, and when they heard stories of sales exceeding five hundred dollars from patches of less than an acre, farmers quickly started setting out strawberries to bolster their income. Grown usually no more than ten miles from point of shipment, the berries went to growers' associations, which set up railside receiving and crating sheds at

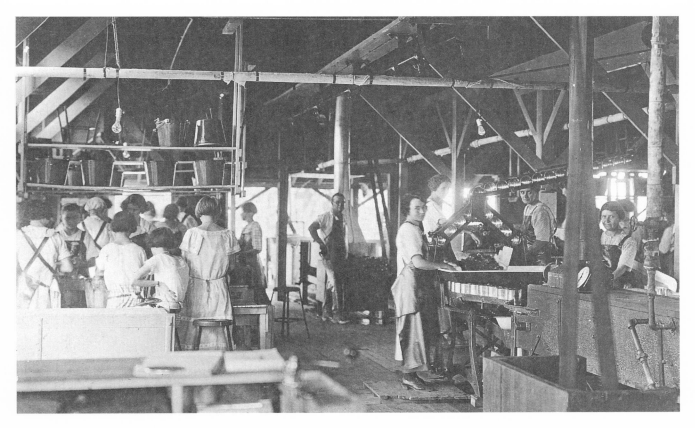

Canning factory at Billings, Missouri. (Courtesy of State Historical Society of Missouri.)

the main shipping points. Where rail facilities were not available, grocery or feed dealers purchased the berries and resold them at these points.[71]

The picking season normally lasted five weeks, from the end of May to the first of July. Since most of the production came from family farms, where women and children could help with the harvest, growers used little outside labor. In a few cases, where large growers planted fields of fifty acres or more, they brought in outside laborers to help with the harvest.

During peak production in the 1920s, strawberry growing had spread throughout the area, and several towns had strawberry warehouses. Any town with a railroad siding was a potential shipping point. Logan, Missouri, a tiny Lawrence County hamlet, was an important market for strawberries. There were two large strawberry barns on the siding at Logan, and it was commonplace for 150 carloads to be shipped during a season.[72] Ozark, Springfield, Marshfield, Aurora, and Monett were other important points of shipment in southwest Missouri, but interior Ozark towns like Mountain View, Cabool, Ava, and West Plains also shipped strawberries. Springdale, Rogers, Bentonville, Farmington, Prairie Grove, and Van Buren were the most important shipping points in Arkansas, but many other towns shipped several carloads each season. Stillwell, Tah-

lequah, and Sallisaw were the chief shipping points in Oklahoma. They transported most of the strawberries to St. Louis and other eastern cities.

The growth and decline of strawberry farming paralleled that of tomato production; the virtual cessation of strawberry growing for distant markets after World War II resulted from labor shortages. Only a few commercial growers remain today, and much of the production is near Stillwell, Oklahoma, where a small growers' association still functions. Some "pick your own" strawberry fields are found near Marionville, Springfield, and in the Fayetteville-Springdale-Rogers urban area, and a few boxes of grower-picked strawberries find their way into local farmers' markets.

VITICULTURE

The growing of grapes is well suited to the climate and soils of the Ozarks. Viticulture was introduced early and was an important step toward the success of the German settlement at Hermann. In 1845 there were fifty thousand vines close to Hermann, and by 1849 the number had grown to seven hundred thousand.[73] By 1850 the grape harvests rivaled hemp in value. The success of grapes at Hermann led to extensive plantings of vineyards at Ste.

Genevieve and Boonville and in Franklin, Warren, and St. Charles counties. Farmers planted the vineyards on loess hillsides, which afforded warm soil, excellent drainage, and protection from unseasonable frosts. The climate was said to be better than that in the Rhine River country because of the sunny fall weather, which permitted the grapes to ripen with high flavor. Before the introduction of viticulture, Hermann had been losing population, but the excellent harvest of 1848 reversed this trend. In 1856, a yield of one hundred thousand gallons of wine was reported for Hermann at a profit of three hundred dollars per acre. The Hermann vintners built a large wine trade; the Stone Hill Winery became one of the sights of Missouri; and the wines gained a wide reputation.

In the 1880s, Catholic Swiss-Germans settled near Altus, Arkansas, on the extreme southern border of the Ozarks. They planted grapes on limestone soils in the Boston Mountain foothills overlooking the Arkansas Valley. The wines became quite popular in central Arkansas, and in recent years, Wiederkehr Wine Cellars has gained a national reputation for its products.[74]

Italian immigrants grew grapes at two widely separated Ozark communities. They settled at Tontitown in Washington County, Arkansas, and at Rosati in eastern Phelps County, Missouri, in 1898 under the leadership of an Italian-born priest.[75] The members of these colonies were fleeing from an ill-fated philanthropic colonization venture in southeastern Arkansas, where malaria had decimated their ranks. One reason for selecting the two Ozarks locations was their suitability for growing grapes. Then, too, the Ozarks reminded them of their homeland in Italy, and the region was free of malaria.

The rise of the grape industry at Tontitown was rapid. The place held no importance for vineyards in 1900, but by 1920, Washington County, with 150,000 vines, had become the chief vineyard county in Arkansas.[76] Similar expansion, but on a smaller scale, occurred at Rosati, and wineries flourished at the two colonies until Prohibition days.

Even before the Italian immigrants began planting vineyards, farmers knew the western Ozarks as excellent grape country. Swiss immigrant Hermann Jaeger settled in Newton County, Missouri, where in 1867 he produced a hardy new grape by crossing Virginia grapes with the wild Ozark variety. Jaeger developed a large vineyard near Neosho with his hybrid, which proved to be very successful. Later, when he learned that grape lice were causing much damage in the vineyards of France, he suggested the adoption of cuttings from the wild Ozark grapes to give more resistance to the French vines. When his suggestions were received favorably, Jaeger sent seventeen carloads of cuttings to France. Jaeger's plan proved successful and won him the Legion of Honor for his service to French agriculture.[77]

The Missouri fruit experiment station at Mountain Grove actively encouraged farmers to plant vineyards and other fruits. The University of Arkansas agricultural extension service also provided technical assistance to farmers who were involved in vitaculture. Not all wine-making ventures were successful. Rose Fulton Cramer in *Wayne County, Missouri* tells of one such ill-fated attempt by a Frenchman, Eleas Flamary, to establish a successful vineyard near Patterson.

Flamary had the love of the grape, the know-how, a large acreage of grapevines, a press, vats, and a cellar of casks of aging wine. But for some reason he sold out. His successor did not care for grape culture. Taylor Putnam bought the vats and used them to water his cattle. So ended Logan Township's famous experiment with wine production.[78]

During the 1920s the Welch Company established several large vineyards in Washington and Benton counties to supply its new grape-juice plant in Springdale.[79] By 1923 the company had sponsored the planting of five thousand acres, of which one thousand were along the Kansas City Southern Railway between the Arkansas Missouri line and Siloam Springs.

During the 1930s and the 1940s, grape production declined throughout the Ozarks. The decline was due to many of the same factors that caused reduction in orcharding and truck farming: labor shortages, drought, and marketing problems. In recent years, viticulture has received a boost from the increasing popularity of wines as opposed to more robust beverages. James and Betty Held purchased the Stone Hill Winery at Hermann, Missouri, and reopened it in 1965. The Maifest and Oktoberfest celebrated there have attracted attention to the excellent wines of the district. The Stone Hill Winery in Branson, Missouri, attracts thousands of visitors and provides another outlet for the Hermann winery. To meet increased demand for wine, plantings of Catawba and other grapes have increased, and the winery buys surpluses from the Rosati district. New wineries have been established at St. James and Rosati. Most of the Concord and other juice grapes in southwest Missouri and northwest Arkansas formerly grown under contract with the Welch Company's grape-juice cannery at Springdale, Arkansas, are now sold to Pappas Foods in Springdale. Grapes are grown near Exeter, Missouri, and at other locations near the Arkansas-Missouri line.

Grapes are grown commercially in only a few counties and most wineries are nearby. Three axes of production are discernible. One extends along the Missouri River west from St. Louis to include the wine producing towns of Augusta and Hermann. The other extends southwest from St. Louis along Interstate 44 and then south along U. S. 71. This axis includes the wineries at Rosati and St. James, the vineyards of Barry County, Missouri, and the vineyards around Tontitown, Arkansas. Though much reduced from its peak years, grape and wine production in the Ozarks has increased in recent years. The popular acceptance of wine as a beverage and the growing tourism industry have helped to increase demand.[80] Any future growth in Ozark vitaculture is highly dependent on the tourism industry and the continued improvement of the wines.

DAIRY FARMING

The pioneers who settled the Ozarks usually led one or more cows to their new home. Most of these animals were nondescript, largely beef cattle, but a few had been crossed with dairy breeds. These cattle supplied both milk and meat; some were used as oxen. Good-quality livestock representing the various dairy breeds did not reach the Ozarks in great numbers until after 1900.

In the early days, trade in dairy products was very limited. About the turn of the century, Springfield began to develop as a major dairy center.[81] In Arkansas, Fayetteville and Springdale also attracted large creameries. Several other larger towns with good railroad connections also attracted dairy businesses. With the end of the Civil War and the coming of the railroads, Springfield grew rapidly, so that a sizable local market developed for milk, cream, and farm-churned butter. By modern standards they conducted the early trade in an extremely crude and unsanitary manner. General stores maintained cream stations that purchased cream from farmers and sent it to market in Springfield or another creamery town every few days. The stores bought churned butter from area farmers and dumped it into a common tub; when the butter was ready for market, they nailed the lid on and shipped it with other products. Tuberculosis and brucellosis testing was unheard of, and dairy items were produced under any number of unwholesome conditions.

Commercial dairying began shortly after 1900. By 1905, several Springfield cream and produce dealers shipped to markets in the East and the South. At the time, four creameries operated in Webster County. Lawrence County also experienced a similar growth in dairying. The first large-scale dairy manufacturer in the area, Springfield Creamery Company, founded in 1910, inaugurated the practice of picking up cream at farms.[82] Similar practices soon were established at Fayetteville and Springdale, where dairying had become established in the level upland prairies and in the valley of the West Fork of the White River. By 1940 most of the larger towns with a railroad had creameries.

Several factors stimulated the growth of the dairy industry. First, good markets became available in St. Louis, Kansas City, and several towns that had sprung up in the

Springfield Creamery Company, circa 1914. First creamery to make pickups at the farm. (Courtesy of State Historical Society of Missouri.)

Tri-State Mining District. High prices for dairy products encouraged its extension. Second, as the area became better settled and landholdings became smaller, farmers looked for ways to make each acre produce more. Dairying provided a means to both ends. Third, the nature of the area's topography made it necessary to keep much of the land in pasture. Most of the grass and forage crops, such as orchard grass, bluegrass, timothy, clover, and sorghum, grew well and furnished an eight- or nine-month grazing season for stock. Innumerable springs supplied plenty of good, clear water.

At first, very few farms made a specialty of dairying, but a number had as many as ten to fifteen cows. Gradually, farmers began to specialize. Because dairying developed before there were large numbers of automobiles and trucks, most of the dairying concentrated close to the railroads. Farmers established dairy farms near Springfield because of its substantial local market and several railroad lines. Thus, in the early years, commercial dairy farming concentrated around Springfield and other larger towns and along the railroads. Each major shipping point on the railroad served as the market for a cluster of dairy farms. Farmers brought their cream and eggs to town on "trading day" to sell to a local creamery, which in turn shipped the products to larger creameries that manufactured butter and cheese. Later, as roads improved and trucks picked up dairy products at the farm, dairy operations became more widely distributed in the interior Ozarks near railroads. However, because of poor roads, the extreme rough topography, and limited forage, dairying did not gain such importance in the Ozark interior.

The demand for dairy products from markets outside the area became more discriminating and competitive, requiring herd improvement, better management, and better feeding. Dairy farmers developed many herds from purebred Holsteins and Jerseys, but other popular dairy breeds were Brown Swiss, Guernseys, and Milking Shorthorns.

Remarkable growth in commercial dairy farming occurred from its inauguration until 1940. In 1910, dairy cattle in the eight-county area surrounding Springfield totaled 64,361, but by 1940 the number had increased to 113,200.[83] Growth during the 1920s was especially rapid. In only three years, Lawrence County rose from twenty-ninth place to third among Missouri counties in the number of dairy cattle. Between 1921 and 1924, the number of dairy cattle in Lawrence County increased from 9,640 to 14,530.[84] By 1924, Springfield ranked fourth in the nation in churned butter, and eleven large creameries in that city employed more than 650 workers. Nearly every town of 1,500 population had creameries, and the larger trade centers began to develop more elaborate milk-processing plants. A second, smaller dairy farming area grew up in Washington and Benton counties in northwest Arkansas.

Dairy farming has declined since the 1950s. A study of a farm in Logan Creek valley in the remote southern Courtois Hills (Reynolds County, Missouri) after a lapse of thirty-five years—1935 to 1970—showed remarkable shifts in land use and farming practices.[85] The farm, operated by N. B. George in 1935, specialized in dairy cattle, but there was considerable diversity in the types of crops and livestock. In 1970 the farm was operated by George's

Large dairy farm of the Bonne Terre Farming and Cattle Company on the property of the St. Joseph Lead Company, circa 1900. (Courtesy of State Historical Society of Missouri.)

son-in-law, Vernon Moore, and emphasis had shifted from mixed livestock-dairy farming to a specialized beef-cattle operation.[86] The restricted number of crops and livestock and the trend toward specialization are shown in Table 10-2.

The trend toward large, more specialized dairy operations has affected remote dairy farms more. This is surely true of the N. B. George/Vernon Moore farm. The shift to larger and more efficient manufacturing plants, along with improvements in farm technology, management, and cooperative marketing, resulted in fewer but larger dairy farms with improved methods of production. In the early days, milk was separated on the farm. They fed the skimmed milk to calves and hogs and sold or "traded" the cream for household and farm supplies. In contrast, modern dairying is geared to cheap, fast, efficient transportation. Today, producers milk cows in inspected milking sheds with most modern equipment. Though still seen occasionally at roadside pickup points in the late 1970s, the cream can is now an antiquarian piece for antique shops. Bulk milk tanks, serviced by fast and efficient tanker trucks, replace it on modern dairy farms.

The marketing of milk has evolved from the small town creamery where farmers dropped off their cans of milk and cream on their weekly market day to large cooperatives involved in milk processing, research and product development, and marketing. The growth of Mid-America Dairymen, now Dairymen of America, is a story of adaptation to a constantly changing dairy industry. The company, headquartered in Kansas City with research and product development offices in Springfield, began as Pro-

ducers Creamery, a regional milk cooperative. By the late 1950s the Producers Creamery operated five manufacturing plants throughout southwest Missouri, processing milk from more than nine thousand producers.[87] Since the production of Grade A milk in southwest Missouri far exceeded the demand in the local market, a series of mergers were undertaken to open markets in Kansas City, St. Louis, Texas, Iowa, Kansas, and other areas. Sometimes Mid-America (Dairymen of America) acquired smaller dairy manufacturing companies by outright purchase. For example, they purchased the Hiland Dairy in Springfield in 1979 when a protracted strike had brought it to the verge of being closed. They made the purchase to protect the market of Mid-Am Southern Division members, by preventing competing dairies in St. Louis and Kansas City from entering the Springfield market.[88] When Mid-America Dairymen formed on July 1, 1968, after multiple mergers during the late 1950s and 1960s, it handled 3.5 billion pounds of milk, both manufacturing grade and Grade A, and represented fifteen thousand dairy farmers.[89] Its manufacturing plants turned out a variety of products, ranging from butter and powdered milk to infant formulas, dietary foods, dips, yogurt, and cottage cheese.

In recent years, milk production in the Ozarks has declined slightly. Most of this has occurred in areas outside the old, established, and highly specialized production areas. Either highly efficient production or strong market orientation seems to be required. Efficiencies of area specialization are apparently more important than cheap labor and underemployment. While milk prices have stayed much the same in recent years, more dairy farms

TABLE 10-2. LAND USE AND LIVESTOCK PRODUCTION ON THE N. B. GEORGE/VERNON MOORE FARM

CROP	(PERCENT OF TOTAL FARM ACREAGE)		LIVESTOCK	(NUMBER OF LIVESTOCK)	
	1936	1970		1936	1970
Woodland	16	24	Dairy cattle	15	6
Woodland pasture	19	26	Beef cattle	6	75
Pasture	17	32	Sheep	20	0
Grass for hay	16	6	Chickens	large flock	0
Alfalfa	8	8			
Red clover	3	0			
Lespedeza	7	0			
Corn	4	0			
Wheat	4	0			

SOURCE: Riggs, "Valley Contrasts in the Missouri Ozarks Region," 351–59; Rafferty and Hrebec, "Logan Creek: A Missouri Ozark Valley Revisited," *Journal of Geography* (October 1973): 7–17, and personal interviews with Vernon Moore. The Vernon Moore farm in 1970 included 460 acres compared to 249 acres on the N. B. George farm in 1936.

are going out of business than new ones starting. At the dawn of the twenty-first century, milk prices plunged to $9 per hundred weight, matching 1980 prices, making the prospects for new dairy farms very bleak. Costs associated with starting a new dairy farm are very high: $1,000 to $1,500 for an adult cow, $100,000 for a dairy barn, plus the cost of land and equipment.[90] Some established farmers have elected to exit milk production and enter a new part of the industry, dairy heifer production.[91] These farmers buy dairy calves from milk producers and raise them in the Ozarks where forage grass is plentiful. When fully developed the heifers go into full-time dairy herds, where they enter milk production on dairy farms throughout the nation. Other farmers have opted to sell their dairy herds and convert to less labor-intensive beef cattle production.

POULTRY FARMING

Developments in poultry production over the past century have been remarkable. There is little similarity between early free-range poultry-handling methods and the increasingly specialized production methods of modern times. The pioneers rarely brought in poultry of distinct breeds. Because they allowed their chickens to run free range in the lots around the house and barn, there was no opportunity to develop pure strains, and mixed breeds were typical. A few farmers had guineas, and some had small flocks of turkeys, geese, and ducks. On many farms the chickens and turkeys had to find their own food. Even in the mid-nineteenth century some farmers built simple poultry houses or sheds, particular for chickens, but often the turkeys and guineas roosted in the trees.

Farmers raised chickens for meat and eggs. Fried chicken, mainly in the summer months, was a favorite food, just as it has been farther south. They ate turkeys on special occasions, such as Thanksgiving and Christmas, along with small numbers of ducks and geese.

Certainly the methods of producing and marketing poultry and poultry products were primitive by modern standards. In the early years, eggs, incubated by setting hens, provided the new stock of fryers and laying hens. The first incubators, which appeared shortly after 1900, were the box type. They were heated with a kerosene lamp and held fifty to one hundred eggs. Later, they increased size and added electric heaters. Thus, modern hatcheries gradually developed with great batteries of egg trays. With the introduction of the incubator, brooders succeeded the setting hen. Small boxes kept in a warm place, often beside the fireplace or stove in the home, first served this purpose. Later brooders used kerosene, natural gas, and electricity for heat.

Ozark poultry farming developed contemporaneously with dairying. Usually farmers combined the marketing of poultry and dairy products. They sold cream, eggs, and poultry to small town creameries, who later shipped the products to large creameries and produce houses in Springfield, Fayetteville, and Springdale and other larger towns.

Farm women usually cared for chickens and turkeys. Children helped in the task of gathering eggs. Because the chickens had the run of the farmyard, the chore consisted of finding all the potential laying spots. Eggs went to market ungraded and rarely cleaned. Because they were marketed irregularly, with little protection from the heat, many of them spoiled.

Before the invention of the egg crate, farmers hauled eggs to market in farm wagons. A heavy layer of straw was placed in the wagon bed, and on this was placed a layer of eggs; layers of straw and eggs were alternated until they filled the wagon to the top. A layer of boards covered the whole, and a boom pole, fastened down in front and back, kept the eggs from jolting around. Almost exclusively farmers exchanged poultry products for groceries, leaving few records of the size of their business.

By 1920, broiler production had become widespread on general farms throughout the Springfield Plain, and poultry production assumed an important place in the agricultural economy. Each farm had at least one small shed which sheltered laying hens or broilers. After the birds went to roost at night, farmers closed the chicken house doors to keep out prowling predators. By 1934, the production of eggs and poultry products had achieved such importance that Springfield adopted the ambitious title of World's Poultry Capital.[92]

Poultry farming has experienced great changes over the past half century. By 1930 the semiwild and nondescript flocks that foraged for themselves and laid eggs in the loft or in the woods had given way to a flock of some one hundred or two hundred hybrid birds. By that time, farmers often housed the flocks in modern poultry sheds built according to plans recommended by state agricultural experiment stations. These small family-size flocks, in turn, yielded to highly specialized production systems with flocks of twenty thousand birds or more.

Most contemporary poultry farmers specialize in one of the modern breeds or hybrids. The principal utility breeds include White Leghorn, White Plymouth Rocks, New Hampshire, Rhode Island Reds, and Inbred Hybrids. The major breeds of turkeys are Bronze, White Holland, and Beltville. The U.S. Department of Agriculture developed the last-named breed to meet the growing demand for smaller turkeys.

Washington and Benton counties in northwest Arkansas

have become the leading center for Ozark broiler production. The area ranks as one of the major broiler districts in the United States. Modern poultry production under contractual agreements between the producers and the processing companies began near Springdale and Rogers in the late 1930s and gradually spread to outlying areas in Missouri and Oklahoma. In the valley of the west fork of the White River, poultry farming replaced lumbering as the chief economic activity. One resident in the Combs, Arkansas, community pointed out that "soon after the Frisco Railroad quit hauling trees from the hills, the trucks started hauling chickens out of the valleys to processors like Campbell Soup in Fayetteville and Tyson Foods in Springdale."[93] Since about 1970, broiler production has spread eastward to the vicinity of Huntsville, into the War Eagle valley, and further east into the Kings River valley, and also into adjacent parts of Oklahoma and Missouri. A second center for poultry farming grew up during the 1960s and 1970s close to Batesville in the southeastern Ozarks. The two Banquet Foods plants in Batesville serve as the primary market for broilers and turkeys grown in that section of the Ozarks. Production of broilers and turkeys is also important in Missouri and Oklahoma. In Missouri, important producing counties—Barry, McDonald, Stone—are in the extreme southwest near the Ozarks poultry hearth in northwest Arkansas. Another area of poultry specialization includes Camden, Miller, and Morgan counties.

Tyson Foods, a member of the *Fortune 500,* had its beginnings in the Ozarks of northwest Arkansas. The corporate headquarters is in Springdale. While John Tyson was hardly the first to produce poultry in northwest Arkansas, the history of Tyson Foods is the story of the transformation of the poultry industry from the farmyard production of chickens and turkeys to huge integrated poultry operations that include production, processing, and marketing of a wide range of processed poultry products.

The beginning of the company was a chance happening. Don Tyson, the present chairman of the board, tells that his father, John Tyson, was led into the chicken trade through trucking.[94] John Tyson had moved to Springdale in 1931 and began hauling chickens. In the spring of 1936, he loaded five hundred Arkansas spring chickens into makeshift crates and drove to Chicago where chickens sold at a higher price than in markets closer to Arkansas.[95] He was prompted to make the trip by a newspaper article he had read about higher poultry prices in distant markets. Following several profitable trips to Chicago, Tyson bought a small hatchery, became a Ralston Purina feed dealer, and put more trucks on the road. In 1943, when World War II created increased demand for chicken, the Tyson company purchased its first farm, a forty-acre tract on U.S. 71. Two years later, Tyson introduced New Hampshire Red Cristy chickens, a select meat-type chicken bred in Missouri. In 1947, when Tyson Feed and Hatchery was incorporated, the company was providing baby

The first Tyson feed store and hatchery in Springdale, Arkansas, with employees Ralph Blythe, Bill Martin, Jack Brashears, and Hiram Knight. (Courtesy of Tyson Foods.)

chicks, feed, and transportation of grown birds for farms in northwest Arkansas.[96]

As other meat-packing companies such as Armour, Swanson, and Swift were locating their processing plants in northwest Arkansas to be closer to the growing areas, Tyson introduced a new financial relationship with growers, allowing them to continue selling their chickens and assuring the growers an equitable payback. Farmers who bought Tyson chicks and feed at a set price were assured that Tyson would purchase the grown birds. This was the beginning of vertical integration of production and marketing in the poultry industry.[97]

The modern vertically integrated poultry company includes production of foundation breeder flocks that produce highly productive lines of breeder hens and roosters; hatchery supply flocks where roosters and hens produce broiler eggs; and commercial hatcheries where the eggs hatch. An integrated company also has feed mills to produce pelletized and mash feed; broiler growout farms, where flocks of chickens are raised in long, narrow houses; processing plants, where birds are processed into poultry staples and byproducts; and finally, distribution channels, which include massive freezer warehouses and trucking fleets that deliver products to the customers.[98] Tyson led the way in the development of many of these steps in the production of poultry. When heavy advertising and national marketing were introduced later, the industry was fully integrated.

The company experienced phenomenal growth during the 1960s, 1970s, and 1980s through expansion of growing, processing, and marketing, and by outright purchase of competing companies. According to the *1999 Tyson Annual Report* the company was concentrating on its major line—chicken—after selling off egg and turkey holdings acquired with the purchase of Hudson Foods.[99] However, if Tyson Foods' January 2001 offer to purchase Iowa Beef Packers, Inc. (IBP), is finalized, the company will be the world's largest producer of poultry, pork, and beef products.

Tyson Foods, like many large corporations, has extended its marketing to foreign countries. Through its International Group, Tyson Foods markets its products in Asia, the Americas, Africa, Russia, Europe, and the Middle East.[100] As the scale of foreign marketing increases there is always the possibility that major food producers could shift production to Mexico or other foreign countries. Possible savings in the cost of labor, transportation, and other production and marketing inputs may be attractive considering the need to compete favorably. Should part of the Ozark poultry industry move to foreign countries, the impact on Ozark communities would likely be similar to the closing of shoe plants, clothing manufacturers, consumer electronics producers, and other Ozark manufacturers that have moved out of the United States to take advantage of reduced production costs.

The changes in poultry farming are strikingly evident in the landscape. The traditional farm chicken house has all but vanished. Many abandoned barns, representing an intermediate stage in the trend toward larger production units, are in various states of disrepair and decay. This anomalous mixture of decaying poultry barns, side by side with apparently prosperous poultry farms, repeats itself again and again through southwest Missouri and northwest Arkansas. Recently poultry farming has added a new element to the rural landscape. This is the large integrated poultry farm that includes a feed mill and a cluster of long, low poultry barns, a management office, and various other support buildings.

LIVESTOCK FARMING AND RANCHING

Before the railroads arrived, animal husbandry was the only feasible system of commercial agriculture. As people moved west into the Appalachian Mountains settlers drove semi-feral horses and cattle from Virginia, Georgia, and the Carolinas west through the mountains and into Kentucky and Tennessee. These animals were the source for the livestock that later settlers drove west into the Ozarks.[101] The Cherokee Indians who settled in Arkansas and Oklahoma brought cattle, horses, and other livestock. When the Reverend Cephas Washburn arrived in Arkansas to establish the Dwight Mission near present-day Russellville, he noted that many Cherokees had become extensive stock holders. He observed that they allowed the cattle, horses, and swine to run at large in forests and prairies and rarely salted them.[102]

For the first settlers, the cost of shipping grain or other bulky products over rough terrain to distant markets outside the Ozarks was prohibitive except in the eastern and northern border areas. Instead, they drove cattle from the prairies in northwest Arkansas and southwest Missouri either to Little Rock or to Springfield.[103] These trips, which usually required six to eight days, provided one of the few opportunities for rural people to experience life in a large town. Occasionally they drove cattle to the western states, even as far as California, where an animal purchased for as little as five dollars in the Ozarks could be sold for fifty dollars.[104] Several hundred cattle were rounded up near Harrison, Arkansas, and accompanied the wagon train of the ill-fated Fancher party, which was destroyed by Mormon raiders in the Mountain Meadows Massacre in Utah.[105]

Angora goats in Arkansas woodland, 1975. (Milton Rafferty Collection, photograph by the author.)

Sometimes farmers banded together and drove herds of cattle from the western Ozarks to St. Louis and even to New Orleans. Before the railroads came, Warsaw, head of navigation on the Osage River, and Boonville, on the Missouri River, served as the main shipping points for livestock and livestock products. Salted meats, cured hides, tallow, and lard were major exports via the river route.

In the 1840s and 1850s, drovers herded longhorn cattle from Texas northeast across the Red River, past Fort Smith, and through northwest Arkansas and southwest Missouri to Independence, Boonville, or St. Louis.[106] Tom Candy of Ponting, Illinois, purchased eight hundred head of Texas cattle in 1853 and drove them back to Illinois. His route went by way of Springfield to Union and St. Louis, where he ferried them across the Mississippi.[107] During the latter half of the 1850s the ravages of the so-called Texas or Spanish fever, which killed thousands of native stock, brought frantic calls for laws prohibiting the driving of longhorns into Missouri. After severe epidemics in 1855 and 1858, the state passed stock laws to attempt to control the disease.[108] Since the Civil War put a stop to the drives north from Texas the laws did not have much effect until the conflict ended and the drives began again. After the Civil War, drovers, including James Daugherty, J. S. Hargus, and R. D. Hunter, established cattle trails to the new railroads at Sedalia and Nevada, Missouri, and at Baxter Springs in extreme southeast Kansas.[109] Cattle driven over the Shawnee Trail, the first of the great western cattle trails, moved north from the vicinity of San Antonio by way of Dallas into eastern Oklahoma, where the mountains were skirted on the west, and then on to Sedalia, Missouri.[110]

Besides the cattle and half-wild hogs that ran at large on unfenced commons, some stock farmers also raised horses and mules. Horses were in strong demand both locally and in northern cities. The mules went to the southern states, where they pulled plows and cultivators in the cotton fields. The major area for mule raising was in the Missouri River area and counties to the north, but breeders established many mule and horse farms near Springfield.[111]

A major influence for the livestock industry in the western Ozarks was the Missouri Land and Livestock Company.[112] This company, owned by Scottish investors, purchased more than 350,000 acres in southwest Missouri from the Atlantic and Pacific Railroad and the University of Missouri. Under the management of John S. Purdy and L. B. Sidway, the company established Sandyford Ranche near Neosho, Missouri, in 1882 as a showplace to promote the region as a livestock ranching area. The managers imported blooded Angus and Hereford cattle from the British Isles to stock the ranch. From this stock, they sold high-bred bulls and blooded heifers to many farmers and ranchers in the western Ozarks.

As open-range livestock farming gave way to general farming, cultivated crops, particularly corn, received more emphasis, and farmers gave more attention to raising hogs and poultry. Stall-feeding cattle to produce a "finished" (fattened) animal became more common. From about 1900 to 1940, general farming reached its zenith, and a Corn Belt-type livestock economy became popular. Farmers raised corn to produce finished hogs and beef cattle. However, beef-cattle production attained its greatest importance in the loess and glacial soils of northern Missouri,

Forest clearing for pasture in the Arkansas Ozarks, 1975. (Milton Rafferty Collection, photograph by the author.)

where natural conditions were better suited to the production of corn and other feeds.

In the Ozarks, since World War II, there has been a marked shift back to a livestock economy based on the production of unfinished feeder cattle (fig. 10-4). During the 1950s, 1960s, and 1970s, the shift in emphasis reached major proportions and became one of the most significant economic changes in the Ozarks.[113] The resulting alterations in land use and landscape patterns promise to continue for some time to come. Higher prices for cattle made conversion of timberland to pasture profitable. Between 1966 and 1969, more than 73,000 acres were defoliated and aerially seeded to pasture by one southwest Missouri farmers' cooperative.[114] In the period 1959 to 1972 in the entire Ozark region, more than 1,453,000 acres of forest were converted to other uses; 955,000 acres were converted to wooded pasture, and 377,000 were converted to improved pasture.

In the late 1960s, landowners were converting wooded land to pasture in two ways. For a time they used aerial spraying with herbicides at a cost of approximately $6.75 per acre, followed by aerial seeding of fescue, lespedeza, and mixed grasses at a cost of fifty cents an acre.[115] This practice was discontinued because of difficulties with controlling brush, low carrying capacity for cattle, and possible environmental risks. The better method employed bulldozing, cultivating, and seeding at a cost of approximately $150 per acre. In the latter case, brush is left in piles to retard water runoff and to serve as wildlife habitat.

Today the Ozarks is a cow-calf region. This means most producers maintain cow herds and produce calves for sale at about seven to ten months of age.[116] When these calves, called feeders or feeder cattle, are sold they go to stocker buyers who grow them until they are ready to enter feed lots for fattening. There are some local buyers for feeder cattle, but most Ozark-raised calves go to the big feed lots in western Kansas, eastern Colorado, the Texas Panhandle, or the Corn Belt. The cow-calf or ranching system seems well suited to the Ozarks where winters are usually mild and where farmers can produce sufficient forage without irrigation under normal conditions. A few ranches graze several hundred head of cattle, but compared with ranches in the West, they are small. Livestock farming also lends itself to part-time operations, and there are many such farms.

Although the trend to beef cattle has been nationwide, the percentage growth rate in the Ozarks beef-cattle operations is substantially above the national average. The numbers of beef cattle in the Ozark counties increased 142 percent from 1959 to 1997, considerably more than the 41 percent increase in the entire United States.[117] The number of beef cattle in the ninety-three counties comprising the Ozarks increased from 890,903 to 2,155,444, while the nation's total increased from 24,751,452 to 34,800,000. Although low beef prices in the mid-1970s caused Ozark cattlemen to reduce the size of herds, the high prices in the late 1970s stimulated another round of herd increase.

The best conditions for livestock farming are in the western Ozarks, especially in the Springfield plain and the level uplands in the Central plateau. The mountain and hill country—Boston Mountains, St. Francois Mountains, Courtois Hills, Osage-Gasconade Hills, and White River

Hills—are heavily forested and not well suited for pastures and the production of hay crops. In the northern and eastern border areas, grain farming and production of finished cattle for slaughter are more important.

PART-TIME FARMING

Part-time farming has increased markedly in the Ozarks over the past few decades. Part-time farms are those that earn at least fifty dollars, but less than one thousand dollars from the sale of farm produce of any kind.[118] Sixty percent of the region's farms are part-time, making it the dominant type of farming. The growth of part-time farming has been most pronounced near St. Louis, Springfield, Joplin, Jefferson City, Fayetteville-Springdale-Rogers, and other larger urban areas. The number of part-time farms in the eight-county area around Springfield increased from 1,593 in 1930 (7 percent of the total number of farms) to 4,393 in 1964 (28 percent of the total number of farms) (fig. 10-5).[119] Since 1964 the number of part-time farms has continued to increase. The increase in number of farms in the Ozark region is most rapid close to growth centers but the desire to own land for recreational or investment purposes has led to increased sales of land for nonfarm purposes even in the less-populated parts of the Ozarks.

Ozarks farmers have always looked to alternate sources of income to bolster their standard of living. The early hunter-woodsman, who gained as much of his living from the wild game and the forests as from agriculture, may be considered as the prototype part-time farmer. Out of necessity the first settlers were largely self-sufficient, so that besides producing nearly all of their food and clothing, they manufactured a large part of their farmstead's furnishings and tools. Some farmers made furniture, tools, leather products, or other essential commodities to supplement their farm income. Tanyards, whiskey distilleries, stave and barrel works, ax-handle and tool works, furniture and coffin shops, sorghum mills, and gristmill were adjuncts to agriculture. In some cases, farm manufacturing persisted through several generations.[120]

Gradually, as towns matured, capital was accumulated by the middle- and upper-income business and professional people, and this led to country-estate farming. Many who occupied such farms were former rural inhabitants who had made good in the city but still yearned for country living. Some of the first country-estate farms in the Ozarks were established in the beautiful Arcadia and Belleview valleys.[121] From 1900 to 1940 and especially after World War II, the number of part-time farms increased near many of the larger Ozark towns. They were used for recreation and casual living and only incidentally for agricultural purposes. Many modern suburban estates, which have little or nothing to do with farming, are included in the Census Bureau's definition of part-time farms.

Part-time subsistence farms increased during the depression between 1930 and 1940. When workers lost their jobs, life in the city became less glamorous, and unemployed workers returned to the farms and small towns they had left, where they hoped to eke out a living. Because of lower land prices, low-cost rural rental property, and more-affordable living costs, the Ozarks became a popular place to establish temporary subsistence homesteads. Strawberry and tomato harvesting, logging, and cannery work provided seasonal employment, which in turn provided money to purchase those things that could not be produced on the farm. Sometimes, people who went back to the cities after the depression returned to the Ozarks to reestablish part-time retirement farms.[122]

In recent years part-time farming has grown throughout the Ozarks. Improved roads allow persons to commute more than fifty miles to off-farm jobs. At the same time, the tightening cost-price squeeze in farming operations encourages seeking supplemental employment. Ozark farmers find enlargement of the farm unit is not always easy because the conditions of slope and topography are not well suited to mechanization. The alternative to expansion has been to earn income from nonfarm employment. This has been particularly true of dairy-farm operators, who, to remain competitive, must have larger farm units and more-expensive equipment.

Many dairy owners throughout the Ozarks have converted their dairy farms to part-time stock farms, a transition that involves no large capital investments and allows more time to be spent off the farm. Also contributing to the increasing number of part-time farms are the farmettes or suburban farms established by people who work in the region's larger towns.[123] Probably, most of these farms serve primarily as places for recreation and casual country living and only incidentally for agricultural purposes. The continued subdivision of productive farms into uneconomic farm units, coupled with increases in land prices, is fraught with risks for continued production from Ozark agricultural land. Farmers are becoming increasingly concerned that land prices are beyond the current levels of profitable economic return from agriculture.

Ozark agriculture appears to have come full circle. The original farmer was a part-time agriculturalist, keeper of livestock, and hunter. The cultivated land was safe and secure in stream bottoms, protected from erosion, and threatened only by occasional floods. The economy was more in tune with the existing natural resources than some subsequent types of farming. Development of commercial agriculture in the Ozarks has been a long and sometimes destructive process replete with experimentation and constant adjustments in the relationships between people and land. Large-scale contemporary agriculture in the Ozarks leans heavily on poultry, beef-cattle, and dairy farming. The general farm has all but disappeared; dairy farming continues under heavy pressure; grape and wine production struggles to hold its own; and only vestiges of fruit and truck farms remain. Like their forebears, the less-progressive Ozark farmers often find greater reward in alternate pursuits than in attempting to wrest a total livelihood from reluctant soils. One can speculate that mutual benefits may accrue to persons and land.

ELEVEN

THE OZARK LUMBER INDUSTRY: DEVELOPMENT AND GEOGRAPHY

The latter part of the 1800s was a time of rapid westward expansion and homesteading. Eastern settlers and European newcomers crowded into the Middle West and Great Plains, where they could claim land with fertile, rock-free soils. This created a vast market for lumber to build houses, barns, and stores. At the same time, railroad construction, which required three thousand crossties for each mile of track, went on at an unprecedented rate. These factors, and the general growth of the population and economy of the United States, created a strong demand for lumber and wood products and accounted for the exploitation of the vast hardwood forests of the Ozarks and of the less-extensive Ozark pine forest.

The timber cutters who entered the Ozarks after the Civil War were pioneers, if the definition of pioneer can be applied to the people who developed untouched natural resources, but they were primarily businesspeople looking for profits. In a free capitalistic society, they bore the same relationships to social and economic development in primitive regions as the cotton farmer, the rancher, the miner, or any individual or group seeking material gain through exploitation of the natural wealth of the wilderness. Nevertheless, the brand of lumbering practiced in the Ozarks, like that across the entire South, was extractive, exploitive, and generally lucrative for only a few. It was "cut out and get out" or "quick-rich, long-poor" lumbering powered by steam and later by gasoline and diesel engines. Unfortunately, only a few were lucky enough to become quick-rich, but when the forests were gone, many people were long-poor.

The lumbering frontier followed a definite pattern of advance from one virgin forest to another. The location of each new milling site depended upon several factors, one of the most important of which was the pressing need for an increased lumber supply to meet the growing demands of a rapidly expanding nation. For the first half of the nineteenth century, the industry centered in New England, with Maine as the principal lumber-producing

state. By 1850, cutting had shifted to western New York, but within ten years Pennsylvania assumed the leading position. During the next decade, penetration of the great white pine forests of the lake states began, and by 1880 the wood cutter's ax began to bite deep into the yellow-pine forests of the South. At this time, southern yellow pine began to replace northern white pine on the nation's markets, and between 1895 and 1910 the southern states produced 30 percent of all the lumber used in the United States.[1] Meanwhile, the advance of the lumber frontier continued, and in the early twentieth century the redwoods and Douglas fir of Washington, Oregon, and California began to compete seriously with the lumber products of the Mississippi Valley.

As far as we know, the first sawmill industry in Missouri was on the Gasconade River, the nearest source of good lumber for the St. Louis district. During his journey into the Ozarks in 1818–1819, Schoolcraft noted that these mills were in operation.[2] Some of them used waterpower, others handpower alone. During the next two decades, however, steam-powered circle mills operated in this region, and the Gasconade River valley was an important source of lumber until the Civil War. By 1880 wood cutters had cut the best timber in the Gasconade region, and St. Louis dealers could not meet the increasing demand for lumber products. Thus, the pine stands of the Ozarks became even more important because of their proximity to the St. Louis market. Until effective transportation was available, however, these forest lands remained untapped (fig. 11-1).

The southern-pine states, including Missouri and Arkansas, played a prominent role in the phenomenal expansion of the lumber industry. As the most northwesterly extension of native southern-pine forest, the Ozarks possessed geographical advantages to tap the market of Nebraska, Kansas, and Indian Territory.

The Ozark timber era began with the arrival of the railroads, which provided easy, low-cost transportation for

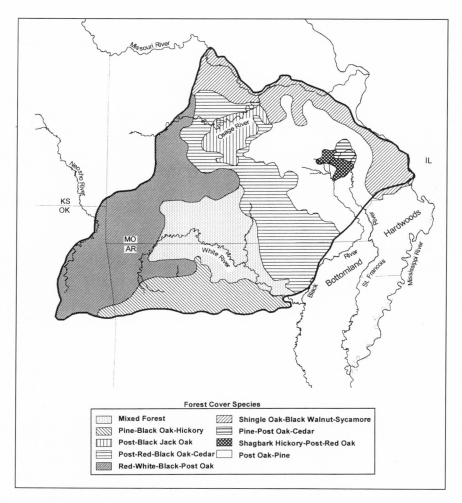

FIGURE 11-1. Forest cover regions of the Ozark Province. Adapted from Arthur B. Cozzens, "Analyzing and Mapping Natural Landscape Factors of the Ozarks Province," *Transactions of the Academy of Science of St. Louis* (Champaign: University of Illinois Press, 1939); with updates from *Forest Inventory and Analysis Data Base Retrieval System,* U.S. Department of Agriculture, Forest Service (Starksville, Miss.: SRSFLA,1999). http://www.srs-fia.usfs.msstate.edu /scripts.ew.html (April 17, 2000).

Forest Cover Species

- Mixed Forest
- Pine-Black Oak-Hickory
- Post-Black Jack Oak
- Post-Red-Black Oak-Cedar
- Red-White-Black-Post Oak
- Shingle Oak-Black Walnut-Sycamore
- Pine-Post Oak-Cedar
- Shagbark Hickory-Post-Red Oak
- Post Oak-Pine

bulky wood products. Two railroads were of unusual significance in stimulating interest in Ozark timberlands. By 1882 the Kansas City, Fort Scott and Memphis Railroad had begun a line southeast from Springfield toward Memphis, Tennessee. When they built through the western part of the pine forests, the St. Louis and Iron Mountain Railroad had already laid tracks southward in the eastern Ozarks through Ironton and Poplar Bluff to the Arkansas line.

Eastern investors purchased large acreages of shortleaf pine and oak. The Ozark forests could clearly supply lumber and railroad supplies for both the Great Plains and the East. The cost of stumpage was low, from a few cents to a dollar per thousand board feet, and the mild winters permitted year-round logging.

Following well-established practices, lumber companies often set up complete manufacturing facilities, constructed logging railroads, and began cutting timber. They exploited shortleaf pine forests for construction lumber, while oak went into flooring, barrel staves, and railroad ties and timbers. The largest sawmills with the most frenzied activity were in the southern Courtois Hills of Mis-

souri in Shannon, Carter, Reynolds, Oregon, Wayne, and Butler counties. Large outfits, such as Missouri Lumber and Mining Company, Cordz-Fisher Company, Ozark Land and Lumber Company, Current River Land and Cattle Company, Clarkson Sawmill Company, Doniphan Lumber Company, and Culbertson Stock and Lumber Company, were founded to exploit the timber resources of the southeast Missouri pineries. Boom towns—Doniphan, Leeper, Grandin, West Eminence, Winona, Birch Tree—grew up around large sawmills that fed on felled timber via tramways built into the forest (fig. 11-2). In the western Ozarks, the Springfield and Southern Railroad built a branch line from Springfield to Chadwick in Christian County. The Hobart-Lee Tie and Timber Company operated shipping docks and company stores at both Sparta and Chadwick.[3]

In areas outside the nearly pure stands of virgin shortleaf pine, lumbering took other forms. Chadwick, formerly known as Log Town, serves as an example. It became an important shipping point for lumber and railroad supplies when the Chadwick Branch of the Springfield and Southern Railroad (later absorbed by Frisco) was completed in 1883.[4] People began to move to Chadwick in larger numbers. New businesses came to the new town —stores, boardinghouses and rooming houses, saloons, and gambling houses reportedly flourished "in the fashion of the western boom towns."[5] Most able-bodied men in the community were earning more cash money tie hacking or working in the sawmills than they ever had before. Newspaper stories, verified by statements of persons who lived in Chadwick at the time, described the town as a hill-country Hell's Half-Acre. Reportedly, it was rough and lawless, like some noted cattle and mining towns of the West.[6]

The most important product of the hardwood forest was the railroad crosstie, which, according to specifications, was to be white oak cut six inches by eight inches by eight feet. Those of good quality brought twenty-five cents at the railhead. Farmers hewed and sold many ties from timber on their own land, but during the most active period of forest exploitation, lumber companies produced most of them. One of the biggest was Hobart-Lee Tie and Timber Company, which in 1890 was one of the largest businesses in southwest Missouri.

Another large concern operated on the Springdale Ranch, an 8,600-acre venture, founded by a Captain Kenna in 1878. It soon furnished much of the timber shipped at Chadwick. The ranch had its own tracks and train to pull carloads of logs across Bull Creek and up Happy Hollow to the foot of Mill Ridge Hill, where a steam hoist lifted the cars to the mill at the top of the hill. Teamsters hauled lumber and ties from the mill to Chadwick in horse-drawn wagons. In later years, strings of wagons were pulled by crawler tractors.

At one time, Springdale Ranch sustained a settlement of 125 people. The property changed hands several times during the timber boom, but the ranch continued to produce important amounts of lumber and ties until the last mill burned in the 1920s. This marked the end of the boom, for they had cut most of the good timber by then. By 1930, Chadwick offered so little trade that, reportedly, the crew of the *Chadwick Flyer* had begun to stop off to shoot quail or pick blackberries along the right of way. In 1934, the railroad stopped service to Chadwick and a short time later removed the tracks between Chadwick and Ozark.[7] However, logging continues lethargically even though the last sawmill in Chadwick closed around 1970.

Likewise in Arkansas and Oklahoma the ax men followed the railroads into the best stands of pine and hardwoods. The Frisco line through Fayetteville on its way from Pierce City, Missouri, to Fort Smith opened new timberlands in the early 1880s. With the railroad came Hugh F. McDaniel, construction man and tie contractor. The railroads had to have ties, hundreds of thousands of them. A branch railroad constructed up the upper White River in Washington and Madison counties in Arkansas opened vast timber tracts to lumbermen such as McDaniel.

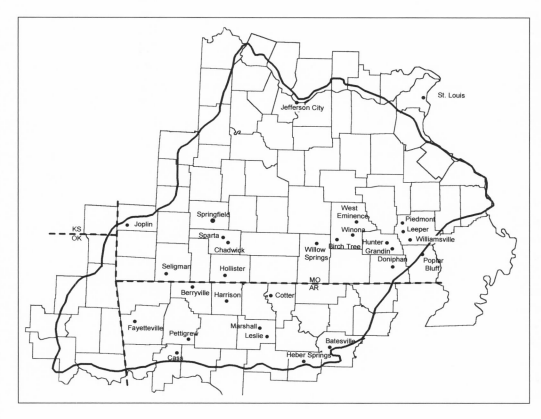

FIGURE 11-2. Ozark lumber mill towns. Prepared by the author with information from several historical and geographical sources, 1979; updated October 2000.

Making whiskey barrels at the Independent Stave Company, Lebanon, Missouri. (Milton Rafferty Collection, photograph by the author.)

Growth began almost immediately. During 1887, the first year of operation, the McDaniel brothers shipped two million dollars' worth of white-oak crossties over the Fayetteville and Little Rock Railroad.[8] Soon the railroad established new stations: Baldwin, Harris, Elkins, Durham, Thompson, Crosses, Delaney, Patrick, Combs, Brashears, and, later, Dutton and Pettigrew. When they extended the railroad to Pettigrew in 1897, more than a dozen lumber and stave mills were built there. Included were the American Land, Timber and Stave Company; Chess and Wymond; Pekin Cooperage Company; J. M. Bryant Company; Kentucky Stave and Heading Company; and W. L. Hillyard Stave Company. Phipps Lumber Company, the largest in northwest Arkansas, also had a mill there. Pettigrew billed itself as the Hardwood Capital of the World.[9]

As the companies cut the timber, they drove railways even farther into the remote hill districts. By 1915, Phipps Lumber Company had cut over thousands of acres in Madison County, and new timber supplies were needed. Phipps constructed its own railroad, the Black Mountain and Eastern, into its large landholdings in the Black Mountain area of Franklin County. The line ended at Cass, which served as the shipping point until logging was completed in the mid-1920s.[10] During the 1930s, after the railroad shut down and salvaged the tracks, the Civilian Conservation Corps (CCC) decided to establish a camp at Frazier, the only settlement on the CC & E between its two ends. To provide transportation to and from the camp, the CCC built an automobile and wagon road on the old railroad bed between Combs and Camp Frazier.

The Missouri and North Arkansas Railroad, which linked Joplin, Missouri, and Helena, Arkansas, cut through the rugged timberlands of the White River Hills and the Boston Mountains. Workers hauled lumber and railroad ties to sidings at Seligman, Missouri, and several Arkansas towns, including Beaver, Freeman, Berryville, Harrison, Pindall, Marshall, Leslie, Edgemont, Heber Springs, Pangborn, and Searcy.[11]

Among the larger lumber dealers were Heber Springs Milling Company, Pangborn Lumber Company, and H. D. Williams Cooperage Company. The last-named furnished employment for nearly everyone in the town of Leslie. The H. D. Williams barrel factory there was reported to be the largest of its kind in the world.[12] They moved it from Poplar Bluff, Missouri, to Leslie in 1907. From Leslie a network of tram lines wound back into the hills to portable "green mills" that supplied staves to the factory. In full operation the mill employed more than a thousand workers. Another major producer, Doniphan Lumber Company, owned eighty-five thousand acres of timberland in Cleburne County and operated several mills in that area.

The Missouri Pacific's White River Line, constructed between 1901 and 1906 at a cost of more than $12 million, opened large acreages of timberland and spawned a host of lumber towns, including Branson and Hollister in Missouri and Cotter and Batesville in Arkansas.[13] Because cedar grows profusely in the glades of the White River drainage basin, several wood-products manufacturers specializing in red cedar grew up in the area. Hanford Cedar Yard at Batesville was one of the largest markets of its kind. Eagle Pencil Company of Branson purchased much of the virgin cedar on the upper White River.[14] The company bought cedar logs by the thousands and processed them into rectangular slats measuring about three by three by eight inches. They shipped the slats to a pencil factory in Batesville where they manufactured the slats into pencils.

Railroads were essential for profitable lumbering; where rails led, lumbermen followed. Sometimes, Ozarks streams were used for transportation of crossties and small timber, but only where conditions were favorable and usually only for short distances from forest to mill. Lumber companies rafted cedar logs and railroad ties down the White River to Batesville and later to Cotter, Arkansas, after the railroad reached that point. Smalley Tie and Timber Company, a subsidiary of Missouri Lumber and Mining Company, floated railroad ties regularly on the Current River. The affairs of this company did not always run smoothly. Tie hackers hewed the ties in the woods during the winter and early spring, then hauled them to the river and stacked them to dry, out of reach of high water. Workers ran them down the river in the fall when the threat of flash floods was least. They either ran the ties loose in the water or fastened them together in small rafts operated by two men. During the fall of 1902 the holding boom at Chicopee on the Current River broke under the pressure of thousands of ties, and about five thousand went downstream. Losses to the swift current in the river were frequent, and John Barber White, president of Missouri Lumber and Mining Company, doubted that he ever profited much from the tie business.[15]

From 1880 to about 1920, lumber companies floated railroad ties down Ozark streams to railheads, where workers loaded them on flatcars to be hauled away. Several large contracting companies were engaged in the business, including the Smalley Tie and Timber Company, the Moss Tie Company, the Hobart-Lee Tie and Timber Company of Springfield, and the largest of all, the Bagnell Brothers of St. Louis. The latter company, with all of its subcontractors, probably was the largest and had the most far-flung operations.

Along the Niangua River, for example, contractors leased large tracts of land and set up tie camps until they ran out of timber, then they moved the camps to new locations. Such camps hired as many as two hundred men. The workers hauled the ties to "bankings" on the Niangua, where they branded them. Contractors usually built stores to supply food and clothing near large tie bankings. There were many bankings, but three were very important: the one at Roach, now on U.S. Highway 54; the one at Mosier Hollow; and the one near Ira close to the Dallas County line.[16]

The tie companies considered three things in selecting banking sites. First, the steepness of the chute had to be such that ties would not bounce and endanger the raft makers below. Second, the landing had to be shallow enough for men to work in but deep enough to float the rafts. Third, the banking, or bank, had to hold enough ties in storage to keep the crews busy.[17]

The men who nailed the tie rafts together worked in the water winter and summer, protected by hip boots. They fashioned the ties into blocks or sections one tie wide and about sixteen feet long, holding about twenty ties. A white-oak pole was split into strips, and the strips were nailed on top as binders. These blocks were joined lengthwise with a larger white-oak strip to form a hinged "snake raft" that could negotiate the sharp bends in the river. The rafts, containing 300 to 700 ties and manned by two men, floated down to old Linn Creek at the mouth of the Niangua, where workers made them up into larger

Million feet of logs in the Current River. Lumberjacks standing on logs. (Courtesy of State Historical Society of Missouri.)

rafts of 2,000 to as many as 4,500 ties before floating them down the Osage River to the railhead at Bagnell.[18]

THE MISSOURI LUMBER AND MINING COMPANY

Leslie G. Hill's doctoral dissertation provides unusual insight into the operations of the Missouri Lumber and Mining Company, the biggest timber cutter in the Ozarks. Its operations were larger and probably better financed than many similar companies, and its organization and purposes will serve to illustrate the character of large-scale lumbering during the era of forest exploitation.

Investors from outside the region founded the Missouri Lumber and Mining Company (MLMC). This type of funding was true of most of the large Ozark lumber companies. In this case, like that of the Maramec Iron Works near St. James, the capital, management experience, and model for operations came from the forested plateau country of western Pennsylvania. By the late 1860s, O. H. P. Williams, a lumberman from Pittsburgh, had cut over most of his timber holdings in Pennsylvania and had begun to look further afield for more timberlands.[19] He heard of the yellow pine in the Ozarks and wrote letters of inquiry to the officers of several southern Missouri counties. Williams purchased tax-delinquent timberlands in the Beaver Dam section of Ripley County for as little as $6.90 a half section.[20] In 1871, he and his son-in-law, E. B. Grandin of Tidioute, Pennsylvania, toured Iron, Reynolds, Shannon, and Wayne counties; Williams purchased thirty thousand acres of timberland in Carter County at an average cost of a dollar per acre.[21] This became the nucleus of the Missouri Lumber and Mining Company's holdings.

The company's business connections and activities are highly significant.[22] E. B. Grandin, its actual founder, had experience in the lumber industry, but Pennsylvania oil was the foundation of his fortune. J. L. Grandin, his brother, was treasurer and manager of the Tidioute and Warren Oil Company. These two men had organized a bank at Tidioute and were able to furnish the capital needed for any new business venture. Another early member of the firm, John Hunter, had a merchandising background and had helped in establishing the Tidioute Savings Bank. Hunter's son, L. L. Hunter, was a retail lumber dealer and operated a sawmill. The last member of the board of directors was H. H. Cumings, another Pennsylvania oil man. This combination represented a concentration of wealth unusual at the time. They selected John Barber White, an aggressive young lumberman, to establish and manage the Missouri Lumber and Mining Company.

Although they purchased land in the 1860s and 1870s, there was no immediate effort to exploit its timber. The successful operation of a sawmill depended on several factors. Even as late as 1880 the population of Carter County was only 2,168, an average of about three per square mile, but fortunately, it was concentrated in a few river valleys, a distribution that made it possible for the company to place some dependence on a local labor supply.[23]

Of equal importance with labor supply as a locational factor were transportation facilities. Local sales of lumber products would be of only slight importance, so there had to be railroads to carry the finished product to market. Thus feeder lines to the St. Louis and Iron Mountain line and the Kansas City, Fort Scott and Memphis were needed. The closest shipping points in the early 1880s were Piedmont and Williamsville on the St. Louis and Iron Mountain, Doniphan on the Doniphan and Neelyville

Mills of the Missouri Lumber and Mining Company at Grandin in Carter County, Missouri. (Courtesy of State Historical Society of Missouri.)

Branch of the St. Louis and Iron Mountain, and Willow Springs on the Kansas City, Fort Scott and Memphis. Until these railroads were built, land held for speculation purposes remained tax delinquent or of low market value.

Another factor that influenced the Pennsylvania capitalists to place their sawmill in southern Missouri was the low cost of stumpage for standing timber in the area. The Fourteenth United States Census estimated the average price of stumpage in the nation at $1.89 per 1,000 board feet as late as 1899.[24] During the same year, white pine stumpage in Michigan and Wisconsin cost more than $3.00 per 1,000 board feet; the pine of Missouri averaged $1.22 for stumpage. The timberlands purchased by MLMC cost much less than the estimated average. The first purchases made by O. H. P. Williams were about $1.00 per acre. This would average about $0.25 per thousand stumpage, since pine in the central Ozarks cut about 4,000 board feet to the acre. They purchased some land at higher prices, but a great deal of stumpage was picked up at tax sales for an average price of $0.25 an acre. This meant a cost of only $0.085 per thousand for stumpage. In 1880, J. B. White managed to buy, at a sheriff's sale in Carter County, two sections of land for $0.125 an acre.[25]

The Ozarks had become a land of opportunity for lumbermen who were wise enough to get in on the ground floor. Native Ozarkers who had patented the timberland from the government were unable to use it effectively. The soil was rocky and unproductive. The only marketable resource on their property was the standing timber, and the only way to reduce it to a salable commodity required an outlay of capital that the ordinary farmer did not possess. Consequently, a large acreage of fine timberland became tax delinquent and ready for purchase by speculators or lumber manufacturers (fig. 11-3). The old adage "It takes money to make money" fit the situation.

Often the title to land was cloudy, and the managers recognized that once they cut the timber, the land was worth very little. Therefore, it was considered a good business practice to remove the timber from land of unsure title as quickly as possible. One of the most important legal cases in which the Missouri Lumber and Mining Company became engaged was the suit involving the B. R. Noble lands, 15,000 acres of pine timber west of the Current River in northern Ripley County. There is probably no better example of the struggle for the big pine in the entire Ozark region. The lands were first purchased by Melvin J. Clark in 1888 as tax-delinquent property. Clark sold the timber to John R. Cook in 1890 and gave a quit-claim deed. B. R. Noble purchased the tract in 1895 and also received a quit-claim deed. Noble sold the lands the same year to Hunter and Grandin, directors of the Missouri Lumber and Mining Company, on a stumpage basis and made a written guarantee of seventy million board feet. Timber cruisers (estimators and purchasing agents) employed by Grandin and Hunter found that the Doniphan Lumber Company, which also claimed the tract, had already begun to remove the timber. When titles to much of the land proved defective, Grandin and Hunter sued Noble. J. B. White, impatient of waiting for legal action, offered to cut the timber if Grandin and Hunter would give the Missouri Lumber and Mining Company a quit-claim deed. The general manager further advised the immediate construction of a tram road directly southwest across the Current River because rivals were cutting the timber. He said:

> They [competitors] have no title and on much of this land our title is so technically imperfect that we could not make ours a basis of action in a suit for damages. The fellow that gets the timber gets it at little or no cost, for not in more than one half the cases will we be able to show up such a title as the court would require for we cannot stand upon the weakness of their title, but have to stand upon the strength of the perfectness of our own. Carter and Culbertson [Doniphan Lumber Company and Culbertson Stock and Lumber Company] are going into this and won't compromise . . . We should push energetically ahead into that territory quick . . . We can get into the best body of timber before they can.[26]

Meanwhile, the Doniphan Lumber Company had ousted Culbertson from the disputed timber and decided to build a tram road from the Current River into the heart of the tract. The Missouri Lumber and Mining Company then bought a farm on the proposed route of the tram and refused to grant the Doniphan concern a right of way. Finally, the two disputing companies compromised by forming the Missouri Tie and Timber Company, which cut the timber.[27] Matters of title to the land were confirmed many years later, long after they had removed the last virgin pine.

The impact of the large lumber companies on the economy, politics, and social life of the region was substantial. The Missouri Lumber and Mining Company built its mills at Mill Creek (Hunter) and Lakewood, later renamed Grandin. Land cruisers purchased land in several surrounding counties, including Reynolds, Butler, Carter, Ripley, Shannon, and Wayne. Grandin was selected as the site for the mill because of Tolliver Pond, a large natural body of water that was a perfect place to preserve the logs until they could saw them in the huge mill.[28] Grandin was

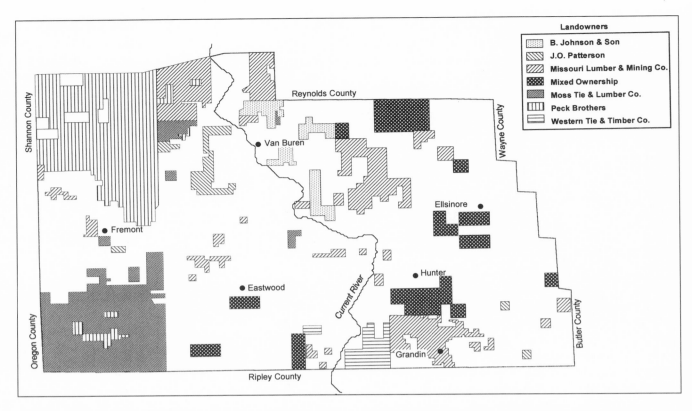

FIGURE 11-3. Large landholdings in Carter County, Missouri, circa 1920. Adapted from *Carter County, Mo. Plat Book* (Rockford, Ill.: W. W. Hixson and Co., circa 1920)

also near the center of the vast amount of land Missouri Land and Lumber Company purchased as a cutting area. The first mill was set up in 1880 and put into operation immediately to cut the lumber for a larger mill and to provide the materials for buildings in the town.

The company eventually built about 475 houses just west and north of the mill site, some of which are still standing. Workers could rent a house in Grandin for a very reasonable fee, a dollar a room per month, and apparently the houses were very pleasing for that particular time. In 1899, 245 houses were rented for $18,597.24, an average of over $6.00 per house per month.[29]

They made most of the tools used in the logging operations at the company-owned blacksmith shop. J. C. Thompson was boss of the shop, which turned out cant hooks, boomers, and various other tools that the workers needed. Reportedly, he patented several pieces of equipment, including an instrument known as a sheep's foot, which workers used to bind the logs down in a way that made it easier to unload the railroad cars when they arrived at the mill. The company owned the store at Grandin and employed six to eight clerks on a full-time basis.

Almost anything that employees needed could be purchased at the commissary. The store was also popular with

other residents of Grandin and vicinity. Wild turkeys sold for $0.15 a pound, potatoes were $1.25 a bushel, and other articles were priced accordingly. The store also sold kerosene, the principal use of which was to provide light for the loggers' homes. Reportedly there were two prices for kerosene, $0.10 and $0.15 per gallon, and a humorous story about it still circulates in the Grandin area. A logger finally discovered that the only difference in the kerosene was the price. The fuel flowed down a long pipe from a tank on the hill. The pipe forked when it reached the commissary, and the same quality kerosene came from both spigots. From that day forward, even the best kerosene sold for $0.10 per gallon.

The Missouri Lumber and Mining Company inaugurated its medical service in 1890. The facilities consisted of a central dispensary at Grandin, staffed by six doctors, a druggist, and two nurses. Field chests, filled with surgical dressings and medicines, were placed with the foremen of small camps so that when the doctor made his regular rounds, usually three times a week, he would have nearby such remedies as were necessary to treat the men. The medical service reduced the number of medical problems in the outlying camps and the mill area to a mere 10 percent of the former level in just two years. This dramatic decrease may or may not have been due in part to the fol-

Loading logs. Ozark Land and Lumber Company. (Courtesy of State Historical Society of Missouri.)

lowing slogans: "Unavoidable accidents rarely occur"; "If a man does not look out for himself, no one else can do it for him"; and "The over use or abuse of hog meat, hot biscuits, black coffee, tobacco and whiskey are precursors of nearly all disorders of the human system."[30] Needless to say, these sayings gave the men something to think about. The charge for the medical service was small. Each family received treatment for $1.25 per month, regardless of the number in the family. They charged single men $0.75 per month, and independent boys and young women $0.40 and $0.25, respectively.[31] These amounts included all medical care; there were no additional charges. In November 1906, about $800 was collected for medical services.

When the Current River Railroad reached Grandin, it helped to open a whole a new aspect of lumber production. The Missouri Lumber and Mining Company expanded its own railroad system, which consisted of tram lines. These short lines hauled timber cut from seventy-five acres of land each day. The logs moved from the tram lines to the main line and then to Tolliver Pond at Grandin to await the sawyer's work. Many men and mules were needed to haul the logs to piling areas near the tram lines, where they were then loaded on the log cars. There were usually ten or eleven wagons in each group, and each wagon was pulled by a four-mule team. Each group had approximately one hundred mules in its "string" so that the animals would not be overworked.

The logging crews went to areas where cutters had felled trees. They carried tents, food and supplies, a portable barn, and hay and grain for their work animals. The Grandin log haulers were hardy and tried to get as much enjoyment from their work as possible. Many of them vied with one another, on various occasions, for the title of Champion Log Hauler. Firmin Sanders of Van Buren claimed to hold the record for hauling the most board feet in one day. The feat was accomplished in 1904, when Sanders hauled 22,744 board feet of logs in nine hours and forty-five minutes.

After workers skidded and hauled the logs to the tram lines, they were loaded onto flatcars and taken to Tolliver Pond at Grandin. A track encircled most of the pond, and the trains unloaded their logs directly into the water. A large sluice ran to the mill from the pond below. The logs were headed into the sluice by lumberjacks, who used pike poles to guide them into the hooks that carried them up the incline to the mill.

The combined capacity of the two mills at Grandin was 220,000 board feet of lumber per day, running two 10-hour shifts to reach it. The mills consumed ninety carloads of logs a day. The plant consisted of two sawmills, four planing mills, fourteen drying kilns, and about thirty warehouses. Herman McKinney of Grandin said he took inventory at the plant one Sunday and tallied 30 million board feet of stockpiled lumber. From its founding until 1902 the Grandin lumber camp produced 648,203,358 board feet of lumber.[32]

The pay at Grandin was $1.50 a day, or $0.15 an hour; but some men made as little as $1.35 daily. The highest wages were paid for top-loading, and people on that particular job received $2.50 a day. The men received their pay on the fifteenth of each month, when the railroad brought in the payroll money. They paid each worker in cash. Coupons (script) were used only in the event a worker needed to borrow money before payday. He could then go to the company store and draw either a $2.00 or a $5.00 coupon. He received his merchandise and his change, and the total amount was charged against his next paycheck.

In 1900 the company employed approximately 1,200 persons, and Grandin's population was about 3,000. The boom continued until September 1910, when the mill whistle blew for the last time. By 1911 MLMC had moved all the equipment to West Eminence, and J. B. White started selling land and houses. The simple shotgun houses fetched fifty dollars, and larger houses sold for one hundred dollars. By 1938 Grandin had shrunk to about 300 persons. In that year the Missouri Highway Department built Highway 21 through the area, providing a better means of travel and helping to connect Grandin to the outside world; however, Frisco found it unprofitable to continue rail service to the town. Nevertheless, Grandin survived. Today the mill site shows but few vestiges of a lost past. One can no longer hear the buzz of the huge saw, the shouts of the workers, the roar of the locomotives.

At the end of the twentieth century, Grandin had about 270 residents, many of whom, were engaged in small-scale timber or farming operations.[33] If one lounges on the store porches today, he may hear the old men talk of the great boom or hear of the fire in the sawdust pile that burned constantly for thirty years. The fire has burned out now; the boom is no more.

The MLMC extended the life of the Grandin mills in 1901 through the acquisition of nearly forty thousand acres of land in Shannon County from J. H. Berkshire.[34] The price of $1.50 per acre was the highest ever paid by the Missouri Lumber and Mining Company, but it added much territory to the firm's holdings. In 1909, Missouri Lumber and Mining built a new mill and the town of West Eminence in Shannon County. A hub mill and a shingle mill were added.

The Missouri Lumber and Mining Company built many new camps to accommodate the workers that would cut and load timber to haul to the mills. Among those in Shannon County were Angelina, Camp Ten, Camp Twelve, Bert George Camp, Camp Five, Camp Six, and Hartshorn-Bryant Camp. Camp Twelve was the largest; it included a grocery store, a doctor's office, a barn, and several houses.[35]

The company operated large stores at Grandin and West Eminence. The latter was particularly striking for the time and place. It had several departments, including dry goods of all kinds, groceries, hardware, a shoe shop, and a butcher shop. A main place of entertainment was the ice-cream parlor next to the general store. Prices and commodities reflect the time and pattern of life: sugar, a nickel a pound; flour, thirty-five cents for a twenty-four-pound bag; work overalls with a bib, fifty cents; blue chambray shirts, fifteen cents and twenty-five cents each; good work gloves, twenty-five cents; and the best calico was six cents a yard, gingham ten.[36]

LAND DISPOSAL

The lumber companies brought people and temporary prosperity. Towns grew up around mills, flourished for a time, passed into rapid decline, then slow attrition. In 1903, Winona, Missouri, had about the same number of people as its present population (1,131), but it declined to less than half that amount when the big sawmills closed.[37] In 1903, people were confident that there would be a Winona long after the Ozark Land and Lumber Company had passed on, and they expected the mill to live at least ten more years because the company was at that time still buying more land.

The principal owner of Ozark Land and Lumber Company was Benjamin Hershey, a successful businessman, lumberman, and land speculator from Muscatine, Iowa.[38] This breed of investor expected high profit margins, from $5.00 to $5.50 per 1,000 board feet. The overall logging cost per 1,000 board feet in 1892 was $2.66, and that year the Ozark Land and Lumber Company sawed 55,529 logs, which gave the mill a tally of 6,454,560 board feet.[39] Records of the Missouri Lumber and Land Exchange, a lumber marketing firm representing several larger Ozark mills, show that by 1902 the mill at Winona had produced 391,209,308 board feet of lumber.[40] Considering the large volume of lumber and the low cost of production, profits were large. When cheap stumpage was no longer available, the mills were closed, the machinery sold, the rails taken up and sold as scrap. Investment capital was withdrawn from the Ozarks for more lucrative ventures in other areas; much was used to purchase timber properties in Louisiana and in the Douglas-fir country of Washington and Oregon.

By 1915 the Ozark Land and Lumber Company had completed the removal of timber from its holdings and had changed its principal business from making lumber to selling real estate. The disposal methods varied, but the most common was selling through the mail. A nationwide advertising campaign describing the Ozarks as sheep and cattle country and as a fruit-growing region was used to good advantage. The owners sold large amounts of land, sight unseen. The Missouri Lumber and Mining Company not only placed newspaper ads widely but published booklets and brochures and employed the services of land agents. A few examples from an advertising booklet for a 28,000-acre tract in Ripley County, Missouri, will serve to illustrate one way in which the lumber companies created Ozark imagery.

The land is to be sold in blocks of 80 to 1,000 acres at $3.50 to $12.50 per acre on terms of one-fifth down, the remainder in four equal annual installments. Those who first come to see the land will have choice selections.

The owners of this vast tract of virgin land offer it to those who will develop it. After studying the resources of the country for 25 years, and witnessing many experiments, they can unhesitatingly recommend this for stock and dairy farms, with small family orchards, vineyards, some alfalfa and forage crops. We sincerely believe that these will make an ideal money making combination and that the buyer will succeed beyond doubt. We do not cater to the land speculator, because we wish to see this country developed.

This is a fertile virgin land. It contains limestone. It has produced trees of wonderful size. It now produces a rank growth of blue stem grass. The rainfall averages 40 inches, the country is not very rough or mountainous, but is undulating, with some high plateaus. There are numerous creeks, springs, small lakes, and one stream of considerable size, the Current River.

Everywhere through the countryside you find peace, happiness, independence and contentment. "It is the country of the little red hen and the much read Bible," said a prominent statesman who spent a vacation on Current River.

Think of getting enough timber on the land to make most of your improvements. Think of having the eternal springs gush forth for your livestock, of not having to erect big barns to protect your stock, of being able to raise just as much on this land, with almost as little labor as on land ten times as valuable.

It will be the means of founding your fortune.

Five hundred acres costs you, say $3,000. In five years you have it developed and paid for. You sell for $25,000. Can you beat it elsewhere? This is our first land opening. The prices are LOW. They will be increased. Terms are EASY. Titles GOOD, your treatment will be FAIR and SQUARE.

Come; let me show you.[41]

Native Ozarkers no doubt scoffed at the land agents' claims, particularly the descriptions of the inherent fertility of the soil. Remarked one Ozarker when they asked him if the lands measured up to the claim: "Yes, and you can go to hell for lying the same as stealing." Yet it is interesting that eighty years later these lands are selling for $300 to $600 an acre and are becoming scarcer each year because people are reluctant to sell as land prices continue to increase. Ozarkers consider themselves sharp traders in land, and it is a face-losing thing to have sold out too cheap.

Sometimes the lumber companies divided the land into lots to sell them. The Ozark Land and Lumber Company even went as far as to lay out a town and sell lots for homes. They established a few demonstration farms that grew wheat, rye, livestock, and fruit, but these were mainly half-hearted efforts designed to dispose of land.

Eventually much of the cutover land became tax delinquent. The U.S. Forest Service purchased much of it in the 1930s. Ozark National Forest in Arkansas included mainly cutover lands in the Boston Mountains. In Missouri the eastern cutover land became Clark National Forest; such land in southwest Missouri formed Mark Twain National Forest. In 1947, the newly formed Missouri Conservation Commission purchased the Peck Brothers holdings in northwest Carter County and adjacent parts of Shannon County, which they later developed as the Peck Ranch Wildlife Area.[42]

THE EFFECTS OF THE LUMBER ERA

The timber boom resulted in a seriously depleted resource base and a greatly increased population, which, to sustain itself, continued to strain the natural resources in the area. Because many people who came to exploit the timber had established close ties in their neighborhoods, they were reluctant to move away when the timber was gone. Many of them remained, purchased cutover tracts, and began farming.

As noted earlier, most of the large holdings that had been cut over were subdivided and sold as farms. The effects of this subdivision in the timbered areas may be seen in census statistics. Stone County, Missouri, had a net loss of only seven farms in the decade 1910 to 1920, and Christian County, where more cutover land was sold, experienced a moderate gain in the number of farms.[43] Most counties outside the timber area had decreases in number of farms. Many large properties were eventually broken up and sold, mainly to former "tie hackers" and mill workers who had been thrown out of work by the clearing of the forest and the closing of the mills.

Contributing to the rapid sale of cutover land were stories that farmers could make a good living raising strawberries and tomatoes on the cleared ridge tops. For a time during the 1920s, strawberry growing became so popular that newcomers lived in tents and raised strawberries at Logan's Ridge, a community in Christian County, Missouri.[44] However, the demand for tomatoes and strawberries declined when more favorably situated areas came into production. When farmers tried corn and wheat and they proved unsuccessful on sterile ridge-top soils, the emphasis shifted to livestock. Open-range grazing on cutover lands became common, and farmers burned regrowth timber to increase forage for livestock. Both practices delayed restoration of the timber.

As crop agriculture proved unprofitable and as forest resources and wildlife were depleted even further, people began to move away. Most of those who remained suffered a reduced standard of living. The overall economy stagnated, and many farmers barely subsisted. The farm supplied milk, meat, and vegetables for the table, but little else. Sometimes farmers could earn money to buy those things that they could not produce on the farm through part-time employment in the small canneries or in the stave mills, and ax-handle factories. Some people found jobs in the few remaining small sawmills that cut scattered, less-accessible timber left behind by the big mills.

The destruction of the forest cover caused serious depletion of related resources. The journals of early travelers and settlers contain many references to the plentiful supply of wild game. By the mid-1930s, they had depleted the populations of many wildlife species. The rapid decline of wildlife stemmed from destruction of their natural habitat and from subsistence hunting. The low level of living encouraged people to engage in unrestricted hunting to supplement their food supply. Just three years before the Missouri Conservation Commission was founded in 1937, the deer population of Missouri had been reduced to an all-time low of "not more than" two thousand animals.[45] Many other species of wildlife experienced similar decreases in population. Researchers estimated that about thirty-five hundred wild turkeys ranged across forty-five Missouri counties, and the numbers of quail, rabbits, raccoons, muskrats, mink, and other wild animals were also decreasing.

Destruction of the forest cover accelerated soil erosion and attempts to convert steep slopes and rocky ridges to cropland further aggravated the problem. The soils of the hillier timber areas are shallow to begin with, being no more than four to eight inches deep, and those of the level areas are only slightly deeper. Destruction of the forests and the successive burning of the woods destroyed the leaf litter and organic matter, which acted to absorb rainfall, prevent excessive runoff, and retard the rate of soil erosion.

By 1935, soil erosion had become serious on much of the cutover lands. The severity of erosion depended primarily upon the intensity of cultivation of the land and the extent to which landowners had burned the woodland. Where landowners practiced burning repeatedly, appreciable erosion had occurred, and where they had cultivated the land, serious sheet and gully erosion had followed. In places where an adequate stand of timber remained, erosion was moderated; probably, slightly more than one-fourth of the original soil had been lost. The unprotected slopes had lost about half their soil.[46] Soil erosion was especially damaging to stream habitats, and the aquatic life was in as precarious a position as land species. The droughts during the 1930s, which further damaged the vegetative cover, also contributed to soil erosion and general depletion of the wildlife habitat and environment.

Reduction of forest cover and organic material that mantled the soil caused many springs to go dry. In the early days, springs were so plentiful that there was little need for dug wells. Almost without exception, homesteaders carried water from nearby springs. Near Chadwick, Missouri, where lumbering was very active, many large springs went dry. One was Bubbling Spring, which supplied water for the settlement and lumber mill on Springdale Ranch. Today it is so choked with rocks, clay, and debris washed from the adjacent slopes that it is hardly visible.[47]

THE ERA OF FOREST MANAGEMENT

The era of forest management dates from the 1920s and 1930s. As early as 1910, there was sufficient concern about the Ozark forest to bring Gifford Pinchot, first chief of the U.S. Forest Service, on a visit to the areas around Grandin, Winona, and Eminence.[48] He was accompanied by Governor Hadley and J. B. White, one of the owners of the Grandin Mill, and a member of the state forestry commission. In 1912, the University of Missouri established a Department of Forestry in the college of Agriculture, but only nineteen people earned degrees over the next nine years. They dropped the program in 1921 and did not start it again until 1936.[49]

The two national forests of the Ozarks—Ozark National Forest in Arkansas and Mark Twain National Forest in Missouri—are made up of several separate districts comprising about 20 percent of the Ozark Upland. They were founded respectively in 1908 and 1933. The Missouri National Forest Association played a major role in lobbying the Missouri legislature to permit the federal government to purchase land in Missouri for the eight purchase areas that became the Mark Twain National Forest.[50] Unclaimed public domain tracts formed the first land acquisitions in the Ozark National Forest. However, the Forest Service purchased most of the land in both national forests after Congress passed the Weeks Act, March 1, 1911. The Weeks Law, as it became known, authorized the federal government to purchase suitable forest areas for national forests to maintain vegetative cover for wildlife and to protect watersheds from floods.[51] The Clarke-McNary Act of 1924 provided additional impetus by enabling the secretary of agriculture to work cooperatively with state officials to bring about better forest protection, chiefly in terms of fire control, water resources protection, and provisions for sustained production of timber.[52]

The Mark Twain National Forest and the Ozark National Forest, like most national forests, contain much private land. Usually, private owners hold the cleared valleys and the land along the well-traveled roads that follow the ridges, and the U.S. Forest Service controls most of the upland area, especially away from the better roads and in rugged areas. The forests and related natural resources have benefited in two ways. The multiple use-sustained yield principle of Forest Service management has improved the condition of the forests on federally owned land significantly. Private owners have, sometimes, begun to adopt better management practices used by the Forest Service. Additional benefits for privately owned forest land are the technical assistance and fire protection provided by the Forest Service.

The purchase of forest land, which began in 1934, reduced the area's population. In Linn Township, Christian County, Missouri, where approximately half the land is federally owned, the population declined from 527 in 1930 to 382 in 1960, a decrease of 45 percent.[53] Although a few residents stayed on the land for a time under special-use permits, the Forest Service required most to move. The decrease in population resulted in a reduction of pressure on the depleted resource base, for many of these people had operated general farms at or near the subsistence level and had relied on the forest to produce a small amount of cash income. At near-subsistence levels of living, proper forest management was impossible. Landowners cut posts, firewood, and stave bolts from immature timber to provide money for necessities. The decline in population also reduced the pressure on wildlife since many rural people traditionally relied on wildlife for part of the meat on their tables.

Fire control was an especially difficult problem in regrowing forests. In 1938, the Missouri Conservation Commission tackled the fire problem by hiring George O. White as state forester in the Division of Fish, Game, and Forestry. He hired four young foresters—William Towell, Arthur Meyer, August Schmidt, Edward Seay—and sent them out to organized districts. Missouri had made some progress before that time under the 1925 state forestry law, which required the Fish and Game Department to use part of its funds for the purchase of state parks.[54] The parks became valuable protected forest areas that later formed the nucleus for the present state forest areas at Deer Run, Indian Trail, and Meramec. In 1926, foresters built Missouri's first lookout tower in what is today Deer Run State Forest with funds from the commissioner of Fish and Game.[55]

Fire-control measures were initiated in the Mark Twain National Forest in 1936. Before that time, landowners had burned over the timbered area now in government ownership in the Mark Twain National Forest an average of about once in every three years. This amounted to an average burn of 280,000 acres per year. Ten years later, they had cut the average annual burn to 8,000 acres. The number of fires dropped from 1,200 in 1940 to 520 in 1944, and continued to decrease in subsequent years.[56] The traditional practice of burning the woods to "green up" the grass hampered early fire-control efforts. This was especially true in the Pine Ridge community in Christian County, where the number of incendiary fires was so high for a time that the area became known outside the Ozarks as a fire-control problem area. The Mark Twain National Forest records show that two hundred to six hundred fires occurred annually in the Ava District until about 1960. Some of these fires were incendiary, set by individuals to obtain work as firefighters.[57] Probably, improved economic conditions and the availability of employment in nonfarm jobs have contributed to the reduction in the number of forest fires. Educational efforts promoting forest conservation and opposing woods burning have helped also. By 1968 the Forest Service had reduced the number of fires in the Ava District to only twenty-three.[58]

The Forest Service inaugurated a new experimental fire-control program, Operation Outreach, in the 1960s.[59] It was designed to give farmers U.S. Forest Service technical advice on the use of fire as a forest and grassland management technique. In particular, the Forest Service provides meteorological and climatological information, and also data on soils and plant life, so that landowners can undertake prescribed burning safely and at times when results will be most beneficial. Usually, fall burning is preferred, since there is less damage to trees and the humus layer than would occur in a spring burn. Indeed, it is paradoxical that firing the woods, which has retarded restoration of Ozark forests and long has been the enemy of the Forest Service, had to be taught to the Ozark farmers. This is especially true when they undertook the education program in a former fire-control problem area.

Fire control is a continuing problem. Strong winds and long droughts can make fire control even more difficult, and malicious arson aggravates the problem. In November 1999 officials with the National Park Service and U.S. Forest Service reported that seven fires discovered in the Buffalo River scenic reserve were intentionally set.[60]

Farmers and other landowners practiced open-range grazing throughout the Ozark region for several years. Gradually, over many years, voters passed laws requiring confinement of animals. Sometimes they passed the laws countywide, and at other times piecemeal, by township. Often, voters enacted laws requiring confinement of small animals, but because landowners had to fence larger tracts to confine the larger animals, they allowed the latter to forage freely several years longer. Voters in Greene County, Missouri, passed the first stock-confinement law in the western Ozarks in 1890; confinement of hogs, goats, and sheep passed 3,364 to 1,980, but confinement of horses, mules, asses, and cattle passed by a narrower margin of 3,095 to 2,164. Voters enacted the last county stock law passed in Missouri in Stone County in 1960. This marked the end of open-range grazing except in some parts of the Mark Twain National Forest. Legislation passed January 1, 1969, by the Seventy-fourth General Assembly repealed all county-option stock laws, and prohibited open-range grazing throughout Missouri.[61] In the Arkansas Ozarks stock laws were nearly nonexistent before World War I and even by the end of the depression most townships enforced no stock laws. A 1938 study of two hundred Ozark farms in Arkansas reported 60 percent of the farmers continued to run cattle on the open range, or free range as they usually called it, and 80 percent of the townships in the study had no stock laws.[62]

The decline of open-range grazing has followed the development of commercial agriculture, especially livestock farming. Well-informed livestock farmers know that open-range grazing and good forage management are incompatible. However, even now, some counties in the interior Ozarks do not enforce livestock confinement laws rigidly.

Open range in the national forest is no longer legal, although most landowners have not practiced it for some time. Since, January 1, 1969, they have impounded stray cattle on Forest Service land, and the person who claimed them has been subjected to fine.[63] Because the national forest contains rocky balds and glades and grassland tracts where the forests have been cleared, the Forest Service leases land to individuals for summer and winter pasturage. Income from this helps support fire control and forest management, but one-fourth of it reverts to the county governments for construction and maintenance of roads.

The Forest Service practices several timber-management practices on government lands. Because most of the timber is slow growing and in some places commercial timber production is not possible, they manage much of the land for aesthetic and recreational purposes. Only on the better land is timber managed for commercial lumber production.

The Forest Service uses salvage and improvement cutting in commercial timber stands. Workers remove fire-damaged and diseased trees to make room for new growth and sell any salvaged usable wood. On good shortleaf pine sites, the Forest Service adopts a reforestation plan. This tree has a faster growth rate than the hardwoods, but it will grow well only where conditions are favorable.

The timber industry is important in Missouri, Arkansas, and Oklahoma. Missouri's more than 450 wood-using mills—sawmills, charcoal mills, cooperage mills, and many others—processed 140.5 million cubic feet of wood in 1997; only 6 percent of the wood came from other states. Most of the wood was cut in the eastern Ozarks region. Bollinger, Butler, Carter, Crawford, Dent, Iron, Madison, Oregon, Reynolds, Ripley, St. Francois, Shannon, Washington, and Wayne counties accounted for more than half the total.[64] They produce stave bolts, pallets, lumber, oak flooring, post and poles, and a small amount of dimension lumber, including some timber from the national forest, sold on the stump to the highest bidder. Trucks haul much of the timber considerable distance for milling. Pulp timber is hauled out of the eastern Ozarks by rail, truck, and river barge to paper mills on the lower Mississippi.

A few large wood products companies continue to operate. One such company is the Independent Stave Company in Lebanon, Missouri. The family-owned and -operated company, founded by T. W. Boswell in 1912 as a white-oak stave mill, has become the world's largest manufacturer of whiskey barrels. The company operates fifteen log buying yards throughout Missouri, Arkansas, Illinois, Indiana, and Kentucky. They ship high-quality white-oak stave bolts from their Missouri green mills at Buick, New Florence, and Salem to the barrel factory at Lebanon. The combined production of the Lebanon, Missouri, plant and a second subsidiary, Kentucky Cooperage, in Lebanon, Kentucky, is approximately four thousand barrels per day. The company also operates sawmills and barrel plants in France and Bulgaria. With its subsidiary, World Cooperage, the Independent Stave Company produces over half the world's oak barrels.[65]

Charcoal manufacturing, once a major industry when charcoal iron furnaces were operating in the region, regained some of its stature following World War II when

Cracking black walnuts by hand at Fordland, Missouri, 1931. (Courtesy of W. A. Hagel, Kansas City, Missouri.)

the backyard barbecue became popular. Much of the supply of wood comes from surplus slabwood (trimmings) from sawmills. Charcoal companies produce the charcoal in low-oxygen furnaces to drive off the water and gasses, without reducing the wood to ash. They haul much of the crude charcoal to the Kingsford Manufacturing Company near Belle, Missouri, where it is processed into briquettes and other marketable forms.

The glade lands, a natural grassy scrub-tree environment distinctive of the Ozarks, require special management, and the Forest Service has conducted research to decide the best long-range management practices for them, primarily for watershed protection, grazing, and aesthetic purposes. Foresters are studying management of red cedar (*Juniperus virginiana)* for market purposes intensively. Cedar's main uses are for fence posts, dimension lumber for closet linings, cedar chests and other special uses, and for tourist novelties.

The Forest Service permits wood harvest for firewood in prescribed areas, usually where thinning is needed. Persons wanting to cut wood must apply for a permit from the Forest Service. When the Forest Service grants a permit, they include a map showing the wood cutter the precise areas where they can harvest wood.

The wildlife and recreational values of the national forests cannot be calculated precisely. However, the forests are free for public use and people from Springfield, Kansas City, Tulsa, Memphis, Little Rock, St. Louis, and places even more distant travel the paved roads heavily on weekends and holidays. This is especially true in the spring, when the new foliage appears and the redbud and dogwood are in bloom, and again in the fall, when the forests

develop their autumn colors. Additional paved roads undoubtedly would facilitate fuller use of the more inaccessible parts of the forests for recreational purposes, but there would be a corresponding loss in aesthetic values. Visitors who choose to travel slow over the steep, rough, forest-crowded hillside trails, often crossing streams on gravel bars, find the least disturbed natural scenery the Ozarks has to offer.

On the whole, private landowners apply a low level of management to their forest lands. The prospects for quality timber are not good in many parts of the Ozarks; in the southwest they are poorer than anywhere else. Forty percent of the trees are culls, and another 30 percent should be harvested soon because they are too old or defective to manage for commercial products; only 30 percent are suitable for future management.[66]

Cutting practices are not conducive to sustained-yield timber production. While the forest is growing faster than they are cutting it—in Missouri regrowth timber volume amounted to 267 million cubic feet compared to 140.5 million cubic feet harvested in 1997—much of the growth is in small trees that may not be of much commercial value when mature.[67] Foresters have to keep a sharp eye on which species, which tree sizes, and which regions the growth and harvesting impact. While the volume in small trees continues to increase, they are cutting larger timber of preferred species, both hardwoods and pine, at a faster rate than it is growing. The supply of high-quality timber has declined steadily over the years, and unless this trend is reversed, local timber industries may encounter a shortage of good-quality timber.

Most owners do not expect to gain sustained revenue from woodlands. They regard the occasional receipts from

Walnut huller at a crossroads store, 1972. (Milton Rafferty Collection, photograph by the author.)

the sale of stave-bolt-quality oak, veneer-quality walnut, or the sale of black walnuts for hulling purposes as windfall money or perhaps as a reserve source of income for emergencies.

A few private owners are vindictive toward the national forest. Often the low regard for the U.S. Forest Service springs from ignorance of the benefits that can accrue through good management techniques and from misinformation concerning the operations of the Forest Service. One property owner whose land borders on the national forest remarked that he was inclined not to like the Forest Service because "they pay no taxes to keep up the roads."[68] He also expressed the belief that forest management, as practiced by the Forest Service, was unprofitable, and he did not like the fire-control crews "to come running every time I burn." He said that he recognized that burning in the spring is not considered a good forest- and range-management practice, but he felt the losses were small and believed burning the woods helped to control ticks, chiggers, and copperheads. Attitudes like this represent an element of persistence of a traditional, if not pioneer, notion of man-land relationships.

Forest management on private lands has been aided by the state conservation departments. Conservation or forest and wildlife management departments were founded in all of the Ozark states by the 1940s to promote wildlife and forest conservation and to furnish fire protection and technical advice to property owners. Throughout the heavily forested parts of the Ozarks, the commissions maintain aerial fire surveillance backed up by trained fire-control crews.

The Farm Forester Program provides technical advice on timber management to private owners in Missouri. Two years after the Missouri Conservation Commission created a forestry division, the state legislature passed the State Forestry Law of 1946.[69] A major part of the law was the forest cropland program, which provides incentives for long-range management of farm woodlands. Woodland tracts that meet certain qualifications may be declared forest cropland and are thereafter subject to small property taxation until the landowner harvests the timber. When they harvest the timber, the state applies a yield tax, based on the value of the stumpage. These acts grant the state additional powers in helping landowners in the enforcement of state laws on timber theft, a continuing problem on both public and private land.

While small owners hold most of the privately owned forest land, large acreages are owned and managed by corporations and other large private owners. For example, the St. Joseph Lead Company and other large mining companies acquired large acreages of forest land in the mineral districts. In years past, when the iron and lead smelting industries relied on charcoal for fuel and reduction of the ores, access to timber was essential. The Doe Run Mining Company still owns and manages large forest tracts in the eastern Ozarks near their lead and zinc mining operations. Private citizens sometimes purchase forest land for their own hunting and recreational use. For example, the St. Louis Game and Agricultural Park in Taney County was founded 1891 by officers of the Liggett and Meyers Tobacco Company in St. Louis.[70] By 1896 they had built a clubhouse and introduced wildlife and forest conservation practices on their five-thousand-acre tract on the White River southeast of Mincy.

Today, the largest private owner of Ozark forest land is Leo Drey. He owns 155,000 acres that he calls the Pioneer Forest. Drey's interest in the outdoors led him to purchase oak and pine forest land in the hills of Dent, Reynolds, Ripley, Shannon, Texas, and Carter counties. The self-taught forester and former stockholder in the Wohl Shoe Company in St. Louis began buying land in the Ozarks when he could buy it for two to five dollars an acre. His largest purchase was in 1954, when he purchased nearly 90,000 acres from National Distillers, a New York company harvesting Ozark white oaks for whiskey barrels. His extensive holdings, which he manages as the Pioneer Forest headquartered in Salem, Missouri, make him the largest landowner in Missouri and the Ozarks.

Drey was concerned about the condition of the Ozark forest after it was stripped of timber and wildlife, burned over repeatedly, and severely eroded. His conservation ethic led him to adopt many practices used in the Mark Twain National Forest and land-management practices recommended by the Missouri Department of Conservation and the Missouri Department of Natural Resources. In an article by Mary Still in the *Missouri Resource Review,* Drey explained, "I wanted to show you could grow timber economically in the Ozarks in a conservation style of land management."[71] The management practices of the Ozark Forest include watchful fire control and selective cutting, rather than the clear-cutting practices of the national forest. With selective cutting or "improvement cutting," as Drey calls it, the property is surveyed tree by tree looking for defective trees.

Drey also founded the LAD Foundation to purchase such natural and historic areas as the Rocky Hollow Petroglyph area, 192 acres in Monroe County, Hickory Creek Canyons in Ste. Genevieve County, and Dillard Mill in Crawford County. The foundation leases the 130-acre Dillard Mill tract to the Missouri Department of Natural Resources for one dollar, enabling the state to manage the land as a state historic site.[72]

Besides a few large private landowners, several not-for-profit groups engage in projects for conservation and preservation of the Ozark forest. For example, the Lucy James Foundation, in cooperation with the Missouri Department of Conservation, manages the Maramec Iron Works properties and forest lands near St. James, Missouri. In 1991, the Nature Conservancy financed the $10 million purchase of 80,819 acres of forest land in Shannon, Carter, and Wayne counties from the Kerr-McGee Corporation, a manufacturer of railroad ties and other forest products.[73] They then sold the land to the Missouri Department of Conservation on a five-year purchase plan. The Missouri Conservation Department will manage the land to protect its natural heritage and to provide uses such as hiking, hunting, timber harvest, and nature study.

Solutions to the problems of managing forest resources and producing and using wood products lie with timber owners and the industries that harvest and process these products. Nonfarm ownership of forest land is increasing steadily. People often purchase land for purposes other than timber production; probably most urban buyers expect higher recreational value in addition to capital gain as land values increase. Advertisements for Ozark recreational land appear daily in the newspapers of Springfield, St. Louis, Joplin, Kansas City, Little Rock, Tulsa, and in smaller places.[74] Buyers purchase it for hunting land, recreational estates or potential home sites in tracts of ten to forty acres, and sometimes in larger acreages. Unless changes in ownership result in consolidation of some of these holdings, the management decisions made by owners of small tracts of timber will largely determine the future of the forest resources of the area.

Three forest-management trends promise increased returns from forest land: (1) *Establishment and management of planted and mature stands of black walnut.* The rate of planting has increased since about 1970. The Forest Service planted many thousands of seedlings each year in the Mark Twain and Ozark national forests as part of a twenty-year improvement program. Improvement and management of seedling walnut are becoming more common on private lands. Hammonds Products Company, a producer of native black walnut kernels, has developed strains of improved black walnuts on their experimental farm near Stockton, Missouri, to ensure a continuing supply of better-quality black walnuts.[75] A small amount of revenue can be earned from walnut trees by gathering and selling the nuts. (2) *More plantings of shortleaf pine.* Nearly all have been on public lands. In Mark Twain National Forest, they plant more than a million pine seedlings each year and another twelve hundred acres per year are direct-seeded to pine. (3) *Conversion of unproductive timberland to grass through aerial spraying and bulldozing.* Aerial spraying proved successful at the Union Gap Experiment Station in the Mark Twain National Forest to convert unproductive timberland to pasture. However, as noted previously, spraying has gone out of favor compared with the 1970s, but farmers and ranchers practice bulldozing of wooded acres on private land widely.

During the 1990s large national forest industry firms introduced a new development in lumbering in the southeastern United States when they built woodchip mills. Woodchip mills turn whole logs into woodchips for making paper, particle board, rayon, and other products. According to one environmental group, the Missouri Coalition for the Environment, in their *1998 Environmental Briefing Book: A Guide for the Missouri State Legislature,* a single chip mill can convert one hundred truckloads of trees a day into woodchips.[76] In 1996 more than 1.2 million acres were clear-cut to feed 140 chip mills in the southeastern states. The largest chip mills can harvest wood from more than one hundred acres per day.

The chip mill frontier is now pushing into the Ozarks. Ozark Wood Fiber, Inc., is operating a small woodchip mill near Goodman in McDonald County. It is a small mill, and some of its activities may even be helpful to forest management by providing a market for salvage wood and small trees cut while thinning the forest. The mill buys mainly slabwood from sawmills and cull logs. In September 2000 the mill was paying five dollars a bundle for slabwood and fourteen dollars each for cull logs.[77] Willamette Industries of Portland, Oregon, is building a large facility in Wayne County at Mill Spring near the site of the first sawmill built by the Missouri Lumber and Mining Company. Other possible chip mill locations include Canal Chip Corporation at Scott City a few miles south of Cape Girardeau.[78] This mill lies just beyond the Ozark border, but since large woodchip mills harvest trees within seventy-five to one hundred miles of the plant, the catchment area for timber purchase would likely include several counties in the southeastern Ozarks. The two largest mills combined can produce close to 600,000 tons of woodchips each year, which is equivalent to harvesting some 30 acres of forest a day.[79] Two additional chip mills are under study by the Georgia Pacific Company at Willow Springs in Howell County and farther north at Belle in Maries County.[80]

Chip mills are controversial because they can strip thousands of acres of forest land in a comparatively short time span. Customarily, the large mills purchase or lease large blocks of land, and then lease the land to loggers. Mill companies pay the loggers for the logs they harvest and deliver to the mill. The system resembles the sharecropping system used in the South and the landowner-miner share practices used in the old Ozark mining districts. At the turn of the twenty-first century, Willamette Industries had already bought some 26,000 acres in Missouri and had requested permission to cut on the Mark Twain National Forest as well. The chip mill industry also buys trees, both pines and hardwoods, from landowners. Since individual landowners control about three-fourths of the region's forests, the potential to harvest large acreages is very high. The temptation of short-term gain will surely be strong for some landowners.[81]

Most objections to chip mills relate to their potential negative environmental impact. Because woodchip mills have no stringent demands as to size and species of trees for pulpwood, clear-cutting is commonly used. Many people have concerns about the impact of removal of all forest cover; namely, soil erosion and the increase in soil load in streams, along with related deterioration of water quality, and damage to aquatic wildlife; problems associated with tannic acid leachate from massive woodchip stockpiles; threats to songbirds, which are already declining; and the destruction of food and habitat for deer, black bear, turkey, and other woodland wildlife. Environmentalists claim that for twenty-five years after a clear-cut, the area can support almost no wildlife since mature, hard mast- (nut-) producing trees are destroyed. Destruction of the scenic beauty of the forest would have a major impact on the attractiveness of the region for tourists and for the local inhabitants. Also, the downstream economic impact of removing young trees that would make tomorrow's lumber is troubling to many industries—sawmills, barrel stave mills, furniture manufacturers, charcoal manufacturers—who depend on the traditional mature timber industry. In Missouri, the growing concern about the potential destructiveness of the woodchip mills prompted several environmental groups and concerned citizens to call for a moratorium on new woodchip mills until the full impact of their operations could be

studied more carefully. There was also a movement to require high-capacity chip mills to apply for Individual Operating Permits rather than the General Operating Permit granted by the Missouri Department of Natural Resources to small timber operators.[82]

The future of woodchip mills in the Ozarks remains a highly charged political issue that will likely require additional study and compromise before the issue of clearcutting is resolved. Currently, the various interest groups concerned with the issue—environmental groups, state and federal agencies, chip mill owners, landowners, and concerned citizens—are involved in lobbying and negotiations with legislators and government officials to develop a workable plan to allow chip mills to operate without doing irreparable harm to the region's natural resources.

An even more intractable threat to the Ozarks forest, particularly to the mighty oaks, is the red oak borer beetle, a drab, easily overlooked insect that blends in with the bark of the trees. This one-inch-long borer has inflicted heavy damage to oaks in Arkansas and is already at home in several counties in Missouri. It is a native insect that has gone beyond its natural controls, mainly woodpeckers and other predators. Sawmill operators claim that borer damage can ruin as much as half the lumber in a log. Foresters in Missouri and Arkansas fear the long-range effects on game habitat, the danger for hunters and hikers from falling dead timber, and even the possibility that oaks will decline as a dominant tree in the Ozark forests. The longrange losses for oak-based wood products industries would likely run into millions of dollars. A June 2001 aerial survey in Arkansas's Ozark National Forest indicated that the beetle has affected 300,000 of the forest's 1.4 million acres.[83] Entomologists are not optimistic about controlling red oak beetle damage since the insect is native and is not a leaf eater and therefore not easily treatable with insecticides. Recent droughts are thought to have made the trees more susceptible to the beetles.

TWELVE

RECREATION AND TOURISM

It is difficult to separate the booming Ozarks tourist-recreation industry into its component parts. Recreation and tourism go hand in hand, and the growing second-home and retirement-home industry is part of the same package. When all the ancillary services and multiplier effects on employment are considered, it is a multi-billion-dollar industry in the Ozarks.

Considered in its popular sense, recreation includes all the leisure-time activities that people pursue for their own pleasure. In all periods of history, men and women probably have spent the greater part of their leisure in informal talk, in visiting and entertaining friends, in casual walks and strolls, and sometimes in reading for their own amusement. These simpler activities are hidden in the obscurity that shrouds private lives, however; organized public recreation consciously has been adopted as the basis for this account.

Before we progress into discussion of the historical geography of Ozark tourism and recreation, reviewing the factors that have influenced the development of these industries in the United States will be helpful.[1] First is the continuing influence of inherent puritanism, which, even today, insists that amusements should at least make some pretense of serving socially useful ends: to keep fit; for education; to promote higher cultural standards; to recapture one's inherited past. Second, our economy has been transformed from the simplicity of the agricultural era to the complexity of the machine age. Concomitantly, cities have grown and the machine has increased the leisure of the laboring masses, simultaneously making life less leisurely.

We will discuss the forms of traditional entertainment practiced by Ozarkers in a later chapter, but at this point we can state that in the years before the Civil War the first Ozark settlers shared a common heritage with most rural Americans. However, while they discouraged dancing, gaming, cockfighting, and horse racing in New England and other sections of the country, these forms of entertainment were common in the more relaxed society on the Ozark frontier.[2] Hunting and fishing were very popular, as were camp meetings and the usual church services.

Professor Robert Gilmore's book illuminated a surprisingly rich body of nineteenth-century Ozark theatrical folkways, which all but disappeared in the twentieth century.[3] In the cities, organized sports become popular, and theater forged ahead. Circuses were very popular. Horse races, foot races, rowing and sailing, and prizefighting became important spectator sports for the masses. If women had any leisure time, they took up embroidery, quilting, painting on glass or china, and waxwork.[4] They often formed women's clubs to further their skills and their social contacts.[5]

By mid-century, pleasure travel had been well established, and the first summer resorts had been built. The new trend had been signaled in 1825 with the appearance of a little booklet called *The Fashionable Tour.*[6] The establishment of summer resorts in the East came as a direct result of improved transportation. New York had the most fashionable of all: Saratoga Springs. In the South, White Sulphur Springs was the place where wealthy plantation owners made their hegira. Many of these visitors were seeking not so much rest or amusement as the establishment of their position in the social world. Wrote one astute observer:

> Hundreds, who, in their own towns could not find admittance into the circle of fashionable society came to Saratoga where . . . they may be seated at the same table, and often side by side, with the first families of the country.[7]

The deep verandahs of the huge, sprawling Congress House and the United States Hotel and the neat gravel walks cutting across Saratoga's spacious, well-mowed lawns served as models for accommodations at resorts that sprung up throughout the United States.[8] The style and grace of the great resorts, with their courting yards, frock-coated gentlemen, and modish ladies in billowing hoop skirts, have never been equaled in the history of American recreation and tourism.

Probably more than any other single factor, the automobile and construction of good roads revolutionized

American tourism and recreation. At first automobiles were for the rich, not so much because of the initial cost, but because of the cost of upkeep. In the early days of auto touring, drivers made vast preparations for a day's run. Among the items of necessary extra equipment were a full set of tools, elaborate tire-changing apparatus, a pail of water for overheated brakes, extra spark plugs, tire chains for muddy roads, and a rear basket with a concealed reserve gasoline supply.[9] Special motoring clothes were both functional and stylish. A hundred miles was considered an excellent day's run, and even then there had to be a lot of "sprinting" at thirty miles an hour to get over such a long distance.

By the 1930s the total number of automobiles on the road had reached twenty-five million, enough that two-thirds of the nation's families had one.[10] The automobile of the 1930s was longer and lower, showing a definite trend toward streamlining, and with a larger more powerful engine it could pull a trailer, which by now had made its appearance as a further boon to vacationists.

After World War II the Sunday-afternoon spin, which had become so popular before the war, became a weekend trip, then the vacation tour that could easily span the continent. Apart from the new freeways, turnpikes, throughways, interstate highways, and the new cars themselves, tourist accommodations underwent spectacular development. Primitive overnight cabins gave way to the luxurious motels demanded by an increasingly affluent society.

At the same time, the automobile continued—in what was called Operation Outdoors—to encourage camping in national parks and forests.[11] Hundreds of thousands of vacationing families in heavily laden sedans, pickup campers, vans, and motor homes set out intrepidly every summer to explore the wilds. Because of the large number of lakes built in all sections of the country, more vehicles now pull boats of assorted types. In the Ozarks, the lakes spawned a growing aluminum boat manufacturing industry. In short, the automobile has given an entirely new dimension to recreation life, which could hardly be more universal in reaching all strata of the nation's population.

TOURISM IN THE OZARKS

From a geographic standpoint, the Ozarks possess unusually good resources for recreation and tourism. The Ozark-Ouachita region is the only major upland area in the midsection of the country west of the Mississippi River. For people traveling by automobile, it is the principal hilly region for many who have only a three- or four-day weekend to spend. Des Moines, Omaha, St. Louis, Kansas City, Memphis, Little Rock, Dallas, Fort Worth, Tulsa,

Oklahoma City, Wichita, and Topeka are all within an easy day's drive of some part of the Ozarks. In a long day's drive, tourists from Chicago can reach the Ozarks. It is from these large cities and their environs that most of the visitors to the Ozarks are drawn.

The region has tremendous variety in scenic beauty. The landscape is remarkably picturesque, with uplands broken into hills by beautiful water courses. Rivers and small streams that flow into the branching arms of more than a dozen large reservoirs have carved bedrock limestones into sharp relief. Hardwoods, mainly oaks, but with scattered clumps of maple, sycamore, and sumac cover most of the hills and lend brilliant color to autumn scenery. Cedar glades, stands of pine, and grassy balds add scenic variety to panoramic views. The climate is mild compared to that of the middle western states, and many of the region's attractions are related to the seasonal change in climate. Automobile touring is especially popular in April, when the dogwood is in bloom, and in the late October, when the varied hardwoods produce their flaming fall display. Nevertheless, the chief climatic disadvantage for the tourism-recreation business is the fact that the winters are too cold for many outdoor activities and snowfall is too light to support winter sports. Many tourist-recreation attractions shut down four or five months and use the slack season to make repairs, build additions, and prepare for the next summer season.

For many the culture and history of the Ozarks is a major attraction. The so-called hillbilly culture, whether real or imagined, has gained wide reputation, and thousands of men and women with hideaway tendencies and preference for casual living have found the Ozarks a pleasant refuge. Furthermore, compared to many other recreation areas, the cost of an Ozarks vacation is usually less.

For purposes of discussion, I have divided tourism and recreation in the Ozarks into seven sections: Nature Tourism; Touring; Health Spas and Springs; Rivers and Float Trips; Hunting and Wilderness Sports; Lakes; and Promotion and Attraction Development. An eighth subdivision is a summary of the tourism-recreation regions of the Ozarks.

NATURE TOURISM

Pinpointing the precise beginning of tourism in the Ozarks is difficult. Several writers have labeled various events as the starting point for the Ozark tourism industry. Most observers would agree that Ozark tourism antedates the great upsurge in country music theaters of the 1970s and 1980s. They recognize that today's live country music phenomenon grew out of a strong base of established tourism. Some see the construction of large dams and reservoirs as the starting point for tourism.[12] For the Branson area, the publication of Harold Bell Wright's novel, *Shepherd of the Hills,* is considered a landmark event that marked the beginning of the tourism era.[13] Others claim that the rapid rise of the automobile and the great road-building boom of the 1920s heralded the beginning of Ozarks tourism.[14] One longtime Ozark resident picked July 1, 1919, as the date for the start of tourism because on that day they threw the switch at Powersite Dam at Lake Taneycomo to send electricity coursing through the Ozarks.[15] He argued that "tourism as we know it today did not begin until electricity and air-conditioning availability made comfortable sleeping quarters a possibility during hot Missouri summers."[16] While it is true that some Ozark towns near Lake Taneycomo were first served by electrical power in 1919, we have seen that many communities were enjoying electricity twenty years before that time. Others had to wait another twenty years or more for electricity and air conditioning.[17]

Like most important industries, modern Ozark tourism has grown out of a number of events and processes of change over more than a century of time, and we cannot tie its origin to a single event or point in time. Tourism clearly began in some parts of the Ozarks well before the beginning of the twentieth century. Much of nineteenth-century tourism was for those who could afford long absences from their work and wanted the experience of a wilderness adventure. They employed guides to navigate streams, to point out the good fishing spots, to find places where deer and turkey were likely to be found, and what was most important, to cook the meals, set up tents, and handle all the logistical matters. Wealthy easterners had worked out the pattern for this type of tourism fifty years before in the Adirondacks and northern Appalachians where they built large hunting estates and great lodges.[18]

Intrepid tourists, those with a liking for semi-frontier conditions in the woods and the solitude of fishing pristine waters, found their way into the Ozarks when railroads penetrated the region and made travel easy. Shortly after the Civil War, by 1869, the St. Louis and Iron Mountain Railroad was promoting tourism in the Arcadia Valley by offering special weekend rates and by publishing information about the beauty and serenity of the St. Francois Mountains. Their promotional literature included mention of the history of Fort Davidson and the battle fought there just five years before. They also gave travelers information about the hotel accommodations in Arcadia and Ironton and about the attractions in the surrounding area.[19]

Tourism for the elite nineteenth-century visitors to the Arcadia Valley was genteel compared with the outdoor adventures in the interior. Popular activities included horseback riding and a coach ride or short bicycle excursions to historical sites and other points of interest, followed by a picnic or dinner at a guest house, a hotel, or a summer house. The first visitors took lodging in the Ironton House Hotel, or the Arcadia Hotel or boardinghouses and private residences. They toured the valley on horseback and by buggy, hiked to the summit of Shepherd Mountain, bicycled to the Elephant Rocks and visited the nearby granite quarries, frolicked in the rapids at Stout's Creek Shut-in, toured the Pilot Knob mine, and traveled north to Iron Mountain where they could view the impressive hydraulic mining operations.[20] Other popular destinations were Taum Sauk Mountain, the highest point in Missouri, and Johnson's Shut-ins on the Black River near Ellington.

Three closely spaced towns—Pilot Knob, Ironton, and Arcadia—offered their own attractions. Pilot Knob, the mining town, attracted Welch, Scotch, German, Italian, and Hungarian miners.[21] Ironton, the county seat and the site of a United States land office, became the chief commercial center in the valley. Arcadia, a "suburban" hamlet, included summer homes for visitors from St. Louis among the houses owned by permanent residents. By the mid-1870s, special Sunday excursion trains brought hundreds of passengers for one-day outings while hotels and sleeping rooms satisfied weekend visitors.[22] Just as Cape May was the summer retreat for Philadelphians, the Arcadia Valley was where St. Louisans found their escape and recreation. Often families would remain in the valley for several weeks at a time while the men commuted by train from their work in St. Louis.

In the 1930s, when roads were better and more of the middle class were driving automobiles, enterprising Ozarkers developed tourist farms and fishing camps. The Meramec River, along with its attractive tributaries—Bourbeuse River, Courtois Creek, and Huzzah Creek—were very popular with St. Louis visitors because of their proximity. Farmers often supplemented their income by constructing and renting out rustic cabins for weekend visitors and summer vacationers.

Professor Donald McInnis grew up on a Huzzah Creek farm that added tourist accommodations to become Cedar Farm Lodge. His father, John Haskell McInnis, moved the family to the Huzzah farm when he lost his teller's job in the Steelville bank. The bank failed during the great rash of bank failures in the 1930s. Years before, probably around 1910, Professor McInnis's grandfather, Donald McInnis, had equipped four upstairs rooms in the large two-story farmhouse with brass numbers on the doors and rented them out to weekend and summer visitors, mainly from St. Louis. To supplement the McInnis family income from the farm and from the Huzzah general store the family operated, John Haskell McInnis reopened the resort business. As business warranted, they built several cabins, the largest of which had four rooms. Professor McInnis recalls:

> Since the cabins had no running water and at best a light bulb, the operative word for them was "rustic." I remember old bedsteads and their springs, some rudimentary furniture, a large water pitcher and matching basin, and underbed chamber pots. There were two outhouses sitting side-by-side on the north bank of the branch which flowed from the hills to the east.[23]

The electric lights were powered by a large gasoline/oil (semi diesel) Delco generator housed in its own building behind the house. The electrical energy was stored in a dozen large batteries hooked in line and when the lights grew dim, the "Delco Plant" had to be started up. A large spring supplied drinking water needs. The spring had its own building and a pump provided running water in the house.

The chief attraction for visitors was the fishing on Huzzah Creek. The McInnis children seined the Huzzah for the "top water" and "shiner" minnows that the anglers used for bait. The Huzzah was a clear stream, and there were some good fishing holes where anglers could catch large bass. The "Blue Hole" upstream from the farm was one of the favorite fishing spots. Cedar Farm Lodge was a summer enterprise only, since there was no heat in the upstairs rooms in the house or in the cabins. Summer was very busy, what with haying, threshing, livestock raising, fence building, silage making, and all the other work of the farm and the Huzzah store and post office. As on all farms, the whole family worked. For a time, when a renter operated the farm, he hired a black man to do the cooking for the guests, but the McInnis family managed to do all the work themselves. The lodge business was abandoned sometime in the 1940s. After a time the cabins were used to house livestock and to store corn and for other general purposes. Years later, Richard "Dick" McInnis, who still resides on the farm, discovered a piece of sheet metal while tearing down a hog house. When he turned it face up he discovered it was the "Cedar Farm Lodge" sign that had directed tourists to Huzzah.[24]

Other summer lodges in the Meramec basin dating from about the same time have continued operating down to the present. Adjoining the Cedar Farm Lodge on the north and south was Eagle-Hurst Ranch, which has operated from the 1930s to the present. Sam Hicks, an executive with the Hobart Company, started the business, and his son and daughter-in-law operated it.[25] The large resort has provided summer employment for young people for more than sixty years. Eagle-Hurst Ranch provided guided fishing "float trips" in johnboats and rented canoes for runs down Huzzah Creek and the Meramec River. Guide service rarely included gigging trips since the city sportsmen were mainly summer visitors and showed little interest in going out on frosty nights to try spearing fish.[26] Gigging remained a sport mainly for the native Ozarkers.

Marian Rymers established an unusual farm resort in 1914 in the wild region near the Devil's Backbone and the Jacks Fork River. The Devil's Backbone is a scenic showplace in one of the wildest sections of Shannon County. Marion Rymers was a young woman when her family purchased a 240-acre tract of wild hill country along the Jacks Fork as a healthful retreat for her blind mother. After hacking out a road to the property, she cut timber and constructed a log house for the family to live in. When friends came to visit, liked the area, and made return visits, she decided to build cabins for guests. The spectacular scenery, the river, and her home-cooked food, especially the fried chicken, which was her specialty, kept the cabins full in the summer. Visitors also came in the fall and spring when hunting and fishing were good. Most of the food for guests—chicken, garden vegetables, ham, bacon, and beef—was produced on the farm. In 1928, when the *St. Louis Globe-Democrat Magazine* ran a feature story on the "cowgirl" who had built a successful mountain resort, the Rymer Ranch had twelve cabins and a large dining hall and could accommodate one hundred guests at a time.[27]

At about the same time that resorts were first founded, wealthy visitors established hunting estates. Midwesterners purchased land in the Ozarks for hunting, hiking, and nature study just as wealthy easterners had purchased land in the Adirondacks and Appalachians half a century before. The rugged terrain, clear streams, and the forests that harbored wildlife—deer, turkey, quail, squirrel, rabbit—were inducements for individuals and groups who wanted a place to hunt or simply to enjoy the outdoors. Often land speculators used their properties for hunting and recreation while waiting for buyers. They could purchase cutover timberland cheap from lumbering companies who were anxious to rid themselves of the tax burden. By the 1890s the largest blocks of remaining government land were in the southern Ozarks, in southern Missouri and northern Arkansas.

The St. Louis Game Park in Taney County, Missouri, was one of the better-known game parks and resorts, and from a conservation standpoint one of the most influential. It was founded in 1891 when a club of St. Louis men, officers in the Liggett and Meyers Tobacco Company, formed the St. Louis Park and Agricultural Company.[28] Game parks were common in the forested eastern states by that time, just as game farms are today in places like the central Texas hill country and the Edwards Plateau where ranchers manage native and exotic animals for both conservation and fee hunting. Following the pattern established in the eastern states, the club hired a game manager, William F. Hunt, and introduced both native and exotic animals. Hunt oversaw the management of several species of deer—native, red, blacktail, and fallow—and introduced Mongolian pheasants to share range with the resident turkey and quail. The native elk and buffalo were no longer ranging the Ozarks, but elk were purchased from an Illinois game park and released in the Taney County game park in 1896, the same year that corporate secretary J. P. Litton announced to readers of *Forest and Stream* that the St. Louis Game Park had grown to include five thousand acres.

A number of dignitaries and men influential in the conservation movement visited the park. Missouri Republican governor Herbert Hadley and Jesse Tolerton, the future Missouri game and fish commissioner, visited the game park and stayed in the eight-room hunting lodge on top of a local bald overlooking the White River. The club president, Moses Wetmore, was heavily involved in Democrat Party politics and was a close friend of William Jennings Bryan, three-time Democrat presidential nominee. When Bryan visited the park in 1896, the party included Governor William J. Stone of Missouri, the Missouri Democratic state chairman Sam B. Cook, Senator James K. Jones of Arkansas, and political dignitaries from as far away as Michigan.[30] Guests customarily traveled by train to Chadwick in eastern Christian County and then traveled by wagon to the game park near Mincy in Taney County. It is reported in *Christian County: Its First Hundred Years* that when Bryan's party arrived at the game park local men in the area took them on a coon hunt. It was a cold and rainy night, and when the hunters and hounds trailed into camp Bryan and the other guests crowded around the crackling campfire to dry out. They soon learned the hillmen's priorities.

Native hunters were astounded and outraged and firmly ordered Mr. Bryan and his entourage to step back from the fire so the wet dogs could come close to its warmth. Proud to entertain a presidential candidate, even a Democratic one, these Republican hillmen might be but not to the point of risking distemper for their hound dogs![31]

Visitors sometimes purchased large properties for sporting clubs. In 1905, a group of investors established one such sporting club in Taney County on the present site of the College of the Ozarks near Hollister. The club moved the impressive Maine Building from the 1904 World's Fair in St. Louis to a magnificent vertical bluff overlooking the White River on the property they had purchased.[32] Because of its unusual clubhouse, the members appropriately named the club the Maine Hunting and Fishing Club. Its members and guests could easily visit the park since the White River Railroad reached Hollister the following year. In 1915 the Maine Club building became the new home of the School of the Ozarks when they moved it from Forsyth.[33]

No doubt the game parks and sporting clubs served many purposes for the members—social, recreational, financial—as well as satisfying their desire to fish and hunt wild game. They also served conservation, for it was on the game parks that some of the first experimentations with game management began. Many biologists and other people interested in game management and restoration visited the parks. It is not too much to say that the game parks helped to give birth to the conservation agencies and government fish and game management departments in the Ozark states.

TOURING

Among the first tourists to visit the Ozarks were bicyclists. The bicycle craze was born in Europe in the 1860s when Pierre and Ernest Michaux, baby-carriage makers in Paris, fitted two pedals to the front wheel of what they then knew as the *velocipede*. By 1875 the ordinary American bicycle had become the one with a very large front wheel, directly driven by pedals, and a very small rear wheel. Manufacturers produced the first Rover safety bicycle in England in 1885. It was smaller and safer, and when John B. Dunlop developed the pneumatic tire, the new safety bicycles soon replaced the old high wheelers.

In the 1880s, midwestern and Ozarks bicycle enthusiasts joined the rest of the country in pushing membership in the National League of American Wheelmen. The league was organized in 1880, and memberships in state chapters had grown to an all-time high just before the turn of the century. St. Louis had the biggest membership in Missouri, but many members were from small towns. By 1895 the Missouri Chapter of the League of American Wheelmen had published a guidebook for Missouri.[34] It had information for each county on road conditions, difficulty of travel, and the names of hotels with prices for accommodations and meals. These intrepid tourists, some still riding their cantankerous high-wheeled bicycles, battled rocky rutted roads and waded bridgeless streams to take in the Ozark scene.

Early bicycle tourism was for the physically fit and adventurous. The divided skirt for female riders was introduced just when some conservative citizens had hopes of curbing the growing tendency of mail-order catalogs to include pictures of men and women in underwear.[35] Of all the tourists who have visited the Ozarks, the early bicyclists, who traveled slow and stopped for rests, sometimes staying in private homes when no commercial lodging was available, witnessed the Ozarks just as it was beginning its transition from a pristine and natural condition to a region of farms, lumber mills, and mines. Mass tourism arrived later when more convenient and comfortable transportation became available to specific areas or to developed tourist sites. Thus the development of tourism has been and continues to be uneven, arriving early in some locations and later in other places.

Only a few Missourians owned automobiles in 1900. At St. Louis in 1901 three automobiles raced a horse at the St. Louis Retail Grocers' picnic and the horse won.[36] Newspapers were reporting that motoring was a "sport for the elite," and the wealthy eastern set called automobile touring "bubbling." By 1904 Washington Boulevard, from Grand to Taylor avenues, had become one of the favorite automobiling spots. It became very popular as ever more companies were founded to produce automobiles—Dorris, Everett, Columbia, Moon, Dragon, Haynes, Peerless, Baker Electric, Richmond, Stoddard-Dayton, Brush, Regal, Chalmers-Detroit, Maxwell-Brisco, Packard, Reo, Pierce-Arrow, Studebaker, Ford, to name a few. By 1914 only Carter, Douglas, Ozark, and Reynolds among Missouri counties had no automobiles, and in 1918 Missouri could claim 170,000 automobiles registered in the state.[37] The automobile soon became a tool for recreation as well as a means of travel for essential things. Carl Sauer, the eminent geographer who grew up near Warrenton, Missouri, recalled the early days of recreational use of automobiles.

When the first automobiles came to my home town there existed a single stretch of eight miles of smooth road to a neighboring town. People who had cars soon formed the habit of evening drives back and forth over this stretch for the sheer exhilaration of rapid motion, not in order to get to another place.[38]

As the number of automobiles and trucks increased so did the agitation for improved roads, and by the 1920s the roads had been improved and interconnected enough that

automobile clubs—the Automobile Association of America, the Automobile Club of Missouri, and automobile clubs in Kansas City and St. Louis—published maps for travelers. The automobile clubs and civic groups began to sponsor organized automobile tours. Groups from Kansas City made the trip to Branson in two days, with an overnight stop in Carthage or Joplin. The Rotary Club of Joplin sponsored a ninety-mile automobile trip to Eureka Springs, Arkansas, in the fall of 1919. The trip took the entire day. In 1919 when William "Coin" Harvey served as president of the Ozark Trails Association, club members laid out a tourist route called the "Ozark Trail" across southern Missouri through Rolla, Licking, Houston, Cabool, Mountain Grove, Mansfield, Seymour, Springfield, Republic, Mount Vernon, Stotts City, and Joplin.[39] The tourist trail then continued to Arkansas passing through Bentonville, Springdale, and Fayetteville. Coin Harvey's Monte Ne resort was just a few miles east of Bentonville.[40]

Boosters proposed a north-south highway called "the Pershing Way" in 1921 to extend from Winnepeg, Canada, to New Orleans, Louisiana. They proposed two routes through the Ozarks, one passing south from Jefferson City through Dent, Shannon, and Oregon counties, the other farther west through Rolla, Houston, Cabool, Willow Springs, and West Plains.[41] In Arkansas the highway continued through Mammoth Spring and Hardy before leaving the Ozarks. The eastern route roughly paralleled today's state Highway 19; the western route, the one that was finally selected, followed the route of U.S. 63. They marked the Pershing Way with large white signs with a large letter "P" emblazoned on them. Towns along the way were expected to benefit from sales of food items, gasoline, cabin and hotel rentals, and tourist souvenirs.

From the 1920s through the 1950s, with a hiatus during the gasoline rationing years during World War II, highway boosterism was very active on the part of associations and individual towns along the various routes. During the same time, many highways leading to the vacation lands in the Rocky Mountains and the West Coast—the Lincoln Highway (U.S. 30), U.S. 40, U.S. 36 (the shortcut to Denver)—became household names. The most famous of all, Route 66, the so-called Mother Road, passed through the Ozarks. During its heyday in the 1930s and 1940s it spawned hundreds of tourist businesses and even small tourist communities like Hooker and Clementine (Basketville) where local craftspeople sold baskets and other hand-made items.[42]

Most travelers found their way to the Ozarks on their own, by rail or by automobile. A few arrived by bus during the period when bus companies served the growing resort areas with good service. Since most visitors had their own vehicles, they did not deem guided tours necessary. One exception was the guided bus tour service established by Pearl Spurlock of Branson, Missouri. The density of attractions was greater in the Branson area, and by the 1920s many people were arriving by rail and needed local transportation. Spurlock started the business with her "Shepherd of the Hills Taxi" in 1923. The tour typically covered Branson, including the waterfront on Lake Taneycomo where the tour boat "Sammy Lane" docked, Hollister, School of the Ozarks, and the many points of interest relating to Harold Bell Wright's novel, *Shepherd of the Hills.* The tour included a nonstop lecture on the various points of interest, the "true" stories of the people who became characters in the novel, and a good measure of local culture, humor, and "hillbilly" sayings.

In 1939 Pearl Spurlock published part of her tour lectures in a book, *Over the Old Ozark Trails in the Shepherd of the Hills Country.*[43] After autographing each book, she wrote "Shepherd of the Hills Guide" beneath her name and often penciled in vignettes on the title page, such as "To those who would give advice. The best advice that I know is, if you can't be kind, be quiet." The book included a photograph of Pearl Spurlock, nicely dressed, standing beside her taxi, with a caption "Pearl Spurlock, typical hillbilly, at Powersite, Mo." For someone so instrumental in shaping the image and substance of Branson tourism, the "hillbilly" name hardly fit. After railroad travel declined and almost everyone arrived in Branson by automobile, the need for a local tour service was greatly diminished. However, guided tours of the Branson area, including Country Music Boulevard and Table Rock Lake, on the amphibious military vehicles called "the Ducks" are still popular. Interestingly, in 1993, seventy years after Pearl Spurlock established her tour service, and following the great blossoming of country music theaters, Branson became the first-ranking tour bus destination in the country.[44]

Still, spur-of-the-moment outings and weekend jaunts in the family car are the most common form of touring today. Automobile touring is very popular, probably more so than ever before, but it is more an individual or family affair. Tours are very popular in the spring and fall for visitors and residents alike. There are many beautiful drives in the Ozarks, and some have attracted national attention. Some visitors find pleasure in driving the stretches of U.S. 66 that remain open alongside Interstate 44. The old gasoline stations, cafes, gift shops, cabin camps, and motels are the main attractions, whether they are still open for business or slowly decaying away. Missouri Highway 94,

which parallels the north bank of the Missouri River from St. Charles to Hermann, passing through the wine country in Missouri's Rhineland region, is another popular tour. Highway 19 from Salem to Eminence in the Big Springs country is traveled by a large number of weekend visitors and by those who come to enjoy canoeing or camping on the Current and Jacks Fork rivers. The Glade Top Trail drive south of Ava, Missouri, in the Mark Twain National Forest follows Forest Road 147 through brilliant panoramic views in autumn, including opportunities to see the glade vegetation, balds, and the famous "smoke trees" that the local people call "yellowwoods."[45] In Arkansas, scenic Highway 7 from Harrison to Russellville on the Arkansas River winds its way through some of the most spectacular scenery in the White River Hills and Boston Mountains.

HEALTH SPAS AND SPRINGS

The growth of health spas in the Ozarks was part of the economic development that followed the Civil War and the emergence of the New South Ozarks. The whole country was experiencing prosperity, and money was becoming more plentiful. Railroads were expanding at a phenomenal rate. The taste for travel had revived, and mountain resorts were serving large crowds. The arts of healing—spiritual, mental, and physical—were influenced by movements never felt before. Faith cures became popular, and in Boston, Mary Baker Eddy published the textbook *Science and Health, With Key to the Scriptures,* which was gaining adherents to the Christian Science movement.[46] In Europe and in the East, thousands made pilgrimages to the various spas that claimed curative properties of water. In retrospect, it is no surprise that the spring water that came out of the ground in such abundance in the Ozarks also healed. Important to the health spas that sprang up there was the yellow-fever epidemic that claimed hundreds of lives in the Mississippi Valley during the 1880s. Many people searched out more healthful locations, high and away from the swamplands along the river.

The mineral waters of the Ozarks may be classified into four major categories: muriatic, containing as their main constituents sodium chloride, or common salt; alkaline, containing sodium carbonade; sulfatic, containing one or more sulfates as their main constituent; and chalybeate, which contain ferrous (iron) carbonate, magnesium carbonate, and sodium carbonate.[47]

The mineral springs of the Ozarks were used to treat a wide range of diseases. Testimonials told of cures, and frequently a particular spring was singled out as having peculiar qualities for a specific disease. The spas recommended both internal and external use of the water in most cases, but usually they mentioned no specific quantities. A report of the time suggested how to drink it.

As to the manner of drinking a mineral water, much depends on time, circumstances and individuality. Quantity, it must be borne in mind, is an important factor, but a just measure of moderation is here likewise necessary. The time-honored custom of rising early and taking before breakfast one to four glasses of water, amounting to not more than a quart in all, is to be recommended. The water should be taken slowly, glass by glass, allowing an interval of a few minutes between the first and second and third; this latter interval should be passed in walking and a walk of a half mile or a mile at the end is recommended. In the case of the stronger mineral waters this morning potion is sufficient and is preferable to taking water at any other time of the day. Chalybeate and other less potent waters may be taken differently and in larger quantity. The time which experience has set for a "cure" with these latter waters, under ordinary conditions, should be reckoned at not less than four weeks; a shortening of this period by greater daily consumption of water is unwise and sometimes even dangerous.[48]

The best known of Ozark spas was Eureka Springs, Arkansas (fig. 12-1). Not only did development go so rapidly that Eureka Springs took on the trappings of a boom town, but the construction of hotels, bathhouses, and summer homes went on in a more substantial and complete manner than at any other place. The pattern was not unlike that at other large resorts: first, a remarkable healing of a well-known figure, in this case Judge L. B. Sanders of nearby Berryville, Arkansas; next, word-of-mouth advertising of the healing powers of the waters; then the attraction of large crowds who camped out or lived in temporary shelters; and, finally, the establishment of grocery stores, hotels, bathhouses, livery stables, and all other necessary conveniences.

Judge Sanders visited the springs in 1879, and by July 4 of that year, four hundred people had visited the waters that had rendered a remarkable cure to the judge's chronic case of erysipelas.[49] Soon, four communities had grown up around the main springs: Basin Spring Community, Harding Spring Community, Evansville, and South Eureka Community. Visitors came by horseback or by daily stage service from Pierce City, Seligman, and Joplin, Missouri, and from Fayetteville and Ozark, Arkansas. Though traveling to the place where water healed was not easy, people wanted to go there and the town grew rapidly. Estimates of the town's population varied greatly.

By April 1880, they estimated the population of the town at various numbers, even as high as fifteen thousand. A federal decennial census that year recorded three thousand residents who could claim permanent residence for voting purposes.[50]

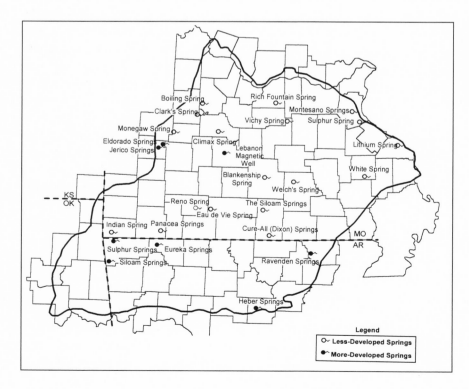

FIGURE 12-1. Ozark spas and mineral springs. Adapted from Paul Schweitzer, "A Report on the Mineral Waters of Missouri," *Geological Survey of Missouri,* 1st series, 3 (1892).

Crescent Hotel, Eureka Springs, Arkansas. (Courtesy of Arkansas History Commission.)

By the early 1880s, a company was bottling and shipping Eureka Water from Basin Spring in all directions. As early as 1881 property owners were replacing the temporary business buildings and boardinghouses with more permanent structures. Several promoters helped to publicize Eureka Springs and to develop hotels and businesses. Foremost among them were the members of the Eureka Springs Improvement Company, some of whom have been mentioned as leaders of the progressive movement that swept through the Ozarks after the Civil War. Powell Clayton, former governor of Arkansas, headed the company's directors. A. H. Foote of St. Louis was secretary, and Logan H. Roots, a prominent Little Rock financier, served as treasurer. These men were instrumental in promoting the Eureka Springs Railroad Company in 1882 and in constructing the elegant Crescent Hotel in 1886. Built of native Ozark stone in American Gothic style, the Crescent was the showplace of northwest Arkansas.

June Westfall and Catherine Osterhage in their book, *A Fame Not Easily Forgotten,* tell of the Crescent's gracious southern hospitality:

An army of white coated servitors catered to the slightest whim of each guest. Meals featured the true Southern cuisine and tall frosty mint juleps were to be had at all times, served on the shady porches and walks.[51]

The Crescent put on gala balls in its elegant ballroom, and picnics, streetcar rides, horseback riding, carriage rides, and hiking were pleasant diversions.

After 1908 the hotel housed a college, and for a time during the 1930s it was a hospital operated by Norman Baker, a flamboyant protégé of the notorious goat-gland healer, Dr. John Brinkley of Milford, Kansas.[52] When tourism expanded during the 1960s, investors restored the Crescent. In recent years its popularity has increased because of its connection with the past splendor of Eureka Springs.

Together, more than fifty hotels of various sizes appeared in Eureka Springs during its first fifty years. Only the Crescent, Basin Park, and New Orleans survive. The hotels and bathhouses built at Eureka Springs and at other springs in the Ozarks were at the end of the era when "taking the waters" was popular. Mental attitudes throughout the United States changed soon after the springs first received publicity. Mandatory free education helped to widen mental horizons and led to critical examination of the actual healing value of the spring water. By the end of World War I the medical profession had a firm hold on the minds of most people, and medicine and surgery seemed the most legitimate means to alleviate pain and suffering. Many visitors continued to return to Eureka Springs out of habit, but as the following passage notes, the scene changed rapidly:

As for the scene in Eureka Springs, the newspapers began to omit the many letters written by grateful people healed by the water from the springs, and in their place appeared what was considered more lucrative advertising. Nationally advertised pills and nostrums were advocated over and over again until they gained a kind of universal acceptance. The water never changed but the acceptance of its therapeutic qualities almost completely died out.[53]

No doubt the success of Eureka Springs contributed to the establishment of resorts, hotels, and bathhouses at many other Ozark springs, particularly those in northwestern Arkansas and southwestern Missouri. In the period 1880 to 1885 a surprising number of springs that had served as sources of water for people and livestock for years were discovered to have amazing health-restoring qualities that had gone unsuspected for years.

One of the largest hotels in northwestern Arkansas was the Park Springs, constructed close by springs at the northeast corner of Bentonville. The huge, rambling two-story brick building with verandahs on all sides had its own railroad line, which connected with the Frisco in Bentonville. Ozark Christian College purchased the hotel in 1940.[54]

In 1885, when the Kansas City, Fort Smith and Southern Railroad built to nearby Splitlog, Missouri, developers laid out the town of Sulphur Springs. Charles Hibler and his wife built a large hotel and several cottages. When the railroad extended tracks to Sulphur Springs in 1889, developers built several additional hotels. When investors built the Sulphur Springs' Kilburn Hotel in 1909, they claimed it was the largest hotel in northwest Arkansas.

The town of Siloam Springs in Benton County, Arkansas, developed around twenty-seven springs in the valley of Sager Creek. Developers sold many lots between 1879 and 1883 when stories of cures at some of the healing springs in the area had people talking of what a great place it would be for a health resort.[55] Most of the development occurred after the Kansas City, Pittsburg and Gulf Railroad built to Siloam Springs in 1894. In 1915, well after the mineral-water rage had passed, Siloam Springs had three hotels in business.

Eldorado (Pactolous), seventeen miles west of Bentonville on Spavinaw Creek, was the first health resort in Benton County. Investors built a large three-story hotel beside several springs in the 1870s, but after a disastrous flood in 1883, the town grew very little.[56] In the 1920s they built a restaurant, dance pavilion, and several summer cabins.

East of Eureka Springs in the Arkansas Ozarks, only a few springs gained other than a local reputation as picnicking and camping areas. The healing power of Ravenden Springs in Randolph County, according to local legend, was first revealed about 1880 to the Reverend William Bailey, who was suffering from a stomach ailment.[57] Three times in one night Bailey dreamed that he had drunk from the waters and had been cured. The next day, he went to the springs and began his treatment. Apparently the waters were helpful, or at least he thought so, for the minister lived until 1909. During the flush times at the springs, investors built the grand Southern Hotel, a showplace for the small community. It was a forty-room frame structure with a double gallery across its wide facade. Wooden stairs led from the hotel down a steep hill to the springs.

Heber Springs, near the Ozarks' southern border, takes its name from the mineral springs in a ten-acre municipal park. The springs, and the nearby settlement that grew up, were at the foot of Sugar Loaf Mountain. Heber Springs was first known as Sugar Loaf Springs.[58] During the spa era, each spring—sulfur, magnesia, and arsenic—was said to have special curative powers. Even today some older residents swear by the health-restoring qualities of the springs, and visitors from Batesville and other nearby towns come to the springs to fill empty milk containers and bottles with the mineral waters.[59]

In the Missouri Ozarks, Eldorado Springs commanded the widest reputation. In 1892, when Eldorado Springs was a flourishing town of fifteen hundred inhabitants, it was reported:

> Less than ten years ago this was a perfect wilderness. A remarkable cure was effected in 1881 by the use of waters issuing from a crevice in the rock at the bottom of a pretty valley, the renown of which spread so rapidly that a town was laid out forthwith and actually built within a very few years.[60]

As often happened, Park Spring, the one that effected the above-mentioned cure, became public property and the townspeople jealously guarded its rights. Other springs in the vicinity, including those at West Eldorado, called the Nine Wonders, attracted visitors. Investors started a rival establishment at West Eldorado, but by 1892 it had become a deserted village. On the other hand, things were flourishing at Eldorado then:

> A number of hotels, the largest of which is the "Forest Grove" have been built in the past few years at an aggregate cost of $50,000. Several bathing establishments with hot and cold water facilities, a Casino hall and similar attractions bring up the total money spent to $80,000. Guests and patients are well taken care of and receive the comforts they have the right to expect. No bottling establishment exists yet on the ground, though a very considered trade is carried on from the sale of the water. Pamphlets, descriptive of the place, are

printed every year, and may be had on application to Mr. W. P. Cruce.[61]

As at many other locations, local people used the mineral residue at the spring to manufacture soap so that after departing the resort visitors could continue treatment until they returned.

People drank the heavily chalybeate waters of Jerico Spring, in southeastern Cedar County, Missouri, for rheumatism, kidney and stomach diseases, and other ailments. The spring, also known as the "Fountain of Youth," was on the property of M. J. Straight, owner of the nearby bathhouse.[62] The spa never attracted large crowds because of scant accommodations and difficulty in reaching the place. The main spring was not large, and a pump was used to supply water to the bathhouse.

Investors built one of the largest resort hotels in the Ozark region, the Gasconade Hotel in Lebanon, Missouri, beside a well that supposedly produced magnetic water. Several months after the city had drilled a deep well they discovered that iron pipes, which exhibited no unusual property while lying in the yard, became strongly magnetized when placed in the well or connected with those previously put down. They found that a pocketknife rubbed on the well pipe would pick up a nail weighing eighty grains and that a compass near the well was powerfully deflected within a radius of three feet. Although people widely believed that the waters from the well were magnetic, they were the same waters now pumped from sandstone aquifers throughout southwest Missouri. Paul Schweitzer, who carefully studied the mineral waters of Missouri in 1892, explained the magnetism of Lebanon Magnetic Well:

It is a well known fact, however, that an iron bar or tube held in a certain position, to be fixed for each place, becomes a magnet; it is further possible that a tube, sunk to great depth, may reach rock formations that are magnetic and will communicate their magnetism to the tube. Such facts have been observed in a number of instances and are not remarkable, because not rare; but even a strong magnet, such as the iron tube of the Lebanon well doubtless is, cannot influence the water flowing through it, to either become magnetic itself or to exhibit by virtue of it any unusual properties; it is a matter of interest, and will remain so, but not one of weight from a medical point of view.[63]

Interestingly, the magnetic survey conducted by the Missouri Geological Survey in the 1930s and the 1960s identified several magnetic highs in the Ozarks. One such location, first discovered with sensitive magnetometers and later core-drilled, was a valuable iron-ore deposit. In the 1960s investors developed it as the Pea Ridge Mine in Washington County.[64] Even more interesting (but not a likely explanation for the magnetic well) is the fact that geologists identified a magnetic high in the Lebanon vicinity.

Although the reputation of magnetic water undoubtedly was a factor in the development of the resort, Lebanon had several geographical advantages. The city's elevation of 1,280 feet established its advantages as a sanitarium as for pure air and freedom from malaria, prevalent in the lower-lying country. It was only 180 miles from St. Louis on the main line of the St. Louis and San Francisco. Schweitzer described the hotel, an imposing structure operated by R. C. Beaty:

A large hotel has been erected at a cost of $100,000 in the usual summer hotel style, with verandahs and pleasant nooks and corners, three stories in height, and altogether of striking appearance. Bath houses for men and women, with sitting and dressing rooms, bowling alleys, billiard halls, an opera house, and other attractions are provided. More than $200,000 may safely be estimated as having been spent on improvements incidental to developing the place as a health resort; pamphlets, descriptive of it, to be had on application to the manager.[65]

In 1892 Beaty appointed a medical staff, with Dr. Paquin as superintendent and physician in charge. Beaty remodeled and enlarged the bathing facilities so that, besides the ordinary cold and hot baths, "turkish, russian, and electric, besides sea-salt baths, with or without massage treatment, and medicated vapor baths, are constantly accessible."[66]

Gasconade Hotel at the Lebanon Magnetic Well, Lebanon, Missouri, *circa* 1892. (Reproduced from Paul Schweitzer, "A Report on the Mineral Waters of Missouri," *Geological Survey of Missouri,* 1st Series, 3 [1892]: 142.)

Paul Schweitzer's 1892 report on the mineral springs of Missouri noted other springs (fig. 12-1) where hotels or summer cottages were built.[67] Investors built a hotel and private homes at *Indian Spring* in McDonald County, six miles west of Wade on the Splitlog Railway. Visitors drank the water to cure rheumatism and kidney disease. Visitors to *Lithium Spring,* about nine miles north of Perryville in Perry County, and to *White Spring,* some six miles south of Fredericktown in Madison County on the St. Louis and Iron Mountain Railroad, hoped to be cured of a variety of illnesses. Accommodations at the latter spring consisted of a few cottages and a boardinghouse that opened during the summer to serve people from neighboring river counties. Apparently, many visitors came from the Mississippi River bottoms because the waters had a reputation for curing malaria besides the usual dyspepsia and stomach troubles. *Montesano Springs* and *Sulphur Spring* in Jefferson County attracted many visitors from St. Louis. The Montesano waters issued into a marshy valley where a resort hotel, built sometime in the 1880s, was in business for about ten years before it burned down. Investors never developed *Sulphur Spring,* perhaps because it was a casual visiting place by excursion parties from St. Louis. *Boling Spring* and *Clark's Spring* in Benton County, though never developed, have muriatic waters that reportedly picnic parties used, as did families and visitors who for health reasons sometimes stayed there several weeks. *Monegaw Spring* in the Osage River valley was the major mineral-water resort of St. Clair County. In the 1880s investors built a twenty-seven-room hotel and several bathhouses to serve visitors, who could reach the place from either Osceola or Clinton.

The town of Vichy, platted in 1880 and named for the French resort, was once a popular spa with a hotel near the springs at the north end of the village. A tornado in 1886 nearly destroyed the town.[68] An Indianapolis group that built a small hotel owned Climax Spring in extreme western Camden County. They tried to make a summer resort of it by advertising but failed because of the inaccessibility of the place. The *Siloam Springs* (Sulphur, Keystone, Rheumatic, Iron, Norman, Siloam, Crooked Ash) of Howell County, about eighteen miles northwest of West Plains, were the best-known mineral springs in south-central Missouri. The owners improved the springs and hired John Johnson, a partner, to manage the property. They built two hotels and a bathhouse for hot and cold baths. Visitors reached the springs over a very rough road from West Plains. Business at *Cure-All (Dixon) Springs,* some fifteen miles south of West Plains, also suffered because of poor road conditions. The site, consisting of five springs (Electric, Eagle, Sore Eye, Potash, Iron), flourished briefly

in the 1880s. The waters of *Panacea Springs,* about seven miles east of Cassville, Missouri, were discovered to be useful in treating rheumatism, kidney diseases, dyspepsia, and bowel troubles. The springs were unimproved in 1892 and were used mostly by area residents. During the 1890s, people from as far away as Erie, Pennsylvania, visited *Blankenship Spring* north of Houston, Missouri. The spring was owned by Dr. John Blankenship, a physician in Houston. Patients were housed in one of the four hotels in Houston on Grand Avenue and would daily take a stagecoach to the springs for treatment of various ailments. Two springs in Christian County, Missouri—*Eau de Vie* and *Reno*—flourished briefly as summer resorts during the 1880s. Investors built hotels at both places.

It is interesting that investors never developed the very large springs of the Courtois Hills region, such as Big Spring and Alley Spring, nor did the springs receive much publicity during the heyday of the health spas. No doubt the reason for this was that to command anything more than area trade a resort had to be no more than a few miles from a railroad over easily traveled roads. By the time railroads had penetrated the most remote sections of the Ozarks, the spa era had passed. One of the last efforts to establish a health resort in the Ozarks was the small sanitarium built by Dr. C. H. Diehl of Roxanna, Illinois, at Welch Cave and Spring in Shannon County, Missouri.[69] He envisioned a resort for asthma sufferers to breathe "the mineral laden air" that came up through the cave tunnel. In 1916 he had workers build a large native-stone building at the entrance to take advantage of the cool air wafting from the cave and the spring pool. He was unable to attract enough patients or picnic parties to the remote area, and in 1933 the county sold the property at a tax sale in Eminence.

As a direct result of the days when taking the waters was popular, many Ozark springs became public property, and many others became the property of watchful private owners who developed and preserved them. During the past half century, the state or federal governments have acquired many of the very large springs. Several larger springs serve as state parks that often include trout hatcheries. One who stands for a moment on a hot summer day under the overhanging alcove of limestone and experiences the cool air rising from water issuing from Meramec Spring (or one of the Ozarks' other large springs) can appreciate the springs' intrinsic value before the arrival of air conditioning.

RIVERS AND FLOAT TRIPS

One of the first attractions for vacationers in the Ozarks was the fishing on clear, spring-fed rivers and streams (fig. 12-2). Hunting parties and float trips became popular at about the same time they built the health spas and for many of the same reasons. Undoubtedly, some visitors to the spas participated in some of the first of these excursions. Not only had the recently constructed railroads opened vast tracts of forest and mineral land, but they also gave access to the scenic and recreational resources of the Ozarks, including the mineral springs and the region's clear, free-flowing streams. The most popular early floats were on the White, Gasconade, Meramec, and Current rivers, but many other streams also were popular.

Some of the first recreational floats were in the eastern Ozarks on the Current, Meramec, Black, and Gasconade rivers where railroads provided transportation and access. The large mining and lumbering companies entertained customers and guests by providing excursions on railroads and company logging trams for hunting and float trips. The Current River played a prominent role in the sales program of the Missouri Lumber and Mining Company. They entertained guests in grand style in the company hotel in Grandin and at their clubhouse on the Current River ten miles west via a logging tram. The company sometimes took guests to Van Buren for a thirty-mile float back to the clubhouse. They sent special trains to the clubhouse to pick up the visitors.[70] J. B. White, the manager at Grandin, provided annual passes for free transportation on the tram lines to the company's best customers. The peak spring and summer buying seasons fortunately corre-sponded with good weather, brilliant autumn colors, blooming dogwoods, good river conditions, and the best hunting seasons.

Perhaps the most important single event to popularize float fishing in the Ozarks was the Current River excursion of Missouri governor Herbert S. Hadley in 1909. Hadley was the first Republican governor since Reconstruction, and many people wanted to see "the Mysterious Stranger."[71] Congressman W. P. Elmer organized the expedition with help from John M. Stephens, Frisco agent in Salem, Sam Hughes, Frisco immigrant agent, and John Curran, head of the Missouri Immigration Commission. The purposes of the jaunt were to publicize the Ozarks and to let the people of the Missouri Ozarks see their governor. The trip, which included a banquet at Salem, the railhead, and a float from Welch's Spring to Round Spring, received wide publicity in the large state and regional newspapers. Representative Elmer wrote of it:

> We blazed the event in the local newspapers, all done free, and soon had $1,000, with which to stage the supper, build ten flat bottom boats to carry our crowd, and one to carry provisions and equipment, hire river guides and transport the crowd to Welch's Cave.[72]

They served, among other things, baked opossum at the $1.50 a head banquet in Salem. It was the first time a

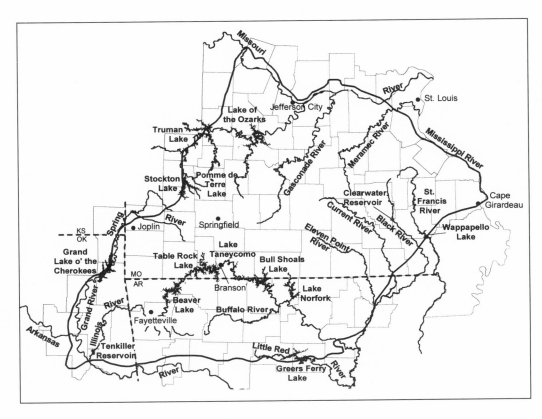

FIGURE 12-2. Ozark rivers and lakes. Adapted from "National Streams Database," U.S. Geological Survey Publications, 1995. U.S. Department of the Interior, U.S. Geological Survey, Rolla, Missouri. http://www. usgs.gov (January 25, 2000).

Govenor Herbert S. Hadley with party on a float trip on the White River, 1909. (Courtesy of State Historical Society of Missouri.)

Missouri governor had visited Salem, and they sold more than three hundred fifty tickets. The next morning, the governor and his party of forty persons, including several state officials and distinguished businessmen from Missouri, traveled by "hacks, buggies, and surries" to Welch's Cave, where they boarded the boats:

> Hadley's boat led the parade and the "grub" boat brought up the rear. He had sandwiches and coffee ready at the Spring. Everybody was in a good humor except a couple of newsmen to whom the trip was a bore and arduous . . . Not a mishap all the way. About 4:30 the guides said "camp" and we did. A tent was provided for the governor and a few others, but most of us slept on the ground in the open.[73]

At Round Spring they made a panoramic photograph of the group and later published it all over the United States. A great deal of national attention was drawn to the "discovery" of the Ozarks by Governor Hadley.

The river float business came later to the western Ozarks. There were fewer large lumber companies with tram lines leading to good river access points, and railroads came later in the White River country. One of the first river float destinations was Arlington, southwest of Rolla, where sportsmen, mainly from St. Louis, arrived on the train. Some brought their own boats and camping gear.

Thomas Hart Benton, who later became Missouri's most famous artist, traveled by train with his father from Neosho to Arlington for a float trip on the Gasconade in 1899 or 1900. Heavy advertising by the Frisco Railroad helped make Arlington known as a vacation spot. Many customers from throughout the Midwest traveled to Arlington by railroad to float down the Gasconade. Perry Andres operated the outfitter's commissary then and provided wagon transportation to fourteen different "put-in" spots on the river.[74]

The float-fishing trip has changed considerably over the years; guides are only rarely used, the canoe far outnumbers the flat-bottom johnboat, and the automobile has opened more streams to floating.[75] Sauer provides a description of the Ozark float trip of the early 1900s:

> At some convenient point the party, usually accompanied by a guide, starts down the river in flat-bottomed boats, which are rowed or poled when desired. The canoe, although well suited to Ozark streams, is almost unknown. The trips are usually taken in a very leisurely fashion, numerous stops being made to fish. Camp is pitched on a gravel bar or at a spring.[76]

Among the more popular floats was the one from Round Spring to Van Buren on the Current River, which was approximately fifty miles long and required nearly a week, depending upon the time spent exploring caves and other attractions. Floaters could travel from Alley Spring to Eminence in one day, but fishing parties often continued downstream past Two Rivers Landing to float the Current River. The Bales Mercantile and Boating Company in Eminence, Missouri, was the best-known outfitter for Current River floats. Occasionally, Bales arranged for floats on the White River as well. The float from Galena to Branson on the James and White rivers was very popular. This was a popular run for group floats because railroad transportation between Galena and Branson was available to transport the boats. As early as 1890, well before the railroad arrived in Branson, a group of Frisco Railroad men in Springfield who called themselves the Molly-joggers, took spring and fall float trips. The expeditions included wagons loaded with gear, bird dogs for short hunting side trips, and a Negro cook.[77]

The whole White River below Powersite Dam in Taney County, Missouri, was considered good for float trips, and Spring River below Arkansas Power and Light Company's Dam No. 3 was a good one. The Illinois River above Tahlequah attracted floaters as did the Elk River, Shoal Creek, and similar small streams in the tri-state area. A few outfitters who provided equipment and guides helped make some floats popular. Bales Mercantile and Boating Company in Eminence, Missouri, and Jim Owen's Float Service at Branson were among the larger and better-known outfitters. Some guides became boat makers. Charles Kinyon of Forsyth built flat-bottomed skiffs for floats down the White River, which he often guided.[78] The Ozark float trip of the late nineteenth and early twentieth century resembled the modern-day hunting or fishing expedition in Canada's northland where limited transportation and remoteness preclude a stop at a convenience store or sporting goods outlet to pick up last-minute supplies. The outfitters planned the trips with all gear, food, and staff provided. They carefully picked guides who knew the river "like the back of their hands." Just as modern tourists in the Canadian northwoods encounter a semi-frontier lifestyle among some native Ojibway and other inhabitants of that vast isolated area, so did floaters and hunters "discover the quaint survivals" of premodern America in the Ozark backwoods. Outfitters soon learned their customers were nearly as interested in the opportunity to socialize with the guides as they were in the sport and scenery. Enterprising guides and outfitters sometimes arranged for good storytellers to be part of the support party.

Float fishing was at first a pastime of the well-to-do vacationer. It was comparatively costly, even at reduced Ozark prices of the time, to mount a float trip with boats,

tents, fishing gear, food, and guides to steer the boats, point out likely fishing spots, and make camp and cook. Stories told around the campfire, sometimes embellished to entertain the visitors, helped "invent" a mythical Ozarks.[79] This was especially true when reporters from newspapers in St. Louis and Kansas City wrote feature articles about their Ozark float trips. Area residents had always float-fished, of course, and for many families the catch provided a welcome relief from a monotonous diet of pork, corn bread, beans, and garden produce. Many local sportsmen from counties near the larger float streams made regular trips, at first by wagon, later by automobile, to their favorite stretches of water. For example, sportsmen from the Springfield area and surrounding counties often traveled to Forsyth to float down the White River to Buffalo Shoals, where they stayed at a well-known fishing camp.[80]

In the years since World War II, particularly the 1960s and 1970s, families have transformed Ozark river floats from a semiwilderness sport for the more fortunate to an activity for adults and children. Several factors are responsible for this change. Better roads and increased use of the automobile have opened nearly all of the floatable Ozark streams. Any location on a stream where the public may enter is a potential put-in or take-out spot. First fiberglass and then aluminum boats replaced the heavier wooden flat-bottomed johnboats. The aluminum johnboat continues to be popular among fishing enthusiasts, but canoes are favored much more today. Two books have helped to make the Ozark float trip popular. The first, *Stars Upstream* by Leonard Hall, is an appealing description of

Johnboats on the Jacks Fork River, 1970. Johnboats are popular for river fishing. (Milton Rafferty Collection, photograph by the author.)

the natural beauty and simplicity of life along the Current and Jacks Fork rivers.[81] The second, *Missouri Ozark Waterways* by Oscar Hawksley, provides specific instructions and detailed maps on how to gain access and run almost every Missouri Ozarks stream capable of floating a canoe or johnboat.[82] In addition to recent guidebooks, various federal and state agencies have published brochures and booklets with information on fishing, floating, and outdoor recreation.[83]

Canoe rental businesses have sprung up to serve visitors from outlying cities, including Kansas City, St. Louis, Springfield, Tulsa, Little Rock, and Memphis. A common sight at popular "put in" spots, such as Hammond Camp on the North Fork, is a cluster of vans or old yellow school buses loaded with enthusiastic paddlers. The vehicles pull specially designed trailers loaded with as many as a dozen canoes. Several Boy Scout troops may make up a single party. Even short-term residents of the Ozarks can feel a bit chagrined and quite nostalgic about "the good old days" when one could float for a day and encounter only a handful of canoes. It is well known that guides are seldom used these days; even a novice would feel out of place with a guide among a pack of canoes carrying inexperienced paddlers less than sixteen years old. Hawksley cites the prime reason for the change from float fishing to pleasure canoeing:

> The special attractiveness to families cannot be overemphasized. Most Ozark rivers, in summer, are so mild that even the family with small children need not fear travelling by canoe. The few places on the average river run which could cause difficulty for the inexperienced paddler occur at places so shallow that the stern paddler can step out and lead the canoe around the trouble spot . . . The gravel bars are nearly all potential campsites and Ozark gravel bars are nearly devoid of noxious insects. To top it all off, no license is required for paddle craft.[84]

Unfortunately, many of the most popular stretches of floating water have been destroyed. The James River, once one of the favorite float-fishing streams, is severely polluted.[85] Downstream from Springfield, the James drains the streets and parking lots of the city and receives the treated but odoriferous sewage water pumped into Wilson's Creek. As recently as August 2000 a sewer line break at Springfield's Southwest Treatment Plant sent an estimated five million gallons of raw sewage into Wilson's Creek and on into the James River.[86] Large man-made lakes have flooded long stretches of other float streams, including the Osage, White, Little Red, Illinois, and Grand

rivers. The float-fishing stream par excellence was the White River, but waters from several large lakes have inundated its shoals and pools. Today floating has shifted to its larger tributaries—Buffalo River, Kings River, North Fork, Little North Fork, and Beaver Creek.

The sport involved in canoeing consists especially of the successful running of a shoal. Where streams cut into a particularly resistant layer of rock, a series of rapids, a shoal, is the result. Most Ozark streams consist of pools with normal water flow broken by shoals between. The large reservoirs interrupt the fast-flowing water and submerge the shoals. The construction of Bull Shoals Dam destroyed some of the best shoals on the White River. Schoolcraft provided what is probably the first written record of a troubled but successful run down the Bull Shoals. Reading it helps us to understand what was lost under the waters of the reservoir:

> In our descent this day, we have passed several hunters' cabins on both banks of the river, but met nothing worth particular note until our arrival at the Bull Shoals, situated twenty miles below M'Gary's. Here the river has a fall of fifteen or twenty feet in the distance of half a mile, and stands full of rugged calcareous rocks, among which the water foams and rushes with astonishing velocity and incessant noise. There are a hundred channels, and the strange navigator runs an imminent risk of being dashed upon the rocks, or sunk beneath the waves, whose whirling boiling and unceasing roar warns him of his peril before he reaches the rapids. There is a channel through which canoes and even large boats pass with a good depth of water, but being unacquainted with it, we ran the hazard of being sunk, and found our canoe drawn rapidly into the suction of the falls, apprehensive of the results. In a few moments, not withstanding every effort to keep our barque headed downwards, the conflicting eddies drove us against a rock, and we were instantly thrown broadside upon the rugged peaks which stand thickly in the swiftest part of the first chute or fall. Luckily it did not fill, but the pressure of the current against a canoe thirty feet in length, lying across the stream, was more that we could counteract, and we had nearly exhausted our strength in vain endeavors to extricate and aright it. For all this time we were in the water, at a depth of two, three, or four feet, at a cool January temperature, but at the length succeeded in lifting it over a ledge of rocks, and again got afloat. We now shot down the current rapidly and undisturbed for 600 yards, which brought us to the verge of a second chute, where we twice encountered a similar difficulty,

but succeeded, with analogous efforts, in passing our canoe and effects in safety.[87]

HUNTING AND WILDERNESS SPORTS

Hunting continues to be as popular in the Ozarks as it was for the first settlers. There is ample written record that they practiced hunting for sport. During his three-month journey in the Ozarks in 1818 and 1819, Schoolcraft wrote that he and his companion killed nine deer, twenty-five turkeys, three wolves (coyotes), one prairie hen, and one goose. They saw bear frequently, and deer herds were large. On Christmas Day, 1818, while Schoolcraft was staying with settlers on Beaver Creek, the hunters killed fourteen turkeys in a matter of two hours.[88] Friedrich Gerstaeker's journal gives ample evidence of the variety and abundance of wild game.[89] Only once, while in the upper White River country, and because of the game, was Gerstaeker tempted to settle in America.

The state conservation departments and the U.S. Forest Service, by regulating hunting and managing habitat, have helped to restore wildlife populations from the low ebb of the 1930s. Deer and wild-turkey seasons attract the largest number of outside hunters. Often hunters come prepared to rough it in the woods for a week or more. They sometimes equip themselves with any number of expensive weapons, including newfangled muzzle loaders; camouflaged clothing; tents or camping vehicles; cooking equipment; and, in one instance reported in a newspaper, an ample supply of beer and spirits and a gasoline-powered electric generator to provide power for a television set so that the group of lusty hunters would not miss the Monday night football telecast.

Other wild game and fish are hunted enthusiastically—rabbit, quail, squirrel, bullfrogs, and so forth—in almost every conceivable fashion: bows, muzzle-loading rifles, gigs (sharp-pointed barbed spears attached to a pole and used in taking frogs and rough fish), and shotguns ranging from .410 to 12 gauge. Various illegal hunting methods are used, including such things as spotlighting and baiting deer (with salt or feed) or noodling (grabbing by hand) for fish along stream banks. Hunting and fishing out of season is also a continuing problem. Conservation agents have arrested some poachers for taking the ancient spoonbill catfish for its eggs, which they sell as "Ozark caviar."

Hunting and fishing are becoming ever more organized and commercialized. Various groups sponsor bass derbies, fishing for prizes, and specialized gear, including such things as special gigging boats equipped with reflected lights and powerful bass boats designed for competitive fishing. Even the dog men, who are among the most tra-ditional of hunters, are well equipped with citizens' band radios and cell telephones as they follow their dogs through the night in search of foxes, raccoons, and coyotes. Hunting, fishing, and other forms of outdoor recreation have spawned many new businesses, including boat manufacturers, dock makers, and companies that design and manufacture fishing tackle and lures.

Bass Pro Shops, one of the most successful sporting goods manufacturing and retailing companies in the United States, had its start in Springfield when Johnny Morris began selling fishing tackle and bait as a sideline in one of the family's Brown Derby liquor stores. Today, in its sprawling headquarters on the corner of Sunshine Street and Campbell Avenue, the company sponsors seminars on hunting, fishing, sportsmanship, and conservation and also other special events related to outdoor recreation. Currently under construction at the site is the new American National Fish and Wildlife Museum, called Wonders of Wildlife, that will include historical exhibits of sports equipment, freshwater and saltwater aquariums, a 220,000-gallon shark tank, live bobcats, a ninety-foot cave, and a Walk in the Ozarks featuring plant and animal life of the region. The 92,000-square-foot museum will surely be a popular tourist attraction. The museum, jointly financed by Bass Pro Shops, the city of Springfield, and the state of Missouri is scheduled to open November 2001.

Many Ozarks residents resent outside hunters. Landowners are likely to allow "local boys" to enter their property, but keep it heavily posted for anyone with whom they are not acquainted. Frontier attitudes regarding wildlife and hunting are slowly waning, but many native Ozarkers consider it their right to take game wherever it may be, even if it means entering posted land.

Private hunting lodges have always been popular, but until recently they were reserved for people who could afford to purchase wild land and use it only for recreation. In recent years, various groups have established cooperative hunting lodges, and they sell memberships for as little as thirty dollars per month. Such lodges are not popular with many residents. One Ozarker put it this way: "Those fellas from St. Louis and Memphis and even Springfield come down here and tear the hell out of things with their fancy four-wheel-drive pickups and kill our deer and turkeys. A lot of them do more boozin' than huntin'."

THE LAKES

Ambussen Hydraulic Construction Company built the first of the great Ozark lakes for the Ozark Power and Water Company.[90] Congress authorized the project on February 4, 1911, and in the fall of that year, Ambussen began to bring in men and machinery. The dam was to be 70 feet high and 1,063 feet long and eventually would create a lake covering 2,080 acres of land, with 52.9 miles of shoreline. It was a small project by modern standards, and the approximate cost of construction and land acquisition amounted to only $2,250,000.[91] Still, the impact of the Powersite Dam project, which created Lake Taneycomo in Taney County, Missouri, both immediately and into the future, was monumental.

Some two hundred to eight hundred men toiled to build the dam, and a little town, called Camp Ozark, grew up near the construction site. The payroll ran about fifteen hundred dollars a day, a large sum considering the time and place. Ozark Power and Water Company purchased land without undue resistance, except a tract owned by Missouri Cook Casey, a widow who had raised eight children, who held out for a higher price than the appraised value. On March 24, 1912, the Ozark Power and Water Company paid the full price for the Casey land, but then the dam had been completed and the lake was filling, leaving no time to clear timber from the Casey property. For many years a sunken forest stood in the lake as a memorial to the widow Casey's persistence.[92]

By 1916, Ozark Power and Water had built power transmission lines to Joplin, Springfield, Monett, Carthage, and Webb City, and soon after that, the company strung lines to the towns in the White River valley. Thus modernity, in the form of electrical power, came to the wild White River hills many years before it reached seemingly more accessible areas. The advantage of a favorable site for the development of hydroelectric power for growing markets in Springfield and the Tri-State Mining District had transformed the geographical disadvantage of rugged hills and remote location.

People recognized the recreation potential of the lake immediately. Three resort towns grew up on its shores: Rockaway Beach, Branson, and Hollister. Ozark Beach, a picnic and resort spot on the site of Camp Ozark, the 1911–1913 construction boom town, never achieved resort town status. Two of the towns, Hollister and Branson, had been established much earlier, but the new lake had a major impact on their economy. Each of these resort settlements offered its own brand of diversion for vacationers. Forsyth, another old town on Swan Creek near the dam site, shared marginally in the prosperity generated by the lake.

Hollister is one of the most unusual towns in the Middle West, since they constructed its buildings to conform with an Old English architectural pattern. William J. Johnson, a landscape architect, platted the town. Johnson developed a plan that drew upon the natural beauty of limestone hills by means of terraces, parks, and supporting walls of stone. The wood, stone, and stucco commercial buildings are of the English half-timbered type. A report written in 1940 characterized it as a planned village "often referred to by sociologists as a good example of the possibilities of the American rural town."[93] Whether Hollister was a rural town then is conjectural, but today it is surely in the midst of a booming tourist-recreation region.

Development progressed rapidly after the lake filled. As early as 1914, several boats cruised on the new lake:

Tucked away on the shores between Branson and Hollister is a "shipyard" where boats are being built entirely of native material. Others are shipped in "knock-down" from factories. A forty-footer known as the "Sammy Lane" was launched only a few days ago. "The Shepherd of the Hills" is another boat well known. The "Sammy Lane" is a mail boat. Sail boats for pleasure are also to be found on the lake.[94]

People praised Lake Taneycomo for working "marvelous" changes in the White River region of the Ozarks, which had so far been without any water impoundments. Even as early as September 1913, Robertus Love, writing in *Technical World,* called attention to the hopeful optimism in the vacation resort area in the hills:

The thrill of the new day is felt everywhere. New hotels have been going up all summer. Fishing and hunting clubs are going up all along the lake. And the good roads boosters are seeing to it that a fine drive will have been finished by the end of the season. This lake is going to make that section of the Ozarks the principal vacation mecca within a few years. Shut in by mountain fastnesses, this land has been, until a few years ago, a little empire to itself. It has lived its own life and gone its own ways. It has had its tragedies and comedies, its thrilling days of feudists and Baldknobbers, bushwhackers and mountain adventures.

But now a change has come and who knows but in a few years electric cars will run up and down the shores of this new lake that promised to revolutionize the entire Ozark region. Already the people of the Ozarks are adapting themselves to the new conditions, which promise not only to attract thousands of sightseers, summer visitors, and permanent residents, but also to develop industries undreamed of in this hitherto sequestered region of romance and mystery, illicit distilling, and honest hillside farming.[95]

Willard and Anna Merriam founded Rockaway Beach. William Merriam, a member of the firm of Merriam, Ellis

Dam and power plant of Ozark Power and Water Company forming Lake Taneycomo at Forsyth, Taney County, Missouri. (Courtesy of State Historical Society of Missouri.)

and Benton Realty and Insurance Company, Inc., Kansas City, Kansas, learned of the plans for the Ozark Water and Power Company dam in Taney County and selected the present location of Rockaway Beach as a good place to build a summer resort.[96] After purchasing more than six hundred acres of land from the Renshaw family along the north shore of the White River, Merriam had the land subdivided and, using as many as fourteen agents in several states, began selling lots. Originally, they named the town Taneycomo, but Mrs. Merriam renamed it after visiting Rockaway Beach in New York.[97] The first tourists traveled to Rockaway Beach via the Missouri Pacific Railroad to Branson or Hollister, then took a boat down the lake. A famous old boat, the *Sadie H,* also delivered mail to the new lake community. The first group of cottages built by the Merriams, now remodeled and called "Brookside Bungalows," were primitive by modern standards. The cottages had no running water, but brochures told guests that every cottage was no more than two blocks from a good well. The Merriams made electric lights available in 1925 when they built a service line from Powersite Dam to Rockaway Beach.[98]

The Merriams' first home, "Whileaway," was on the site known today as Eden Rock Motel. The red Oriental peaked roof on the Taneycomo Hotel, which burned in the 1970s, was Anna Merriam's idea. The old hotel had pillars of cedar trees, little changed so that their branches interlaced, reaching to the ceiling. Although on ground level, each room was elevated because the hotel was on the hillside. This style of multilevel architecture continues to be popular for resorts and housing developments on the steep slopes around Ozark lakes.

Lake Taneycomo has undergone continuous change since the completion of Powersite Dam in 1913. It was a warm-water lake until the 1950s, when the U.S. Army Corps of Engineers built Table Rock Dam. Rockaway Beach and other resorts underwent certain changes as a result. The traditional style of vacation, which included visits lasting from two weeks to a whole summer, was popular before water from Table Rock entered Lake Taneycomo. The temperature of cold water feeding from the bottom of Table Rock is less than 60 degrees Fahrenheit always. The cool temperature discouraged swimming and proved unsuited for many kinds of fish. Fortunately, as a cold water body, Lake Taneycomo was good trout habitat. As a result, Rockaway Beach became a trout fisherman's resort and a quiet home base for vacationers who like to tour the region.

In 1929, Union Electric and Power Company began construction on the second major dam in the Ozarks. Bagnell Dam, built on the Osage River, was completed in October 1931, becoming the largest hydroelectric plant in the Ozarks and impounding one of the largest man-made lakes in the United States. Interest in the dam was first expressed in 1912, and extensive engineering and feasibility studies followed in the early 1920s. Financial complications forced the original investors to sell the land and plans for the dam to Union Electric, a power company based in St. Louis. When the Public Service Commission approved the project on July 27, 1929, Union Electric got the project underway immediately.[99] Stone and Webster Engineering Corporation constructed the dam at a cost of thirty million dollars.

The dam formed the Lake of the Ozarks. The large

Main street in old Linn Creek, Camden County, Missouri. The site of the original town was flooded by Lake of the Ozarks. (Courtesy of State Historical Society of Missouri.)

lake, sometimes called the "Ozark Dragon" because of its unusual shape outlined by the S-shaped meanders of the Osage River, has more than thirteen hundred miles of shoreline. It was, very likely, the last of the major lakes built by private capital in the United States. The contractor extended a rail line to the site and, as at Lake Taneycomo, a workers' camp, known as Bagnell, was established nearby. The construction company brought in skilled workers from outside, but they hired many laborers locally, providing an opportunity for outside corporations to see that the Ozarker's image as a listless worker was more fancy than fact. The dam was finished in eighteen and a half months. They poured the first concrete on April 21, 1930, and in less than ten months the lake began to form. Traffic began to cross the dam on Highway 54 on October 19, 1931, the same day the turbines began to produce electricity.[100]

This time, there was much more resistance to those responsible for purchasing the property in the river bottoms. They moved the entire town of Linn Creek, the county seat of Camden County, from its site on the Osage River near the mouth of the Niangua. Powersite Dam was small, mainly a river-channel dam that flooded a comparatively small acreage, but Bagnell Dam extended from bluff to bluff, backing water across the fertile Osage River flood plain and into tributary valleys. T. Victor Jeffries, a native of Linn Creek, came home as the lawyer representing Union Electric. In his book, *Before the Dam Water,* he describes how it felt to help destroy the homes and force residents to move.[101] Many residents were reluctant to leave old Linn Creek, but once started, the project went

ahead relentlessly. Some residents moved up the hollow to what would be new Linn Creek; others moved to Camdenton, the new town built to be the new county seat; still others took the money received for their property and moved far away. Before the waters began to rise above the dam, the town of Linn Creek began to disappear piece by piece. Workers tore down houses, moved others to higher ground, and burned the remaining structures. They moved more than three thousand graves from the old town cemetery to a new cemetery on high ground.

Camdenton, the current seat of Camden County, is a comparatively new town. It grew out of the business acumen of John Thomas Woodruff, a Springfield lawyer, builder, and developer. Persuaded by his brother, William, that a new county seat for Camden County would have to be built, John Woodruff joined with his brother and two businessmen from Linn Creek, Clinton Webb and James Banner, to accomplish that goal. The four men "formed a little syndicate . . . and acquired 310 acres of land" at the intersection of the newly relocated U.S. 54 and Missouri Highway 5.[102] Shortly afterward they petitioned the county court of Camden County to call an election to vote on the move of the county seat from Linn Creek to the new town of Camdenton. The business buildings formed a large landscaped circle. For a time the money from the construction project helped stimulate the economy in the small towns around the dam site, but when the project was complete, the boom passed. Even so, after the citizens of Camden County voted to move the county seat to Camdenton, the sale of lots was brisk enough to make the new town a financial success. Camdenton, with a 1999 estimated population of 3,173, rivals Osage Beach (3,349) for leadership in the Lake of the Ozarks area.

Among the foremost opponents of the dam was the Snyder family, owners of Hahatonka, a summer place built by R. M. Snyder of Kansas City.[103] Snyder purchased a 3,500-acre estate and began building a gray limestone, three-story, twenty-eight-room mansion of modified Late English–Renaissance design. It was never fully completed. The structure, begun in 1905 and worked on intermittently to 1922, perched on the flat summit of a crag known as Deer Leap Hill. At the base of the hill was Hahatanka Spring, which the lake partly flooded. At the time R. M. Snyder was killed in an auto accident October 31, 1906, improvements at Hahatonka were well underway, but far from completed. The total project when completed was to have cost more than $300,000. The payroll reportedly amounted to $1,200 per week at one time.[104] The Snyder family used the estate very little, but they contended before the Missouri Supreme Court that the construction of Bagnell Dam caused extensive damage to the property.

Hahatonka Castle, Camden County, Missouri. Country estate of the Snyder family of Kansas City, Missouri. (Courtesy of State Historical Society of Missouri.)

People recognized the recreation potential of Lake of the Ozarks immediately, especially because its northern Ozarks location was accessible from both Kansas City and St. Louis. Investors planned to develop elaborate resorts and summer homes. As we have seen, Camdenton, built on the upland and established in 1929 as the seat of Camden County, is by virtue of its youthfulness something of an anomaly in Camden County. Near the dam, a community called Lake Ozark, composed of a single row of cabins, restaurants, dance halls, taverns, and shops, grew up to cater to tourists. Osage Beach, a tiny resort village, was one of the earliest projects planned by lake real-estate developers. They platted a town and sold a few lots when Bagnell Dam was first proposed in 1928. However, the depression halted development, and many lots remained unsold until prosperity resumed during and after World War II.[105]

Oddly, during the 1960s and 1970s, when environmentalists fought bitterly against a proposed new U.S. Army Corps of Engineers dam[106] on the Meramec River, a new history of Baxter County, Arkansas,[107] told of the great benefits derived from an earlier dam and lake. The book included a chapter titled "The Dreams Come True —Norfork and Bull Shoals Dams." Attitudes toward harnessing the power of rivers had changed in the years since Ben Kantor of Peer International Corporation wrote this ditty about man and Nature:

You've all heard the story, that's covered with glory.
A story about Uncle Sam.
How old Mother Nature was challenged and changed
By the building of Boulder Dam.[108]

By 1938 the Federal Power Commission had rescinded the rights of all private power companies—including Dixie Power Company and White River Power Company, which dated back to 1916—pending the determination of future projects by the United States in the White River Basin. In 1941, construction began on Norfork Dam on the North Fork River in Baxter County, Arkansas. It was one of six reservoirs that the Comprehensive Flood Control Act of 1938 authorized for construction in the White River Basin. The government rushed it through to completion during World War II for its electric-power production, although they had not included generation facilities in its authorization.

Community groups met in Harrison, Arkansas, in 1940 in an attempt to get hydroelectric power included in the project purpose. The reasons were basic:

Those areas were not adequately served [by electrical power] at the time and the sparseness of population could not justify any expansive companies. On the other hand, the population growth which usually came with the construction and completion of the dams and reservoirs could make it feasible for private power companies to move in. Some feared the cost-benefit ratio would not justify Congressional expenditure unless hydroelectric power was included. Privately, most citizens would have accepted any government project with open arms . . . Depression gripped the communities. Farms were being abandoned and communities were drying up . . . Even a partial solution to their economic problems was met with hopeful enthusiasm.[109]

The U.S. Army Corps of Engineers established its headquarters at Mountain Home to administer the affairs of Norfork Dam and to begin the construction of Bull Shoals Dam. Construction villages, similar to those at Powersite and Bagnell dams, sprang up around Corps of Engineers dams built before the mid-1950s. When Norfork Dam was under construction, many area residents quit low-paying jobs to work at the dam for thirty cents an hour, "a fabulous common labor wage for the area." The social impact of the two dams was substantial as men sought to learn new jobs and work habits and as they became familiar with new machinery and materials. Even the children felt the glamour of the projects:

Remember those orange colored "hard hats" the workers wore? How I secretly envied the children of our neighborhood when he [one of the fathers] swaggered into the Monkey Run Store wearing his hard hat. The roads leading to the dam site carried a constant stream of trucks laden with strange looking machinery and material.[110]

As soon as construction began, Norfork Dam became an attraction. The Morrison-Knudsen Company, the principal contractor, built an overlook that became a popular Sunday-afternoon sightseeing stop until the site was closed in January 1942 because of the "fear of war sabotage." Charles Bivan, who promoted Disney, Oklahoma, on Lake o' the Cherokees, promoted Spencer, the main town next to the dam. Mary Ann Messick's recollection of Norfork Dam's impact vividly describes the dramatic changes in land and life:

Actually there was not one—but three boomtowns. Spencer, at the dam site, Salesville (also known as Ellis) on Highway 5, and in between the two false front towns was Hutcheson. In all three towns, businesses sprung up overnight—lumberyards, hotels, boarding houses, trailer parks, rent houses and cabins, stores, department stores, garages, cafes, pool halls, beauty shops, and a restaurant. In March, '41, even before the contract was let, the Arkansas Employment Service opened an office in Spencer. One thousand people applied for jobs the first week. Since local people were to have first chance at the jobs, applicants had to show a Baxter County Poll Tax Receipt. . . . The building of Norfork Dam was our first mass encounter with the outside world—including the gaudy, bright-light world of dance halls, scantily clad show girls, and gamblers. Sheriff Harvey Powell and his deputies had their work cut out—but before long they had Spencer "cleaned up." The Chef—a café featuring beer, wine, and illegal gambling—was closed and padlocked.[111]

Today, visualizing a brightly lit Las Vegas–type strip in the Baxter County of the early 1940s stretches one's imagination, but the infusion of money and new people probably spawned a few beer joints where workers could gamble wages away. The dedication of Norfork Dam on May 23, 1941, attracted a large crowd, estimated at twelve thousand people. The organizers arranged for special trains from Springfield and Little Rock. The event included a parade, with bands from Springfield, West Plains, Little Rock, Harrison, and Cotter, which wound from the Salesville junction to the dam. There were few critics of the U.S. Army Corps of Engineers in those days.

By 1970, however, in the midst of the national environmental movement and after completion of a dozen Corps of Engineers dams in the region, a more affluent Ozark population paused to reflect and to criticize proposed corps projects. The large lakes seem to have spawned the doom of future impoundments. The Corps of Engineers canceled two dam projects—one on the Meramec River, the other on the upper James River—in the 1970s because of widely based opposition.[112] A third Corps of Engineers project, the Gilbert Reservoir project on the midsection of the Buffalo River, was withdrawn after strong opposition from environmentalist groups and after Governor Orval Faubus issued an official statement strongly opposing the dam and supporting the national river proposal.[113] No doubt the corps dams promoted much of the prosperity and attracted many of the new people who were among the opponents of future projects.

Norfork Dam was completed in 1944, the first of a series of large Corps of Engineers reservoirs that eventually amounted to an investment of more than one billion dollars when they had constructed all of the power installations, boat docks, public-access roads, and parks. The Corps of Engineers lakes and reservoirs in the Ozarks along with the dates of completion, cost, and number of visitors in 1998 are given in Table 12-1.[114] Public use of the lakes for recreation continues to increase, although in a given year the number of visitors may decline if the water levels are too high or too low for optimum recreational use.[115]

PROMOTION AND ATTRACTION DEVELOPMENT

As with most business enterprises, promotion and development of Ozark tourism and recreation have progressed hand in hand; it is a cumulative process by which devel-

TABLE 12-1. U.S. ARMY CORPS OF ENGINEERS LAKES

Lake	Completed	Est. Cost	1976 Visitors	1998 Visitors
Wappepello	1941	$.	1,825,000	1,995,300
Norfork Lake	1944	9,372,960	1,673,993	
Clearwater Lake	1948	69,390,000	3,842,398	. . . .
Bull Shoals Lake	1951	93,400,000	3,885,000	5,717,345
Tenkiller Ferry Lake	1953	23,713,000	5,668,200	1,272,170
Fort Gibson Lake	1953	42,494,000	3,570,200	2,676,320
Table Rock Lake	1958	70,382,000	6,379,163	6,181,672
Pomme de Terre Lake	1861	17,129,120	1,380,811	1,474,343
Greers Ferry Lake	1962	51,174,000	4,224,088	5,646,760
Beaver Lake	1962	49,403,000	3,842,398	3,268,104
Webbers Falls Lake	1969	83,688,000	863,600	. . . .
Stockton Lake	1974	75,531,000	1,785,247	1,213,272
H. S. Truman Lake	1979	550,900,000	. . . .	1,806,000

SOURCE: Regional U.S. Army Corps of Engineers offices in Kansas City, Missouri; Tulsa, Oklahoma; Little Rock, Arkansas; and Memphis, Tennessee.

opment begets promotion and additional promotion leads to further development. The early health spas were among the first tourist attractions, and, as we have seen, they published brochures and placed advertisements in newspapers. The railroad companies also were important promoters of the Ozarks as a place for recreation. Newspaper accounts of float trips and hunting retreats helped to promote the Ozarks as a tourism destination. Construction of Lake Taneycomo was a landmark event; as the first of the Ozarks lakes, it opened a new aspect of recreational development. Few events or developments of great importance can be explained by a single cause, and the development of Ozark tourism is a case in point. The process is ongoing even today. Lynn Morrow and Linda Myers-Phinney, in *Shepherd of the Hills Country: Tourism Transforms the Ozarks, 1880s-1930s,* a thoroughgoing study of the historical development of tourism in the Branson area, pointed out many causative factors leading to the present tourism landscape of the White River country.[116]

One milestone in the promotion of Ozark tourism was the founding of the Ozark Playgrounds Association on November 25, 1919. This organization, one of the first of its kind in the United States, carried on national and regional promotional campaigns for the recreation and tourism industry of northwest Arkansas and southwest Missouri until 1979. The 1977 *Official Directory of the Ozark Playgrounds Association* consisted of 101 pages of color advertisements, descriptions, and maps from hundreds of businesses, including motels, resorts, marinas,

historical attractions, caves, fishing docks, and canoe rentals. The Ozark Playgrounds Association sprang from an automobile tour to Eureka Springs, Arkansas, in the fall of 1919 by the Rotary Club of Joplin. The ninety-mile trip required a full day. After the tour, they decided to form an association to promote Ozark attractions, the foremost of which were Lake Taneycomo and vicinity; Springfield; Eureka Springs, Arkansas; Monte Ne, a resort near Rogers, Arkansas; and Bella Vista, a resort near Bentonville, Arkansas.

With construction of the large lakes from the 1950s to the 1970s, the Ozark Playgrounds Association grew rapidly as developers built more boat docks and lake-front attractions. Perusing the back issues of the *Official Directory* of the Ozark Playgrounds Association is a good way to assess the evolution of the tourism and recreation industry. Advertisements in the 1930s and 1940s emphasized scenic drives, historic attractions, caves, overnight and weekly cabin rentals, and fishing. From the 1950s to 1979, the *Official Directory* carried, increasingly from year to year, advertisements related to water sports, resorts, motel accommodations, convention activities, country-music shows, and second-home and retirement-home developments. Each year businesses placed more advertisements for recreational services that appeal to the whole family. The trend continues as ever increasing emphasis is placed on activities for women and children. Advertising in all of its various forms—postcards, brochures, booklets, roadside signs, newspapers, radio, television, the Internet—

has been very effective in attracting visitors to the region and allowing tourism to grow. As one informant put it, "the only thing that has gotten smaller in this business are the bathing suits."

The Ozark Playgrounds Association served as a model for state tourism commissions in Missouri, Arkansas, and Oklahoma. These agencies became especially active in publicizing the Ozarks in the 1970s. At the local level, each major lake or reservoir had its own promotional association. For the larger lakes, various clusters of attractions, usually along a developed stretch of highway or an arm of a lake, have their own promotional associations intended to attract visitors. When combined with chamber-of-commerce advertising in most of the nearby lake towns, the result is an intricate geography of tourism and recreation promotion that is well designed to entice the visitor to the Ozarks and then direct him to various attractions.

A complete historical geography of current tourism-recreation attractions of the Ozarks would be most useful and interesting, but it is beyond the immediate purposes of this account. However, sketching briefly the development of selected tourist-recreation businesses to provide historical perspective is useful.

MONTE NE

One of the most interesting stories, not just because of its size and influence, concerns the resort built by William "Coin" Harvey near Rogers, Arkansas. Harvey constructed Monte Ne at a place called Silver Springs, where he had retired after an active life in the real-estate business and in politics.

William Hope Harvey was born in 1851 in Buffalo, West Virginia. A child prodigy in matters of finance, he was admitted to the bar at the age of twenty-one. In 1884 he opened real-estate offices in Denver and Pueblo, Colorado, and in a relatively short time amassed considerable property and other wealth. He returned to Chicago, where he had practiced law, and immediately entered the political brouhaha over free coinage of silver. His lectures in favor of free coinage of silver were published in a book called *Coin's Financial School,* which sold more than one million copies.[117] It was from this book that he got his nickname. Harvey became a close friend of William Jennings Bryan, the champion of free silver, and was a close advisor when Bryan ran for president in 1896.

Coin Harvey's retirement was brief. By 1901 he had become actively engaged in the construction and promotion of Monte Ne, and in 1902 the railroad was extended to the resort from Lowell. Bryan and U.S. senator Ben "Pitchfork" Tillman of South Carolina were on hand for the dedication:

The little one- or two-car trains arrived at the impressive log station with a reverberating blast from the engines' whistle and a tolling of its bell. Passengers alighted from coaches and were met with a royal welcome. Upon naming their destination, they were escorted to the nearby lagoon, where deep blue-green waters from Big Spring reflected stately trees of the forest. At the lagoon visitors were ceremoniously ushered aboard a long, low Venetian gondola in which they were leisurely transported to the hotel or cottage of their choice. The gondoliers were dressed in colorful costumes, and the final minutes of the journey were made as pleasant and inviting as possible.[118]

The resort was impressive. In 1904 Harvey organized the Monte Ne Club House, Hotel and Cottage Company, Inc., to build a hotel 220 feet long and four stories high.[119] The "cottages," constructed of logs for a rustic effect, were between 300 and 350 feet long. They knew them as Arkansas, Texas, Louisiana, Missouri, and Oklahoma rows, no doubt a good identification of the home states of most of the visitors. In 1904 a newspaper and a bank opened for business. Other attractions for guests included a splendid golf course, an enclosed swimming pool, and a rustic pavilion that attracted large crowds.

Reportedly, Harvey had considerable trouble with organized labor and stopped construction on the large stone hotel. It seems strange that organized labor was strong enough at that time and place to influence his decision, but perhaps his national reputation in politics had some influence in the matter. In any case, Coin's untiring efforts to develop the resort and to promote tourism—in 1913 he started promoting the Ozark Trails, an association devoted to getting more and better roads in the four-state area—were doomed to failure.

Coin was born thirty years too soon as a developer of the resort trade. Two teams of the Western Baseball Association were brought to Monte Ne aboard a special train for an exhibition game. Again the good people frowned upon such goings-on on Sunday. The attraction was not repeated. Then Harvey and the Frisco agreed to disagree on several problems, whereupon the Frisco refused to handle the special excursions.[120]

By 1920 the summer resort at Monte Ne had become a lost dream to Coin. He lost the railroad, the bank, and the newspaper. He had trouble with the stockholders, and people just did not come to Monte Ne as they once had. The financial loss and the loss of his eldest son a few years earlier apparently drove Coin into retirement again.[121]

Harvey spent his last years attempting to build a pyramid at Monte Ne to house the secrets of "our civilization." Work was started in 1925, but the project was never completed. A metal plate on the top of the pyramid was to read, "When this can be read, go below and find a record of and the cause of the death of a former civilization." Several items were to have been placed in the pyramid, including a four-hundred-page book telling of "our civilization."

The last big event held at Monte Ne was the national convention of the Liberty Party in 1932. Coin Harvey helped launch the party and served as editor of the *Liberty Bell,* its newspaper. Its slogan, "Prosperity in Ninety Days," was to be realized by initiating many of Coin's old free-silver ideas. In many ways, the convention was a gathering of political eccentrics. They laid plans for a crowd of 10,000, but only 390 voting members were on hand for the nomination:

> The crowd and delegates were made up with a sprinkling of Reformers, Socialists, Populists, and disgruntled Democrats and Republicans. Many of them were selling books and giving out tracts with their own beliefs.[122]

Among the delegates aspiring for nomination were the likes of Dr. John Brinkley of Milford, Kansas, he of goatgland rejuvenation fame, and Alfalfa Bill Murray of Oklahoma. Nevertheless, Coin Harvey, at the age of eighty-two, was nominated as the standard-bearer of the Liberty Party.

Voters soundly rejected the Liberty Party in the fall election, and Coin spent the last four years of his life attempting to raise money to build the pyramid. He died in 1936 at age eighty-five and was buried in a mausoleum beside the lagoon at Monte Ne. Shortly after the Corps of Engineers closed the dam to form Beaver Lake they moved the mausoleum to a spot high above the lake waters encroaching on the old resort.[123]

BELLA VISTA

The development of Bella Vista in extreme northern Benton County, Arkansas, is one of the most significant stories related to the Ozark tourism recreation industry. Developers introduced many innovations that have proved successful at other locations at Bella Vista. Much of what is included in modern second-home and retirement-home development and promotion was tried at Bella Vista several years ago.[124]

The story of Bella Vista began on November 11, 1918, when two large touring cars drove into Bentonville. The drivers were two brothers from Dallas, Texas, one with his wife, the other with his wife and small son. The end of the war could not have been a better omen for the two brothers, Forest W. and Clarence A. Linebarger, for the year before, with a third brother, Clayton C. Linebarger, they had invested three thousand one hundred dollars in six hundred acres of land in Sugar Creek Valley seven miles north of Bentonville. This purchase included bluff-rimmed East Mountain and spectacular Big Spring. The three Linebargers had been engaged in the real-estate business in Texas, townsiting they called it, and had just completed a very successful real-estate venture with the then new town of Tomball, Texas.[125] At Bella Vista they planned to build a resort.

The idea of building a resort on Sugar Creek originated with another owner, William S. Baker, a Presbyterian minister in Bentonville. He and his wife, Mary, inherited property in Sugar Creek that included springs and caves. The Bakers laid out a subdivision and sold a few lots, but when the task seemed too formidable they formed the Smith-Baker Land Company in 1916, and a few months later decided to sell out.[126] They had already built a dam, forming a lake on the creek, and had named the spot Bella Vista.[127] In spite of his selling a few lots to local people, financial difficulties set in and the Baker-Smith Land Company sold the property to the Linebarger brothers.

In contrast to the former owner's policies, the Linebargers immediately set out to gain regional sales. They spent the first year selling Bella Vista lots to families from such centers of new oil prosperity as Dallas, Fort Worth, Bartlesville, and Tulsa. Their most successful sales agent, Dallas Rupe of Dallas, Texas, soon joined the Linebargers. Rupe sold the "staggering amount" of $80,000 worth of property "to Tulsa families in the spring of 1918, resulting in the first row of cottages at Bella Vista: Tulsa Row.[128] When oilmen discovered a new oil field, the Linebarger sales agents were not far behind. By 1926 the sales booklet *Bella Vista, Nature's Gem of the Ozarks,* enticed oil men with the assurance that "Bella Vista, on account of its nearness to the Midcontinent Fields, is properly called the Summer Capitol and Playground of the Oil Men of the Southwest."[129]

Among all the oil families at Bella Vista were several Osage Indians, who made a lasting impression on the people of Bentonville as they drove about in their big cars, sometimes bedecked in traditional dress. There were as many as forty or fifty Osage families at Bella Vista in the 1920s.

The Linebargers used a technique long practiced by real-estate promoters: sell property to prominent citizens and use their inherent prestige to sell additional lots. One of the most appealing aspects of living at Bella Vista was the opportunity to rub shoulders with the very rich or socially prominent. Doctors, bankers, university presidents, ministers, and businesspeople were especially sought after by Bella Vista sales agents. A list of Bella Vista owners and their occupations showed who was making money in the Southwest: W. W. Patterson, coal-mine owner, Pittsburg, Kansas; T. E. Braniff, insurance, Oklahoma City; Walter Harrison, business manager of the *Daily Oklahoman,* Oklahoma City; T. S. Terry, wholesale and retail jewelry, Bartlesville, Oklahoma; Mrs. Camilla Davis, Texas Farm Loan Mortgage Company, Dallas.[130] Many Bella Vista owners were wealthy enough to have servants, most of whom were black. Among the property owners of national prominence were Congressman Sam Rayburn and Will Rogers. Will Rogers's wife's parents lived in nearby Rogers, Arkansas.

The real-estate promoters priced the lots modestly, considering the wealth of many purchasers. The Linebargers' sales booklet, *Bella Vista: Nature's Gem of the Ozarks,* in about 1918 advertised the terms for lots at "$300 or $250 Summer Homesite, $15.00 cash, $15.00 a month. $200, $150, or $100 Summer Homesite, $10 cash, $10 per month. No interest, discount 8 percent for all cash."[131] By the mid-1920s, they no longer specified prices in *Nature's Gem,* Bella Vista's newsletter, but simply said they were reasonable. In the summer of 1926, six hundred cottages were occupied, and there were seven hundred cottages owned by people from ten states. Most of the guests came from Oklahoma, Texas, Mississippi, Louisiana, and Kansas.[132]

When the brothers built the Sunset Hotel in 1929 on a mountain overlooking Lake Bella Vista, they designed it for the elite. Its sixty-five guest rooms each had a private bath with hot and cold running water.[133] They also had quarters for servants. Besides hosting vacationers at the hotel, the Linebargers invited prospective purchasers of lots and houses to stay there, a practice now used at time-share resorts near Branson and the Lake of the Ozarks. The hotel thrived for only a short time because the depression nearly ended lot sales and expensive vacations. Today, what was once the fanciest hotel in the region is an office building. It is known as the Village Hall, and houses the administrative offices of Cooper Communities, Inc., including the *Weekly Vista* newspaper.

The Linebargers were innovative. Each year, they made new improvements to extend the line of services. Perhaps the most popular entertainment was dancing. They held the dances in a large pavilion every night except Sunday. For a time, in the 1920s, the radio station KVOO in Tulsa broadcast Bella Vista's dances several nights a week. Various bands, including Doc Miller and the Quadrangle Orchestra, Marshall Hayes's Bella Vista Orchestra, Ockly Pittman's Bella Vista Blue Bonnet Orchestra, and Carl Wortz' Ozark Smile Girl Band, played for the dances.[134] C. A. Linebarger watched every person, every night, for infractions of the posted rule: "Anyone dancing with heads together or doing the 'shimmy' or like dancing will be ejected from the floor. Polite dancers welcome." The Wonderland Cave nightclub opened in May 1930. For opening night, it had a top band, and more than eight hundred people came. This cave became very famous as one of the top night spots in Arkansas.

Sunset Hotel overlooking Sugar Creek Dam with dancehall in the foreground, Bella Vista, Arkansas, circa 1930. (Courtesy of Rogers Museum, Rogers, Arkansas.)

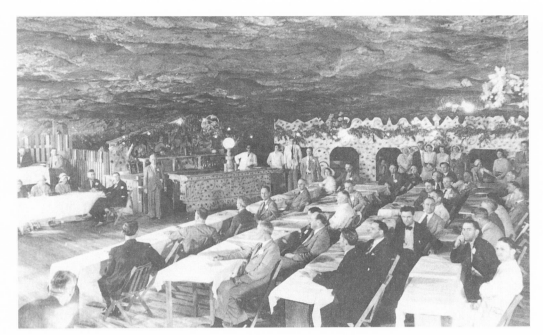

Arkansas legislature at Wonderland Cave Nightclub, Bella Vista, Arkansas, circa 1930. (Courtesy of Rogers Museum, Rogers, Arkansas.)

Bridge was popular for wives, but hiking, tennis, horseback riding, fishing, and swimming at "the Plunge" were popular with almost everyone. When, in 1919, they converted a cornfield in the Sugar Creek bottoms into a nine-hole golf course, the men of Bella Vista could emulate the popular new president Warren G. Harding, playing the rising new game for the middle class in the twenties.[135] The brothers arranged to equip the swimming pool with electric lights in the 1920s. They arranged special events nearly every week: air shows, pony races, fireworks displays, bucking-horse contests, boxing matches, and open-air theater.

The Linebargers participated enthusiastically in another hallmark of boosterism. Beginning in the 1920s, the Ozarks was promoted as the Land of a Million Smiles, which gave rise to the popular "Smile Girl" contest. Bella Vista, a flourishing Benton County city, always sponsored a candidate for the contest.

Bella Vista was the Ozarks' most advanced pioneer second-home and retirement-home development. Eventually, the Linebarger brothers established nearly all phases of the present system at Bella Vista. Purchasers of lots had the privilege of using the facilities at Bella Vista whether they built a home or not. Most buyers preferred to let the Linebargers build for them rather than exercise their option to build their own cottages. Because most lots were narrow and steep, the cottages frequently extended from the hillside on open foundations enclosed with lattice work. Lattice work, widely used in India, had become popular in England in the 1800s and became popular in the United States in the 1920s for the construction of summer resorts. The cottages built by the Linebargers compared favorably with city dwellings of that time. They had hardwood floors, plasterboard ceilings and walls, stone fireplaces, kitchens with a sink and cabinets, and the most prized of all, a bathroom with tub, shower, lavatory, and toilet. Some cottages had a servant's room. By the mid-1920s a battery of rams pumped water from Big Spring into reservoirs, where gravity forced it through pipes into the cottages. Briefly, a water-powered generator at a small dam on Sugar Creek supplied erratic electrical power for the resort, but by 1920 the Linebargers had arranged to tap Bentonville's electrical system for twenty-four-hour service to each cottage.[136]

After a time, many owners found that they could not use their cottages as frequently as they wished to, so many of them were empty much of the time. The Linebargers provided a rental service under which, for a fee, they would rent the cottage to visitors for periods ranging from a few days to several months. They also engaged in reselling cottages and lots for those who wanted to divest themselves of their holdings at Bella Vista. Thus, by 1930 most of the administrative, organizational, and operating procedures of modern second-home and retirement-home development had been well explored at Bella Vista.

To continue the story of Bella Vista, one must begin at West Memphis, Arkansas, and then follow the career of John Cooper from West Memphis to the Spring River country near Hardy, Arkansas, and finally to Bella Vista. John Cooper was born in Earle, Arkansas, in the delta country, the eldest of eight children, and after attending Vanderbilt University at Nashville, Tennessee, and Cumberland Law School at Nashville, he entered practice in West Memphis.[137] Cooper's career as a practicing attorney lasted only one year. Very soon he was engaged in several enterprises, including farming; trading in cotton, soybeans, rice, and cattle; selling farm machinery; heavy construction; sawmilling; cotton ginning; and banking.

As a young man, Cooper had made several trips to the southeast Ozarks in the Spring River country. As his business ventures prospered, he was unable to forget the Ozark hill country, and in 1943 he went by boat from Hardy up the South Fork of Spring River to Otter Creek. This spot intrigued him so much that in 1948 he purchased four hundred acres and named it Otter Creek Ranch. He had a small house on the river bank enlarged as a summer home for the family. Cooper subdivided part of the tract into lots to sell to others who wished to build a weekend cottage. Summer camps, cottages, and inns had been popular in the Spring River area for many years. Ravenden, the elegant old health resort some twenty miles east, had prospered for many years before it finally closed. Many summer places had Indian names, so the Coopers selected the name *Cherokee Village* for their development.

In 1953, at a time when Sharp County, Arkansas, was down to about sixty-five hundred people—or about half what it was in 1940—Cooper formed the Cherokee Village Development Company to subdivide the tract into smaller lots and sell them. From the beginning it was a family corporation, with all the brothers and sisters of John and Mildred Cooper as stockholders.

The development company sold the first property in the summer of 1954. Governor Orval Faubus, Burl Ives, and an obscure Cherokee Indian chief were invited to the dedication of the village on June 11, 1955. The ceremony was arranged to attract attention to the new development and to assist in the sale of lots. The major amenities with the early properties were all-weather roads, electricity, man-made Lake Cherokee with three parks, and access to the river for swimming and fishing. Cooper Communities, Inc., was one of the first Ozark second-home developers to invite prospective buyers to view the properties with all expenses paid.

In 1960 the concept of the village changed from weekend place to year-round residence. The goal was now to be a recreation and retirement community. At this time the company employed land planners to study the situation to figure out the villages' growth pattern and its need for recreation, businesses, schools, churches, and utilities. They have followed this plan since then with very little variation.

In 1977 the village consisted of fifteen thousand acres and approximately twenty-five thousand lots. By 1979,

they had sold more than 95 percent of the lots, and Cooper Communities, through a subsidiary company, engaged in a lively resale business of both lots and properties. The village has seven man-made lakes, a town center for shopping, a community center for civic and social events, and hundreds of modern homes and townhouses to accommodate guests and permanent residents. Although property owners have built houses on less than half the lots, mainly those close to the lakes, Cherokee Village has a population of approximately forty-five hundred, making it the largest town in the tri-county area: Sharp, Fulton, Izard. The October 9, 2000, Internet home page for Cherokee Village listed the following community services and shopping facilities: two championship golf courses, seven lakes, all the school buildings in the Highland School District, and a town center with all the shopping and services to be found in a city of forty-five hundred. Other businesses and services include Village Rentals; Cooper Communities, Inc.; the Chamber of Com-merce; a recreation department; a sanitation department; a security department; the *Cherokee Villager* newspaper; Quapaw Water Service; a U.S. Post Office; and a medical clinic.

Cooper Communities has established similar developments at Bella Vista, where they purchased and expanded the property of the Linebarger brothers, and at Hot Springs Village in the Ouachita Mountains. The latter communities are larger than Cherokee Village.

One can only speculate about the consequences of full development of the villages into communities of forty-five thousand to sixty thousand residents if property owners developed and occupied all the lots. The requirements in energy would be substantial, and if local or state governments no longer permitted on-lot sewage disposal, the cost of development on the rocky hillsides would be very high. However, the village plans incorporate many modern subdivision concepts, including clustered services and commons that serve as buffers from contiguous developed land. Probably, the planned communities—and there are several others, Horseshoe Bend, Fairfield Bay, Holliday Island—would be, if they grew to full planned size, environmentally more sound than unplanned communities of similar size.

THE SHEPHERD OF THE HILLS HOMESTEAD

The cumulative effect of a variety of types of attractions is perhaps best exhibited near Branson and Table Rock Reservoir. Even before nearby Lake Taneycomo formed in 1913, Harold Bell Wright's book *The Shepherd of the Hills*, which was an immediate success after publication in 1907, had made that area in western Taney County a popular tourist haunt. Wright, a minister-author who made his home in Lebanon, Missouri, for several years, had visited the vicinity of Dewey Bald on numerous occasions, camping on the farm of John K. Ross. While there, he wrote a fictional account about the people and the area. In Wright's story, Uncle Matt and Aunt Molly Matthews are near portraits of John Ross and his wife, Anna.[138] The book was a turning point in Wright's literary career. Millions of copies were sold in several languages, and four movie versions were filmed. Wright's forty-year career as a writer resulted in nineteen books, many scripts for stage plays, and a number of magazine articles before his death in 1944.

As early as 1910, vacationers started coming into the area to see where the book was written and the places and people about whom it was written. The Matthews' (Ross) farm was the original setting of the *Shepherd of the Hills* story, and the old cabin still stands today. Lizzie McDaniel, the daughter of a Springfield banker, bought the Ross farm after the deaths of John and Anna Ross. When she visited Low Gap in 1926, she found the Ross homestead "overrun with pigs and squatters."[139] Visitors had removed parts of the old cabin for souvenirs. She restored the cabin and lived in it while collecting furnishings and memorabilia connected to the Ross family and Wright. Dr. Bruce Trimble, a professor at the University of Kansas, and his wife, Mary, with their son Mark, acquired the homestead in 1946 after Lizzie McDaniel's death. The Trimbles developed the Shepherd of the Hills Farm and the Old Mill Theatre (1960) into a multifaceted operation.

In 1985 the Trimble family sold the property to Gary Snadon, a Branson real-estate developer. Snadon gave the property its present name, the Shepherd of the Hills Homestead. In 1988, the Inspiration Tower at Inspiration Point opened as part of a continuing effort to develop the property and its popular outdoor reenactment of Harold Bell Wright's story into one of the prime tourist attractions in the Ozarks (fig. 12-3). Its link with history and early settlement has given it an important place in the tourism-recreation blend of the area, so much so that the Branson-Table Rock Lake area is sometimes called the Shepherd of the Hills Country.

SILVER DOLLAR CITY

Only a few miles west of Shepherd of the Hills Farm on Missouri Highway 76 is Marvel Cave, which was opened to the public by William Henry Lynch. He became interested in the cave, in Stone County, Missouri, when he helped explore its twenty-two passages and three streams.

Lynch bought the cave property and devoted a large part of the remaining years of his life to it, opening it to public touring in 1894. He called it Marble Cave because he thought it contained marble; the name has since been changed to Marvel Cave.

When the Lynches opened the cave to visitors, they attracted a hardy but small clientele who had to journey to the spot from the Missouri Pacific railroad stop on Roark Creek, northwest of the cave, or make a two-day trip from Branson, staying overnight in cabins at the Lynch homestead. In 1946, Hugo and Mary Herschend of Wilmette, Illinois, visited the Ozarks and became interested in the cave. A ninety-nine-year lease on the property, secured in 1950 from Lynch's daughter, provided the basis for what was to be the Ozarks' largest tourist attraction.

Silver Dollar City, located over Marvel Cave, opened in May 1960 on the site of the abortive 1880s mining community of Marmaros, which was founded to exploit the bat guano in the cave.[140] In 1961, in its second year of operation, park personnel were expecting 250,000 visitors.[141] In 1999, more than three million visitors enjoyed the Silver Dollar City's attractions. Today it is one of the nation's most popular entertainment facilities of its kind. Its distinction as an attraction lies in Mary Herschend's concept of a middle-western Williamsburg, with native craftspeople displaying their skills. The city keeps alive more than twenty historic crafts once commonly found in the hills. Visitors can chat with the craftspeople as they work and see, at first hand, their methods.

In 1963 the first Missouri Festival of Ozark Craftsmen marked the beginning of an activity that would eventually draw to Silver Dollar City a quarter of a million people and more than sixty craft displays yearly. At this festival, held each October, the visitor can see everything from glassblowing to log hewing to cane-bottomed chair weaving to fiddle making. Each year additional attractions, crafts, and accommodations are added to serve the ever-increasing number of visitors. The concept, which involves a pleasant blend of commercial activities with traditional crafts and historical-cultural activities, has proved so popular that the management of Silver Dollar City opened a similar attraction near the entrance to the Great Smoky Mountains National park in eastern Tennessee. Because of the success of the Ozarks attraction, personnel from Silver Dollar City are in demand as consultants for other theme-park developments throughout the United States. The Herschend family has maintained a strong management position as Silver Dollar City has diversified into other entertainment and tourism businesses.[142] The company also operates five other tourist attractions in the Branson area: the showboat *Branson Belle*; White Water, a popular

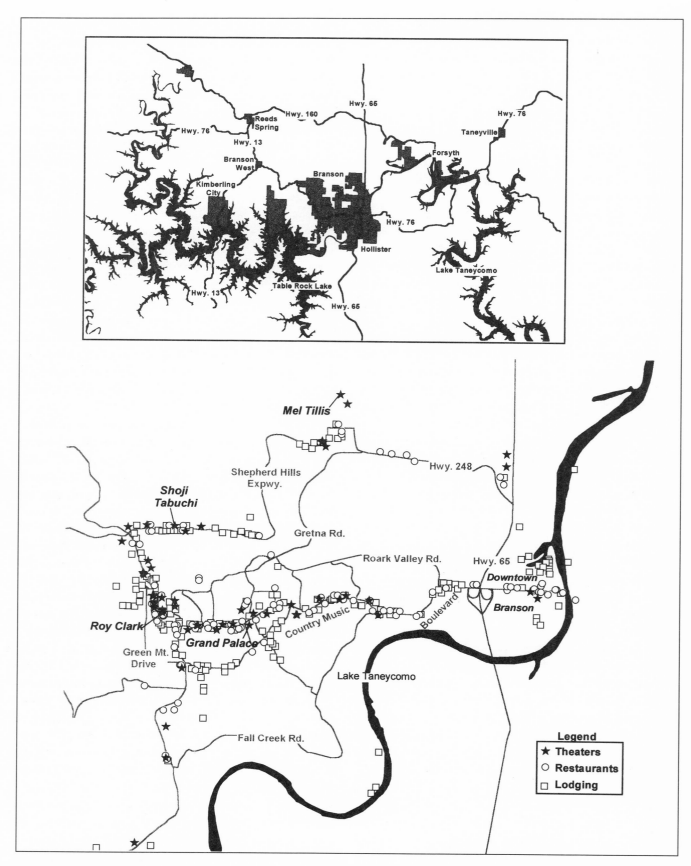

FIGURE 12-3. Branson-Table Rock Lake tourism area, 2000. Adapted from City of Branson, Missouri, Engineering and GIS Division, *Digital Geographic Information Systems (GIS)Files* (Branson, Mo.: City of Branson Press, 2000).

water park; Grand Village Shopping Center; Silver Dollar City Campground; and Radio City Christmas, a two-month Christmas season show at the Grand Palace featuring the Radio City Rockettes.

COUNTRY MUSIC

If you ask almost anyone what made Branson what it is today, they will respond, "Country music." Undoubtedly country music has played an important part in the phenomenal growth of Branson and the attractions along the stretch of Missouri Highway 76 leading west of the city. Before country music, Branson was primarily a resort town consisting of cafes, taverns, novelty shops, and motels and tourist cabins. Lake Taneycomo and Table Rock Lake provided opportunities for water-based recreation—swimming, boating, fishing. West of Branson along Highway 76 was Old Matt's Cabin, Uncle Ike's Post Office, Shepherd of the Hills Farm, all connected with Harold Bell Wright's 1907 novel, *Shepherd of the Hills,* and the Silver Dollar City theme park where tourists could visit spectacular Marvel Cave. However, as we have seen, there were many important developments in tourism that set the stage for the growth of "Branson" as it is today. First-time visitors are struck with awe at the impressive tourist and shopping developments, but perhaps not as much as the local people who remember Highway 76 as a two-lane highway winding through a pastoral landscape astride the ridge tops above the north shore of Table Rock Lake.

In truth, old Branson, including the downtown area, retains some ambiance of the past. There is the old railroad station where tourists wait in wooden bench chairs to board the *Ozark Zephyr,* a special train operated by the Branson Scenic Railroad for a short run down the old Missouri Pacific White River line (now the Missouri and Arkansas Railroad). A block east is the boat dock on Lake Taneycomo, where the newest model *Sammy Lane* tour boat docks at the same spot other boats by the same name docked for three-quarters of a century. Northwest of the boat docks are the early tourist courts where third-generation tourists stay in the same cabin their grandparents once occupied. Up the hill a block west of the railroad station is the old business district, now spiced up with T-shirt shops, novelty stores, and other places selling tourist bric-a-brac.

The transformation of the Branson scene has been rapid with the greatest development occurring since the mid-1970s. The new "Branson" grew up along Highway 76 and has spread to Shepherd of the Hills Expressway and other expanding hilltop roads. Two-lane Highway 76 has been widened with a turning lane to adapt to auto-

mobiles and busses carrying visitors to Silver Dollar City theme park, Shepherd of the Hills Homestead, White Water water park, and more than forty theaters, the majority featuring country music. The theaters have a combined seating capacity of more than fifty thousand, making the Branson area the nation's largest center for live performances by nationally known performers such as Mel Tillis, Andy Williams, Bobby Vinton, and Roy Clark. Many established local musical groups—the Bald Knobbers, the Presleys, and a popular Japanese-American fiddle player, Soji Tobuchi—draw crowds as large as the nationally known performers. Some theaters, like the four-thousand-seat Grand Palace, are nearly as brightly lighted as Las Vegas casinos. The theaters have comfortable seats, air conditioning, and professional stage personnel and equipment. Many theaters feature three shows each day—breakfast shows, matinees, and after-dinner shows—during an eight- or nine-month season. The attractions along "Country Music Boulevard," the locally coined name for Highway 76, attracted more than five million visitors in 1991. By 1992, with the christening of the showboat *Branson Belle,* country music had taken to the waters of Table Rock Lake.

The Branson country-music phenomenon evolved in three stages.[143] It began with the use of local talent from 1959 to 1982. A group of local performers from Christian County, the Mabe Brothers, after singing live at a Springfield radio station and at Silver Dollar City, opened in a fifty-seat auditorium in the basement of the Branson community building in 1959. The Mabes, known professionally as the Bald Knobbers, then purchased the town's skating rink in 1965, which may be the first bona fide country-music theater in the Branson area. By 1968 the Bald Knobbers had outgrown the theater in Branson and built a new theater on Highway 76, just east and across the road from the Presley Mountain Music Jubilee theater, which was built in 1966 by another local musical group from the Brighton area north of Springfield, the Presley family. The Presleys lay claim, correctly, to the first country-music show (1966) on "the strip" (Country Music Boulevard), while the Mabes (Bald Knobbers) rightly claim to be the first country-music show (1959) in Branson. After several additional local groups—Foggy River Boys (1974), Plummer Family (1974), Bob-O-Links Country Hoedown Theater (featuring Bob Mabe) (1977), the Wilkinson Brothers (1981), and the Ozark Jubilee (1981)—moved to the strip and drew good audiences, the stage was set for the second phase.

The second stage in Branson's country-music development began in 1983 when nationally known Roy Clark, a native of Tulsa, Oklahoma, opened a large theater on

Country Music Boulevard on the site of the old Branson airport. Clark, longtime and popular host of the "Hee Haw" television show, brought name recognition to Branson, which helped to attract other performers with national reputations, including the likes of Boots Randolph, T. G. Sheppard, and Boxcar Willie.[144] Box Car Willie, a longtime Grand Old Opry star, was the first of the visitors to build a theater and move to Branson. Several factors attracted the big stars. The drug-free atmosphere, early closing time for the theaters, and attentive and enthusiastic audiences drawn from farms and towns in Middle America were inducements for some entertainers. Several big-name performers cited the opportunity to perform nightly in one location, thereby avoiding long bus trips and one-night stands as the most attractive feature. Veteran country-music performer Johnny Cash put it this way, "We are tired of putting on a million smiles on the road."[145] Other performers liked the easy-going, laid-back lifestyle, where a beautiful forested setting with large lakes, golf courses, and good restaurants had attracted a colony of performers that provided opportunities for social contacts with other country-music stars that could not be had elsewhere. For some performers—Mel Tillis, Loretta Lynn, Mickey Gilley, Charley Pride, Moe Bandy—for example, Branson was an investment opportunity as they built theaters and contributed to the more than $25 million in new construction and $5 million in remodeling during the 1980s.[146]

The third stage of development, from about 1990, has seen some older performers retire or move on, while a new generation of performers have come to Branson. The new performers, including Country Music Association award winners Vince Gill, Randy Travis, and Reba McEntire, see Branson as a place to have direct contact with fans, while continuing to record in Nashville. Some performer-investors did not stay in Branson. Nationally known Kenny Rogers, who had established a partnership with Silver Dollar City in the Grand Palace theater and reportedly planned to invest more than $100 million in Branson developments, sold his interests and moved on.[147] Others, like Mel Tillis, have put down roots and built new, even larger theaters. As Tillis put it, "You go to Nashville, you see the stars' homes. You come to Branson, you see the stars."[148]

Country music, especially the traditional or "old-timey" substyle, was deeply rooted in the culture of the Ozarks from the very outset of settlement. Nurtured at family get-togethers, community picnics, festivals, county fairs, and Saturday night dances and "hoe downs," it blossomed commercially in the 1920s and 1930s on radio stations, notably on KWTO (Keep Watching the Ozarks) in Springfield, which gained a longstanding reputation as one of the major country-music radio stations west of the Mississippi River.[149] Additional attention was focused on Ozark musical talent when KY-3 TV broadcast Red Foley's Ozark Jubilee on the ABC national television network. Country-music theaters featuring local talent have operated for many years at tourist centers other than Branson, namely, the Highway 54 "strip" near Lake of the Ozarks, and in Arkansas at Mountain View and Mountain Home. Many people continue to play their music just for the joy of it. For more than two generations, people have gathered on the courthouse square in Mountain View, Arkansas, on Friday and Saturday nights to play and hear "old-timey" country music. Several small communities near Springfield have nights set aside for country music, square dancing, and clogging. The pattern repeats itself across the Ozarks.

TOURISM-RECREATION REGIONS OF THE OZARKS

In delimiting eight tourism-recreation regions in the Ozarks, the concentration and linkages between specific points of interest, such as lakes, caves, state parks, national forests, resorts, and historical sites, were taken into account (fig. 12-4). The regions are broadly generalized to include much open and wild land that is essential for scenic tours, but areas that are undeveloped or have less potential for tourism-recreation were not included. In this way the regions are different from the recreation regions that the three state tourism commissions define, which include, for reasons of maintaining good public relations, all sections of the respective states in the tourism-recreation regions. The names that I have applied to the various regions were taken from striking physical features, historical or cultural traditions, or they are the names that have been popular during long periods of use.

LAKE OF THE OZARKS REGION

This region, about equidistant from St. Louis and Kansas City, features the 65,000-acre Lake of the Ozarks, with 1,300 miles of shoreline behind Bagnell Dam. The hills, creeks, bluffs, natural bridges, caves, springs, and the lake make this area one of the outstanding recreation regions of the Ozarks. It is heavily used, attracting vacationers not only from the large urban centers of St. Louis, Kansas City, and Chicago, but also from other areas, especially Missouri, Illinois, Iowa, and Kansas.

A resort economy extends throughout most this region. Businesspeople in Camdenton estimate that retail volume

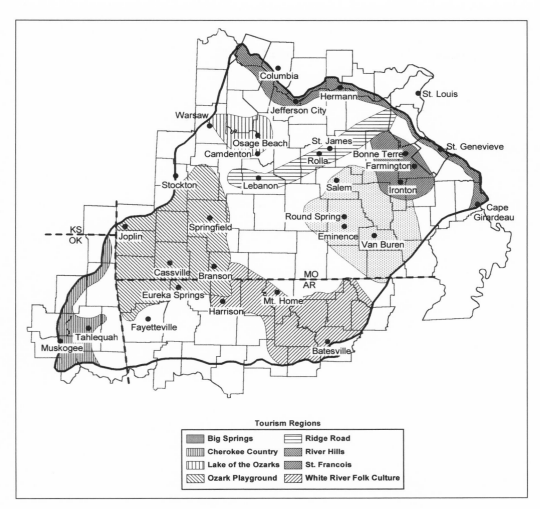

FIGURE 12-4. Ozark tourism-recreation regions. Adapted from Milton D. Rafferty. *The Ozarks Outdoors: A Guidebook for Fishermen, Hunters, and Tourists* (Norman: University of Oklahoma Press, 1980).

Tourism Regions

▓ Big Springs	☰ Ridge Road
▥ Cherokee Country	▨ River Hills
▥ Lake of the Ozarks	▧ St. Francois
▩ Ozark Playground	▨ White River Folk Culture

has increased many fold since tourism development began. In Eldon, another trade center, retail volume is said to have increased four times between the completion of Bagnell Dam in 1931 and 1940 and to have expanded at an even more accelerated rate since 1940. Within this region is Lake of the Ozarks State Park, the largest state park in Missouri. It contains a deer preserve, beach, boat dock, airport, and picnic, camping, and riding facilities. A second state park, Hahatonka, encompasses twenty-five hundred acres on the Niangua arm. It is known for its "karst" topography, characterized by sinkholes, caves, underground streams, and natural bridges. There are two commercially operated caves: Bridal and Jacob's. Hahatonka Spring and the ruins of Hahatonka Castle are attractions, as are the many resorts and roadside gift shops. Lee Mace's venerable Ozark Opry and the Main Street Music Hall are popular country-music shows in the area.[150] Shopping is popular at the Factory Outlet Village where more than 110 top-name manufacturers are represented. Big Surf, the area's only water park, is one of the newer attractions. Developers and individuals have built second homes and retirement homes in large numbers. AmerenUE (formerly

Union Electric), the lake's owner, permits building on the waterfront. Boating is very popular, but because the lake is so popular, heavy boat traffic creates problems during holiday weekends. Another problem surfaced during the 1990s on "Party Cove," where drinking, nudity, and loud parties have brought complaints from boaters and lakeside residents. There were over ten thousand boats on the Lake of the Ozarks during Memorial Day weekend 2001, and more than eight hundred of those were crowded into "Party Cove."

Probably the best-known resort on Lake of the Ozarks is Tan-Tar-A, which covers more than four hundred acres. Burton Duenke of St. Louis founded the resort, which is now operated by the Mariott Corporation. The 930-room resort started in 1960 when Duenke had twelve cottages built overlooking the lakefront. Its central location in the state of Missouri makes it a convenient and popular place to hold statewide meetings. The Windgate Center's convention accommodations include twenty-six meeting rooms. The 23,160-square-foot Grand Ballroom holds up to thirty-five hundred for receptions. Over the years, increasing emphasis has been placed on sports activities.

Water-sports activities continue to be popular, but the resort now advertises itself as a golf and tennis center. It is a complete resort in that it operates twelve months a year, offers package plans for guests, and provides an extensive range of activities and services. Among them are these: marina, fishing docks, swimming pools, sauna and health spa, several eating places, golf courses, bowling, billiards, tennis, ski slope, and horseback riding. An October 2000 price quotation from the resort's Internet home page listed the rate for the "honeymoon package" of two nights, including luxury accommodations with dinner and champagne each evening and various sports activities, at $396 fall through spring or $544 in the summer. A second large resort and golf center, Lodge of the Four Seasons, opened in 1964. Harold Koplar, a St. Louis banker who often vacationed in the area, founded it.

The Lake of the Ozarks region is one of the most maturely developed tourism areas in the Ozarks. The stretch of U.S. Highway 54 from Camdenton to the Osage River below Bagnell Dam is a nearly continuous strip of motels, restaurants, fast-food establishments, children's rides, boat docks, resorts, country-music halls, antique shops, bric-a-brac stores, realty offices, and assorted other commercial activities that cater to both transients and residents.

THE RIDGE ROAD REGION

Interstate 44 from Sullivan to the vicinity of Lebanon is the focus of this region. The existence of this well-traveled highway and U.S. Highway 66, which preceded it, have been important in developing the natural attractions of this region. In fact, I selected the name *Ridge Road* over *I-44 Region* as the proper designation for this tourism-recreation area because entrepreneurs developed some attractions, including the once-popular Gasconade Hotel at Lebanon and Onondaga Cave, when most people traveled by railroad.[151]

The hills, streams, and caves are the major attractions. At the northeast end of the region is Meramec State Park and at the southwest extremity Bennett Spring State Park, two of Missouri's best-developed parks. Two of the Ozarks' most outstanding caves, Meramec Caverns and Onondaga Cave, are near Stanton and Sullivan, respectively. The Meramec, Gasconade, Big Piney, and Little Piney rivers and the lower reaches of Huzzah and Courtois creeks are popular float streams.

At St. James, Missouri, the James Memorial Library houses an excellent collection of nineteenth- and early-twentieth-century photographs of the life and work of Ozark people. East of St. James is the Italian settlement at Rosati and several extensive vineyards. The wineries at Rosati and St. James are popular tourist attractions. Southeast of St. James is Meramec Springs, historic Maramec Iron Works, and public trout fishing. The property is operated jointly by the Lucy James Foundation and the Missouri Department of Conservation.[152] It included the spring and a trout hatchery, the ruins of the Maramec Iron Works, a historical museum, and inviting picnic grounds. Lucy Wortham James, descendant of the founding fathers of St. James and the ironworks and heir to large stockholdings in the financial firm of Dun and Bradstreet, purchased the spring and ironworks and sixteen hundred acres of surrounding land. She willed much of her estate to the care and maintenance of the property and gave these directions to the New York Community Trust, the administrator of her estate: "As this is considered to be the most beautiful spot in Missouri, it is my great hope that you will arrange that it may ever be in private, considerate control and ever open to the enjoyment of the people."[153]

Other attractions include the University of Missouri at Rolla, one of the foremost mining and engineering universities in the United States; Fort Leonard Wood, near Waynesville; and many resorts, camps, and float services along the Gasconade River and the Big Piney and Little Piney rivers. One of the more unusual attractions is the Caveman Restaurant near Richland, Missouri. The restaurant, built, owned, and operated by David and Connie Hughes, is off Route W near Interstate 44 in a very wild and scenic area. Vans carry visitors from the parking lot to an elevator that takes them to the cave entrance in a bluff overlooking a scenic valley. The restaurant, popular for anniversaries and parties, attracts local patrons and visitors from St. Louis, Springfield, and other cities.

ST. FRANCOIS REGION

This important recreation area in eastern Missouri is centered in the oldest geological formations outcropping anywhere in the Ozarks. The U.S. Forest Service is preserving much of the forest land in the Mark Twain National Forest. There are also six state parks: Washington, St. Francois, Hawn, Elephant Rocks, Johnson Shut-ins, and St. Joe. The St. Joe Mineral Corporation donated the latter park to the state after it closed down mining operations in the Old Lead Belt. Many picturesque gorges cut through granite and dark rhyolite enhance the scenery. At Graniteville are the widely known Elephant Rocks, huge boulders eroded into fantastic shapes. Also in the region are four well-known isolated mountain peaks that attract tourists: Iron Mountain, Pilot Knob, Buford Mountain, and Taum Sauk Mountain. The last-named is the highest

Trout fishing at Bennett Springs State Park, Dallas County, Missouri, 1973. (Milton Rafferty Collection, photograph by the author.)

point in Missouri. At the base of the St. Francois Mountains are scenic Arcadia and Belleview valleys.

Historically, this region was among the first settled areas in the entire Mississippi Valley. Place names show the early French influence, and a handful of older residents can still speak an old French dialect around Old Mines, a settlement north of Potosi. At Potosi, former center for the mining of lead and barite, is the tomb of Moses Austin. Huge chat piles of waste rock from the lead mines around Flat River and Bonne Terre Mine are reminders of mining's importance. The mining museum and tours of the old Bonne Terre Mine are popular tourist attractions.

The tourist-recreation blend in the St. Francois region, like that of most of the northeastern Ozarks, is different from that of the bustling lake districts in the southern and western Ozarks. Camping, picnicking, horseback riding, canoeing, and touring are very popular. There are no amusement parks, and only a few motels and restaurants. Many visitors bring their own camping gear and food and stay in one of the state parks or camping areas.

Visitors who tour the pleasant and picturesque Belleview and Arcadia valleys find a different style and a more leisurely pace than in the western lakes country. As we have seen, these valleys were discovered early by visitors from St. Louis. By the 1870s wealthy families were building summer homes. Because they could reach the region easily on the St. Louis and Iron Mountain Railroad, the St. Francois Mountains became a popular vacation spot for St. Louisans. Individuals purchased tracts of the most desirable land for private estates, and churches bought properties for summer camps and rest homes. For example, the United Methodist church operates the Blue Mountain camp and the Epworth Among the Hills camp in the Arcadia Valley. The meeting building at the latter camping area was once the Japanese pavilion at the 1904 World Fair in St. Louis.[154] Adding to the attractiveness of the setting are the appealing rest areas, scenic overlooks, and bridges built of native granite and rhyolite by the Civilian Conservation Corps during the 1930s. Because the streams are mainly small, the dams and lakes are small. Stewardship of aesthetic and scenic values of the land has produced a remarkable pleasant cultural landscape.

BIG SPRINGS REGION

Many clear streams drain this rugged, forest-covered area, and several large springs add to the region's attractiveness. There are five state parks. Big Spring State Park contains one of the biggest springs in the United States. Three other state parks, Montauk, Alley Spring, and Round Spring, also feature large springs, while Sam A. Baker State Park is known for encompassing some of the wildest country in Missouri.

Not all of the large springs are in state parks. Greer Spring, north of Alton, the most outstanding of these, is part of the Eleven Point Wild and Scenic Riverway System. Leo Drey, Missouri's largest landowner and long-time patron of environmental efforts, served as an intermediary purchaser and facilitator in moving the Greer Spring property from private to public ownership. Several large caves have commercial potential, but, because they are far from major highways, their owners have not been successful in developing them for commercial tours.

The Big Springs region is the retreat of the intrepid canoe enthusiast and camper. Semi-wilderness tourism has characterized the Big Springs region for more than a hundred years. Large parties with canoes or johnboats would set out from Montauk Spring or Round Spring on the Current River or Alley Spring or Eminence on the Jacks Fork and end up at Van Buren. Rose Cliff Lodge on the Current River overlooking Van Buren was the final destination of many of these parties. The lodge was host to a number of leaders in the movement to preserve the natural beauty of the Ozarks, including journalist Leonard Hall, botanist Julian Steyermark, artist Thomas Hart Benton, and others.[155] The decaying remains of the old lodge clung to the bluff overlooking Eminence for many years after it closed.

The establishment of a national scenic riverway on the Current and Jacks Fork rivers has attracted national attention to the formerly isolated region. As a result, considerable development is taking place as motels, camping areas, canoe rentals, and supply stores. However, the federal government controls development along the riverway to preserve the riverfront and natural and cultural resources in the area. Thus far, real-estate developers have attempted only a few small housing developments near private lakes or on tributary streams.

Included in the area are large acreages of the Mark Twain National Forest. The heavily forested national lands along with thousands of square miles of private property support some of the largest deer herds in the Ozarks. Texas and Shannon counties are normally among the leaders in the number of deer killed during the autumn hunting season. Two medium-sized reservoirs—Lake Wappapello and Clearwater Lake—attract visitors from nearby counties in the Ozarks and from the lowlands to the southeast.

The distance to major highways is probably the most important limiting factor in the tourism-recreation development of the region. As the Missouri Department of Transportation makes improvements to roads connecting with U.S. Highways 60, 63, and 67 and Interstate 44, travel to and from the area will require less time. However, with increased accessibility, the wilderness character of the region—its fundamental asset—will, ultimately, be changed.

OZARK PLAYGROUND REGION

This large recreation region covers the southwestern corner of Missouri and extends well into Arkansas. Its name is derived from the Ozark Playgrounds Association, an early business association created for the advancement and advertisement of Ozark tourism. In recent years the Ozark Marketing Council, an association of several prominent tourist attractions, has promoted much of the area as Ozark Mountain Country.[156] Besides the many interesting scenic features, larger cities like Springfield, Joplin, and Fayetteville-Springdale-Rogers attract many visitors. Much of the area is in the Mark Twain National Forest. More than any other district of the Ozarks, this is the core area of Ozark tourism and recreation. It was here that developers and investors built the great spas and some of the first large lake resorts and retirement-home communities.

For purposes of description, it is convenient to subdivide this region into six subregions: the Beaver Lake Area, the Eureka Springs Area, the Shepherd of the Hills Area, the Springfield Area, the Joplin Area, and the Stockton-Pomme de Terre Area.

The *Beaver Lake Area* features approximately 880 private and public-use campsites, outstanding fishing in the 28,000-acre lake, and the winding waters of the White River. The area has several championship golf courses and a wide range of hotels, motels, and restaurants. Thousands of visitors with a liking for history visit the Pea Ridge and Prairie Grove battlefields.

West of Beaver Lake is "the Strip," nearly thirty miles of commercial establishments along U.S. Highway 71B. The Strip begins near the Missouri state line and extends beyond Fayetteville, Arkansas. Included in it are the communities of Bella Vista, Bentonville, Rogers, and Springdale. At Tontitown, an Italian settlement, the restaurants that serve traditional Italian food are popular, as is the annual grape festival. Bella Vista Village is the largest of the Ozark second-home and retirement-home developments. The campus of University of Arkansas rambles over the hills of Fayetteville, a popular tourist town, which also serves as a jumping-off place for "shunpiking" into the Boston Mountains.[157] This popular Ozark diversion consists of traveling the winding back roads to discover tiny communities and to view houses and farms in the more-remote sections of the region.

The *Eureka Springs Area* consists primarily of the old resort town. Eureka Springs calls itself the Little Switzerland of America because of the stylish homes and old hotels perched on precarious ledges and hillsides. Eureka Springs claims to be "a Victorian showplace where artists and writers congregate," and the town and surroundings offer a wide range of attractions: Blue Spring, Onyx Cave, the Passion Play outdoor theater, the Christ Only Art Gallery, Miles Mountain Music Museum, and the Holiday

Christ of the Ozarks, Eureka Springs, Arkansas, 1972.
(Milton Rafferty Collection, photograph by the author.)

Island Exotic Animal Park. The Christ of the Ozarks statue is situated on Magnetic Mountain overlooking Eureka Springs. The Elna M. Smith Foundation in 1967 constructed this seven-story-high white-washed concrete statue. The late Gerald L. K. Smith, a minister and some-times controversial figure in politics, established the foun-dation.[158] Country-music theaters can be found along the Highway 62 "strip." Visitors find accommodations at one of the old resort hotels—Crescent, Basin Park, New Orleans—or in one of more than a dozen bed and break-fasts or at one of the several new motels and inns along U.S. Highway 62 at the edge of town.

In nearby Berryville, Saunders Memorial Museum offers an outstanding display of firearms. The old Grand View Hotel at Berryville still stands. Constructed in 1902, when the coming of the Missouri and North Arkansas Railroad promised a lively future for Berryville, the hotel is an imposing brick building with prominent wooden galleries. The impressive steamboat-Gothic–style galleries girdle each of its three floors. It has a high-peaked roof with a pointed tower.

The *Shepherd of the Hills Area* has a highly developed resort economy, especially around Lake Taneycomo and Table Rock Lake. The name derives from the popularity of Harold Bell Wright's book[159] and the much-visited Shepherd of the Hills Homestead.[160] The outstanding attractions for visitors are Silver Dollar City and the country-music theaters. Trout fishing, boat excursions, and camping are the chief activities on Lake Taneycomo. Anglers take trout, raised by the Missouri Department of Conservation at the hatchery below Table Rock Dam, from the bank or by drifting down the lake. Table Rock Lake has many camping sites and marinas. Warm-water fish, particularly bass, crappie, and channel catfish, make Table Rock Lake one of the most popular fishing spots in the Ozarks.

Rockaway Beach, Branson, and Hollister offer individ-ual brands of diversions for vacationers. The region next to the lakes is especially desirable as a location for retirement and second homes. As seen at night, the lights of the lake district resemble those of a sprawling city. Investors have built many retirement- and second-home subdivisions over the past several years. More recently they have built several time-share resorts. The latter industry has been stimulated by the expansion of the country-music theaters and the national attention it has brought. Thousands of new visitors to the area are prospective time-share vacation buyers. The week-long vacation provides exceptional oppor-tunity to showcase several luxury condominium develop-ments in the hills near Branson. Whether or not new time-share owners spend much time in Branson, they have

Jig dancers performing at College of the Ozarks, Point Lookout, Missouri, 1977. (Milton Rafferty Collection, photo-graph by the author.)

a major impact on the area's economy. In 1999, time-share owners invested an estimated $62 million in the city's 750 time-share units. Of sixteen time-share projects in Branson, some have multiple locations, and at least 1,000 more units, a mix of time-share and whole-ownership condo-miniums, are on the drawing boards.[161] The increasing number of upscale condos reflect the maturing of Branson.

A stretch of Missouri Highway 76 west of Branson has become known as the Branson Strip or Country Music Boulevard (fig. 12-3). Included in the thirteen-mile sec-tion between Branson and Missouri Highway 13 are motels, inns, restaurants, antique shops, dozens of gift and souvenir shops, a shopping center, a factory outlet mall, more than two dozen country-music theaters, White Water water park, Shepherd of the Hills Home-stead, Silver Dollar City, and a collection of lesser attrac-tions. The country-music theaters, and the motels, restaurants, and gift and souvenir shops that follow them, have spread onto nearby streets so that Country Music Boulevard is no longer the sole attraction. When a new street or road is built to relieve traffic congestion, it soon attracts commercial development. To bypass the built-up areas near the lake, a new road—the Highline Road (cur-rently under construction)—will pass north of the lakes to connect U.S. 65 with U.S. 160 west of the heavy traf-fic areas.

Roaring River State Park, near the western headwaters of Table Rock Lake, is one of the most completely devel-oped in Missouri. Roaring River Spring supports a trout hatchery operated by the Missouri Department of Con-servation. Much of the 3,403-acre park is preserved in its natural state, although the site has a swimming pool, hik-ing trails, more than two hundred campsites, rental cabins,

Anchor Travel Village tourist court in Branson, Missouri, *circa* 1945. (Courtesy of State Historical Society of Missouri.)

a store for fishing and camping supplies, and a stable for horse rental. The park's new inn and conference center offers dining and lodging facilities and a scenic setting for conferences.

The *Springfield Area* has many tourist-recreation attractions. Approximately ten miles southwest of the city is Wilson's Creek Battlefield National Park. Northwest of Springfield is Fantastic Caverns, which features a cavern tour by vehicle. To the east on Interstate 44 is Exotic Animal Paradise, which features automobile tours of the property, where various animals from all parts of the world are kept.

Within the city are several important attractions: the Springfield National Cemetery, Springfield Art Museum, the Landers Theater and the Juanita K. Hammons Hall for the Performing Arts, Bass Pro Shops, and the American National Fish and Wildlife Museum. Even before the wildlife museum opened in 2001, nearby Bass Pro Shops claimed to be Missouri's largest attraction for tourists. Cultural and sports events at Southwest Missouri State University, and at the city's smaller colleges and universities —Drury University, Evangel University, Central Bible College, Baptist Bible College—draw large crowds. The International Headquarters of the Assemblies of God Church holds many large conventions. The Battlefield Mall is the largest regional shopping mall in the Ozarks. The Shrine Mosque, built in 1923, also is host to many meetings and musical productions. A growing downtown entertainment and restaurant district attracts numerous visitors for the Jazz Fest and other special events. The Jordan Valley Park, currently under construction, will include convention and sports facilities when it is completed. As one of the oldest towns in the Ozarks, Springfield has an interesting history, including two periods under Confederate rule and several historic homes and commercial buildings. The Walnut Street Historic District features many historic homes now occupied by attorneys' offices, restaurants, and other businesses.

Springfield, self-styled Queen City of the Ozarks, provides an important ingredient for the tourism-recreation blend of the Ozark Playground Region. It has the most comprehensive range of services available in the Ozark region, including two large and well-equipped hospitals; a large regional shopping mall besides the downtown area and other shopping centers; a wide range of motel and convention accommodations; a selection of movie theaters; the Juanita K. Hammons Center for the Performing Arts and other theaters; the Springfield Symphony orchestra; dozens of restaurants to suit varied tastes; and many evening-entertainment and cultural attractions.

The *Joplin Area* is particularly popular with history buffs and mineral collectors. The city calls itself "the town that Jack built" because it is built literally upon the now-abandoned mines that produced the zinc ore known as "jack." The mineral museum in Schiffendecker Park, walking tours among the chat piles, and auto tours to old mining camps are popular pastimes. Mining tycoons built some of the most elegant houses in the Ozarks in a residential district west of downtown Joplin. Many homes, which included servants' quarters and carriage houses, are opened during a house tour in the fall of the year. Missouri Southern State College holds a large number of cultural and sports events. Shoal Creek Parkway, at the south edge of Joplin, includes 220 acres and five parks—McClelland, Witmer, McIndoe, Barr, and Bartlett. Grand Falls, the largest waterfall in the Ozarks, is on Shoal Creek at the west edge of the parkway. The ledge of cherty limestone that forms the falls is about twenty-five feet high, and a dam from a former mill further increases the height of the falls.[162]

Outlying attractions in the Joplin area include the George Washington Carver National Monument near Diamond; Truitt's Cave at Lanagan; Rockhound Paradise at Anderson; Ozark Wonder Cave at Noel; the tiff mines near Seneca; and the Carthage marble quarry and plant at Carthage. Pineville, the county seat of McDonald County, Missouri, is one of the most undisturbed and picturesque towns of the courthouse-square type. Here, under storefront canopies, Vance Randolph collected from residents many of the stories he incorporated into several books on Ozark folklore. In the summer of 1938, actors Henry Fonda and Tyrone Power and a complete technical and camera crew moved in to film the movie *Jessie James*. More than any other county seat town on busy U.S. 71, Pineville has retained its mid-twentieth-century appearance.

The *Stockton-Pomme de Terre Area*, compared with the other districts of the Ozark Playground Region, is in its youthful stage of development. Stockton and Hermitage are the chief towns, located, respectively, north of the dams. There are two additional physical similarities: each lake has two major arms; and two state parks—Stockton and Pomme de Terre—are each located on the point of land where the arms of the lakes meet. Both lakes have good reputations for fishing and water sports. Construction of marinas, visitor accommodations and services, and residential subdivisions continues, but not at the same frantic pace as Branson or Lake of the Ozarks.

WHITE RIVER FOLK CULTURE REGION

Investors and businesspeople are developing tourism and recreation attractions very rapidly in this region. Beyond three large lakes—Norfork, Bull Shoals, Greers Ferry—the region possesses superb float streams, including the Buffalo, Spring, and North Fork rivers. For convenience in description, I have subdivided the region into five sections: the Harrison Area, the Twin Lakes Area, the Mountain View Area, the Hardy Area, and the Greers Ferry Area.

The *Harrison Area* includes the scenic Buffalo River, one of the most popular Ozark float streams and, according to local residents, the last of the good warm-water float-fishing streams. South of Harrison is Scenic Highway

7, a popular route through the Boston Mountains for those who enjoy driving the back roads. Along Highway 7 south of Harrison is the now-abandoned theme park Dogpatch U.S.A.[163] Conceived in 1967 by O. J. Snow and nine other Harrison businesspeople, the park, developed on an 825-acre tract known as Marble Falls, depicted Al Capps's comic strip "Li'l Abner." Actors, mainly recruited locally, dressed in the costumes of Daisy Mae, Li'l Abner, Mammy and Pappy Yokum, Marryin' Sam, Moonbeam McSwine, and other characters from the comic strip, welcomed visitors and served as hosts. Next door was Arkansas's only ski resort, Marble Falls Resort and Convention Center. Dogpatch closed and reopened more than once before finally being abandoned in 1992. The motel has closed but the chalets are still occupied. Most of the camping facilities at the approximately 452 private and public-use campsites remain open to serve the sizable number of visitors in the area. South of Harrison off Highway 7 near the town of Deer, Arkansas, is Alum Cove Natural Bridge. Visitors must park their vehicles at the entrance to the 220-acre natural area and hike to the 130-foot long natural bridge, the largest in the Ozarks.[164] Other attractions in the area include Diamond Cave, Lost Valley, and the Limestone Valley, a little known but geologically and historically interesting solution valley.

The *Twin Lakes Area* surrounds mammoth Bull Shoals and Norfork lakes. Canoe floats are popular on the North Fork River. Trout fishing is available on the river and on private trout farms at several large springs that issue into the North Fork. Besides the many resorts and marinas on the lake, there are a number of other attractions and accommodations: Bull Shoals State Park, Penrod's Museum, Mountain Village 1890, Norfork Federal Fish Hatchery, the oldest home in the White River country (Wolf House), and the resort communities of Mountain Home, Bull Shoals, and Lakeview. Historically interesting Norfork, a community of less than five hundred people southeast of Mountain Home on Arkansas 5, was the normal head of navigation for steamboats that plied the White River. Trout fishing is popular on the North Fork and White River below the hatchery at Norfork Dam.

The *Mountain View Area* has enjoyed a profitable increase in visitors because of the $3.4 million Ozark Folk Culture State Park and the opening of Blanchard Springs Caverns as a recreation area. Mountain music is the theme at Mountain View. Visitors at the Folk Culture Center listen to music played by area residents on the dulcimer, fiddle, or pickin' bow. The Rackensack Society musicians assemble informally on Friday and Saturday nights to play their music on the courthouse square in Mountain View. Artisans at the Folk Culture State Park have preserved many local crafts. Lodging is available at the park for visitors to stay overnight or for longer periods. Many weekend visitors spend a day in the antique stores, then attend a country-music show at a theater or at the folk center, and spend nights in a bed and breakfast or motel.

At Blanchard Springs Caverns, guides lead visitors every twenty minutes along Dripstone Trail, which leads them through three-fourths of a mile of caverns, including the giant Cathedral Room, which measures 180 by 1,200 feet and has a 65-foot Giant Column. Above ground are opportunities to hike or camp in the Sylamore District of Ozark National Forest. Canoeing and float fishing are popular on the White River.

The *Hardy Area* calls itself the "land just made for tranquillity." Besides the motels in Hardy and other nearby towns there are excellent accommodations at the resort developments at Horseshoe Bend and Cherokee Village. As we have seen, Cherokee Village, one of the successful retirement-home developments of Cooper Communities, opened in 1954. The Arkansas Traveler Dinner Theatre is west of Hardy in an isolated wooded area off U.S. 62 and Arkansas 167. The theater features old-time country music, humor, hill-country legends, and a salt pork and beans dinner.[165] Camping is available at approximately 400 private and public campsites, including those at

Folk musician at the Ozark Folk Culture Center, Mountain View, Arkansas, 1976. (Courtesy of Arkansas Department of Parks and Tourism.)

Mammoth Spring State Park. Spring River is one of the better cold-water canoe and float-fishing streams in the Ozarks. Horseshoe Bend, another Arkansas Ozarks resort community, is an incorporated 14,000-acre town operated by the Horseshoe Bend Development Corporation. The town, on a spectacular bend of the Strawberry River, has churches, schools, civic clubs, a shopping center, restaurants, and the Hillhigh Lodge and Health Spa, featuring spas, saunas, exercise equipment, and a small convention center.

Much of the recent tourism-recreation development and other commercial growth has occurred along U.S. Highway 167 between Hardy and Ash Flat. Sharp County is one of those Arkansas Ozark counties that, because of poor roads and local politics, had two county seats. The new courthouse, a sprawling one-story structure of contemporary architectural style, is at Ash Flat, about midway between the former county seats at Hardy and Evening Shade.

The *Greers Ferry Area,* on the south slope of the Boston Mountains, focuses on the forty-thousand-acre Greers Ferry Lake. The lake is popular for sailing, water skiing, scuba diving, swimming, and fishing. The Little Red River below the dam vies with the lake for fishing trophies. Popular activities include tours of the federal fish hatchery, hikes on Sugar Loaf Nature Trail, and the Ozark Frontier Trail Festival and Crafts Show in October. The resort communities of Quitman, Clinton, Edgemont, Heber Springs, and Brownsville provide ample services and lodging. Fairfield Bay, another planned resort community on the north shore of the lake, features a full package of recreation, second-home, and retirement living.

THE RIVER HILLS REGION

The River Hills Region borders the Missouri and Mississippi rivers. White settlers entered this area before any other part of the Ozarks. The history and cultural traditions include French, American, and German elements. Many historical and tourist attractions relate to the commerce and travel along the two great waterways, the Mississippi and Missouri rivers. For convenience of description, I have divided the region into two subregions: the Mississippi River Border Area and the Missouri River Border Area.

The *Mississippi River Border Area* consists of many attractions scattered along the river between Cape Girardeau and Ste. Genevieve.[166] The river border is an important transportation corridor—water, rail, and highway—and much of the history and culture of the area is connected with commerce and trade. The most visited place is Ste. Genevieve, where historical groups have preserved elements of French culture dating to the eighteenth century.[167] Points of interest include Ste. Genevieve Catholic Church, which casts its afternoon shadow across the square. The stained-glass windows captioned with the names of priests and important parishioners tell of the dominance of French and then German culture. Nearby are a historical museum and the Old Brick House Restaurant, said to be the first brick building west of the Mississippi River. Other houses dating from the late 1700s and early 1800s include Vital de St. Gemme de Beauvais House, Jean Baptiste Valle House, Bolduc House, Meilleur House, Francois Valle House, Green Tree Tavern, and Misplait House.[168] In the old cemetery, weathered gravestones record, often in French, the memory of many early residents of Ste. Genevieve.

Other attractions in the Mississippi River Border Area include East Perry, a string of German communities—Uniontown, Frohna, Altenburg, Wittenburg—where descendants of immigrants who settled in the 1840s have retained their language and customs to some degree; Bollinger Mill and Covered Bridge; and Trail of Tears State park, which overlooks the Mississippi River. A suitable base for tours is Cape Girardeau, an old waterfront town where people from the Ozarks mingle with flatlanders from the Mississippi alluvial plain. At Cape Girardeau are Southeast Missouri State University and many early nineteenth-century buildings and homes.

The *Missouri River Border Area* is rich in history and culture. The section between Washington and Jefferson City is part of a region called the Missouri Rhineland because of the large number of people of German descent. The section along the river above Jefferson City is the historic Boonslick country, where Daniel Boone and his sons first established saltworks and opened the area to settlement. At Washington in Franklin County is the Missouri Meerschaum Company, billed as the world's leading manufacturer of corncob pipes. Traveling upriver, along the scenic Missouri Highway 100 on the bluffs overlooking the fertile Missouri River valley, one enters the town of Hermann. Because many German immigrants who settled there in the 1840s and 1850s were well educated, people came to know Hermann as the cultural capital of the Missouri Rhineland. The town has several examples of German architecture in the commercial and residential buildings. In autumn and spring, the houses are opened to the thousands of visitors who crowd the streets of the town for the Maifest and Octoberfest.

At Jefferson City, locally known as Jeff City, are the state capitol and the large cluster of state office buildings required to administer programs to provide services for Missouri's 5.4 million people. Other points of interest include the Executive Mansion, the old Missouri State Penitentiary, the national cemetery, and Lincoln University.

Upstream in the heart of Boonslick country is Boonville, built on the crest of the bluffs and encircled by hills. In the residential section are antebellum brick homes with generous rooms, wide halls, and modest Classic-Revival details, flamboyant houses of the "gingerbread" era, and modern bungalows and ranch-style homes.

The entire town of Arrow Rock, situated on the Missouri River bluffs at the extreme northern point of the Ozarks, became a National Historic Landmark in 1964. An integral part of this historic town is Arrow Rock State Historic Site. The site's visitor center museum features exhibits that tell about Arrow Rock and the historic "Boone's Lick Country." The Bingham Home, built by Missouri's preeminent artist of the 1800s, George Caleb Bingham, has been restored and furnished as it might have been when he lived there. The Huston Tavern, dating back to 1834, stands ready to serve visitors its traditional hearty fare. The old courthouse, a town doctor's home, a stone jail, and other historic buildings are part of a walking tour offered at the site.

In a rural historic district located nearby is the home of Dr. John B. Sappington, frontier doctor and patriarch of a prominent Missouri family. The district, which includes several houses, a school, a black cemetery, and the Missouri Department of Natural Resources Sappington State Park cemetery, was created in large part through the efforts of international real-estate developer and current owner of the Sappington house, Whitney Kerr.

The *Cherokee Country Region,* situated on the extreme southwest border of the Ozarks, focuses especially on water sports, canoeing on the rivers, and fishing in the lakes on the Neosho (Grand) and Illinois rivers.[169] The Illinois, by far Oklahoma's most popular float stream, is convenient and commercialized—the perfect place to develop canoe skills. Spring Fork of the Neosho River, near Quapaw, offers commercial canoe outfitters, and many other streams await the aggressive canoeist. Flint and Barren Fork creeks, tributaries of the Illinois, can be floated with minimum portage during the high-water seasons, early spring and late fall.

For purposes of description, the lake areas may be subdivided into the Spavinaw–Lake o' the Cherokees Area and the Fort Gibson–Tenkiller Area.

The *Spavinaw—Lake o' the Cherokees Area* includes a number of marinas and motel and resort accommodations at recreation areas on the three lakes. Notable concentrations are found in developed recreation areas: Twin Bridges,

Honey Creek, Cherokee, Spavinaw, Upper Spavinaw, and Salina. The communities of Grove, Jay, Spavinaw, and Salina serve the east shore, or Ozark side, of the two large lakes. Shangri-La Resort and Lakemont Shores are probably the best known of the large resort developments. As in the other Ozark lake recreation areas, the resorts advertise widely and offer package plans for visitors.

The region is rich in history: Salina was the site of the Chouteau Trading Post, established in the early nineteenth century by the same French family that figured in the founding of St. Louis, Missouri; near Jay is Oak Hills Indian Center, where Cherokee artisans produce crafts; and ten miles above Upper Spavinaw Lake is the site of Fort Wayne, headquarters of Captain Nathanial Boone, son of Daniel Boone, who conducted the Indian boundary surveys.[170] Immediately to the north are the old lead-zinc mining towns of Commerce, Picher, and Cardin, Oklahoma, and Baxter Springs and Galena, Kansas. These towns and backwoods hills provide interesting areas for touring.

The *Fort Gibson–Tenkiller Area* includes the two large reservoirs by the same names, the channeled and improved sections of the Grand and Arkansas rivers, including Greenleaf Lake, and the rugged Brushy Mountain section of the Boston Mountains. In addition to the various resorts, marinas, and fishing docks, the region is rich in historical attractions. Resort communities include Fort Gibson, Hulbert, Cookson, and Blackgum. At Tahlequah, the capital of the Cherokee Nation, are Northeastern Oklahoma University and the Cherokee Museum. Southeast of the city is Park Hill, where Chief John Ross established his home in 1839 near the Presbyterian Mission. The Ross family cemetery and the John Murrell mansion are nearby. At Fort Gibson, many of the buildings of the old army post have been restored and opened to the public.

ENVIRONMENTAL EFFECTS OF TOURISM AND RECREATION

The development of tourist and recreation attractions necessarily affects the landscape and environmental quality. Increases in population inevitably produce change. As outsiders are attracted to a region, the residents encounter different lifestyles, and established patterns of life are gradually altered. Over the years, some of the visitors have become permanent residents, so that the character of the resident population has itself evolved.

The large variety of tourist attractions along Ozark highways often gives a Coney Island appearance to the landscape. Go-carts, bumper cars, minibikes, country-

Sequiota cave and spring, Springfield, Missouri, 1975. Water from the spring formerly supplied a state trout hatchery, but the water has been polluted by septic drainage from residential subdivisions. (Milton Rafferty Collection, photograph by the author.)

music theaters, and other attractions designed for family entertainment are mixed with antique shops, drive-in food establishments, restaurants, gift and souvenir shops, and signs and billboards. Two notable tourist string or strip developments have grown along the section of U.S. Highway 54 between Camdenton and Osage Beach in the Lake of the Ozarks region and along Highway 76 west of Branson in Taney County. Some observers have recommended that certain recreation services having nuisance value be grouped and located where they do not mar aesthetic values or other tourist attractions. In Missouri, a proposition to regulate the size and number of highway signs was narrowly defeated by voters in November 2000.

The construction of second homes and retirement homes has progressed rapidly around the lakes. There was little nuisance at the outset, but as the development became intensive, several problems cropped up. The most critical problem is the danger of serious pollution of ground-water supplies and the large lakes. The risk has increased as more on-site sewage treatment facilities (septic tanks) have been installed without proper construction methods or inspection. In an effort to gain speculation profits, the acreages that are subdivided for homes often exceed demand. Developers are sometimes allowed to put in access roads meeting minimum engineering standards and turn them over to the county for maintenance. Often this results in covering scenic hills with many crisscrossing access roads but few houses; equally important, there is little tax base for maintenance of the roads. An extra burden is placed on community facilities, such as highways, hospitals, and schools, by increases in seasonal and permanent population.

Even in the white-hot real-estate market in the Branson area in the 1990s several large projects failed, and developers discovered that it takes more than a bright idea to succeed. A recent article in the *Springfield News-Leader* listed fifteen large projects that failed between 1992 and 1998. Among the largest were Branson South, which was to include luxury hotels, a 10,000-seat conference center, golf courses, five theaters, and homes on sixteen hundred acres; the Branson Monorail, a $5 million project that was supposed to solve Branson's traffic congestion problem; Heartland America, a 1993 proposal to construct a 265,000-square-foot shopping mall; Branson Hills, a hotel and resort; and Frontier Town-Missouri a $38 million western theme park near Reeds Spring Junction in Stone County.[171] Most of the projects, now grown over with grass, lacked solid financing. As the *Springfield News-Leader* reporter Jennifer Barnett put it, to be successful in the maturing Branson tourism scene, "It takes creativity and boldness. It takes an understanding of the region's history and personality—what will and what won't fly in the down-home, family-oriented culture of the Ozarks. And it takes money."[172]

The problems created by the sale of cheap land are not new to the Ozarks. Carl O. Sauer described the basic dilemma that existed about 1920 as follows:

> The large areas of cheap land have given rise from time to time to promotion schemes. For this business the region possesses unusual inducements. The Ozarks are near large centers of population. They have an attractive climate, especially to northern people. The region delights city people who think of country life in romantic terms. In the hands of skillful manipulators, well-selected illustrations and half-truths are elaborated artfully from these points of attraction. Visions of comfortable country homes are held out to city clerks and tradesmen who have tired of the precariousness and routine of their present occupations. Fruit orchards, chicken farms, cattle and hog ranches are the very favorite projects promoted. Usually the very poorest land, which even the natives have avoided, is chosen. This is either laid out in small tracts of five to forty acres, or a stock company sells shares in a very large tract. In either case the profits are figured on the basis of a high per acre pro-

ductiveness. In this way land has been sold for fruit orchards on which trees could have been planted only by blasting holes, chicken ranches have been promoted in inaccessible locations where the production of grain is an impossibility and even grass grows with difficulty. Some of the land which has been sold for purposes of intensive farming is so rough that it is impossible to drive a wagon over it. If properly managed, the companies clear many hundred percent, and the investor is left with a tract of land that is nearly worthless because it is poor and is too small to be put to any practical use. Much of the land is sold for taxes after the owners are disillusioned. In numerous cases the owner, who has not seen the land, has decided to quit his position and move to his "farm." By the time he is established on the place a large part of his savings is gone, and in the course of a short time the remainder is lost in the hopeless effort to produce a living there. Finally, the settler is reduced to doing odd jobs in the vicinity at very low wages, or, if fortunate, returns to the city to begin over. The promotion of these schemes has not only unloaded on the region families who have become its wards, but has discredited the Ozarks entirely in the minds of many people, in spite of their not inconsiderable possibilities of successful development.[173]

The image of the Ozarks as a place for cheap retirement living is not entirely false, but certainly there have been many mistakes in land use. It behooves both the newcomer and the longtime Ozark resident to embrace a philosophy of conservation and wise use of natural resources. Even today many immigrants, particularly those who have come to gain a livelihood wholly from a small tract of land as part of the back-to-the-land movement, do not understand the limited productivity of Ozark soils. There are some who, either from their own misunderstanding or in a frantic effort to make a living or to speculate in land investment, misrepresent the region and its possibilities. The following advertisement that I picked up in a crossroads general store when the back-to-the-land movement was at its zenith in the early 1970s is interesting because of its resemblance to Sauer's remarks and to advertisements by lumber companies that were disposing of cutover land in the early 1900s.

WANTED: "NATURAL" FAMILIES

We are presently farming organically, in the heart of the Ozarks, our 600 acre farm overlooking Bryant Creek south of Mansfield, Missouri. This is one of the seven pollution free areas left in the United States. To enable us to secure a better market for our livestock and produce, we are selling 5 acre homesteads to people who want a better way of life. There is employment in Mansfield and Ava; both are 6 miles from the farm by blacktop. The homesteads are in timber because they've not been farmed for over 25 years. The ground is rock free, level, farmable, and has never been "Pesticided" or chemically fertilized. Some tracts have fruit trees.

Buy 5 acres, subdivide it into acre homesites and pay for your own land, sell to retiring couples, a friend, anyone who wants to live in a clean community, and have natural foods available. Choose your own neighbors, or keep and farm your own homestead. We're not selling any parcel smaller than 5 acres. Five acres of anything would support and supply a family with all produce, grain, poultry, small meats, and dairy products. What you don't want to raise, someone else can supply.

Two and three bedroom homes with full basements are available for under $20,000, 5 acres included. There are some reasonable restrictions for your own protection. Within the year, if we have enough marketables raised here, a marketing co-op will be formed to secure a steady outlet for surplus commodities.

Aerie Acres wants doers, the now people, whether you're 8 or 80. Each of us has something to offer others from apples or bees to yucca or zucchini, so extend a helping hand and be part of this community.

Visit us; stay for supper.[174]

The world energy crisis casts a pall over the tourism-recreation industry, just as it does over the entire American economic system. It is impossible to predict what the future of the tourism-recreation industry will be if gasoline is rationed or its price increases to a prohibitive level. Although the higher cost of fuel might discourage some visitors, it could attract others. Some tourists, who normally might select a vacation on the East or West coast or in Europe, might opt for a less-expensive Ozark vacation, thereby helping to offset the visitors who cancel vacation plans altogether.

The settlements scattered about the lakes and along highways are not energy efficient. It is expensive to provide services of the everyday type—health care, education, electricity, sewage treatment—when the houses are scattered several hundred yards or even a mile a more apart. Many of the people who live in the lake areas work in growth centers, such as Springfield, Joplin, Miami, Fayetteville, Springdale, Rogers, Muskogee, or in the burgeoning lake towns nearby. The future of such long-distance commuting depends on economic factors that cannot be accurately predicted.

THIRTEEN

NONMATERIAL CULTURAL TRAITS

Although a complete analysis of the cultural traits of an area as large as the Ozarks would require all the detail of a mail-order catalog and an organization comparable to that of the federal census, something can be done to convey the idea to the reader. In his history of pioneer life, Wiley Britton gave us a picture of the material culture of the pioneer in southwest Missouri.[1] Vance Randolph elaborated on it in several books to present to the world the isolated hill man and his family.[2] In recent years writers have produced many books, mainly of the reminiscent type dealing with everyday life in the rural Ozarks.[3]

The Ozark resident's belated reflection has nourished recent local histories and memorabilia on his past. The belated interest in local history was accompanied by the national bicentennial and a host of centennial celebrations in towns founded during the railroad-building boom of the 1870s and 1880s. The telling and retelling in redundant detail of hog killings, fiddle making, moonshining, quilting bees, cabin raisings, rail splitting, tie hacking, food preserving, hayrides, spelling bees, party playing, long walks to rural schools in all kinds of inclement weather, revivals, fistfights, pie auctions, shootings, trials, hangings, funerals, family reunions, Fourth of July celebrations, kangaroo courts, drawing water from the well, carrying water from the spring, and churning homemade butter tell of the passing of the cultural isolation of rural America. Little of this was unique to the Ozarks; much the same rural lifestyle, with variations, once existed throughout the Midwest, the Great Plains, and the South and in virtually every other rural section of the United States. A simple subsistence lifestyle perhaps lasted longer in the Ozarks and is therefore fresher in memory. Undoubtedly, the Ozark tourism industry has played an important role in preserving the country image of the region even to the point of nurturing crafts and skills that were little known by early residents of the region.

EDUCATION

Strictly speaking, the whole of the process by which one becomes adjusted to culture is part of the individual's education. This naturally includes both the unconscious adjustment and education provided consciously and purposely by society. Although it is probably true that the school is the most effective agency of change in an isolated area, the ability to teach culture through radio and television has removed the buffer of isolation from formerly remote sections. It is perhaps arguable whether the two media accurately reflect the existing cultural mores or encourage higher levels of cultural achievement.

In former times, Ozarkers did not regard education as highly as they do now. The family-farm institution was particularly strong, and many people thought that very little of that taught in the schoolroom would be important in making a living.[4] This attitude is not completely absent, but it is far less prevalent today. Farming is a vocation that offers a livelihood to fewer people each year, and successful farming in any terms requires a number of skills taught in schools.

Education in the Ozarks has lagged behind that of more prosperous sections. In 1925, St. Louis journalist Harry Bundidge and Ozark County school superintendent Samuel Megee described the plight of education in the central Ozarks.[5] Though 1,102 young people were not attending school, the county court refused to hire a truant officer, stating, "We don't believe the compulsory education law is a good law." Ozark County had ninety school districts, eighty-five of which supported only one-room, one-teacher schools. Four districts had a term of less than four months each year, twenty held school four to six months, forty-five less than eight months, twenty maintained an eight-month schedule, and only one had a nine-month schedule. The average length of the school term was 129 days, while in St. Louis the schools were open 200 days. Thirty of the ninety teachers had no equipment, not even a dictionary, and forty-five had no map or globe. Twenty schools had no desks, thirty had no toilet, and in eighteen schools drinking water had to be carried a quarter-mile or more. Eighty percent of the schools had blackboards, but these were made by painting the rough inner walls of the school with black carriage paint.

In the 1930s, when an eight-month session was considered minimal for elementary education in Missouri, many Ozark counties had shorter terms. In Missouri 10 of the 17 districts that provided less than four months of school were in the Ozarks. The Ozarks also had 95 of 114 districts that provided four to six months of school, and 756 of the 875 that provided between six and eight months. In all, 86 percent of the school districts in Missouri that provided less than the standard eight-month term were in the Ozarks, as were only 11 percent of those that provided more than eight months.[6]

Although education has improved much, the Ozarks continues to lag behind more prosperous regions. In only Cole, Pulaski, Greene (Missouri), and Washington (Arkansas) counties had the median school year completed risen to twelve years or more by 1972. Cole, Greene, and Washington counties have universities, and in Pulaski County the officers, staff, and some enlisted personnel from Fort Leonard Wood may contribute to a higher educational level. Still, in more than half the interior Ozark counties, less than 40 percent of persons twenty-five years old and over had completed high school in 1972. Percentages ranged from 29.1 in Gasconade County to 58.4 in Greene County. Education lagged even more in the Arkansas and Oklahoma Ozarks. The federal government established schools in the Cherokee Nation schools at an early date, but those schools served only a small part of the potential student population.

There continues to be some resistance to formal education, much of it expressed in an unconscious way. Although most natives express interest in supporting schools, those who place great store in traditional values believe that formal education draws native youths out of the shelter of families, out of churches, and out of participation in the family and community. Frequently, one hears about college-educated young people who no longer closely associate with their family because "they got ruined by too much education."

In a column in the *White River Leader* (Branson, Missouri), "Uncle Bill from Kirbyville" expresses, humorously, some native beliefs about the nature and worth of a higher education:

> Ed asked if the government has ever given serious study to the groundhog, and nobody didn't know that either, Ed allowed that a Government that can spend hundreds of thousands of dollars on researching hawks wings, owls eyes and the navigation equipment of bats and porpoises had ought to be able to appropriate a few thousand for groundhogs. Bug Hookum has agreed with Ed that folks get too carried away with useless learning.

While the schools of higher learning are doing research in pinup calendars and comic books, and the younguns is taking courses in movie appreciation and ping pong, Bug said, bricklayers and plumbers in this country get more work than they can do at $11 a hour. It ain't no wonder, declared Bug, that the educated is the ones out of work.

Clem Webster was agreed with Bug that students in what they call the liberal arts has plenty to be liberal with. They got all the time in the world while they spend money their folks earned a lifetime to save up. They got no responsibility in life but to take their bodies to a room to be talked to, and if they want to take part in a riot somewhere they get excused from that. With nothing to do but look down their noses at the working world, Clem said, it ain't no wonder the students get restless and burn down the schools.[7]

Evidence of increased sophistication of instruction in schools is plentiful, particularly concerning computers and other technological areas. For example, the *2000 Missouri School District Computing Census* reported that 99 percent of Missouri school districts have a technology plan, and 90 percent of the plans covered such items as hardware and peripherals, software, internal connections, staff training, and curriculum integration.[8] It is also clear that some poor school districts do not provide the same number of computers or the same levels of instruction as wealthier urban school districts.[9] Even so, the ratio of students to computers dropped from 7 to 1 in 1997 to 4.2 to 1 in 2000, and the ratio of students to Internet-connected computers dropped from 24 to 1 to 6.6 to 1.[10] Some taxpayers are concerned that schools teach too many nonessential courses and fail to teach essential courses well. Some school patrons criticize across-the-board goals. Setting goals to purchase a computer for every classroom may appear wasteful and even pedagogically unsound, because some classes may not be well-adapted to computer instruction. As the cost of education increases, some taxpayers want schools to cut perceived frills and to concentrate on basics. However, there are strong supporters of education who argue schools should provide a wide range of inter-school athletics and extra-class activities, in addition to strong instruction in computers and technology, college preparatory courses, and instruction in the arts and music.

For many, however, education is, primarily, a means of getting a job. Second, it is essential for successful interactions with nonnatives. Although a regional accent is considered unimportant, bad grammar is considered to be a disadvantage in dealing with outsiders. The native Ozarker who secures a good education may attain a managerial or ownership position or gain a position in the legal and political system. In these situations, he or she is often in a superior competitive position compared with a nonnative with equal talents and education.

Until about 1960, education beyond the eighth grade was not considered essential. The decision to attend high school not only had important implications for one's future, it also meant contact with a different lifestyle for many. Professor Donald Holliday tells of his brother Gerald's decision to attend high school in Hollister:

> When Gerald started to high school in 1944, he started after having faced and made a serious decision —whether to go to high school, for in the community of Pine Top, the common thing for a young man to do after he finished the eighth grade, somewhere between the ages of thirteen and twenty-one or so, was to begin to farm with his father. To make the decision to attend high school, Gerald was forced to decide that he wanted a higher education. The younger brothers never faced that decision; consolidation and universal public school laws made it for them. Thus, when they started to high school, they did so with their goals yet undefined. Not until they graduated and were faced with the decision to go to college or not to go were they forced to consciously consider objectives.[11]

Education is usually not a thing to be displayed. Speech habits are indicative. The form of dialect is both geographical and individual. Geographical patterns are no longer as important as family and associates in determining dialect. However, in a few remote sections dialect may be so pronounced that even an occasional departure from it stamps the speaker as an outsider; in the more accessible sections it is confined to the ignorant or the occasional lapse of the educated. A person of education may seem to have two languages: one to meet the formal and more stilted demands of polite society, the other for ordinary discourse with those he considers his equals or inferiors. Professor Waldo Cralle related an interesting example told by one of his students:

> You know, when I'm up at college I believe I can talk about as well as any of them. But let me get down here in these hills again, get on a pair of overalls and about three days' growth of beard, and I'll be talking just like a hill-billy.[12]

A more recent example of this dualism surfaced during the 1970s with the language usage of educated individuals who joined the citizens' band radio rage. The requisite singsong CB jargon sometimes becomes mixed with throwback rural colloquial expressions. While eavesdropping on a CB radio, I was entertained by a "really countrified" dialogue between two young women, only to hear one of them suddenly speak in ordinary conversational tones, "Mary, I really can't believe I'm talking like this."[13] Undoubtedly, the educational level and social standing of individuals influence word usage in spoken language. It is common to hear a food server in a Springfield restaurant say "I hope you-uns enjoy your food," or to ask "You-alls enjoy your food?" It seems "you-uns" and "you-all" are used whether the situation calls for singular or plural. Some people say "you-alls" only when speaking to two or more.[14] While one hears both "you-uns" and "you-all" frequently, "you-uns" is the more common Ozark usage.[15]

Little research has been done on Ozark dialect. However, Vance Randolph suggested that the source of the unusual wealth of literary words in the Ozarks is sixteenth- and seventeenth-century English.[16] Professor Cralle pointed out that the old Blue Back Spelling Book and the King James Version of the Bible are two other possible sources.[17] A few examples of Old English words sometimes used by natives are *agile, admired, bemean, beguile, candidly, cavil, caucus, contentious, careen, dilatory, diligent, disfellowship, docile, denotes, exhort, forsake, fray, jaunt, genteel, lavish, meander, proffer, ponder, partake, peruse, rectify, reconcile, ridiculous, tragedy, warysome, wrest,* and *loiter.*[18]

Dale Freeman's *How to Talk Pure Ozark in One Easy Lesson* is a popular collection of old Ozark terms.[19] Probably, the meaning of 80 percent of the "pure Ozarks" words in the collection would be familiar to most Kansas or Iowa farmers who have reached the age of sixty-five. They are rural colloquialisms sometimes modified by geographic surroundings. *Afore* (before), *ary* (singular of any), *bulge* (advantage), *born days* (life), *cut the mustard* (succeed), *woods colt* (illegitimate child; this expression is rendered as *pasture colt* in the Plains states), *hear to* (to agree), *hog wild* (excited), and *honin'* (eager) are examples of rural middle-western terms taken from the book. These homespun "Ozark" expressions, and many others of the type, were very familiar to me when I moved to the Ozarks from north-central Kansas thirty-five years ago.[20] Professor E. Joan Wilson Miller's effort to identify an Ozark cultural hearth revealed that many times the same type of tale told in the Ozarks had been collected outside the region, although sometimes with slightly different embellishments to fit the surroundings.[21]

Many similes in Vance Randolph's volumes of folktales reveal an intense relationship between the Ozarks environment and its inhabitants. Examples compiled by Professor Miller include "enough to physic two horses; it looks like they were both gone goslings for sure; fighting like wildcats; thick as crows at a hog killing; shake all over like a dog getting rid of a peach stone; run like a quarter horse; squeal like a young pig; solemn as a tree full of owls, squealed like a stuck pig; the crowd scattered like quails; roaming around like a bug in a hot night; naked as a jay bird; run like turkeys; as common as hoot owls on Bull Creek . . ."[22]

The homespun usages illustrate how language evolved from everyday life in the hills.

The scholars who work with language usage put the Ozarks in the South Midland speech grouping.[23] Although there has been little systematic study of speech patterns, preliminary investigations show that important differences occur where Germans or people from Yankee or North Midland background settled. It was the social predominance of Yankees, or Germans, rather than a numerical predominance, that influenced speech habits. Professor Timothy Framer suggests that the German immigrants in the Illinois counties next to the Ozarks patterned their speech habits after the socially prominent northerners who settled there:

> It thus seems likely, at least from the slight amount of information available, that the Germans did adopt the Northerners as a cultural and language model, and that the Germans themselves were great enough in number and status to account for the spread of their adopted English to become standard for the region.[24]

Thus, in the northern and eastern Ozark borders, where northern and German influences have been strongest, a North Midland speech pattern is predominant. Such phrases as *school leaves out, sick to the stomach,* and *quarter to* (as opposed to school lets out, belly ache, and quarter of) are considered indicators of North Midland dialect.[25]

Traditional speech habits die slowly. Daily human interaction at work, in school, in church, at social events, and most important, in the family tends to perpetuate the traditional language usages. Nevertheless, speech habits are changing. American culture is becoming more homogeneous. Through education, travel, the printed word, and television and movies, new speech forms have become part of everyday usage. Not all of the change has been positive. The younger generation of Ozarkers has adopted modern slang and street language nationally broadcast daily. In my own classes at Southwest Missouri State University I heard more expressions of "cool" (affirmative) and "dude" (good fellow) than any of the homespun Ozark expressions. The

nearly universal sentence break, "you know," is heard far more than any other expression. More recently, a new doggerel sentence break, "know'm say'n?" (Do you know what I am saying?), has crept into the speech of young people via television and movies from the inner-city streets. Much of the slang is transitory, what is "in" or current today is shortly out of favor, and the use of out-of-date slang is a sure sign of one's aging.

The traditional Ozark dialect, or at least the historical Ozark dialect as they often portray it, has become a theater museum piece, preserved by Branson comedians and hillbilly theatrical presentations. Yet, there are forums where one can hear genuine contemporary Ozark speech. Local talk radio is a readily accessible listening post where call-in guests provide a broad spectrum of dialects representing the diverse backgrounds of people who live in the Ozarks.[26]

ENTERTAINMENT

Traditional Ozark entertainment was much different from today's. We have seen how technological advances have worked to reshape the economy and transportation network of the region. The impact of technology, combined with constant social change, has been to modify entertainment forms. Old forms have persisted to some extent, mainly in the sections where roads and rails did not penetrate until later, but for the most part, current entertainment is similar to that of other sparsely populated rural sections of the United States.

Professor Robert Gilmore studied the traditional entertainment in the Ozarks and compiled an interesting and surprisingly varied array of entertainment forms.[27] Gilmore found that by 1900 elaborate entertainment activities had evolved. Literary society meetings were held regularly in almost every community throughout the Ozarks, usually held on Friday nights at the schoolhouse. Attendance often meant an inconvenient if not hazardous trip after dark, and stream crossing could be dangerous after dark. A respondent in Howell County complained:

> All along one of the largest and most traveled roads in the south part of the county the large loose stones or boulders are so numerous that it is dangerous to drive faster than a walk with a buggy or carriage and also very hard on a loaded wagon as well as dangerous.[28]

Because the literaries provided something to do and a break from the work routine, they were well attended. They included debates, spelling bees, ciphering matches, and kangaroo courts. In the spelling bees and ciphering matches the excitement of a contest combined with tangible learn-

NONMATERIAL CULTURAL TRAITS

ing that stimulated pride in the school patron. Debates on topics of every conceivable nature, ranging from speculation about the future of the world to the universal and unresolvable problem of the relative usefulness of the broom and the dishrag, occupied the whole interest of an audience. Gilmore used newspaper accounts of debates to compile a most interesting list of topics that included whiskey and war, love, the Indian, education, personalities, the printing press, man's nature, women, religion, morals, and prospects for the future.[29] Even the intrepid and educated German hunter-woodsman Friedrich Gerstaeker joined a debate before a large crowd in Arkansas. Gerstaeker's selected debate topic was "Which enjoys life most, has fewer cares, and lighter sorrows—a short or a long-tailed dog."[30]

A kangaroo court[31] combined the drama of a courtroom trial with the ribaldry of a practical joke that contained for the audience "all the interest, suspense, and humor of a stage play."[32] Elaborate stage settings were rare at literary performances, but costuming was an important element in the presentation of many entertainments. At times, participants fired colored flash powder to illuminate dramatic tableau scenes. Sometimes the performers at the literaries were schoolchildren, but often, especially in the instances of debates and kangaroo courts, the adult members of the community acted for their fellow citizens.

School closing programs were among the most obvi-

ously theatrical of all Ozark folk entertainments. The performers were the students, and their performances consisted of plays, dialogues, recitations, speeches, Delsarte drills, or whatever other mode of entertainment the particular district had come to expect.[33] Even the drill in lessons for examination period served as entertainment for the proud parents and patrons of the school. Frequently they decorated the schoolhouse for the occasion with flowers, evergreens, and students' work. Preparation for the closing-of-school event occupied a large part of the last two months of school, and many teachers felt that their chances of being rehired for the following year depended upon their producing a program that not only would entertain their patrons but also would compare favorably with previous programs.

Religious gatherings of all kinds were extremely important in the life of the Ozarker, as they are today. When families were more isolated, religious gatherings gave people the opportunity to "participate in fellowship with neighbors, engage in group singing, witness the emotional performances of his fellows or to participate in such performances himself, and most important, be entertained by a minister or ministers."[34] Churchgoers enjoyed these entertainments in the knowledge that they were part of a religious service and therefore appropriate. Ministers often gained reputations for their ability to preach an interesting and entertaining sermon, sometimes acquiring near-star

---

status in the eyes of their admirers. Preachers' messages were often emotional, lengthy, and fundamentalist, often enlivened with pantomimic action and humorous anecdotes.[35] Camp meetings added the extra dimension of a spectacle, of crowds of people, of camping out, and of an intensified emotional atmosphere.

Religious debates were usually conducted in an atmosphere of intense partisan emotion and at times extended over several days. Baptisms drew large crowds to witness the converts filing into waist-deep water, where a minister totally immersed them. Although usually carried out in the spring of the year, church members sometimes had to break ice to accomplish the feat.[36] Members of rural churches still regard river baptisms highly and occasionally use them. The author has witnessed several river baptisms while canoeing or fishing, especially near the Easter season.

Many people attended box and pie suppers. They enjoyed the good food and the entertainment as well. Much of the enjoyment derived from the time-honored ritual of identifying the supposedly unmarked boxes or pies and of purchasing the desired one at the best possible price. Beauty-cake contests always generated good-natured rivalry when the prettiest young woman was selected.

Picnics were always popular, as they are today. Shady groves and cold springs were abundant, and it was a simple matter for a family to pack a basket lunch and slip from work and worries for a few hours or for a day. Communities held large picnics to celebrate special occasions. Intense notes of patriotism and sentiment pervaded the celebration of the Fourth of July, Memorial Decoration Day, veterans' encampments, and old settlers' reunions. Attractions at the organized picnics often included balloon ascension, orators, circle swings, lemonade stands, the popping of firecrackers, recitations, songs, and instrumental music.

Ozarkers in the horse-and-buggy era were especially fond of baseball, and they cheered their town team on, win or lose. Traveling teams, such as the Nebraska Indians, provided special entertainment and drew large crowds.[37] Ministers preached vigorously against the Sunday baseball craze, but writers proudly recorded scores of sixty-five to five in the winning town's newspaper. Baseball was more than a big-city game, but the St. Louis Cardinals, the westernmost "Big League" team, generated strong fan loyalty in the region. To this day, the Cardinals enjoy strong fan allegiance in the Ozark region. Over the past forty years, the Kansas City Royals have captured the loyalty of many fans in the western Ozarks.

The strongest fan allegiance was reserved for the local town teams. The game itself, which many say embodied the American character, contributed to baseball's popularity in small-town Ozarks. In *America through Baseball,* David Voigt asserts that the dominant value of American social history is the celebration of individualism, and baseball provided a means to achieve individual recognition.[38] Many young Ozark men—Bill Dickey, Lon Warneke (the Arkansas Hummingbird), Jay Hanna (Dizzy) Dean—began playing baseball in the Ozarks before eventually becoming members of the Major League Baseball Hall of Fame.[39] The towns had good reason to identify with their teams because the players were, for the most part, local citizens. Using imported players, a practice usually reserved for championship games, was often a contentious issue, especially between intense rivals.[40]

Large crowds attended court trials, which they usually held in the fall and spring. As with hangings, their very rarity added to their desirability as entertainment. At times, the hangings took a macabre turn, with the convicted man participating to make the event a gruesomely festive occasion. Once, at the hanging of Jodia Hamilton in Texas County, Missouri, the condemned man gave an oration and sang several verses of a song. When someone in the crowd asked the condemned man, "Is that you, Jodia?" he replied, "I told you I would try to be here."[41] Reportedly, on May 17, 1872, a crowd of seven or eight thousand formed a procession from the jail in Marshfield, Missouri, to the gallows on Bald Hill for the public hanging of Charles Waller, a man convicted of committing three murders in 1867.[42] At Fort Smith, Arkansas, on the southwest Ozarks border, Judge Isaac Parker presided for the trials of nearly ten thousand persons between 1875 and 1896. Parker's court convicted many of the accused for capital crimes and put 168 of them to death.[43] Large crowds attended when the courts hanged as many as six condemned men at once.[44] The last public hanging in Missouri drew a large crowd to witness the event at Galena, Missouri, on May 21, 1938. Roscoe "Red" Jackson was hanged from an outside gallows for the murder of Pearl Bozarth. Four hundred people received tickets to view the outdoor event held behind a high fence, but hundreds of people watched from trees and buildings. Afterward, onlookers received as souvenirs bits of rope used in the hanging.[45]

Political gatherings drew enthusiastic crowds. The arrival of a governor, senator, or representative from Washington, D.C., always attracted large crowds. Politicians with a national reputation seldom spoke at towns other than Springfield, Jefferson City, or Fayetteville. When Governor Herbert Hadley spoke at a banquet in Salem, Missouri, in 1909, it was the first time a governor had visited the town. Because of the large crowd, many people were turned away at the entrance.[46] Band concerts were especially appealing

"Men Who Rode for Parker," deputy U.S. marshals who served in Indian Territory for the Hanging Judge at Fort Smith, Arkansas. (Courtesy of Arkansas History Commission.)

because of the setting under the stars. The gaily decorated community Christmas tree was a lure to many.

Hunting and fishing were tied closely to the business of making a living. They were carried on in very much the same way as plowing the corn, simply a matter of augmenting the family larder with game and fish. Noodling and gigging were popular means of taking fish, as they are even today.[47] A few people took fish by dynamiting, and the more simple expedient of mashing a sack of green walnuts to pulp, weighting it, and sinking it in a likely deep hole filled with fish.[48] Whatever chemical action took place, it was well known that every fish in the hole came to the top of the water on his back and were then easily taken.

Collective work, such as road repair and threshing, provided an opportunity to socialize. When the thresher came into the neighborhood, all who had grain to thresh met it at the first stand and followed its progress through the neighborhood until the crew threshed the last bundles of wheat. Neighbors also gathered for hog butchering and apple peelings. These gatherings served as social functions and helped to preserve the fine art of conservation.

CONTEMPORARY ENTERTAINMENT

Contemporary entertainment in the Ozarks is not greatly different from that of other rural sections of the Middle West. Outdoor sports, particularly hunting and fishing, are still very popular. Much of the entertainment is the "canned" variety; rock and country-western music are played on stereos, tape players, and radios; soap operas dominate daytime television schedules; situation comedies, charismatic detectives, court dramas, and news and sports events fill the prime television slots. Television and movies have replaced the Friday night "literary" and the Saturday night band concert. Cable and satellite television has expanded the range of choices to include educational, self-help, political, and other programs. Videocassette recorders and rental videotapes, as well as DVD players and disks, have added to the choice and variety of sedentary entertainment.

Craft festivals are very popular, but this is mainly a nonnative thing. Many quilts, tablecloths, bedspreads, rugs, dolls, pots, and articles of clothing are made from craft kits. While some residual knowledge of native crafts remains, festivals, craft stores, and tourist businesses have helped stimulate interest in crafts.

Support of school activities continues to be strong. Basketball is especially popular, and a town's reputation rides on the outcome of the Christmas-season tournament and league championship. Girls' and women's softball have been popular for many years. In recent years the national emphasis on women's activities has created new interest and support for intramural and interscholastic women's athletics. Passage of federal Title 9 legislation in 1972, which reallocated (among other things) tax-funded budgets for equality between the sexes in the participation of sports, had an important impact on women's high school and college sports. Thus, Ozark schools, just like schools throughout the United States, have enjoyed budgets that account for predictable schedules and teams for the participation of women and the enjoyment of audiences. Fan loyalty for the Southwest Missouri State University *Lady*

Bears basketball team has become so strong that attendance at their games often exceeds that of the men's team.[49] The women's team frequently plays before capacity crowds exceeding eight thousand in Hammons Student Center. In the 2000–2001 basketball season, when All-American Jackie Stiles set a new Women's Division National Collegiate Athletic Association scoring record with 3,393 career points and led the SMSU Lady Bears to the "Final Four" in the Women's NCAA tournament, Southwest Missouri State University ranked sixth in the nation in attendance for women's basketball.

Over the past twenty-five years several other sports—soccer, field hockey, volleyball, to name a few—have become popular intramural and interscholastic sports. Men's football, which requires more players, has less historical tradition in the small Ozark schools, but with school consolidation, football has increased in popularity. The large enrollments and improved tax base in consolidated schools made it easier to field and equip an eleven-man football team.[50] The widespread support of college and professional teams throughout the United States has probably helped to stimulate more interest in football. The strongest fan loyalty for professional football teams lies with the St. Louis Rams, the Kansas City Chiefs, and the Dallas Cowboys. Fan support is also strong for college athletic teams, including the Missouri Tigers, the Arkansas Razorbacks, the Southwest Missouri State University Bears, and other regional college and university teams.

Theatrical productions continue to be popular. In high schools, junior and senior plays are traditional. Some area colleges have very strong theater departments. Some graduates have become nationally known performers. Larger towns—Springfield, Fayetteville, Joplin, and others—support civic theatrical groups. Traveling Broadway shows and other professional groups attract large crowds.

School events still attract large crowds. School proms and parties are popular, but they still hotly contest the propriety of dancing at school events in some communities. School patrons often scrutinize books assigned as required reading carefully to seek out profane or "inappropriate" passages. Occasionally, the issue of controversial books is the subject of emotional debates at meetings of the school board. School dress codes at Ozark, Missouri, were the subject of discussion in July 2000, as reported in the *Springfield News-Leader.*

> Spiked collars and clothing with satanic references have never been acceptable student attire in the Ozark School District.
>
> But now it's spelled out in the 2000–2001 Ozark student handbook.

The new dress code, recently approved by the Ozark school board, also prohibits miniskirts, see-through shirts, underwear worn as outer clothing and knee-length coats worn during school hours.

Superintendent Leo Snelling said the revised dress code is not much different than the earlier code. . . .

"We try to maintain a code that will be comfortable and conducive to learning."

Snelling said the changes, based on the recommendations of an advisory committee made up of parents, targeted clothing that "exposed inappropriate parts of the body or too much of the body."[51]

Religion continues to be an important part of life for many Ozarkers, as it has been since the first settlement. Catholicism began with the first eighteenth-century French settlements in the lead mines in the eastern Ozarks. Several Protestant denominations were founded during the first years of the twentieth century in southeast Missouri and a few years later in Arkansas.[52]

Probably, a smaller proportion of the population attends church regularly than in the past because of the many outdoor activities and other alternatives. Float trips, picnics, camping out, swimming, boating, and hunting are regular Sunday fare for many Ozark residents. Some churches combine recreational activities with church activities, but usually not. Many urban churches maintain strong youth recreation programs, including summer softball and baseball teams and other outdoor recreation. A few affluent churches have basketball courts and other indoor recreational facilities. Revivals may be regaining some of their appeal, particularly the open-air brush-arbor event. Music, singing, and vigorous preaching continue to be the main attractions, as in times past. Occasionally, spectators park nearby to take in the revival, but the rowdies, imbibed with white lightning, who harassed the congregations in former times have since found other outlets for their style of entertainment. The number of rural churches has declined over the years, probably because of a combination of the decline of religious influence in the rural area and partly because of the decline in population below the level that can support a church. Professor Cralle describes the problems of maintaining churches at Birch Tree in Shannon County in the 1930s (1930 population, 505):

> Six different denominations about the same time originally built churches in Birch Tree: The Methodist Episcopal, Methodist Episcopal-South, Missouri Baptist, Christian, Presbyterian, and the Roman Catholic. At this time the mills were thriving and the population was above 500. About 1925 a Pentecostal

(Holiness) Church was established and they also erected a building. With the closing of the large lumber mill all but three families of the Roman Catholic faith left the town and since that time these three families have gone and by 1920 their building was sold and wrecked. The Methodist Episcopal (North) membership meanwhile dwindled and all efforts at church and Sunday School were dropped, this building finally being sold and wrecked in 1928. Some of the members have affiliated with the Methodist Episcopal Church, South. The Presbyterians abandoned and sold their church in 1914, and for a long time the Christian Church was active. A revival meeting in 1922 resulted in 50 additions to the church, and a full time pastor. Within two years the full time pastor was cut to twice a month, later to once a month, and for three years they had no regular church service. They maintained a small Sunday School until recently. The Missionary Baptist and the Methodist Episcopal Church, South, have service twice a month. They hold an occasional union service at Christmas or Easter and arrange their regular meetings on different Sundays to avoid competing with each other. Denominational friction is breaking down; a large number of each denomination attend the services of the other when their own church has no service. Each maintains a small Sunday School. The Pentecostal seems to be the most flourishing Church remaining and their membership is gaining.[53]

Thus, except for loss in population, the example of Birch Tree in the 1930s contains most of the conditions being faced by many religious leaders in the Ozarks today: competitive denominationalism from a period of church building, the breakdown of a degree of social isolation in which the church was almost the only place to go, and half or more of the churches having given up the struggle to maintain regular services.

Although many rural churches are plagued with declining memberships, church organization continues to be strong in the growth centers of the Ozarks. In Springfield, Cape Girardeau, Joplin, Fayettville, Batesville, in the towns in the lake districts, and in smaller towns with only modestly increasing population, the churches are at least moderately healthy, if not prosperous. The new town of Viburnum (population 750) in Iron County, built in the 1960s and 1970s to house the workers in the lead mines, included a shopping district, a large new school, modern contemporary-style houses, and no less than five new churches to meet the sectarian needs of the inhabitants. Apparently, sectarianism surfaces wherever economic conditions permit. Although churches in the population growth areas tend to prosper, those in the sparsely settled areas often hold services in a union church shared by two or more denominations.

NATIVES VERSUS OUTSIDERS

Much is made of the native Ozarker's reluctance to accept outsiders, or "furriners." Elizabeth Herlinger has likened this to the behavior of distinct ethnic groups.[54] According to Herlinger, about 1900 was the latest point in time that any new settlers were incorporated folklorically into the Anglo-Saxon population of the remote sections of the Ozarks.[55] Herlinger notes clear differences in the way Taney County, Missouri, residents recount their heritage.

Natives (those who settled, or whose ancestors settled, in the hills prior to about 1890) think of heritage in terms of group survival. The past is thought to have been a physical and spiritual struggle to make a life in the frontier. Talk commonly concerns the close dependence of families upon each other, the hard work involved, the wide variety of crafts and skills natives possessed, and community expression of Christianity at camp meetings and revivals. Commonly natives of any age are anxious to place themselves in the context of their ancestors; they were eager to show me pictures of family ancestors and of historic family outings.

Non-natives (those who settled, or whose ancestors settled, in the hills after about 1890) seem more often to understand the past in terms of the frustrations of poverty. Settlement for these families was primarily in little towns, small settlements, or on semi-developed farm land. The emphasis in their talk today is upon past inconvenience (for example, no toilets, dirt floors, no electricity) and upon the adaptation, change, and growth that the area has experienced since 1900. These people tended to show me pictures that illustrated how roads, stores, bridges, and towns had changed. They only rarely seemed concerned with their family ancestry or their place in it (outside their own nuclear family).[56]

Birthright, then, is the basis for being a native Ozarker. Time does not make one a native, though longtime association with the land and its people may make one more nativelike. The highest compliment a native can pay a nonnative is that he is "really just an old hillbilly like me." The peculiarities of Ozark birthright rival the complexities of claiming citizenship in the United States. The birthright is not passed through women:

A native's mother need not be a native. Having a native mother does not make one any more native than merely having a native father. But one who does not have a native father is "not really native." . . . Another peculiarity of individual native inheritance is that birth in the hills is not required for native status. Many young natives marry and then temporarily leave the hills to seek their fortune elsewhere . . . The children of native parents are native, no matter where they are born.[57]

To say that native Ozarkers refer to themselves as hillbillies and to nonnative as foreigners or outsiders is too sweeping a generalization. Likewise, the distinction by natives between a stranger (a native Ozarker from another part of the region) and a "furriner," or non-Ozarker, is more fancy than fact. As discussed in chapter 1, the term *hillbilly*, which apparently came into popular use about 1900, has been much stereotyped, and many native Ozarkers object to it altogether. One's attitude toward use of the word is largely a matter of personal preference and individual situation. Some, particularly those who have attained a good education, reject the word outright.[58] Others of equal stature may accept it themselves, so long as it is recognized that they really do not fit the popular stereotype. Still others have become attached to the word and apply the name hillbilly to anyone who lives in the Ozarks, regardless of ancestry, circumstances, or place of residence (town or country). One native, Jerry Lee, of Branson, Missouri, sells hillbilly dolls and markets gag gifts and hillbilly novelties over the Internet.[59] Other natives, who genuinely hope to preserve Ozark culture and tradition through readings and theatrical presentations, may convey the same folksy image when they dress in overalls and red bandannas to depict the old time Ozarkers. Outsiders may see little difference in the images.

LIFESTYLE

Except for the small amount of influence of foreign immigrants, mainly among the Germans who live in the northern and eastern borders of the Ozarks, and recent Asian and Hispanic immigrants, the people of the Ozarks have a wholly American lifestyle. This is not to say that there is one lifestyle, for as we have seen, the region has experienced almost continuous change throughout its history. Although it is assumed that very little is known about Ozarks culture and lifestyle, actually, researchers have accomplished an important amount of inquiry into the agriculture, economic activities, customs, beliefs, education, settlement, ethnicity, and pioneer life of the people.

The references for this volume alone is a fair indicator of the substantial amount of work done.

Herlinger pointed out the two general patterns of human behavior or lifestyle among native Ozarkers: the traditionalist and the progressive (or, less pejoratively, nontraditional).[60] Neither of these lives up to the aspirations of the tourists who are seeking to see the folkloric Ozarker, a type of person to whom traditional values, such as honesty, morality, purity, and closeness to nature, can be attributed.

The traditionalist believes that rural values and life are superior to those found in an urban setting. This includes, or at least it did once, the belief that the people who inhabit the isolated small towns that served as trade centers are less moral, less forthright, and therefore less native than rural people. To the traditionalist, the city is a place of crime and pollution, and its population is believed to be largely immoral and ungodly. Conversely, the progressive Ozarker's view of city life is more likely tempered by what one has read or learned in school or from television and radio broadcasts. He or she is less likely to reject city life and city values out of hand.

Traditionalists view themselves with high regard. Their assessment of their fellow Ozark hill person is in many ways similar to those held by tourists. Herlinger found that the traditionalist characterizes himself in the pattern of the folkloric hill man, even to the point of switching verb tense: "The hill people were honest, kind, skilled craftsmen. They are goodly, pure, and live close to nature."[61] Traditionalists believe themselves to be different from nonnatives because of their heritage:

I'm a native because I'm a descendant of a special person—a man who would subject his family to the special hardship of pioneer life in these hills, for the special reasons of freedom and independence. That makes me, or any native, different from you.[62]

This folkloric view of ancestry ignores the fact that some settlers escaped to the Ozarks as dropouts seeking a place where competition was unnecessary or at least a place where land could be obtained free or at little cost. A few native Ozarkers followed the first of the eastern Indians into the Ozarks where they made their living selling illegal rotgut whiskey to the tribes.[63]

The traditionalist places strong emphasis on knowing family genealogy. I recall stopping at a house in Grandin, Missouri, to ask directions to a place and, after a while, the conversation somehow was sidetracked into family history. A son, about forty years old, recently returned from fifteen years of military service, gave a recitation on the family tree, including several divorces, stepchildren, half-brothers and sisters, cousins, nephews, and nieces, while his mother looked on, nodding her head in approving fashion. In many rural areas it is common for young people to identify themselves in terms of their relatives who have a better established community identity, but in the Ozarks it is common for young and adults alike to identify themselves as "I'm Jim and Mary Matthews's boy." Knowledge of all the family names in the community is expected, and older traditionalists will sometimes be familiar with most of the family names in the county.

Traditionalists believe that their ancestors were individualistic, self-reliant, self-sufficient, capable, well rounded, and proud. Traditionalists believe they have inherited these traits: "Natives have inherited the knack of adjustment to any hardships that come their way. That's why they're really all hillbillies just like the ones who settled these hills."[64]

The land has special meaning for the traditional Ozarker. Natives feel strongly that they are the only ones who know how to wrest a living from it. It is a place of refuge, a place to come back to. They presume they gain intrinsic values from the land. Professor Donald Holliday speaks of growing up in Taney County's Pinetop Community in the 1940s and 1950s.

All of the boys reaped tremendous rewards from the simple fact that they knew, intimately, their woods environment, because they knew well enough the various characteristics of their habitat that they could reap almost anything that nature had to offer. That they knew enough about wild animals, their skill in tracking, hunting, trapping attested. Their knowledge of trees and plants, and their uses, gave them added assurance that nature would support them.[65]

The traditionalist places great store in being handy at a great many tasks, of being self-reliant and able to do for himself what others must hire done. This is a belief they share with farm people throughout the United States. Farm life demands that a degree of skill be learned in many different but necessary farm activities:

By accretion, from the time the boys were very young until they were grown, until they left home they learned the thousand tricks of shoeing horses and breaking them. They learned how to castrate a calf or a hog without letting either bleed to death. They learned all the details of the eleven-month season of growing tobacco. They learned their father's belief in planting by signs, the hundreds of home remedies for man and ani-

mal, and many of the superstitions and potions for counteracting not-quite-physical maladies. They all sawed and hammered their way into being fair carpenters, and they mixed mortar and laid rock. Bicycles, plows, tractors, trucks, cars, haymakers, and machines made mechanics of them, capable, determined, ingenious enough to repair a machine or to get it unstuck and back on the road. Double-batted axes, crosscut saws, and mall and wedges made timbermen of them, too.[66]

Traditional Ozarkers think that legal matters are best handled according to local community standards. The sheriff and deputies in nearly all the rural counties are local men from long-line families. The most common violations of the law are traffic violations, including many arrests for drunk driving, disturbing the peace, burglary, theft, and domestic violence. Fines or imprisonment in the county jail is considered ample punishment for most crimes, and judges often assign penalties according to one's family background and history of scrapes with the law.

Occasionally, confrontations require outside assistance to establish order. In the instance on July 14, 1917, at the time the United States was becoming involved in World War I, when local miners, mainly from old-line families, rounded up most of the foreign workers and shipped them out of the Lead Belt with only the few possessions they could carry, the sheriff did not make any arrests.[67] To bring the situation under control, military units were brought in.

The tourist postcard caricature of mountain hillbillies working a moonshine still was never an accurate portrayal of Ozark life. It was another element of fabricated Appalachian culture that was somehow stamped on the Ozarks without any real basis. There was no "Whiskey Rebellion" in the Ozarks, and while Ozark pioneers sometimes made illicit homemade whiskey for their own use, and occasionally for sale to the immigrant Indians, moonshining was never a really important part of the economy or culture. Even during prohibition days when urban Ozarkers, like many other Americans, had their bathtub beer and white lightning, and occasionally sold some to tourists, the Ozarks had no worse reputation regarding the production and use of alcohol than many other sections of the United States. However, as we have seen, since about 1960, the drug culture has found its way into the Ozarks. It has resulted in a deterioration in family life, an increase in criminal activity, and a great increase in the need for social services and law enforcement.

A common belief is that natives "take care of their own." Natives expect to be taken care of in times of physical or spiritual need. They are aware of the impersonal condition of the poor in the city slums, and they regard Ozark poverty as decidedly different from city slum conditions, mainly because it is not associated with lack of identity. Some traditionalists believe that government assistance is a native right. In certain localities where divisions of the federal government (for example, the U.S. Army Corps of Engineers and the U.S. Forest Service) have been especially active, some individuals hold the government responsible for existing conditions today and therefore it owes certain financial support. The inflationary price rises through the 1960s, 1970s, and 1980s was further justification for federal assistance. Although there is a certain stigma attached to poverty, particularly when they attribute it to laziness, some Ozarkers accept government assistance programs readily. Occasionally, there are complaints that the "new people" know more about the federal assistance programs and can therefore take better advantage of them. Some administrators have asserted that the food-stamp program (for people with lower incomes), in particular, has been a factor in encouraging immigration to the Ozarks.[68]

Some Ozark towns—Springfield, for example—have grown to the point that a homeless population has become a problem. Businesspeople on Commercial Street (old North Springfield) fear that a skid row will develop along the street where various church relief groups provide food, clothing, housing, and other services for the homeless.[69] This large-scale big-city "soup kitchen" social aid is new and foreign to the Ozarks. Formerly the needy were cared for by family or by individuals, and in some counties they sent the homeless and needy to county-supported "poor farms."[70] This is not to say that Ozarkers were not generous or philanthropic. In the years following the Civil War, several women's' clubs became interested in the downtrodden. As early as 1889 the Progressive Workers' Club of Springfield, composed of a group of women, added to their desire for intellectual advancement a deep interest in the welfare of the unfortunate.[71] In 1906, when the Springfield City Federation of Women's Clubs was formed its membership included the Saturday Club, Friends in Council, Home Economics, Progressive Workers, Political Equality, and South Side Women's Christian Temperance Union.[72] Several of the clubs engaged in philanthropic and social assistance projects.

According to the traditionalist views, the native Ozarker is sharp in land dealings. One tale has become legendary. It is the story of a clever farmer who sold property at a high value to an outsider, bought it back "for a song," and resold it, not once, but several times. No doubt buyers have defaulted many land contracts, but the story is largely apocryphal. In fact, land prices have increased so rapidly since World War II that it would have been difficult for anyone to have lost money in farm real estate if they had held property more than a few years. One informant in Shannon County near the Ozark National Scenic Riverways stated that landowners in the area were reluctant to sell their property, almost at any price, for fear the buyer would resell it soon at a much higher price, thereby making them "look bad" coming out on the short end of a land deal. Then there is the case of a student in one of my classes who researched her family history and discovered that her grandparents, who had sold their farm for ten thousand dollars in 1947, still had the money in a *checking account,* at no interest, nearly twenty years later.

Traditionalists define sex roles strongly. There is women's work, not to be done by a man: mending clothes, washing dishes, cooking (other than wild game for special occasions), and all the other household chores. However, there is no particular aversion to women doing men's work: helping when needed in the hayfield, working in a clothing or shoe factory or hefting one-hundred-pound barrels in a whiskey-barrel factory. It is a common joke among Ozarkers themselves that "Ozarkers are real go-getters. They take her to work in the morning and 'go get her' in the afternoon." This image of the traditional lifestyle is not without some basis in fact. One informant, a teacher married to a traditional Ozarker but who herself would belong to the progressive-lifestyle group, said the go-getter image was not only correct but strongly resented:

> Oh, he likes it fine. He takes me to work and then drives down to the café where they all sit around in their Caterpillar caps and drink coffee all day. Then when he comes to get me and we go home, I have to cook supper, wash the dishes, and do whatever else needs to be done. I'll tell you I'd trade jobs with him.[73]

A final cultural trait of the traditional Ozark lifestyle is the adherence to fundamentalistic religious belief. The Baptist Bible, Assembly of God, Church of Christ, Full Gospel, and various other Pentecostal-revivalist churches serve people of all backgrounds, but their membership is strongly weighted with those of the traditional lifestyle. Herlinger found that those of the progressive lifestyle were more likely to attend Episcopal, Presbyterian, Methodist, Christian, Lutheran, or Catholic churches. These churches, sometimes called social-gospel Christianity, are more popular among people with middle-class values.[74]

Although social factors, particularly family tradition, are important in determining the lifestyle of individuals, geographical considerations are important. The most obvious geographical factor influencing lifestyle is whether one lives in town or in the country. Town life, particularly in the towns that early on received technology and ideas because of their location on railroads or the more traveled highways, has always been different from rural life. Likewise, the people in the mining districts received modernizing influences in the form of rail and road transportation, steam and electrical power, improved schools, and social services. These factors, and the fact that many people found employment in the mines, mills, and smelters, influenced lifestyles. Most important, the larger towns have been centers for diffusion of ideas and technology that have had profound influence on lifestyles. But even this spatial difference is rapidly changing as living conditions, mobility, and communications make rural living much the same as living in a city.

Ethnicity has had various degrees of influence, depending on the cultural level of the ethnic group. The French of Washington County, Missouri, have clung to a close-knit traditional lifestyle that centers around the Catholic church and the extended family group. For generations they eked out a bare existence working part-time in the barite diggings. Traditional craftsmanship, including that of constructing log cabins persisted past the mid nineteenth century. Here, too, is found one of the highest unemployment rates in the Ozarks.[75]

The traditional lifestyle of the Cherokees, particularly those who have clung to the old ways, the followers of the secret societies, has had an adverse influence on their level of living.[76] Longtime status as wards of the government, coupled with low-paying jobs, reduced family income for generations. For many families the main source of income came from part-time work picking strawberries and tomatoes, working in sawmills, or, for the young men, catching on as a harvest hand in the Wheat Belt or as a roughneck in the nearby oil fields. Traditional lifestyles became fixed in the culture and even today established patterns of economic pursuits are followed, so that only slowly are the cultural barriers broken down as young Cherokee men and women discover new opportunities. Overall, the mixed bloods have faired better economically and socially. They are more likely to have learned skills and sought higher education and to have accepted city life. While full bloods and mixed bloods may move in different social circles and have greatly different lifestyles and widely varying political views, they have a common bond. Grace Steele Woodward in her book, *The Cherokees,* put it this way:

A common ancestry promotes understanding between Cherokee full bloods and the mixed bloods. They are poles apart in many respects but, under the skin, are still brothers. For one thing, they have Cherokee traditions in common, and no amount of white blood can dilute the remembrance of what happened in centuries past to the Cherokee people.[77]

The Germans on the farms of the northern and eastern Ozarks border have practiced a traditional lifestyle of progressive small farms. The mark of successful parenthood has been to equip sons and daughters with the knowledge, skills, and mental attitude to be successful farmers. This traditional lifestyle, which incorporated ready acceptance of new agricultural methods resulting in a successful technology and high levels of production, has, nevertheless, resulted in smaller farms that have some difficulty competing in the increasingly competitive agricultural marketplace.

Thus, the traditional Ozark lifestyle is that accepted mainly by descendants of the original Scotch-Irish immigrants. Although it is most persistent in the rugged, wooded hill districts—the Osage-Gasconade Hills, the Courtois Hills, the White River Hills, and the Boston Mountains—it may be found near the major growth centers. Scarcely thirty miles from Springfield, in the breaks along the Eureka Springs Escarpment, there are families who live in quite isolated valleys, where in one instance they must sometimes park the family automobile nearly a half mile from the house because the stream crossing is so poor. Even within the larger towns small neighborhoods occur where clusters of ramshackle houses surrounded by vintage automobiles symbolize a nonprogressive "Ozark ghetto" lifestyle.

In recent years there has been much speculation about how the large number of new immigrants may affect politics, attitudes, and beliefs of the larger Ozark community. This is not only because the newcomers themselves comprise a large share of the population, but because the new immigrants influence longtime residents through everyday contact. Most of the statements of this matter are conjectural, but there is a small amount of information to support the idea.

A study of ten southwest Missouri counties, sponsored by the Southwest Missouri Local Government Advisory Council, produced data showing that Ozarkers are far less conservative than is commonly believed regarding questions of land use and environmental issues.[78] For example, more than 91 percent of a random-sample population believed that tourism and related businesses should be promoted while maintaining and preserving the same environment that tourists come to see; 87 percent believed that local, state, and federal agencies should be required to include affected landowners in recreational-resource expansion plans; 53 percent believed the Corps of Engineers should not discontinue all further development projects, while 28 percent believed corps projects should be terminated; more than 88 percent believed landowners should have greater influence, by law, regarding government purchase of land for recreation use; slightly more than 50 percent (versus 25 percent opposed) thought government recreation developers had given insufficient consideration to the conservation of resources; more than two-thirds of the respondents regarded as too stringent the state and federal government regulations regarding decisions made by private landowners; more than 70 percent favored increased financing for sanitary landfills, sewage treatment facilities, water treatment, and extension of farm-to-market roads; there was overwhelming support for controls to reduce the threat of pollution of surface and ground-water resources; and more than two-thirds of the respondents believed that population growth and industrial and commercial development should be encouraged.

The attitudes regarding land ownership and private property are traditional rural beliefs, but the strong support for conservation of land and water resources may reflect nationwide publicity on environmental issues. Support for commercial and industrial expansion likely will continue as a natural outgrowth of desire for jobs and economic well-being. Support for population growth shows that Ozarkers are willing to accept growth to support economic viability. Some recent immigrants, many of whom moved to the Ozarks for its quietude, express strong concerns about further population growth. Longtime residents sometimes accuse newcomers of wanting to be "the last person to immigrate to the Ozarks."

FOURTEEN

OZARK TOWNS AND CITIES

Transportation routes have always been paramount in the establishment of towns in the Ozarks. The earliest towns were along the major navigable streams: the Mississippi, Missouri, and Arkansas rivers. St. Louis, St. Genevieve, Cape Girardeau on the Mississippi River; Washington, Hermann, Jefferson City, Boonville, and Glasgow on the Missouri River; and Batesville on the White River are all old river towns. Little Rock and Fort Smith, just beyond the Ozark border on the Arkansas River, were also important river ports for the region. These towns owe their existence to favorable sites for river wharfage or crossing, or to a situation that commanded a productive hinterland. As discussed previously, the White River was also an important transportation artery for northern Arkansas and southwest Missouri. Batesville was the gateway city for boats operating on the White River. The only other navigable stream of consequence was the Osage River. Warsaw was for a time an important river port, and under favorable circumstances steamboats could navigate the Osage as far as Osceola. Still, the Osage River was never a reliable route of commerce.

Because interior Ozark streams were not navigable, the larger interior towns are on railroads. When railroads were built, towns were about six to ten miles apart along the right of way. While many newly founded towns failed to grow, many others became growth centers, and the railroads linked these corridors of growth and development.[1] Many early railroad towns were paper towns; that is, they were planned but never built, either because the planned railroad was never completed, or because of commercial competition from adjacent towns, or, perhaps, because they were purely fraudulent real-estate promotions. These early villages had two purposes: to serve as trade and service centers for the agricultural community and to serve as watering and fueling stops for the locomotives. The population during this time was mainly engaged in agriculture and was dispersed throughout the countryside. Hamlets, villages, and towns grew up closely spaced because the principal transportation beyond the railroad was by horseback, wagon, or shank's mare. Comparatively few towns

have been founded since the 1850–1910 railroad construction era.[2]

In the ensuing years, major technological changes have occurred, causing changes in settlement patterns. One major change is the continuing agricultural technology revolution, which has enabled a much smaller percentage of the population to produce more than the necessary amount of food and fiber. The percentage of the population engaged in agriculture has declined continuously. A second significant change is in transportation and communication. *Time distance* is a convenient term used as a measure of the distance a person travels in one hour.[3] On foot, people can travel four or five miles, on horseback ten or twelve, but with today's system of highways and motorvehicles, traveling fifty miles in an hour is easy. Thus, today, an hour's time distance is fifty miles or more. In recent years, the industrialization of the region's economy has stimulated population growth in the medium-size and larger towns. In combination these changes have worked to modify the region's communities. Many villages and towns have become functionally obsolete, and others have grown into important centers of industry and population.

Construction of new highways has brought growth and prosperity to many interior Ozark towns, while at the same time highways have sometimes affected small hamlets and villages adversely. In fact, highways affect Ozark towns in several ways. A new highway may bring some formerly remote towns into reasonable commuting distance to places of employment. The location of new highways may either help or hinder a town's central business district. Towns may become more attractive as industrial locations because of improved transportation routes. Convenience stores, restaurants, motels, and other travel-related services may grow up at centralized or preferred locations. New growth centers may emerge at highway intersections. Improved federal highways attract area residents to the large centers where they find a wider selection of goods and services. Villages and small towns may suffer economic stagnation as the rural population declines and the remaining residents bypass smaller places to shop in larger towns.

In a recent study of three southwest Missouri towns—Nixa, Sarcoxie, Rich Hill—community leaders identified factors that influence the economy, growth, and livability of small towns.[4] Factors deemed to have had a negative influence on town growth included loss of a basic industry; location between two competing growing towns; poor leadership and citizen involvement; an aging population; a transient population with no ties to the community; old, deteriorating, low-income housing; lack of jobs; lack of retail stores; limited personal and professional services; and lack of community planning.

In the Ozarks, the critical population range is five hundred to fifteen hundred; that is, until about the mid-1960s, most communities with fewer than five hundred people declined; those with more than fifteen hundred seemed to have a better chance for growth. Since the 1960s, which marks the beginning of recent immigration to the Ozarks, many small places have experienced population increases.[5] We may group Ozark trade centers according to population and the number and range of services available. Geographers usually classify central places into four categories: hamlets, villages, towns, and cities.[6] Hamlets, the most rudimentary trade centers, consist of about five to twenty-five residential, cultural, or functional structures, but usually fewer than half a dozen retail units. A regional sample of Ozark hamlets showed that grocery stores, elementary schools, churches, convenience stores, and taverns are the most typical services.[7] Unplanned in form, they occur as crossroads, clusters, and as sparse strings of assorted buildings. The populations of the hamlets surveyed ranged from twenty to one hundred fifty with a mean of sixty-five.

Villages are larger. The population range is from approximately one hundred fifty to about one thousand. They have commercial nuclei with a minimum of ten retail and service businesses. Grocery stores, taverns, convenience stores, elementary schools, lumberyards, hardware stores, and feed dealers are typical retail outlets. Banks and post offices are the usual services. Ozark villages have few governmental services, personal services, professional services, and little commercial entertainment.

Towns have more specialized services and range in population from about one thousand to about seven thousand. In the Ozarks, most towns have maintained or increased their population. The faster-growing towns are near major highways or where tourist attractions or large-scale urbanization has taken place. Ozark towns usually have a well-defined business district with about fifty retail units or more. Represented are all types of schools and professional services, such as medical, legal, and veterinary. Towns frequently support some warehousing, distributing,

Buffalo Shoals, Arkansas, on the White River. (Courtesy of Arkansas History Commission.)

and wholesaling and also highway-oriented businesses such as motels and fast-food restaurants. A county courthouse is most often (but not always) found in a town rather than in a hamlet or village.

Functional change is most notable in hamlets and villages, largely because many have regressed as trade centers.[8] Old signs and abandoned buildings tell of the passing of hotels, blacksmith shops, lumberyards, farm-implement dealers, automobile agencies, and so on. Occasionally one sees community libraries housed in abandoned corner service stations and restaurants, taverns, or beauty shops in abandoned bank buildings. Many residents of hamlets and villages are reluctant to leave even when their standards of living must suffer. Because of close social and family ties, they are willing to maintain several jobs to earn a living. Until recently, one tavern owner in Altenburg, a small German hamlet in eastern Perry County, Missouri, sold groceries and operated a one-chair barbershop in the front of the tavern.[9] Some villages and towns in the tourist-recreation areas in the Ozarks offer a large range of services for the summer population, which is sometimes several times the number of permanent residents. For example, the number of restaurants, gift shops, convenience stores, and shopping places in Branson, Missouri, far exceeds the average for towns of five thousand population.[10] Likewise, regional trade towns, such as Rolla, Lebanon, West Plains, Harrison, Mountain Home, and Tahlequah, have larger-than-normal ranges of services because of the extensive trade areas they serve.

The form and appearance of Ozark towns is quite variable. Many towns, particularly those founded on the level uplands, have grid systems with the streets usually running north-south and east-west. Many county seat towns have a grid plan with the courthouse within an open square. West Plains, Van Buren, Marshfield, Salem, Houston, Galena, and Carthage are examples of courthouse square towns, a common town plan throughout the United States.[11] Among the courthouse square towns in the Arkansas Ozarks are Mountain Home, Salem, and Jasper. Some county seats are small. Lesterville, the tiny seat of Reynolds County, Missouri, has too few businesses to form a complete business square around the courthouse. Highway travelers in the Ozarks, just as in much of the Middle West and South, must thread their way through a busy town square every forty or fifty miles. For example, in Mountain Grove, Missouri, Highway 95 passes through the main business square and then zigzags through half a dozen turns as it finds its way through the south part of town. On busy U.S. 60 at the north edge of Mountain Grove is a cluster of motels, fast-food restaurants, and gasoline-convenience stores, the tell-tale markers of a modern growth town. Similar highway clusters, sometimes called by the acronym GEMs for gas-eats-motels, have grown up throughout the Ozarks, especially during the last two decades of the twentieth century.[12] When a Wal-Mart store moves to a bypass highway site, the increased traffic can attract other businesses and by doing so reduce business activity in the downtown business district of a small town.

REGIONAL GROWTH CENTERS

I have said that the most striking geographic change in Ozark population during the past half century or more has been movement of people from farm to city. Over the years, several growth centers have emerged. The influence of these cities is much greater than that of smaller places. Each commands a trade area, the size of which varies according to the range of services offered, the distance to competing growth centers, the condition of roads and required travel time, and the density of population in the hinterland (fig. 14-1). They have several things in common: good rail and highway transportation and some type of scheduled airline service; educational institutions beyond high school; a regional hospital; professional services; federal, state, and county governmental services; and better retail shopping than in smaller hinterland towns. A Wal-Mart store or a Wal-Mart Supercenter is typically found in such cities. A brief description of the historical development, chief functions, and trade areas of eight of the larger regional centers follows.

Jefferson City, the capital of Missouri and the seat of Cole County, is on the steep southern bluffs of the Missouri River. Its location, midway between St. Louis and Kansas City on the river and a direct railroad route, has attracted several important industries. It is, however, primarily a political city, with state government, for which it was created, its principal business. Besides 16,368 Missouri state government employees, there are several other large employers: St. Mary's Health Center (1,250 employees), Capital Region Medical Center (1,200), Jefferson City Public Schools (1,081), Lincoln University (500), the Maytag Company (500), Scholastic, Inc. (1,600), and the Wal-Mart Supercenter (577).[13]

The selection of a capital site was one of the first matters taken up by the Missouri General Assembly when they met in the Missouri Hotel in St. Louis in September 1821. After considering several towns, they agreed temporarily to place the state government in St. Charles until a permanent capital could be selected. The General Assembly appointed five commissioners from various parts of the state to select a capital site. Jefferson City was one of several sites on the Missouri River, "within forty miles of the mouth of the Osage," under consideration.[14] Cote Sans Dessein was the front runner in the competition, but in early 1822, without full explanation of their decision, the General Assembly directed the commissioners to lay out the town that it had already named, the City of Jefferson, which through common usage soon became Jefferson City.[15]

In its first years, the capital site's growth was slow. In 1828 voters elected to move the Cole County seat from Marion to Jefferson City. After completion of the state penitentiary in 1836 and the new capitol in 1839, Jefferson City grew faster. It was incorporated in 1839, and according to the federal census, it had 1,174 inhabitants, including 262 slaves in 1840. In 1849, the steamboat *Monroe,* carrying west-bound Mormons, stopped at Jefferson City and discharged cholera-stricken passengers. Sixty-three of them died, and for the next two years the plague curtailed immigration and commerce.[16]

Railroad service to St. Louis began in 1856, but the Civil War soon dampened the enthusiasm brought by the railroad. Expansion of business activities did not progress rapidly until the 1880s. Three shoe factories were opened in the early 1880s to supplement an already healthy printing industry. The drawbridge built across the Missouri River in 1895 and the construction of a new capitol in 1917 helped to establish a pattern of slow but steady growth.

Over the years, the city spread inland across the narrow ridges and valleys that parallel the river. High Street, following the first of the ridges east and west, became the axis of the community. The business buildings consist of blocks of brick and stone structures. A block north of

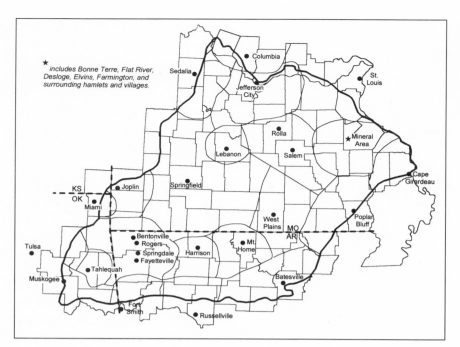

FIGURE 14-1. Ozark growth centers and trade areas. Adapted from Milton D. Rafferty, *Historical Atlas of Missouri* (Norman: University of Oklahoma Press, 1982), plate 76, with updates for Arkansas and Oklahoma.

★ *includes Bonne Terre, Flat River, Desloge, Elvins, Farmington, and surrounding hamlets and villages.*

High Street, atop a bluff overlooking the river, the governor's mansion sits opposite the capitol. The residential sections lie east, west, and south of the business district. Blacks, comprising almost 10 percent of the population, live especially in the southeastern portion of the city close to Lincoln University, formerly a state-supported Negro college but now open to all races. The Capitol Mall, west of the central business district and state capitol, has attracted considerable new commercial and residential development. Many of Jefferson City's attractions—the Missouri Capitol, the Governor's Mansion, Jefferson Landing State Historical Site, the Union Hotel, and the Lohman Building—are near the downtown area.

Compared with most state capitals, Jefferson City is small; its population, 32,407 in the census of 1970, had grown to 34,911 in 1998.[17] Much of the recent growth has occurred outside the city. Cole County's population increased from 46,228 to 69,512 during the same time span.[18] While an interstate highway does not serve Jefferson City directly, I-70 is only thirty miles north via U.S. Highway 63. Commercial airlines serve Columbia-Jefferson City Regional Airport, situated between the two cities. Government and finance continue to play the largest role in the city's economy.

No other places in the Jefferson City's Ozark hinterland exceeded 3,500 people in 1980, but by 1998 two towns, California (3,760) and Eldon (4,626), had surpassed that mark.[19] Owensville is the third-ranking outlying town. The *Missouri Manufacturers Register 2000* listed the following types of manufacturers employing more than 100 workers in the outlying towns: saddler, poultry processing,

shoe manufacture, clothing, charcoal briquettes, electric motors, fishing boats, wooden novelties, and aluminum and copper tubular parts.[20] The pattern from town to town is similar to that of other rural trade centers; several small manufacturers or service companies that supply the needs of local or regional farms and agri businesses, and one or two larger manufacturers of products distributed to a larger regional or national market. The latter are often of the footloose type taking advantage of less-expensive, nonunion labor in rural communities. Two types of manufacturing—clothing and shoes—have continued to decline throughout the Ozarks since about 1960.

St. Louis lies just outside the Ozarks, but as one of America's great cities it has always had a profound influence on the region. St. Louis radio and television stations dominate the northeastern Ozarks and the *St. Louis Post-Dispatch* is the leading daily newspaper well into the Current River country. Although the city of St. Louis has experienced declines in population for the past five census periods, down from 856,796 in 1950 to 339,316 in 1998, the Metropolitan Statistical Area (MSA) continues to grow, and much of the growth is spreading into the northeast Ozark border.[21] The population of the St. Louis MSA increased from 1,681,281 in 1950 to 2,653,801 in 1998, an increase of more than the 2,506,511 living in the ninety-three-county Ozark region.[22]

Several outlying towns in the Ozarks have profited from the proximity to St. Louis. Many manufacturing plants have moved to the outlying towns, and the larger companies have found it profitable to build plants in these towns and centralize warehousing and sales facilities in St.

Louis. Washington, Union, Pacific, Boone Terre, and Farmington are the larger and more important towns for manufacturing employment. An inventory of manufacturers in the outlying towns shows that shoes, clothing, light metals, and mining and mineral processing are important. A complete inventory of manufacturing plants that employ more than one hundred workers include women's clothing, men's clothing, shoes, piston rings, vinyl advertising items, carburetor tune-up kits, aircraft parts, dairy equipment, tents and tarpaulins, lime and stone, toy telephones, electric motors, iron pellets, and lead smelting. The Missouri Meerschaum Company at Washington manufactures an unusual product, corncob pipes. Crystal City, founded as a company town by the Pittsburgh Plate Glass Company, is on the extreme northeast Mississippi border. The Doe Run Company's massive lead smelter is at Herculaneum.

The northeast border possesses the best transportation network in the Ozarks. Besides good railroad facilities, and year-round navigation on the Mississippi River, workers, materials, and manufactured products can reach St. Louis in about an hour from the most-distant points in the trade area by the way of I-44, I-55, U.S. 67, and U.S. 61.

Cape Girardeau, called "Cape" by many inhabitants, overlooks the Mississippi from the rocky ledge that forms the Ozark escarpment. As the site of Southeast Missouri State University, the town has been the educational and commercial center of southeast Missouri for more than a hundred years. About 1720, a French soldier named Girardot, from the French post near Kaskaskia (Illinois) settled on the Cape, a rocky promontory north of the city.[23] Shortly afterward, maps designated the point as Cape Girardot (or Girardeau). Actual farm settlement did not occur until Americans from the eastern uplands discovered the location in the late 1700s. Uncertainty of land titles retarded the growth of the town after the U.S. Land Commission rejected Louis Lorimer's Spanish land title.[24] In 1815, Jackson became the county seat and Cape Girardeau languished.

Nevertheless, the geographic location of Cape Girardeau pointed toward its growth as a commercial town.[25] Its location on the first high ground above the confluence of the Ohio and the Mississippi rivers gave it strategic importance in the river trade. Rivermen floated logs, grain, and livestock down to Cape Girardeau's sawmills, flour mills, and packing houses. The trail that followed Crowley's Ridge north from the Arkansas swamps brought trade to "Cape."[26] In 1880, Louis Houck organized the Cape Girardeau Railway Company, which eventually became the Gulf System, and placed Cape Girardeau on a main line connecting with St. Louis.[27]

Cape Girardeau is served by I-55 and U.S. 61. Barge traffic on the Mississippi is important, and several airlines serve the city. The *Missouri Manufacturers Register 2000* listed eighty-six manufacturing establishments.[28] Companies employing more than 300 workers included Dana Corporation, Spicer Light Vehicle Axle Division (386; axle parts), Florsheim Shoe Company (325; men's dress shoes), and Thorngate, Ltd., Division of Hart, Schaffner & Marx (500; men's clothing).

Today, Cape Girardeau is a regional hub for education, commerce, and medical care. Although the city's population is 35,596, planners estimate that as many as 90,000 commute to the city daily to work, shop, go to school, or to visit the many doctors' offices or two hospitals.[29] The new Bill Emerson Memorial Bridge, scheduled for completion in 2004 at a cost of $100 million, will make travel from the east side of the Mississippi River easier. In 1998, Southeast Missouri State University and the municipal government collaborated to secure funding for a new River Campus performing arts center. The new arts center will occupy the site of the old St. Vincent's academy on the Mississippi River.

Poplar Bluff has a geographic site similar to that of Cape Girardeau. It is perched on the Ozark escarpment where the Black River exits from the Ozarks onto the Southeast Alluvial Plain. The older business district lies on the flood plain, and the better residential districts stretch back across the upland to the north. Some neighborhoods appear as pages out of a nineteenth-century picture book with their brick-paved streets bordered by huge oaks and grand old houses. A commercial strip with the usual array of convenience stores, gasoline stations, eating places, motels, and assorted businesses has grown up along the stretch of U.S. 60–67 leading north through the west part of the city.

Founded in 1850 as the county seat of Butler County, Poplar Bluff grew slowly until 1873 when the Iron Mountain Railroad linked its trade area with St. Louis and points east. The town has been supported at various times by the lumber industry, mining of sink-fill iron deposits, and trade with farms and smaller towns. Employment in the Missouri Pacific and St. Louis and San Francisco (Frisco) switching yards and shops was important until the mid-twentieth century. Manufacturing continues to be an important employer.

Poplar Bluff benefited from its selection as the site of the Three Rivers Community College in 1966. Classes began in 1967 in a downtown storefront campus, but now the college occupies a seventy-acre campus and has an enrollment of thirty-five hundred students. The city of 17,029 people is an important retailing, medical, and service center for Butler County and surrounding counties.[30] There are approximately fifty manufacturing plants in Poplar Bluff, but most have fewer than fifty employees and serve primarily the city and its trade region. The larger "basic" or "city-building"[31] manufacturers include the Briggs and Stratton Corporation (751 employees; industrial engines), Rowe Furniture Corporation (750; upholstered furniture), the Gates Rubber Company (525; automotive hoses), Plastic Engineered Components, Inc. (200; plastic molding parts), and the Smiley Container Corporation (160; candy boxes).[32]

Springfield is Missouri's third-largest city and self-proclaimed Queen City of the Ozarks.[33] Its population of 120,000 in the 1970 census had grown to an estimated 142,898 in 1998. Much of the growth over the past twenty-five years has occurred outside the city.[34] The Springfield Metropolitan Statistical Area (as defined by the U.S. Census Bureau) includes Greene and Christian counties.[35] In 1998, it encompassed an estimated population of 304,863 making it the largest urban place in the Ozarks.[36] Because of rapid population growth and close economic linkages with Springfield, Census Bureau plans call for the addition of Webster County to the Springfield MSA for the 2000 census. For several years, the Springfield MSA has had the fastest growth rate among Missouri's Metropolitan Statistical Areas and the addition of Webster County to the MSA should push the total over 320,000 in the 2000 census. The rapid growth of Branson and Taney County and the continued southward growth of the Springfield metropolitan area along U.S. 65 and Missouri 160 could result in the inclusion of Branson and Taney County in the Springfield MSA by the 2010 federal census.

Education is an important part of the Springfield economy. Its five 4-year colleges—Southwest Missouri State University (17,388 enrollments), Evangel University (2,932), Drury University (2,779), Central Bible College (1,834), and Baptist Bible College (1,604)—had a combined enrollment of 26,537 in the fall semester 1998.[37] Ozark Technical Community College enrolled an additional 5,922 students. Additionally, proprietary business and technical schools enrolled hundreds of students.

Springfield's four television stations, several radio stations, and the widely read *Springfield News-Leader* enhance the city's role as a cultural and commercial center in the Ozarks. Rural Ozarkers have always called Springfield an "Ozark town," where people are "just plain folks and are friendlier than in other big places." Many immigrants to Arkansas and the Cherokee Ozarks in the later decades of the nineteenth century came through Springfield. The federal land office attracted many people to Springfield to file land claims. It was a jumping-off place, a trade center, and

a place to conduct other government business in the offices of county, state, and federal agencies. Springfield still performs most of these functions.

Reports that Delaware and Kickapoo Indians established villages on the present site of Springfield in the 1820s[38] are arguable, but there is conclusive evidence that they built villages just a few miles south at the mouth of Wilson's Creek.[39] The first white families, those of John Campbell, Joseph Miller, William Fulbright, and A. J. Burnett, settled at the site of Springfield in 1829 and 1830. The origin of the name *Springfield* is uncertain, but it was probably named after Springfield, Tennessee.[40] Springfield became the seat of Greene County when they organized the county in 1833 and was incorporated as a town in 1838.[41] In 1835 the federal government established a land office for southwest Missouri in Springfield, and by 1859, the town of twenty-five hundred was the main trade center in southwest Missouri. In 1870 the Atlantic and Pacific Railroad built north of Springfield, and the Ozark Land Company platted a rival town, North Springfield, along what is today Commercial Street. The two towns were first linked by a trolley line, and in 1887, after the old town got its own rail depot (Kansas City, Fort Scott and Memphis), the two towns were consolidated.[42]

The Public Square, near the center of the city, is the core of Springfield's downtown central business district (fig. 14-2).[43] North of the square is the Jordan Creek Industrial District, which extends for several blocks east and west. North of Jordon Creek, northeast of the intersection of Boonville and Trafficway, is a cluster of government buildings, including the city hall, Busch Municipal Building, City Utilities, police headquarters, Greene County courthouse, judicial center and jail, the old Carnegie library, the Social Security office building, and newly remodeled Central High School. East of the central business district, around the intersection of St. Louis and John Q. Hammons Parkway, in what was once an old black neighborhood called the "East End," is another cluster of high rise buildings built by Springfield developer John Q. Hammons.[44] This center includes the University Plaza Hotel and Convention Center, the twenty-two-story Hammons Tower office building (the tallest building in the Ozarks), the University Plaza Trade Center, the United States Courthouse, the John Q. Hammons Building, and One Parkway Place, a high-rise condominium. Ten blocks north of the central business district, Boonville Avenue intersects Commercial Street, the focus of the old North Springfield commercial and industrial district, which extends east-west parallel to the Frisco tracks. The extensive Burlington Northern-Santa Fe Railroad switching yards are at the west end of this district.

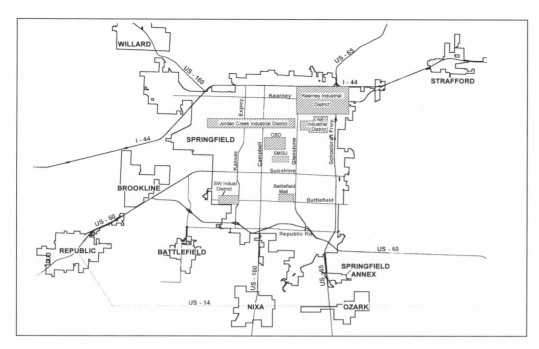

FIGURE 14-2.
Springfield, Missouri,
and surrounding towns.
Adapted from Bill
Weaver and Mike
Fonner, *Digital
Geographic Information
Systems (GIS) Files*
(Springfield: City of
Springfield, Missouri,
2000).

Several outlying commercial centers grew up over the years. Small retail centers developed earlier at trolley transfer points. Some of these small clusters of grocery stores, drugstores, and laundromats continued in business many years partly because the bus lines followed the routes of the streetcar lines after the last streetcar ran in 1937.[45] These small centers are now all but gone.

As with most cities, federal and state highways have helped shape the commercial geography of the city. Businesspeople laid out the city's older highway commercial districts along St. Louis and College streets, where U.S. 66 found its way through the city.[46] U.S. 66 also attracted commercial growth along Kearney Street when it later followed that route through the city. Since about 1980, Kearney Street has experienced steady commercial rejuvenation as property owners replace small false-front buildings, formerly houses, with modern commercial buildings. Many businesses along East Kearney Street, from Glenstone Avenue to Schoolcraft Expressway (U.S. 65 Bypass) and beyond, serve the trucking industry. Here, Kenworth (truck sales and repair), Mack Trucks, Mitsubishi Fuso Trucks, Volvo Trucks, Cummins Diesel, Diesel Exchange, Inc., and other trucking-related businesses established themselves to take advantage of easy access to Interstate 44 at the Glenstone and Schoolcraft Expressway interchanges. Farther east on State Highway 744 (Historic U.S. 66) beyond the city limits is the sprawling Roadway truck terminal. In May 2000, the Greyhound Bus Terminal moved from its former downtown location on St. Louis Street to a new terminal building on East Kearney.

Today's busiest commercial thoroughfares were formerly bypass or business route highways. Heavily developed Sunshine and Campbell streets are also highway business routes. Glenstone Avenue is the city's most remarkable string shopping street: eleven miles of service stations, eating establishments, motels, grocery stores, discount stores, insurance agencies, automobile dealerships, and off-street shopping centers.[47] One major shopping node is the motel, restaurant, and service station cluster on Glenstone between Kearney Street and I-44.

A second major commercial node is the group of off-street shopping centers developed at the intersection of Sunshine Street and Glenstone Avenue and then north on Glenstone to Bennett. The Plaza on the southeast corner of Sunshine and Glenstone is the oldest; a Ramey supermarket was built there in the early 1950s. Developers built Katz City (now Osco Drugs), Glen Isle, and Country Club shopping centers in the 1960s.

Rapid growth on South Glenstone began in 1972 when Simon and Associates (now the Simon Property Group) completed the Battlefield Mall, the Ozarks' largest regional shopping center. The mall helped tilt Springfield's commercial activity and traffic pattern to the southeast. In 1974, there were sixty-one businesses operating in the Battlefield Mall, including Montgomery Ward, J. C. Penney Company, Dillard's, Century 21 Theater, Osco Drugs, and Piccadilly Cafeteria. After a major expansion in 1982, one hundred and fifty businesses operated in the mall, a level that had increased to one hundred and seventy by 2000. Other anchor stores, including Sears and Famous Barr, were added after the expansion. The mall

NORTHWEST CORNER SQUARE 1879

could possibly support more stores if sufficient parking were available.

With the Battlefield Mall acting as a retail magnet, heavy commercial development continued to develop along Battlefield Road and especially farther south on Glenstone. When a sprawling Wal-Mart Supercenter opened about a mile farther south along Glenstone in September 1996 the traffic it generated triggered another round of commercial growth. Development became so intense that by 1999 the Springfield Department of Community Development placed a moratorium on further development along Glenstone Avenue until they could formulate new traffic plans.[48] Wal-Mart will operate five Supercenters in Springfield when it completes construction of a new Supercenter at Sunshine Street and West Bypass and remodeling and enlargements at two other locations, including their North Town Mall property.

Commercial development along north Kansas Expressway near Interstate 44, includes Springfield's first Wal-Mart Supercenter (1993), a Lowe's Home Improvement Warehouse, a strip shopping center, and other businesses. On the city's south side, at the intersection of Kansas Expressway and James River Expressway is Chesterfield Village, a planned commercial and residential development featuring a turn-of-the-twentieth-century motif in a commercial district of brick two-story buildings.

The Frisco passenger terminal closed after the last passenger train left the city in 1966. Frisco razed the shops, the old southwestern-style terminal, and most of the switching

tracks in the lower Jordon Creek valley. A concrete-mix plant occupies part of the land; the remainder, except for stacks of open storage railroad supplies, is idle, what planners call "brown space." During the 1980s and 1990s, after the Burlington Northern Railroad (now BNSF) absorbed the St. Louis and San Francisco, more than fourteen hundred railroad jobs were lost when Frisco's management offices and diesel shops closed.[49] In 1972, Missouri Pacific closed its line to Crane and removed the track. Ozark Greenways converted part of the Missouri Pacific roadbed to a hiking and bicycling trail, which will extend all the way to Wilson's Creek National Battlefield Park when completed.

Until the middle of the twentieth century, railroads had a dominant influence on the location of manufacturing in Springfield. By that time well-defined manufacturing districts had developed.[50] The *Missouri Manufacturers Register 2000* listed 394 manufacturers in the city.[51] Those with more than 1,000 employees included Aaron's Automotive Products (1,800; automotive engines and transmissions), Kraft Foods (1,500; cheese and pasta processing), and Willow Brook Foods, Inc. (1,625; turkey processing). Manufacturing companies employing 500 to 999 employees included Advanced Circuitry (700; printed circuits), Loren Cook Company (500; ventilation equipment), GE Motors (750; electric motors), Interstate Brands Corporation (500; baked bread), Paul Mueller Company (800; steel tanks and equipment), Positronics Industries (549; utility connectors), and Sweetheart Cup Company, Inc. (850; paper and plastic cups). Other major employers included the national headquarters of Assembly of God Churches; two large hospitals—St. John's Regional Health Center and Cox Medical Center—and the Federal Medical Center for prisoners; the U.S. Post Office; the Springfield Public Schools; and the city's colleges and universities.

Manufacturing has changed considerably in Springfield since the 1930s. Just as the Ozark region has been modernized and transformed economically, the city of Springfield has become much less dependent on agricultural manufactures. The U.S. Census Bureau, *County Business Patterns: Missouri, 1997,* classification of manufacturing according to the Standard Industrial Classification (SIC) shows Springfield to be high in Food and Kindred Products (3,882 employees), but Electronics and Other Electrical Equipment is nearly as important with 3,201 employees. Other leading manufactures include Printing and Publishing, Transportation Equipment, Fabricated Metals, Industrial Machinery, and Paper and Allied Products.[52] A 1968 telephone survey by students at Southwest Missouri State University found a rapid increase in manufacturing plants in the period 1940 to 1960. The companies reported their founding years as follows: before 1900, 7; 1900 to 1909, 5; 1910 to 1919, 8; 1920 to 1929, 21; 1930 to 1933, 13; 1940 to 1949, 45; 1950 to 1959, 29; 1960 to 1967, 13.[53] Many plants founded after World War II are larger than the older manufacturing plants.

Some of the city's oldest manufacturers are in the Jordan Creek Industrial District, notably feed mills and food wholesale houses, furniture and fixture manufacture, and printing and publishing. In the 1960s, new plants began to spring up in the Northeast Industrial District and at other scattered outlying locations. Several long-established industries have built facilities in the new industrial parks, taking advantage of lower-priced land, better accessibility, and less congestion. They also ridded themselves of the disadvantages of obsolete buildings and equipment. Chestnut Expressway carries heavy truck traffic serving the upper and lower Jordan Creek industrial districts. Telltale evidence of one facet of the city's economy is the chicken feathers scattered along the road shoulders on West Chestnut Expressway. They are blown from poultry trucks entering the city from the southwestern Ozark counties bound for processing plants in the Jordan Creek valley. The Partnership Industrial Park, located off East Kearney Street, has attracted both new and old industries. The city of Springfield and City Utilities of Springfield (city owned) had invested, by midyear 2000, an estimated $8.1 million in the land, roads, utilities, and other infrastructure for the city's newest industrial park.[54] A new city-financed partnership industrial park is currently under development near the Springfield-Branson Airport.

Many industries that were important in the 1930s have closed, and others have moved to new locations. The Marblehead Lime Quarry was a central city brush dump for many years. Then, after a persistent fire that burned for several months in 1972, it became a sump for washing concrete trucks. It has been drained and will be part of the new Jordan Valley municipal park. The Springfield Wagon and Tractor Company closed many years ago and most of the buildings were razed. The Harry Cooper Supply Company now occupies the site. After razing the stockyards on Mill Street long ago, investors built new stockyards on Commercial Street east of Kansas Expressway.

Work began in late 1999 to redevelop much of the Jordan Creek Industrial District as a major civic park.[55] When completed, most of the valley between National Avenue and Kansas Expressway will be incorporated into the Jordan Valley Park. Planners hope the park will enhance the development of downtown Springfield as a restaurant, shopping, and governmental center. Now, city leaders are negotiating with developers for a new civic center. It will be a capstone development in the new Jordan Valley Park. The 1970s effort to convert Springfield's Public Square into pedestrian-only Park Central Mall was abandoned due to agitation from downtown businesspeople. The Public Square has been opened to traffic again and the encircling one-way streets restored to two-way streets again to make the area more accessible to visitors. Opening the area to traffic seems to have stimulated additional traffic and the founding of new businesses. Springfield's economic planners are optimistic about the continued development of the downtown area as an entertainment and restaurant center.

Sparse settlement accounts, in large part, for Springfield's large trade area. Its size is comparable to the trade hinterlands of some larger cities. Springfield is an important railroad center and a focus for several highways, including Interstate 44, U.S. Highway 60 and 65, and Missouri highways 13, 160, and 266. The Springfield-Branson Regional Airport is the busiest in the Ozarks. The airport had 705,882 departures and arrivals on 12,292 commercial flights in 1999.[56] Plans call for the construction of a new terminal on the west side of the main runways within ten years. The *Springfield News-Leader* is the major daily newspaper eastward halfway across Missouri to Shannon and Dent counties. It is also read in the northern two tiers of counties in Arkansas.[57]

Like most cities its size, Springfield has a highly diversified economy. The largest employment category in Greene County is the service sector. In 1997, services accounted for 43,862 of the labor force of 124,252 or 35 percent.[58] Health services alone accounted for 18,680 employees with the largest numbers employed in Cox Medical Center and St. John's Regional Health Center. Other leading employment categories are retail trade (28,276), including 10,504 employed in eating and drinking places; manufacturing (21,355); wholesale trade (10,883); transportation and public utilities (7,352); finance, insurance, and real estate (6,786); construction (5,204); and educational services (3,133).

The Springfield trade area includes five towns with populations exceeding five thousand: Rolla, Lebanon, West Plains, Monett, and Mountain Home, Arkansas. Four towns show abnormal growth curves. Aurora and Pierce City were mining camps that followed the boom-and-bust growth patterns so typical in the Joplin area.[59] Like many other towns in the old Tri-State Mining District, these towns are now growing steadily. Republic, Nixa, and Ozark experienced abnormally sharp upturns beginning in the 1960s because of overspill from Springfield. These three towns, all among the fastest growing in the Ozarks, have become satellite cities and along with smaller growth centers—Willard and Strafford—are becoming part of metropolitan Springfield. In the Central Plateau, Lebanon and West Plains have experienced steady population increases.

West Plains, the biggest town in a large area of south-central Missouri, increased in population from 6,500 in 1974 to 11,135 in 1998.[60] It has been the leading town in south-central Missouri for more than a hundred years. By 1900 the courthouse square was ringed by businesses that served customers from beyond the limits of Howell County. Besides being one of only a handful of towns in the interior Ozarks that could boast of municipal electric lights, West Plains had a college, a waterworks, an opera house, a public library, and a Chautauqua circle.[61] Today, it has an unusually large range of services for a town of its size.

The growth of Southwest Missouri State University at West Plains has helped to stimulate economic growth. The expanding one-thousand-student campus northwest of the courthouse square has added vitality to the downtown area. However, much of the new commercial development is along Porter Wagoner Boulevard extending beyond the northern limits of the town.[62]

Lebanon (pop. 11,704) has profited from its location on I-44, one of Missouri's growth corridors. Good rail and highway transportation and a location in a major recreation area with many rivers and lakes has enabled Lebanon to attract large aluminum boat manufacturing plants. Boat manufacturing began with the establishment of the Appleby Manufacturing Company in 1960. J. B. Appleby founded the company following several years working for

the Richline Boat Company in Richland.[63] Current boat manufacturers listed in the *Missouri Manufacturers Register 2000* include G-3 Boats (200 employees), Landau Boats, Inc. (115), Lowe Aluminum Boats (300), Osagian Boats, Inc. (13), Sundancer Pontoons (25), and Tracker Marine, L.P. (600).[64] Other leading manufacturing employers are Copeland Corporation (1,000; air compressors), Detroit Tool and Engineering Co. (700; industrial machinery), and Detroit Tool Metal Products (305; metal fabrication).

As mentioned previously, a longtime employer in Lebanon is the Independent Stave Company, which employs seven hundred workers in its Lebanon plant.[65] Lebanon is also a popular shopping town and a place with good medical and professional services.

Rolla (pop. 16,027) is the primary city of the Osage-Gasconade Hills section. Rolla's future as a trade center was assured when the Pacific Railroad reached the city in 1860. Its role as a federal supply center and military base during the Civil War helped stimulate trade and business. Rolla was a popular overnight stop on Historic U.S. 66, and it continues to profit from travelers and trucking along Interstate 44. Institutional expansion explains much of its modern growth. The University of Missouri-Rolla, the Missouri Division of Geology and Land Survey, the Missouri Department of Water Resources, and the U.S. Geological Survey Mapping Center are some larger government employers. Visits by military personnel and their dependents from Fort Leonard Wood help boost Rolla's economy.

Mountain Home, Arkansas (pop. 10,129), the governmental seat of Baxter County, owes much of its prosperity to its location between lakes Norfork and Bull Shoals. Until the U.S. Army Corps of Engineers built the dams, Mountain Home was not unlike many small mountain county seats. The growth of lakeside communities and subdivisions bordering Bull Shoals and Norfork lakes has contributed to the growth of retail trade and services in Mountain Home. North Arkansas Community College also has contributed to the city's growth and cultural attractiveness. The two-year college offers programs and preparatory courses for transfer to four-year colleges, registered nursing and licensed practical nursing programs, and several technical educational programs.

Beyond serving nearby tourist and second-home communities—Bull Shoals, Lake View, Fairview—Mountain Home attracts customers from several counties in north-central Arkansas and south-central Missouri to its retail stores and medical facilities. The major employers for residents and commuters include the hospital; local, state, and federal government services; and manufacturing. The *Arkansas Manufacturers Register 2000* lists more than forty

Mountain Home companies. The Baxter Healthcare Corporation, which employs thirteen hundred workers in the manufacture of medical supplies and equipment, is the largest employer. The Aeroquip Corporation (hydraulic hoses), the second-ranking manufacturer, employs three hundred workers. Five boat and dock makers in Mountain Home—Bass Cat Boats; Champion Boats, Inc.; Lakeland Industries, Inc.; Ozark Boat Docks, Inc.; Viper Boats—have an aggregate employment of three hundred and twenty workers.[66]

Harrison, Arkansas, incorporated in 1876, grew slowly until the beginning of the century, when the Missouri and North Arkansas Railway built through from Eureka Springs. As headquarters for the railroad's offices and shops, Harrison grew rapidly. The railroad brought cheaper freight rates enabling the town to attract several industries. In 1933, five stave mills and a branch of the Lansing Motor Wheel Corporation, a manufacturer of wooden wheels for automobiles, operated in the town.[67] When the railroad shut down in 1960, Harrison's economy suffered only briefly as the general economic upsurge in the Ozarks led it to recovery.

Since about 1970, Harrison joined the group of growing northern Arkansas cities. Its population increased from 7,239 in 1970 to 11,594 in 1998.[68] Its service area now encompasses a population of about 70,000. Harrison has good accessibility. U.S. 65, U.S. 62, and Arkansas 7 provide access to regional tourist attractions and also travel to and from regional centers like Little Rock, Fayetteville, Mountain Home, and Springfield. Today, Harrison's economy is well diversified with retailing, services, and manufacturing. North Arkansas Community College's two

campuses provide employment for faculty and staff, plus college preparatory and technical courses for students from Harrison and surrounding counties, and many cultural events. Another cultural attraction in the city is the three-story Boone County Heritage Museum at the corner of West Central Avenue and North Cherry Street.

Manufacturing (750 employees) and retail trade (750) are Harrison's largest employment categories. Health care ranks third, and the majority work in the North Arkansas Regional Medical Center (550).[69] Harrison's labor force of 7,881 comprises 4,497 women and 3,384 men.[70] The

Tower Inn, Salem, Missouri, 1979. High-rise buildings are landmarks in the small Ozark growth centers. (Milton Rafferty Collection, photograph by the author.)

imbalanced sex ratio, common in many other Ozark towns, stems from the fact that many farm women often take a job in town to supplement family income. The largest manufacturing plants are west of town off Industrial Park Road. Among nearly seventy-five small establishments are several plants that employ more than 250 workers: White-Rogers, Division of Emerson Electric Co., Inc. (air cleaners and transformers); Wabash Wood Products, Inc. (laminated hardwood flooring for trucks); Pace Industries, Inc. (aluminum die castings); Claridge Products and Equipment, Inc. (aluminum extrusions and products).[71]

Branson has the reputation of a fast-growing tourist center. However, the city itself experienced only modest growth during the 1960s and 1970s because much of the growth was outside the corporate limits of the town. Income from tourists has made it possible for Branson to provide services comparable to those in larger towns. The steady increase in new businesses—restaurants, hotels, motels, factory outlet malls, and the usual personal and professional services—has made Branson a popular shopping and service center for surrounding towns. For example, in 1979 Branson was similar to Neosho, Missouri, in the range and number of services available for permanent and transient residents. Today, it is more like Jefferson City in the range and number of services.[72] Branson's population increased significantly during the 1980s and 1990s. A more active real-estate market, including increased residential and commercial construction, an increased number of time-share resorts, a greater tendency for visitors to move to the Branson area, and more active annexation, are factors that account for most of Branson's growth.

As in other sections of the Ozarks, manufacturing provides many jobs in the outlying towns of the Springfield trade area. Though the plants are small by big city standards, the opening or closing of an industry that employs as many as three hundred workers can have a marked impact on a town of two or three thousand people. Even in prosperous Buffalo, Missouri, the closing of the Petit Jean Company poultry processing plant in March 2000 caused economic hardship for employees and loss of income for the town.[73] The manufacturing directories for Missouri and Arkansas for the year 2000 list the following diversified plants employing one hundred workers or more in outlying towns in the Springfield trade area: turkey and chicken processing, children's shoes, aluminum extrusions, aluminum boats, metal products, prepared feeds, gas and electric furnaces, women's uniforms, hospital supplies and laboratory instruments, evaporated milk, men and boys' clothing, electric motors, automotive fans, bread production, women's clothing, camping trailers, machine tools, white-oak barrels, electric controls, men's shoes, truck bod-

ies and suspensions, custom woodcarving, artificial flowers, charcoal briquettes, printing and publishing, plastic products, and women's shoes.[74] Before foreign competition caused the decline of shoe and clothing manufacturing plants, some larger companies—Brown Shoe Company, International Shoe Company, and H. D. Lee Company—had several manufacturing plants that were close enough together to share warehousing and technically trained personnel. By the turn of the twenty-first century, the few remaining shoe and textile plants were struggling to remain in business. Recently, Hagle Industries, the largest Ozark clothing manufacturer, has had to close some plants and reduce the work force in others. Hagle's manager credited their highly trained workers with the company's ability to remain in business in a highly competitive market.[75] However, in January 2001 Hagle Industries had to declare bankruptcy and attempt to reorganize to remain in business.

Joplin (pop. 44,612) is one of the Ozarks' most distinctive towns. Thomas Hart Benton, a native son of the Tri-State District, captured much of its history in a mural that graces the municipal building in Joplin. The mural depicts the mines and miners and the gaudy saloons, dance halls, and gambling halls that once strung out along Main Street. The city grew up, literally, upon the mines, straddling the boundary of Jasper and Newton counties.

The first settler, John C. Cox, built a home on Turkey Creek near the end of what is now Mineral Avenue.[76] Shortly after that, the Reverend Harris C. Joplin, a Methodist minister from Greene County, settled on an eighty-acre tract. Reportedly, they discovered lead in 1849, but only a few diggings were opened before the Civil War. After the war the Atlantic and Pacific Railroad built to Joplin and the mining boom was on. Two towns grew up on either side of Joplin Creek: Murphysburg to the west and Joplin to the east. In 1873 they were incorporated as the city of Joplin.[77] As prospectors discovered additional ore bodies, more mining camps grew up around the mines so that by the turn of the century small mining towns surrounded Joplin.

As the miners removed the best ores and production declined in the mines, the city turned to other businesses: buying and selling lead and zinc, processing and smelting ores, manufacturing of explosives and mining equipment, providing services for mining companies and workers. Joplin became the primary city of the Tri-State Mining District, but, as the ores gradually petered out, the city relied increasingly on other manufacturers and commerce. Now, the huge tailings piles have been hauled away for road macadam, railroad ballast, and dozens of other uses. Still, the small tailings dumps and mine shafts scattered about the town are reminders of the mining era. The elegant homes just west of the downtown area are also reminders of the glory days in the Tri-State Mining District. Range Line Road, a five-mile commercial strip extending north from Interstate 44 through the east edge of the city, is a manifestation of the new Joplin. The large shopping mall and the usual assortment of restaurants, motels, services stations, and fast-food outlets along the street indicate the city has recovered its commercial vitality.

Within a fifty-mile radius of Joplin is a population of more than 350,000. Joplin has long been the marketing, commercial, financial, cultural, educational, recreational, and transportation hub of this economically important area, which covers parts of Missouri, Kansas, and Oklahoma. Joplin benefits from its situation in the southwest corner of Missouri near the intersection of Interstate 44 and U.S. 71. The Joplin Metropolitan Statistical Area's top employers range from transportation, food service, and health care to manufacturing of precision bearings and electronics. Eagle-Picher Industries, Inc., once the principal producer of lead and zinc when the mines were open, still has a major presence in Joplin. It operates several plants with a combined employment of more than eleven hundred workers. The plants produce pistons, batteries, and sheet metal products.[78] Joplin is also an important transportation hub. Four major motor carriers, employing six thousand people, operate from Joplin.

The growth patterns of towns in the Joplin area are among the most distinctive in Missouri. This is in keeping with the rise and fall of mining in the Tri-State Mining District. Only two large towns, Carthage and Neosho, both outside the main mining areas, show a normal development pattern. The fortunes of Webb City, Carterville, and Granby, all former mining towns, waxed and waned with the good times and bad times in the mines. They grew fast about the turn of the century but experienced a rapid population decline between 1920 and 1940.[79]

The *Fayetteville-Springdale-Rogers Metropolitan Statistical Area* encompasses Benton and Washington counties. The MSA includes the fast-growing cities of Fayetteville, Springdale, Rogers, Bentonville, Siloam Springs, the retirement town of Bella Vista, and the many rural subdivisions in the two counties. The two counties, among the fastest growing in the Ozark region, grew in population from 92,069 to 272,616 between 1960 and 1998.[80] The Fayetteville-Springdale-Rogers MSA is the second-largest urban agglomeration in the Ozark region, close behind the Springfield MSA. Unlike Springfield, which dominates its MSA, the northwest Arkansas urban agglomeration is an urban chaparral with no dominant city. Most residents of the communities in the urbanized area would prefer to be identified with their home towns, but these three communities are becoming one functional unit. This amalgamation is expressed in very practical ways. The owners of the shopping mall midway between Fayetteville and Springdale chose to name it Northwest Arkansas Mall. Also, the *Washington County History,* published in 1989, includes a chapter titled, "Northwest Arkansas City."[81]

Perhaps the best way to appreciate the dimensions of Northwest Arkansas City is to drive the length of it along its "main street," U.S. 71 Business route. To do this, one should avoid the rush hours when vehicles carrying workers to their jobs in hundreds of retail stores, services, and manufacturing plants jam the highway. Unlike the flow of traffic in large cities, where traffic crowds the inbound lanes in the morning hours and then the outbound lanes in late afternoon, the traffic on U.S. Highway 71B through the northwest Arkansas strip has the steady roar and frenzy of a big-city commercial street.

A twenty-five-mile stretch of Business 71, from the Missouri state line through Bella Vista, Bentonville, Rogers, Springdale, and Fayetteville, is the main street and core area of the metropolitan area. It is a good example of a commercial "strip" or string business street. Each town has its special character: Bella Vista is a sprawling retirement community; Bentonville is the home and main headquarters of Wal-Mart and the seat of Benton County; Rogers is a grown-up farm trade center with fast-growing residential neighborhoods; Springdale is an industrial town and headquarters of Tyson Foods; and Fayetteville, the largest city, is the Washington County seat, a governmental center, and the home of the University of Arkansas. U.S. 71 is fronted on both sides by a nearly continuous string of businesses in almost random order. A windshield inventory includes the following: lumberyards, bowling alleys, off-street shopping centers, carpet shops, paint stores, building suppliers, antique shops, supermarkets, convenience stores, garden shops, fruit stands, motels, electrical co-ops, well drillers, liquid petroleum gas distributors, automobile sales, mobile home dealers, savings and loans, farm machinery dealers, boat sales, orchards, food-processing plants, motorcycle sales, trucking companies, the Veterans Administration hospital, a regional medical center, and many restaurants and franchised fast-food outlets, including such familiar names as Pizza Hut, Taco Bell, Sonic, Burger King, Wendy's, and McDonald's.[82] In Springdale, feed mills punctuate the landscape near Business 71, "forming an Arkansas poultry skyline."[83] There is little else to distinguish the strip from scores of others that have grown up throughout the United States except that feathers from semitrailer loads of chickens bound for Springdale's processing plants litter the roadsides. Nevertheless, from the heights in Fayetteville, lights on the strip present an interesting nighttime panorama. Since 1979, when I first surveyed the area, a new bypass highway has been built from Fort Smith to the Missouri state line. It is four-lane I-540, a closed-access highway, which avoids the congested traffic in the urban centers in Benton and Washington counties. Business 71 continues to carry the local commercial traffic and part of the commuting traffic.

Fayetteville, the largest of the five towns, is the seat of Washington County and the site of the main campus of the University of Arkansas. It has been the leading town in northwest Arkansas since the first lots were sold in 1828. Fayetteville became a center for education when the Fayetteville Female Seminary, a pioneer girls' school, was founded in 1836.[84] Other small colleges opened in the 1840s and 1850s. General McCulloch's Confederate troops burned the colleges, along with stores and many homes, during the Civil War. The city fell alternately to Union and Confederate forces during the course of the war. Fayetteville's location midway between the Union base at Springfield and the Confederate encampments along the Arkansas River placed it in the midst of the Ozarks battleground. Almost 30 percent of all Union casualties in Arkansas occurred within a thirty-five-mile radius of Fayetteville.[85]

The city of 53,300 residents sprawls across several hills that form a northern outlier of the Boston Mountains.[86] The town's founders built the main business district around the Washington County courthouse square and several other adjacent streets. Three courthouses occupied the square, the first a log structure, followed by two brick structures. A fourth courthouse, an elegant towered structure, was built in 1904 on College Avenue, which later became U.S. 71. Yet another Washington County Courthouse, the county's fifth, was built in 1986 north of the previous courthouse on College Street. Northwest of the courthouse and business district is the University of Arkansas campus. The university has been an important cog in the economic machinery that powers Fayetteville. It has grown from an enrollment of 642 in 1900 to 15,226 in 1999.[87]

The most striking building in the city is "Old Main," the university's newly remodeled administration building. It is an imposing four-story brick structure with a mansard roof and dormer windows and two corner towers that are visible for miles. The handsome Walton Arts Center, built with funds donated by Sam and Helen Walton (Wal-Mart founders) and many other people in the community, is on West Dickson Street between the downtown square and the university.

As with other cities, roads and rails shaped the urban form of Fayetteville. The city's industrial fathers built their businesses near the railroad that passed north-south through the city between the central business district and the university. Since about 1950, manufacturing plants have selected sites in industrial parks in outlying areas with good rail and highway access. The commercial strips follow the business routes of state and federal highways. New motels and other highway service businesses are moving near accesses to the new controlled-access I-540 (U.S. 71). Many newer retail businesses have found space north of the city along Business 71 and in the new Northwest Arkansas Mall. Commercial strips also have spread south along Business 71 toward Greenland and West Fork, west along U.S. 62 toward Farmington, and east along Arkansas 16. Residential subdivisions have grown outward along these same highways to form an irregular-shaped geographic city.[88]

Besides good highway and rail transportation, Fayetteville is well-served by air service. The new (1998) Northwest Arkansas Regional Airport in Highfill (Benton County) serves Fayetteville and adjacent parts of northwest Arkansas, southwest Missouri, and northeast Oklahoma. American Eagle, TWExpress, Delta Connection, and Northwest Link fly out of the regional airport, while Bentonville Municipal Airport and Drake Field in Fayetteville provide commercial air charter service.

Although Fayetteville enjoys a reputation as a university town, and the University of Arkansas employs more than 2,500 faculty and staff, manufacturing employment is substantial. The plants with more than 1,000 employees include Campbell Soup Company (frozen dinners) and Superior Industries (cast aluminum wheels). Nine additional companies employ between 200 and 599 workers: Tyson's Mexican Original (Mexican food products), Tyson's Entree Division (frozen dinner entrees), McClinton-Anchor Company (limestone and hot mix), American Air Filter (air filters), Baldwin Piano and Organ (electric organs), Elkhart Products (pipe fittings), Marshalltown Tools (cement finishing tools), and Standard Register (business forms).[89] The Fayetteville Veterans Administration Medical Center, the Washington Regional Medical Center, and several clinics and health-care centers employ many people in Fayetteville and from other towns within commuting distance.

Springdale has grown rapidly in recent years, from 16,783 in 1970 to 40,282 in 1998.[90] Since the 1940s, it has had a reputation as a small industrial town. It is a center for the canning and preparation of frozen foods. Over the years, as general farming gave way to production of small fruits and vegetables in northwest Arkansas, commercial canning prospered. As we have seen, several small canneries in southwest Missouri and northwest Arkansas packed beans, spinach, poke greens, strawberries, blackberries, apples, grapes, and potatoes, but many more packed tomatoes.[91] Over the years, Springdale became the chief center for consolidated and enlarged canneries. In the 1950s and 1960s, several companies built plants to process poultry products and to produce prepared frozen foods. This industry continued to expand through the rest of the twentieth century.

Large feed companies that serve poultry farms in northwest Arkansas round out agribusiness manufacturing in Springdale. The largest poultry processor, Tyson Foods, employs approximately two thousand office workers in its international headquarters and fifteen hundred production workers in its Springdale processing plants.[92] The Honeysuckle White Turkey Processing plant employs one thousand workers, and Georges, Inc., employs another twelve hundred production workers in two poultry processing plants. Manufacturing plants employing five hundred to one thousand employees are Ball Metal Food Container Corporation, Danaher Tool Group (hand tools), and Kawneer Co., Inc. (aluminum windows). Other noteworthy manufacturers include Cargill, Inc. (poultry products and feed), Dayco Products, Inc. (automotive parts), J. V. Manufacturing Co. (solid waste processing equipment), Multicraft Contractors (sheet metal fabrication), and Pratt and Whitney PSD, Inc. (jet aircraft engine parts).[93]

A unique feature of Springdale is the Jones Center for Families that opened to the public October 29, 1996. The Jones Center, in the former Jones Truck Lines Building, has 220,000 square feet of new and remodeled space for educational, recreational, and community events. The Center is a personal gift from Harvey and Bernice Jones, former owners of the Jones Truck Line (JTL). The company grew from a dray service with two mules and a wagon to become one of the largest privately owned truck lines in the United States. Springdale is also the site of the Shiloh Museum, which features display rooms and historical and educational materials gathered from throughout northwest Arkansas and beyond.

Rogers, the largest town in Benton County, has shared in northwest Arkansas's growth and prosperity during the last three decades of the late twentieth century. Its population increased from 13,189 in 1970 to 37,073 in 1998.[94] As in Springdale, agri businesses are the largest employers, but metal and wood products manufacturing also are important. Manufacturers with more than five hundred employees include North Arkansas Poultry (poultry processing), Rogers Tool Works, Inc. (cutting tools), Tyson Foods, Inc. (poultry processing). Other large employers include Tysons of Rogers (poultry processing) and First Brands Corporation (plastic bags).[95]

Another employer is the Daisy Outdoor Products, manufacturer of Daisy air rifles. This company, which began as the Plymouth Iron Windmill Company in Plymouth, Michigan, has manufactured air rifles since 1889. The company introduced the Daisy Red Rider air rifle in 1939, and over nine million have been sold to date, making it the most famous BB gun ever made. The corporation's decision to move to Rogers in 1957, as described by Cass S. Hough, helps to explain the increase in Ozarks manufacturing during the past forty-four years.

My travels had taken me to nearly every section of the country except the far west and the far east, in search of a new home for Daisy. First, I narrowed the choice down to an area, and that was the Arkansas-Oklahoma-Kansas-Missouri one. Not only was it centrally located for the shipment of Daisy products nationwide, but in the main, people who would constitute Daisy's work force seemed to be several cuts above what I found in other areas. The time I spent in choosing *the* spot in this four-state area was spent in evaluating the people themselves . . . The people of northwest Arkansas, by and large, are "pioneer" types, probably the last stronghold of those who want no handouts and are not only willing but eager to give a day's work for a day's pay, who take a long time making up their minds about newcomers, are cooperative and courteous.[96]

The Daisy Outdoor Products company on Highway 71B (South 8th Street) was sold in 1999, but Daisy continues to manufacture and pack BBs and pellets there. Daisy moved the corporate offices to a new building in Rogers. In 1997 the assembly, packaging, and shipping operation was moved to a new facility in nearby Neosho, Missouri, as part of the company's transition to becoming a fully outsourced manufacturer.

Bentonville, the smallest of the six cities that make up Northwest Arkansas City, is the seat of Benton County. It has tripled in size over the past thirty years, increasing from 5,391 to 19,691.[97] Bentonville is well known for being the starting place and headquarters for Wal-Mart. It was here in 1950 that Sam Walton bought Luther Harrison's Variety Store and opened the first store in what was to become the world's largest retailer—Wal-Mart. He paid $15,000 for the Harrison store, $20,000 for the building, and $20,000 for remodeling.[98] Today acres of parking lots, jammed with workers and customers' vehicles surround the sprawling Wal-Mart Stores, Inc., headquarters and Wal-Mart Supercenter, which straddle South Walton Avenue (U.S. 71B). Considering the growing subdivisions inside and outside the city, many of them filled with houses costing more than $300,000, it is not too much to say that modern Bentonville is the town that Sam Walton built. Besides the customary retail and commercial activities and the usual governmental services found in county seats, Bentonville has more than thirty manufacturers. Tyson Foods of Bentonville (poultry processing), which employs 450 workers, is the largest.[99]

Bella Vista, the northernmost town in the northwest Arkansas urban agglomeration, extends north from Bentonville and bumps against the Missouri state line. As we have seen, Bella Vista is an unincorporated residential community first developed by the Linebarger brothers and now owned and expanded by Cooper Communities, Inc. It is a carefully planned, private community of homes, townhouses, churches, commercial centers with business and professional services, medical clinics, library, and $35,500,000 in recreational amenities, including eight lakes and 117 holes of golf. There is a wide variety of housing options available in Bentonville, from executive homes to one-bedroom apartments. Bella Vista and Bentonville are closely linked and share the same chamber of commerce.

Siloam Springs, the sixth of the coalescing cities in northwest Arkansas, began as a resort on Sager Creek. By 1900, businesses serving apple and dairy farms soon dominated the declining hotels and spas near the salt and sulfur springs. Siloam Springs is the home of John Brown University, which enrolls approximately fourteen hundred students. The university, founded in 1919, is named for John E. Brown Sr., a Salvation Army leader. The university continues to emphasize interdenominational Christian education in a small-town setting.

Four-lane U.S. 412 connects Siloam Springs with the U.S. 71B corridor; the Cherokee Turnpike leads west to Tulsa, Oklahoma. The Kansas City Southern Railroad provides freight service to Kansas City and New Orleans. Siloam Springs's strategic location next to the booming cities to the east has attracted several manufacturers. The major manufacturing plants along the Highway 59 corridor in western Benton County include Franklin Electric, Gates Rubber Company, Baldor Electric, La-Z-Boy, Hudson Foods, Syrocon of Arkansas, and Jet Stream Plastic Pipe. Companies with multiple manufacturing sites that have headquarters in the Siloam Springs area include Simmons Foods, McKee Foods (Little Debbie), Peterson Industries, Allen Canning Company, and DaySpring Cards.

Batesville, seat of Independence County, Arkansas, is the major growth center of the southeastern Ozarks. The city has grown steadily since the 1970 census reported 7,209 residents. The U.S. Census Bureau estimates that its 1998 population is 9,595. Batesville grew up on the bluff where the White River exits the Ozarks. When Henry Schoolcraft and Levi Pettibone arrived in Batesville in October 1819, after their celebrated tour through the Ozarks, the small settlement was called Poke Bayou after the name for the creek that entered the White River there. The red brick buildings of Lyon College (formerly Arkansas College), high on the ridge north of the city, are visible for miles. Founded in 1872, it ranks among the oldest active universities in the Ozarks. The city and region also benefit from liberal arts and technical courses offered by the University of Arkansas Community College at Batesville.

Batesville is sharing in the rapid growth and development of northern Arkansas. National trends account for part of this: the shift of industries to the South, faster growth of the service sector of the national economy, the accelerated growth of population in areas that have amenities. One resident explained it this way: "It's the water, scenery, environment, and people that will work. Batesville is developing into the chief regional shopping and distribution center for the fast-growing north-central Arkansas counties."[100]

Manufacturing is important, particularly the sprawling Con-Agra Poultry Plant, which employs 1,360 in the production of frozen poultry products. Another large poultry processor, Townsends of Arkansas, employs another 1,000 workers. These plants are important markets for the expanding poultry industry in the southeastern Ozarks. Other manufacturing plants include Arkansas Eastman (chemicals), GenCorp Automotive (industrial automotive products), Life Plus (vitamins), Pro-Dentec (tooth brushes), White Rogers Company (electrical controls), and White River Materials (ready-mix concrete).[101] In all, nearly fifty manufacturers call Batesville home.[102]

The growth of Batesville and the Ozark counties to the north has been so rapid in recent years that some residents are becoming concerned about its overall effects. More than twenty years ago, in 1979, Leo Rainey, area development agent at Batesville, put it this way:

The things that are happening today are the things people hoped would have happened twenty years ago, or even ten years ago. There were few jobs to be had then and there were political fights over committee representation on the ASCS [Agricultural Stabilization and Conservation Service] and over who would get a $150 per month job as a school bus driver. Now the people aren't as concerned about such things because there are other jobs in the manufacturing plants, in the construction business, or in the tourist business. People are now beginning to think about restraining some of this growth. We've not reached the point where no growth is the majority, but people aren't as anxious for growth as they were.[103]

Lyon College is a highly selective liberal arts college associated with the Presbyterian Church. It provides educational opportunities and cultural enrichment for much of the southeastern Ozarks. Batesville also has a branch campus of the University of Arkansas Community College. Towns in the southeastern Ozarks—Mountain View, Heber Springs, Fairfield Bay—and many smaller towns look to Batesville for education, entertainment, medical services, and employment opportunities.

Tahlequah, the largest city in the Oklahoma Ozarks, is also the most Indian city in the region. Twenty-eight percent of the population reports Native American ancestry, mainly Cherokee.[104] More than two-thirds of the population is white, and only 2 percent is black. Tahlequah's location in the Cookson Hills near the scenic Illinois River and Lake Tenkiller is ideal to serve the many outdoor sports enthusiasts and tourists who visit the area. Summer visitors take advantage of canoeing the river, singing along with the River City Players at the Northeastern Oklahoma State (NSU) Playhouse, and visiting Tsa-La-Gi village. Progressive cities—Tulsa, Muskogee, Fort Smith–Van Buren MSA, Fayetteville-Springdale-Rogers MSA—hem in Tahlequah, leaving a trade area confined mainly to Cherokee County. The city has a thirty-year history of modest growth, increasing from 9,254 in 1970 to 12,336 in 1998.[105]

Tahlequah became the permanent capital of the Cherokee Nation on September 6, 1839, when the Eastern and Western Cherokees met on the site of the present square to sign the new constitution.[106] They platted the town in 1843 and removed several houses to form the public square in 1845. In 1846 the Cherokees established two schools: the Male Seminary southwest of town and the Female Seminary at Park Hill, approximately four miles south of Tahlequah. Both schools burned, but the Female Seminary was rebuilt in Tahlequah and later (in 1909) purchased by the state of Oklahoma to form the nucleus of Northeast Oklahoma University. The Cherokee County courthouse occupies the old Cherokee Capitol, which the Cherokee Nation built on the square in 1869.

Tahlequah is primarily a retailing and service center and college town with remarkably little manufacturing employment. The list of manufacturers is short: two clothing factories, two or three wood-products manufacturers, several small printing establishments, and a ready-mix concrete plant. The twenty-odd small manufacturing plants employ only 152 workers.[107] The city's largest employer is the Indian Services department of the Cherokee Nation (1,100 employees), which provides various services to the Native American population in the area. Other large employers include these businesses and institutions: Northeastern Oklahoma State University (900), the City Hospital (350), W. W. Hastings Hospital (350), the Wal-Mart retail store (190), and Reasor's Inc. (120), a retail grocery.[108] Tahlequah calls itself the Nursery Capital of the Midwest. Two nearby commercial nurseries, Greenleaf Nursery and Mid-Western Nursery, cultivate flowers and ornamentals to supply Wal-Mart, K-Mart, and other large retail outlets. These two nurseries together employ more than 600 workers.

FIFTEEN

THE CULTURAL LANDSCAPE

A description of the complete Ozark scene would challenge the capacity of a computer and the lucidity and expository ability of a Shakespeare. As we have seen, the region possesses several physical settings over which have been laid, layer upon layer, a century and a half of American settlement and development. To sort out the landscape milieu and to understand it, geographers have conceived a cultural landscape:

> The cultural landscape is fashioned from a natural landscape by a cultural group. Culture is the agent, the natural area is medium, the cultural landscape the result. Under the influence of a given culture, itself changing through time, the landscape undergoes development, passing through phases, and probably reaching ultimately the end of its cycle of development. With the introduction of a different—that is, an alien-culture—a rejuvenation of the cultural landscape sets in, or a new landscape is superimposed on the remnants of an older one. The natural landscape is of course of fundamental importance, for it supplies the materials out of which the cultural landscape is formed. The shaping force, however, lies in the culture itself.[1]

The number of possible cultural landscapes that might be produced, through time, in a region—such as the Ozarks —that is so varied in physical resources and in cultural background of its people, is very large. There are almost innumerable possible permutations and combinations of physical landscape features, including bedrock, slope, soils, vegetation, rivers and creeks, and man-made landscape features, including houses, barns, fences, cultivated fields, pastures, orchards, roads, bridges, lakes and reservoirs, utility lines, and airports, and also the complete ensemble that makes up the urban landscape.

Included in the cultural landscape of the Ozarks are the people themselves, not only the permanent inhabitants but also the seasonal or occasional visitors as well. The various physical types, their food, and their habit of dress not only add variety to the Ozark scene but also tell of the style and conditions of life in the region.

Material culture consists of those things that make up the standard of life of the people, among them housing and house furnishing, together with food and habits of dress. Though broadly similar to rural America overall, the material culture of the Ozarks includes important differences. The true material culture probably lies somewhere between the generalized descriptions published by local chambers of commerce and those of the Sunday feature writer in search of interesting material. Marked differences in material culture exist even within the Ozark region. Some of these differences are obvious and strike the eye of the visitor on his first contact with the region, while others are much less apparent.

HOUSES

Houses are especially rewarding objects of study for students of landscape because they provide clues to the cultural background of the people and their approximate level of technology at the time of their construction.[2] The construction materials often provide insight into the local resource base and the level of living.[3] Building materials and form may provide some general indication of age, although the practice of remodeling and adding rooms complicates definitive chronological classification. Study of houses and other structures can help to fill gaps in the record of culture that are not recorded in written accounts of the region. Also, for many, the houses and outbuildings of Ozark farms are picturesque and provide an additional scenic attraction.

My interest in Ozark houses began as a casual observation of the differences in types from place to place as I traveled the region on field trips. On one of my first forays into the interior Ozarks in 1966, the great amount of variation in the size, style, and building materials of houses, and also their care and upkeep, interested me. Barns and outbuildings also exhibited great variation, although less than houses. Farmsteads seemed to tell their own story of fertile uplands and rich bottomlands versus the poverty of hardscrabble hillsides. Their state of repair and general condition told of hard times and good times. This led me to observe systematically and record the condition of houses and barns and many other features of the rural farming landscape.[4] The variability of the built environment piqued my curiosity and led me to look into other aspects of the physical and cultural geography of the Ozarks.

My first effort to describe Ozark houses used a simple classification scheme developed by Robert A. Finley and E. M. Scott to survey houses along a traverse from the Great Lakes to the Gulf Coast.[5] Over the past twenty years several researchers have published studies of Ozark single-family dwellings. The works of Jean Sizemore, Charles Van Ravenswaay, Howard W. Marshall, Lynn Morrow, Robert Flanders, and David Quick have been especially helpful in pulling together a picture of the Ozark built environment.[6] These sources provide descriptions of the styles and building materials and insight into the cultural influences and origins of the dwellings, with information about the builders who produced them. In combination with well-respected studies of regional and national scope these new studies form the basis to describe the single-family houses of the Ozarks as they evolved over more than two hundred years of occupancy.

FOLK HOUSING

Before railroads provided cheap and efficient means for transporting bulky construction materials such as lumber, brick, and quarried stone, house builders constructed simple dwellings of local materials. When railroads expanded in the last half of the nineteenth century, builders far from water transportation no longer had to depend on local materials. Lumberyards in towns along the railroads could buy lumber from distant sawmills. By 1900, pre-railroad building traditions survived only in isolated areas, far from the nearest rail service.

By the time the first immigrants settled west of the Mississippi River three building traditions had evolved along the eastern seaboard, namely, New England, Tidewater South, and Midland.[7] Frontiersmen carried the Midland log house tradition across the Appalachians, where it became the dominant pre-railroad folk housing over much of the heavily wooded eastern half of the country, including the Ozarks.[8] The Midland building tradition began in the Middle Colonies (Pennsylvania, New Jersey, Delaware, and Maryland), where Germanic immi-

grants from heavily wooded areas of central and northern Europe introduced techniques of building with logs hewn square and then placed horizontally, one on top of the other, to make a solid wooden wall. Various systems of carefully interlocking or notching the squared timbers, where they joined at the corners, held these hewn log buildings together. Such log construction contrasted sharply with the frame buildings of the adjacent English colonies to the north and south, where they constructed houses covered by lighter planks or shingles to make them weatherproof.[9]

Log houses. The first Ozark settlers constructed log houses. These early log houses, like others of the Midland tradition, are generally made up of room-sized square or rectangular units called "pens." The simplest log houses have only a single unit or pen. Two-unit houses were common, and it was very common for a second room or pen to be added on when the need and resources permitted. Very frequently they built the second room so that a breezeway or open space separated the two pens. These houses are called "dogtrot" houses. Usually double-pen houses (two-room log houses) had two chimneys, one at each end gable, but when there was a large central chimney, they were known as saddlebag houses.[10] Sometimes they built three-unit and two-story log houses. The Jacob Wolf House at Norfork, Arkansas, is a rare two-story dogtrot house.[11] Built in the 1820s, the Arkansas Historic Preservation Program now owns it.

Framed additions, often as a "lean-to" or shed room, and porches were added to pre-railroad houses as local sawmills provided nearby sources of dimension lumber. Wood or asphalt shingles, or sometimes sheet metal, gradually

Jacob Wolf House, Norfork, Arkansas, 1999. (Milton Rafferty Collection, photograph by the author.)

Log cabin in a French settlement, Washington County, Missouri, 1976. The house was constructed in 1951. (Milton Rafferty Collection, photograph by the author.)

replaced hand-split oak or hickory shake shingles. The tradition of building with horizontal logs persisted in the Ozarks long after cut lumber was locally available. The workmanship and quality of the log houses were variable. This variability in workmanship and quality is readily visible in the Clark-King single-pen log house near Mountain View, Arkansas.[12] The original single-pen log house, built by P. C. Clark in 1885, is constructed of massive hand-hewn oak timbers precisely locked together with clean-cut dovetails. In 1889, a second owner, the Reverend Jacob King, built a second single-pen log house a few feet to the south and attached it to the existing house with a roofed breezeway, which he later enclosed to form another room. King also constructed the newer part of the house of squared oak logs, but they are fitted together less precisely at the corners with simple notches.[13] Sometimes the later generations of log houses are distinguishable from the older log houses by imprecise squaring of the logs, less-precise notching at the corners, and other details of handicraft.

A distinction is usually made between *log houses,* such as those discussed so far, and *cabins,* in which the timbers are left rounded and join at the corners by overlapping saddle notches. Because chinking between the logs was difficult, cabins were usually used for temporary dwellings. Near the old French communities of Old Mines, Fertile, and Cadet, in Washington County, Missouri, a few simple log cabins are still in use. Some were built as late as the 1950s.[14]

I-Houses. The I-house, like the one-story hall and parlor plan (two rooms wide and one room deep), is a traditional British folk form that was common in pre-railroad America, particularly in the Tidewater South. They were also found in the Midland area of log houses, but because constructing two-story walls of solid hewn logs was diffi-

cult, they were not common. They were popular folk dwellings in the midwestern states where the long winters made large houses more of a necessity than farther south. Post railroad I-houses are common in the South where builders dressed them up with porches, chimneys, and rearward extensions to make them more pretentious for affluent gentry.[15] In fact, the name I-house was coined in 1936 by the geographer Fred Kniffen in his landmark study, *Louisiana House Types.* After observing that midwestern immigrants from Indiana, Illinois, and Iowa built many of the houses in Louisiana, three states whose names begin with the letter *I,* he named the house the Midwestern type, or I-house.[16] Architectural historian Michael Southern has asserted that the I-house was the "dominant folk house type throughout the Upland South from the late eighteenth century to the early twentieth century."[17] In her field study of the vernacular houses of the Arkansas Ozarks, Jean Sizemore documented a range of dates for I-houses from 1855 to 1912.[18]

In all its various forms, including the one-story and two-story types, and the "L" and "T" forms created by constructing a wing at the end or at the center of one gable side of the house, either as original construction or as an add-on, the I-house is the most ubiquitous ordinary folk house of the rural Ozarks, although in many areas the bungalow-style and ranch-style houses are more numerous. Except for the historically significant large estate houses in the Arcadia valley, and a few other isolated historical examples, and some modern suburban dwellings, it is also the most pretentious rural dwelling. It is an indicator of agrarian prosperity and is most commonly found in the better agricultural districts in the region. Sizemore found a close correlation between the Arkansas Ozarks subregions and the I-house type. The densest concentrations are in the prosperous farmlands around Prairie Grove and Cane Hill in Washington County. Only a few occur in the Boston Mountains and the White River hills.[19] My own fieldwork conducted in 1979, and on many subsequent field trips through 1996, showed a close correlation between the I-house and other two-story houses and the better farming districts in the Missouri Ozarks. The larger, more elaborate houses are found in the Springfield Plain, in the loess soil belts along the eastern and northern Ozark borders, and in the larger interior upland "prairies."[20]

Central Hall Cottage. Various groups brought the *Central Hall Cottage* style from Europe to the American colonies, notably the English and the Scotch-Irish in the Chesapeake and Tidewater South. They were single-pile (one room deep) one-story houses with two rooms of equal size separated by a central hall. Its gable-end roof and exterior chimneys are similar to other traditional houses, but it differs in having a central hall and only one door. Vernacular architecture scholars attribute its symmetrical form to the influence of Georgian architectural style.[21]

All the Arkansas central-hall cottages documented by Jean Sizemore were one story high and one room deep, and like the I-houses they were mainly in the more prosperous areas of the Springfield Plain.[22] They are not a common type, probably because families who could afford the formality of a central hall preferred to build a two-story I-house instead. The date range for the houses surveyed in the Arkansas Ozarks extended from 1851 to 1895.[23]

Romantic, Victorian, and Eclectic Houses. The era of the Romantic houses in America was 1820 to 1880. These houses—Greek Revival, Gothic Revival, Italianate, and various other exotic revivals—were popularized by publication in 1842 of the first popular pattern book of house styles, Andrew Jackson Downing's *Cottage Residences.*[24] Carpenter's guides and pattern books helped to spread the styles. The most influential of these were written by Asher Benjamin (*The Practical Carpenter: The Builder's Guide*) and Minard Lafever (*The Modern Builder's Guide; The Beauties of Modern Architecture*). Most Victorian houses date from the period 1860 to 1900 and were based on Medieval prototypes. Multitextured or multicolored walls, strongly asymmetrical facades, and steeply pitched roofs with stylistic details freely adapted from both Medieval and classical precedents are common features.[25] This popular style with all of its variations—Second Empire, Stick, Queen Anne, Shingle, Richardson Romanesque, and Folk Victorian—was so-named because of its popularity during the last decades of Britain's Queen Victoria, which lasted from 1837 to 1901. During this period, industrialization

McGuire House in the valley of the Middle Fork of the White River, 1999. (Milton Rafferty Collection, photograph by the author.)

and the growth of the railroads led to dramatic changes in American house design and construction. Virginia and Lee McAlester in *A Field Guide to American Houses* sum up the many changes.

> The balloon frame, made up of light two-inch boards held together with wire nails, was rapidly replacing heavy-timber framing as the standard building technique. This, in turn, freed houses from their traditional box-like shapes by greatly simplifying the construction of corners, wall extensions, overhangs, and irregular ground plans. In addition, growing industrialization permitted many complex house components—doors, windows, roofing, siding, and decorative detailing—to be mass-produced in large factories and shipped throughout the country at relatively low cost on the expanding railway network.[26]

Balloon framing, quite different from standard eight-foot platform framing, employed studs twelve, fourteen, or sixteen feet long, depending upon the height of the second floor, and the exterior walls were assembled on the ground and then raised.[27] Nowadays, balloon framing is rarely used except for framing around tall windows and for other special needs on large architect-designed houses and then only when firestops are added between the studs to meet fire code requirements. For ordinary framing eight- and ten-foot platform framing requires less labor and shorter dimension lumber can be used.

American eclectic houses occupy the historical niche from 1880 to 1940. Their stylistic inspiration draws on the full spectrum of architectural tradition. The eclectic styles began when European-trained architects began to design landmark houses for wealthy clients. The main styles were Italian Renaissance, Neoclassical, Tudor, Chateauesque, Beaux arts, and French Eclectic.[28] After inexpensive techniques were perfected for adding a thin veneer of brick or stone to the exterior of the traditional balloon-framed house, modest cottages began to mimic, in brick veneer, the masonry facades of Old World landmarks.

For the most part Romantic, Victorian, and Eclectic houses were large and, as styles dictated, trimmed with columns, multipane windows, patterned moldings, vergeboards, and other intricate details. Consequently, these large houses were built mainly in the larger Ozark towns and cities where there was sufficient wealth to afford them. While the region was mostly without the large Romantic style houses, there were exceptions. For example, the leading families of the high Scotch-Irish who settled in the Belleview Valley in the St. Francois Mountains, with the help of their slaves, shaped a remarkable cultural landscape of productive farms, iron furnaces and forges, and stately houses.[29] The magnificent Bellevue Collegiate Institute, a Methodist college founded by the valley residents, failed in 1902. After years of neglect, the once-elegant building finally fell to the wrecking ball in 1955. The remarkable 1850s Greek Revival manses along Main Street in tiny Caledonia still stand as a tribute to their perseverance and industry.

Springfield, Joplin, Rolla, Cape Girardeau, and Fayetteville and Batesville in Arkansas all have their grand Romantic houses. Even small towns like Bentonville, Arkansas, had their "Silk Stocking Row" where many community leaders lived.[30] Joplin in particular, because of the wealth created by the lead and zinc mines, had a larger than normal collection of grand houses. The counties in the Boonslick country, one of the earliest settled parts of Missouri, have a rich architectural heritage. Like the tiny Belleview Valley, a large contingency of propertied high Scotch-Irish settled the fertile Boonslick. Some planters owned slaves who were skilled carpenters and brick layers. The leading families of the Boonslick country, in keeping with their wealth and social standing, built large houses in the Romantic styles.[31]

During the latter two decades of the nineteenth century, new, wealthy immigrants settled the Arcadia valley and built large Victorian and Eclectic houses on sprawling country estates. The prosperous years following the Civil War triggered a great expansion in tourism. The Arcadia valley in Iron County, Missouri, became a summer retreat for wealthy St. Louis families. Unionist settlers from Missouri, Illinois, and Indiana, including some who had served at Fort Davidson near Pilot Knob, had already begun to shape a culture far different from the backwoods.

The St. Louis and Iron Mountain Railroad, which had reached Ironton before the war, encouraged tourism to the area. By 1869 the railroad had begun to advertise a special "Summer Arrangement" schedule to the valley, which by the 1880s had become the "Arcadia Accommodation."[32] At about the same time, wealthy visitors from St. Louis and from the plantations in the Mississippi Delta began to build permanent homes in Ironton and Arcadia and on rural valley estates. Massachusetts-born Colonel John W. Emerson became the chief spokesman and promoter for the valley. Emerson served as a judge in Iron County and had legal offices in St. Louis, substantial business interests in the Arcadia valley and southeast Missouri, and the Emerson Electric company in St. Louis. In 1877 he rebuilt a large Italianate brick-and-stone eleven-room house on a six-acre estate.[33] Other grand houses soon followed. In 1881 William H. Thomson, cashier of Boatmen's Bank of St. Louis, built Valley Home, a rustic estate that included a lake and rustic summer cottages for guests. In 1891 he remodeled the Greek Revival house in a dual-wing stick style.[34]

General John W. Turner, son of John B. Turner who promoted the Western Railway, was a frequent guest in the valley during the 1880s. Like many others, he and his family began their summer retreats in one of the Arcadia House cottages. In 1887 he purchased a brick Italianate house from a Mississippi County cotton farmer and remodeled it with the help of St. Louis architects into a rambling shingle style house. When Mrs. Ulysses S. Grant and her party visited in 1894, the estate included its own spring-fed pond stocked with trout, a bath house, irrigated lawns, and a Victorian cottage on Stout's Creek.[35] Other large opulent estates included Maple Grove, developed by Scotsman Alexander Gray Simpson; the Maples, developed by Clarence Jones, secretary of the Drummond Tobacco Company; and the estate of Joseph G. Clarkson, a veteran of the Virginia Confederacy and prominent lumberman in the eastern Ozarks. By the 1920s estates and model farms very nearly filled the Arcadia Valley.

The great Arcadia Valley estates have all but disappeared. Fire claimed most of the great houses. George Middleton's Arcadia Valley Farms, once known as "El Jane of the Ozarks," still provides a visible Arcadia Valley landscape that connects the St. Louis-Arcadia Valley estate building tradition with the present.[36]

Bent Houses. The term *bent house,* employed by the architectural historian Dell Upton, is but one of several used to describe houses whose exterior appearance depended upon the positioning of two gabled perpendicular wings. Other terms used include "L" house, "T" house, "cross-wing," "upright-and-wing," and "gable-front-and-wing" house, depending on the geographical area.[37] These houses, descended from styled Greek Revival houses, became common in the Midwest.[38] An additional side-gabled wing was added at right angles to the gable-front plan to give the house an *L-* or *T*-shaped ground plan or gable-front-and-wing shape. Builders typically constructed a shed-room porch within the *L* made by the two wings.[39] Sometimes carpenters modified traditional gable-front houses to bent houses when gable-front wings were added to hall-and-parlor and I-house plans. In the Ozarks, both two-story and one-story bent houses occur widely, although the smaller one-story *L-* and *T*-shaped houses are much more common.[40] In the Boonslick country, where they are not common, they call them "Yankee houses," because of their widespread occurrence in New England and the upper Midwest.[41]

The *shotgun house* is a narrow, one-story, gable-fronted house one room wide and usually three rooms deep. It is said to have been named because one could open the front door and the back door and fire a shotgun through the house without hitting an intervening wall. They are common in cities throughout the South, but are also found in old lumber towns and the oil fields of Louisiana, Oklahoma, and Texas. The origin of the shotgun house is uncertain. Some architectural scholars link it to Haitian influences that spread first to New Orleans, and later to the cotton fields, mining camps, and oil patches.[42] Other scholars think it is but another form of the familiar one-room deep, hall-and-parlor plan of the rural South turned sideways to fit city lots.[43]

Few shotgun houses still stand in the Ozarks, although they were once common in some lumber camps. When the Missouri Lumber and Mining Company built company towns at Grandin and West Eminence, Missouri, they built shotgun houses and simple square houses with pyramid roofs to house the workers. When they built the houses with lumber from the mills, they did not paint them, but let them weather to a dull gray color. The company rented or sold the houses at very reasonable prices. When the company closed their operations at Grandin in 1909 and at West Eminence in June 1927, they sold most of the houses.[44] Nevertheless, some were loaded on flatcars and hauled to new mill sites in Louisiana. Two weathered shotgun houses still stand in Grandin, Missouri, but nothing remains in West Eminence.

Craftsman (Bungalow) Houses. Craftsman houses have low-pitched, gabled roofs (occasionally hipped) with a

Shotgun house, Grandin, Missouri, 1975. (Milton Rafferty Collection, photograph by the author.)

wide, unenclosed eave overhang leaving roof rafters exposed. Decorative false beams or braces were commonly added under gables. The porches, either full or partial width, sometimes placed asymmetrically and occasionally with a trellised roof, were supported by tapered square columns, usually resting on stone or masonry pedestals. Two California brothers who practiced together in Pasadena—Charles Sumner Greene and Henry Mather Greene—inspired them primarily.[45] About 1903 they began to design and build Craftsman-type bungalows, and by 1909 they had built several exceptional landmark examples. These and similar houses received extensive publicity in such magazines as the *Western Architect,* the *Architect, House Beautiful, Good Housekeeping, Architectural Record, Country Life in America,* and *Ladies' Home Journal.*[46] A flood of pattern books appeared for local builders. These books, and the precut kits of instructions and materials marketed by such retailers as Sears, Roebuck, and Company, eventually made the one-story Craftsman-style bungalow the most popular and fashionable of the nation's smaller houses.[47]

Craftsman bungalows are common in the Ozarks in towns and cities. They are also common in the countryside, especially in the more prosperous areas where people could afford to replace older houses with the more modern and stylish bungalows. One may see many noteworthy examples of Craftsman houses in the Arcadia Valley in Iron County, Missouri. Lynn Morrow, who has studied the valley intensively, credits the valley's architectural excellence to the unbeatable combination of a propertied gentry eager to build fine homes and a cadre of master builders to build them.[48]

Louis Miller was one such "master builder." From the

Native-stone bungalow, 1969. Many houses and public buildings are constructed with rough field stones. (Milton Rafferty Collection, photograph by the author.)

mid-1870s until the mid-1920s, Miller designed and built structures throughout southeast Missouri, from St. Louis to the Missouri Bootheel, throughout the eastern Ozarks and especially in the Arcadia Valley of Iron County.[49] Drawing on blueprints, pattern book plans, and his own creativity, Miller worked with wood, brick, rock, and the native Missouri Red granite from nearby quarries in the St. Francois Mountains to build and remodel fashionable summer homes for St. Louisans and homes for local year-round residents. As the number of tourists arriving on the Iron Mountain Railroad increased, Miller added several Craftsman-style bungalows as rental units for his Arcadia Hotel and Resort. Beyond the usual Craftsman features popularized by designer William Morris in the *Craftsman* magazine, the bungalows also included Miller's own distinctive cobblestone-style construction.[50]

As noted previously, Craftsman houses were very popular, and because of very strong demand following World War I, many builders soon learned to build in that style. One distinctive Craftsman style was the bungalow built from local slab rock or sandstone that could be split along strata lines with a chisel. There were countless slab-rock bungalows built throughout the Ozarks.[51] The greatest densities are near readily accessible supplies of good slab rock. For example, builders sought after the easily split sandstones in the Roubidoux formation because they often include ripple marks and mud cracks, which added decorative appeal.[52] Workers nailed rough wood siding to a wood-frame house, then attached the rock slabs to the wood siding with nails, which they then clinched (bent over) to hold the slabs. They then applied a concrete grout

to seal the cracks. Frequently, skilled stonemasons textured or beaded the grout material and painted it. Slab-rock houses were known by other names, including "Ozark Mosaic," "native stone," and "giraffe rock" houses.[53] The latter name applied to houses in which the builder or homeowner painted the grout between the slabs either white or black, which, with the brown sandstone, presented a large irregular pattern resembling the skin of a giraffe. Some builders used slab rock only for trim or "skirting" around the lower exterior walls. They also constructed commercial buildings of slab rock. One still may see slab-rock motels, gasoline service stations, and other commercial buildings along preserved sections of historic U.S. 66 that parallel Interstate 44. They are also common along other Ozark highways. Slab rock was also used to construct buildings in business districts of Ozark towns, mainly in smaller places. For example, some slab-rock commercial buildings in Bakersfield, Missouri, have impressive filled mud cracks weathered in bas-relief.[54] Some builders also built "field stone" houses or "cobble" houses. In these houses they built the walls of rough stones concreted together.

The larger towns and sometimes even small communities had their builders; sometimes they were highly skilled, experienced workers who had learned their trade working with master builders, but often they were simply men with tools and a need to make a living. In the latter case, the building quality suffered.[55] Sometimes whole families, through two or three generations, became builders. For example, many slab-rock bungalows of Thayer, Missouri, and in a few other Ozark railroad and highway towns were built by the Eders family, whose reputation for building high-quality houses was widely known.[56] Charles Green, another Thayer builder, founded another dynasty of builders who built houses throughout south-central Missouri, but especially in Greentown, a subdivision on the south edge of Thayer. The Greens built slab-rock Craftsman-style bungalows and other house types. They also perfected a system of building houses with solid cobblestone walls held together by concrete.[57]

Modern-Style Houses. Drawing upon the architectural designs of the Craftsman bungalows and the less-popular Prairie-style houses, a more elaborate style designed by Frank Lloyd Wright and other architects from Chicago, and also other styles, the era of Modern houses began in the 1930s. Comparatively few were built before the outbreak of World War II, which, except housing built for the war effort, caused construction of domestic houses to cease between 1941 and 1945. When construction resumed in 1946, builders largely abandoned historical houses in favor of the Modern styles.[58] The earliest form was the *Minimal*

Traditional style, a small, simplified house loosely patterned on the popular Tudor houses of the 1920s and 1930s. By the early 1950s the Ranch-style house with its low-pitched roof, broad facades, and attached garages was replacing them. Ranch-style houses are still popular in some sections of the country, including the Ozarks. By the 1960s split-level–style houses had made their way from California and the West to the Ozarks. Since about 1970, builders have constructed a few *Contemporary-style* houses. These have very low-pitched roofs, and wide overhanging eaves, but because they were often architect designed, they were never popular outside the larger Ozark cities. The most recent of the modern styles is the *Shed style,* which, like the Contemporary, eschews traditional detail and is also most common in architect-designed houses.

Recently, in the newer subdivisions and in outlying Ozark suburbia, there has been a return to the Romantic, Victorian, and Eclectic styles, but with the addition of new materials, including improved prefabricated building materials. The newer materials include high-efficiency multipane windows, massive entrance doors and patio doors, vinyl lap siding, and trim materials to adapt to a wide range of historical and modern styles. Porches, after regaining popularity, are found on many contemporary house styles. A nearly ubiquitous addition to contemporary houses since about 1980 is the picketed deck, which usually attach to the rear of the house. Chemically treated (CCA) pine and Western Red Cedar lumber are the usual building materials for decks, but the former is most common. Decks on houses sometimes wrap around one or more sides of the house.

Among the pre-railroad Ozark houses are some well-preserved houses built by the French during the Spanish regime in Missouri. The handsome French houses in Ste. Genevieve represent one of the finest collections of French colonial architecture between Quebec and the French Quarter and the older Creole suburbs in New Orleans.[59] These rural tradition houses have extensive porches supported by slender wooden columns under the main roofline. Most old French houses have steeply pitched, hipped, or side-gabled roofs raised on high masonry foundations. However, in Ste. Genevieve some are of the peculiarly French upright-log construction, now weather boarded. The wide galleries or porches, a style believed to be of Caribbean origin, sometimes encircle the entire house. Many French colonial houses were constructed, at least in part, with half-timbered walls, although it is not a common style among the houses in Ste. Genevieve. The Bolduc House, dating from about 1785, is the best preserved of the houses using vertical-log or "post-in-ground" construction.[60] Other well-preserved French colonial houses in Ste. Genevieve include the Amoureaux house, the St. Gemme Beauvais house (bed and breakfast), and the Felix Valle House State Historic Site.

The Germans who settled in and around the Missouri cities of Ste. Genevieve, St. Louis, St. Charles, Washington, Hermann, and Jefferson City often built their homes of brick.[61] Although less frequently seen in a rural setting, the German brick house is common in the eastern and northern Ozark towns. German craftsmen often embellished these impressive two-story structures with ironwork, decorative brickwork, and colored shingles laid in ornamental

Bolduc House, Ste. Genevieve, Missouri, 1975. The house, constructed with logs placed in the wall vertically in the French style, was built about 1785. (Milton Rafferty Collection, photograph by the author.)

design. A bell-shaped lower slope and a double false chimney often outline the gambrel roof at each end of the house.

Mobile homes, formerly known as trailer houses, are very popular in the Ozarks, as are manufactured houses. This is in line with the continuing need for basic economical shelter without great concern for fashionable stylistic design. The mobile home's adaptability to the needs and level of living of many people accounts for its increasing popularity since about 1940.[62] Mobile homes and manufactured houses are usually less expensive on a square-foot basis than conventional housing, and in the Ozarks owners may tow them to parcels of land that are still comparatively inexpensive. Inexpensive rural living holds a strong attraction for many Ozark residents.

There are many homemade houses with unpredictable house plans. For want of a better name, they may be called vernacular houses.[63] The homemade character of most of these Ozark houses accounts for most of their variation from standard plans. Regional builders continue to construct their own versions of modern houses. Vernacular builders use various building materials—stone, concrete block, brick, stucco, and other materials—but most are wood-frame construction.

Unusual idiosyncratic house styles also may be found in the Ozarks. This includes dwellings adapted from World War II–era Quonset huts, geodetic domes styled after the prototypes designed by Buckminster Fuller, alpine style A-frame houses, and, very rarely, makeshift cabins constructed of packing crates and other cast-off materials. Even rarer are the old school buses that become temporary dwellings.

GEOGRAPHY OF HOUSE TYPES

The maps of house types (fig. 15-1) should be read and interpreted as one would read and interpret any other map of the same scale, with recognition that the differentiated areas are generalizations of features observed in the field. Each part of the Ozarks includes some houses of almost every type, but I have identified on the maps areas where certain types of houses are most numerous. Several interesting associations are evident. The most active areas for new house construction are near the larger towns and in the lake resort areas, especially along bituminous-surface secondary roads, federal highways, and state farm-to-market roads. These are the areas where population has grown most rapidly in recent years. The fringes of the national forest lands, when within commuting distance of a larger city, also have become hot spots for new house construction. Permanent open space and attractive scenery are important magnets for new suburbanites.

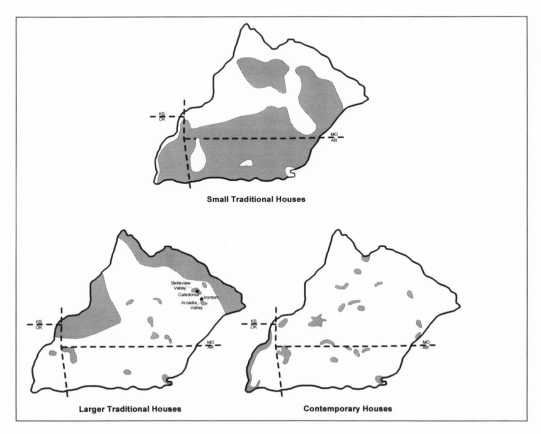

FIGURE 15-1. Geography of house types. Prepared by the author using house type maps and data from Milton D. Rafferty, "Persistence Versus Change in Land Use and Landscape in the Springfield Missouri, Vicinity of the Ozarks" (Ph.D. diss., University of Nebraska, 1970), and data from house type surveys along selected traverses across the Ozarks, 1969–1990 and 1999. Original map, 1980. Updated, October 2000.

Small Traditional Houses

Larger Traditional Houses

Contemporary Houses

Bonniebrook, home of Rose O'Neill. From left are Rose O'Neill, Clarence O'Neill (brother), Vance Randolph, and Kallista O'Neill (sister.) (Courtesy of State Historical Society of Missouri.)

Smaller houses are associated with areas of steep slopes and stony soils where farms and towns produced little surplus to afford larger dwellings. Even so, large houses, sometimes with exotic styles, occur as erratics in the remote hilly districts. For example, Bonniebrook, the elegant residence of artist Rose O'Neill, was singularly anomalous when her father built it in the 1890s in the rugged and isolated White River country in Taney County, Missouri.[64] Later, after Rose O'Neill had spent most of the fortune she earned from the popular Kewpie doll, other artwork, and her books, she moved back to the Ozarks and spent the final years of her life at Bonniebrook. In 1982, more than thirty years after the house burned, and following Rose O'Neill's death, the Bonniebrook Historical Society laid the foundation for a restoration of Bonniebrook.[65] Today the house is the centerpiece for Bonniebrook Park, a tourist attraction, including a gift shop, a nature park, and a hiking trail.

Another such anomalous house, Curtis Fletcher Marbut's rambling Cape Cod, is tucked away in northern Barry County, Missouri. Marbut patterned the house after the home of Clark University's president Wallace Atwood, where he was a frequent guest. Workers cut the oak and walnut lumber from timber on the Marbut farm. Marbut, a nationally known soil scientist, had the house built on the family estate for his retirement years, but died while doing soil survey work in China without seeing the house completed.[66]

The most arresting and celebrated house of all was Hahatonka, a twenty-eight-room mansion of modified Late English-Renaissance style. R. M. Snyder, wealthy Kansas City banker, speculator, and businessman, had the house built as the capstone of his Niangua River retreat in Camden County, Missouri. Due to the owner's early death in an automobile accident, the grand retreat was never fully completed.

As mentioned previously, larger two-story houses are associated with more level and productive agricultural land. Farmers and city dwellers built large two-story houses, notably the I-houses, along the railroads where cities and farms were more prosperous.[67] This relationship still holds true in a general way today, except that in recent years other factors have become more important, namely, a rural setting close to a larger town or city where individuals or builders can purchase small acreages or attractive building sites in a scenic area close to good highways. More than a few opulent houses have been built along the shores of the large lakes, notably Table Rock, Beaver, and Lake of the Ozarks.

Rural houses are mainly old, except those built in more recent years by commuters and resort developers. The construction of most rural dwellings dates before World War I, and only a small percentage was constructed after World War II. As in many hill districts east of the Mississippi River, much of the housing of the rural Ozarks is of poor quality, although recently remodeling and new construction have improved the region's housing stock. Small traditional houses are still numerous in the more isolated sections, where rugged terrain and poor soils limit the possibilities for agriculture. They are the main dwellings in sections of the White River drainage basin, in the rugged Courtois Hills and the St. Francois Mountains, in the rocky hills drained by the Osage and Gasconade rivers, and throughout the hidden coves and lonely mesas in the Boston Mountains of Arkansas. Modular houses and mobile homes in these districts have replaced many substandard houses over the past twenty years. In the Springfield Plain and the better agricultural districts of the northern and eastern Ozarks, small traditional houses are mainly in the hilly belts along larger streams.

Professor Hewes's study of the Cherokee country of the Oklahoma Ozarks showed that most of the houses of that district were small, unpretentious, and often in poor repair.[68] Likewise, farm buildings in the Cherokee Ozarks are of poorer construction than those immediately to the east. The explanation for retardation lies in cultural history, rather than in deficient natural resources, since rocks, landforms, soils, water resources, natural vegetation, and climate are much the same as they are immediately to the east. Since the Cherokees long held land as tribal property until they distributed it to private owners under the Dawes Act, there was little incentive to invest in large homes and farmstead accouterments. In the 1940s, the contrasts were of sufficient amount to form a sharp cultural boundary at the Oklahoma border.[69]

The colonial French houses of Ste. Genevieve, as well as the large pre–Civil War houses of the Belleview Valley and the elegant summer homes in the Arcadia Valley built by wealthy St. Louisans, represent cultural islands. The architecture of these cultural islands speaks strongly of their history and culture, which were surely worlds apart from the stereotyped backwoods Ozarks. Likewise, the architecture of the larger Ozark towns and cities reveal a cultural history far different from the tiresome hand-to-mouth portrayal of the region.

The houses in Ozark towns and cities are even more varied than in the countryside. As previously noted, the merchants and businesspeople built larger and more elegant houses. The larger Victorian homes built by the mining-rich in Joplin and in Bonne Terre included marble porticos and carriage houses. Almost any community of ten thousand population has its neighborhood of upscale houses that tell of middle-class affluence and a refined lifestyle. Some small towns have neighborhoods of fine homes. Bentonville, Arkansas, long before its Wal-Mart days, had its sedate, aristocratic Silk Stocking Row, a short section of West Central Avenue only a few blocks from the courthouse square.[70]

HOUSE FURNISHINGS

The life of pioneers in America has often been misrepresented. Reconstructions and memorials often depict those aspects of life that, because we have lost them, we mistakenly suppose our forebears enjoyed. Historians have shown that isolation and monotony, scarcities and shortages, hard work and early death were the common fare for frontier men and women. Although the people who first settled the Ozarks no doubt were skilled in fashioning a surprising number of useful tools and household implements from the forest, they constantly endured scarcities.

As for household wares, except furniture, most probably were brought by the settlers when they moved to the Ozarks. As happens today, one did not start completely anew when they made a move. What they could put away in a pack, load in a wagon, or stow on a flatboat they carried along. Cynthia and James Price's archeological excavations at the Widow Harris cabin in the southeast Missouri Ozarks discovered many fragments of household tools bearing the names of manufacturers in the East or in Europe, but there were few hand-crafted artifacts.[71]

There is a considerable historical record of the material culture of the first settlers. Houses were usually one-room log structures set in a clearing and surrounded by "innumerable quantities of deer, bear, and other skins" stretched and hung up to dry on poles and trees.[72] In spring the settlers planted a patch of corn for bread and for feeding horses. "No cabbages, beets, onions, potatoes, turnips, or other garden vegetables are raised. Gardens are unknown," wrote Schoolcraft.[73] Barking dogs announced a visitor's approach to the cabin. Men wore deerskin garments that served as a shirt and jacket; women frequently dressed in buckskin frocks "abundantly greasy and dirty."[74] Schoolcraft's description of the interior of a house in the White River country in 1818 points up the primitive conditions of life:

> Around the walls of the room hung horns of deer and buffalo, rifles, shot pouches, leather coats, dried meat, and other articles composing the wardrobe, smokehouse, and magazine of our host and family, while the floor displayed great evidence of his own skill in the fabrication of household furniture. A dressed deerskin, sewed up much in the shape the animal originally possessed, and filled with bear's oil, and another filled with wild honey, hanging on opposite sides of the fireplace, were too conspicuous to escape observation, for which indeed, they appeared to be principally kept, and brought forcibly to mind the ludicrous anecdote of potatoes and point. "As in some Irish houses where

things are so-so, one gammon of bacon hangs up for show."[75]

A generation later, in 1839, Gerstaeker, the intrepid German wanderer, described the house of a Pole who had somehow chanced to settle along the Little Red River in the extreme southeastern Ozarks:

The Pole's dwelling was nothing but a simple rough log-house, without any window, and all the chinks between the logs were left open, perhaps to admit fresh air, but probably from neglect. Two beds, a table, a couple of chairs, one of them with arms, some iron saucepans, three plates, two tin pots, one saucer, several knives, and a coffee-mill, formed the whole of his furniture and cooking utensils.[76]

Gerstaeker's account of a midnight snack at the Pole's house is an amusing record of the inconveniences and work involved in preparing a meal:

Being deeply interested in our conversation, we forgot to prepare any supper, and it was not till the cold made itself felt that we went to bed. It may have been about half-past twelve, when Turoski woke up, and swore by all the saints, that he could lie no longer in bed for ravenous hunger, and that he must have something to eat, even if it were a piece of raw meat. I laughed, and told him to draw his hunger-belt tighter, but he jumped up and gave me no more rest. We made up the fire, which was nearly burnt out, and then held a council as to what we should cook. We had shot nothing, the bread was all gone, and we had eaten our last bit of pork for dinner. What was to be done? Turoski decided the point. The Indian corn of last harvest was in a small building in a field by the river; I was to go and fetch an armful, while he would prepare something in the meantime. The night was dark as pitch; I was often obliged to feel with my feet for the path like a blind man, that I might not lose myself in the forest. When, in the course of half an hour, I returned with the maize, Turoski had killed one of the fowls that were roosting on a low tree, plunged it in hot water, and while he cleaned it I fried the corn; then, while the fowl was being grilled, I ground the corn in the coffee-mill, which by no means reduced it to the consistence of flour. I moistened the grist with water, added a little salt, made a cake of it about three-quarters of an inch thick, and set it in a saucepan cover to bake. So far so good; but I wanted a couple of eggs. There was a kind of shed attached to the house, in which leaves of Indian corn, plucked green, and then dried, were kept as fodder, and here the hens came to lay their eggs. Turoski crept in, and feeling about, soon came to a nest with five, of which he brought away only two, having broken the others in his hurry. Coffee was then made and we had a very good supper, or rather breakfast, for it was not past two o'clock. But we were not yet to repose in safety; the monster log of hickory, that we had laid on the hearth, flared up and set fire to the chimney: Turoski mounted on the roof while I handed him some buckets of water, and the fire was soon extinguished. At last we got to sleep, and remained so till the sun was high in the heavens.[77]

No doubt the construction of railroads was the most important single factor in bringing change in lifestyles to the nineteenth-century Ozarks. Until railroads arrived, town life was not greatly different from living in the country. Railroads brought commerce, introduced a money economy, and brought in new people and the trappings of town life. Brick buildings replaced rough-sawed clapboard stores, and sometimes merchants who enjoyed the prosperity fostered by the railroads built large townhouses. In the immediate hinterland of the railroad towns, settlers built new farmhouses and they remodeled and enlarged old ones. Cralle recorded the contrasting conditions of life and the material culture of the mid-1930s.[78] He noted the substantial contrast in material culture in isolated versus nonisolated communities. James Wood's inventory of the material culture of Mentor, near Springfield, shows the striking changes in conditions of life over the two generations from the time Cralle studied it in 1930 to 1978.[79] Most of the data in Tables 15-1, 15-2, and 15-3 speak for themselves. The material culture as represented in household furnishings is much improved. Houses are better painted, better furnished, and better heated, and eight out of ten have air conditioning. Floors are mainly carpeted, windows are curtained, and drywall, wallpaper, and paneling are used liberally for interior walls. The telephone, which was installed in only 16 percent of the homes in Mentor in 1935, is now considered essential. Television, unknown in the Ozarks until the 1950s, is now in every home. Washers, dryers, freezers, lawn mowers, and garbage disposals are as common in Mentor as in cities and towns throughout the United States. Since Wood and Rafferty made their survey in 1975, computers and many other electronic devises have added to the inventory of conveniences in most homes. At the dawn of the twenty-first century, Springfield's urban fringe has very nearly engulfed Mentor, and an upscale planned residential development—Highland Springs—complete with an Arnold Palmer golf course, is but two miles away.

TABLE 15-1. HOUSE FURNISHINGS, MENTOR, MISSOURI

	Cralle Survey, 1935	Wood Survey 1975
Rug on living-room floor	54%	84%
Rag carpet on living-room floor	18	13
Living-room floor bare	28	2
Windows curtained	64	100
Fireplace	6	40
Living-room stove	81	1
Furnace	3	99
Interior wall finish		
Paint	———	20
Paneling	———	30
Wallpaper	70	50
Storm windows	———	48

Total number of houses surveyed in 1935 study, circa 100
Total number of houses surveyed in 1975 study: 32

TABLE 15-2. MISCELLANEOUS HOUSE FURNISHINGS, MENTOR, MISSOURI

	Cralle Survey, 1935	Wood Survey 1975
Oil Stove	32%	1%
Coal stove	4	———
Electric stove	———	3
Ice box	5	———
Refrigerator	———	100
Telephone	16	100
Sewing machine	53	23
Loom	1	———
Washer	———	96
Dryer	———	81
Freezer	———	30
Garbage disposal	———	50
Television	———	100
Air Conditioner		
Room	———	30
Central	———	50
Automobile	6	100
Truck (including pickups)	———	20
Lawn Mower (power)	———	94
Boat	———	6

Total number of houses surveyed in 1935 study: circa 100
Total number of houses surveyed in 1975: 32

The survey of houses revealed a few surprises. For example, the percentage of homes with iceboxes should obviously be greater in 1935 than in 1968, but only 5 percent of the homes in a community only ten miles from Springfield had them. Another example is the sewing machine. Not only were there fewer sewing machines in the late 1970s, but they are hardly the ostentatious piece of parlor furniture that they were in the mid-1930s.[80]

Fireplaces, essential to log-cabin settlers but out of fashion by the 1930s, are again popular as aesthetic components of new houses. Possibly the most intriguing data are those for musical instruments. In 1935 only 25 percent of the homes had musical instruments, and this was a time when much entertainment was of the home type.[81] Some popular accounts of early days in the Ozarks convey the message that virtually everyone played a musical instrument and sang colorful folk songs. The second and perhaps more interesting point is that only 11 percent of the homes had a musical instrument in 1975. As has been noted, much of today's home entertainment is provided by radio, television, CD players, and the many forms of entertainment now available through computers and the Internet. If one wants to get away, the automobile provides ready access to a wide range of entertainment. Two generations of modernization, especially in the form of electrical power and the widespread use of automobiles, have eliminated most of the disagreeable aspects of rural Ozark life. Ozarks' culture and lifestyle have been homogenized to the point that they are barely distinguishable from the rest of America. To some this seems sad; to others it is a sign of progress. As one native Ozark observer of the contemporary scene put it, "I love the Ozarks, but I would not have wanted to live here a hundred years ago."[82]

For young people of high-school age the automobile has become a form of entertainment in itself. Much socializing focuses on the automobile, and cruising the main drag past the local Sonic drive-in, the movie, or other hangouts for teenagers is a popular pastime in small towns. Each town seems to have its "cruising street"—Springfield has Kearney Street and Battlefield Road, West Plains has Porter Wagoner Boulevard, Cape Girardeau has Broadway Street, and in Ozark, Missouri, and many other county seats, it is the courthouse square. Whether or not they have had a positive effect on cultural standards, these technological advances, more than any other thing, prepared the Ozarks for the modern era of immigration.

TABLE 15-3. MUSICAL INSTRUMENTS AND PLAYERS

	Cralle Survey, 1935	Wood Survey 1975
Talking machine (record player)	22%	2%
Radio	17	100
Stereo Player	—	43
Piano	11	5
Organ	4	—
Banjo	3	—
Violin	7	—
Horn	—	2
Guitar	—	2
Miscellaneous Instruments	—	2

Total number of houses surveyed in 1935 study: circa 100
Total number of houses surveyed in 1975: 32

WATER MILLS

Water mills are one of the most picturesque and fascinating features of the Ozark landscape. There was a great abundance of water mills in the Ozarks in the nineteenth and early twentieth centuries. Fire has destroyed many old mills. Even more slowly decayed after they no longer served a purpose. Many hamlets owed their existence to the business generated by water mills. A number of factors account for the large number of mills in the Ozarks. The many large steady-flowing springs and streams provided a reliable power source. Most of the streams are small and easily dammed to divert the water to a mill site. The rough terrain made hauling grain for milling or timber for sawing both time-consuming and expensive, so nearby mills were a great convenience.

Fire was the great destroyer of water mills, and some mill sites have had two and sometimes three or more mills, each being replaced in turn after a fire. During the Civil War both Union and Confederate forces destroyed many mills for strategic reasons, to preclude their use by the opposing forces.[83]

About mid-twentieth century, just as the last mills were closing, interest in preserving the old mills increased. Today, many mills are still standing, and a few are operated as tourist and historical attractions. The largest Ozark mill is at Burfordville in Cape Girardeau County. Unlike most Ozark water mills, the impressive Bollinger mill is a three-story brick structure. The War Eagle Mill on War

Eagle Creek in Madison County, Arkansas, surely one of the most photographed mills, is well known because of the large craft festival held nearby each year.

South-central Missouri is rich in water mills and a popular driving tour, the Ozark Water Mill Trail, attracts a number of tourists to the mills.[84] Rockbridge Mill in Ozark County is the centerpiece of a quiet trout fishing resort with a popular restaurant that serves both visitors and local people. Dawt Mill on the North Fork of the White River in Ozark County has long been a popular take-out spot for floaters, and the recent addition of a motel and restaurant has increased its attractiveness. The picturesque spring-powered Hodgson Mill, also in Ozark County, is slowly deteriorating for lack of maintenance. Hammond Mill on the North Fork has received some restoration. Zanoni Mill, built in 1905 by "Doc" Morrison, is one of the few remaining overshot mills. Dave Morrison, grandson of the mill's builder, restored the mill and old store building. They also built the Zanoni Mill Bed and Breakfast, which features an indoor swimming pool. Topaz Mill and store in Douglas County are well preserved but are not open for visitors. Greer Mill in Oregon County is near the entrance to the famous Greer Spring.[85] Greer Mill was something of an engineering marvel because the mill dam and turbine were in the deep ravine of Greer Spring Branch, and the power generated was transferred three-quarters of a mile uphill to the mill by cables and contraptions known as shiftstands. The mill was once owned by John Greer and his son Samuel.

SAWMILLS

Sawmills are ubiquitous and transient features of the landscape. Since they vary greatly in size, their landscape imprint is highly variable. As we have seen, some large sawmills operating around the turn of the nineteenth century covered many acres and included several separate mill buildings. The Missouri Lumber and Mining Company operations at Grandin and West Eminence boasted several large mill buildings, hotels, hospitals, general stores, and company-owned housing for employees as well as sidewalks and other infrastructure for the towns. Modern sawmills are smaller, with usually only three or four buildings for the sawmill, planing mill, and for storage of high-grade planed lumber. Some sawmills, such as Smith Flooring Company in Mountain Grove, Missouri, have been in business for more than fifty years. The sawmill site, with its large buildings, drying kilns, sawdust piles, and sprawling woodyard, is a landmark along U.S. 60. Spider Smith founded it in the early depression years.[86]

BARNS AND OTHER FARMSTEAD BUILDINGS

Compared with the great barns in New England and the western dairy belt in Wisconsin and Minnesota, most Ozark barns are simple structures.[87] They are usually multipurpose buildings once used for sheltering work horses, mules, and milk cows and for storing hay and feed. Barns, no matter the type, generally have two levels, the upper level is a haymow where farmers stored and later pitched hay down into stanchions or bunks for livestock. Log barns were once the dominant type of barn, and many are still in use.[88] Pioneer settlers built log barns as units with square or rectangular rooms or "cribs," similar to the "pens" in log houses. When the farmers constructed larger log barns, they added up to six additional pens or units to the original barn.

When railroads brought sawmills and lumberyards, builders constructed barns of lighter framing lumber. Several different types of barns are found in the region— English barns, transverse crib, bank barns, Pennsylvania Dutch or German barns, diminutive mountain stable barns, modern one-story barns, specialized hog and poultry barns, and a handful of idiosyncratic round and hexagonal barns.

Mountain stable, Limestone Valley, Arkansas, 1976. (Milton Rafferty Collection, photograph by the author.)

The transverse crib barn is gable-fronted with one or two side sheds. It is the most common barn type in the Ozarks. The size and condition of barns vary with age and the relative prosperity of the farm. Large transverse crib barns, sometimes with attached silos and milking sheds, are found in the better dairy areas in the Springfield Plain of southwest Missouri and northwest Arkansas and in the more fertile northern and eastern Ozark border areas. Small transverse crib barns also are found in the hilly districts. The English-style barns are smaller and easy to identify because of their gable-sided orientation and central runway, which presents a frontal appearance similar to the dogtrot house.[89] The English-style barn is widely distributed, but not common. Bank barns have one end built into the side of a hill. These barns are rare in the rocky interior Ozarks, perhaps because hard limestones discourage digging. They are most numerous, but still rare, in the eastern and northern Ozark border areas. Pennsylvania Dutch or Swiss-Mennonite barns, often called German barns in Missouri,[90] may be identified by their large size, propensity for hillside locations, and overhanging forebays.[91] These barns are also rare, but a 1977 survey by Charles van Ravenswaay, discovered several in the German areas of the northern and eastern Ozark borders.[92]

The mountain stable is a small barn type found in the more rugged parts of the upland South and in the very hilly districts in the Ozarks. Its floor plan is reminiscent of the transverse crib barn, but much smaller. Sometimes, when they needed additional space, farmers attached a shed to one or both sides. They are not common, even in the hilly districts, and are extremely rare in other sections.

Today, farmers seldom build traditional barns. Nevertheless, modern barns are going up all over the United States and the Ozark region. The modern or contemporary barn is often overlooked in landscape studies, probably because they have not achieved sufficient antiquarian appeal. Also, because builders often construct them with prefabricated materials, modern barns lack the uniqueness and charm of hand-constructed log or sawed-lumber barns. The typical modern barn is a low rectangular, shed-like structure designed for general purpose use. Often barn builders include removable internal subdivisions so that the buildings can house livestock or store hay or machinery. Sheet metal construction is very common, and even when the sides are wood, the roof is usually sheet metal. Molded plastic skylights or roof windows, which permit sunlight to enter, are common features. These barns may be found anywhere in the Ozarks, but they are most numerous in the more favored agricultural districts.

One of the fastest-growing Ozark barn types is the modern poultry barn. These are highly specialized structures that have replaced the old farm chicken houses. They have a history of their own. Beginning in the 1920s, poultry farmers built small one-story, gable-fronted, long, rectangular shed structures, with few specialized interior features and equipment. With each passing year, they constructed still larger and yet more specialized barns. The larger poultry barns, which nowadays often cluster in groups near a large feed mill and mixing plant, have heating and cooling facilities, automated feeding and watering stations, and features to simplify cleaning. Even modest-sized poultry barns, with dimensions of 40 feet by 240 feet, can house fifteen to seventeen thousand birds.[93]

New features in the Ozarks landscape since about 1980 are the large integrated poultry and hog farms. These sprawling "factory farm" operations, like the poultry farm operated by Tyson Foods north of Westville, Oklahoma, are often situated on railroad sidings so that they can offload carloads of grain and supplies. The large operation at Westville includes Tyson Mills' feed mill and poultry growout complexes 1, 2, and 3, thirty poultry barns in all. The Westville operation is capable of handling 200,000 chickens in one growout period or 600,000 in a year's time. It is one of sixteen company farms, a truck shop, a farm maintenance operation, a hatchery at Stilwell, Oklahoma, and a poultry processing plant at Noel, Missouri . . . all part of the Tyson Foods' Noel Complex. The towering four-tube feed mill and office building backed by thirty large poultry barns arranged in rows to allow access for the eighteen-wheel tractor trailers that haul the chickens to be processed gives the Westville operation the appearance of a small city.

To keep up with the constant growth and innovation in the poultry business, farmers have built new barns and allowed old barns to waste away. Therefore, it is not surprising that one of the common landscape features in the Ozarks is the dilapidated, older-style poultry barn. Modern poultry barns are common throughout northern Arkansas, northeastern Oklahoma, and southwestern Missouri, but especially in the Arkansas counties of Madison, Washington, Stone, and Independence, and in the Missouri counties of Barry, McDonald, and Stone. These counties are leaders in the production of broilers and turkeys. A secondary concentration of modern poultry barns is in the south-central Missouri counties of Miller, Camden, Morgan, and Moniteau, where turkey production is important.

The condition of barns and the number of outbuildings vary greatly within the Ozarks. In the better agricultural areas, many farms have eight or more buildings, but in areas of steep slopes and poorer soils, barns are very scarce and outbuildings often consist of a wretched shed or two. Data on Ozark barns show that most of the large barns are in the three agricultural border districts, three-fourths are constructed of sawed lumber, most of the remainder being covered with sheet metal, and comparatively few stone, brick, or log barns are to be found; 85 percent have composition shingles and of those that are painted, about half are red and half are white; two-thirds of the barns need major repair and paint.[94]

The fact that older-style barns are generally in poor condition throughout the region results from their decreasing functional utility. Mild winters make barns unnecessary for the protection of stock. In the hill country, where deep valleys and wooded slopes afford ample protection for stock, barns have never been highly regarded. Over the past half century, the traditional frame barn with an overhead loft, milking stanchions, and horse stalls has become largely nonfunctional.[95] Farms are now less self-sufficient, and tractors have replaced the horse and mule. If used for anything besides storage, traditional barns have been renovated and equipped with modern machinery. Some serve as milking parlors or storage places for machinery or hay, functions that the single-story contemporary barns or sheds can serve more efficiently. In recent years a movement to preserve and restore barns has swept across the nation, but unfortunately little has been done to preserve barns in the Ozarks.[96] The barn on the farm owned by Joe Patton near Mount Vernon, Missouri, is a noteworthy exception.[97] The transverse crib barn, a Victorian house, and several other buildings have been restored to turn-of-the-twentieth-century condition. A few barns near growing urban centers have been remodeled and converted for storage and assorted business uses on urban fringes.

Silos are associated with dairy and livestock farming. They are most numerous in the more prosperous border districts, where livestock feeding and dairying gain stature. Farmers built many tall silos between 1900 and 1920, a time of rapid expansion in dairy farming.[98] Nearly all are concrete. The farmers usually built silos near the barn, and about half the time they built them attached to or inside the barn. Rotted roofs, cracked and chipped concrete, and weed-grown lots suggest that many silos have fallen into disuse as the number of dairy farms and general farms has declined. The trench silo, which is more readily adaptable to machine handling of silage, has come into wider use. The old wooden silos are rare. Metal tank-type silos are associated with dairy farms. These structures have the advantage of being adaptable to the storage of either dry silage or commercial livestock feeds. A few abandoned silos, those fortunate enough to be along a major highway, have been repainted for advertising as super-size beer or soft-drink cans.

The assortment of smaller outbuildings is highly variable from farmstead to farmstead. The small chicken houses, which were important and functional structures when farms were more self-sufficient and when commercial poultry farming was in its infancy, are rare and almost never used to house chickens. These small shed-type structures, now used for incidental storage, are often in a pitiful state of repair.

The first modern milk sheds date mainly from the 1940s. They are of quite uniform architectural style, most being patterned after plans drawn at the agricultural colleges. Most are simple rectangular concrete-block buildings attached to the barn, although sometimes farmers built them detached. In recent years a few dairy farmers have constructed elaborate glassed-in milking parlors.

About 50 percent of the rural houses have small one-car garages, the kind they built for older, smaller automobiles. Many old garages now serve as shops or for general storage. Newer houses have attached garages for one, two, or more vehicles.

Grain storage bins and corn cribs are conspicuously absent. The few grain bins are small, round, galvanized sheet-metal structures with conical roofs. Corn cribs, buildings with open slat construction to allow free movement of air, are rare indeed. These old wooden structures apparently have not been used for sometime. They are relics of a different time and a different agricultural economy. Today, Ozark farmers raise little grain, and they chop most of the corn for silage. Some modern farms have machine sheds and repair shops. These structures, along with assorted small sheds, round out the assembling of farm buildings.

Fences in the Ozarks are mainly woven wire (hog wire) or barbed wire, with the latter prevalent. Split-log worm fences, which were dominant shortly after the turn of the century and still common in remote areas in the mid-1930s, have disappeared from the landscape except as occasional ornamental fences.[99] Wood-panel fences are found near the larger towns, such as Springfield, Joplin, and Fayetteville, where they add to the appearance of affluence on country estates and riding stables. Such fences serve to inform passersby that the occupants of the enclosed "farmstead" really need not farm for a living.

Stone fences are rare. Because the soils are often shallow and stony, farmers in earlier times constructed stone fences at the margins of the fields as they periodically cleared their crop land of chert and limestone. Today, most of these stone fences are overgrown with brush and tumbling down. In very stony areas, farmers pile field stones at the base of trees or in sinkholes. Another distinctive and unusual stone feature is the rock crib post. It is a cylinder of woven wire, approximately three feet in diameter, filled with field stones. Cribs are usually supported with posts and sometimes girdled with discarded iron wagon tires.

Barbed-wire fences range from two to six strands, with four-strand fences the most common. Timbered land in remote areas is usually fenced poorly; two or three strands of loosely strung barbed wire are considered sufficient where free range persisted until the mid-1960s. Woven-wire (hog-wire) fences account for three-fourths of the fencing along the highways but is less common along the byroads. Along the well-traveled roads, woven-wire is a safety factor, protecting against straying livestock, and where persimmon sprouts and brush were once "goated down," farmers preferred woven-wire because it is a goat-tight fence. Steel posts most commonly support fences, but cedar, hedge, and oak posts are also used. Because post holes are difficult to dig in the rocky soils, fence builders sometimes sharpen the wooden posts on one end so they can drive them with a mallet.

Propane tanks, gardens, and fruit trees are associated with many rural dwellings. Propane (liquid petroleum, or LP gas) or electricity are almost universally used for cooking purposes, even where wood is still used for heating the home. Propane also is widely used for heating purposes and has continually gained favor over wood and fuel oil because of its convenience and cleanliness. Recently the rising cost of propane has slowed the conversion from wood for heating purposes.

Wood is still widely used as fuel, as witnessed by the many cords of stacked wood and woodpiles.[100] This is especially true in outlying areas, but since many urban houses have fireplaces, the woodpile is ubiquitous. Pickups and trailers loaded with split-oak for sale are commonplace in shopping center parking lots throughout the Ozarks. Wood-burning heating stoves have become popular in recent years, mainly because of rising prices for natural gas and electricity but also because of a heightened concern about energy supplies. Wide porches on the older houses, especially in the more remote locations, serve as places to keep a supply of dry kindling close at hand. Natural-gas lines serve only the larger cities in the border districts, so the interior towns depend on bottled gas, electricity, or wood for heating and cooking purposes. The restrictions on extension of natural-gas service, coupled with the rising cost of LP, have caused many rural home builders to install electric furnaces with heat pumps.

A comparatively long growing season and adequate precipitation make the production of garden truck patches fairly easy. Backyard gardens, although probably less popular than in earlier times, are still highly regarded. They are used mainly to produce fresh cucumbers, tomatoes, lettuce, radishes, onions, beans, and other assorted vegetables for the table. Some large gardens are set out to supply vegetables for home-canning purposes. Some people plant potatoes, and raise sweet corn for both the table and the home freezer. The Amish families that settled in the Ozarks during the 1960s and 1970s grow especially large gardens to be as self-sufficient as possible.[101]

Fruit trees are less common than gardens, but some houses have from one to half a dozen fruit trees. The few remaining large farm orchards are usually well tended. Apples and peaches are the most common fruits, but cherries, pears, and apricots also are grown. Grapes do well but are not as popular as the tree fruits. Many grape arbors are poorly kept and may be considered relics of a time when farm families were more self-sufficient and the home canning of jams and jellies was a more widely practiced art. Still, the abundant display of home-canned jams, jellies, and fruits at the Ozark Empire Fair and other regional fairs and craft festivals attest that berry and fruit growing and preservation persists.

Cellars are associated with older houses. Because bedrock is often near the surface, the cellars are shallow and appear as grass-covered mounds with limestone entranceways. In former times, people stored potatoes in cellars, and homemakers filled the shelves with home-canned vegetables and fruits. On farmsteads where there was no spring, the cellar was the poor man's spring house, serving as a cool place to store crocks of milk, cream, butter, and eggs. Many new cellars reportedly were constructed shortly after the Marshfield tornado of 1880; today they serve mainly as places of refuge during storms, most of their other uses having been lost.[102]

Windmills are scarce. With so many permanently flowing streams and springs, there was little need for windmills except on the level uplands. Rural electrification reduced the number of windmills even further as farmers installed pumps with electric motors to provide pressure water systems for the house and barnyard. Most windmill towers have been dismantled. Occasionally, they serve as supports for television antennas. The scarcity of windmills presented a problem for the Old Order Amish who immigrated to Webster County, Missouri, in the 1960s. These newcomers purchased their windmills in Indiana because they could not obtain repair parts or adequate service in Missouri.[103] Over the past thirty-five years the colony of Amish has grown to the point that one can see a cluster of windmills from U.S. highway 60 west of Seymour, Missouri.

The water bucket and dipper have passed entirely into oblivion. A few cisterns still provide water, but functional cisterns are very rare. The wells with windlass, rope, and

Shed-room house, one of several small house types in the Ozarks, 1969. (Milton Rafferty Collection, photograph by the author.)

bucket are even rarer, if they exist at all. Because settlers occupied the eastern Ozark border before well drilling technology was available, cisterns were very popular in the German communities in Perry and Cape Girardeau counties in Missouri.[104] Even there, where cisterns are still numerous, they are seldom used. Cistern pumps, with their cranks and chain of water cups, are still common on farms and in small communities like Altenberg and Frohna.

Sturdy stone springhouses, though rarely used, remain common features of the rural landscape. Typically, they are at the base of a hill where springs of adequate and constant flow are found. The cold spring water served to keep perishable foods fresh for a time. Farm families customarily stored milk, cream, butter, meats, and other perishables inside. Today, their rotted doors and muddy, hoof-marked surroundings divulge their role as a source of water for livestock.

Apparently, more attention is given to the beautification of the yard than in former times. One observer in the 1930s noted that farmers customarily fenced the yard to keep out livestock, but allowed chickens and geese to range freely.[105] Frequently the grass was completely worn away around the front of the house, and the painstaking homemaker swept this area as faithfully as she swept the front porch.

More than thirty years ago when I first surveyed Ozark farmsteads along preselected traverses there was more evidence of poverty and primitive lifestyles. Along the poorest roads, and especially in the rough land in the interior districts and in the Boston Mountains, poorly tended farmyards were common. There are far fewer today. During the summer months the small bench with basin and water bucket could be seen on the porches of some houses. A mirror and a wash basin on the porch added a certain traditional charm. Such small houses could not easily hold many larger appliances, which rural electrification and income from off-farm employment had made available to many Ozark residents. As a result, old wringer washing machines often occupied a space on the back porch, and if no back porch existed, the front porch served as well. Refrigerators or freezers sometimes found their place on one of the porches. Television antennas were ubiquitous or nearly so; inside, the television set had replaced the sewing machine as the most conspicuous piece of parlor furniture. Today, satellite dishes provide much better television reception and have largely replaced the tall antennas.

The number of these occupied dwellings has declined precipitously in recent years due to abandonment or replacement.[106] Wildfires have played their part in destroying many of these old traditional dwellings, most of which were already abandoned. The eighteen houses destroyed by fire during high winds on March 5, 2000, in heavily wooded sections of Camden County, Missouri, were valued at only $130,000 or an average of $7,222 each.[107] A more likely explanation for the decline of substandard housing has been the improvement in the Ozarks economy. Rising levels of income and off-farm employment have enabled many families to build new homes or to purchase mobile homes or modular houses. Income from off-farm employment has contributed to remodeling and enlarging of many rural houses.

Visitors and tourists are often struck by the unkept appearance of many sections of the Ozarks. Unkept farmsteads stand in stark contrast to the striking beauty of the natural landscape. There is a long tradition for the unkept "laissez faire" landscape. The very first visitors called attention to this phenomenon. Schoolcraft's unflattering comments on the appearance of wilderness settlements balance his eloquent descriptions of the natural beauty of the White River country. Schoolcraft described the scene November 9, 1818, when he approached the cabin of Lem "Buck" Coker at the Sugarloaf Prairie settlement near present-day Diamond City, Arkansas:

> Our approach to the house was, as usual, announced by the barking of dogs, whose incessant yells plainly told us, that all who approached that domain, of which they were the natural guardians, and whether moving upon two, or upon four legs, were considered as enemies, and it was not until they were peremptorily, and repeatedly recalled, that they could be pacified. Dried skins, stretched out with small rods, and hung up to dry on trees and poles around the house, served to give the

scene the most novel appearance. This custom has been observed at every hunter's cabin we have encountered, and, as we find, great pride is taken in the display, the number and size of the bear-skins serving as a credential of the hunter's skill and prowess in the chace [*sic*].[108]

Professor Robert Flanders has suggested that the unkept appearance of homesteads may be deep seated, traceable to the transatlantic Scotch-Irish, where a "clarty" (unkept) landscape was a longstanding cultural trait.[109] Perhaps it is less complicated, a simple matter of remotenesss, isolation, and level of living. Could it be that the careless attitude regarding the appearance of houses, buildings, and yards stems from the scattered and isolated settlement in sparsely populated rural areas? When few people pass by on lonely roads and visitors stop in only occasionally, mowing the lawn, painting the house, and planting flowers and hedges may seem an expensive waste of time. Then too, many of the seemingly cast-off materials—fencing material, posts, and scrap iron—around rural residences may have considerable utility on a working farm.

A distinctive feature of today's remote Ozark farmsteads is the assemblage of old abandoned automobiles; seeing as many as half a dozen vehicles scattered about a single farmyard is common. Apparently, the resident of the rougher parts of the region seldom purchases a new automobile, either because of the cost or because the roads are unsuited for a quality vehicle. When a car or pickup is no longer serviceable, they abandon it on the farmstead. At first it may serve as a source of repair parts for other vehicles, and later, the old vehicles serve as storage or as places of shelter for hogs, goats, or poultry. Some rural homesteads are very unkept. A single rural dwelling yielded this inventory of cast-off material: four abandoned (unlicensed) automobiles, another dismantled automobile chassis, and a pickup truck rolled on its side to make scavenging of parts easy. Scattered about were several automobile tires, a refrigerator, two window air conditioners, two washing machines, a cast-off television set, several broken children's toys, a roll of woven wire, several rolls of rusty barbed wire, three lawn mowers, two of which appeared partially dismantled, part of a cream separator, and several crumbling cardboard boxes filled with material that I could not identify. All this lay about the yard in random fashion.[110]

On the whole, however, rural yards and farmyards are well tended. Homeowners mow their yards regularly and prune flowers and shrubbery. They tend the yards along the highways better than those along the byroads.[111] The general upkeep of yards and the attention paid to landscaping and horticultural plantings and to painting and building maintenance has improved over the past thirty years. This is especially true of the suburban fringes of the larger cities and towns.

Farm machinery is small, and a simple line of equipment is kept on most farms. Tractors are two- and three-plow types that are comparatively inexpensive to operate, versatile, and well suited for powering light hay equipment. Plows, disks, harrows, drills, hay swathers, mowing machines, rakes, balers, manure spreaders, and field choppers are evidence that crop agriculture has given way to livestock farming and ranching.[112] One seldom sees grain combines and cultivators outside the more fertile border districts.

In the border districts, where crop farming has persisted to a greater degree, the line of machinery kept on farms is more elaborate and generally newer. Dairy farms often have a larger line of machinery, and because milking schedules shorten the time that can be spent in the field, two or more tractors are usually kept. On stock farms, where demands on machinery are not as heavy, equipment, except hay machinery, is often old. On many farms in the interior hill districts, only a tractor and mower are kept to mow weeds around the farmyard. On one stock farm I visited in Christian County, Missouri, the complete equipment inventory consisted of a four-wheel drive pickup and a lawn mower.[113] The owner used the pickup to haul custom-baled hay to the cattle and for a dozen other general purposes. The lawn mower served to keep the lawn short "to keep down ticks and chiggers."

OTHER SETTLEMENT FEATURES

Improvements in roads and the economies of size have virtually put an end to the country school. By 1967 the Missouri Department of Education reported only thirty-three one-room rural schools in twenty-two southwest Missouri counties.[114] Rural residents have come to realize that schools can operate, even at minimum accepted levels, only when there is adequate financial support. Local pride and sentiment have temporarily preserved the high school in some small towns, and many more small towns have clung to their elementary schools. However, the one-room rural school has largely passed from the scene. The fate of abandoned school buildings has been variable. As rural school districts dissolved, residents tore down some buildings for the lumber that they could salvage. Neighboring farmers sometimes bought the abandoned schools and converted them to hay barns. A few rural schools have been converted to homes, and the remainder stand empty to fall apart slowly. A few small-town schools have caught the eye of preservationists and have been converted to commercial use. For example, the seven-thousand-square-foot school at

McHaffie Church, Christian County, Missouri, 1968. McHaffies were among the first immigrants to Christian County. (Milton Rafferty Collection, photograph by the author.)

Prosperity, Missouri, has been converted to a bed and breakfast. The C & M Electric Company remodeled the Eugene Field Elementary School in Carthage to rent to local businesses. Small towns are anxious to divest themselves of the expense of maintaining schools. After the school at Alba was consolidated into the Webb City school system, city leaders sought a buyer who could "put it to good use and possibly create a few jobs."[115]

A half century of depopulation of the countryside has had less-marked influence on country churches. While abandoned churches may be seen, most rural churches show signs of use. A few appear dilapidated, but near larger towns, where population is increasing, they are well cared for, and some churches have built additions to hold growing memberships. Churches near cemeteries and along the better roads also have fared better. Often, small independent churches place little emphasis on the type of building used for services. Abandoned stores or service stations are considered adequate, even preferable, to big churches, which are considered showy. Some Pentecostal churches have colorful names, such as Church of the Bread of Life or Temple of Deliverance.

In recent years the urban "mega church" has appeared on the Ozark scene as they have throughout the United States. What accounts for the recent growth of very large churches? Perhaps it is the personal mobility provided by automobiles in combination with the power of television and other media to reach large audiences of potential churchgoers. Maybe it is the desire by some people to belong to ever-larger groups with strong identities. Perchance the attraction is the sheer size of the new churches, the elaborate programs and services they can provide, and the arousing sermons delivered by charismatic ministers. The mega churches tend to locate on belt highways or major thoroughfares where they can attract membership from an entire city or large area. Examples of very large beltway churches in Springfield include the High Street Baptist Church and the James River Assemblies of God. In 1978, the High Street Baptist Church in Springfield outgrew the church building on North High Street and moved to a new three-thousand-seat church off Schoolcraft Freeway at the east edge of the city. In March 2000, a second three-thousand-seat church, the James River Assemblies of God, moved from their building on U.S. Highway 65 to a new church complex five miles farther south, beyond the city limits. They effected the move to provide space for a growing congregation and to avoid problems with parking and increasing complaints from neighbors about the heavy traffic in the neighborhood.

Community cemeteries have persisted, although they are sometimes neglected. Some of them receive grooming only once a year, before Memorial Day, when relatives of the interred return from distant places. The small family burial plot is less well cared for, and in cases where the families have moved away, the burial plots are sometimes grown over with brush and weeds. Pinetop Cemetery in Taney County, Missouri, consists of a cluster of homemade and commercial headstones scattered more or less randomly among pine and oak trees, completely hidden from view of passersby on a nearby road. Sunken spots among the trees and forest scrub attest to several unmarked graves.[116]

Country stores and crossroads filling stations continue to decline. The filling station, which provided gasoline, oil, kerosene, white gas for Coleman lanterns, and tire repair for the surrounding neighborhood, has fared poorly. As farm delivery of gasoline became nearly universal and as roads and automobiles improved, rural filling stations declined in favor of major oil company service stations, which provided a comprehensive line of goods and services. These in turn yielded to the convenience store, which in fact has many attributes of the old country general store. These purveyors of canned and packaged food and snacks, soft drinks, candy, assorted household goods, and gasoline are spreading from urban intersections to the urban fringes and to heavily traveled roads near the region's large lakes. Their colorful names—Git and Go, Stop and Shop, Fast N Friendly—mark them as different from the old "crossroads store" with its potbellied stove and circle of chairs and benches for loiterers and hangers-on.

The old breed of country stores lingers on, probably because they can continue to afford some convenience to the surrounding population. Stores in sparsely settled areas usually carry a more varied line of merchandise than those in more populated areas. The typical country store occupies a false-fronted frame building with a wide covered porch. Sturdy porch benches provide a place for customers to pass time in a shady place. The old ramshackle stores often have a single gasoline pump and, sometimes, a walnut huller for the convenience of customers who gather nuts in the fall.

Store owners stock the shelves with canned goods, packaged food, and sundry items; in a small refrigerated display case are assorted prepared meats and cheeses. A soft-drink machine just inside the front door is easily accessible to those who frequent the verandah. The remaining complement of goods—work clothing and gloves; frequently used hardware items, such as hammers, nails, and bolts; assorted pliers and wrenches; rope and barbed wire; bagged livestock feed and livestock salt; and a small assortment of veterinary supplies—are often dusty and dated from having been on the shelves for a long time. Adding to the appearance of antiquity in one country store in southern Christian County, Missouri, is a potbellied stove, nearly circled by a group of rickety chairs, and on the wall, a large framed picture of Franklin D. Roosevelt, which gives every appearance of having hung undisturbed since New Deal days. Occasionally, when business prospects warrant, new owners have converted abandoned stores and filling stations to other uses. In the recreation regions, they have remodeled some old stores to house a variety of types of retail and service establishments. Each year, the number of country stores grows smaller as roads are improved, reducing the time required for the trip to town. When the old stores finally expire, the shelves are emptied and the goods auctioned along with the antique gas pumps, old signs, and other memorabilia accumulated over the years. The old store buildings then stand empty to deteriorate as rustic reminders of a past economy.

PEOPLE AS LANDSCAPE

The people themselves comprise the final element of the Ozarks landscape. This includes all who move upon the Ozark scene, permanent residents and transients, in all their various social and economic conditions, habits of dress, and personal paraphernalia.

Selecting a characteristic physical type is difficult. In the northern and eastern borders, where the German element is strongest, there are many tall, heavy-built men and

Huzzah, Missouri. Abandoned rural store and post office in Crawford County, Missouri, 1977. (Milton Rafferty Collection, photograph by the author.)

women with fair complexions. In the Oklahoma Ozarks, one may see the Cherokee bloodline in various degrees, ranging from tall, copper-skinned people with jet black hair and dark eyes to fairer-skinned types with dark hair and eyes. The old-line Ozark residents, descended from Scotch-Irish stock, are most often medium to tall in stature, usually slender when young, fair-skinned, blue-eyed, and often with hair that is sandy or reddish-tinged.

Although the region is not known for producing people of national importance, more than a few, either natives or longtime residents, have achieved a measure of fame. Edwin Hubble, a native of Marshfield, Missouri, graduated from the University of Chicago and made outstanding contributions in the study of the universe.[117] His observations with the one-hundred-inch telescope at Mount Wilson Observatory led him to classify the nebulae and to confirm the theory of the expanding universe. Curtis F. Marbut grew up on a farm near Monett, Missouri, and later studied under the eminent geologist William Morris Davis. Marbut achieved recognition as a geologist and geographer, but his greatest fame is for his monumental work in the study and classification of soils.[118] Carl O. Sauer, a native of Warrenton, Missouri, on the northern Ozark border, achieved wide renown as a geographer.[119] His publications on geographic methodology, historical geography, and the origins of domestic grains are landmarks in the profession. As chair and professor in the Department of Geography at the University of California at Berkeley, Sauer spawned a genre of geographic inquiry known as landscape geography, or the Berkeley School, which focuses on the form and function

of landscape. Several Ozarkers achieved distinction in politics. John S. Phelps and John Ashcroft of Springfield, Joseph W. McClurg of Linn Creek, Mel Carnahan of Ellsinore, and Phil M. Donnely of Lebanon served as governors of Missouri. Richard P. Bland of Lebanon was a contender for the 1896 Democratic nomination for the presidency. Archibald Yell of Fayetteville, Isaac Murphy of Huntsville, Elisha Baxter of Batesville, William R. Miller of Batesville, James H. Berry of Bentonville, and Orval Faubus of Combs were Ozarkers who served as governors of Arkansas.[120] J. William Fulbright of Fayetteville, Arkansas, was an influential member of the U.S. Senate until his retirement in 1974.

Several Ozarkers have attained recognition in art, literature, and music. Rose O'Neill gained attention for her designs, the most important of which, the Kewpie doll, became a national rage.[121] Her elegant home, Bonnie-brook, in Taney County, Missouri, was a showplace of style and comfort in its day. A native of Neosho, Missouri, Thomas Hart Benton, achieved international acclaim for his vigorously realistic paintings of Missouri and Ozark life. Vance Randolph, a native of Kansas but a longtime resident of Fayetteville, Arkansas, is the best-known collector of Ozark folklore. Otto Rayburn, another Kansan who moved to the Ozarks, became regionally known through his newspaper columns and books about the Ozarks.[122] More recently, Jimmie Driftwood, who lived on a farm near Timbo, Arkansas, achieved national fame for his folk songs, particularly "The Battle of New Orleans" and "The Tennessee Stud."[123] Driftwood aided in obtaining federal assistance to establish the Ozark Folk Culture

Center at Mountain View, and he continued to be active in the Rackensack Society until his death in 1998. The Rackensack Society is an informal gathering of folk musicians who play traditional music in Mountain View. Porter Wagoner began as a country-music performer in West Plains and other Ozark towns near his home in Howell County, moved on to sing on radio in Springfield, before gaining national prominence on the Grand Old Opry in Nashville. Laura Ingalls Wilder, after settling in Mansfield, Missouri, wrote *Little House on the Prairie* and other best-selling books about her life experiences.[124] Tess Harper, Kathleen Turner, and John Goodman, all from the Speech and Theater Department in Southwest Missouri State University, became nationally known movie and television stars.

Also, in recent times, several Ozarkers have achieved great fame and fortune in the business world. Foremost among these is the late Sam Walton, founder of the Wal-Mart stores. Born near Kingfisher, Oklahoma, Walton lived in several Missouri communities during the period when his father moved from town to town while working for his brother's mortgage company. The Waltons' ancestral ties extended back to Webster County in the Ozarks.[125] After several business ventures, Walton launched the Wal-Mart empire from a single store in Bentonville, Arkansas. John Tyson, after relocating in Springdale, Arkansas, established a trucking business hauling chickens to Chicago, and then branched into the production and processing of poultry. Today, Tyson Foods operates internationally and is the world's leading producer of poultry products. John Q. Hammons, born in 1918, received a bachelor's degree from Southwest Missouri State College, taught two years in the Cassville, Missouri, schools, then spent a year in Alaska before entering construction and real-estate development in Springfield. Hammons's enterprises spread from real-estate developments in Springfield to other cities in the Ozarks, including the resort and retirement town of Kimberling City; hotels and convention centers in Springfield, Jefferson City, and Fort Smith; and the grand Chateau on the Lake hotel on Table Rock Lake. Hammons is a major owner in the Holiday Inn company and has developed hotels and motels throughout the United States.

This list of notables is hardly complete, but simply serves notice that the Ozarks has produced talented and energetic people. Nevertheless, examining its celebrated can hardly identify the character of a population. No single Ozark type represents a median or mode, just as there is no typical New Yorker. Ozarkers are as varied as middle westerners can be. One who moves about the region at various functions and meetings will gradually accumulate a memory full of bits and pieces from which, ever so slowly, emerges an image of the fabric of life.

A Sunday drive on a highway leading to an Ozark lake provides a view of a cross-section of permanent and transient residents. Huge motor coaches chock-full of senior citizens roar down U.S. 65 toward Branson. Vehicle license plates identify out-of-state tourists. Baggage and gear tell a bit more about vacationers. A young couple in a sports utility vehicle with a canoe on top and the rear seat loaded with camping gear are headed for one of the region's many float streams. A Winnebago motor home with motorcycle, lawn chairs, and water skis tied on wherever possible, driven by a fiftyish man, will seek out a lakeside camping spot where all the requisite utilities are available. A new automobile pulling a twelve-thousand-dollar bass boat weaves through traffic in a hurry to get to a boat dock in time to allow its occupants to spend a few hours on the lake before returning home. An old auto with no hubcaps and blue smoke pouring out of the exhaust pipe, loaded with inner tubes, fishing poles, and youngsters, is headed for a nearby river or creek where the occupants will spend an afternoon wading, swimming, and fishing. The new four-wheel-drive pickup equipped with West Coast mirrors, buggy-whip citizens' band radio antenna, heavy mudflaps—and with a lever action .30-30 carbine and a coiled bullwhip displayed in the rear-window gun rack—is occupied by a pleasant-looking couple who appear thirtyish. He wears a medium-brimmed cowboy hat, Levis, and a western-cut shirt; she wears stylish-cut blue jeans. They are just out for a ride in what one of my Ozark friends calls a genuine "Ozark convertible," otherwise known as a pickup truck.

Country music, the Nashville sound, popular with a wide cross-section of Americans, still attracts a cosmopolitan crowd. Twenty years ago capacity crowds were attracted to the Shrine Mosque or Hammons Student Center on the campus of Southwest Missouri State University in Springfield for concerts featuring popular country-music entertainers, such as Buck Owens, Tammy Wynette, Johnny Cash, Johny Rodriguez, or Merle Haggard. Today even more people crowd into the more than forty theaters in Branson to attend performances by a new generation of musical artists.

The appearance of the crowd has changed over the past twenty years. The pale pastel leisure suit has gone to join the beaver hat in the graveyard of sartorial style, but a few older men and a sprinkling of bright young college young women still wear overalls. There are men dressed to the teeth in Levi jeans, western-cut cowboy shirts with white piping, wide-brimmed cream-colored cowboy hats and hand-tooled cowboy boots accompanied by women in similar attire. Other men show up wearing Cargo pants with side pockets, "Dockers," or other casual trousers, open-necked shirts, and a ball cap bearing an advertisement from their hometown, a professional sports team, or one of the Branson shows they have attended. It is a crowd that is on hand wherever they play country music in the United States.

The styles of the inner city are making inroads among the younger set. Baggy pants, spiked hair, earrings (sometimes in rows) and other facial piercings, along with a noticeable amount of skin graffiti (tattoos), bespeak the influence of movies, television, print advertising, and peer pressure. Perhaps the days are past when one could spot amongst the crowd in Springfield's Shrine Mosque a matronly woman wielding a 10X rifle scope as an opera glass.

The country-music scene is but one part of Ozark life. The four-room house on a lonely gravel road is another. Yet another scene is the busy dairy farm, where days are spent cutting and putting up hay, mending fences, and milking cows. Evenings are spent keeping records and balancing accounts. Some Ozark residents live in apartment buildings and spend their days working in a shopping mall, a school, or an office building. Others live in $300,000 houses with three- and four-car garages and landscaped lawns. They spend their days managing factories, consulting and counseling, offering technical advice, and providing professional services. Evenings are spent at a country club or attending Little Theater, the civic opera, or whatever may be playing at the Juanita K. Hammons Center or the Walton Arts Center, or some other cultural venue. There are homeless people who in the summer find shelter under bridges, in abandoned buildings wherever a door is left unlocked, or in vacant wooded lots in modern-day "hobo jungles." In the winter they seek haven in shelters provided by churches and community groups. Some have mental problems; many have abused their bodies with drugs and alcohol; others have had a run of bad luck. There are numerous lifestyles in the Ozarks, perhaps almost as many as there are individuals. To try to characterize the typical Ozark resident is futile.

The stereotyped postcard hillbilly is a caricature of a lifestyle that sprang from poverty, lack of skills and education, and underemployment rather than inherent laziness or lack of ambition. There is ample evidence that Ozarkers readily accepted assistance from state and federal agencies and most of the material goods of modern America. The image of the region as a backwater area isolated from the mainstream of society overlooks the fact that some sections of the Ozarks had electrical power a generation before it came into common use in the Corn Belt or in the Plains states. The image of the carefree woodsman-farmer living in peaceful bliss in the midst of the Ozark forest is equally false. Little about poverty is picturesque.

It is the persistence of fragments of departed lifestyles that holds intrinsic fascination for visitors. Traditional speech patterns, habits of dress, agricultural practices, family ties, and community social bonds have persisted a little longer in some Ozark communities. This peculiar resistance to change reminds one of the little patches of snow that linger, protected by the shade of rocks and overhanging banks of the north slope of a hill, long after spring has come to the southern slopes. And like the melting drifts of snow, it seems unlikely that even this is retained in its original purity, but is more probably colored by experiences that have happened since it was laid down. Thus, the attraction of the Ozarks lies in its superlative scenic beauty and its cultural tradition. It is one of the few remaining places where one can not only view but also can participate in selected dwindling fragments of America's past.

The Ozarks has been washed over by several waves of immigration and change. Some sections were better suited to receive the benefits of the forces of change at various stages of time. Some individuals have succeeded more than others, and some give better promise than others. But all the land and people of the Ozarks are worth knowing, and in all cases an understanding of their history and geography goes far toward explaining their contrasting conditions. My earnest hope is that this volume will contribute to the understanding of a region that I have learned to appreciate in the same way I do my own homeland in the plains of Kansas.

NOTES

CHAPTER 1: THE OZARKS: WHAT AND WHERE

1. Rhoads Murphey, *The Scope of Geography*, 3d ed. (London: Methuen and Co., 1982), 8–22.

2. William D. Thornbury, *Regional Geomorphology of the United States* (New York: John Wiley and Sons, 1965), 202; Nevin M. Fenneman, *Physiography of the Eastern United States* (New York: McGraw-Hill Book Co., 1983), 631. Both Fenneman and Thornbury place the Shawneetown Hills in the Interior Low Plateaus province. In newspaper and popular magazine articles the Shawneetown Hills are sometimes referred to as the Illinois Ozarks. Similar rugged limestone plateau terrain in the Interior Lowlands province extends into southern Indiana.

3. There are many books dealing with cultural regions in the United states. Two respected examples are Howard W. Odum and Harry Estill Moore, *American Regionalism* (New York: Henry Holt and Co., 1938); and Raymond D. Gastil, *Cultural Regions of the United States* (Seattle: University of Washington Press, 1975). Joel Garreau's *Nine Nations of North America* (Boston: Houghton Mifflin Co., 1981) is a popular discussion of North American regions based on the "new realities of power and people."

4. The United States Bureau of the Census defines urban as places with a population of 2,500 or more. Using this definition, forty of the ninety-three counties in the Ozarks have no urban population. Twenty-four additional counties with fewer than 20,000 residents include only one or two towns that exceed 2,500 in population.

5. This topic is explored more fully in chapter 5.

6. Wilbur Zelinsky, *Cultural Geography of the United States* (Englewood Cliffs, N.J.: Prentice Hall, 1992), 13–14.

7. The term *semi-arrested frontier* is used by historians to designate regions that have lagged in their economic and cultural development. Professor Robert Flanders, emeritus professor and former director of Southwest Missouri State University's Center for Ozark Studies, has used this term to describe the late-nineteenth-century Ozarks.

8. Several explanations for the origin of the word *Ozark* have been offered. Carl O. Sauer, in his *Geography of the Ozark Highland of Missouri*, offered the most likely explanation. He explained that the abbreviation of place names was common with the French in America. The French post on the Arkansas, and the river, were shortened to Aux-Arcs or Aux-arcs (pronounced *Ozark*). The term means, literally, "to the Arkansas" or "to Arkansas Post." When travelers headed for Arkansas or Arkansas Post applied the name to the region, it soon became the accepted name. Sauer also noted that the region first received a distinctive name in its most rugged portion, although this was not the first part to be explored nor to be settled. Bill McNeil, writing in *Ozark Country* (pp. 1–2), offers other hypotheses for the origin of the word involving the French tendency to abbreviate followed by careless Anglicization. The first suggestion is that the word *Ozarks* is a corruption of the French phrase *bois aux arcs* (also, *bois d'arc*), which refers to the common hedge tree, a wood used for bows. The second suggestion is that the word stems from the American corruption of the French terms *aux Os* and *aux Arks,* which were used to refer to excursions into the territory of the Osage and Arkansas Indians. Still another postulation is that the name *Ozark* evolved from the Azoic (Precambrian) rocks exposed in the St. Francois Mountains. Given that to understand this possible origin for the name Ozarks would require a fairly sophisticated level of understanding, it is probably the least likely. See Lynn Morrow, "Ozark/Ozarks: Establishing a Regional Term," *White River Valley Historical Quarterly* (Fall 1996): 4–11, for a complete discussion of the origin and use of the term.

9. *Southwestern Bell Springfield-Branson Telephone Directory,* 1999–2000 (St. Louis, Mo.: Southwestern Bell, 1999), 117–20.

10. *Gladden, Mo. Quadrangle,* 7.5 minutes (Washington, D.C.: U.S. Geological Survey, 1967).

11. County allegiance is still strong in the Ozarks, but local residents recognize regional differences even within a given county. Townships (minor civil divisions) once had a stronger regional identity when they provided certain public services such as road maintenance. Often stream valleys—the Bull Creek and Swan Creek valleys, for example—are recognized as subregions in Christian County, Missouri.

12. George R. Stewart, *Names on the Globe* (New York: Oxford University Press, 1975), 19.

13. John W. Yolton, ed., *John Locke: Problems and Perspectives* (Cambridge: Cambridge University Press, 1969). See the State of Nature and the Nature of Man, 99–136. John Locke, an English philosopher, taught that the beauty and solitude of the natural landscape could shape man's thinking.

14. Ruth F. Hale, "A Map of the Vernacular Regions of the United States" (Ph.D. diss., St. Paul: University of Minnesota, 1971). See also Milton D. Rafferty, *Historical Atlas of Missouri* (Norman: University of Oklahoma Press, 1982), plate 33, for a discussion of the historic regions of Missouri.

15. Harold Bell Wright, *The Shepherd of the Hills* (New York: Gossett and Dunlop, 1907; reprint, McCormick-Armstrong Company, 1987).

16. John Q. Wolf, *Life in the Leatherwoods* (Fayetteville: University of Arkansas Press, 1999). John Quincy Wolf, born in 1864 in the backwoods in Izard County, Arkansas, became a banker and a prominent citizen of Batesville. His diary of life in the "Leatherwood Mountains" of Izard, Stone, and Independence counties is the basis for the book. The name for the region derives from the hardy shrub, Leatherwood (*Dirca palustris*), that grows in the area. Leatherwood Creek near Ponca, Arkansas, also derives its name from the plant. The Leatherwood is quite common along streams in northern Arkansas and southern Missouri. It is one of the earliest blooming shrubs in the spring, and its branches are so supple that they can be tied in a knot without breaking. Indians used its bark and branches to make baskets.

17. Bonnie Eagans Russell, "Life in Booger County" (Springfield, Mo.: Unpublished manuscript, 1999), 1. The manuscript is in the archives of SMSU Ozarks Studies Institute. The author listed "Booger County" among fourteen titles that had been suggested for her story of forty years living on a farm in Douglas County, Missouri. This is evidence that the name is used by Douglas County residents as well as non-residents. One can speculate that the name may have origi-nated from children's stories and admonitions like, "the booger will get you if you don't watch out," or "the booger lives down in those hills and he might get you." Certainly, Douglas County has a great wealth of hills and hollows for a "booger" to hide in.

18. Russel L. Gerlach, *Immigrants in the Ozarks: A Study in Ethnic Geography* (Columbia: University of Missouri Press, 1976), 123–25.

19. Rebecca T. Kirkendall, "Who's a Hillbilly," *Newsweek*, November 27, 1995, 22.

20. Ibid.

21. William L. Shea, "A Semi-Savage State: The Image of Arkansas in the Civil War," *Arkansas Historical Quarterly* 48 (Winter 1989): 309–28.

22. John F. Bradbury Jr., "Good Water & Wood but the Country Is a Miserable Botch: Flatland Soldiers Confront the Ozarks," *Missouri Historical Review* 90 (January 1996): 166–86.

23. Ibid., 172.

24. Foy Lisenby, "A Survey of Arkansas's Image Problem," *Arkansas Historical Quarterly* 30 (Spring 1971): 60–71.

25. The double-wide mobile home episode occurred when Governor Huckabee and his wife were interviewed by Jay Leno on the *Tonight Show*, August 13, 2000. Excerpts were shown on the NBC *Morning Show*, August 14, 2000.

26. Louis E. Brister, "The Image of Arkansas in the Early German Emigrant Guidebook: Notes on Immigration," *Arkansas Historical Quarterly* 36 (Winter 1977): 338–45.

27. Lee A. Dew, "'On a Slow Train Through Arkansaw': The Negative Image of Arkansas in the Early Twentieth Century," *Arkansas Historical Quarterly* 39 (Summer 1980): 125–35.

28. Leslie Hewes, "Cultural Fault Line in the Cherokee Country," *Economic Geography* 19 (April 1943), 136–42.

29. John S. Otto, "Reconsidering the Southern 'Hillbilly': Appalachia and the Ozarks," *Appalachian Journal* 12 (Summer 1985): 327.

30. Ibid.

31. M. J. Gilbert, *1995 Road and Handbook of the Missouri Division of the League of American Wheelmen* (Columbia, Mo.: E. W. Stephens, Printer and Binder, 1896), 112.

32. Allison Graham, "Remapping Dogpatch: Northern Media on the Southern Circuit," *Arkansas Historical Quarterly* 56 (1997): 334–40.

33. "What Orval Hath Wrought," *Time Magazine*, September 23, 1957, 11–13.

34. Otto, "Reconsidering the Southern 'Hillbilly,'" 328.

CHAPTER 2: LANDFORMS AND GEOLOGY

1. William D. Thornbury, *Regional Geomorphology of the United States* (New York: John Wiley and Sons, 1965), 262–63.

2. The preferred spelling for the mountain district in southeast Missouri is St. Francois, but the English spelling, St. Francis, has been used in some publications. The French spelling is used for the mountains, and for St. Francois County, Missouri. The English spelling is used for the St. Francis River. Both spellings are pronounced the same.

3. Geographers differentiate between mountains and hill country based on the amount of local relief and steepness of slopes. To be considered mountainous, the relief, or distance between the valley bottoms and ridgetops, must be at least 2,000 feet. Areas with steep slopes with vertical relief between 325 feet (100 meters) but less than 2,000 feet (600 meters) are considered hill districts. Using this arbitrary criterion, no part of the Ozarks is truly mountainous. Both the St. Francois Mountains and the Boston Mountains, the only parts of the region that might reasonably be considered to be mountains, have less than 2,000 feet of local relief. See Arthur N. Strahler, *Physical Geography*, 3d ed. (New York: John Wiley and Sons, 1969), 389.

4. J. Harlan Bretz, "Geomorphic History of the Ozarks of Missouri," *Missouri Geological Survey and Water Resources*, 2d Series, vol. 41 (Rolla, Mo.: 1965).

5. Nevin M. Fenneman, *Physiography of the Eastern United States* (New York: McGraw-Hill Book Co., 1938).

6. Carl O. Sauer, *The Geography of the Ozark Highland of Missouri*, Geographical Society of Chicago Bulletin no. 7 (Chicago: University of Chicago Press, 1920), 50.

7. Fenneman, *Physiography of the Eastern United States,* 642.

8. Sauer, *The Geography of the Ozark Highland of Missouri,* 50–51.

9. Fenneman, *Physiography of the Eastern United States,* 640–45.

10. Sauer, *The Geography of the Ozark Highland of Missouri,* 26.

11. Robert Marchi, park manager, H. S. Truman Dam and Reservoir. Telephone conversation with the author, September 13, 2000.

12. Milton D. Rafferty, *The Ozarks: A Guide for Fishermen, Hunters, and Tourists* (Norman: University of Oklahoma Press, 1985), 78. Compiled from lake maps and brochures.

13. Robert L. Bates and Julia A. Jackson, eds., *Glossary of Geology,* 2d ed. (Falls Church, Va.: American Geological Institute, 1980), 337.

14. Rafferty, *The Ozarks: A Guide for Fishermen, Hunters, and Tourists,* 182–98.

15. Ibid., 185–87.

16. The author served as co-chair for the national meeting and arranged for the banquet in Fantastic Caverns. National Council for Geographic Education members from throughout the United States were served dinner and local wines from the Ozark region.

17. Curtis F. Marbut, *Soil Reconnaissance of the Ozark Region of Missouri and Arkansas* (Washington, D.C.: Field Operations of the Bureau of Soils, 1913), 140.

18. Ibid., 139–41.

19. Thomas R. Beveridge, *Geological Wonders and Curiosities of Missouri* (Rolla, Mo.: Missouri Division of Geology and Land Survey, Educational Series no. 4, 1978), 335–37.

20. While visiting the Vernon Moore farm north of Ellington, Missouri, on a cloudless day in April 1967 the author crossed the dry bed of Logan Creek on a bedrock ford, but upon returning to the farm four hours later, the stream was flowing "running board" deep with runoff from rains upstream. Logan Creek is a losing stream in that section, and the normal flow of water at the ford is below the surface in the gravel and in underground channels, but overnight rains upstream had filled the subsurface drainage channels and caused the creek to rise. Mr. Moore informed the author that it was his customary practice after storms to telephone neighbors upstream to determine the amount of rainfall upstream before making a day-long trip away from the farm.

21. Sauer, *The Geography of the Ozark Highland of Missouri,* 53–56.

22. Edward M. Shepard, *U.S. Geological Survey, Water Supply and Irrigation Paper 195* (Washington, D.C.: U.S. Government Printing Office, 1907), 214.

23. Jerry Vineyard and Gerald L. Feder, *Springs of Missouri* (Rolla, Mo.: Missouri Geological Survey and Water Resources, 1982), 12.

24. Ibid., 12.

25. Sauer, *The Geography of the Ozark Highland of Missouri,* 81–82, 110.

26. J. A. Steyermark, "Phanerogamic Flora of the Freshwater Springs in the Ozarks of Missouri," in *Studies of the Vegetation of Missouri, II* (Chicago: Field Museum of Natural History, Botanical Series, vol. 9, no. 6, 1941), 481–618.

27. Vineyard and Feder, *Springs of Missouri,* 5–16.

28. Arthur B. Cozzens, "Analyzing and Mapping Natural Landscape Factors of the Ozark Province," *Transactions of the Academy of Science of Saint Louis* 30 (May 31, 1939): 50–51.

29. One of the boldest sections of the Boston Mountain front is south of Jasper, Arkansas, in Newton County. Scenic Arkansas Highway 7 traverses the escarpment in a series of switchbacks and steep grades. The overlook at the top is over 1,300 feet above the town of Jasper. See *Jasper, Ark. Quadrangle,* 7.5-minute series (Denver, Colo.: U.S. Geological Survey, 1967); *Parthenon Quadrangle,* 7.5-minute series (Denver, Colo.: U.S. Geological Survey, 1980).

30. The Burlington Escarpment is formed by the outcrop of the Burlington formation, which includes beds of very pure and massive limestones. In the western Ozarks the same rock units form the Eureka Springs Escarpment, also known as the Burlington Escarpment.

31. Curtis F. Marbut, *The Physical Features of Missouri* (Jefferson City, Mo.: Tribune Printing Co., State Printers and Binders, 1896). Extracted from *Reports of the Missouri Geological Survey* 10 (1896).

32. Sauer, *The Geography of the Ozark Highland of Missouri.*

33. James F. Collier, "Geographic Regions of Missouri," *Annals of the Association of American Geographers* 45 (1955): 368–92.

34. Thornbury, *Regional Geomorphology of the United States,* 264.

35. The Central Plateau is the more level part of the Salem Plateau delimited by both Fenneman, *Physiography of the Eastern United States,* and Thornbury, *Regional Geomorphology of the United States.* The Salem Plateau includes the hilly districts surrounding the Central Plateau without differentiating them.

36. Bretz, *Geomorphic History of the Ozarks of Missouri,* 114–15.

37. Ibid., 70–72.

38. Sauer, *The Geography of the Ozark Highland of Missouri,* 40.

39. Bretz, *Geomorphic History of the Ozarks of Missouri,* 126–28.

40. Thornbury, *Regional Geomorphology of the United States,* 56–59. See also Bretz, *Geomorphic History of the Ozarks of Missouri,* 72–76.

41. Henry Rowe Schoolcraft, early Ozarks explorer, noted that prominent balds were used by hunters and trappers as landmarks in their travels. For example, Sugarloaf Knob near Lead Hill, Arkansas, guided frontiersmen to their cabins located on Sugarloaf Prairie. See Henry R. Schoolcraft, *Rude Pursuits and Rugged Peaks: Schoolcrafts 1818–19 Ozark Journal,*

ed. Milton D. Rafferty (Fayetteville, University of Arkansas Press, 1996), 62.

42. L. E. Schroeder, "The Battle of Wilson's Creek and Its Effect upon Missouri," *Missouri Historical Review* 71 (January 1977): 159.

43. *Metropolitan Area Population Estimates for July 1, 1998.* Population Estimates Program, Population Division, U.S. Census Bureau, Washington, D.C., http://www.census.gov/population/estimate/metro-city/ma98-01.txt (June 2, 2000).

44. Sauer, *The Geography of the Ozark Highland of Missouri,* 67.

45. Ibid., 11–12, Sauer used "shut-in" to describe the places where the streams cross igneous barriers and noted that "the shut-ins isolate the valley settlements above them very effectively . . ." See also Bretz, *Geomorphic History of the Ozarks of Missouri,* 27. Bretz uses the term *narrows* to describe the shut-ins in his discussion of the geomorphology of the St. Francois Mountains. The term was also used by Henry Rowe Schoolcraft in describing the "Narrows of St. Francis" southwest of Fredericktown, Missouri, on the Little St. Francis River. See Schoolcraft, "Rude Pursuits and Rugged Peaks," 122–23. This name still appears on the *Fredericktown Quadrangle, 7.5-minute series.*

46. The French name *Courtois* is pronounced *Cour-twah* in the native tongue, but the local pronunciation is *Cur'-te-we.*

47. *Gladden, Mo. Quadrangle,* 7.5-minute series (Denver, Colo.: U.S. Geological Survey, 1958).

48. The Irish Wilderness is a poorly defined region in southern Missouri in Ripley and Oregon counties. About 1858 a small colony of poor Catholic Irish from St. Louis was settled along the tributaries of the Current and Eleven Point rivers, about twenty miles north of Arkansas, where land could be purchased for as little as twelve and a half cents an acre. The Right Reverend John Joseph Hogan, Bishop of Kansas City, and Reverend William Walsh, pastor of St. Peter's church, Jefferson City, assisted with purchasing land and making arrangements for actual settlement on land purchased and donated by the Reverend James Fox of Old Mines, Missouri. The settlement failed due to unsettled conditions during the Civil War, but the name lingers on. The Catholic Irish left no cultural imprint. See John J. Hogan, Rt. Rev., *On the Mission in Missouri: 1857–1868* (Glorieta, N.M.: Rio Grande Press, 1976), ch. 7, 8, and 12.

49. Beveridge, *Geological Wonders and Curiosities of Missouri,* 310.

50. Ibid., 193–95.

51. The Central Plateau is the central part of the Salem Plateau as defined by Thornbury's *Regional Geomorphology of the United States* and Fenneman's *Physiography of the Eastern United States.* These authors designate four main subdivisions of the Ozarks—the St. Francois Mountains, Boston Mountains, Springfield Plateau, Salem Plateau—and do not divide the Salem Plateau into smaller subdivisions.

52. Vineyard and Feder, *Springs of Missouri,* 131–33.

53. Beveridge, *Geologic Wonders and Curiosities of Missouri,* 334–44.

54. Henry Rowe Schoolcraft, *A View of the Lead Mines of Missouri Including Some Observations on the Mineralogy, Geology, Geography, Antiquities, Soil, Climate, Population and Productions of Missouri and Arkansas, and Other Sections of the Western Country* (New York: C. Wiley and Co., 1819), 248.

55. *Harrison, Ark.-Mo., 1: 250,000 Series U.S.G.S. Map* (Denver, Colo.: U.S. Geological Survey, 1985); *Russellville, Ark., 1: 250,000 Series U.S.G.S. Map* (Denver, Colo.: U.S. Geological Survey, 1985).

56. *Parthenon, Ark. Quadrangle,* 7.5-minute series (Denver, Colo.: U.S. Geological Survey, 1980); *Jasper, Ark. Quadrangle,* 7.5-minute series (Denver, Colo.: U.S. Geological Survey, 1967).

57. *Harrison, Ark.-Mo., 1: 250,000 Series U.S. G. S. Map* (Denver, Colo.: U.S. Geological Survey, 1985); *Russellville, Ark., 1: 250,000 Series U.S. G. S. Map* (Denver, Colo.: U.S. Geological Survey, 1985).

58. Marbut, *Soil Reconnaissance of the Ozark Region,* 139–41.

59. Carbonate rocks are derived from sediments formed by organic or inorganic precipitation from aqueous solution of carbonates of calcium, magnesium, or iron. Limestones are formed mainly of calcium carbonates ($CaCO_3$). Dolomites are carbonate sedimentary rocks containing more than 90 percent dolomite, or magnesium carbonate ($CaMg(CO_3)_2$). See Robert L. Bates and Julia A. Jackson, eds., *Glossary of Geology,* 2d ed. (Falls Church, Va.: American Geological Institute, 1980), 183.

60. A. G. Unklesby and Jerry D. Vineyard, *Missouri Geology: Three Billion Years of Volcanoes, Seas, Sediments, and Erosion* (Columbia: University of Missouri Press, 1992), 76. Precambrian time, which lasted about three billion years, is divided into an older part called *Archaean* and a younger part called *Proterozoic.* The oldest Ozark rocks are *Proterozoic* and are about two billion years old as determined by uranium half-life dating methods. While it is often said that the rocks of the Ozarks are the oldest in North America, the deep-seated rocks in the Canadian Shield near Hudson Bay are much older.

61. Beveridge, *Geologic Wonders and Curiosities of Missouri,* 45–48. A shut-in occurs where a stream cuts into the more resistant igneous granites and felsite porphories which form a barrier at which the stream channel narrows as a gorge, and the resistant bedrock forms rapids. Above and below the shut-in the stream flows in a wider valley underlain by softer limestones and dolomites.

62. Geologic time is divided into broad time spans called *eras,* which are subdivided into *periods.* The periods are further subdivided into *epochs.*

63. John W. Koenig, *The Stratigraphic Succession in Missouri* (Rolla, Mo.: Geological Survey and Water Resources, 1961), 13–14.

64. Ibid., 15.

65. Unklesby and Vineyard, *Missouri Geology,* 81–83.

66. Ibid., 83.

67. Koenig, *The Stratigraphic Succession in Missouri,* 19–20.

68. E. B. Branson and W. D. Keller, "Geology," in Noel P.

Gist et al., *Missouri: Its Resources, People, and Institutions* (Columbia: Curators of the University of Missouri, 1950), 21.

69. Charles van Ravenswaay, *The Arts and Architecture of German Settlements in Missouri: A Survey of a Vanishing Culture* (Columbia: University of Missouri Press, 1977), 179.

70. Unklesby and Vineyard, *Missouri Geology*, 72–73.

71. James Penick Jr., *The New Madrid Earthquake of 1811–12* (Columbia: University of Missouri Press, 1976), 6.

72. A. C. Johnston, "A Major Earthquake Zone on the Mississippi," *Scientific American* 246 (April 1982): 60–68.

73. Myron L. Fuller, *The New Madrid Earthquake* (Cape Girardeau, Mo.: Ramfre Press, 1966), 16–31.

74. The earthquake in 1967 produced tremors over a wide area. In Springfield it produced a noticeable tremble and an audible rumble similar to an underground dynamite blast. Shortly after the earthquake, the author received a telephone call from a former student, then living in St. Louis, inquiring whether the earthquake had also been felt in Springfield. The earthquake of 1975 produced no audible sound and little tremor in Springfield. However, students in the high-rise dormitories at Southwest Missouri State University reported that the buildings swayed.

75. Johnston, "A Major Earthquake Zone on the Mississippi," 60–68.

76. *Late Quaternary Faulting and Earthquake Liquefaction Features in Southeast Missouri: The Identification of New Earthquake Hazards.* Prepared for the Forty-third Annual Meeting and Field Trip of the Association of Missouri Geologists, Missouri Department of Natural Resources, Division of Geology and Land Survey, Cape Girardeau, Mo.: September 21–22, 1996, 1–44.

77. F. A. McKeown et al., *Investigations of the New Madrid, Missouri Earthquake Region* (Washington, D.C.: U.S. Geological Survey, Professional Paper 1236, 1982), 2–3.

78. Sue Hubbell, "Earthquake Fever," *New Yorker*, February 11, 1991, 84.

79. Frank G. Snyder et al., *Cryptoexplosive Structures in Missouri.* Missouri Geological Survey and Water Resources Report of Investigations no. 30 (Rolla, Mo.: 1965). Cryptoexplosion structure is a nongenetic, descriptive term that designates a roughly circular structure formed by the sudden, explosive release of energy and exhibiting intense, often localized rock deformation with no obvious relation to volcanic or tectonic activity.

80. T. W. Offield and H. A. Pohn, *Geology of the Decaturville Structure, Missouri,* U.S. Geologicial Survey Professional Paper 1042 (Washington, D.C.: U.S. Government Printing Office, 1979).

81. Unklesby and Vineyard, *Missouri Geology*, 43.

CHAPTER 3: WEATHER AND CLIMATE

1. Glenn T. Trewartha, *An Introduction to Climate,* 4th ed. (New York: McGraw-Hill Book Co., 1968), 237–52.

2. Springfield, Missouri, has the most variable climate in the United States as determined by the National Oceanographic and Atmospheric Sciences Administration.

3. Mid-latitude cyclones or low-pressure cells regularly migrate through the region from west to east. These low-pressure cells draw in winds blowing from anticyclones or high-pressure cells.

4. *Local Climatological Data, Annual Summary: Springfield, Missouri, 1999* (Asheville, N.C.: National Climatic Data Center, 1999).

5. *Storm Data Base.* National Oceanic and Atmospheric Administration, National Climatic Data Center, Asheville, N.C. December, 1999. http://www4.ncdc.noaa.gov/cgi-win/wwcgi.dllwwevent-storms (May 8, 2000).

6. *Tornadoes—Greene County.* Typewritten record of tornadoes abstracted by the author from the Springfield Weather Station records, March 2000. The record is in the possession of the author.

7. Floy W. George, *History of Webster County,* Historical Committee of the Webster County Centennial (Springfield, Mo.: Roberts and Sutter Printers, 1955), 27–33. See chapter 14 for a discussion of the Marshfield Tornado.

8. Mike O'Brien, "Storm Rips County, Kills One," *Springfield News-Leader,* December 15, 1971, A1, A3, A4.

9. Harlan Stark, "Killer Tornado Leaves Three Dead in Neosho," *Neosho Daily News,* April 25, 1975, D7, 1, 9. See also, "Special Storm Edition," *Neosho Sunday News,* April 27, 1975, 1.

10. Samuel T. Bratton, "Climate," in Noel P. Gist, ed., *Missouri: Its Resources, People, and Institutions* (Columbia: Curators of the University of Missouri, 1950), 12.

11. Jefferson Strait and Claudette Riley, "Ozarks Buried," *Springfield News-Leader,* December 14, 2000, A1, 6–9.

12. Frank Farmer, "Ozarks on Skids: Ice Paralysis Stuns Wide Area," *Springfield News-Leader,* December, 12, 1972, 1A, A2.

13. Bill Sutherland, "Holiday Storm Darkens Ozarks," *Springfield News-Leader,* December 26, 1987, A1, A7.

14. "Arkansas Ice Storm," KY-3 television, Springfield, 10:00 P.M. news report, January 16, 2000. The news report included interviews with Searcy County, Arkansas, farmers who had lost cattle in the ice storm.

15. Committee on Atmospheric Science, Assembly of Mathematical and Physical Sciences, National Research Council, *The Atmospheric Sciences: Problems and Prospects* (Washington, D.C.: National Academy of Sciences, 1977), 24–28.

16. Eugene M. Poirot, *Our Margin of Life* (Raytown, Mo.: Acres U.S.A., 1978), 27–28.

17. Photos taken by the author in September 1975, show the ampitheater and stone bridges that were built on the small lake at Monte Ne. The bridges and most of the ampitheater are normally inundated by the water of Beaver Lake.

18. Mike Penprase, "Fires Storm through Ozarks," *Springfield News-Leader,* March 9, 2000, 1B, 2B.

19. Observed by the author July 4, 1973, in the Finley River valley two miles west of the Missouri Highway 160 bridge. Colluvial deposits washed from the hillsides filled the road to the level of the second strand of barbed wire on the roadside fences. Rock rubble washed from the hillside covered five or six acres of prime bottomland. For further description of this unusual rain episode, see "Now That's What You Call a Rain," *Springfield News-Leader,* July 2, 1973, A1, A17.

20. Roger Logan, ed., *History of Boone County, Arkansas.* Boone County Historical and Railroad Society (Paducah, Ky.: Turner Publishing Co., 1998), 76–77.

21. J. E. Dunlap, "Harrison Survives '100 Year Flood' Damage," *Harrison Daily Times,* Sesquicentennial edition, July 4, 1986, 2.

22. "Engineer's Report Traces Crooked Creek Floods," *Harrison Daily Times,* Sesquicentennial edition, July 4, 1986, 4.

23. Robert Keys, "Rain Swamps City: More Than 100 People Are Chased from Their Homes," *Springfield News-Leader,* July 13, 2000, 1A, 5A-7A.

24. Trewartha, *An Introduction to Climate,* 123–33.

25. Henry R. Schoolcraft, *Rude Pursuits and Rugged Peaks: Schoolcraft's 1818–19 Ozark Journal,* ed. Milton D. Rafferty (Fayetteville: University of Arkansas Press, 1996), 50.

26. Margaret Ray Vickery, *Ozark Stories of the Upper Current River* (Salem, Mo.: Salem News, n.d.), p. 29.

27. *Farmers Almanac* (Greensburg [Westmoreland], Pa.: Snowden and M'Corkle, 1799).

28. "Ward's Weather: Heavenly," *Springfield Leader and Press,* December 11, 1977. John Ward, "The Ozark Weather Prophet," passed away on December 9, 1977. Mr. Ward based his predictions on the planets and other astronomical observations.

29. Vance Randolph, *Ozark Magic and Folklore* (New York: Columbia University Press, 1964); see ch. 2, "Weather Signs," 10–33.

30. Ibid., 18

31. Ibid., 21–22.

CHAPTER 4: INDIANS OF THE OZARKS

1. Duane Meyer, *The Heritage of Missouri: A History* (St. Louis: State Publishing Co., 1970), 30–32.

2. Universities actively engaged in archaeological excavation and research in the Ozarks include the University of Missouri, Southwest Missouri State University, and the University of Arkansas.

3. George Sabo III, ed., *Contributions to Ozark Prehistory.* Arkansas Archaeological Survey Research Series no. 27 (Fayetteville: Arkansas Archaeological Survey, 1966). This work reports on several excavations of shelters, mounds, and other sites.

4. Carl H. Chapman, *The Archaeology of Missouri,* vol. 1 and 2 (Columbia: University of Missouri Press, 1975).

5. Michael J. O'Brien and Raymond Wood, *The Prehistory of Missouri* (Columbia: University of Missouri Press, 1998).

6. O'Brien and Wood, *The Prehistory of Missouri;* Chapman, *The Archaeology of Missouri,* vol. 1; Neal H. Lopinot and Jack H. Ray, "Brief Summary of Ozarks Prehistory," *OzarksWatch* 11 (Fall 1998): 5–7; Charles R. McGimsey, "Indians of Arkansas," *Arkansas Archaeological Survey Popular Series,* 1 (1969); John P. Newton, "Paleo-Indians in the Arkansas Ozarks: A Preliminary Statement," *Arkansas Archaeologist* 16–18 (1975–1977): 89; and George Sabo III et al., *Human Adaptation in the Ozark and Ouachita Mountains,* Arkansas Archaeological Survey Research Series no. 31 (Fayetteville, Ark., 1990).

7. Neal H. Lopinot and Jack H. Ray, "Brief Summary of Ozarks Prehistory," *OzarksWatch* 11 (Fall 1998): 1.

8. Russell W. Graham and Marvin Kay, "Taphonomic Comparisons of Cultural and Noncultural Faunal Deposits at the Kimmswick and Barnhart Sites, Jefferson County, Missouri," in R. S. Laub, N. G. Miller, and D. W. Steadman, eds., *Late Pleistocene and Early Holocene Paleoecology and Archeology of the Eastern Great Lakes Region.* Bulletin of the Buffalo Society of Natural Sciences, 33 (Buffalo, N.Y.: Buffalo Society of Natural Sciences, 1988), 230–33. For further discussion of late Pleistocene vertebrates in the Ozarks, see Jeffery J. Saunders, *Late Pleistocene Vertebrates of the Western Ozark Highland.* Illinois State Museum Reports of Investigations no. 33 (Springfield: Illinois State Museum, 1977).

9. James A. Brown, *Prehistoric Southern Ozark Marginality: A Myth Exposed.* Missouri Archaeological Society Special Publication no. 6 (Columbia: Missouri Archaeological Society, 1984).

10. Chapman, *The Archaeology of Missouri,* vol. 1, 69–71.

11. Ibid., 2.

12. Carol Diaz-Granados and James R. Duncan, *The Petroglyphs and Pictographs of Missouri* (Tuscaloosa: University of Alabama Press, 2000), 5–22.

13. Chapman, *The Archaeology of Missouri,* vol. 1, 2.

14. Sabo, *Human Adaptation in the Ozark and Ouachita Mountains,* 57–60.

15. Newton, "Paleo-Indians in the Arkansas Ozarks: A Preliminary Statement," 89.

16. Gayle J. Fritz, "Prehistoric Ozark Agriculture: The University of Arkansas Rockshelter Collections" (Ph.D. diss., University of North Carolina-Chapel Hill, 1986); Gayle J. Fritz, "In Color and in Time: Prehistoric Ozark Agriculture," in *Agricultural Origins and Development in the Midcontinent.* ed. William Green (Iowa City: University of Iowa, 1994), 105–26.

17. Gary A. Wright, "Ohio Hopewell Trade," *Missouri Archaeological Society Newsletter* 269 (1973).

18. J. Mett Shippee, "Archaeological Remains in the Area of Kansas City: The Woodland Period, Early, Middle, and Late," *Missouri Archaeological Society Research Series* (1967).

19. Lee M. Adams, "Archaeological Investigations in Southwest Missouri," *Missouri Archaeologist* 20 (December 1958): 84–93.

20. Neal H. Lopinot, Jack H. Ray, and Michael D. Conner, *The 1997 Excavations at the Big Eddy Site (23CE426) in*

Southwest Missouri, Special Publication no. 2 (Springfield: Center for Archaeological Research, Southwest Missouri State University, 1998), 1–424.

21. Louis Houck, *A History of Missouri,* vol. 1 (Chicago: R. R. Donnelly and Sons Company, 1908), 178.

22. Ibid.

23. Ibid., 181–82.

24. Ibid., 179.

25. Ibid., 180.

26. Henry R. Schoolcraft, *Rude Pursuits and Rugged Peaks: Schoolcraft's 1818–19 Ozark Journal,* ed. Milton D. Rafferty (Fayetteville: University of Arkansas Press, 1996), 23, 60.

27. Principal chief John Ross, who led the main body of Cherokees over the Trail of Tears to what is today Oklahoma, was only one-eighth Cherokee. His father, Daniel Ross, was a Scotsman and his mother, Anna, was one-quarter Cherokee, the daughter of Scotsman John McDonald and a half-blood mother. See Stanley W. Hoig, *The Cherokees and Their Chiefs: In the Wake of Empire* (Fayetteville: University of Arkansas Press, 1998), 124–32.

28. John M. Faragher, "'More Motley than Mackinaw': From Ethnic Mixing to Ethnic Cleansing on the Frontier of the Lower Missouri, 1783–1833," in *Contact Points, American Frontiers from the Mohawk Valley to the Mississippi, 1750–1830,* ed. Andrew Cayton and Fredricka Teute (Chapel Hill: University of North Carolina Press, 1998), 304–5.

29. Houck, *A History of Missouri,* vol. 1, 208–19.

30. Faragher, "'More Motley than Mackinaw,'" 307.

31. Houck, *A History of Missouri,* vol. 1, 209.

32. Faragher, "'More Motley than Mackinaw,'" 310.

33. Houck, *A History of Missouri,* vol. 1, 214.

34. Ibid., 217–18.

35. Schoolcraft, *Rude Pursuits and Rugged Peaks,* 24.

36. Houck, *A History of Missouri,* vol. 1, 219.

37. Lynn Morrow, "Trader William Gilliss and Delaware Migration in Southern Missouri," *Missouri Historical Review* 75 (January 1981): 147–67.

38. Ibid., 153.

39. Ibid., 157.

40. Ibid., 159.

41. Houck, *A History of Missouri,* I, 208–19.

42. Elmo Ingenthron, *Indians of the Ozark Plateau* (Point Lookout, Mo.: School of the Ozarks Press, 1970), 115–16.

43. Jonathan Fairbanks and Clyde E. Tuck, *Past and Present of Greene County, Missouri* (Indianapolis, Ind.: A. W. Bowen and Co., 1915), 40–41.

44. Morrow, "Trader William Gilliss," 153.

45. Emmet Starr, *History of the Cherokee Indians* (Oklahoma City, 1921), 38.

46. Houck, *A History of Missouri,* vol. 1, 221.

47. Ibid., 221–22.

48. Ralph R. Rea, *Boone County and Its People* (Van Buren, Ark.: Press-Argus, 1955), 17.

49. George E. Lankford, "The Cherokee Sojourn in North Arkansas," *Independence County Chronicle* 18 (1977): 2–3.

50. Ibid., 5.

51. R. S. Cotterill, *The Southern Indians* (Norman: University of Oklahoma Press, 1954), 131. See also Grace S. Woodward, *The Cherokees* (Norman: University of Oklahoma Press, 1963), 127–29.

52. Lankford, "The Cherokee Sojourn in North Arkansas," 5.

53. Dallas T. Herndon, ed., *Centennial History of Arkansas,* vol. 1 (Chicago: S. J. Clarke Publishing Company, 1922), 63.

54. Ibid., 6.

55. Mary Ann Messick, *History of Baxter County, 1873–1973* (Mountain Home, Ark.: Mountain Home Chamber of Commerce, 1973), 63.

56. Cotterill, *The Southern Indians,* 205.

57. Lankford, "The Cherokee Sojourn in North Arkansas," 10.

58. Ibid., 13–14.

59. Ibid., 10–11.

60. *Batesville Quadrangle,* 7.5-minute series (Denver, Colo.: U.S. Geological Survey, 1943; photorevised 1981).

61. Charles C. Royce, "The Cherokee Nation of Indians," *Fifth Annual Report of the Bureau of Ethnology* (Washington, D.C.: Government Printing Office, 1887), 218.

62. J. Dickson Black, *History of Benton County, 1836–1936* (Little Rock, Ark.: International Graphics Industries, 1975), 15–17.

63. Schoolcraft, *Rude Pursuits and Rugged Peaks,* 110.

64. Josiah H. Shinn, *Pioneers and Makers of Arkansas* (Baltimore: Genealogical Publishing Company, 1967), 294.

65. Lankford, "The Cherokee Sojourn in North Arkansas," 15.

66. Messick, *History of Baxter County,* 9.

67. Lankford, "The Cherokee Sojourn in North Arkansas," 17.

68. Ingenthron, *Indians of the Ozark Plateau,* 140.

69. Schoolcraft, *Rude Pursuits and Rugged Peaks,* 78.

70. Leslie Hewes. "Cultural Fault Line in the Cherokee Country," *Economic Geography* 19 (April 1943): 136–42.

CHAPTER 5: SETTLEMENT: THE FIRST PHASES

1. Robert Flanders, "Shannon County of the Ozarks," Development Grant proposal (Southwest Missouri State University, Springfield, 1977), 10.

2. Carl H. Moneyhon, *Arkansas and the New South, 1874–1929* (Fayetteville: University of Arkansas Press, 1997), 3–40.

3. Ibid., 41–60.

4. Flanders, "Shannon County of the Ozarks," 13–14.

5. Ibid., 14.

6. Louis Houck, *A History of Missouri,* vol. 1 (Chicago: R. R. Donnelly and Sons Company, 1908), 149–62.

7. American State Papers, Public Lands, II, 182. See also John R. Henderson, "The Cultural Landscape of the French Settlement in the American Bottom" (Master's thesis, Illinois State University, 1966), 27–30.

8. Thomas B. Costain, *The Mississippi Bubble* (New York: Random House, 1955).

9. Duane Meyer, *The Heritage of Missouri: A History* (St. Louis: State Publishing Company, 1970), 33.

10. Houck, *A History of Missouri*, vol. 1, 274.

11. Ibid., 249.

12. Louis Houck, *The Spanish Regime in Missouri,* vol. 1 (Chicago: R. R. Donnelly and Sons Company, 1909), 279–80.

13. Houck, *A History of Missouri*, vol. 1, 282. Philip Francois Renault, to whom the grants were made, was a native of Picardy, France, and was appointed director-general of the mining operations of the Royal Company of the Indies. He was a man of fortune and enterprise, and a stockholder in the Royal Company. He carried on his mining operations until 1742, when he returned to France.

14. Ibid., 281.

15. Ibid., 281–82. Houck asserts that from the language of the grants, the mines had been worked prior to Renault receiving the grant in 1723.

16. Ibid., 337–39. Louis Houck suggests the founding of Old Ste. Genevieve was about 1830. Houck mentions that in 1881 an old stone well was discovered on the site of Old Ste. Genevieve, about three miles south of the present town. One of the stones in the hand-dug well bore the inscription "1832."

17. Carl Ekberg, *Colonial Ste. Genevieve: An Adventure on the Mississippi Frontier* (Gerald, Mo.: Patrice Press, 1985), 2–25. Chapter 1 includes a thorough discussion of the various theories on the founding of Ste. Genevieve. After exhaustive research, Ekberg placed the most reliable founding year at about 1750.

18. Houck, *The Spanish Regime in Missouri,* vol. 1, 53–54.

19. Ibid., 235.

20. Houck, *A History of Missouri*, vol. 1, 284.

21. Eugene M. Violette, *A History of Missouri* (Boston: D. C. Heath and Co., 1918), 12–13.

22. Morris S. Arnold, *Colonial Arkansas, 1686–1804 : A Social and Cultural History* (Fayetteville: University of Arkansas Press, 1991), 5–6.

23. Houck, *The Spanish Regime in Missouri,* vol. 1, 76–83.

24. Ekberg, *Colonial Ste. Genevieve,* 178–96.

25. Sauer, *Geography of the Ozark Highlands,* 92–93.

26. Ibid.

27. John Fraser Hart, "The Middle West," *Annals of the Association of American Geographers* 62 (June 1972): 258. During World War II the American soldiers, in order to introduce some light-hearted humor into their terrifying existence, created a mythical character, "Kilroy," and they wrote the phrase, "Kilroy was here," as graffiti on buildings, military equipment, and any other available surface. Soldiers in the vanguard wrote "Kilroy was here," to inform the following support and logistical troops that they were the followers.

28. Houck, *A History of Missouri*, vol. 2, 93.

29. Ibid., 109–24.

30. Sauer, *Geography of the Ozark Highlands,* 100–101. Landowners whose property had been damaged by the earthquakes were issued certificates which could be used to relocate on new land. Because the New Madrid certificates could be sold or exchanged for goods, they circulated from hand to hand much like money. Counterfeit certificates were produced which introduced many instances of fraud and illegal land claims. For example, at about the same time that Moses Austin, and his son Steven, were closing out their business ventures in Missouri, they attempted to claim land on the site of Little Rock with New Madrid land certificates. The land was also claimed by William Russell, a St. Louis land speculator, who's preemption claim proved to be the better claim. The Austins moved on to Texas. See David B. Gracy II, *Moses Austin: His Life* (San Antonio, Tex.: Trinity University Press, 1987), 81, 198–200.

31. Houck, *A History of Missouri*, vol. 2, 169–74.

32. Henry M. Brackenridge, *Views of Louisiana; Together with a Journal of a Voyage Up the Missouiri River, in 1811* (Pittsburgh: Cramer, Spear and Eichbaum, 1814), 131.

33. Sauer, *Geography of the Ozark Highlands,* 105–6.

34. Henry R. Schoolcraft, *A View of the Lead Mines of Missouri* (New York: Arno Press, 1972), 19–20.

35. Henry R. Schoolcraft, *Scenes and Adventures in the Semi-Alpine Region of the Ozark Mountains* (Philadelphia: Lippincott, Grambo and Co., 1853), 65–67.

36. Sauer, *Geography of the Ozark Highlands,* 107.

37. The Spanish land grants still appear on U.S.G.S. topographic maps. When the U.S. land survey was undertaken in Missouri and Arkansas, beginning in 1815 with the survey of the Fifth Principal Meridian by Prospect K. Robbins and the Arkansas Base Line by Joseph C. Brown, the surveyors left the Spanish grants intact by surveying the rectangular township and range system around them. The Spanish grants were assigned numbers to identify them. See Milton D. Rafferty, *Missouri: A Geography* (Boulder, Colo.: Westview Press, 1983), 39–48.

38. Houck, *A History of Missouri*, vol. 2, 93–94.

39. Sauer, *Geography of the Ozark Highlands,* 110. See also Walter A. Schroeder, "Settlement in Howard County, Missouri, 1810–1839," *Missouri Historical Review* 63 (1968): 2. Schroeder locates the salt spring called Boon's Lick in the NW 1/4 of Section 6, T 49 N, R 17 W, although salt seeps occur for some distance along the valley of Salt Creek. Part of the area is now in a state park. See Douglas Hurt, *Nathan Boone and the American Frontier* (Columbia: University of Missouri Press, 1998), for descriptions of activities and difficulties in the manufacture of salt.

40. Walter A. Schroeder, "Spread of Settlement in Howard County, Missouri, 1810–1839," *Missouri Historical Review* 63 (1968): 2.

41. Sauer, *Geography of the Ozark Highlands,* 110–11.

42. Ibid., 112.

43. Thomas Jefferson, *Travels in the Interior Parts of America; communicating discoveries made in exploring the Missouri, Red River and Washita, by Captains Lewis and Clark, Doctor Sibley, and Mr. Dunbar; with a statistical account of the countries adjacent. As laid before the Senate, by the President of the United States in February, 1806, and never before published in Great Britain* (London: Phillips, 1807).

44. Zebulon M. Pike, *The Journals of Zebulon Montgomery Pike, With Letters and Related Documents,* edited and annotated by Donald Jackson (Norman: University of Oklahoma Press, 1966).

45. Thomas Nuttall, *A Journal of Travels into the Arkansas Territory During the Year 1819* (Ann Arbor, Mich.: University Microfilms, 1966).

46. David B. Gracy II, *Moses Austin: His Life* (San Antonio, Tex.: Trinity University Press, 1987), 198–200.

47. Jonathan Fairbanks and Clyde E. Tuck, *Past and Present of Greene County, Missouri* (Indianapolis, Ind.: A. W. Bowen and Co., 1915), 129–30.

48. Ibid., 131.

49. Ibid., 682–84. The sinkhole spring is on Phelps Street north of the public square between Jefferson and Campbell. The spring, buried beneath a large warehouse, is identified by a marker in the building placed by the Rotary Club of Springfield in 1921.

50. Ibid., 685–86.

51. Sauer, *Geography of the Ozark Highlands,* 148–49.

52. Henry R. Schoolcraft, *Rude Pursuits and Rugged Peaks: Schoolcraft's 1818–1819 Ozark Journal,* ed. Milton Rafferty (Fayetteville: University of Arkansas Press, 1996), 116–20.

53. Workers of the Writers' Project of the Works Projects Administration in the State of Arkansas, *Arkansas: A Guide to the State* (New York: Hastings House, 1941), 385.

54. George E. Lankford, "The Cherokee Sojourn in North Arkansas," *Independence County Chronicle* 18 (1977): 6.

55. Schoolcraft, *Rude Pursuits and Rugged Peaks,* 67–68.

56. Friedrich Gerstaeker, *Wild Sports in the Far West* (Durham, N.C.: University Press, 1968), 157. Gerstaeker noted that the soil in the White River bottomland called the "Oiltrove bottom." was even more fertile than the American Bottom along the Mississippi River, after "having seen from sixty to seventy bushels of maize to the acre, and pumpkins larger than a man can lift."

57. Robert B. Walz, "Migration Into Arkansas, 1834–1880" (Ph.D. diss., University of Texas, 1958).

58. Ibid., 111.

59. Ibid., 75–76.

60. Sauer, *Geography of the Ozark Highlands,* 101.

61. Ibid., 158.

62. John J. Jones, "The Morrill Lands of the University of Missouri," *Missouri Historical Review* 51 (January 1957): 126.

63. Harbert L. Clendenen, "Settlement Morphology of the Southern Courtois Hills, Missouri, 1820–1860" (Ph.D. diss., Louisiana State University, 1973), 28–29.

64. Ibid.

65. A slipoff slope is the long, low, relatively gentle slope on the inside of a stream meander, produced on the downstream face of the meander spur by the gradual outward migration of the meander as a whole. It is located opposite of the *cutbank* where the stream cuts into the bank or bluff on the outside bend of the meander. Slip-off slopes, due to their more gradual slopes, offered the advantage of easier access in and out of deeply entrenched Ozark stream valleys.

66. Ibid., 30.

67. Grant Foreman, *The Five Civilized Tribes: Cherokee, Chickasaw, Choctaw, Creek, Seminole* (Norman: University of Oklahoma Press, 1934), 22.

68. Leslie Hewes, "Occupying the Cherokee Country of Oklahoma," *University of Nebraska Studies* (New Series, No. 57, 1978): 2–5.

69. B. B. Lightfoot, "The Cherokee Immigrants in Missouri, 1837–1839," *Missouri Historical Review* 56 (January 1962): 156.

70. Woodward, *The Cherokees,* 158–59.

71. John Ross was born October 3, 1790, at Turkeytown on the Coosa River in Alabama. Because of his small stature as a boy, he was given the Cherokee name *Tsan Usdi,* or Little Boy; later he would acquire the adult name of *Kooweskoowe,* reflecting the image of a migratory bird. His father, Daniel Ross, was a Scotsman and his mother, Anna, was one-quarter Cherokee, the daughter of Scotsman John McDonald and a half-blood mother. Ross was well educated and because of his good command of English, considerable business skills, and honesty, he gained substantial wealth and political stature among the Cherokees. Although only one-eighth Cherokee and almost entirely Caucasian in appearance, Ross was elected principal chief in 1828 under the new Cherokee constitution. He was for many years the Cherokees' leading chief and a determined opponent of removal to the West. As a young man, Ross operated a trading post called Ross's Landing at the north end of Lookout Mountain on the south bank of the Tennessee River, now in the city of Chattanooga, Tennessee. He was the leader of the Late Arrivals or Ross Party that migrated to Indian Territory (Oklahoma) over the Trail of Tears in the winter of 1838–39. John Ross died August 1, 1866, in Washington, D.C. His final burial place is at the old Cherokee cemetery (Ross cemetery) near Tahlequah, Oklahoma. See Stanley W. Hoig, *The Cherokees and Their Chiefs: In the Wake of Empire* (Fayetteville: University of Arkansas Press, 1998), 124–32.

72. Woodward, *The Cherokees,* 129 ff.

73. Ibid., 195–96.

74. Ibid., 196.

75. Lightfoot, "The Cherokee Immigrants," 156–67.

76. Tom Holm, "Cherokee Colonization in Oklahoma," *Chronicles of Oklahoma* 54 (Spring 1976): 60.

77. Woodward, *The Cherokees,* 208–9.

78. Ibid., 216.

79. Ibid., 218.

80. Foreman, *The Five Civilized Tribes,* 297–98.

81. Morris L. Wardell, *A Political History of the Cherokee Nation,* 1838–1907 (Norman: University of Oklahoma Press, 1977).

82. Josiah H. Shinn, *Pioneers and Makers of Arkansas* (Baltimore: Genealogical Publishing Company, 1967), 107.

83. Henry J. Ford, *The Scotch-Irish in America* (New York: Arno Press, 1969), 1–3.

84. Ibid., 115.

85. Ibid., 301, 305.

86. Russel Gerlach, "The Ozark Scotch-Irish," *Cultural Geography of Missouri,* ed. Michael Roark (Cape Girardeau: Department of Earth Sciences, Southeast Missouri State University, April 1983), 11–29.

87. Lynn Morrow, "A Preliminary Survey of Richwoods Township, Miller County, Missouri, 1870." Fiscal Year 1980–81 Historic Preservation Program, Center for Ozarks Studies, Southwest Missouri State University, Springfield, Missouri, 1981.

88. Ekberg, *Colonial Ste. Genevieve,* 199.

89. Schoolcraft, *A View of the Lead Mines of Missouri,* 15; Houck (*A History of Missouri,* vol. 1, 282) notes that Renault purchased 500 slaves in San Domingo, then a French colony and way station for ships sailing to Louisiana. The slaves were purchased to work the Missouri mines he expected to find. The number of slaves is probably exaggerated. The 1737 census of the Illinois Country listed a total of 314 blacks and according to earlier 1726 census Renault had only 20 black slaves. See Ekberg, *Colonial Ste. Genevieve,* 199–201.

90. Houck, *The Spanish Regime in Missouri,* I, 53–54.

91. Nuttall, *A Journal of Travels into the Arkansas Territory,* 87.

92. John S. Otto, "Slavery in the Mountains," *Arkansas Historical Quarterly* 39 (1980): 35–52.

93. S. C. Turnbo, "A Long Time Ago," Turnbo Manuacript Collection, Springfield-Greene County Public Library, Springfield, Missouri. Document 615, vol. 21, 19. Transcribed by library staff and indexed by James F. Keefe and Lynn Morrow.

94. Billy D. Higgins, "The Origins and Fate of the Marion County Free Black Community," *Arkansas Historical Quarterly* 54 (Winter 1995): 431.

95. Ibid., 432.

96. Ibid., 437.

97. C. W. Cathey, "Slavery in Arkansas" (Master's thesis, University of Arkansas, 1936), 19.

98. Higgins, "The Origins and Fate of the Marion County Free Black Community," 439.

99. Ibid., 440.

100. Cathey, "Slavery in Arkansas," 94.

101. Census Office, U.S. Department of the Interior, *Eighth Census of the U.S., 1860: Census of Population,* I, Table II, 1862; Census Office, U.S. Department of the Interior, *Ninth Census of the U.S., 1870: Census of Population,* I, Table II, 1872.

102. Carl L. Schiefer Jr., "Washington County, Arkansas: A Geography of Population Change, 1840–1970" (Master's thesis, University of Arkansas, 1976), 26–27.

103. Milton D. Rafferty, "Edward Frink Returns to Boyhood Home after 69-Year Absence," *Kanhistique* 24 (January 1999): 8–10. See also Nell Irvin Painter, *Exodusters: Black Migration to Kansas after Reconstruction* (New York: Knopf, 1977).

104. Katherine Lederer, *Many Thousands Gone: Springfield's Lost Black History* (Springfield: Missouri Committee for the Humanities and the Gannett Foundation, 1986), 13.

105. Gary Kremer, professor of history, William Woods, University, e-mail correspondence, January 29, 2001.

106. Gordon D. Morgan et al., "Black Hillbillies in the Arkansas Ozarks" (Fayetteville: A report of the Department of Sociology, University of Arkansas, 1973), 25–26.

107. Philip V. Scarpino, "Slavery in Callaway County, Missouri: 1845–1855, Part II," *Missouri Historical Review* 71 (April 1977): 267.

108. Gary Kremer, ed., *George Washington Carver in His Own Words* (Columbia: University of Missouri Press, 1987).

109. James D. Norris, *Frontier Iron: The Story of the Maramec Iron Works: 1826–1876* (Madison: State Historical Society of Wisconsin, 1964), 39.

110. Edward T. Price, "The Melungeons: A Mixed-Blood Strain of the Southern Appalachians," *Geographical Review* 41 (1951): 256–71. See also Melanie Lou Sovine, "The Mysterious Melungeons: A Critique of the Mythical Images" (Ph.D. diss., University of Kentucky, 1982), and C. S. Everett, "Melungeon History and Myth," *Appalachian Journal* 26 (Summer 1999): 358–409. Melungeons were said to be neither red nor black nor white, but possessed physical characteristics of all three racial types. Until recent scholarship contradicted such notions, it was widely accepted that these people were a distinct race with a mysterious origin. Melungeons in the Newman's Ridge area of eastern Tennessee sued successfully to be classified as white. The traditional Melungeon surnames in Tennessee are Goins, Collins, Mullins, and Gibson. No Marion County mulattoes had these surnames. However, since some of the Marion County mulattoes were light in skin color and originally came to Arkansas from Tennessee, the Melungeon designation may have been applied to them at times by their white neighbors.

111. Mary Ann Messick, *History of Baxter County, 1873–1973* (Mountain Home, Ark.: Mountain Home Chamber of Commerce, 1973), 7.

112. Morgan, "Black Hillbillies in the Arkansas Ozarks," 38.

113. Alphonso Pinkney, *Black Americans,* (Englewood Cliffs, N.J.: Prentice-Hall, 1969), 26.

114. Morgan, "Black Hillbillies in the Arkansas Ozarks," 60–67.

115. Ibid., 60.

116. "Three Negroes Lynched by Mad Mob," *Springfield Republican,* April 15, 1906, 1, 5.

117. Census Office, U.S. Department of Interior, *Eighth Census of the United States: 1860. Population of the United States: 1860* (Washington, D.C.: U.S. Government Printing Office, 1864); U.S. Bureau of the Census, *Fifteenth Census of the United States: 1930. Population,* vol. 3, pt. 1 (Washington, D.C.: U.S. Government Printing Office, 1932).

118. Morgan, "Black Hillbillies in the Arkansas Ozarks," 44–45.

119. Ibid., 47.

120. Ibid.

121. U.S. Bureau of the Census, *United States Census of Population: 1960. Characteristics of the Population, Arkansas,*

Missouri, Oklahoma, Kansas, vol. 1, (Washington, D.C.: U.S. Government Printing Office, 1963); *Black population, 1998,* www.census.gov/population/www/estimates (June 8, 2000).

122. Lederer, *Many Thousands Gone,* 13.

CHAPTER 6: SETTLEMENT: THE LATER STAGES

1. Census Office, U.S. Department of the Interior, *Eighth Census of the United States, 1860: Census of Population,* 1, table 2 (Washington, D.C.: U.S. Government Printing Office, 1862).

2. Ibid.

3. Census Office, U.S. Department of the Interior, *U.S. Census of Population, 1850* (Washington, D.C.: Robert Armstrong, Public printer, 1853).

4. U.S. Department of Interior, *Eleventh Census of the United States: 1890, Population of the United States* (Washington, D.C.: U.S. Government Printing Office, 1895).

5. Russel L. Gerlach, *Immigrants in the Ozarks: A Study in Ethnic Geography* (Columbia: University of Missouri Press, 1976), 171–77.

6. Louis Houck, *A History of Missouri,* vol. 2 (Chicago: R. R. Donnelly and Sons Company, 1908), 187–88. The Americans found the German name "Deutche" difficult to pronounce so the Germans along the Whitewater River came to be known as the Whitewater Dutch.

7. Carl O. Sauer, *The Geography of the Ozark Highland of Missouri,* Geographical Society of Chicago Bulletin no. 7 (Chicago: University of Chicago Press, 1920), 165.

8. Gottfried Duden, *Berict uber eine Rise nach den westlichen Staaten Nordamerika,* translated in English, ed. James W. Goodrich (Columbia: State Historical Society of Missouri and University of Missouri Press, 1980).

9. Sauer, *The Geography of the Ozark Highland,* 166.

10. Ibid.

11. Ibid.

12. Ibid.

13. Houck, *A History of Missouri,* vol. 1, 187–88.

14. Sauer, *The Geography of the Ozark Highland,* 167.

15. Ibid.

16. Gerlach, *Immigrants in the Ozarks,* 41–42.

17. Sauer, *The Geography of the Ozark Highland,* 171.

18. Ibid., 171.

19. Census Office, U.S. Department of Interior, *Ninth Census of the United States: 1870. The Statistics of the Population of the United States.* vol. 1 (Washington, D.C.: U.S. Government Printing Office, 1872).

20. Ibid.

21. Hildegard B. Johnson, "The Location of German Settlements in the Middle West," *Annals of the Association of American Geographers* 41 (1941): 1–41.

22. *Greater St. Louis Telephone Directory* (St. Louis, Mo.: Southwestern Bell Company, 1999), 1029–57.

23. Gerlach, *Immigrants in the Ozarks,* 48, map, 134.

24. "Immigrant Guidebook" (St. Louis, Mo.: St. Louis and San Francisco Railroad, 1895).

25. Larry A. McFarlane, "The Missouri Land and Livestock Company, Limited, of Scotland: Foreign Investment on the Missouri Farming Frontier, 1882–1908" (Ph.D. diss., University of Missouri-Columbia, 1963), 198–235.

26. Gerlach, *Immigrants in the Ozarks,* 132; map, 57.

27. Leslie Hewes, "Tontitown: Ozark Vineyard Center," *Economic Geography* 29 (April 1953): 125–43.

28. Gerlach, *Immigrants in the Ozarks,* 57.

29. Leslie Hewes, "The Oklahoma Ozarks as the Land of the Cherokees," *Geographical Review* 32 (April 1942): 276–77.

30. Carl H. Schiefer Jr., "Washington County, Arkansas: A Geography of Population Change 1840–1970" (Master's thesis, University of Arkansas, 1976), 18–22.

31. Milton D. Rafferty, *The Ozarks Outdoors: A Guidebook for Fishermen, Hunters, and Tourists* (Norman: University of Oklahoma Press, 1980); Arkansas State Planning Board and the Writers Project of the Work Progress Administration, *Arkansas: A Guide to the State* (New York: Hastings House, 1941), 290.

32. Mary Ann Messick, *History of Baxter County, 1873–1973* (Mountain Home, Ark.: Mountain Home Chamber of Commerce, 1973), 313.

33. Carolyn G. LeMaster, *A Corner of Tapestry: A History of the Jewish Experience in Arkansas, 1820s-1990s* (Fayetteville: University of Arkansas Press, 1994), 22.

34. Ibid., 22.

35. Ibid., 46.

36. Ibid., 150.

37. Ibid., 152.

38. Ibid., 296.

39. Ibid., 370.

40. Marc Cooper and Julie Hennigan, "Brief History of the Springfield, Missouri Jewish Community," *OzarksWatch* 12 (1999): 9.

41. Mara C. Cohen Ioannides, "Bearing Witness: Documenting the Jews of the Ozarks," *OzarksWatch* 12 (1999): 2.

42. "Jewish Renewal Growing in Joplin," *Springfield News-Leader,* October 15, 2000, 8B.

43. Glen Jeansonne, *Gerald L. K. Smith: Minister of Hate* (New Haven, Conn.: Yale University Press, 1988).

44. Kelly Heierman, "Winrod Trial Moves Rapidly," *Springfield News-Leader,* January 31, 2001, 1A, 4A.

45. Linda Leicht, "Nazi Symbols Painted on Gravestones," *Springfield News-Leader,* Feburary 7, 2001, 1A, 9A.

46. Donald B. Kraybill, *The Riddle of Amish Culture* (Baltimore: The Johns Hopkins University Press, 1989).

47. John A. Hostetler, *Amish Society* (Baltimore: The Johns Hopkins University Press, 1968).

48. Angela R. Seffker, "Understanding a Planners Role: A Case Study of the Amish Community in Webster County, Missouri" (Master's thesis, Southwest Missouri State University, 1992), 12–13.

49. Gerlach, *Immigrants in the Ozarks,* 54–55.

50. Milton D. Rafferty, "Persistence Versus Change in the Economy and Landscape in the Springfield, Missouri, Vicinity of the Ozarks" (Ph.D. diss., University of Nebraska, 1970), 192–200.

51. Seffker, "Understanding a Planners Role: A Case Study of the Amish Community," 24.

52. The author purchased a made-to-order Amish doll in Seymour, Missouri to fit in an Amish buggy (modified baby buggy) of his own creation. The doll was purchased in a liquor store that sold Amish-made products.

53. Rafferty, "Persistence Versus Change," 194–200.

54. Kelly Heierman, "Victim Left Behind 13 Children," *Springfield News-Leader,* January 16, 2000, 1A, 8A.

55. "Man Dies in Buggy Accident: Was Nephew of Woman Killed in a Similar Accident," *Springfield News-Leader,* August 27, 2000, 1A, 12A.

56. Peggy Stepp, "Jonathan Fairbanks: 'Mr. Springfield Public Schools'" (Master's seminar paper, Department of History, Southwest Missouri State University, 1972).

57. Ibid.

58. "The History of St. Joe," *St. Joe Headframe,* Special Edition (Bonne Terre, Mo.: St. Joe Minerals Corp., 1970).

59. William H. Burnside, *The Honorable Powell Clayton* (Conway: University of Central Arkansas Press, 1991).

60. June Westfall and Catharine Osterhage, *A Fame Not Easily Forgotten: An Autobiography of Eureka Springs* (Conway, Ark.: River Road Press, 1970), 28–29.

61. Ibid., 97–99.

62. William A. Neilson, ed., *Webster's Biographical Dictionary* (Springfield, Mass.: G. & C. Merriam Co., 1974), 317.

63. Helmi R. Tadros, "Return Migration to Selected Communities in the Ozarks: A Predominantly Rural, Economically Depressed Region" (Ph.D. diss., University of Missouri-Columbia, 1968), 7–8.

64. Harry Vanderheide, personal interview with the author, August 10, 1969. Mr. Vanderheide, a retired machinist, resided near Christian Center, Christian County, Missouri. He purchased an eighty-acre farm in the 1920s while working as a machinist in Detroit. When he lost his job during the Great Depression he moved back to the farm "to weather the Depression." He later returned to work at Detroit, but upon retirement returned to the Christian County farm.

65. Green mills are sawmills, sometimes portable, where logs are sawed into barrel staves and other rough lumber. The product of green mills go to barrel manufacturing plants or planing mills for further processing.

66. Tadros, "Return Migration to Selected Communities in the Ozarks," 97–108.

67. Ibid., 92–96.

68. U.S. Bureau of the Census, *United States Census of Population: 1960. Missouri,* 1, pt. 27 (Washington, D.C.: U.S. Government Printing Office, 1963); *Population Estimates for Places: Annual Time Series, July 1, 1990, to July 1, 1998, Missouri* (Washington, D.C.: Population Estimates Program, Population Division, U.S. Census Bureau, 1999). http://www.census.gov/population/estimates/metro-city/sets/SC98T_MO-DR.txt (May 15, 2000). The municipal boundaries of St. Louis, like many inner cities in large metropolitan areas are fixed by bordering suburbs. While the metropolitan areas continue to grow, the growth is mainly on the fringes while the inner cities tend to decline in population.

69. "Counties Ranked by Hispanic Population, July 1, 1998." Washington, D.C.: Population Estimates Program, Population Division, U.S. Census Bureau, 1999. http://www.census.gov/population/estimates/county/rank/hisp-a.txt.

70. Diane Ott, "Vietnamese Celebration Descends on Carthage: Tens of Thousands Join in the City for the Annual Religious, Cultural Event," *Springfield News-Leader,* August 27, 2000, 1A,11A.

71. Jefferson Strait, "An Incredible Appetite," *Springfield News-Leader,* August 13, 2000, 1B.

72. Ibid.

73. Kathy O'Dell, "Refugees," *Springfield News-Leader,* August 12, 2000, 1A, 8A.

74. Willard Woods, "Is Springfield Ready for Yet Another Cashew-Chicken Restaurant," *Springfield News-Leader,* June 17, 1990, 1A, 9A.

75. *Southwestern Bell Springfield-Branson Telephone Directory, 2000/2001* (St. Louis, Mo.: Southwestern Bell, May 2000), 497–506.

76. The population of the Ozarks was calculated by apportioning the population of the border counties according to the percent of land area in each county that is in the Ozark region. One hundred percent of the population of interior counties was included. The data were taken from the 1960 federal decennial census and census bureau estimates for 1998. The United States population increased from 179,323,175 in 1960 to an estimated 270,299,000 in 1998. The Ozark region increased from 1,385,726 in 1960 to an estimated 2,506,511 in 1998.

77. U.S. Census Bureau, *Census of Population, 1970,* Number of Inhabitants, U.S. Summary (Washington, D.C.: U.S. Census Bureau, 1971); *Rand McNally 1999 Commercial Atlas and Marketing Guide,* 130th ed. (Chicago: Rand McNally and Co., 1999). The central cities of Los Angeles, Houston, and Dallas increased while New York, Chicago, Boston, Philadelphia, Washington, D.C., Detroit, and Atlanta declined in population. When the Metopolitan Statistical Areas are considered, only New York declined. The other nine MSAs increased in population.

78. U.S. Bureau of the Census, *United States Census of Population: 1960. Missouri,* vol. 1, pt. 27 (Washington, D.C.: U.S. Government Printing Office, 1963), and "County Population Estimates, 1998: Missouri," Population Estimates Program, Population Division, U.S. Census Bureau. http://www.census.gov/population/estimates/county/co-99–1/99_29.txt (May 15, 2000).

79. Ravindra G. Amonker and Russel L. Gerlach, *The

Changing Population of Missouri: Trends and Patterns (Springfield: Center for Social Research, Southwest Missouri State University, 1988), 123.

80. Kathleen Morrison, "Poverty of Place: A Comparative Study of Five Rural Counties in the Missouri Ozarks" (Ph. D. diss., Memphis State University, 1999). The relationship and comparison of West Plains and Howell County with four surrounding counties is discussed at length.

81. New towns are defined as those founded after about 1900 or after the period of town founding that accompanied the construction of railroads. While most of the new towns are resort-retirement towns or towns that were moved to upland locations when the great dams were built, Viburnum, Missouri, is a new town built during the 1960s by the St. Joe Mineral Corporation to house its workers.

82. H. B. Stroud, "Problems Associated with the Regulation of Recreational Land Development in Arkansas," *Arkansas Journal of Geography* 1 (1985): 12–25.

83. *General Highway Map: Shannon County,* Scale one-half inch equals 1 mile (Jefferson City: Missouri Highway and Transportation Department, Division of Planning, 1988). See T28N, R25W. No dwellings are shown in this thirty-six square-mile U.S. Land Survey township. Other large areas in Shannon County, like many other heavily forested Ozark counties, are also sparsely settled.

84. U.S. Bureau of the Census, *United States Census of Population: 1960. Missouri,* vol. 1, pt. 27 (Washington, D.C.: U.S. Government Printing Office, 1963), and "County Population Estimates, 1998: Missouri," Population Estimates Program, Population Division, U.S. Census Bureau. http://www.census.gov/population/estimates/county/co-99–1/99_29.txt (May 15, 2000).

85. Milton D. Rafferty, "Population and Settlement Changes in Two Ozark Localities," *Rural Sociology 38* (Spring 1973): 46–56.

86. C. O. Bridges, retired stock farmer, Ozark, Missouri. Personal interview with the author, August 24, 1968. Mr. Bridges accompanied the author while driving the roads of Linn Township and provided employment information and approximate length of tenancy for the occupants of each house.

87. Harry Vanderheide, retired machinist, Ozark, Missouri. Personal interview with the author, August 10, 1968.

88. Brooks R. Blevins, "Fallow Are the Hills: A Century of Rural Modernization in the Arkansas Ozarks" (Master's thesis, Auburn University, 1994), 69–72.

89. Milton D. Rafferty, "Field Reconnaissance of Settlement Patterns in Linn Township, Christian County, Missouri, 1992" (Unpublished research paper. Department of Geography, Geology, and Planning, Southwest Missouri State University, December, 1992).

90. Earl W. Kersten Jr., "Changing Economy and Landscape in a Missouri Ozarks Area," *Annals of the Association of American Geographers 48* (December 1958): 398–418.

91. Milton D. Rafferty and Dennis Hrebec, "Logan Creek: A Missouri Ozark Valley Revisited," *Journal of Geography 72* (October 1973): 7–17.

CHAPTER 7: THE CIVIL WAR AND ITS CONSEQUENCES

1. Duane Meyer, *The Heritage of Missouri: A History* (St. Louis: State Publishing Co., 1970), 357–59.

2. Ibid., 358.

3. Eugene M. Violette, *A History of Missouri* (Boston: D. C. Heath and Co., 1918), 308.

4. R. Halliburton Jr. "Origins of Black Slavery among the Cherokees," *Chronicles of Oklahoma* 52 (Winter 1974–1975): 483–96.

5. Ibid., 483–84.

6. Violette, *A History of Missouri,* 278–79.

7. William Baxter, *Pea Ridge and Prairie Grove; or, Scenes and Incidents of the War in Arkansas* (Fayetteville: University of Arkansas Press, 2000), 69–70.

8. See Robert E. Shelhope, *Sterling Price: Portrait of a Southerner* (Columbia: University of Missouri Press, 1971), 116–19, for Price's pro-slavery and pro-union views.

9. Isaac Murphy, a Pennsylvania Irishman, born near Pittsburgh, Pennsylvania, October 16, 1799, lived most of his life in Washington and Madison counties in Arkansas. He taught school, practiced law, and served in the state Senate. He was a strong Unionist, as were the majority of his constituents. In February 1861 he was elected by Madison County voters as their representative to the convention to vote for or against secession. He got all but 114 votes out of more than 1,000 votes cast. He displayed courage, strength, sound common sense, scrupulous honesty, and determination long before he became Arkansas's eighth governor under the Amnesty and Reconstruction proclamation of President Abraham Lincoln, December 8, 1863. At the end of his term as governor, Murphy went back to Madison County where he purchased two small farms, one for $30 and the other for $195. He died September 8, 1882. See John I. Smith, *The Courage of a Southern Unionist* (Little Rock, Ark.: Rose Publishing Co., 1979).

10. Ralph Wooster, "The Arkansas Secessionist Convention," *Arkansas Historical Quarterly* 13 (1954): 183–84.

11. Thomas A. Belser, "Military Operations in Missouri and Arkansas, 1861–1865" (Ph.D. diss., Vanderbilt University, 1958), 221–22.

12. Ibid., 503–5.

13. W. Craig Gaines, *The Confederate Cherokees: John Drew's Regiment of Mounted Rifles* (Baton Rouge: Louisiana State University Press, 1989), 13.

14. Daniel E. Sutherland, "Guerrillas: The Real War in Arkansas," in *Civil War in Arkansas: Beyond Battles and Leaders,* ed. Anne J. Bailey and Daniel E. Sutherland (Fayetteville: University of Arkansas Press, 2000), 133–54. Reprinted from the *Arkansas Historical Quarterly* 52 (Autumn 1993): 257–85.

15. Sterling Price was born in Virginia, in 1809, and was a graduate of Hampden-Sydney College. He was twenty-two years old when he migrated to Missouri. He ran for a seat in the General Assembly of Missouri as a Democrat and served from 1836 to 1844, when he was elected to Congress. After serving with distinction in the Mexican War, Price returned to Missouri and reentered politics and was elected governor in 1852. In politics he was a conservative and an ardent Union man when elected president of the convention to decide on the issue of Missouri's succession from the government of the United States (Belser, *Military Operations in Missouri and Arkansas,* 75). He was appointed brigadier general of the state militia and was highly regarded by his troops, but Jefferson Davis, president of the Confederate States of America, called him, simply, "the vainest man I ever met" (Albert Castel, *General Sterling Price and the Civil War in the West* [Baton Rouge: Louisiana State University Press, 1968], 90). Price was a striking figure "over six-feet two inches in stature, of massive proportions, but easy and graceful in his carriage and his gestures . . . his hair and whiskers which he wore in the old English fashion, were silver white; his face was ruddy and very benignant, yet firm in its expression . . . his voice was clear and ringing, and his accentuation singularly distinct" (Dabney H. Maury, "Recollections of the Elkhorn Campaign," *Southern Historical Society Papers,* 2 [1876]: 181–83.)

16. Robert U. Johnson and Clarence C. Buel, eds., *Battles and Leaders of the Civil War* (Secaucus, N.J.: Castle, 1887), vol. 1, 269–70.

17. Ibid.

18. Belser, "Military Operations in Missouri and Arkansas," 127.

19. Ibid., 131. See also Albert Castel, *General Sterling Price and the Civil War in the West* (Batton Rouge: Louisiana State University Press, 1968), 33.

20. Ibid., 14–15.

21. John Gould Fletcher, *Arkansas* (Chapel Hill: University of North Carolina Press, 1947), 150.

22. Nathaniel Lyon, a native of Connecticut, was of Puritan stock, and a graduate of West Point, eleventh in the class of 1841. Unlike most "Old Army" officers, he was a staunch abolitionist and a strong believer in national sovereignty. Although his political beliefs may have made him unpopular in officers messes, he was a splendid soldier, and extremely energetic. He was a veteran of both the Seminole and the Mexican wars, and as a career officer, he continued in active service on the frontier. He was forty-two years old when he arrived in St. Louis with reinforcements for the arsenal. See Christopher Phillips, *Damned Yankee: The Life of General Nathaniel Lyon* (Columbia: University of Missouri Press, 1990).

23. Claiborne Fox Jackson was born in Kentucky in 1806, but moved to Missouri in 1822. He gained military experience serving in the Black Hawk War and was a prominent politician for more than twenty-five years, serving in both houses of the state Assembly, and as a member of the constitutional convention. He resigned as state bank commissioner to accept the nomination for governor. Shortly after he led a party of Missourians into Kansas to vote in the territorial elections, in 1855, he took the oath of office for governor of the state of Missouri. Although a Douglas Democrat, Jackson was an outspoken advocate for the South. See Christopher Phillips, *Missouri's Confederate, Claiborne Fox Jackson and the Creation of Southern Identity in the Border West* (Columbia: University of Missouri Press, 2000).

24. Thomas L. Snead, *The Fight for Missouri* (New York: Charles Scribner and Sons, 1886), 196–97.

25. Franz Sigel was an educated German, a graduate of the military college at Carlsruhe, who had served as chief adjutant in the army of the Grand Duke of Baden. He joined the German revolutionaries in 1847, and after their defeat by Prussian forces, Sigel fled to the United States, settling in St. Louis as a teacher of mathematics. Because he had great influence with the German people of that city, he was selected by Congressman Francis Blair and Col. Nathaniel Lyon to organize German regiments for the Union army. Sigel was given command of one of the regiments. His experience in European warfare gave him a great military reputation, which he did not live up to in the American Civil War. See Stephen Engle, *Yankee Dutchman: The Life of Franz Sigel* (Fayetteville: University of Arkansas Press, 1993).

26. Belser, "Military Operations in Missouri and Arkansas," 116–22.

27. Ibid., 122.

28. Ibid., 107–9.

29. Ibid., 50–51.

30. Jesse N. Cypert, "Secession Convention," in *Publications of the Arkansas Historical Association,* vol. 1 (1906): 319. Cypert was, in 1906, one of the four surviving delegates.

31. Castel, *General Sterling Price and the Civil War in the West,* 33–34.

32. Benjamin McCulloch was born in Rutherford County, Tennessee, and grew up in Dyer County, where he was known as an expert hunter, raftsman and flatboatman. In 1835 he joined Colonel David Crockett's expedition for the relief of Texas, but fell ill and was not in the Alamo when it fell. After recovering, he joined Houston's army and commanded a gun in the artillery at the battle of San Jacinto. Following the war, he served for a time in the Congress of the Republic of Texas. When Texas joined the Union, McCulloch was appointed to command all state military units west of the Colorado River. He served with distinction in the Mexican War and earned the rank lieutenant colonel. McCulloch was called "Ben" or "Black Ben" by his troops. Belser, *Miltitary Operations in Missouri and Arkansas,* 57–58.

33. The Battle of Wilson's Creek was called the Battle of Oak Hills by Confederates. See Gaines, *The Confederate Cherokees,* 9.

34. Johnson and Buel, *Battles and Leaders of the Civil War,* vol. 1, 303.

35. N. Bartlett Pearce, "Arkansas Troops in the Battle of Wilson's Creek," in *Battles and Leaders of the Civil War,* I, ed.

Robert U. Johnson, and Clarence C. Buel (Secaucus, N.J.: Castle, 1887), 303.

36. Ibid., 306.

37. Belser, *Military Operations in Missouri and Arkansas,* 1.

38. William G. Piston, "'Springfield is a Vast Hospital,': Dead and Wounded at the Battle of Wilson's Creek," *Missouri Historical Review* 93 (July 1999): 345–66.

39. Belser, *Military Operations in Arkansas,* 156–57.

40. Gaines, *The Confederate Cherokees,* 9.

41. Castel, *General Sterling Price,* 49.

42. Ibid., 50–56.

43. Ibid., 62–65.

44. Major General Earl Van Dorn was the Confederate president Jefferson Davis's third choice for the trans-Mississippi command. He was a Mississippi-born West Pointer who, in addition to being a personal friend of the Confederate President, had a high military reputation, considerable experience in the West, a desire for an independent command, and boldness that bordered on rashness. He proved to be popular with the Missouri Militia, and acceptable to Price, although he would have liked to have had the command (Castel, *General Sterling Price,* 67–68).

45. Belser, "Military Operations in Missouri and Arkansas," 259.

46. In Cherokee Nation politics Stand Watie headed the Watie party, or Southern Rights party, in opposition to the Ross party. Watie earned considerable respect as a military leader during the Civil War. He preformed well as the leader of a Cherokee unit at Pea Ridge and in later battles. He was elevated to the rank of brigadier general in the Confederate army on June 15, 1864. After Lee's surrender at Appomattox on April 9, 1865, Watie held off from surrender until June 23, 1865. By this action, he went down in history as the last Confederate general to give up the fight. Grace S. Woodward, *The Cherokees* (Norman: University of Oklahoma Press, 1963), 288–89.

47. Woodward, *The Cherokees,* 280.

48. Thomas Carmichael Hindman was born in Tennessee in 1818 and studied law there before moving to Mississippi in 1845, where he practiced law. After serving in the Mexican war he moved to Helena, Arkansas where he practiced law and was elected to congress. An ardent secessionist, Hindman resigned from congress and returned to Helena when Arkansas joined the Confederacy. He helped raise the Second Arkansas Infantry regiment and was elected colonel in June 1861. After service in northeastern Arkansas and southeastern Missouri he was promoted to brigadier general in September 1861. Following distinguished service at Shiloh, he was promoted to major general. Belser, "Military Operations in Missouri and Arkansas," 370–71.

49. James Gilpatrick Blunt was born in Maine and had served five years as a common seaman by the time he was twenty. Having overcome the sea fever, he studied medicine and graduated from Starling Medical College, Columbus, Ohio in 1849. He practiced medicine in Ohio until 1856 when he

moved near Greeley, Kansas. He became deeply interested in the antislavery movement and the Kansas crisis and was one of the first to enlist when the Civil War broke out. Within a short time he was appointed colonel of the Third Kansas Volunteers, and in April, 1862, he was promoted to brigadier general and placed in command of the Department of Kansas (Belser, "Military Operations in Missouri and Arkansas," 409).

50. Belser, "Military Operations in Missouri and Arkansas," 464–65.

51. Ibid., 474.

52. *War of the Rebellion: A Compilation of the Official Records of the Union and Confederate Armies.* 70 volumes in 128 parts, atlas (Washington, D.C.: Government Printing Office, 1880–1901).

53. Castel, *General Sterling Price and the Civil War in the West,* 197.

54. Ibid., 198–99.

55. Ibid., 200.

56. Belser, *Military Operations in Missouri and Arkansas,* 699.

57. Castel, *General Sterling Price,* 210.

58. Belser, *Military Operations in Missouri and Arkansas,* 705.

59. Ibid., 710.

60. Castel, *General Sterling Price,* 226.

61. Belser, *Military Operations in Missouri and Arkansas,* 739.

62. Richard L. Brownlee II, "Guerrilla Warfare in Missouri, 1861–1865" (Ph.D. diss., University of Missouri, 1955), 9–20.

63. George E. Lankford, "Jayhawker Narratives as Treasure Legends," *Kentucky Folklore Record* 32 (1986): 111.

64. Leo E. Huff, "Guerrillas, Jayhawkers and Bushwhackers in Northern Arkansas during the Civil War, *Arkansas Historical Quarterly* 24 (Summer 1965): 129.

65. Ibid., 127–28.

66. Daniel E. Sutherland, "Guerrillas: The Real War in Arkansas," in *Civil War in Arkansas: Beyond Battles and Leaders,* ed. Anne J. Bailey and Daniel E. Sutherland(Fayetteville: University of Arkansas Press, 2000), 257. Reprinted from the *Arkansas Historical Quarterly* 52 (Autumn 1993).

67. Huff, "Guerrillas, Jayhawkers and Bushwhackers," 127.

68. Ibid., 132–33.

69. Ibid., 132.

70. Kenneth C. Barnes, "The Williams Clan: Mountain Farmers and Union Fighters in North Central Arkansas," *Arkansas Historical Quarterly* 52 (Autumn 1993): 287.

71. Ibid., 286–317.

72. Ibid., 311–12.

73. Michael A. Hughes, "Wartime Gristmill Destruction in Northwest Arkansas and Millitary Farm Colonies," in *Civil War Arkansas: Beyond Battles and Leaders,* ed. Anne J. Bailey and Daniel E. Sutherland (Fayetteville: University of Arkansas Press, 2000), 38.

74. Baxter, *Pea Ridge and Prairie Grove,* 24–31.

75. Ibid., 61.

76. Duane Schultz, *Quantrill's War: The Life and Times of William Clarke Quantrill, 1837–1865* (New York: St. Martin's Press, 1996), 255–59.

77. Lucille M. Upton, *Bald Knobbers* (Caldwell, Idaho: Caxton Printers, Ltd., 1939), 26–27.

78. Barnes, "The Williams Clan," 294.

79. Margaret Gilmore Kelso, "Margaret Gilmore Kelso: A Memory Story, Part II, Bushwhackers and Wilson's Creek," *OzarksWatch* 4 (Spring/Summer 1991), 7.

80. Ibid.

81. Ibid., 8.

82. Baxter, *Pea Ridge and Prairie Grove,* 99–100.

83. Ibid., 17–18.

84. Carl H. Moneyhon, *The Impact of the Civil War and Reconstruction on Arkansas* (Baton Rouge: Louisiana State University Press, 1994), 176–77.

85. John F. Bradbury Jr., "'Buckwheat Cake Philanthropy': Refugees and the Union Army in the Ozarks," *Arkansas Historical Quarterly* 3 (Autumn 1998): 234.

86. Kelso, "Margaret Gilmore Kelso: A Memory Story, Part II," 9.

87. Bradbury, "'Buckwheat Cake Philanthropy': Refugees and the Union Army in the Ozarks," 239.

88. Ibid., 236.

89. Ibid., 238.

90. Ibid., 240–42.

91. Elmo Ingenthron, *The Land of Taney* (Point Lookout, Mo.: School of the Ozarks Press, 1974), 227.

92. Jonathan Fairbanks and Clyde Edwin Tuck, *Past and Present of Greene County, Missouri,* vol. 1 (Indianapolis, Ind.: A. W. Bowen and Company, 1915), 377.

93. Ibid., 225–26.

94. Ibid., 226.

95. The Bald Knobbers were active in both Christian and Taney counties. Harold Bell Wright incorporated the Bald Knobbers as a theme in his popular novel, *Shepherd of the Hills,* thereby ensuring longevity for the name. The story of the Shepherd of the Hills played in the outdoor Shepherd of the Hills Theater on highway 76 west of Branson is still dramatized during the tourist season. The dramatic scenes of Bald Knobber activity are crowd pleasers. For the story of the Bald Knobbers, see L. M. Upton, *Bald Knobbers.*

96. Ingenthron, *The Land of Taney,* 231.

97. L. M. Upton, *Bald Knobbers,* 233–43.

98. J. Trenton Kostbade, "Geography and Politics in Missouri" (Ph.D. diss., University of Michigan, 1957), 212–16.

99. Robert S. Wiley, *Dewey Short: Orator of the Ozarks* (Cassville, Mo.: Litho Printers and Bindery, 1985).

100. Ibid., 32.

101. Ibid., 137.

102. Laura B. Menner, "Merritt Ends Pierpont's Reign," *Springfield News-Leader,* August 9, 2000, 1A, 4A. After a hard-fought primary election, the newly nominated Republican candidate handily defeated the Democrat nominee in the general election, 8–9.

103. Denny Pilant, ed., *Reinventing Missouri Government: A Case Study in State Experiments at Work* (Fort Worth, Tex.: Harcourt Brace College Publishers, 1994).

104. Patricia W. Lockwood, "The Legacy of Caleb Starr," *Chronicles of Oklahoma* 61 (Fall 1983): 288–307.

105. "Moonshine" and "white lightning" are vernacular names for illicitly distilled alcohol. They are generic names that include several illegal alcoholic beverages including whiskey. Since producers did not license the stills and pay taxes on their products, the stills were hidden away in remote locations. Often the distilling and transport of the alcohol were at night by the light of the moon. Hence the product was called "moonshine" and the manufacturing process was known as "moonshining."

106. "Mobile Meth Lab Found in SUV," *Springfield News-Leader,* January 13, 2001, 1B.

107. The list of news stories was copied from the SWAN electronic library catalog system at Southwest Missouri State University, September 24, 2000.

108. Laura Bauer Menner, "Missouri Town Worried, Intrigued," *Springfield News-Leader,* December 31, 1999, 11A. See also Laura Bauer Menner, "Police Scour Rural Fields for Carjacking Suspect," *Springfield News-Leader,* December 31, 1999, 1A, 11A; Laura Bauer Menner, "Fugitive Linked to Second Death; Manhunt Continues," *Springfield News-Leader,* January 2, 2000, 1A, 12A.

CHAPTER 8: TRANSPORTATION, TECHNOLOGY AND CULTURAL TRANSFORMATION

1. Duane Huddleston, Sammie Cantrell Rose, and Pat Taylor Wood, *Steamboats and Ferries on the White River: A Heritage Revisited* (Fayetteville: University of Arkansas Press, 1998), 3–4.

2. Ibid.

3. Ibid., 9.

4. Duane Meyer, *The Heritage of Missouri: A History* (St. Louis: State Publishing Company, 1970), 245.

5. Ibid., 247.

6. Floyd C. Shoemaker, *Missouri and Missourians: Land of Contrasts and People of Achievements,* vol. 2 (Chicago: Lewis Publishing Company, 1943), 598.

7. Huddleston, Rose, and Wood, *Steamboats and Ferries on the White River,* 67.

8. Meyer, *The Heritage of Missouri,* 247.

9. Shoemaker, *Missouri and Missourians,* vol. 2, 598.

10. James D. Norris, *Frontier Iron: The Story of the Maramec Iron Works, 1826–1876* (Madison: State Historical Society of Wisconsin, 1972), 96.

11. Ibid., 99.

12. Ibid., 101.

13. Eugene M. Violette, *A History of Missouri* (New York: D. C. Heath and Co., 1918), 185.

14. Grace S. Woodward, *The Cherokees* (Norman: University of Oklahoma Press, 1963), 217.

15. Huddleston, Rose, and Wood, *Steamboats and Ferries on the White River,* 72.

16. Ibid., 69.

17. Ibid., 89. Includes a map of landings in 1876.

18. Ibid., 37.

19. Ibid., 86.

20. Ibid., 51–57.

21. Ibid., 112–13.

22. Ibid., 131.

23. Ibid., 125.

24. A. C. McGinnis, "Pearl Search Began in 1897," *Independence County Chronicles* 9 (July 1968): 26.

25. Elmo Ingenthron, *The Land of Taney* (Point Lookout, Mo.: School of the Ozarks Press, 1974), 308.

26. Hugh P. Williamson, "Restrictions and Rights of the Missouri Sportsman" (Missouri Department of Conservation Publication, n.d.).

27. Milton D. Rafferty, *Historical Atlas of Missouri* (Norman: University of Oklahoma Press, 1982), plate 67.

28. A. L. Story, owner of Wolf Island Farms. Personal interview with the author, May 15, 1994.

29. Shoemaker, *Missouri and Missourians*, vol. 2, 757–61.

30. Ibid., 802.

31. Ibid., 752.

32. Nancy H. Self, "The Building of the Railroads in the Cherokee Nation," *Chronicles of Oklahoma* 49 (summer 1971): 180–205.

33. Jonathan Fairbanks and Clyde E. Tuck, *Past and Present of Greene County, Missouri* (Indianapolis, Ind.: A. W. Bowen and Company, 1915), 178–82.

34. Dallas County Historical Society, *The Dallas County, Missouri Story* (Cassville, Mo.: Litho Printer, 1974), 221–23.

35. For additional information on the complex corporate history of various Ozark railroads during their growth, expansion and eventual consolidation the reader is referred to a massive collection of documents and records held by the University of Missouri-Rolla. See Brenda Brugger, compiler, *Guide to the Historical records of the Frisco: St. Louis-San Francisco Railway Comapny and its Predecessor, Subsidiary and Constituent Companies* (Rolla: University of Missouri Western Historical Manuscript Collection, 1989).

36. Rafferty, *Historical Atlas of Missouri*, plate 63.

37. *Biennial Report of the Public Service Commission, 1943–1944* (Jefferson City: Missouri Public Service Commission, 1944), 52.

38. Ozark Greenways, Incorporated, a not for profit group, has established five greenway trails in the Springfield vicinity: Frisco Highline Trail, Sac River Trail, Volunteer Nature Trail, Galloway Creek Greenway, and South Creek-Wilson's Creek Greenway.

39. Christian County History Committee, *Christian County: Its First Hundred Years* (Ozark, Mo.: Christian County Centennial, 1959), 152.

40. Ibid., 17.

41. Delbert Cook, "Abandoned Railroads in Missouri" (Research Paper, Department of Geography and Geology, Southwest Missouri State University, 1977), 6.

42. *Biennial Report of the Public Service Commission, 1953–1954,* 39–40.

43. Ibid., 9.

44. Rose F. Cramer, *Wayne County, Missouri* (Cape Girardeau, Mo.: Ramfre Press, 1972), 282–92.

45. Norbert Sacklet, "Trackage Abandonment, 1948–1974" (Unpublished notes held by the Missouri Public Service Commission, 1974).

46. Ibid.

47. Clifton E. Hull, *Shortline Railroads of Arkansas* (Norman: University of Oklahoma Press, 1969), 53.

48. Lawrence R. Handley, "A Geography of the Missouri and North Arkansas Railroad" (Master's thesis, University of Arkansas-Fayetteville, 1973). Handley's thesis records the full development, decline and demise of the railroad. See also Hull, *Shortline Railroads of Arkansas.*

49. Lawrence R. Handley, "Settlement across Northern Arkansas as Influenced by the Missouri and North Arkansas Railroad," *Arkansas Historical Quarterly* 33 (Winter 1974): 273–92.

50. Ibid.

51. Hull, *Shortline Railroads of Arkansas,* 242–47.

52. Ibid., 250.

53. Ibid., 351–52.

54. Ibid., 254–56.

55. Ibid., 354.

56. Mark Wiehe, "Abandon 700 Miles of Missouri Rails?" *Today's Farmer* 71 (November 1979): 6–7.

57. *Missouri Rail Plan 1995 Update* (Jefferson City: Missouri Highway and Transportation Department, Transportation Division, June 1995), 1–1.

58. Wiehe, "Abandon 700 Miles of Missouri Rails?" 8.

59. *Missouri Rail Plan 1995 Update,* 2–23.

60. "Midwest Regional Rail System: A Transportation System for the Twenty-first Century," Missouri Department of Transportation, Jefferson City. http://www.modot/state.mo.us./ trans/mwrailsum.pdf

61. David Moser et al., *Missouri's Transportation System: Condition, Capacity, and Impediments to Efficiency* (Jefferson City, Mo.: Office of Administration, Division of Budget and Planning, 1976), 155–61.

62. Michal Dale, "Katy Trail Runs between Sedalia and St. Charles," *Springfield News-Leader,* July 27, 1998, 8B.

63. "Ozark Greenways Going for the Gold: Group to Start Fund Campaign to Finish Off the Frisco Trail," *Springfield News-Leader,* April 27, 2000, 3B.

64. G. C. Broadhead, "Early Missouri Roads," *Missouri Historical Review* 8 (January 1914): 90.

65. George A. Makris, "A Survey of Transportation in the State of Arkansas" (Master's thesis, University of Arkansas, 1933), 5–6.

66. Houck, *History of Missouri,* vol. 2, 150–53.

67. Houck, *History of Missouri,* vol. 3, 163–64.

68. Fairbanks and Tuck, *Past and Present of Greene County, Missouri,* 145–46.

69. Shoemaker, *Missouri and Missourians,* vol. 1, 588. See also Fairbanks and Tuck, *Past and Present of Greene County, Missouri,* 43.

70. Fairbanks and Tuck, *Past and Present of Greene County, Missouri,* 186.

71. Odie B. Faulk, *Muskogee: City and County* (Muskogee, Okla.: Five Civilized Tribes Museum, 1982), 23, 41. West of Joplin, one branch of the Texas Road turned south through the Cherokee country, passing through Fort Gibson and Muskogee on the way to Texas. The other branch continued west skirting both the Ozarks and the Ouachita Mountains. Today, the latter route is followed closely by U.S. 69.

72. Lynn Morrow, "Trader William Gilliss and Delaware Migration in Southern Missouri." *Missouri Historical Review* 75 (January 1981): 154–55.

73. James D. Norris, *Frontier Iron: The Story of the Maramec Iron Works, 1826–1876* (Madison: State Historical Society of Wisconsin, 1964), 103–5.

74. Sauer, *The Geography of the Ozark Highland,* 127. Plank roads were common in the pre-railroad era. Because of the cost of construction and maintenance, plank roads were usually toll roads. When railroads were built the plank roads were soon abandoned. See Shoemaker, *Missouri and Missourians,* vol. 2, 509. The forty-two-mile plank road constructed from Iron Mountain to Ste. Genevieve to haul iron and lead ore was the longest in the Ozarks. Plank and stump roads were also used as the first hard-surfacing for city streets. See Fairbanks and Tuck, *History of Greene County, Missouri,* 699.

75. Ibid., 127.

76. Shoemaker, *Missouri and Missourians,* vol. 2, 509.

77. Arthur B. Cozzens, "The Iron Industry of Missouri," *Missouri Historical Review* 35 (October–July 1940–1941): 532–34.

78. These early state road maps and their survey notes are in the Missouri State Archives, Jefferson City.

79. Broadhead, "Early Missouri Roads," 90–91.

80. David L. Loberg, "The Mapping of Arkansas: 1541–1900" (Master's thesis, University of Arkansas, 1976), 85.

81. Houck, *A History of Missouri,* vol. 1, 227.

82. Terry G. Jordan, "Population Origins in Texas, 1850," *Geographical Review* 59 (1969): 83–103.

83. Descriptions of the early landscape and human occupancy along the Natchitoches Trace are documented in three works: George W. Featherstonhaugh, *Excursion Through the Slave States, From Washington on the Potomac to the Frontier of Mexico; With Sketches of Popular Manners and Geological Notices.* (New York: Negro Universities Press, 1968); Henry Rowe Schoolcraft, *Rude Pursuits and Rugged Peaks: Schoolcraft's 1818–1819 Ozark Journal,* ed. Milton Rafferty (Fayetteville: University of Arkansas Press, 1996); Frederich Gerstaeker, *Wild Sports in the Far West* (Durham, N.C.: University Press, 1968).

84. Featherstonhaugh, *Excursion Through the Slave States,* 8.

85. John Gould Fletcher, *Arkansas* (Chapel Hill: University of North Carolina Press, 1947), 80–81.

86. Shoemaker, *Missouri and Missourians,* vol. 1, 608–9.

87. Robert A. Campbell, *Campbell's Gazetteer of Missouri* (St. Louis: R. A. Campbell, 1875), 304.

88. *History of Dade County and Her People* (Greenfield, Mo.: Pioneer Historical Company, 1917), 246.

89. Lee A. Dew, "From Trails to Rails in Eureka Springs," *Arkansas Historical Quarterly* 41 (Autumn 1982): 203–4.

90. James E. Vance Jr., *Capturing the Horizon* (New York: Harper and Row, Publishers, 1986), 485–87.

91. Ibid., 496.

92. M. J. Gilbert, *1995 Road and Handbook of the Missouri Division of the League of American Wheelmen* (Columbia, Mo.: E. W. Stephens, Printer and Binder, 1896), 216–17.

93. "Stepping Stones Over 75 Years of Service," *Midwest Motorist* 48 (February 1977): 12–13.

94. Shoemaker, *Missouri and Missourians,* vol. 2, 307, provisions of the Centennial Road Act of 1921, 526.

95. Shoemaker, *Missouri and Missourians,* vol. 2, 528–29.

96. Judge (Commissioner) Fred Schaeffer, Greene County Court (Commission). Personal interview with the author, September 6, 1968.

97. Information office, Greene County Highway Department. Telephone Interview with the author, August 17, 2000.

98. In 1968, while driving traverses to collect data on land use, the author had three flat tires in one day, all punctures from sharp chert in the roadbeds. The routes, all within thirty miles of Springfield, were purposely selected to traverse rugged terrain over poor roads.

99. "Two-Year-Old Girl Drowns after Truck Swept Away," *Springfield News-Leader,* February 28, 1997, 1B.

100. Mike Penprose, "Recent Rains Helped Open Sinkholes," *Springfield News-Leader,* August 5, 2000, 1B, 6B.

101. John K. Hulston, *An Ozark Lawyer's Story, 1946–1976* (Republic, Mo.: Western Printing Company, 1976), 285.

102. Vance, *Capturing the Horizon,* 556.

103. Hulston, *An Ozark Lawyer's Story,* 288.

104. Ibid., 289.

105. Featherstonhaugh, *Excursion Through the Slave States,* 96.

106. Floy W. George, *History of Webster County* (Marshfield, Mo.: Historical Committee of the Webster County Centennial, 1955), 78–80.

107. Maurice Tudor, *Pictorial Crackerbarrel: Some of the Better-Told Tales of Searcy Countains and News Scenes as They Appeared in the Marshall Mountain Wave Newspaper, 1972–1976* (Marshall, Ark.: Marshall Wave, 1976).

108. James Ira Breuer, *Crawford County and Cuba, Missouri* (Cape Girardeau, Mo.: Ramfre Press, 1972), 122.

109. When the author moved to Springfield in 1966, a two-party telephone line was still an option. Many customers chose the two-party hookup to reduce costs.

110. Rugged terrain and distance from cell phone communications, can effect the quality of cell telephone commu-

nication. Cell telephone communication may be poor or impossible in some hilly, sparsely settled parts of the Ozarks.

111. Edgar McKinney, "Images, Realities, and Cultural Transformation in the Missouri Ozarks, 1920–1960" (Ph.D. diss., University of Missouri, 1990), 172–201.

112. Ibid., 195.

113. Robert C. Glazier, "When Springfield Television Was Young," *Springfield! Magazine,* February 1983, 44.

114. McKinney, "Images, Realities, and Cultural Transformation," 371.

115. Glazier, "When Springfield Television Was Young," 44.

116. Milton D. Rafferty, "The Golden Age of Mass Transit in Springfield, part I," *Springfield! Magazine* 3 (March 1982), 13–16.

117. E. F. Chesnutt, "Rural Electrification in Arkansas: The Formative Years." *Arkansas Historical Quarterly 46* (Autumn 1987): 222.

118. Ibid., 221–22.

119. The first large dams with hydroelectric stations were built by private power companies. In 1913, Ozark Power and Electric Company completed Powersite Dam on the White River near Forsyth impounding Lake Taneycomo. Union Electric Company's Bagnell Dam on the Osage River formed Lake of the Ozarks in 1931.

120. Chesnutt, "Rural Electrification in Arkansas," 219.

121. Leslie G. Hill, " History of the Missouri Lumber and Mining Company, 1800–1909" (Ph.D. diss., University of Missouri, 1949), 240.

122. Mary Ann Messick, *History of Baxter County, 1873–1973* (Mountain Home, Ark.: Mountain Home Chamber of Commerce, 1973), 287–89.

123. J. E. Curry, *A Reminiscent History of Douglas County Missouri, 1857–1957* (Ava, Mo.: Douglas County Herald, 1957), 136.

124. Chesnutt, "Rural Electrification in Arkansas," 235–36.

125. George, *History of Webster County,* 104.

126. Chesnutt, "Rural Electrification in Arkansas," 257.

127. "About Us: Ameren Corporation," Ameren Corporation. http://www.amerenenergy.com.

128. Robert Bergland, "Deregulation," Ozarks Electric Coop Connection, http://www. ozarkssecccom/Newsletter3.html

129. Rafferty, *Historical Atlas of Missouri,* plate 73.

130. Shortly after gasoline prices increased to $1.70 per gallon in June 2000, a Lowry City resident who applied to rent a house from the author, said the increased cost of commuting to his work was the chief reason for relocating from Lowry City to Springfield. While he was renting a house for $395 in Lowry City and would have to pay $550 for a similar house in Springfield, he thought the gasoline costs and the time-cost of driving seventy miles (one hour and a half each direction) to Springfield warranted the move. Although he preferred the small town lifestyle in Lowry City, economic considerations had forced him to make the "sacrifice" to live in a larger city.

CHAPTER 9: MINING: ITS GEOGRAPHY AND HISTORY

1. Louis Houck, *A History of Missouri,* vol. 1 (Chicago: R. R. Donnelly and Sons Company, 1908), 274.

2. Pierre Francois Xavier de Charlevoix, *Letters to the Duchess of Lesdiquieres . . .* (London: R. Goadby, 1763).

3. Carl Ekberg, *Colonial Ste. Genevieve: An Adventure on the Mississippi Frontier* (Gerald, Mo.: Patrice Press, 1985), 199. It was earlier thought that Renault brought as many as five hundred black slaves to work in the mines. He was probably one of the largest slave owners when the 1726 census of Illinois Country listed twenty blacks in his possession.

4. Henry Rowe Schoolcraft, *A View of the Lead Mines of Missouri* (New York: Arno Press, 1972), 72.

5. Houck, *A History of Missouri,* vol. 1, 276.

6. Le Page du Pratz, *Histoire de la Louisiane . . .* (Paris: De Bure, l'Aine. La Beuve Delaguette, et Lambert, 1858), *I:* map opposite p. 138.

7. Houck, *A History of Missouri,* vol. 1, 277.

8. Ekberg, *Colonial Ste. Genevieve,* 12–25.

9. Houck, *A History of Missouri,* vol. 1, 351.

10. Ibid., 284–85.

11. Christian Schultz, *Travels on an Inland Voyage Through the States of New York, Pennsylvania, Virginia, Ohio, Kentucky and Tennessee and Through the Territories of Indiana, Loouisiana, Mississippi and New Orleans Performed inthe years 1807 and 1808,* vol. 2 (New York: Isaac Riley, 1810), 49.

12. Moses Austin, *Description of the Lead Mines in Upper Louisiana,* vol. 1 (Philadelphia: American State Papers, 1834), 190.

13. Houck, *A History of Missouri,* vol. 1, 285.

14. John Bradbury, *Travels in the Interior of America* (London: Sherwood, Neely and Jones, 1817), 251.

15. Ibid., 251–53.

16. Henry C. Thompson, *Our Lead Belt Heritage* (Flat River, Mo.: News-Sun, 1955), 32.

17. Henry R. Schoolcraft, *Rude Pursuits and Rugged Peaks: Schoolcraft's 1818–19 Ozark Journal,* ed. Milton D. Rafferty (Fayetteville: University of Arkansas Press, 1996), 19.

18. Houck, *History of Missouri,* vol. 2, 228–29.

19. Cheryl M. Seeger, "Ozark-Ouachita Highlands Assessment" (Unpublished report, Missouri Department of Natural Resources, Division of Geology and Land Survey, Rolla, Mo., 1999), 3.

20. J. Wyman Jones, *A History of the St. Joseph Lead Company* (New York: St. Joseph Lead Company, 1892), 5.

21. Irwin J. Cornell, "How the St. Joseph Lead Company Grew," *Mining and Metallurgy* 28 (August 1947): 363.

22. Moses Austin, *A Summary Description of the Lead Mines in Upper Louisiana,* 9. See Schoolcraft's *View of the Lead Mines of Missouri,* Section IV, Methods of Working the Mines, 90–112, for a description of early smelters and smelting technology.

23. Cornell, "How the St. Joseph Lead Company Grew," 363–64.

24. A disseminated ore deposit (especially metals) is one in which the desired minerals occur as scattered particles in the rock, but in sufficient quantity to make the deposit an ore. Much of the lead ore in the Bonneterre formation is scattered throughout the dolomite.

25. Cornell, "How the St. Joseph Lead Company Grew," 363.

26. Seeger, "Ozark-Ouachita Highlands Assessment," 37.

27. Cornell, "How the St. Joseph Lead Company Grew," 364.

28. Charles C. Roome, "Selected Aspects of the Southeast Missouri Mining Region" (Master's thesis, University of Missouri-Columbia, 1962), 52.

29. Jones, *A History of the St. Joseph Lead Company,* 39.

30. "The History of St. Joe," *St. Joe Headframe,* Special Edition (Fall 1970): 7.

31. In 1984 St. Joe Mineral Co. merged with the Doe Run Mining Company. In this move Doe Run Mining Company, a former subsidiary of St. Joe, gained control of the lead mines and other St. Joe properties in the Viburnum Trend or New Lead Belt.

32. Seeger, "Ozark-Ouachita Highlands Assessment," 2.

33. W. L. Bouchard, *St. Joseph Lead Company and Affiliated Companies in Southeast Missouri.* A reprint of articles published by *The Lead Belt News,* Flat River, Missouri, following visits to various operating plants, February through August, 1949 (Flat River, Mo.: St. Joseph Lead Company, 1950), 3–113.

34. Roger W. Forsythe, "City of Park Hills History: A New Union for Progress," http://www.pacific-pages.com/parkhill/history.htm (August 20, 2000).

35. Seeger, "Ozark-Ouachita Highlands Assessment," 3.

36. Several studies during the 1930s, which focused on language, folklore, school attendance, and child labor, describe the barite mining area of Washington County, Missouri, as a small, isolated homogeneous community of French Creoles. See Ward A. Dorrance, "The Survival of French in the Old District of Ste. Genevieve," *University of Missouri Studies,* 10 (Columbia, Mo., 1935); Joseph M. Carriere, "Tales from the French Folklore of Missouri," *Northwestern University Studies* (Evanston, Ill., 1937); Mary Boland Taussig, "Factors Influencing School Attendance in the Missouri Barytes Fields" (Master's thesis, Washington University, 1938); Charles E. Gibbons, *Child Labor in the Tiff Mines* (New York: National Child Labor Committee, 1938). For a collection of French folklore from Missouri, see Rosemary Thomas, *It's Good to Tell You: French Folktales from Missouri* (Columbia: University of Missouri Press, 1981).

37. "Creole" refers to descendants of the French settlers of Louisiana territory, including Missouri.

38. Carl O. Sauer, *The Geography of the Ozark Highland of Missouri,* Geographical Society of Chicago Bulletin no. 7 (Chicago: University of Chicago Press, 1920), 92–93.

39. Dick Steward, *Frontier Swashbuckler: The Life and Legend of John Smith T* (Columbia: University of Missouri Press, 2000).

40. Henry Rowe Schoolcraft, *Scenes and Adventures in the Semi-Alpine Region of the Ozark Mountains* (Philadelphia: Lippincott, Grambo and Co., 1853), 253.

41. David F. McMahon, "Tradition and Change in an Ozark Mining Community" (Master's thesis, St. Louis University, 1958), 23.

42. Henry R. Lieberman, "Les Miserables in Missouri," *Ken* 9 (March 1939): 26.

43. Carriere, *Tales from the French Folklore of Missouri,* 2.

44. Clarence R. Keathley, "Reflections on Public Welfare in Washington County, Missouri, 1939–1941," *Missouri Historical Review* 82 (October 1987): 51–70.

45. Hayward M. Wharton et al., *Missouri Minerals-Resources, Production, and Forecasts* (Rolla: Missouri Geological Survey and Water Resources, 1969), 5.

46. Seeger, "Ozark-Ouachita Highlands Assessment," 4.

47. Arthur B. Cozzens, "The Iron Industry of Missouri, Part I," *Missouri Historical Review* 35 (October–July 1940–1941): 509.

48. Ibid., 513–14.

49. James D. Norris, *Frontier Iron: The Story of the Maramec Iron Works 1826–1876* (Madison: The State Historical Society of Wisconsin for the James Foundation, 1972), 105.

50. Truman A. Hartshorn and John W. Alexander, *Economic Geography,* 3d ed. (Englewood Cliffs, N.J.: Prentice-Hall, 1988), 198–200.

51. Jo Burford, "Underground Treasures: The Story of Mining in Missouri," in *Official Manual State of Missouri 1977–1978,* ed. Kenneth M. Johnson (Jefferson City, Mo.: Office of the Secretary of State, 1978), 1–33.

52. Early ironworks were known as plantations, and like the early agricultural plantations, they were nearly self sufficient. Workers usually lived on the property.

53. Seeger, "Ozark-Ouachita Highlands Assessment, 1999," 3.

54. *Missouri Iron Company: An Act to Charter the Missouri Iron Company* (Jefferson City, Mo.: John Jamison, Speaker of the House of Representatives; Franklin Cannon, President of the Senate, 1837), 20–24. For a map of Missouri City, see Milton D. Rafferty, *Historical Atlas of Missouri* (Norman: University of Oklahoma Press, 1982), plate 106.

55. G. C. Broadhead, "Early Missouri Roads," *Missouri Historical Review* 8 (January 1914): 90–92.

56. Hugh N. Johnson, "Sequent Occupance of the St. Francois Mining Region" (Ph.D. diss., University of Missouri-Columbia, 1950), 187.

57. Ibid.

58. M. J. Gilbert, compiler, *Road and Hand-Book of the Missouri Division of the League of American Wheelmen* (St. Louis: Missouri Division of the League of American Wheelmen, 1896), 128–29.

59. Seeger, "Ozark-Ouachita Highlands Assessment," 43.

60. Schoolcraft, *Rude Pursuits and Rugged Peaks,* 82.

61. F. A. North, *The History of Jasper County, Missouri* (Des Moines, Iowa: Mills and Company, 1883), 607.

62. Earnest R. Buckley and H. A. Buehler, "The Geology of the Granby Area," *Missouri Bureau of Geology and Mines,* 2d Series, vol. 4 (1905): 80.

63. Arrell M. Gibson, *Wilderness Bonanza: The Tri-State District of Missouri, Kansas, and Oklahoma* (Norman: University of Oklahoma Press, 1972), 20.

64. Ibid., 21.

65. Ibid., 24.

66. Miners called zinc ore, or sphalerite, by other names. The most common alternative names were "blende," "zinc blende," and "jack."

67. Gibson, *Wilderness Bonanza,* 27.

68. Ibid., 28.

69. Ibid., 147–48.

70. Ibid., 165.

71. Ibid., 123.

72. Mary Megee, "The Geography of the Mining of Lead and Zinc in the Tri-State Mining District" (Master's thesis, University of Arkansas, 1950), 38–44.

73. Gibson, *Wilderness Bonanza,* 99.

74. Richard S. Thoman, *The Changing Occupance Pattern of the Tri-State Area of Missouri, Kansas, and Oklahoma,* University of Chicago Department of Geography Research Paper no. 21 (Chicago, 1953), 82.

75. Gibson, *Wilderness Bonanza,* 81.

76. Schoolcraft, *Rude Pursuits and Rugged Peaks,* 82.

77. Lynn Morrow, "Joseph Washington McClurg: Entrepreneur, Politician, Citizen," *Missouri Historical Review* 78 (January 1984): 168–201.

78. Edward M. Shepard, "A Report on Greene County," *Geological Survey of Missouri,* vol. 12, pt. 1, Sheet Report no. 5 (Jefferson City, Mo.: Tribune Printing Co., 1898), 181.

79. G. W. Featherstonhaugh, *Excursion through the Slave States, From Washington on the Potomac to the Frontier of Mexico; With Sketches of Popular Manners and Geological Notices* (New York, 1968), 88.

80. David D. Owen, *First Report of a Geological Reconnaissance of the Northern Counties of Arkansas, Made During the Years 1857 and 1858* (Little Rock, Ark., 1858), 136.

81. Dwight Pitcaithley, "Zinc and Lead Mining along the Buffalo River," *Arkansas Historical Quarterly* 37 (Winter 1978): 296.

82. Ibid., 297.

83. Lawrence Handley, "Settlement across Northern Arkansas as Influenced by the Missouri & North Arkansas Railroad," *Arkansas Historical Quarterly* 33 (Winter 1974): 286.

84. Mary Ann Messick, *History of Baxter County, 1873–1973* (Mountain Home, Ark.: Mountain Home Chamber of Commerce, 1973), 93.

85. W. L. Lane and T. R. Yanske, "Pillar Extraction and Rock Mechanics at the Doe Run Company in Missouri," *Proceedings of the Thirty-seventh U.S. Rock Mechanics Symposium* (Vail, Colo., June 6–9, 1999): 285.

86. Seeger, "Ozark-Ouachita Highlands Assessment," 39.

87. "Indian Creek—The Prototype Operation," *Engineering and Mining Journal* 165 (April 1964): 89.

88. U.S. Bureau of the Census. *United States Census of Population: 1980. General Population Characteristics, Missouri,* 1, chap. B (Washington, D.C.: U.S. Government Printing Office, 1982); "County Population Estimates, 1998, Missouri." Population Estimates Program, Population Division, U.S. Census Bureau. http://www.census.gov/population/estimates/county/co-99-8/99c8_29.txt.

89. Seeger, "Ozark-Ouachita Highlands Assessment," 20–21.

90. Ibid., 28.

91. *Missouri's Environment* 3 (March 1977): 4.

92. Seeger, "Ozark-Ouachita Highlands Assessment," 13–16.

93. Larry W. Casteel, mining executive, St. Joe Mineral Company. Personal interview with the author, June 11, 1978.

94. *Population Estimates for Places, Missouri, Block 1 of 2.* Annual Time Series, July 1, 1990, to July 1, 1998 (Washington, D.C.: Population Division, U.S. Census Bureau, 1999). http://www.census.gov/population/estimates/metro-city/scful/SC9F_MO.txt.

95. Thomas Yanske, "Missouri Lead Mining Information," Typewritten document provided by the Doe Run Company (Viburnum, Mo., November 22, 1999), 1.

96. W. L. Lane and T. R. Yanske, "Pillar Extraction and Rock Mechanics," 285–92.

97. Ibid., 285.

98. G. W. Crane, "The Iron Ores of Missouri," *Missouri Bureau of Geology and Mines,* 2d Series, vol. 10 (1912): 98–99.

99. Ibid., 55, 64–82, 84–96.

100. Norris, *Frontier Iron,* 45.

101. Ibid., 46.

102. Ibid., 168–70.

103. Arthur B. Cozzens, "The Iron Industry of Missouri, Part II," *Missouri Historical Review* 36 (July–October 1941): 49.

104. Ibid., 44–58.

105. Ibid., 58.

106. "Meramec Iron Ore Project Starts Production at Pea Ridge," *Engineering and Mining Journal* 165 (April 1964): 93–108.

107. Seeger, "Ozark-Ouachita Highlands Assessment," 43.

108. Ibid., 16.

109. Ibid., 44.

110. Milton D. Rafferty, *Historical Atlas of Missouri* (Norman: University of Oklahoma Press, 1981), plate 86.

111. "Unimin Corporation," http://www.cisa.org/members/unimin.htm.

112. William D. Spier, "Farming and Mining Experience: Independence County, Arkansas, 1900–1925" (Ph.D. diss., Washington University, 1974), 81.

113. William Spier, "A Social History of Manganese Mining in the Batesville District of Independence County," *Arkansas Historical Quarterly* 36 (Summer 1977): 132–33.

114. Ibid., 136.

115. Ibid., 133.

116. Ibid., 132.

117. Spier, "Farming and Mining Experience," 111.

118. Workers of the Writers' Program of the Works Progress Administration in the State of Missouri, *The WPA Guide to 1930s Missouri* (Lawrence: University Press of Kansas, 1986), 539.

119. *Rand McNally Commercial Atlas and Marketing Guide, 1999* (Chicago: Rand McNally and Co., 1999), 405.

120. H. A. Buehler, "The Lime and Cement Resources of Missouri, Missouri," *Bureau of Geology and Mines,* vol. 6, 2d Series (Jefferson City, Mo.: Hugh Stephens Printing Co., 1907), xv.

121. Shepard, *A Report on Greene County,* 205–6.

122. Rafferty, *Historical Atlas of Missouri,* plate 85.

123. Field observations by the author, April 30, 2000.

124. Charles van Ravenswaay, *The Arts and Architecture of German Settlements in Missouri* (Columbia: University of Missouri Press, 1977), 221.

125. Seeger, "Ozark-Ouachita Highlands Assessment," 5.

126. Clarence N. Roberts, "History of the Structural Brick Industry in Missouri," *Missouri Historical Review* 47 (July 1953): 320. For a discussion of the architecture, construction, and history of Missouri courthouses, see Marion M. Ohman, *Encyclopedia of Missouri Courthouses* (Columbia: University of Missouri Press, 1981).

127. Ibid., 320.

128. Shiloh Museum Board of Trustees, *Washington County History.* (Springdale, Ark.: Shiloh Museum, 1989), 220–21.

129. van Ravenswaay, *The Arts and Architecture of German Settlements in Missouri,* 221.

130. Ibid., 223.

131. Roberts, "History of the Structural Brick Industry in Missouri," 326.

132. Ibid., 325.

133. William C. Breckenridge, "Early Gunpowder Making in Missouri," *Missouri Historical Review* 20 (October 1925): 85.

134. Schoolcraft, *A View of the Lead Mines,* 43.

135. Richard M. Clokey, *William Ashley: Enterprise and Politics in the Trans-Mississippi West* (Norman: University of Oklahoma Press, 1980), 28–29.

136. Ibid., 36.

137. Ibid.

138. Breckenridge, "Early Gunpowder Making in Missouri," 85–95.

139. Ibid.

140. Ibid., 90.

141. Owen, *First Report,* 53–55, 224–26.

142. James J. Johnston, "Bullets for Johnny Reb: Confederate Nitre and Mining Bureau in Arkansas," *Arkansas Historical Quarterly* 49 (Summer 1990): 124–25.

143. Duane Huddleston, Sammie Cantrell Rose, and Pat Taylor Wood, *Steamboats and Ferries on the White River: A Heritage Revisited* (Fayetteville: University of Arkansas Press, 1998), 51.

144. Johnston, "Bullets for Johnny Reb," 140.

145. Ibid., 63.

146. Frederick F. Simonds, "The Geology of Washington County," in *Geological Survey of Arkansas Annual Report for 1888* 4 (1891), 1–154.

147. *History of Washington County, Arkansas,* 33.

148. Ibid., 34.

149. Robert G. Winn, "Coal in the Ozarks," *Washington County Observer* (April 21, 1977).

150. *History of Washington County, Arkansas,* 33.

151. Mary Ann Messick, *History of Baxter County, 1873–1973* (Mountain Home, Ark.: Mountain Home Chamber of Commerce, 1973), 291.

152. Gloria A. Young and Michael P. Hoffman, eds., *The Expedition of Hernando de Soto West of the Mississippi, 1541–1543* (Fayetteville: University of Arkansas Press, 1993).

153. Messick, *History of Baxter County,* 291.

154. *The WPA Guide to 1930s Missouri,* 507.

155. J. Dickson Black, *History of Benton County, 1836–1936* (Little Rock, Ark.: International Graphics Industries, 1975), 69–70.

156. Ibid., 73–74.

157. Margaret Ray Vickery, *Ozark Stories of the Upper Current River* (Salem, Mo.: Salem Publishing Company, n.d.), 71.

158. The Lost Silver Mine Theater at Branson West advertised that the Yocum Silver Mine was on the property. A booklet authored by Artie Ayres, owner of the theater and real estate developer, explained the traditional legend of the "lost Yocum silver mine" and the "Yocum Dollar." In 1985, the Yocum dollar story resurfaced with a new element of mystery. J. R. Blunk of rural Stone County authored a typewritten story, "History of Missouri and the Yoachum Silver Dollar, 1822," in which he claimed to have discovered the "lost" dyes for molding the Yocum silver dollars. The location of the buried molds came to his son in a dream. The typescript manuscript is in the hands of the author.

159. "The Yoachum Dollar of 1822," *World Exonumia* (September 4, 1984): 453.

160. Lynn Morrow and Dan Saults, "The Yocum Silver Dollar: Sorting Out the Strands of an Ozarks Frontier Legend," *Gateway Heritage* 5 (Winter 1984–1985): 8–15.

161. Ibid., 11.

162. Messick, *History of Baxter County,* 295.

163. Thomas R. Beveridge, *Geologic Wonders and Curiosities of Missouri,* 2d ed. (Rolla: Missouri Department of Natural Resources, Division of Geology and Land Survey, 1990), 50–51.

164. *Silver Mines Self-Guided Trail,* brochure (Fredericktown, Mo.: District Ranger, Mark Twain National Forest, n.d.).

CHAPTER 10: OZARK AGRICULTURE: PATTERNS OF TRIAL AND ERROR

1. Tilth is the physical condition of the topsoil after tillage. A fine tilth consists of small clods and loose, crumbling soil particles. In a course tilth, comparatively large clods constitute most of the broken material.

2. Arthur N. Strahler, *Physical Geography*, 3d ed. (New York: John Wiley & Sons, 1969), 299–303.

3. In soil science, a pan is a hard, cement-like layer, crust, or horizon within or just beneath the surface soil. Being strongly compacted, indurated, or high in clay content, it usually impedes the movement of water and air and the growth of plant roots. It is sometimes called a hardpan or fragipan. Many upland Ozark soils have pans that prevent trees from growing to their largest size.

4. Chert is a hard, dense, dull to semivitreous sedimentary rock, consisting dominantly of interlocking crystals of quartz. It occurs as nodular masses in limestones and dolomites and sometimes as thin layered deposits between beds of limestone. Because of its resistance to weathering, chert remains as a residual material in soils as the softer limestones and dolomites decay. Its hardness and smooth concoidal fracture made it a prized commodity for scrapers, knives, and other tools fashioned by Native Americans.

5. Carl O. Sauer, *Geography of the Ozark Highland of Missouri*, Geographical Society of Chicago Bulletin no. 7 (Chicago: University of Chicago Press, 1920), 38–39.

6. Curtis F. Marbut, "Soil Reconnaissance of the Ozark Region of Missouri and Arkansas," *Field Operations of the Bureau of Soils, 1911* (Washington, D.C.: Bureau of Soils, U.S. Department of Agriculture, 1914), 139–41.

7. E. B. Branson and W. D. Keller, "Geology," ch. 2 in Noel P. Gist et al., *Missouri: Its Resources, People, and Institutions* (Columbia: Curators of the University of Missouri, 1950), 26.

8. Curtis F. Marbut, "Soils of the Ozark Region: A Preliminary Report on the General Character of the Soils and Agriculture of the Missouri Ozarks," *Research Bulletin no. 3* (Columbia: University of Missouri College of Agriculture, Agricultural Experiment Station, 1910), 195. There are numerous accounts about the selection of bottomland soils by the first settlers. See also Carl O. Sauer, *The Geography of the Ozark Highland of Missouri*, Geographic Society of Chicago Bulletin no. 7 (Chicago: University of Chicago Press, 1920); Earl W. Kersten Jr. "Changing Economy and Landscape in a Missouri Ozarks Area," *Annals of the Association of American Geographers* 48 (December 1985): 298–418; Harbert L. Clendenen, "Settlement Morphology of the Southern Courtois Hills, Missouri, 1820–1860" (Ph.D. diss., Louisiana State University, 1973), 61–85; Ruth Rowe, "The Geographic Saga of an Ozark Family" (Master's thesis, Washington University, 1939), 63–70.

9. Henry R. Schoolcraft, *Rude Pursuits and Rugged Peaks:*

Schoolcraft's 1818–19 Ozark Journal, ed. Milton D. Rafferty (Fayetteville: University of Arkansas Press, 1996), 82.

10. Ibid., 62. Sugarloaf Knob north of Lead Hill, Arkansas, described by Schoolcraft as a high hill covered with grass, is now heavily wooded.

11. Julian A. Steyermark, *Vegetational History of the Ozark Forest*, University of Missouri Studies no. 31 (Columbia: 1959).

12. Marbut, *Soils of the Ozark Region*, 254–55.

13. Undesirable shrubs and scrubby trees, such as sumac, persimmon and oak sprouts, are commonly removed by mowing pastures with large tractor-mounted rotary mowers called brush hogs.

14. Schoolcraft, *Rude Pursuits and Rugged Peaks*, 41–43.

15. Walter P. Webb, *The Great Plains* (New York: Grosset and Dunlap, 1931), 290–95. Osage Orange, *Maclura pomifera*, is sometimes called hedge, hedge apple, or bois d'arc because the Indians made their hunting bows from it. It is native to the Black Prairie region of northeast Texas, and also western Arkansas and southeast Oklahoma. The Osage Orange tree was taken to the tall grass prairies of western Missouri and Illinois where timber for fencing was in short supply. Later it was taken to the treeless western plains where it grew well in the dry climate. Its thorns made it a "horse high, bull strong, hog tight" fence. After barbed wire made hedge fences obsolete, the trees still found use as a source of unbeatable fence posts. In the Great Plains many miles of Osage Orange fences and windbreaks have been removed for various reasons over the past half century, with great detriment to wildlife habitat.

16. Dennis Figg, "Is Every Grassland a Prairie" (Presentation, Missouri Natural Resources 2000 Conference, Tan-Tar-A Resort, Lake of the Ozarks, February 2–4, 2000).

17. Morris E. Austin, *Land Resource Regions and Major Land Resource Areas of the United States*. Agricultural Handbook No. 296 (Washington, D.C.: Soil Conservation Service, U.S. Department of Agriculture, 1965).

18. Gloria Salberg, "The New Madrid Land Claims in Howard County, Missouri," *Missouri Mineral Industry News* 7 (May 1967): 69–79. See also Louis Houck, *History of Missouri*, vol. 1, 34–54; and Milton D. Rafferty, *Historical Atlas of Missouri* (Norman: University of Oklahoma Press, 1983), plate 32.

19. U.S. Department of the Interior, *U.S. Census of Wealth and Industry, 1870*, vol. 3 (Washington, D.C.: U.S. Government Printing Office, 1872).

20. Lee A. Dew, "From Trails to Rails in Eureka Springs," *Arkansas Historical Quarterly* 41 (Autumn 1982): 206.

21. Brooks R. Blevins, "Fallow Are the Hills: A Century of Rural Modernization in the Arkansas Ozarks" (Master's thesis, Auburn University, 1994), 13.

22. Jonathan Fairbanks and Clyde E. Tuck, *Past and Present of Greene County, Missouri* (Indianapolis, Ind.: A. W. Bowen and Co., 1915), 196.

23. Tomatoes, native to South America, were taken to

Europe where they gained wide acceptance as a food. However, in the British Isles they were thought to be poisonous. In the United states tomatoes did not gain wide acceptance until about the middle of the nineteenth century.

24. Miles W. Eaton, "The Development and Later Decline of the Hemp Industry of Missouri," *Missouri Historical Review* 43 (October–July 1948–1949): 344–54.

25. Ibid., 344. Ropes and other cordage were manufactured in businesses called "rope walks."

26. Dew, "From Trails to Rails in Eureka Springs," 206.

27. Fairbanks and Tuck, *Past and Present of Greene County, Missouri,* 198.

28. Margaret Riggs, "Valley Contrast in the Missouri Ozarks Regions," *Journal of Geography* 35 (December 1936): 351–59.

29. Marbut, "Soil Reconnaissance of the Ozark Region of Missouri and Arkansas," 139.

30. John Q. Wolf, *Life in the Leatherwoods* (Fayetteville: University of Arkansas Press, 1999), 132–37.

31. Fairbanks and Tuck, *Past and Present of Greene County, Missouri,* 198.

32. Ibid.

33. Census Office, U.S. Department of Interior, *Eleventh Census of the United States: 1890, Statistics of Agriculture* (Washington, D.C.: U.S. Government Printing Office, 1895); Census Office, U.S. Department of Interior, *Twelfth Census of the United States: 1900, Agriculture,* 6, pt. 2 (Washington, D.C.: U.S. Government Printing Office, 1902).

34. Larry A. McFarlane, "The Missouri Land and Livestock Company, Limited, of Scotland: Foreign Investment on the Missouri Farming Frontier, 1882–1908" (Ph.D. diss., University of Missouri-Columbia, 1963), 120–22.

35. Fairbanks and Tuck, *Past and Present of Greene County, Missouri,* 198.

36. Leslie Hewes, "Cultural Fault Line in the Cherokee Country," *Economic Geography* 19 (April 1943): 136–42.

37. Grace Steel Woodward, *The Cherokees* (Norman: University of Oklahoma Press, 1963), 325.

38. U.S. Bureau of the Census, *Fifteenth Census of the United States: 1930. Agriculture,* 2, pt. 1 (Washington, D.C.: U.S. Government Printing Office, 1932); U.S. Bureau of the Census. *United States Census of Agriculture: 1964. Statistics for the State and Counties, Missouri,* 1, pt. 17 (Washington, D.C.: U.S. Government Printing Office, 1967). The U.S. Bureau of the Census did not continue the type of farm classification beyond 1964, but instead classified farms as to size.

39. Milton D. Rafferty, "Agricultural Change in the Western Ozarks," *Missouri Historical Review* 69 (April 1975): 305.

40. Blevins, "Fallow Are the Hills"; Brooks R. Blevins, "A Social History of the Arkansas Ozarks" (Ph.D. diss., Auburn University, 1999).

41. Edgar McKinney, "Images, Realities, and Cultural Transformation in the Missouri Ozarks, 1920–1960" (Ph.D. diss., University of Missouri, 1990).

42. Blevins, "Fallow Are the Hills," 24–25.

43. Otis T. Osgood, "Farm Planning in the Eastern Ozarks," *Arkansas Agricultural Experiment Station Bulletin no. 435* (Fayetteville: University of Arkansas College of Agriculture, 1943), 13.

44. Blevins, "Fallow Are the Hills," 28.

45. Kersten, "Changing Economy and Landscape in a Missouri Ozarks Area," 398–418.

46. Blevins, "Fallow Are the Hills," 38.

47. Walter B. Stevens, *Missouri, The Center State* (Chicago: S. J. Clarke Publishing Company, 1915), 617.

48. Robert Flanders, "Preservation Corner: The Hazeltine Orchards," *OzarksWatch* 9 (1996): 2.

49. Hewes, "Cultural Fault Line in the Cherokee Country," *Economic Geography* 19 (April 1943): 136–42. As defined by Professor Hewes, a cultural fault line is a break in continuity of the geographic patterns of cultural features that comprise a cultural landscape. The terminology is derived from the geologic term "fault line" which connotes the break in continuity of rock types resulting from a fault or crustal disturbance. In Hewes' study, the Oklahoma Ozarks displayed a retarded stage of development which resulted in the retention of older patterns of economy and landscape than in the more progressive areas immediately east of the eastern boundary of Indian Territory (Oklahoma).

50. A. T. Sweet and Howard V. Jordan, *Soil Survey of Lawrence County, Missouri* (Washington, D.C.: U.S. Department of Agriculture, Soil Survey, 1928), 1150.

51. Thomas Rothrock, "A King That Was," *Arkansas Historical Quarterly* 33 (Winter 1974): 329.

52. Flanders, "Preservation Corner: The Hazeltine Orchards," 5.

53. Rothrock, "A King That Was," 332.

54. Ibid., 328–29.

55. Clarence W. Olmstead, "American Orchard and Vineyard Regions," *Economic Geography* 32 (July 1956): 213–27.

56. Rothrock, "A King That Was," 330.

57. Rafferty, "Agricultural Change in the Western Ozarks," 308.

58. Rothrock, "A King That Was," 332.

59. "Vollenweider Pioneer Grower Makes Seymour Apple Capital of the Ozarks," *Ozarks Mountaineer* (October 1955): 5.

60. Rafferty, "Agricultural Change in the Western Ozarks," 309–10.

61. The author frequently visited the Speas Vinegar Plant in Marionville while on field trips with students in the late 1960s and early 1970s. In the final years of operation, local apples were no longer used; the vinegar was produced from condensed apple syrup shipped from Washington state.

62. Rafferty, "Agricultural Change in the Western Ozarks," 145–49.

63. J. A. Drake and A. T. Strahorn, *Soil Survey of Webster County, Missouri* (Washington, D.C., 1904), 17.

64. Irene A. Moke, "Canning in Northwestern Arkansas:

Springdale, Arkansas," *Economic Geography* 28 (April 1952): 154.

65. The author witnessed the auction of the machinery taken from a small "shade tree cannery" in August, 1969. The total inventory of equipment, including pressure cookers, canners, and other miscellaneous equipment, was loaded into a single pickup truck and hauled away.

66. Rafferty, *Agricultural Change in the Western Ozarks,* 311.

67. Paul Johns, "Tomato Canning Memories," *Missouri Life* 8 (March–April 1980): 32.

68. Blevins, "Fallow Are the Hills," 36.

69. Ibid.

70. Rafferty, *Agricultural Change in the Western Ozarks,* 311–12.

71. Finus Carver, fruit farmer, Marionville, Missouri. Personal interview with the author, August 1, 1968.

72. Ibid. Mr. Carver mentioned that the last strawberry shipping shed at Logan, Missouri was destroyed by a tornado in 1955. Strawberry shipping by railroad had ceased several years previously.

73. Michael Poeschel, "The Vineyards of Hermann, Missouri," *Western* 3 (October 1849): 54.

74. John J. Baxevanis, *The Wine Regions of America: Geographical Reflections and Appraisals* (Stroudsburg, Pa.: Vinifera Wine Growers Journal, 1992), 184.

75. Russell Gerlach, *Immigrants in the Ozarks: A Study in Ethnic Geography* (Columbia: University of Missouri, 1976), 142–48. A detailed review of the early history of Rosati, Missouri, and Tontitown, Arkansas, may be found in Joseph Velikonja, "The Italian Contribution to the Geographic Character of Tontitown, Arkansas and Rosati, Missouri," trans. Don Fisher (Southwest Missouri State College, Springfield, 1971). The manuscript is available in Meyer Library, Southwest Missouri State University.

76. Leslie Hewes, "Tontitown: Ozark Vineyard Center," *Economic Geography* 29 (April 1953): 139.

77. Leon D. Adams, *The Wines of America,* 2d ed. (New York: McGraw-Hill Book Co., 1978), p. 178. See also Peter J. Poletti, "An Interdisciplinary Study of the Missouri Grape and Wine Industry, 1650 to 1989" (Ph.d. dissertation, St. Louis University, 1989), 122–25.

78. Rose F. Cramer, *Wayne County, Missouri* (Cape Girardeau, Mo.: Ramfre Press, 1972), 344–45.

79. Hewes, "Tontitown," 140–41.

80. Peter J. Poletti, "An Interdisciplinary Study of the Missouri Grape and Wine Industry: 1650–1989" (Ph.D. diss., Saint Louis University, 1989), 238–46.

81. Virginia Hogg, "Urban Pattern of Springfield, Missouri" (Master's thesis, Washington University, 1934), 55–56.

82. Fairbanks and Tuck, *Past and Present of Greene County, Missouri,* 680.

83. U.S. Bureau of the Census, *Thirteenth Census of the U.S., 1910, Agriculture,* 6: 896–900; U.S. Bureau of the Census, *Sixteenth Census of the U.S., 1940, Agriculture,* 1, pt. 2: 274–82.

84. Sweet and Jordan, *Soil Survey of Lawrence County, Missouri,* 1129.

85. Milton D. Rafferty and Dennis J. Hrebec, "Logan Creek: A Missouri Ozark Valley Revisited," *Journal of Geography* 72 (October 1973): 7–17.

86. Ibid.

87. James L. Reeves, *The First Twenty Years: The Story of Mid-America Dairymen* (Springfield, Mo.: Mid-America Dairymen, 1989), 11.

88. Ibid., 215.

89. Ibid., 34.

90. Sandy Z. Poneleit, "Dairy Industry in Danger," *Springfield News-Leader,* February 6, 2000, 10b.

91. Ibid.

92. Hogg, *Urban Pattern of Springfield,* 51.

93. Omer A. Combs, Combs, Arkansas. Personal interview with the author, April 6, 2001. For maps and a discussion of the distribution of poultry farms in the Kings River drainage basin, see Jason W. White, "Spatial Assessment of Nonpoint Phosphorus Sources Using Streambed Sediment Monitoring in the Kings River Basin, NW Arkansas" (Master's thesis, Southwest Missouri State University, 2001).

94. Marvin Schwartz, *Tyson: From Farm to Market: The Remarkable Story of Tyson Foods* (Fayetteville: University of Arkansas Press, 1991), 3.

95. Ibid., 4.

96. Ibid., 6.

97. Ibid., 7.

98. Ibid., 65.

99. *To Get to the Other Side,* Tyson Foods 1999 Annual Report (Springdale, Ark.: Tyson Foods, 1999), 17.

100. *To Get to the Other Side,* 22.

101. C. J. Brown, *Cattle on a Thousand Hills: A History of the Cattle Industry in Arkansas* (Fayetteville: University of Arkansas Press, 1996), 1–2.

102. Ibid., 7.

103. Ibid., 26.

104. Ibid., 18.

105. Ibid., 19.

106. Clifford D. Carpenter, "The Early Cattle Industry in Missouri," *Missouri Historical Review* 47 (April 1953): 203–4.

107. Ibid., 204.

108. Ibid., 205.

109. "Missouri's War against Texas Herds," *Springfield News-Leader,* January 30, 1977, F1.

110. Brown, *Cattle on a Thousand Hills,* 22.

111. Fairbanks and Tuck, *Past and Present of Greene County, Missouri,* 202.

112. McFarlane, "The Missouri Land and Livestock Company," 96–130.

113. Kersten, "Changing Economy and Landscape in a Missouri Ozarks Area," 398–418.

114. O. C. Claxton, area community development agent, Ava, Missouri. Personal correspondence with the author, July 18, 1969.

115. C. O. Bridges, stock farmer, Christian County, Missouri. Personal interview with the author, August 24, 1968.

116. Brown, *Cattle on a Thousand Hills,* 41.

117. U.S. Bureau of the Census, *1987 Census of Agriculture: Historical Highlights,* 1, pt. 51 (Washington, D.C.: U.S. Government Printing Office, 1988); U.S. Department of Agriculture, National Agricultural Statistical Service, *1997 Census of Agriculture* (Washington, D.C.: U.S. Government Printing Office, 1998).

118. U.S. Bureau of the Census, *Census of Agriculture, 1997: Missouri, State and County Data,* 1, Geographic Area Series, pt. 25 (Washington, D.C.: U.S. Department of Agriculture, 1999), v–11. The definition of a farm for census purposes was first established in 1850. It has been changed nine times since. The current definition, first used for the 1974 census, is any place from which $1,000 or more of agricultural products were produced and sold, or normally would have been sold during the census year. Part-time farms are those places that produce and sell at least $50 but less than $1,000 of agricultural products during the census year.

119. U.S. Bureau of the Census, *Fifteenth Census of the United States: 1930, Agriculture,* 2, pt. 1 (Washington, D.C.: U.S. Government Printing Office, 1932); U.S. Bureau of the Census, *United States Census of Agriculture: 1964, Statistics for the State and Counties, Missouri,* 1, pt. 17. (Washington, D.C.: U.S. Government Printing Office, 1967).

120. Christian County History Committee, *Christian County: Its First Hundred Years* (Ozark, Mo.: Christian County Centennial, 1959), 143.

121. Lynn Morrow, "Estate Builders in the Missouri Ozarks: Establishing a St. Louis Tradition," *Gateway Heritage* 2 (Winter 1981–1982): 42–48.

122. Harry Vanderheide, retired machinist, Ozark, Missouri. Personal interview with the author, August 10, 1968.

123. Farmettes are small "farms" that meet the U.S. Census Bureau's definition of a farm, but are not truly economically viable farms. Part-time farms would also fall in this category. Other names include "country estate farms," "commuter farms," and "suburban farms."

CHAPTER 11: THE OZARK LUMBER INDUSTRY: DEVELOPMENT AND GEOGRAPHY

1. Ruben L. Parson, *Conserving American Resources* (Englewood Cliffs, N.J.: Prentice-Hall, 1964), 180–82.

2. Henry R. Schoolcraft, *Rude Pursuits and Rugged Peaks: Schoolcraft's 1818–1819 Ozark Journal,* ed. Milton D. Rafferty (Fayetteville: University of Arkansas Press, 1996), 34.

3. Christian County History Committee, *Christian County: Its First Hundred Years* (Ozark, Mo.: Christian County Centennial, 1959), 144.

4. Ibid., 16.

5. Ibid., 136.

6. Ibid.

7. Ibid., 152.

8. Clifton E. Hull, *Shortline Railroads of Arkansas* (Norman: University of Oklahoma Press, 1969), 350.

9. Ibid., 351.

10. Ibid., 356.

11. Ibid., 55, map. See also, Lawrence R. Handley, "Settlement across Northern Arkansas as Influenced by the Missouri and North Arkansas Railroad." *Arkansas Historical Quarterly* 33 (winter 1974): 273–92.

12. Hull, *Shortline Railroads of Arkansas,* 66.

13. Gerald W. Dupy, "Two Determined Freight Lines Ply Historic Rails of the Ozarks," *Ozarks Mountaineer* 42 (June 1994): 30–31.

14. Elmo Ingenthron, *The Land of Taney* (Point Lookout Mo.: School of the Ozarks Press, 1974), 193.

15. Leslie G. Hill, "History of the Missouri Lumber and Mining Company, 1800–1909" (Ph.D. diss., University of Missouri, 1949), 259.

16. Lela Cole, "The Early Tie Industry along the Nianqua River," *Missouri Historical Review* 48 (Fall 1953): 265.

17. Ibid., 267.

18. Ibid., 268–69.

19. Hill, "History of the Missouri Lumber and Mining Company," 10.

20. Ibid.

21. Ibid., 11.

22. Ibid., 11–13.

23. Census Office, U.S. Department of Interior, *Tenth Census of the United States: 1880, Census of Population,* 1, table 5 (Washington, D.C.: U.S. Government Printing Office, 1882).

24. Hill, "History of the Missouri Lumber and Mining Company," 18.

25. Ibid.

26. Ibid., 282–83.

27. Ibid., 180–81.

28. Tolliver Pond is in a large sink hole. The pond remains, but all buildings, conveyors, and other evidence of the large sawmills were removed shortly after the mills closed.

29. Hill, "History of the Missouri Lumber and Mining Company," 153.

30. Ibid.

31. Ibid., 168.

32. Ibid., 78.

33. *Population Estimates for Places, Missouri,* Block 1 of 2. Annual Time Series, July 1, 1990, to July 1, 1998. Population Division, U.S. Census Bureau, Washington, D.C., 1999. http://www.census.gov/population/estimates/metro-city/sets/SC98T_MO-DR.txt (May 15, 2000).

34. Hill, "History of the Missouri Lumber and Mining Company," 259.

35. Judy Ferguson, *The Boom Town of West Eminence and Its Lumbering Days* (Rolla, Mo.: Rolla Printing Company, 1969), 37.

36. Ibid., 17.

37. *Population Estimates for Places, Missouri,* Block 1 of 2. Annual Time Series, July 1, 1990, to July 1, 1998. Population Division, U.S. Census Bureau, Washington, D.C., 1999. http://www.census.gov/population/estimates/metro-city/sets/SC98T_MO-DR.txt (May 15, 2000).

38. James W. Martin and Jerry J. Presley, "Ozark Land and Lumber Company: Organization and Operations" (Unpublished manuscript, School of Forestry, University of Missouri, January 31, 1958), 8.

39. Ibid., 28.

40. Hill, "History of the Missouri Lumber and Mining Company, 78.

41. Jerry Ponder, *Grandin, Hunter, West Eminence and the Missouri Lumber and Mining Company* (Doniphan, Mo.: Ponder Books, 1989), 64–65.

42. James F. Keefe, *The First Fifty Years* (Jefferson City: Misouri Department of Conservation, 1987), 172.

43. U.S. Bureau of the Census. *Thirteenth Census of the United States: 1910, Agriculture,* 6 (Washington, D.C.: U.S. Government Printing Office, 1913); U.S. Bureau of the Census. *Fourteenth Census of the United States: 1920. Agriculture.* 4, pt. I (Washington, D.C.: U.S. Government Printing Office, 1922).

44. Percy Bridges, retired teacher, Ozark, Missouri. Personal interview with the author, April 30, 1968.

45. Rudolph Bennitt and Werner O. Nagel, "A Survey of Resident Game and Furbearers of Missouri," *University of Missouri Studies* 13 (April 1937).

46. Leonard D. Baver, "Soil Erosion in Missouri," *University of Missouri Agricultural Experiment Station Research Bulletin no. 349,* 1935.

47. The condition of Bubbling Spring has improved somewhat from its condition when the author first observed it in 1969. The volume of water appears to have increased slightly, perhaps in response to improved forest cover in its catchment area. Field observations by the author, August 1969 and July 1999.

48. Bruce Palmer, "Back from the Ashes," *Missouri Conservationist* 61 (September 2000): 10.

49. Ibid.

50. Ibid., 11.

51. Mark J. Boesch, "History of Mark Twain National Forest" (Unpublished manuscript, Rolla, Mo.: Mark Twain National Forest, 1968), 2.

52. Ibid.

53. U.S. Bureau of the Census, *Census of Population, Missouri, 1930* (Washington, D.C.: U.S. Department of Interior, Bureau of the Census, 1932); U.S. Bureau of the Census, *Census of Population, Missouri, 1960,* 1, pt. 27 (Washington, D.C.: U.S. Department of Interior, Bureau of the Census, 1963).

54. Palmer, "Back from the Ashes," 10.

55. Ibid.

56. Boesch, "History of Mark Twain National Forest," 7.

57. Roger Hatch, fire control officer, Mark Twain National Forest. Personal interview with the author, March 5, 1969.

58. Ibid.

59. Rafferty, "Persistence Vs. Change in Land Use and Landscape in the Springfield, Missouri, Vicinity of the Ozarks," 106.

60. Jennifer Portman and Traci Bauer, "Forest Land Burns by Buffalo River," *Springfield News-Leader,* November 19, 1999, 1A, 6A.

61. *Laws of Missouri, 1967* (Jefferson City: Committee on Legislative Research, General Assembly of Missouri, 1967), 375–76.

62. W. T. Wilson and J. W. Reid, "Livestock and Forestry Enterprises on Farms in the Ozark Region," *Arkansas Agricultural Experiment Station Bulletin no. 419* (Fayetteville: University of Arkansas College of Agriculture, 1942), 22.

63. Roger Hatch, fire control officer, Mark Twain National Forest. Personal interview with the author, March 5, 1969.

64. Thomas Trieman, "The State of Missouri's Forests: Tracking the Well-being of Our Trees," *Missouri Conservationist* 61 (September 2000): 6.

65. *Company Profile, World Cooperage Company* (Napa, Calif.: World Cooperage Company, 2000).

66. David A. Ganser, Timber Resources of Missouri's Southwestern Ozarks, *University of Missouri Bulletin B845* (January 1966).

67. Trieman, "The State of Missouri's Forests," 6–7.

68. Personal interview with a property owner in Linn Township, Christian County Missouri, July 14, 1968. The property owner was surprised to learn that a percentage of the sale of timber and grazing revenues from the national forest went to the county road fund. This information did not appear to sway his long-held suspicion of the United States Forest Service.

69. Palmer, "Back from the Ashes," 12.

70. Lynn Morrow, "The St. Louis Game Park: Experiments in Conservation and Recreation," *White River Valley Historical Quarterly* (Spring 1997): 7–19.

71. Mary Still, "Leo Drey: Land Magnate of the Ozarks," *Missouri Resource Review* 2 (Winter 1983–1984): 25.

72. Ibid., 26.

73. "Forest Land Bought," *Wake Up to Missouri* 22 (March 1992): 6.

74. Classified Advertisements, Real-Estate section, *Springfield News-Leader,* September 10, 2000.

75. James Jones, Director of Research, Hammons Products Company. Orientation and field trip at the Hammons Products Company Experimental Farm, July 1995, for administrators in the College of Natural and Applied Sciences, Southwest Missouri State University. Attended by the author.

76. *Environmental Briefing Book: A Guide for the Missouri State Legislature* (St. Louis: Missouri Coalition for the Environment, 1998), 14.

77. Ozark Wood Fiber, Inc., Goodman, Missouri. Personal interview by the author with mill personnel, October 4, 2000.

78. *Environmental Briefing Book: A Guide for the Missouri State Legislature,* 14.

79. Doug Johnson, "Chip Mills Investigated," *Springfield News-Leader,* April 18, 2000, 3B.

80. *Environmental Briefing Book: A Guide for the Missouri State Legislature,* 14.

81. Ibid.

82. Ibid.

83. Mike Penprase, "Borer Beetle Could Harm Local Forests," *Springfield News-Leader* (July 1, 2001), 1A, 13A.

CHAPTER 12: RECREATION AND TOURISM

1. Foster R. Dulles, *A History of Recreation: America Learns to Play* (New York: Meredith Publishing Co., 1965). Dulles's discussion of the history of recreation includes a wealth of information on the underlying causes.

2. Ibid., chap. 1, "In Detestation of Idleness," 3–21.

3. Robert K. Gilmore, *Ozark Baptizings, Hangings, and Other Diversions: Theatrical Folkways of Rural Missouri, 1885–1910* (Norman: University of Oklahoma Press, 1984).

4. Dulles, *A History of Recreation,* 96.

5. Jonathan Fairbanks and Clyde E. Tuck, *Past and Present of Greene County, Missouri* (Indianapolis, Ind.: A. W. Bowen and Company, 1915), 560–78.

6. Gideon M. Davison, *The Fashionable Tour* (New York: G. & C. & H. Carvil, 1833), 149.

7. Dixon Wecter, *The Saga of American Society* (New York: C. Scribner's Sons, 1973), 437.

8. Ibid., 150.

9. Foster R. Dulles, *A History of Recreation,* 315.

10. Ibid., 318

11. Ibid., 324.

12. Mary A. Messick, *History of Baxter County: 1873–1973.* Centennial Edition (Mountain Home, Ark.: Mountain Home Chamber of Commerce, 1973), 328.

13. Lynn Morrow and Linda Myers-Phinney, *Shepherd of the Hills Country: Tourism Transforms the Ozarks, 1880s–1930s* (Fayetteville: University of Arkansas Press, 1999), 26–28, 31–36.

14. Edgar McKinney, "Images, Realities, and Cultural Transformation in the Missouri Ozarks, 1920–1960" (Ph.D. diss., University of Missouri, 1990), 276.

15. Ibid., 277–78.

16. Ibid.

17. Messick, *History of Baxter County,* 287–90.

18. Milton D. Rafferty, *A Geography of World Tourism* (Englewood Cliffs, N.J.: Prentice Hall, 1993), 109–10.

19. Lynn Morrow, "Louis Miller: Master Craftsman and Folk Artisan of Southeast Missouri," *Gateway Heritage* 4 (Winter 1983), 30.

20. M. J. Gilbert, ed., *Road and Handbook of the Missouri Division of the League of American Wheelmen* (Columbia, Mo.: E. W. Stephens, Printer and Binder, 1896), 128.

21. Lynn Morrow, "Estate Builders in the Missouri Ozarks: Establishing a St. Louis Tradition," *Gateway Heritage* 2 (Winter 1981–1982): 43.

22. Morrow, "Louis Miller: Master Craftsman," 31.

23. "Cedar Farm Lodge" (Unpublished manuscript of recollections of Professor Donald H. McInnis, Springfield, Missouri, August 28, 2000), 1. The manuscript is in possession of the author.

24. Ibid.

25. Ibid., 2.

26. James P. Jackson, *Passages of a Stream: A Chronicle of the Meramec* (Columbia: University of Missouri Press, 1984), 61.

27. Louis La Coss, "How the Hand of a Girl Carved an Alluring Home out of an Ozark Mountain Fastness," *St. Louis Globe-Democrat Magazine* (July 22, 1928), 1, 15.

28. Morrow and Myers-Phinney, *Shepherd of the Hills Country,* 62.

29. Ibid., 63.

30. Ibid., 63–65.

31. Christian County History Committee. *Christian County: Its First Hundred Years* (Ozark, Mo.: Christian County Centennial, 1959), 138.

32. Morrow and Myers-Phinney, *Shepherd of the Hills Country,* 68.

33. Ibid.

34. M. J. Gilbert, *Road and Handbook of the Missouri Division of the League if American Wheelmen* (St. Louis, Mo.: League of American Wheelmen, 1895).

35. Lewis Atherton, *Mainstreet on the Middle Border* (Bloomington: Indiana University Press, 1984), 25.

36. Floyd C. Shoemaker, *Missouri and Missourians: Land of Contrasts and People of Achievements,* vol. 2 (Chicago: Lewis Publishing Company, 1943), 1012.

37. Ibid., 1013.

38. Carl O. Sauer, "Status and Change in the Rural Midwest-a Retrospect," *Metteilungen der Osterreichischen Geographischen Gesellschaft* (Band 105, Heft III, 1963), 365.

39. McKinney, "Images, Realities, and Cultural Transformation in the Missouri Ozarks, 1920–1960," 279–80.

40. Clara B. Kennan, "The Ozark Trails and Arkansas' Pathfinder, Coin Harvey," *Arkansas Historical Quarterly* 7 (Winter 1948): 299–316.

41. McKinney, "Images, Realities, and Cultural Transformation in the Missouri Ozarks, 1920–1960," 280–81.

42. Elbert I. Childers and John F. Bradbury Jr., "Basketville and the Roadside Craftspeople on Route 66," *Missouri Historical Review* 91 (October 1996): 25.

43. Pearl Spurlock, *Over the Old Ozark Trails in the Shepherd of the Hills Country* (Branson, Mo.: The White River Leader, 1939). The author's autographed copy of the book has two hand-printed vignettes by Pearl Spurlock on the title page.

44. "First There Was Nashville . . . Then Came Branson," *Atlanta Journal-Constitution* (July 4, 1993): 4N.

45. Elizabeth L. Newhouse, ed., *National Geographic's Guide to Scenic Highways and Byways* (Washington, D.C.: National Geographic, 1995), 165.

46. Mary B. Eddy, *Science and Health: With Key to the Scriptures* (Boston: First Church of Christ, Scientist, 1994).

47. Paul Schweitzer, "A Report on the Mineral Waters of Missouri," *Geological Survey of Missouri,* 1st Series, 3 (1892): 1–10.

48. Ibid., 30.

49. Jane Westfall and Catherine Osterhage, *A Fame Not Easily Forgotten* (Conway, Ark.; River Road Press, 1970), 2.

50. Ibid., 7.

51. Ibid., 98–99.

52. Ibid., 100–101. Dr. John Romulus Brinkley established a medical practice in Milford, Kansas, in 1916. He soon attracted a national following by the performance of "goat gland" transplantations, which were advertised as being able to restore masculine virility. His practice soon reached a volume of $10,000 a week, and he built a clinic and a powerful radio transmitter. In 1923 his name became linked to a diploma mill, and it was discovered that he had had no formal medical training. The American Medical Association, the *Kansas City Star,* the Federal Communications Commisssion, and the Kansas Medical Society were soon after him, but their activities only seemed to attract a bigger following of sympathizers. In 1930 he became an independent candidate for governor of Kansas and was narrowly defeated in a three-way election that resulted in the election of Harry Woodring, a Democrat. As usual the Republicans carried every other position on the state ticket. See Don B. Slechta, "Dr. John R. Brinkley: A Kansas Phenomenon" (Master's thesis, Fort Hays State College, 1952); Walter Davenport, "Gland Time in Kansas," *Colliers* 79 (January 16, 1932), 12–13; William F. Zornow, *Kansas: A History of the Jayhawk State* (Norman: University of Oklahoma Press, 1957), 245–47.

53. Westfall and Osterhage, *A Fame Not Easily Forgotten,* xii.

54. Workers of the Writers' Project of the Works Projects Administration in the State of Arkansas, *Arkansas: A Guide to the State* (New York: Hastings House, 1941), 307–8.

55. Arkansas State Planning Board and the Writers Project of the Work Progress Administration. American Guide Series, *Arkansas: A Guide to the State* (New York: Hastings House, 1941), 311.

56. J. Dickson Black, *History of Benton County, 1836–1936* (Little Rock, Ark.: International Graphics Industries, 1975), 293–94.

57. *Arkansas: A Guide to the State,* 290.

58. Evalena Berry, "Sugar Loaf: The Mountain, the Springs, the Town," *Arkansas Historical Quarterly* 42 (Spring 1942): 27.

59. Observed by the author, June 1979. A couple from Little Rock had removed the rear seats from a large van and the entire cargo area behind the front seats was filled with one-gallon milk jugs to be filled with water. The couple, both in their late 70s, credited their good health to the mineral waters from Heber Springs.

60. Schweitzer, "Mineral Waters of Missouri," 155.

61. Ibid.

62. Ibid., 153.

63. Ibid., 143.

64. Cheryl M. Seeger, "Ozark-Ouachita Highlands Assessment" (Unpublished report, Missouri Department of Natural Resources, Division of Geology and Land Survey, Rolla, Mo., 1999), 3.

65. Schweitzer, "Mineral Waters of Missouri," 143.

66. Ibid.

67. Ibid., 41–182.

68. Workers of the Writers' Project of the Works Projects Administration in the State of Missouri, *The WPA Guide to 1930s Missouri.* (Lawrence: University Press of Kansas, 1986), 468–69.

69. Margaret R. Vickery, *Ozark Stories of the Upper Current River* (Salem, Mo.: Salem News, [1969]), 29.

70. Leslie G. Hill, " History of the Missouri Lumber and Mining Company, 1800–1909" (Ph.D. diss., University of Missouri, 1949), 85.

71. Vickery, *Ozark Stories of the Upper Current River,* 35–38.

72. Ibid., 37.

73. Ibid.

74. Lynn Morrow, "The Arlington Hearth: St. Louisans, Perry Andres, and Commercial Tourism," *Newsletter of the Phelps County Historical Society* 18 (October 1998): 3–18.

75. Lynn Morrow, "What's in a Name, like Johnboat?" *White River Historical Quarterly* 37 (Winter 1998): 9–24.

76. Carl O. Sauer, *Geography of the Ozark Highland of Missouri (*Chicago: University of Chicago Press, 1920), 230. The first float trips were largely just as Sauer described. Flat-bottomed johnboats were launched for a leisurely float following the current with little paddling. The modern float is most commonly a canoe trip, which often involves a great deal of paddling to stay in the lead or to catch up with a group of canoes. For Ozarkers, a canoe trip is still called a "float," rather than canoeing.

77. Morrow and Myers-Phinney, *Shepherd of the Hills Country,* 123.

78. Ibid., 121

79. Ibid.

80. Ibid., 122.

81. Leonard Hall, *Stars Upstream* (Columbia: University of Missouri Press, 1958).

82. Oscar Hawksley, *Missouri Ozark Waterways* (Jefferson City: Missouri Department of Conservation, 1965).

83. Representative guidebooks on the Ozark region include Milton D. Rafferty, *The Ozarks Outdoors: A Guidebook for Fishermen, Hunters, and Tourists* (Norman: University of Oklahoma Press, 1980); and *The Branson-Ozark Mountain Country Sourcebook* (Branson, Mo.: Alliance Press, 1994).

84. Hawksley, *Missouri Ozark Waterways,* 7.

85. Mike Penrose, "Threat to Water Sinking In," *Springfield News-Leader,* July 30, 2000, 1A, 8A–9A. See also Mike Groves and Angela Wilson, "Sewage Rushes into Creek," *Springfield News-Leader,* July 30, 2000, 1B.

86. Angela Wilson, "Workers Start Repairing Pipe," *Springfield News Leader,* August 7, 2000, 1A.

87. Henry R. Schoolcraft, *Rude Pursuits and Rugged Peaks: Schoolcraft's 1818–19 Ozark Journal,* ed. Milton D. Rafferty (Fayetteville: University of Arkansas Press, 1996), 99–100.

88. Ibid., 73. The data on the number of birds and animals killed were compiled from Schoolcraft's journal by the author.

89. Friedrich Gerstaeker, *Wild Sports in the Far West* (Durham, N.C.: Duke University Press, 1968).

90. At least two other Ozark lakes—Iron Mountain Lake and Lake Killarney—predate Lake Taneycomo. Iron Mountain Lake, in western St. Francois County was built to supply water for hydraulic mining operations at Iron Mountain, but was also used for recreational purposes. Lake Killarney, near Ironton, was promoted by the Iron Mountain Railroad and corporate business investors in St. Louis to provide more varied recreation and home sites for people moving into the Arcadia valley. See Morrow, "Estate Builders in the Missouri Ozarks," 42–48.

91. Elmo Ingenthron, *The Land of Taney: A History of an Ozark Commonwealth* (Point Lookout, Mo.: School of the Ozarks Press, 1974), 283.

92. Ibid., 285–86.

93. *The WPA Guide to 1930s Missouri,* 486–87.

94. Robertus Love, "Making Niagaras in the Ozarks," *Technical World Magazine* 20 (September 1913): 139–40.

95. Ibid., 40.

96. Stephen Burton, "The Origin and Growth of Rockaway Beach, Missouri," *White River Valley Historical Quarterly* 1 (Spring 1963): 16.

97. The first post office was established January 31, 1919, with the name Taneycomo. One source states that the first postmaster, Jacob Mueller, "figured the name of the resort might be duplicated elsewhere in Missouri" so he petitioned the postal service to change the name to Rockaway Beach. This account seems flawed since the name "Taneycomo," derived from "Taney County, Missouri," is very unusual and not likely to be duplicated. See Burton, "The Origin and Growth of Rockaway Beach, Missouri," 16.

98. Burton, "The Origin and Growth of Rockaway Beach, Missouri," 18.

99. Carolyn Callison, "The Great Lake of the Ozarks Was Just a Small River Fifty Years Ago," *Midwest Motorist* 51 (March-April 1980): 9.

100. Ibid.

101. T. Victor Jeffries, *Before the Dam Water: Story and Pictures of old Linn Creek, Ha Ha Tonka, and Camden County* (Lebanon, Mo.: Jeffries Abstract and Title Insurance Company, 1974).

102. John T. Woodruff, *Reminiscences of an Ozarkian and Early Tourism Developments,* ed. Steve Illum (Springfield: Office of Leisure Research, Southwest Missouri State University, 1994), 146–47.

103. Because of its size and distinctive architecture, the structure was sometimes called Hahatonka Castle.

104. "The Beauties of Ha-Ha-Tonka," *Forty-third Annual Report of the Missouri Sate Board of Agriculture: A Record of the Work for the Year 1910* (Jefferson City, Mo.: Hugh Stephens Printing Company, 1911), 398.

105. *The WPA Guide to 1930s Missouri,* 565.

106. James P. Jackson, *Passages of a Stream: A Chronicle of the Meramec* (Columbia: University of Missouri Press, 1984), 91–107.

107. Mary Ann Messick, *History of Baxter County, 1873–1973* (Mountain Home, Ark.: Mountain Home Chamber of Commerce, 1973).

108. Messick, *History of Baxter County,* 315.

109. Ibid., 316–18.

110. Ibid., 320.

111. Ibid., 320–23.

112. Jackson, *Passages of a Stream,* 91–107.

113. Kenneth L. Smith, *The Buffalo River Country: In the Ozarks of Arkansas* (Fayetteville, Ark.: Ozark Society, 1967), 155.

114. Lake visitation varies greatly from year to year due to weather and lake levels. When the lakes are at flood stage and the water covers dock approaches, recreational facilities, and parking areas fewer people visit the lakes. During very low water stages, some boat docks and recreational areas have limited use. Also, the statistical data for annual visitors for 1978 and 1998 are not comparable because the data collection criteria varied considerably.

115. Robert Marchi, Park Manager, H. S. Truman Dam and Reservoir. Telephone conversation with the author, September 13, 2000.

116. Morrow and Myers-Phinney, *Shepherd of the Hills Country.*

117. William H. Harvey, *Coin's Financial School* (Chicago: Coin Publishing Company, circa 1894).

118. Clifton E. Hull, *Shortline Railroads of Arkansas* (Norman: University of Oklahoma Press, 1969), 244–45.

119. Kennan, "The Ozark Trails and Arkansas' Pathfinder, Coin Harvey," 299–316.

120. Hull, *Shortline Railroads of Arkansas,* 245.

121. "Death of Monte Ne," *Springfield Leader Press,* December 10, 1961, 3D.

122. Black, *History of Benton County,* 151.

123. "Rennaissance of Monte Ne," *Springfield News-Leader,* February 27, 1977, 3B.

124. Gilbert Fite, *From Vision to Reality: A History of Bella Vista Village, 1915–1993* (Rogers, Ark.: Ro-Ark Printing, 1993).

125. *The Bella Vista Story* (Bella Vista, Ark.: Bella Vista Historical Society, 1980), 16.

126. *The Bella Vista Story,* 15.

127. Ibid. C. A. Linebarger told the Bella Vista Historical Society that the name "Bella Vista" was submitted to William and Mary Baker by Mrs. George Crowder, proprietor of the old Park Springs Hotel in Bentonville.

128. Ellen C. Shipley, "The Pleasures of Prosperity, Bella Vista, Arkansas, 1917–1929," *Arkansas Historical Quarterly* (Summer 1978): 102–3.

129. Ibid., 103.

130. Ibid., 104.

131. Ibid.

132. Ibid., 105.

133. *The Bella Vista Story,* 29.

134. Shipley, "The Pleasures of Prosperity," 112–13.

135. Ibid., 113.

136. Ibid., 119–20.

137. *The Bella Vista Story,* 2.

138. Morrow and Myers-Phinney, *Shepherd of the Hills Country,* 196.

139. Kathleen van Buskirk, *In the Heart of Ozark Mountain Country: A Popular History of Stone and Taney Counties, Including Branson, Missouri* (Reeds Spring, Mo.: White Oak Press, 1992), 30.

140. "Silver Dollar City Bonanza in the Ozarks," *Springfield Leader-Press,* June 25, 1961, 2D.

141. "250,000 Visitors Expected This Year," *Springfield Leader-Press,* June 25, 1961, 3D.

142. "Herschend Brothers Run Business by Complimentary Efforts," *Springfield News-Leader,* March 1, 1981, 1C.

143. George O. Carney, "Branson: The New Mecca of Country Music," *Journal of Cultural Geography* 14 (1994): 44–50.

144. Ibid., 47.

145. *USA Today* (June 17, 1992), D1.

146. Carney, "Branson: The New Mecca of Country Music," 49–50.

147. Ibid., 50.

148. "Move Over Nashville," *St. Louis Post-Dispatch,* September 11, 1988, 12.

149. George C. Carney, "From Down Home to Uptown: The Diffusion of Country-Music Radio Stations in the United States," *Journal of Geography* 76 (March 1977): 4–10.

150. "Mace's Show in Thirtieth Year," *Sun Scenes: The Lake's Entertainer* 6 (May 20, 1983), 14.

151. The name Ridge Road applies to the great migration and trade route stretching across the Ozarks from St. Louis to Joplin and beyond. It has been the great east-west transportation route across the central Ozarks, followed by trails, roads, and railroads. The transportation routes—the Osage Trace, the Springfield to St. Louis wagon road, the Old Wire (telegraph) Road, the St. Louis and San Francisco Railway (Burlington–Santa Fe), venerated U.S. 66, and modern Interstate 44—all took advantage of the great upland ridge that approximates the drainage divide between the drainage basins of the Missouri and Arkansas rivers. Construction costs were lower because of the advantages of moderate grades and the small number of large streams to bridge. Travel time and costs are reduced because the roads and railroads are straighter and climb fewer steep hills. The branch transportation corridor follows U.S. 71 south from near Joplin, Missouri, through Fayetteville, Arkansas, and on to Fort Smith. The heaviest regional air traffic, connecting some of the Ozarks largest cities follows the same approximate route.

152. Jerry Giffen, "The Town Lucy Loved," *Missouri Life* 2 (May–June 1974): 9–15.

153. Ibid., 15.

154. For more than twenty years the author led an Ozark field trip in conjunction with a course on the geography of the Ozarks in the Department of Geography, Geology, and Planning at Southwest Missouri State University with one of the overnight stops at Epworth Among the Hills Methodist camp. Evening presentations were held in the old Japanese Pavilion.

155. Lynn Morrow, "Rose Cliff Hotel: A Missouri Forum for Environmental Policy," *Gateway Heritage* 3 (1982): 38–48.

156. According to the Ozark Marketing Council, the organization that created, advertised and promoted the name, Ozark Mountain Country includes four counties in southwest Missouri: Greene, Christian, Taney, and Stone.

157. The term *shunpiking* appears frequently in the American Guide Series, a series of travel books supported by the Works Progress Administration and local state governments. The term applies to the practice of driving the backroads through small towns and rural landscapes, that is, shunning the major roads or pikes. See *Arkansas: A Guide to the State* and *The WPA Guide to 1930s Missouri.*

158. "Gerald L. K. Smith Helped Cultivate Racism's Deep Roots," *Springfield News-Leader,* June 26, 1966, 20A. Born Feb 27, 1898, at Pardeeville, Wisconsin, Gerald Lymann Kenneth Smith came from hardy rock-ribbed Republican stock. He was a descendant of English pioneers who had emigrated from Virginia to southern Wisconsin. A gifted orator at an early age, Smith began preaching while studying at Valparaiso University. While pastoring at Kingshighway Christian Church in Shreveport, Louisiana, he began broadcasting controversial radio sermons over a powerful station owned by W. K. Henderson, a millionaire and personal friend of Huey P. Long. Smith's demagoguery peaked in 1935 and 1936, when he won an audience of millions by promoting Huey Long's gospel of sharing the wealth and the controversial proposals of Dr. Francis E. Townsend and Father Charles E. Coughlin. His mass popularity was short lived but he had managed to accumulate a personal fortune that enabled him to employ a small staff and attract enough support to mail out millions of pieces of propaganda, publicizing such anti-Jewish publications as *The International Jew* and *the Protocols of the Learned Elders of Zion,* and his own reactionary hate-sheet *The Cross and the Flag.* In his later years he retired in Eureka Springs, Arkansas, where he became involved in tourism developments with religious themes, including the *Passion Play* and the *Christ of the Ozarks.* He died April 15, 1976, and was buried on Magnet Mountain in Eureka Springs near the *Christ of the Ozarks* statue. See Glen Jeansonne, *Gerald L. K. Smith: Minister of Hate* (New Haven, Conn.: Yale University Press, 1988).

159. Harold Bell Wright, *The Shepherd of the Hills* (New York: Gossett and Dunlop, 1907; reprint, McCormick-Armstrong Company, 1987).

160. See Morrow and Myers-Phinney, *Shepherd of the Hills Country,* for a full history of the historical background of the Shepherd of the Hills Tourism Region.

161. Kathryn Buckstaff, "Time-share Packages Increasing in Popularity," *Springfield News-Leader,* February 28, 2000, 6A.

162. Rafferty, *The Ozarks Outdoors,* 242.

163. Ibid., 252–53.

164. Ibid., 252.

165. Ibid., 266–67.

166. See Rafferty, *The Ozarks Outdoors,* 305–13, for a more complete discussion of the tourist attractions in the Mississippi River Border tourism region.

167. Ibid.

168. Lucille Basler, *A Tour of Old Ste. Genevieve* (Ste. Genevieve, Mo.: Wehmeyer Printing Co., 1975), 1–26.

169. See Rafferty, *The Ozarks Outdoors,* 272–86, for a more complete discussion of the Cherokee Country tourism region.

170. Douglas Hurt, *Nathan Boone and the American Frontier* (Columbia: University of Missouri Press, 1998).

171. Cathryn Buckstaff, "Ride the Monorail to the Land of Never-was Ideas," *Springfield News-Leader,* February 28, 2000, 1A, 6A.

172. Jennifer Barnett, "Wanted: Ideas Built to Last," *Springfield News-Leader,* February 28, 2000, 1A.

173. Sauer, *Geography of the Ozark Highland,* 186–87.

174. Aerie Acres Advertisement Leaflet (Ava, Mo.: Aerie Acres, n.d.). The leaflet, picked up at a store in Ava, Missouri, about 1975, is in possession of the author.

CHAPTER 13: NONMATERIAL CULTURAL TRAITS

1. Wiley Britton, *Pioneer Life in Southwest Missouri* (Kansas City: Smith-Grieves Company, 1929).

2. Vance Randolph, *Down in the Holler: A Gallery of Ozark Folk Speech* (Norman: University of Oklahoma Press, 1953). In addition to *Down in the Holler,* Randolph authored many books on Ozark folk tales and customs which also include traditional speech and language usage.

3. Contrary to popular belief there is a substantial body of literature and other source material available for those who wish to research the Ozark region. However, because much of it is of the unedited reminiscent type, the quality of the local historical accounts is highly variable. Furthermore, because many of the accounts are based on personal recollections and word of mouth transfer, they vary widely in reliability. Even so, there is no shortage of reliable evidence about living conditions and lifestyles. These sources include census data and the manuscript census, various reports produced by federal, state, and local governmental agencies, master's theses, doctoral dissertations, and several reliable edited books. For a useful guide to Ozark folklore, see Vance Randolph and Gordon McCann, *Ozark Folklore: An Annotated Bibliography* (Columbia: University of Missouri Press, 1987).

4. Donald R. Holliday, "Autobiography of an American Family" (Ph.D. diss., University of Minnesota, 1974), 144–47.

5. Lynn Morrow, "Fighting Flat, Carriage Paint, and Toilets in the Brush," *White River Valley Historical Quarterly* (Winter 1988): 3. Condensed and edited by Lynn Morrow from "Conditions of Schools in Ozark County," *St. Louis Star,* January 22, 1925.

6. Waldo O. Cralle, "Social Change and Isolation in the Ozark Mountain Region of Missouri" (Ph.D. diss., University of Minnesota, 1934), 248.

7. "Uncle Bill from Kirbyville Says Groundhog Deserves Research?" *Branson* (Mo.) *White River Leader,* January 31, 1972, 2.

8. "2000 Missouri School District Computing Census," Missoui Department of Education. http://www.dese.state.mo.us/computing census/2000/, Oc

9. Deborah S. Sutton, director of Instructional Technology, Missouri Department of Elementary and Secondary Education. E-mail correspondence with the author, September 19, 2000.

10. Ibid.

11. Holliday, "Autobiography of an American Family," 146.

12. Cralle, "Social Change and Isolation," 64.

13. Overheard by the author on a citizens' band radio, January 18, 1978.

14. Recorded by the author, 1982 to 2000. Beginning in 1982, the author kept notes on fequently heard colloquial expressions during trips and everyday life in Springfield.

15. Personal observations by the author over a period of more than thirty years.

16. Randolph and Wilson, *Down in the Holler,* 70–94.

17. Cralle, "Social Change and Isolation," 61.

18. Randolph and Wilson, *Down in the Holler,* 222–301.

19. Dale Freeman, *How to Talk Pure Ozark In One Easy Lesson* (Kimberling City, Mo.: Ozark Postcard Publishers, 1991).

20. The author was born in 1932 in Jewell County, Kansas, attended school, and worked in Kansas and Nebraska until 1964. Many, if not most, so-called Ozark terms were in common use by residents of rural Kansas and Nebraska.

21. E. Joan Wilson Miller, "The Ozark Culture Region as Revealed by Traditional Materials," *Annals of the Association of American Geographers* 58 (March 1968): 58–64.

22. Ibid., 57–58.

23. Timothy C. Frazer, "American Dialect Acquisition in Foreign Settlement Areas" (Paper delivered to the American Dialect Society, Western Illinois University, Macomb, Ill., November 1976).

24. Ibid.

25. Ibid.

26. Sports enthusiasts come from all walks of life. "Sports Talk," a popular radio talk show broadcast on KWTO, 560 AM, from Springfield, Missouri, provides a good listening post to hear the many different types of English spoken in the Ozarks, including "pure Ozark."

27. Robert K. Gilmore, "Theatrical Elements in Folk Entertainment in the Missouri Ozarks, 1886–1910" (Ph. D. diss., University of Minnesota, 1961). Published as Robert K. Gilmore, *Ozark Baptizings, Hangings, and Other Diversions: Theatrical Folkways of Rural Missouri, 1885–1910* (Norman: University of Oklahoma Press, 1984).

28. *West Plains Journal* (January 19, 1899).

29. Gilmore, *Ozark Baptizings, Hangings, and Other Diversions*, 33–35.

30. Friedrich Gerstaeker, *Wild Sports in the Far West* (Durham, N.C.: Duke University Press, 1968), 327–29.

31. Kangeroo courts are staged trials popular at community celebrations. People in the community, often businessmen or prominent citizens, were "arrested," tried before the "court" and always convicted. The usual sentence was a douse in a horse tank filled with water or some other humorous punishment. Kangaroo courts were popular throughout much of rural America. The author recalls kangaroo trials at celebrations in his home town in Mankato, Kansas, following World War II. The staged trials were used for student celebrations on the campus of Southwest Missouri State University in the 1960s and 1970s. Unsuspecting faculty members were sometimes put on trial and dunked in a horse tank on the campus green.

32. Gilmore, "Theatrical Elements," 38–41.

33. Francoise Delsarte, a teacher in France, developed a popular system of calisthenics or physical exercises. The exercises, used widely in schools, were called Delsarte drills.

34. Gilmore, *Ozark Baptizings, Hangings, and Other Diversions*, 33–35.

35. Ibid., 76–77.

36. Ibid., 90.

37. Ibid., 145.

38. David Q. Voigt, *America through Baseball* (Chicago: Nelson-Hall, 1976), 7, 10.

39. David D. Dawson, "Baseball Calls: Arkansas Town Baseball in the Twenties," *Arkansas Historical Quarterly* 54 (Winter 1995): 413.

40. Ibid., 413–19.

41. Gilmore, *Ozark Baptizings, Hangings, and Other Diversions*, 160.

42. Floy W. George, *History of Webster County*, Historical Committee of the Webster County Centennial (Springfield, Mo.: Roberts and Sutter Printers, 1955), 18–22.

43. Glenn Shirley, *Law West of Fort Smith: A History of Frontier Justice in the Indian Territory, 1834–1896* (Lincoln: University of Nebraska Press, 1968), 209–31.

44. Ibid., 226.

45. "Hundreds Watched Hanging in 1938," *Springfield News-Leader*, January 26, 2000, 3B.

46. Margaret Ray Vickery, *Ozark Stories of the Upper Current River* (Salem, Mo.: Salem News, [1969]), 29–31.

47. Both noodling and gigging are practiced at night. Noodling (hand fishing) is illegal. Noodling is accomplished by wading into shallow pools and feeling along the stream banks and under tree roots until a large fish is encountered. The fish is then caught by hand, sometimes with the aid of the legs and body to entrap it. Gigging is legal for some less desirable species such as carp, gar, and suckers as well as frogs. Long-shafted barbed spears are used to spear the fish. Lanterns were used to identify the fish in the early days, but today boats are equipped with special lights designed to penetrate deep into the water.

48. C. C. Cavender, manager of Hammons Products Company, a black walnut processing plant in Stockton, Missouri. Personal interview with the author, November 20, 1967. Cavender stated that Indians and pioneer settlers used walnut hulls to stun fish. Ozarkers also used dynamite and other explosives to stun fish, causing them to rise to the top of the water where they could be taken by hand. See Milton D. Rafferty, "Missouri's Black Walnut Kernel Industry," *Missouri Historical Review* 63 (January, 1969): 214–26.

49. Sarah Overstreet, "Determined Women Played Role in Lady Bears' Success," *Springfield News-Leader*, February 11, 2001, 1B.

50. Balys H. Kennedy, "Half a Century of School Consolidation in Arkansas," *Arkansas Historical Quarterly* 27 (Spring 1968): 59–67.

51. Claudette Riley, "Ozark Schools Get List of Attire No-Nos," *Springfield News-Leader*, July 28, 2000, 1A.

52. Earl T. Sechler, *Our Religious Heritage: Church History of the Ozarks, 1806–1906* (Springfield, Mo.: Westport Press, 1961), 1–14.

53. Cralle, "Social Change and Isolation," 236.

54. Elizabeth Herlinger, "Historical, Cultural, and Organizational Analysis of Ozark Ethnic Identity" (Ph. D. dissertation., University of Chicago, 1972).

55. Ibid., 77.

56. Ibid., 80–81.

57. Ibid., 83–84.

58. Doug Johnson, "Hillbilly Jokes Start Opinion War in Ozarks," *Springfield News-Leader*, January 14, 2001, 6B.

59. Ibid.

60. Herlinger, "Historical, Cultural, and Organizational Analysis of Ozark Ethnic Identity," 80–83.

61. Ibid., 120.

62. Ibid.

63. Lynn Morrow, "Trader William Gilliss and Delaware Migration in Southern Missouri," *Missouri Historical Review* 75 (January 1981): 147–67.

64. Herlinger, "Historical, Cultural, and Organizational Analysis of Ozark Ethnic Identity," 146.

65. Holliday, "Autobiography of an American Family," 138.

66. Ibid., 113.

67. V. Lonnie Lawson, *The Lead Belt Mining Riot of 1917* (Flat River, Mo.: Susan D. Lawson, 1976). See also Christopher Gibbs, *The Great Silent Majority: Missouri's Resistance to World War I* (Columbia: University of Missouri Press, 1988).

68. Leo Rainey, area development agent, Batesville, Arkansas. Personal interview with the author, June 16, 1977.

69. Paul A. Rollinson and Suzanne Goldsmith-Hirsch, "Reason for Hope: A Framework for Resolving Conflict between Homeless Shelters and Their Neighbors," *Dig* 2 (Fall 1999), 1–14.

70. Jonathan Fairbanks and Clyde E. Tuck, *Past and Present of Greene County, Missouri, I* (Indianapolis, Ind.: A. W. Bowen and Company, 1915), 177–78.

71. Ibid., 564.

72. Ibid., 570.

73. Notes recorded by the author at a summer workshop for teachers, Alley Spring, Shannon County, Missouri, June 1979.

74. Herlinger, "Historical, Cultural, and Organizational Analysis of Ozark Ethnic Identity," 134–37.

75. For many years Washington County has had high unemployment rates and frequently leads the state in the percent unemployed. In 1997, when near record low unemployment rates of under 4 percent were common, Washington County's percent unemployed ranged from 9.8 in July to 12.1 in January. See *Employment Record* (Jefferson City: Missouri Department of Labor and Industrial Relations, August 19, 1997).

76. The Keetoowah or Nighthawk societies are conservative groups within the Cherokee nation who have various goals, including the preservation of Cherokee tradition. In 1859, Evan Jones, a Baptist missionary, reorganized the Keetoowah Society, giving as his motive the desire to assist the Cherokees in preserving the best of their traditions. Jones's critics claim his real motive was to originate an abolitionist society which could be counted on to support the Union if it became divided by civil war. Today the Keetoowah Society is split into several factions, each having its own chief or headman. See Grace S. Woodward, *The Cherokees* (Norman: University of Oklahoma Press, 1963), 7–9.

77. Woodward, *The Cherokees,* 9.

78. *Citizens Recommendations Regarding Formulation of Area Development Program* (Republic, Mo.: Southwest Missouri Local Government Advisory Council, 1977).

CHAPTER 14: OZARK TOWNS AND CITIES

1. John R. Stilgoe, *Metropolitan Corridor: Railroads and the American Scene* (New Haven, Conn.: Yale University Press, 1983).

2. Milton D. Rafferty, "Population Trends of Missouri Towns," in *Cultural Geography of Missouri,* ed. M. O. Roark (Cape Girardeau: Southeast Missouri State University, 1983), 59–76.

3. Raymond E. Murphy, *The American City: An Urban Geography* (New York: McGraw-Hill Book Co., 1966), 72–81.

4. Wally Schrock, "Varying Fortunes of Small Towns: Case Studies in Rich Hill, Sarcoxie, and Nixa, Missouri" (Master's thesis, Southwest Missouri State University, 2000).

5. Rafferty, "Population Trends of Missouri Towns," 59–76.

6. A great deal has been written about the hierarchy of towns and cities. Representative examples of published material dealing with American central places include Glenn T. Trewartha, "Types of Rural Settlement in Colonial America," *Geographical Review* 36 (1946): 568–96. See also J. E. Brush, "The Hierarchy of Central Places in Southwestern Wisconsin," *Geographical Review* 43 (1953): 414–16; Glenn T. Trewartha, "The Unincorporated Hamlet: One Element of the American Settlement Fabric," *Annals of the Association of American Geographers* 33 (1943): 32–81; Harold M. Mayer, "Urban Geography," in *American Geography: Inventory and Prospect,* ed. Preston E. James and Clarence F. Jones (Syacuse, N.Y.: Syracuse University Press, 1954), 149–50. For a straightforward explanation of Walter Christaller's central place theory, see Murphy, *The American City: An Urban Geography,* 72–81.

7. Milton D. Rafferty, "Central Places in Southwest Missouri" (Springfield: Department of Geography, Geology, and Planning, Southwest Missouri State University, 1970), 1–14. This paper summarizes the fieldwork of the Geography of Missouri class, spring 1970. The paper is in the possession of the author.

8. Harley E. Johansen and Glenn V. Fuguitt, *The Changing Rural Village in America: Demographic and Economic Trends since 1950* (Cambridge, Mass.: Ballinger Publishing Company, 1984), 107–36.

9. Personal observation of the author. In the 1960s, 1970s, and 1980s, the author led student field trips to the eastern Ozarks. The tavern-grocery in Altenburg was a frequent stop to purchase food for a noon lunch on the bank of the Mississippi River at Wittenburg.

10. A survey of telephone directories for Branson and Jefferson City provides a simple measure of Branson's prowess in the service sector. The telephone directory for Branson, a city of 4,911, listed 131 restaurants, while Jefferson City, with a population of 34,911, had 88. Data sources: *Branson-Tri-Lakes Telephone Directory* (St. Louis, Mo.: GTE Midwest, May 1999), 225–36; and *Sprint Yellow Pages* (Shawnee Mission, Kans.: Sprint, June 1999), 318–25.

11. Edward T. Price, "The Central Couthouse Square in the American County Seat," *Geographical Review* 58 (1968): 29–60.

12. Milton D. Rafferty, *A Geography of World Tourism* (Englewood Cliffs, N.J.: Prentice Hall, 1993), 52–53. For a discussion of the growth of a highway business district in an Ozark county seat town, see Stuart A. Smith, "Houston, Missouri: An Example of a Changing Cultural Landscape in the Rural Missouri Ozarks" (Master's thesis, University of Missouri, 1991), 94–111.

13. "Jefferson City Chamber of Commerce," Jefferson City, Missouri. http://www.jcchamber.org/ (July 10, 2000).

14. Eugene M. Violette, *A History of Missouri* (Boston: D. C. Heath and Co., 1918), 131.

15. Perry McCandless, *A History of Missouri, II, 1820–1860,* ed. William E. Parrish (Columbia: University of Missouri, 1972), 21–22.

16. Workers of the Writers' Project of the Works Projects Administration in the State of Missouri, *The WPA Guide to 1930s Missouri.* Originally published by Duell, Sloan and Pearce in 1941. Reprint. (Lawrence: University Press of Kansas, 1986), 227.

17. *Population Estimates for Places, Missouri,* Block 1 of 2. Annual Time Series, July 1, 1990, to July 1, 1998. Population Division, U.S. Census Bureau, Washington, D.C., 1999. http://www.census.gov/population/estimates/metro-city/sets/SC98T_MO-DR.txt (May 15, 2000).

18. "County Population Estimates, 1998: Missouri." Population Estimates Program, Population Division, U.S. Census Bureau, Washington, D.C. http://www.census.gov/population/estimates/county/co-99–1/99C1_29.txt (May 15, 2000).

19. *Population Estimates for Places, Missouri,* Block 1 of 2.

20. *Missouri Manufacturers Register 2000* (Evanston, Ill.: MNI Manufacturers' News, 1999), 177–81.

21. *Population Estimates for Places, Missouri,* Block 1 of 2.

22. "Metropolitan Area Population Estimates for July 1, 1998." Population Estimates Program, Population Division, U.S. Census Bureau, Washington, D.C. http://www.census.gov/population/estimates/metro-city/ma98–01.txt (May 15, 2000).

23. Houck, *A History of Missouri,* vol. 2, 168.

24. Houck, *A History of Missouri,* vol. 3, 48.

25. Lynn Morrow, "Cape Girardeau and Its Hinterland: 1736–1826," *Missouri Historical Society Bulletin* 36 (July 1980): 251–50.

26. Milton D. Rafferty, "Crowley's Ridge: An Ozarks Outlier?" *Ozark Mountaineer,* 4 parts (March–April, June–July, August–September, October–November 1989).

27. William T. Doherty Jr., *Louis Houck: Missouri Historian and Entrepreneur* (Columbia: University of Missouri Press, 1960).

28. *Missouri Manufacturers Register 2000* (Evanston, Ill.: MNI Manufacturers' News, 1999), 241–43.

29. City of Cape Girardeau, Missouri. http://www.showme.net/capecity/welcome/ (July 10, 2000).

30. *Population Estimates for Places, Missouri,* Block 1 of 2.

31. The urban economic base as commonly defined, consists of all activities that export goods and services to points outside the community or that market their goods and services to persons who come from outside. Basic manufacturers and service companies are considered "city-building" because they bring new revenues into the city to provide new jobs, and to make the city grow. Non-basic or "city-serving" manufacturers and service companies tend to sell or serve primarily the people of the city itself, and therefore do not bring in new revenues. See Raymond E. Murphy, *The American City: An Urban Geography* (New York: McGraw-Hill, 1966), 98–111.

32. *Missouri Manufacturers Register 2000,* 248–50.

33. The origin of the appellation "Queen City of the Ozarks" is obscure. It probably originated in promotional material for the city and its businesses. Authors Jonathan Fairbanks and Clyde E. Tuck referred to Springfield as the "Queen of the Ozarks"in their 1915 history of the county. (Jonathan Fairbanks and Clyde E. Tuck, *Past and Present of Greene County, Missouri I.* (Indianapolis, Ind.: A. W. Bowen and Company, 1915), 682.) Even earlier, in 1906, the *Merchants and Manufacturers Record of Springfield Missouri* (Springfield: A. Owen Jennings, 1906) included the subtitles, "The Queen City of the Ozarks," and "The Metropolis of the Southwest." Listed in the publication are two "Queen City" companies—the Queen City Restaurant and Queen City Ice and Refrigeration Company. Although authors E. F. Perkins and T. M. Horne did not mention "Queen City" in connection with Springfield in their 1883 history of Greene County, the Queen City Milling Company had been incorporated earlier, in 1879. See E. F. Perkins and T. M. Horne's *History of Greene County, Missouri, Including a History of Its Townships, and a Brief History of Missouri* (St. Louis, Mo.: Western Historical Society Company, 1883). In December 2000, 211 active and inactive businesses that included "Queen City" in there names were registered with the Missouri secretary of state. The majority had Springfield addresses.

34. For a discussion of the historical geography of Springfield, Missouri, in the context of theoretical models of city structure, see Milton D. Rafferty, *Missouri: A Geography* (Boulder, Colo.: Westview Press, 1983), 185–96.

35. The general concept underlying definitions of Metropolitan Areas is that of a core area containing a large population nucleus together with adjacent communities having a high degree of economic and social integration with that core. In effect, the definitions specify a boundary around each large city that includes most or all suburbs in addition to the city itself. Most definitions also include smaller satellite communities and some open country since, in general, entire counties form the Metropolitan Area building blocks. Some areas are defined around two, three, or more central cities. The Metropolitan Statistical Area is the smallest in the heirarchy of U.S. Census Bureau metropolitan areas. Springfield MSA, Fayetteville-Springdale-Rogers MSA, and Joplin MSA constitute the Ozarks' three Metropolitan Statistical Areas. There are no higher order metropolitan areas in the Ozarks. See "Federal Information Processing Standards Publication 8–6." Announcing the Standards for Metropolitan Areas, March 1995. http://www.itl.nist.gov/fipspubs/fip8–6–0.htm (August 6, 2000).

36. "Metropolitan Area Population Estimates for July 1, 1998."

37. Registrars' Offices, Southwest Missouri State University, Drury University, Evangel University, Ozark Technical Community College, Baptist Bible College, and Central Bible College. Telephone interviews by the author with registrars' office personel, July 5, 2000.

38. Fairbanks and Tuck, *Past and Present of Greene County, Missouri,* vol. 1, 40–41.

39. Lynn Morrow, "Trader William Gilliss and Delaware Migration in Southern Missouri," *Missouri Historical Review* 75 (January 1981): 147–67.

40. Fairbanks and Tuck, *Past and Present of Greene County, Missouri,* vol. 1, 686.

41. Ibid. 156.

42. Ibid., 190.

43. In the1970s the city of Springfield closed the Public Square to automobile traffic in their effort to create a pedestrian mall and to stimulate growth in the downtown area. Public officials gave the Public Square a new name, Park Central Mall. In the late 1990s, urged by downtown businessmen, the city opened the square to traffic. In the city map published in the year 2000, the name Public Square reappeared with no mention of Park Central Square.

44. Katherine Lederer, *Many Thousand Gone: Springfield's Lost Black History* (Springfield: Missouri Committee for the Humanities and the Gannett Foudation, 1986), 13.

45. Milton D. Rafferty, "The Golden Age of Mass Transit in Springfield, pt. II," *Springfield Magazine,* April 1982, 39–48.

46. Karen E. Culp, "College Street Banks on Business Revival," *Springfield News-Leader,* July 6, 2000, 1A. Parts of U.S. 66 in Springfield have been designated Historic Route 66 and marked as such.

47. In American cities commercial streets often form along former trolley lines, city thoroughfares, and bypass highways. Urban geographers call such commercial thoroughfares "string shopping streets." Due to the heavy traffic, former residential streets developed into commercial streets with diverse retail stores and off-street shopping centers. Retail nodes or agglomerations often develop where two string shopping streets intersect. See Raymond E. Murphy, *The American City: An Urban Geography* (New York: McGraw-Hill Book Co., 1966), 261–67.

48. Robert Keyes, "Council Sees Four Plans for Glenstone," *Springfield News-Leader,* June 21, 2000, 1A, 7A.

49. "Burlington Northern-Santa Fe to cut 1,400 Jobs," *Springfield News-Leader,* May 25, 1999, 4A.

50. Virginia Hogg, "Urban Pattern of Springfield, Missouri" (Master's thesis, Washington University, 1934), 37–90.

51. *Missouri Manufacturers' Register 2000,* 273–86.

52. U.S. Bureau of the Census, *County Business Patterns: Missouri, 1997* (Washington, D.C.: U.S. Government Printing Office, 1999), 55.

53. "Springfield Manufacturers' Survey, 1968" (Department of Geography, Geology, and Planning, Southwest Missouri State University, Springfield, Mo., 1968). A report based on a telephone survey by the urban geography class. The report is in the possession of the author.

54. Karen Culp, "Industrial Park's Impact Praised," *Springfield News-Leader,* June 27, 2000, 1A, 8A.

55. Robert Keyes, "City Focuses on Buying Land," *Springfield News-Leader,* August 31, 2000, 1A, 4A.

56. Springfield-Branson Regional Airport, Marketing Department. Telephone interview with the author, June 30, 2000.

57. Milton D. Rafferty, *Historical Atlas of Missouri* (Norman: University of Oklahoma Press, 1982: plate 77.

58. U.S. Bureau of the Census, *County Business Patterns: Missouri, 1997,* 55–59.

59. Rafferty, *Missouri: A Geography,* 218–23.

60. *Population Estimates for Places, Missouri,* Block 1 of 2.

61. Walter Williams, *The State of Missouri: An Autobiography* (Columbia, Mo.: Press of E. W. Stephens, 1904), 407.

62. Porter Wagonner Boulevard is a portion of Business Route U.S. 63. It was named for country-music performer, Porter Wagoner, who grew up near West Plains.

63. Sue Griffith, "Lebanon, Missouri, Home of Thriving Appleby Boat Plant," *Ozarks Mountaineer* (July 1965): 4, 14.

64. *Missouri Manufacturers Register 2000,* 378–80.

65. "Welcome to Independent Stave Company," Independent Stave Company, Lebanon, Missouri. http://www.cooperage.com/welcome.html (July 12, 2000).

66. *Missouri Manufacturers' Register 2000,* 204–6.

67. Workers of the Writers' Project of the Works Projects Administration in the State of Arkansas, *Arkansas: A Guide to the State* (New York: Hastings House, 1941), 267.

68. *Population Estimates for Places, Arkansas.*

69. "Welcome to Harrison, Arkansas," Development Information Network of Arkansas. http://harrison.dina.org/ (July 8, 2000).

70. Ibid.

71. *Arkansas Manufacturers' Register 2000* (Evanston, Ill.: MNI Manufacturers News, 1999), 152–55.

72. *Branson-Tri-Lakes Telephone Directory* (St. Louis, Mo.: GTE Midwest, May 1999); *Jefferson City Telephone Directory* (Shawnee Mission, Kans.: Sprint, June 1999). Data on the number of motels, eating establishments, and professional services were collected for comparison.

73. Jennifer McDonald, "Plant Closings Change Ozarks," *Springfield News-Leader,* January 9, 2000, 1A, 4A.

74. *Arkansas Manufacturers' Register 2000; Missouri Manufacturers' Register 2000.*

75. Karen E. Culp, "Hagale Losing to the World," *Springfield News-Leader,* August 23, 2000, 10A.

76. Arrell M. Gibson, *Wilderness Bonanza: The Tri-State District of Missouri, Kansas, and Oklahoma* (Norman: University of Oklahoma Press, 1972), 17–20.

77. Ibid., 35.

78. *Missouri Manufacturers' Register 2000,* 325–32.

79. Rafferty, *Missouri: A Geography,* 120–21.

80. U.S. Bureau of the Census. *United States Census of Population: 1960. Missouri,* vol. 1, pt. 27 (Washington, D.C.: U.S. Government Printing Office, 1963); "Metropolitan Area Population Estimates for July 1, 1998."

81. Shiloh Museum Board of Trustees, *History of Washington County, Arkansas* (Springdale, Ark.: Shiloh Museum, 1989), ch. 6, 271–373.

82. Land use information collected along U.S. 71 by the author in August 1979, April 2000, and September 2000.

83. *History of Washington County, Arkansas,* 273.

84. Ibid., 130.

85. Michael A. Hughes, "Wartime Gristmill Destruction in Northwest Arkansas and Military Farm Colonies," in *Civil War in Arkansas: Beyond Leaders and Battles* (Fayetteville: University of Arkansas Press, 2000), 31.

86. *Population Estimates for Places, Arkansas.*

87. "University of Arkansas Stats," University of Arkansas. http://www.uark.edu/admin/ urelinfo/info/briefing-book/stats.html (August 5, 2000).

88. Geographers recognize both a geographic city and a political city. The geographic city is often larger than the political city because it includes the heavily built up residential, commercial and manufacturing areas that lie outside the political boundaries of a city. In some instances, when cities are allowed to annex large areas of rural land, the political city may be larger than the actual built up geographical city. Two large political cities not far distant from the Ozarks, Kansas City and Oklahoma City, serve as examples of the latter case. See Rhoads Murphey, *The Scope of Geography,* 3d ed. (London: Methuen and Co., 1982).

89. "Fayetteville, Arkansas Economic Data," Fayetteville Chamber of Commerce, Fayetteville, Arkansas. http://www.fayettevillear.com/data.htm (July 13, 2000). See also, *Arkansas Manufacturers Register 2000* (Evanston, Ill.: MNI Manufacturers News, 2000), 128–34.

90. *Population Estimates for Places, Arkansas,* Block 1 of 2.

91. Poke greens are the leaves of the pokeberry plant. Pokeberry, sometimes called pokeweed, grows wild in the Ozarks and over much of the southeastern United States. Because the mature plant is slightly toxic, the leaves are picked in the spring while immature. It was formerly cultivated commercially for canning purposes, but has gone out of favor. It is still grown in gardens and eaten fresh, mainly in salads, during the spring and early summer.

92. *Arkansas Manufacturers' Register 2000,* 248.

93. Ibid., 243–48.

94. *Population Estimates for Places, Arkansas,* Block 1 of 2.

95. *Arkansas Manufacturers' Register 2000,* 230–33.

96. Cass S. Hough, *It's a Daisy* (Rogers, Ark.: Daisy Division Victor Comptometer Corporation, 1976), 159.

97. *Population Estimates for Places, Arkansas,* Block 1 of 2.

98. Vance H. Trimble, *Sam Walton: The Inside Story of America's Richest Man* (New York: Penquin Books USA, 1990), 76.

99. *Arkansas Manufacturers' Register 2000,* 103–4.

100. Leo Rainey, area development agent, Batesville, Arkansas. Personal interview with the author, June 16, 1977.

101. "Batesville, Independence County, Arkansas," Development Information Network of Arkansas. http://batesville.dina.org/industry/majemp.html (July 10, 2000).

102. *Arkansas Manufacturers' Register 2000,* 96–98.

103. Leo Rainey, area development agent, Batesville, Arkansas. Personal interview with the author, June 16, 1977.

104. "General Information for Tahlequah," Oklahoma Department of Community Development, Data and Statistics. http://www.odoc.state.ok.us/oknet/.

105. *Population Estimates for Places, Oklahoma.* Annual Time Series, July 1, 1990, to July 1, 1998. Population Estimates Program, Population Division, U.S. Census Bureau, Washington, D.C., 1999. http://www.census.gov/population/estimates/metro-city/sets/SC98T_MO-DR.txt. (May 15, 2000).

106. Grace Steel Woodward, *The Cherokees* (Norman: University of Oklahoma Press, 1963), 229.

107. "General Information for Tahlequah."

108. Ibid.

CHAPTER 15: THE CULTURAL LANDSCAPE

1. Carl O. Sauer, "The Morphology of Landscape," in *Land and Life,* ed. John Leighly (Berkeley and Los Angeles: University of California Press, 1963), 343.

2. Michael A. Williams, *Homeplace: The Social Use and Meaning of the Folk Dwelling in Southwestern North Carolina* (Athens: University of Georgia Press, 1991). A good reference for the style, construction, materials, use, and modification of folk housing in the Appalachian hill country.

3. Fred Kniffen, "Folk Housing: Key to Diffusion," *Annals of the Association of American Geographers* 55 (December 1965): 549–77.

4. Milton D. Rafferty, "Persistence Versus Change in Land Use and Landscape in the Springfield, Missouri Vicinity of the Ozarks" (Ph. D. diss., University of Nebraska, 1970). See chap. 6, 223–320.

5. Robert A. Finley and E. M. Scott, "A Great Lakes-to-Gulf Profile of Dispersed Dwelling Types," *Geogaphical Review* 30 (July 1940): 412–18.

6. Several important studies of Ozark houses have been published since *The Ozarks: Land and Life* first appeared in 1980. Jean Sizemore's *Ozark Vernacular Houses: A Study of Rural Homeplaces in the Arkansas Ozarks, 1830–1930* (Fayetteville: University of Arkansas Press, 1994) is a comprehensive study of Arkansas Ozarks. Several articles by Robert Flanders and Lynn Morrow trace the origins of house and the architects who built them: Robert Flanders, "Caledonia: Ozarks Legacy of the High Scotch-Irish," *Gateway Heritage* 6 (Spring 1986): 34–52; Lynn Morrow, "Louis Miller: Master Craftsman and Folk Artisan of Southeast Missouri," *Gateway Heritage* 4 (Winter 1983): 26–30; Lynn Morrow, "Estate Builders in the Missouri Ozarks: Establishing a St. Louis Tradition," *Gateway Heritage* 2 (Winter 1981–1982): 42–48; Lynn Morrow and Robert Flanders, "An Overview of Seven Ozark Counties" (West Plains: South Central Ozarks Council of Governments, 1989), 33–81; and David Quick and Lynn Morrow, "The Slab Rock Dwellings of Thayer, Missouri," *Proceedings of the Pioneer America Society,* 13 (1990): 36–37. A useful reference on the German house and barn architecture in

the northern Ozarks is Charles C. van Ravenswaay, *The Arts and Architecture of German Settlements in Missouri: A Survey of a Vanishing Culture* (Columbia: University of Missouri Press, 1977). Howard W. Marshall's *Folk Architecture in Little Dixie: A Regional Culture in Missouri* (Columbia: University of Missouri Press, 1981) includes useful information on early folk architecture, although its principal focus was outside the Ozarks.

7. Virginia McAlester and Lee McAlester, *A Field Guide to American Houses* (New York: Alfred A. Knopf, 1984), 75–86.

8. McAlester and McAlester, *A Field Guide to American Houses,* 76–77, 84.

9. McAlester and McAlester, *A Field Guide to American Houses,* 82.

10. Sizemore, *Ozark Vernacular Houses,* 62.

11. Sizemore, *Ozark Vernacular Houses,* 63.

12. Ibid., 57.

13. Field observations by the author, June 19, 1972.

14. Miss Ladonna Hermann, associate of the Rural Parish Workers of Christ the King, St. Louis Catholic Diocese. Personal interview with the author, Fertile (Washington County), Mo., March 29, 2001. Miss Ladonna Hermann was an associate of the Rural Parish Workers when they first established residency at Fertile in 1949 to serve the people of St. Joachim Parish. She still lives at the Rural Parish Workers residence and works in the parish. In 1951, Miss Ladonna Hermann and fellow Rural Parish Worker, Miss Alice Widmer, employed a local resident, Elmer Govero, to build the rustic log cabin as a place of residence for members of the Rural Parish Workers. He built the cabin from timber cut on the property.

15. McAlester and McAlester, *A Field Guide to American Houses,* 96.

16. Fred Kniffen, "Louisiana House Types," *Annals, AAG* 26 (December 1936): 190.

17. Michael Southern, "The I-House as a Carrier of Style in Three Counties of the Northeastern Piedmont," in Doug Swaim, ed., *Carolina Dwelling: Toward Preservation of Place; In Celebration of the Vernacular Landscape.* Student Publication of the School of Design, vol. 26 (Raleigh: North Carolina State University, 1978), 71.

18. Sizemore, *Ozark Vernacular Houses,* 76.

19. Ibid.

20. Rafferty, "Persistence Versus Change," 266–75.

21. Doug Swaim, "Carolina Dwelling: Toward Preservation of Place," in *Celebration of the Vernacular Landscape,* ed. Doug Swaim. Student Publication of the School of Design, vol. 26 (Raleigh: North Carolina State University, 1978), 38.

22. Sizemore, *Ozark Vernacular Houses,* 89.

23. Ibid.

24. McAlester and McAlester, *A Field Guide to American Houses,* 178. See also Andrew Jackson Downing, *Cottage Residences: A Series of Designs for Rural Cottages and Cottage Villas, and their Gardens and Grounds* (New York: J. Wiley and Son, 1873).

25. Ibid., 239.

26. Ibid.

27. Fred W. Peterson, *Homes in the Heartland: Balloon Frame Farmhouses of the Upper Midwest, 1850–1920* (Lawrence: University Press of Kansas, 1992). This volume is includes a thorough discussion of balloon framing and its applications.

28. McAlester and McAlester, *A Field Guide to American Houses,* 319.

29. Flanders, "Caledonia: Ozarks Legacy of the High Scotch-Irish," 34–52.

30. Vance H. Trimble, *Sam Walton: The Inside Story of America's Richest Man* (New York: Penquin Books USA, 1990), 79.

31. Howard W. Marshall, *Folk Architecture in Little Dixie: A Regional Culture in Missouri* (Columbia: University of Missouri Press, 1981), 30–71.

32. Morrow, "Louis Miller: Master Craftsman," 30.

33. Morrow, "Estate Builders in the Missouri Ozarks," 45.

34. Ibid.

35. Ibid.

36. Ibid., 48.

37. McAlester and McAlester, *A Field Guide to American Houses,* 95.

38. Ibid., 92.

39. Ibid.

40. Rafferty, "Persistence Versus Change," 266–75.

41. Marshall, *Folk Architecture in Little Dixie,* 35.

42. John Vlatch, "The Shotgun House: An African Architectural Legacy," in *Readings in American Vernacular Architecture,* ed. Dell Upton and John M. Vlatch (Athens: University of Georgia Press, 1986), 58–78.

43. McAlester and McAlester, *A Field Guide to American Houses,* 9.

44. Judy Ferguson, *The Boom Town of West Eminence and Its Lumbering Days* (Rolla, Mo.: Rolla Printing Company, 1969), 10.

45. Randell L. Makinson, *Greene & Greene: Architecture as a Fine Art* (Salt Lake City, Utah: Peregrine Smith, 1977). Makinson traces the building careers of Charles Sumner Greene and Henry Mather Greene in southern California and their influence on bungalow style houses. For national and world perspective on bungalow houses, see Anthony D. King, *The Bungalow: The Production of a Global Culture* (New York: Oxford University Press, 1995).

46. McAlester and McAlester, *A Field Guide to American Houses,* 454.

47. Ibid. See Catherine Cole Stevenson and H. Ward Jandl, *Houses by Mail: A Guide to Houses from Sears, Roebuck and Company* (New York: John Wiley and Sons, 1986), for a discussion of the houses that Sears, Roebuck and Company sold through their Modern Homes Department between 1908 and 1940.

48. Morrow, "Louis Miller: Master Craftsman," 42–48.

49. Ibid., 42–48.

50. Ibid., 35–36.

51. Morrow and Flanders, "An Overview of Seven Ozark Counties," 33–81.

52. Professor Vincent Kurtz, geologist, Southwest Missouri State University. Personal interview with the author, April 15, 1978.

53. Milton D. Rafferty, *Ozark House Types* (Springfield, Mo.: Aux-Arc Book Co, 1979), 4. A primer on Ozark house types for student field trips.

54. Personal observations of the author. The author has in his possession several color slides of commercial buildings in Bakersfield, Missouri, which are built of local stone with prominent mud-filled cracks raised in relief. The sandstone, red to yellow in color and probably quarried from the Roubidoux formation, has numerous darker colored, denser, and more resistant pentagonal sandstone bands protruding above the ripple-marked sandstone slabs. The protruding bands represent former mud cracks that were subsequently filled with sand when the area was part of a coastal environment. The sand in the mud cracks was cemented more tightly than the main slab sandstone, which accounts for the fact that they extend above the surface of the slabrock. Ripple marks are very common in many Ozark sandstones, mud cracks are less common.

55. A friend of the author tells an apocryphal story about the time he and his neighbor were each building a new house in Greene County. When he stopped by one day to see how his neighbor was progressing, he noticed how the door and window openings were obviously out of square and most everything appeared "catty-wampus." As they were talking, my friend asked his neighbor whether he had used a carpenter's square while lining things up. His neighbor replied, "What's that?"

56. Quick and Morrow, "The Slab Rock Dwellings of Thayer, Missouri," 36–37.

57. Ibid., 37–42.

58. McAlester and McAlester, *A Field Guide to American Houses,* 477.

59. Ibid, 122.

60. Ibid., 124.

61. van Ravenswaay, *The Arts and Architecture of German Settlements in Missouri,* 221.

62. McAlester and McAlester, *A Field Guide to American Houses,* 497.

63. Morrow and Flanders, "An Overview of Seven Ozark Counties," 56–57.

64. Shelley Armitage, *Kewpies and Beyond: The World of Rose O'Neill* (Jackson: University Press of Mississippi, 1994).

65. Robert Gibbons, founder and first president of the not-for-profit Bonniebrook Historical Society. Telephone interview with the author, August 17, 2000.

66. Milton D. Rafferty, "The Marbut Place: A Touch of New England in the Ozarks," *Springfield News-Leader,* July 22, 1973, 1C–2C, 7C.

67. Morrow and Flanders, "An Overview of Seven Ozark Counties," 48–56.

68. Leslie Hewes, "Cultural Fault Line in the Cherokee Country," *Economic Geography* 19 (April 1943): 136–37.

69. Ibid., 136–42.

70. Trimble, *Sam Walton,* 79.

71. Cynthia R. Price, "Patterns of Cultural Behavior and Intra-site Distributions of Faunal Remains at the Widow Harris Site," *Historical Archaeology* 19 (1985): 40–56.

72. Henry R. Schoolcraft, *Rude Pursuits and Rugged Peaks: Schoolcraft's 1818–19 Ozark Journal,* ed. Milton D. Rafferty (Fayetteville: University of Arkansas Press, 1996), 52.

73. Ibid., 63. Professor George Lankford has suggested that the reason Schoolcraft may not have seen gardens was because he traveled in the winter months. Even though Schoolcraft's descriptions of the foods eaten by the settlers includes no mention of garden produce, it seems likely that they would have planted potatoes and other vegetables. In any case, the second wave of immigrants certainly planted gardens. See George E. Lankford, "Beyond the Pale: Frontier Folk in the Southern Ozarks," in *The Folk: Identity, Landscapes and Lore,* ed. Robert J. Smith and Jerry Stannard (Lawrence: University of Kansas Studies in Anthropology no. 17, 1989).

74. Ibid., 53.

75. Ibid.

76. Friedrich Gerstäker, *Wild Sports in the Far West* (Durham, N.C.: Duke University Press, 1968), 89.

77. Ibid., 89–91.

78. Waldo O. Cralle, "Social Change and Isolation in the Ozark Mountains Region of Missouri" (Ph.D. diss., University of Minnesota, 1935).

79. James Wood and Milton D. Rafferty, "Mentor Missouri: Forty Years Later," *Missouri Geographer* (Fall 1976): 21–26.

80. Cralle, "Social Change and Isolation," 296.

81. Ibid.

82. Martha Gilmore. Videotaped interview for "Just That Much Hillbilly in Me," a video production by Mark Biggs, associate professor of Media, Southwest Missouri State University, Springfield, 1999.

83. Michael A. Hughes, "Wartime Gristmill Destruction in Northwest Arkansas and Military Farm Colonies," in *Civil War Arkansas: Beyond Battles and Leaders,* ed. Anne J. Bailey and Daniel E. Sutherland (Fayetteville: University of Arkansas Press, 2000), 31–46. Originally published in the *Arkansas Historical Quarterly* 47 (Summer 1987): 167–86.

84. "The Ozark Watermill Trail," *Ozarks Mountaineer* 16 (June 1968): 21; For paintings, drawings and descriptions of Ozark watermills, see George G. Suggs Jr., *Water Mills of the Missouri Ozarks.* Paintings and illustrations by Jake K. Wells. (Norman: University of Oklahoma Press, 1990).

85. Morrow and Flanders, "An Overview of Seven Ozark Counties," 66.

86. Ibid., 64.

87. Loyal Durand Jr., "Dairy Barns of Southeastern Wisconsin," *Economic Geography* 19 (January, 1943): 37–44.

88. Sizemore, *Ozark Vernacular Houses,* 118.

89. Ibid., 119–22.

90. Marshall, *Folk Architecture in Little Dixie,* 84.

91. Ibid., 84–85. See also chap. 2, "Classification of the Pennsylvania Barn," in Robert M. Ensminger, *The Pennsylvania Barn: Its Origin, Evolution, and Distribution in North America* (Baltimore: The Johns Hopkins University Press, 1992), 51–106. Note: Forebays are the eave side overhang of the upper level of a Pennsylvania barn (*vorbau* or *vorschuss* in German).

92. Charles van Ravenswaay, *The Arts and Architecture of German Settlements in Missouri: A Survey of a Vanishing Culture* (Columbia: University of Missouri Press, 1977), 263–94.

93. Rafferty, "Persistence Versus Change," 174.

94. Milton Rafferty, "Ozark House Types: A Regional Approach," *Proceedings of the Pioneer America Society* 2 (1973): 93–106.

95. Ensminger, *The Pennsylvania Barn,* 181.

96. *Barn Again* is a national program devoted to the preservation of historical farm buildings sponsored by the National Trust for Historic Preservation and *Successful Farming* magazine. See also chap. 5, "The Future of the Pennsylvania Barn," in Robert M. Ensminger, *The Pennsylvania Barn,* 181–200, for a discussion of preservation and new uses for restored barns. Note: Some farmers are reluctant to make improvements and repairs to barns because the buildings are seldom used and painting and repairs often result in higher tax assessments.

97. Kay Hively, "An Ozarks Farm Is Barn Again," *Ozarks Mountaineer* 39 (November–December 1991): 38–39.

98. H. H. Krusekopf and F. Z. Hutton, *Soil Survey of Greene County, Missouri* (Washington, D.C.: U.S. Department of Agriculture, Bureau of Soils, 1915), 15.

99. Sauer, *Geography of the Ozark Highland of Missouri,* 206. Sauer observed that rail fences were almost universal, except in the Springfield Plain and on the interior prairies. Several types of split-log fences were built, including the worm fence or zig-zag fence and the post-and-rider fence.

100. Randall O. Herberg, "Fuelwood-Using It Wisely," *Missouri Conservationist* 45 (January 1984): 24–27.

101. Rafferty, "Persistence Versus Change," 196.

102. The Marshfield Tornado, or "cyclone" as it became widely known, was very destructive and tales were told for generations about its catastrophic peculiarities. It struck Marshfield on Sunday, April 18, 1880, shortly after 6:00 P.M. and virtually destroyed the business district and a major part of the town. Sixty people were killed outright, thirty-two died later from wounds received, and eight had limbs amputated. The Marshfield *Chronicle* and many other newspapers carried feature stories about the storm which included accounts that letters and deeds were found many miles away in Phelps and Miller counties. Reportedly it caused the discovery of Medical Spring in the north part of the town when the storm inexplicably changed the path of a small stream which uncovered the spring. For a time visitors stayed in hotels on the town square and frequented the spring for health purposes. One of the most interesting anecdotes connected with the tornado is the story of Blind Boone, a blind Negro youth residing in Columbia, who wrote a song entitled "The Marshfield Cyclone," which launched a lifelong career as a touring pianist. See Floy W. George, *History of Webster County, 1855 to 1955,* Historical Committee of the Webster County Centennial (Springfield, Mo.: Roberts and Sutter Printers, 1955), ch. 8, "The Great Cyclone, April 18, 1880," 27–33.

103. Samuel C. Swartz, Old-Order Amish spokesman, rural Webster County. Personal interview with the author, August 31, 1968.

104. Large companies and municipalities were drilling wells by the 1870s in the Ozarks. In 1870, the St. Louis and San Francisco Railroad (Frisco) sunk a well in Springfield using a churn drilling tool north of the intersection of Commercial Street and Washington Avenue to a depth more than 600 feet. The well produced water from the Roubidoux sandstone. See Edward M. Shepard, *U.S. Geological Survey, Water Supply and Irrigation Paper 195* (Washington, D.C.: U.S. Government Printing Office, 1907), 132.

105. Cralle, "Social Change and Isolation," 285.

106. Rafferty, "Persistence Versus Change," 267–75.

107. Mike Penprase,"Fires Storm through Ozarks," *Springfield News-Leader,* March 9, 2000, 1B, 2B.

108. Schoolcraft, *Rude Pursuits and Rugged Peaks,* 64.

109. Robert Flanders, "The Places We Call Home: Ozarks Dwellings," *Ozark Watch* 9 (Summer 1988): 2–7.

110. Compiled by the author. The list of materials strewn about the yard was compiled from photographs of a farmstead in Dent County, Missouri. The photographs were taken by the author, July 1983.

111. Rafferty, "Persistence Versus Change," 280. In 1979 thirteen traverses were surveyed on roads extending thirty miles in all directions from Springfield; seven along highways and six along rural roads. Three of the same traverses along rural roads were surveyed again in August 1999. The general upkeep of yards improved by 14 percent. Quality ratings for houses and barns improved by 11 percent. The data were collected by the author in both surveys. See Rafferty, "Persistence Versus Change," 7–15.

112. Ibid., 303–4.

113. C. O. Bridges, Christian County stock farmer, Ozark, Missouri. Personal interview with the author, June 16, 1968.

114. *Comprehensive Report on Missouri Schools, 1967* (Jefferson City: Missouri Department of Education, 1967.

115. "Towns, Entrepreneurs Breathe New Life into Old Schools," *Springfield News-Leader,* September 28, 2000, 1B, 3B.

116. Personal observations of the author, August 18, 1978.

117. Gale E. Christianson, *Edwin Hubble: Mariner of the Nebulae* (New York: Farrar, Straus, Giroux, 1995).

118. Milton D. Rafferty, "Curtis F. Marbut: Geographer," *Soil Survey Horizons* 26 (Spring 1985): 13–15. Volume 26, No. 1, is a special issue devoted to the work of Curtis Fletcher Marbut in the fields of soil science, geology and geography. See also H. H. Krusekopf, ed., *Life and Work of C. F. Marbut: Soil*

Scientist (Columbia, Mo.: Soil Science Society of America, 1942).

119. John Leighley, *Land and Life: A Selection from the Writings of Carl Ortwin Sauer* (Berkeley and Los Angeles: University of California Press, 1969), 1–8.

120. Timothy P. Donovan, Willard B. Gatewood Jr., and Jeannie M. Whayne, *The Governors of Arkansas: Essays in Political Biography,* 2d ed. (Fayetteville: University of Arkansas Press, 1995).

121. Shelley Armitage, *Kewpies and Beyond: The World of Rose O'Neill* (Jackson: University Press of Mississippi, 1994). For Rose O'Neill's edited autobiography, see Rose O'Neill, *The Story of Rose O'Neill: An Autobiography,* ed. Miriam Formanek-Brunell (Columbia: University of Missouri Press, 1997).

122. Otto E. Rayburn, *Forty Years in the Ozarks: An Autobiography* (Eureka Springs, Ark.: Ozark Guide Press, 1957.)

123. James Morris (1908–1998), stage name Jimmie Driftwood, the folk musician and songwriter wrote over 6,000 songs during his career, and over three hundred were recorded and/or published. His best-known songs included "The Battle of New Orleans," "The Tennessee Stud," "Down in Arkansas," and "He Had a Long Chain On." He got his start as a high school teacher and used his songs to help teach his classes. "The Battle of New Orleans" was written to help explain to his high school history students that the Battle of New Orleans was fought during the War of 1812. It was written eighteen years before it became famous. Jimmie and his wife, Cleda, welcomed and entertained literally hundreds of visitors each year in their home near Timbo, Arkansas. In the 1970s, he founded the Rackensack Folklore Society in Mountain View and then was instrumental in getting the funds appropriated to build the Ozark Folk Center in Mountain View, Arkansas. James Morris (a.k.a. Jimmie Driftwood), folk musician and songwriter. Personal interview with the author, Timbo, Arkansas, July 23, 1977. See also, "Jimmie Driftwood Obituary," Bill Slater Webpage, http://billslater.com/drift-wood.htm.

124. John E. Miller, *Becoming Laura Ingalls Wilder: The Woman behind the Legend* (Columbia: University of Missouri Press, 1998).

125. Trimble, *Sam Walton,* 23–25.

REFERENCES

BOOKS

Adams, Leon D. *The Wines of America,* 2d ed. New York: McGraw-Hill Book Company, 1978.

Arkansas Manufacturers Register 2000. Evanston, Ill.: MNI Manufacturers News, Inc. 2000.

Arkansas State Planning Board and the Writers Project of the Works Progress Administration. American Guide Series. *Arkansas: A Guide to the State.* New York: Hastings House, 1941.

Armitage, Shelley. *Kewpies and Beyond: The World of Rose O'Neill.* Jackson: University Press of Mississippi, 1994.

Arnold, Morris S. *Colonial Arkansas, 1686–1804: A Social and Cultural History.* Fayetteville: University of Arkansas Press, 1991.

Atherton, Lewis. *Mainstreet on the Middle Border.* Bloomington: Indiana University Press, 1984.

Austin, Moses. A Summary Description of the Lead Mines in Upper Louisiana; Also an Estimate of their Produce for Three Years Past; Also: A Table Shewing the Increase of Population in their Vicinity Since the Year 1799. Drawn at the Request of Captain Amos Stoddard, First Civil Commandant of Upper Louisiana, 1804. City of Washington: A and G Way, Printers, 1804. Typescript copy in the archives of the State Historical Society of Missouri, Columbia.

Austin, Moses. *Description of the Lead Mines in Upper Louisiana.* Vol. I and II. Philadelphia: American State Papers, 1834.

Bailey, Anne J., and Daniel E. Sutherland. *Civil War in Arkansas: Beyond Battles and Leaders.* Fayetteville: University of Arkansas Press, 2000.

Basler, Lucille. *A Tour of Old Ste. Genevieve.* Ste. Genevieve, Mo.: Wehmeyer Printing Co., Inc., 1975.

Bates, Robert L., and Julia A. Jackson, eds. *Glossary of Geology,* 2d ed. Falls Church, Va.: American Geological Institute, 1980.

Baxevanis, John J. *The Wine Regions of America: Geographical Reflections and Appraisals.* Stroudsburg, Pa.: Vinifera Wine Growers Journal, 1992.

Baxter, William. *Pea Ridge and Prairie Grove; or, Scenes and Incidents of the War In Arkansas.* Introduction by William Shea. Fayetteville: University of Arkansas Press, 2000.

The Bella Vista Story. Bella Vista, Ark.: Bella Vista Historical Society, Inc., 1980.

Beveridge, Thomas R. *Geologic Wonders and Curiosities of Missouri,* 2d ed. Rolla: Missouri Department of Natural Resources, Division of Geology and Land Survey, 1990.

Black, J. Dickson. *History of Benton County, 1836–1936.* Little Rock, Ark.: International Graphics Industries, 1975.

Bouchard, W. L. *St. Joseph Lead Company and Affiliated Companies in Southeast Missouri.* A reprint of articles published by the *Lead Belt News,* Flat River, Missouri, following visits to various operating plants, February through August, 1949. (Flat River, Mo.: St. Joseph Lead Company, 1950).

Brackenridge, Henry M. *Views of Louisiana; Together with a Journal of a Voyage Up the Missouri River, in 1811.* Pittsburgh, Pa.: Cramer, Spear and Eichbaum, 1814.

Bradbury, John. *Travels in the Interior of America.* London: Sherwood, Neely, and Jones, 1817.

Branson, E. B., and W. D. Keller. "Geology," in Noel P. Gist et al., eds., *Missouri: Its Resources, People, and Institutions.* Columbia: Curators of the University of Missouri, 1950, chap. 2.

The Branson-Ozark Mountain Country Sourcebook. Branson, Mo.: Alliance Press, 1994.

Bratton, Samuel T. "Climate," in Noel P. Gist et al., eds., *Missouri: Its Resources, People, and Institutions.* Columbia: Curators of the University of Missouri, 1950.

Breuer, James Ira. *Crawford County and Cuba, Missouri.* Cape Girardeau, Mo.: Ramfre Press, 1972.

Britton, Wiley. *Pioneer Life in Southwest Missouri.* Kansas City, Mo.: Smith-Grieves Company, 1929.

Brown, C. J. *Cattle on a Thousand Hills: A History of the Cattle Industry in Arkansas.* Fayetteville: University of Arkansas Press, 1996.

Brown, James A. *Prehistoric Southern Ozark Marginality: A Myth Exposed.* Missouri Archaeological Society Publication No. 6. Columbia: Missouri Archaeological Society, 1984.

Burford, Jo. "Underground Treasures: The Story of Mining in Missouri." In Kenneth M. Johnson, ed., *Official Manual State of Missouri 1977–1978.* Jefferson City: Office of the Secretary of State, 1978.

Burnside, William H. *The Honorable Powell Clayton.* Conway: University of Central Arkansas Press, 1991.

Campbell, Robert A. *Campbell's Gazetteer of Missouri.* St. Louis: R. A. Campbell, Publisher, 1875.

Castel, Albert. *General Sterling Price and the Civil War in the West*. Baton Rouge: Louisiana State University Press, 1968.

Chapman, Carl H. *The Archaeology of Missouri*, Vol. I and II. Columbia: University of Missouri Press, 1975.

Charleviox, Pierre Francois Xavier de. *Letters to the Duchess of Lesdiquieres, Giving an Account of a Voyage to Canada, and Travels through that vast Country and Louisiana, to the Gulf of Mexico, Undertaken by Order of the President King of France*. London: R. Goadbly, 1673.

Christian County History Committee. *Christian County: Its First Hundred Years*. Ozark, Mo.: Christian County Centennial, Inc., 1959.

Christianson, Gale E. *Edwin Hubble: Mariner of the Nebulae*. New York: Farrar, Straus, Giroux, 1995.

Clokey, Richard M. *William H. Ashley: Enterprise and Politics in the Trans-Mississippi West*. Norman: University of Oklahoma Press, 1980.

Committee on Atmospheric Science, Assembly of Mathematical and Physical Sciences, National Research Council. *The Atmospheric Sciences: Problems and Prospects*. Washington, D.C.: National Academy of Sciences, 1977.

Costain, Thomas B. *The Mississippi Bubble*. New York: Random House, 1955.

Cotterill, R. S. *The Southern Indians*. Norman: University of Oklahoma Press, 1954.

Cramer, Rose F. *Wayne County, Missouri*. Cape Girardeau, Mo.: Ramfre Press, 1972.

Curry, J. E. *A Reminiscent History of Douglas County, Missouri*. Ava, Mo.: Douglas County Herald, 1957.

Dallas County Historical Society. *The Dallas County, Missouri, Story*. Cassville, Mo.: Litho Printer, 1974.

Davison, Gideon M. *The Fashionable Tour*. New York: G. & C. & H. Carvil, 1833.

Diaz-Granados, Carol, and James R. Duncan. *The Petroglyphs and Pictographs of Missouri*. Tuscaloosa: University of Alabama Press, 2000.

Doherty, William T., Jr. *Louis Houck: Missouri Historian and Entrepreneur*. Columbia: University of Missouri Press, 1960.

Donovan, Timothy P., Willard B. Gatewood Jr., and Jeannie M. Whayne. *The Governors of Arkansas: Essays in Political Biography*, 2d ed. Fayetteville: University of Arkansas Press, 1995.

Downing, Andrew Jackson. *Cottage Residences: A Series of Designs for Rural Cottages and Cottage Villas, and their Gardens and Grounds*. New York: John Wiley and son, 1873.

Duden, Gottfried. *Berict uber eine Rise nach den westlichen Staaten Nordamerika*. Translated in English. James W. Goodrich, ed. Columbia: State Historical Society of Missouri and University of Missouri Press, 1980.

Dulles, Foster Rhea. *A History of Recreation: America Learns to Play*. New York: Meridith Publishing Company, 1965.

Du Pratz, Le Page. *Histoire de la Louisiane. . . .* Paris: De Bure, l'Aine, la Beuve Delaquette, et Lambert, 1958.

Eddy, Mary B. *Science and Health: With Key to the Scriptures*. Boston: First Church of Christ Scientist, 1994.

Ekberg, Carl. *Colonial Ste. Genevieve: An Adventure on the Mississippi Frontier*. Gerald, Mo.: Patrice Press, 1985.

Engle, Stephen. *Yankee Dutchman: The Life of Franz Sigel*. Fayetteville: University of Arkansas Press, 1993.

Ensminger, Robert F. *The Pennsylvania Barn: Its Origin, Evolution, and Distribution in North America*. Baltimore: The Johns Hopkins University Press, 1992.

Fairbanks, Jonathan, and Clyde E. Tuck. *Past and Present of Greene County, Missouri*. Indianapolis, Ind.: A. W. Bowen and Company, 1915.

Faragher, John M. "'More Motley than Mackinaw,' From Ethnic Mixing to Ethnic Cleansing on the Frontier of the Lower Missouri, 1783–1833," in *Contact Points, American Frontiers from the Mohawk Valley to the Mississippi, 1750–1830*. Andrew Cayton and Fredricka Teute, eds. Chapel Hill: University of North Carolina Press, 1998: 304–26.

Farmers Almanac. Greensburg (Westmoreland), Pa.: Snowden and M'Corkle, 1799.

Faulk, Odie B. *Muskogee: City and County*. Muskogee, Okla.: Five Civilized Tribes Museum, 1982.

Featherstonhaugh, George W. *Excursion Through the Slave States, From Washington on the Potomac to the Frontier of Mexico; With Sketches of Popular Manners and Geological Notices*. New York: Negro Universities Press, 1968.

Fenneman, Nevin M. *Physiography of the Eastern United States*. New York: McGraw-Hill Book Company, Inc., 1938.

Ferguson, Judy. *The Boom Town of West Eminence and Its Lumbering Days*. Rolla, Mo.: Rolla Printing Company, 1969.

Fite, Gilbert. *From Vision to Reality: A History of Bella Vista Village, 1915–1993*. Rogers, Ark.: Ro-Ark Printing, Inc., 1993.

Fletcher, John Gould. *Arkansas*. Chapel Hill: University of North Carolina Press, 1947.

Ford, Henry J. *The Scotch-Irish in America*. New York: Arno Press, 1969.

Foreman, Grant. *The Five Civilized Tribes: Cherokee, Chickasaw, Choctaw, Creek, Seminole*. Norman: University of Oklahoma Press, 1934. Sixth printing, 1977.

Freeman, Dale. *How to Speak Pure Ozark in One Easy Lesson*. Kimberling City, Mo.: Ozark Postcard Publishers, 1991.

Fritz, Gayle J. "In Color and in Time: Prehistoric Ozark Agriculture," in *Agricultural Origins and Development in the Midcontinent*. William Green, editor. Iowa City, Iowa: University of Iowa, 1994.

Fuller, Myron Leslie. *The New Madrid Earthquake*. A reprint of U.S. Geological Survey Bulletin 494. 1912. Cape Girardeau, Mo:. Ramfre Press, 1958.

Gaines, W. Craig. *The Confederate Cherokees: John Drew's Regiment of Mounted Rifles*. Baton Rouge: Louisiana State University Press, 1989.

Garreau, Joel. *Nine Nations of North America*. Boston: Houghton Mifflin Co., 1981.

George, Floyd W. *History of Webster County, 1855 to 1955.* Historical Committee of the Webster County Centennial. Springfield, Missouri: Roberts and Sutter Printers, Inc., 1955.

Gerlach, Russel L. *Immigrants in the Ozarks: A Study in Ethnic Geography.* Columbia: University of Missouri Press, 1976.

———. "The Ozark Scotch-Irish." *Cultural Geography of Missouri.* Michael Roark, ed. Cape Girardeau: Department of Earth Sciences, Southeast Missouri State University, April 1983.

Gerstaeker, Frederich. *Wild Sports in the Far West.* Durham, N.C.: University Press, 1968.

Gibbons, Charles E. *Child Labor in the Tiff Mines.* New York: National Child Labor Committee, 1938.

Gibbs, Christopher. *The Great Silent Majority: Missouri's Resistance to World War I.* Columbia: University of Missouri Press, 1988.

Gibson, Arrel M. *The Kickapoos.* Norman: University of Oklahoma Press, 1963.

———. *Wilderness Bonanza: The Tri-State District of Missouri, Kansas, and Oklahoma.* Norman: University of Oklahoma Press, 1972.

Gilbert, M. J. *1995 Road and Handbook of the Missouri Division of the League of American Wheelmen.* Columbia, Mo.: E. W. Stephens, Printer and Binder, 1896.

Gilmore, Robert K. *Ozark Baptizings, Hangings, and Other Diversions: Theatrical Folkways of Rural Missouri, 1885–1910.* Norman: University of Oklahoma Press, 1984.

Gist, Noel P. et al., eds. *Missouri: Its Resources, People, and Institutions.* Columbia: Curators of the University of Missouri, 1950.

Gracy, David B., II. *Moses Austin: His Life.* San Antonio, Texas: Trinity University Press, 1987.

Graham, Russell W., and Marvin Kay. "Taphonomic Comparisons of Cultural and Noncultural Faunal Deposits at the Kimmswick and Barnhart Sites, Jefferson County, Missouri." In R. S. Laub, N. G. Miller, and D. W. Steadman, eds., *Late Pleistocene and Early Holocene Paleoecology and Archeology of the Eastern Great Lakes Region.* Bulletin of the Buffalo Society of Natural Sciences, no. 33. Buffalo, N.Y.: Buffalo Society of Natural Sciences, 1988.

Greater St. Louis Telephone Directory. St. Louis, Mo.: Southwestern Bell Company, 1999.

Hall, Leonard. *Stars Upstream.* Columbia: University of Missouri Press, 1958.

Hartshorn, Truman A., and John W. Alexander. *Economic Geography,* 3d ed. Englewood Cliffs, N.J.: Prentice-Hall, 1988.

Harvey, William H. *Coin's Financial School.* Chicago: Coin Publishing Company, circa 1894.

Hawksley, Oscar. *Missouri Ozark Waterways.* Jefferson City: Missouri Department of Conservation, 1965.

Herndon, Dallas T., ed. *Centennial History of Arkansas,* vol. 1. Chicago: S. J. Clarke Publishing Company, 1922.

History of Dade County and Her People. Greenfield, Mo.: Pioneer Historical Company, 1917.

Hogan, John J., Rt. Rev. *On the Mission in Missouri, 1857–1868.* Glorifta, N.M.: Rio Grande Press, Inc., 1976. A reprint of a 1892 edition published by J. A. Heilmann, Kansas City, Missouri.

Hoig, Stanley W. *The Cherokees and Their Chiefs: In the Wake of Empire.* Fayetteville: University of Arkansas Press, 1998.

Hostetler, John A. *Amish Society.* Baltimore: The Johns Hopkins University Press, 1968.

Houck, Louis. *A History of Missouri,* vol. 1, 2, 3. Chicago: R. R. Donnelly and Sons Company, 1908.

———. *The Spanish Regime In Missouri,* vol. 1, 2. Chicago: R. R. Donnelly and Sons Company, 1909.

Hough, Cass S. *It's a Daisy.* Rogers, Ark.: Daisy Division Victor Comptometer Corporation, 1976.

Huddleston, Duane, Sammie Cantrell Rose, and Pat Taylor Wood. *Steamboats and Ferries on the White River: A Heritage Revisited.* Fayetteville: University of Arkansas Press, 1998.

Hughes, Michael A. "Wartime Gristmill Destruction in Northwest Arkansas and Military Farm Colonies." In *Civil War Arkansas: Beyond Battles and Leaders.* Anne J. Bailey and Daniel E. Sutherland, eds. Fayetteville: University of Arkansas Press, 2000. Originally published in the *Arkansas Historical Quarterly* 47 (Summer 1987): 167–86.

Hull, Clifton H. *Shortline Railroads of Arkansas.* Norman: University of Oklahoma Press, 1969.

Hulston, John K. *An Ozark Lawyer's Story, 1946–1976.* Republic, Mo.: Western Printing Company, 1976.

Hurt, Douglas. *Nathan Boone and the American Frontier.* Columbia: University of Missouri Press, 1998.

Immigrant Guidebook. St. Louis, Mo.: St. Louis and San Francisco Railroad, 1895.

Ingenthron, Elmo. *Indians of the Ozark Plateau.* Point Lookout, Mo.: School of the Ozarks Press, 1970.

———. *The Land of Taney.* Point Lookout, Mo.: School of the Ozarks Press, 1974.

Jackson, James P. *Passages of a Stream: A Chronicle of the Meramec.* Columbia: University of Missouri Press, 1984.

Jeansonne, Glen. *Gerald L. K. Smith: Minister of Hate.* New Haven, Conn.: Yale University Press, 1988.

Jefferson, Thomas, *Travels in the Interior Parts of America; communicating discoveries made in exploring the Missouri, Red River and Washita, by Captains Lewis and Clark, Doctor Sibley, and Mr. Dunbar; with a statistical account of the countries adjacent. As laid before the Senate, by the President of the United States in February, 1806, and never before published in Great Britain.* London: Phillips, 1807.

Jeffries, T. Victor. *Before the Dam Water: Story and Pictures of Old Linn Creek, Ha Ha Tonka, and Camden County.* Lebanon, Mo.: Jeffries Abstract and Title Insurance Company, 1974.

Johansen, Harley E., and Glenn V. Fuguitt. *The Changing Rural Village in America: Demographic and Economic Trends since 1950.* Cambridge, Mass.: Ballinger Publishing Company, 1984.

Johnson, Robert U., and Clarence C. Buel, eds. *Battles and Leaders of the Civil War*, vol. 1. Secaucus, N.J.: Castle, 1887.

Jones, J. Wyman. *A History of the St. Joseph Lead Company.* Published for private circulation. New York: St. Joseph Lead Company, 1892.

Keefe, James F. *The First Fifty Years.* Jefferson City: Missouri Department of Conservation, 1987.

———, and Lynn Morrow, eds. *The White River Chronicles of S. C. Turnbow: Man and Wildlife on the Ozarks Frontier.* Fayetteville: University of Arkansas Press, 1994.

King, Anthony D. *The Bungalow: The Production of a Global Culture.* New York: Oxford University Press, 1995.

Kraybill, Donald B. *The Riddle of Amish Culture.* Baltimore: The Johns Hopkins University Press, 1989.

Kremer, Gary, ed. *George Washington Carver in His Own Words.* Columbia: University of Missouri Press, 1987.

Krusekopf, H. H., ed. *Life and Work of C. F. Marbut: Soil Scientist.* Columbia, Mo.: Soil Science Society of America, 1942.

Lankford, George E. "Beyond the Pale: Frontier Folk in the Southern Ozarks." In *The Folk: Identity, Landscapes and Lore.* Robert J. Smith and Jerry Stannard, eds. Lawrence: University of Kansas Studies in Anthropology No. 17., 1989.

Laws of Missouri, 1967. Jefferson City: Committee on Legislative Research, General Assembly of Missouri, 1967.

Lawson, V. Lonnie. *The Lead Belt Mining Riot of 1917.* Flat River, Mo.: Susan D. Lawson, 1976.

Lederer, Katherine. *Many Thousand Gone: Springfield's Lost Black History.* Springfield, Mo.: Missouri Committee for the Humanities and the Gannett Foundation, 1986.

Leighley, John. *Land and Life: A Selection from the Writings of Carl Ortwin Sauer* (Berkeley: University of California Press, 1969): 1–8.

LeMaster, Carolyn G. *A Corner of Tapestry: A History of the Jewish Experience in Arkansas, 1820s–1990s.* Fayetteville: University of Arkansas Press, 1994.

Logan, Roger, ed. *History of Boone County, Arkansas.* Boone County Historical and Railroad Society. Paducah, Ky.: Turner Publishing Co., 1998.

McAlester, Virginia, and Lee McAlester. *A Field Guide to American Houses.* New York: Alfred A. Knopf, 1984.

McCandless, Perry. *A History of Missouri, 1820–1860,* vol. 2. William E. Parrish, general ed. Columbia: University of Missouri Press, 1972: 21–22.

McGimsey, Charles R. "Indians of Arkansas." *Arkansas Archaeological Survey Popular Series,* 1, 1969.

McNeil, W. K. *Ozark Country.* Jackson: University Press of Mississippi, 1995.

Makinson, Randell L. *Greene & Greene: Architecture as a Fine Art.* Salt Lake City, Utah: Peregrine Smith, 1977.

Marbut, Curtis F. *The Physical Features of Missouri.* Jefferson City, Mo.: Tribune Printing Co., State Printers and Binders, 1896. Extracted from *Reports of the Missouri Geological Survey* 10 (1896).

Marshall, Howard W. *Folk Architecture in Little Dixie: A Regional Culture in Missouri.* Columbia: University of Missouri Press, 1981.

Mayer, Harold M. "Urban Geography." Chapter 6 in *American Geography: Inventory and Prospect.* Preston E. James and Clarence F. Jones, eds. Syracuse, N.Y.: Syracuse University Press, 1954: 149–50.

Messick, Mary Ann. *History of Baxter County, 1873–1973.* Mountain Home, Ark.: Mountain Home Chamber of Commerce, 1973.

Meyer, Duane. *The Heritage of Missouri: A History.* St. Louis: State Publishing Co., 1970.

Miller, John E. *Becoming Laura Ingalls Wilder: The Woman behind the Legend.* Columbia: University of Missouri Press, 1998.

Missouri Manufacturers Register 2000. Evanston, Ill.: MNI Manufacturers' News, 1999.

Missouri Rail Plan 1995 Update. Jefferson City: Missouri Highway and Transportation Department, Transportation Division, June 1995.

Moneyhon, Carl H. *The Impact of the Civil War and Reconstruction on Arkansas.* Baton Rouge: Louisiana State University Press, 1994.

———. *Arkansas and the New South, 1874–1929.* Fayetteville: University of Arkansas Press, 1997.

Morrow, Lynn, and Linda Myers-Phinney. *The Shepherd of the Hills Country: Tourism Transforms the Ozarks, 1880s–1930s.* Fayetteville: University of Arkansas Press, 1999.

Murphey, Rhoads. *The Scope of Geography,* 3d ed. London: Methuen and Co., 1982.

Murphy, Raymond E. *The American City: An Urban Geography.* New York: McGraw-Hill Book Company, 1966.

Neilson, William A. ed.-in-chief. *Webster's Biographical Dictionary.* Springfield, Mass.: G. & C. Merriam Co., 1974.

Newhouse, Elizabeth L., ed. *National Geographic's Guide to Scenic Highways and Byways.* Washington, D.C.: National Geographic, 1995.

Norris, James D. *Frontier Iron: The Story of the Maramec Iron Works, 1826–1876.* Madison: State Historical Society of Wisconsin, 1964.

North, F. A. *The History of Jasper County, Missouri.* Des Moines, Iowa: Mills and Company, 1883.

Nuttall, Thomas. *A Journal of Travels Into the Arkansas Territory During the Year 1819.* Ann Arbor: University Microfilms, 1966.

O'Brien, Michael J., and Raymond Wood. *The Prehistory of Missouri.* Columbia: University of Missouri Press, 1998.

Odum, Howard W., and Harry Estill Moore. *American Regionalism.* New York: Henry Holt and Co., 1938.

Ohman, Marion M. *Encyclopedia of Missouri Courthouses.* Columbia: University of Missouri Press, 1981.

O'Neill, Rose. *The Story of Rose O'Neill: An Autobiography.* Miriam Formanek-Brunell, ed. Columbia: University of Missouri Press, 1997.

Owen, David D. *First Report of a Geological Reconnaissance of the Northern Counties of Arkansas, Made During the Years 1857 and 1858*. Little Rock, Ark.: Johnson & Yerkes, State Printers, 1858.

Painter, Nell Irvin. *Exodusters: Black Migration in Kansas after Reconstruction*. New York: Knopf, 1977.

Parson, Ruben L. *Conserving American Resources*. Englewood Cliffs, N.J.: Prentice-Hall, 1964.

Pearce, N. Bartlett. "Arkansas Troops in the Battle of Wilson's Creek." In *Battles and Leaders of the Civil War*, I. Robert U. Johnson, and Clarence C. Buel, eds. Secaucus, N. J.: Castle, 1887.

Penick, James, Jr. *The New Madrid Earthquake of 1811–12*. Columbia: University of Missouri Press, 1976.

Perkins, E. F., and T. M. Horne's *History of Greene County, Missouri, Including a History of Its Townships, and a Brief History of Missouri*. St. Louis, Mo.: Western Historical Society Company, 1883.

Peterson, Fred W. *Homes in the Heartland: Balloon Frame Farmhouses of the Upper Midwest, 1850–1920*. Lawrence: University Press of Kansas, 1992.

Phillips, Christopher. *Damned Yankee: The Life of General Nathaniel Lyon*. Columbia: University of Missouri Press, 1990.

———. *Missouri's Confederate, Claiborne Fox Jackson and the Creation of Southern Identity in the Border West*. Columbia: University of Missouri Press, 2000.

Pike, Zebulon M. *The Journals of Zebulon Montgomery Pike, With Letters and Related Documents*. Edited and annotated by Donald Jackson. Norman: University of Oklahoma Press, 1966.

Pilant, Denny, ed. *Reinventing Missouri Government: A Case Study in State Experiments at Work*. Fort Worth, Tex.: Harcourt Brace College Publishers, 1994.

Pinkney, Alphonso. *Black Americans*. Englewood Cliffs, N.J.: Prentice-Hall, 1969.

Poirot, Eugene M. *Our Margin of Life*. Raytown, Mo.: Acres U.S.A., 1978.

Rafferty, Milton D. *The Ozarks Outdoors: A Guidebook for Fishermen, Hunters, and Tourists*. Norman: University of Oklahoma Press, 1980.

———. *Missouri: A Geography*. Boulder, Colo.: Westview Press, 1983.

———. "Population Trends of Missouri Towns." In *Cultural Geography of Missouri*. Michael Roark, ed. Cape Girardeau: Department of Earth Sciences, Southeast Missouri State University, April 1983.

———. *A Geography of World Tourism*. Englewood Cliffs, N.J.: Prentice-Hall, 1993.

Randolph, Vance. *Down in the Holler: A Gallery of Ozark Folk Speech*. Norman: University of Oklahoma Press, 1953.

———. *Ozark Magic and Folklore*. New York: Columbia University Press, 1964.

———, and Gordon McCann. *Ozark Folklore: An Annotated Bibliography*. Columbia: University of Missouri Press, 1987.

Rayburn, Otto E. *Forty Years in the Ozarks: An Autobiography*. Eureka Springs, Ark.: Ozark Guide Press, 1957.

Rea, Ralph R. *Boone County and Its People*. Van Buren, Ark.: Press-Argus, 1955.

Reeves, James L. *The First Twenty Years: The Story of Mid-America Dairymen*. Springfield: Mid-America Dairymen, 1989.

Royce, Charles C. *The Cherokee Nation of Indians*. Fifth Annual Report of the Bureau of American Ethnology. Washington, D.C.: Government Printing Office, 1887.

Sabo, George, III, ed. *Contributions to Ozark Prehistory*. Arkansas Archaeological Survey Research Series No. 27. Fayetteville: Arkansas Archaeological Survey, 1966.

——— et. al. *Human Adaption in the Ozark and Ouachita Mountains*. Arkansas Archaeological Survey, Research Series No. 31. Fayetteville: Arkansas Archaeological Survey, 1990.

Sauer, Carl O. *The Geography of the Ozark Highland of Missouri*. Geographical Society of Chicago Bulletin no. 7. Chicago: University of Chicago Press, 1920.

———. "The Morphology of Landscape." In *Land and Life: A Selection from the Writings of Carl Ortwin Sauer*. John Leighly, ed. Berkeley: University of California Press, 1963, 315–350.

Saunders, Jeffery J. *Late Pleistocene Vertebrates of the Western Ozark Highland*. Illinois State Museum Reports of Investigations No. 33. Springfield: Illinois State Museum, 1977.

Schoolcraft, Henry Rowe. *A View of the Lead Mines of Missouri: Including Some Observations on the Mineralogy, Geology, Geography, Antiquities, Soil, Climate, Population and Productions of Missouri and Arkansas, and Other Sections of the Western Country*. New York: C. Wiley and Co., 1819.

———. *Scenes and Adventures in the Semi-Alpine Region of the Ozark Mountains*. Philadelphia: Lippincott, Grambo and Co., 1853.

———. *Rude Pursuits and Rugged Peaks: Schoolcraft's Ozark Journal, 1818–1819*. Milton Rafferty, ed. Fayetteville: University of Arkansas Press, 1996.

Schultz, Christian. *Travels on an Inland Voyage Through the States of New York, Pennsylvania, Virginia, Ohio, Kentucky and Tennessee and Through the Territories of Indiana, Louisiana, Mississippi and New Orleans Performed in the years 1807 and 1808*, vol. 2. New York: Isaac Riley, 1810.

Schultz, Duane. *Quantrill's War: The Life and Times of William Clarke Quantrill, 1837–1865*. New York: St. Martin's Press, 1996.

Schwartz, Marvin. *Tyson: From Farm to Market: The Remarkable Story of Tyson Foods*. Fayetteville: University of Arkansas Press, 1991.

Sechler, Earl T. *Our Religious Heritage: Church History of the Ozarks, 1806–1906*. Springfield, Mo.: Westport Press, 1961.

Shelhope, Robert E. *Sterling Price: Portrait of a Southerner*. Columbia: University of Missouri Press, 1971.

Shiloh Museum Board of Trustees. *History of Washington County, Arkansas*. Springdale, Ark.: Shiloh Museum, 1989.

Shinn, Josiah H. *Pioneers and Makers of Arkansas.* Baltimore: Genealogical Publishing Co., 1967.

Shippee, J. Mett. *Archaeological Remains in the Area of Kansas City: The Woodland Period, Early, Middle, and Late.* Missouri Archaeological Society Research Series. Columbia, 1967.

Shirley, Glenn. *Law West of Fort Smith: A History of Frontier Justice in the Indian Territory, 1834–1896.* Lincoln: University of Nebraska Press, 1968.

Shoemaker, Floyd C. *Missouri and Missourians: Land of Contrasts and People of Achievements,* Vols. 1 and 2. Chicago: Lewis Publishing Company, 1943.

Simonds, Frederick F. *The Geology of Washington County.* Little Rock: Geological Survey of Arkansas Annual Report for 1888, 1891: 1–154.

Sizemore, Jean. *Vernacular Houses: A Study of Rural Homeplaces in the Arkansas Ozarks, 1830–1930.* Fayetteville: University of Arkansas Press, 1994.

Smith, John I. *The Courage of a Southern Unionist.* Little Rock, Ark.: Rose Publishing Co., 1979.

Smith, Kenneth L. *The Buffalo River Country: In the Ozarks of Arkansas.* Fayetteville, Ark.: Ozark Society, 1967.

Snead, Thomas L. *The Fight for Missouri From the Election of Lincoln to the Death of Lyon.* New York: C. Scribner's Sons, 1886.

Southern, Michael. "The I-House as a Carrier of Style in Three Counties of the Northeastern Piedmont." In Doug Swaim, ed., *Carolina Dwelling: Toward Preservation of Place; In Celebration of the Vernacular Landscape.* Student Publication of the School of Design, Vol. 26. Raleigh: North Carolina State University, 1978.

Spurlock, Pearl. *Over the Old Ozark Trails in the Shepherd of the Hills Country.* Branson, Mo.: White River Leader, 1939.

Starr, Emmet. *History of the Cherokee Indians.* Oklahoma City: Warden Company, 1921.

Stevens, Walter B. *Missouri: The Center State.* Chicago: S. J. Clarke Publishing Company, 1915.

Stevenson, Catherine Cole, and H. Ward Jandl. *Houses by Mail: A Guide to the Houses by Sears, Roebuck and Company.* New York: John Wiley and Sons, 1986.

Steward, Dick. *Frontier Swashbuckler: The Life and Legend of John Smith T.* Columbia: University of Missouri Press, 2000.

Stewart, George R. *Names on the Globe.* New York: Oxford University Press, 1975.

Steyermark, Julien A. "Phanerogamic Flora of the Fresh-water Springs in the Ozarks of Missouri." In *Studies of the Vegetation of Missouri,* vol. 2. Chicago: Field Museum of Natural History, Botanical Series, vol. 9, no. 6, 1941, 481–618.

———. *Vegetational History of the Ozark Forest.* University of Missouri Studies No. 31. Columbia: University of Missouri Press, 1959.

Stilgoe, John R. *Metropolitan Corridor: Railroads and the American Scene.* New Haven, Conn.: Yale University Press, 1983.

Strahler, Arthur N. *Physical Geography,* 3d ed. New York: John Wiley & Sons, 1969.

Suggs, George G., Jr. *Water Mills of the Missouri Ozarks.* Paintings and illustrations by Jake K. Wells. Norman: University of Oklahoma Press, 1990.

Sutherland, Daniel E. "Guerrillas: The Real War in Arkansas." In *Civil War in Arkansas: Beyond Battles and Leaders,* Anne J. Bailey and Daniel E. Sutherland, eds. Fayetteville: University of Arkansas Press, 2000, 133–54. Reprinted from the *Arkansas Historical Quarterly* 52 (Autumn 1993): 257–85.

Swaim, Doug, ed., *Carolina Dwelling: Toward Preservation of Place; In Celebration of the Vernacular Landscape.* Student Publication of the School of Design, Vol. 26. Raleigh: North Carolina State University, 1978.

Thoman, Richard S. *The Changing Occupance Pattern of the Tri-State Area of Missouri, Kansas, and Oklahoma.* University of Chicago Department of Geography Research Paper no. 21. Chicago: University of Chicago Press, 1953.

Thomas, Rosemary. *It's Good to Tell You: French Folktales from Missouri.* Columbia: University of Missouri Press, 1981.

Thompson, Henry C. *Our Lead Belt Heritage.* Flat River, Mo.: Flat River *News-Sun,* 1955.

Thornbury, William D. *Regional Geomorphology of the United States.* New York: John Wiley and Sons, 1965.

Trewartha, Glenn T. *An Introduction to Climate,* 4th ed. New York: McGraw-Hill Book Co., 1968.

Trimble, Vance H. *Sam Walton: The Inside Story of America's Richest Man.* New York: Penquin Books, 1990.

Tudor, Maurice. *Pictorial Crackerbarrel: Some of the Better-Told Tales of Searcy Countians and New Scenes as They Appeared in the Marshall* Mountain Wave *Newspaper, 1972–1976.* Marshall, Ark.: Marshall *Wave,* 1976.

Unklesbay, A. G., and Jerry D. Vineyard. *Missouri Geology: Three Billion Years of Volcanoes, Seas, Sediments, and Erosion.* Columbia: University of Missouri Press, 1992.

Upton, Lucille M. *Bald Knobbers.* Caldwell, Idaho: Caxton Printers, 1939.

Van Buskirk, Kathleen. *In the Heart of Ozark Mountain Country: A Popular History of Stone and Taney Counties, Including Branson, Missouri.* Reeds Spring, Mo.: White Oak Press, 1992.

Vance, James E., Jr. *Capturing the Horizon: The Historical Geography of Transportation.* New York: Harper and Row, 1986.

Van Ravenswaay, Charles. *The Arts and Architecture of German Settlements in Missouri: A Survey of a Vanishing Culture.* Columbia: University of Missouri Press, 1977.

Vickery, Margaret Ray. *Ozark Stories of the Upper Current River.* Salem, Mo.: Salem News, circa 1969.

Vineyard, Jerry D., and Gerald L. Feder. *Springs of Missouri.* Water Resources Report No. 29. Missouri Department of Natural Resources, Division of Geology and Land Survey in cooperation with the U.S. Geological Survey and the Missouri Department of Conservation, Rolla, Mo., 1982.

Violette, Eugene M. *A History of Missouri*. Boston: D. C. Heath and Co., 1918.

Vlatch, John. "The Shotgun House: An African Architectural Legacy." In *Readings in American Vernacular Architecture*. Dell Upton and John M. Vlatch, eds. Athens: University of Georgia Press, 1986, 58–78.

Voigt, David Q. *America through Baseball*. Chicago: Nelson-Hall, 1976.

War of the Rebellion: A Compilation of the Official Records of the Union and Confederate Armies. 70 volumes in 128 parts, atlas. Washington, D.C.: Government Printing Office, 1880–1901.

Wardell, Morris L. *A Political History of the Cherokee Nation, 1838–1907*. Norman: University of Oklahoma Press, 1977.

Webb, Walter P. *The Great Plains*. New York: Grosset and Dunlap, 1931.

Wecter, Dixon. *The Saga of American Society*. New York: C. Scribner's Sons, 1937.

Westfall, June, and Catherine Osterhage. *A Fame Not Easily Forgotten: An Autobiography of Eureka Springs*. Conway, Ark.: River Road Press, 1970.

Wiley, Robert S. *Dewey Short: Orator of the Ozarks*. Cassville, Mo.: Litho Printers and Bindery, 1985.

Williams, Michael A. *Homeplace: The Social Use and Meaning of the Folk Dwelling in Southwestern North Carolina*. Athens: University of Georgia Press, 1991.

Williams, Walter. *The State of Missouri: An Autobiography*. Columbia, Mo.: Press of E. W. Stephens, 1904).

Wolf, John Q. *Life in the Leatherwoods*. Fayetteville: University of Arkansas Press, 1999.

Woodruff, John T. *Reminiscences of an Ozarkian and Early Tourism Developments*. Steve Illum, ed. Springfield: Office of Leisure Research, Southwest Missouri State University, 1994.

Woodward, Grace Steel. *The Cherokees*. Norman: University of Oklahoma Press, 1963.

Workers of the Writers' Project of the Works Projects Administration in the State of Missouri. *The WPA Guide to 1930s Missouri*. Lawrence: University Press of Kansas, 1986. Originally published as *Missouri: A Guide to the "Show Me" State* by Duell, Sloan and Pearce in 1941.

Wright, Harold Bell. *The Shepherd of the Hills*. New York: Grossett and Dunlap, 1907. Reprinted by the McCormick-Armstrong Company, 1987.

Yolton, John W., ed. *John Locke: Problems and Perspectives*. Cambridge, U.K.: Cambridge University Press, 1969.

Young, Gloria A., and Michael P. Hoffman, eds. *The Expedition of Hernando de Soto West of the Mississippi, 1541–1543*. Fayetteville: University of Arkansas Press, 1999.

Zelinsky, Wilbur. *Cultural Geography of the United States*. Englewood Cliffs, N.J.: Prentice Hall, 1992.

Zornow, William F. *Kansas: A History of the Jayhawk State*. Norman: University of Oklahoma Press, 1957.

ARTICLES

Adams, Lee M. "Archaeological Investigations of Southwestern Missouri." *Missouri Archaeologist* 20 (December 1958): 3–195.

Barnes, Kenneth C. "The Williams Clan: Mountain Farmers and Union Fighters in North-Central Arkansas." *Arkansas Historical Quarterly* 52 (Autumn 1993): 286–317.

Berry, Evalena. "Sugar Loaf: The Mountain, the Springs, the Town." *Arkansas Historical Quarterly* 42 (Spring 1942): 27–35.

Bradbury, John. "'Good Water & Wood but the Country is a Miserable Botch': Flatland Soldiers Confront the Ozarks." *Missouri Historical Review* 90 (January 1996): 166–86.

———. "Buckwheat Cake Philanthropy: Refugees and the Union Army in the Ozarks." *Arkansas Historical Quarterly* 57 (Autumn 1998): 233–54.

Breckenridge, William C. "Early Gunpowder Making in Missouri." *Missouri Historical Review* 20 (October 1925): 85–95.

Brister, Louis E. "The Image of Arkansas in the Early German Immigrant Guidebook: Notes on Immigration." *Arkansas Historical Quarterly* 36 (Winter 1977): 338–45.

Broadhead, G. C. "Early Missouri Roads." *Missouri Historical Review* 8 (January 1914): 90–92.

Brush, J. E. "The Hierarchy of Central Places in Southwestern Wisconsin." *Geographical Review* 43 (1953): 414–16.

Burton, Stephen. "The Origin and Growth of Rockaway Beach, Missouri." *White River Valley Historical Society Quarterly* (Spring 1963): 16–21.

Callison, Carolyn. "The Great Lake of the Ozarks Was Just a Small River Fifty Years Ago." *Midwest Motorist* 51 (March–April 1980): 8–13.

Carney, George C. "From Down Home to Uptown: The Diffusion of Country-Music Radio Stations in the United States." *Journal of Geography* 76 (March 1977): 4–10.

———. "Historic Resources of Oklahoma's All-Black Towns." *Chronicles of Oklahoma* 69 (Summer 1991): 116–33.

———. "Branson: The New Mecca of Country Music." *Journal of Cultural Geography* 14 (1994): 17–32.

Carpenter, Clifford D. "The Early Cattle Industry in Missouri." *Missouri Historical Review* 47 (April 1953): 201–15.

Carriere, Joseph M. "Tales from the French Folklore of Missouri." *Northwestern University Studies* (1937).

Chesnutt, E. F. "Rural Electrification in Arkansas, 1935–1940: The Formative Years." *Arkansas Historical Quarterly* 46 (Autumn 1987): 215–60.

Childers, Elbert I., and John F. Bradbury Jr. "Basketville and the Roadside Craftspeople on Route 66." *Missouri Historical Review* 91 (October 1996): 24–34.

Cole, Lela. "The Early Tie Industry along the Nianqua River." *Missouri Historical Review* 48 (Fall 1953): 264–72.

Collier, James F. "Geographic Regions of Missouri." *Annals of the Association of American Geographers* 45 (1955): 368–92.

Cooper, Marc, and Julie Hennigan. "Brief History of the Springfield, Missouri Jewish Community." *OzarksWatch* 12 (1999): 9–11.

Cornell, Irwin H. "How the St. Joseph Lead Company Grew." *Mining and Metallurgy* 28 (August 1947): 362–65.

Cozzens, Arthur B. "Analyzing and Mapping Natural Landscape Factors of the Ozark Province." *Transactions of the Academy of Science of Saint Louis* 30 (May 31, 1939): 37–63.

———. "The Iron Industry of Missouri, Part I." *Missouri Historical Review* 35 (October–July 1940–1941): 509–38.

———. "The Iron Industry of Missouri, Part II." *Missouri Historical Review* 36 (October–July 1941–1942): 48–59.

Crane, G. W. "The Iron Ores of Missouri." *Missouri Bureau of Geology and Mines* 10, 2d ser. (1912).

Cypert, Jesse N. "Secession Convention." *Publications of the Arkansas Historical Association,* I, 1906.

Davenport, Walter. "Gland Time in Kansas." *Colliers* 79 (January 16, 1932), 12–13.

Davison, Gideon M. *The Fashionable Tour.* New York: G. & C. & H. Carvil, 1833.

Dawson, David D. "Baseball Calls: Arkansas Town Baseball in the Twenties." *Arkansas Historical Quarterly* 54 (Winter 1995): 409–26.

Dew, Lee A. "'On a Slow Train Through Arkansaw': The Negative Image of Arkansas in the Early Twentieth Century." *Arkansas Historical Quarterly* 39 (Summer 1980): 125–35.

———. "From Trails to Rails in Eureka Springs." *Arkansas Historical Quarterly* 41 (Autumn 1982): 203–14.

Dorrance, Ward A. "The Survival of French in the Old District of Ste. Genevieve." *University of Missouri Studies* 10 (1935).

Dupy, Gerald W. "Two Determined Freight Lines Ply Historic Rails of the Ozarks." *Ozarks Mountaineer* 42 (June 1994): 30–31.

Durand, Loyal, Jr. "Dairy Barns of Southeastern Wisconsin." *Economic Geography* 19 (January 1943): 37–44.

Eaton, Miles W. "The Development and Later Decline of the Hemp Industry of Missouri." *Missouri Historical Review* 43 (October–July 1948–1949): 344–54.

Everett, C. S. "Melungeon History and Myth." *Appalachian Journal* 26 (Summer 1999): 358–409.

Finley, Robert A., and E. M. Scott. "A Great Lakes-to-Gulf Profile of Dispersed Dwelling Types." *Geographical Review* 30 (July 1940): 412–18.

Flanders, Robert. "Caledonia: Ozarks Legacy of the High Scotch-Irish." *Gateway Heritage* 6 (Spring 1986): 34–52.

———. "The Places We Call Home: Ozarks Dwellings." *OzarkWatch* 9 (Summer 1988): 2- 7.

———. "The Kith and Kin of Caledonia." *OzarksWatch* 5 (Spring 1992): 24–31.

———. "Preservation Corner: The Hazeltine Orchards." *OzarksWatch* 9 (1996): 2–5.

"Forest Land Bought," *Wake Up to Missouri* 22 (March 1992): 1–6.

Giffen, Jerry. "The Town Lucy Loved." *Missouri Life* 2 (May–June 1974): 9–15.

Glazier, Robert C. "When Springfield Television Was Young." *Springfield Magazine!* 3 (February 1983): 4.

Graham, Allison. "Remapping Dogpatch: Northern Media on the Southern Circuit." *Arkansas Historical Quarterly* 56 (1997): 334–40.

Griffith, Sue. "Lebanon, Missouri: Home of Thriving Appleby Boat Plant." *Ozarks Mountaineer* (July 1965): 4, 14.

Haliburton, R., Jr. "Origins of Black Slavery among the Cherokees." *Chronicles of Oklahoma 52* (Winter 1974–75): 483–96.

Handley, Lawrence R. "Settlement across Northern Arkansas as Influenced by the Missouri and North Arkansas Railroad." *Arkansas Historical Quarterly* 33 (Winter 1974): 273–92.

Hart, John Fraser. "The Middle West." *Annals of the Association of American Geographers,* 62 (June 1972): 258–82.

Herberg, Randall O. "Fuelwood—Using It Wisely." *Missouri Conservationist* 45 (January 1984): 24–27.

Hewes, Leslie. "The Oklahoma Ozarks as the Land of the Cherokees." *Geographical Review 32* (1942): 269–81.

———. "Cultural Fault Line in the Cherokee Country." *Economic Geography 19* (April 1943): 136–142.

———. "Tontitown: Ozark Vineyard Center." *Economic Geography 29* (April 1953): 125–43.

———. "Occupying the Cherokee Country of Oklahoma." *University of Nebraska Studies,* New Series, no. 57, 1978.

Higgins, Billy D. "The Origins and Fate of the Marion County Free Black Community." *Arkansas Historical Quarterly* 54 (Winter 1995): 427–42.

"The History of St. Joe." *St. Joe Headframe* (Fall 1970): 1–20.

Hively, Kay. "An Ozarks Farm Is Barn Again." *Ozarks Mountaineer* 39 (November–December 1991): 38–39.

Holm, Tom. "Cherokee Colonization in Oklahoma." *Chronicles of Oklahoma* 54 (Spring 1956): 60–76.

Hubbell, Sue. "Earthquake Fever." *New Yorker,* February 11, 1991, 75–84.

Huff, Leo E. "Guerrillas, Jayhawkers and Bushwhackers in Northern Arkansas during the Civil War." *Arkansas Historical Quarterly* 24 (Summer 1965): 127–48.

"Indian Creek—The Prototype Operation: After a Century of Successful Operation, St. Joseph Lead Company Plans for the Next." *Engineering and Mining Journal* 165 (April 1964): 87–92.

Ioannides, Mara Cohen. "Bearing Witness: Documenting the Jews of the Ozarks." *OzarksWatch* 12 (1999): 1–2.

Johns, Paul. "Tomato Canning Memories." *Missouri Life* 8 (March–April 1980): 32.

Johnson, Hildegard B. "The Location of German Settlements in the Middle West." *Annals of the Association of American Geographers* 41 (March 1941): 1–41.

Johnston, A. C. "A Major Earthquake Zone on the Mississippi." *Scientific American* 246 (April 1982): 60–68.

Johnston, James J. "Bullets for Johnny Reb: Confederate Nitre and Mining Bureau in Arkansas." *Arkansas Historical Quarterly* 49 (Summer 1990): 124–65.

Jones, John J. "The Morrill Lands of the University of Missouri." *Missouri Historical Review* 51 (January 1957): 126–38.

Jordan, Terry G. "Population Origins in Texas, 1850." *Geographical Review* 59 (1969): 83–103.

Keathley, Clarence L. "Reflections on Public Welfare in Washington County, Missouri, 1939–1941." *Missouri Historical Review* 82 (October 1987): 51–70.

Kelso, Margaret Gilmore. "Margaret Gilmore Kelso: A Memory Story, Part II, Bushwhackers and Wilson's Creek." *OzarksWatch* 4 (Spring/Summer 1991): 7–9.

Kennan, Clara B. "The Ozark Trails and Arkansas' Pathfinder, Coin Harvey." *Arkansas Historical Quarterly* 7 (Winter 1948): 299–316.

Kennedy, Balys H. "Half a Century of School Consolidation in Arkansas." *Arkansas Historical Quarterly* 27 (Spring 1968): 59–67.

Kersten, Earl W., Jr. "Changing Economy and Landscape in a Missouri Ozarks Area." *Annals of the Association of American Geographers* 48 (December 1958): 398–418.

Kirkendall, Rebecca T. "Who's a Hillbilly?" *Newsweek*, November 27, 1995, 22.

Kniffen, Fred. "Louisiana House Types." *Annals of the Association of American Geographers* 26 (December 1936): 179–96.

———. "Folk Housing: Key to Diffusion. " *Annals of the Association of American Geographers* 55 (December 1965): 549–77.

La Cross, Louis. "How the Hand of a Girl Carved an Alluring Home out of an Ozark Mountain Fastness." *St. Louis Globe-Democrat Magazine,* July 22, 1928, 1–15.

Lankford, George E. "The Cherokee Sojourn in North Arkansas." *Independence County Chronicle* 18 (1977): 2–19.

———. "Jayhawker Narratives as Treasure Legends." *Kentucky Folklore Record* 32 (1986).

Lieberman, Henry R. "Les Miserables in Missouri." *Ken* 9 (March 1939): 26.

Lightfoot, B. B. "The Cherokee Immigrants in Missouri, 1837–1839." *Missouri Historical Review* 56 (January 1962): 156–67.

Lisenby, Foy. "A Survey of Arkansas's Image Problem." *Arkansas Historical Quarterly* 30 (Spring 1971): 60–71.

Lockwood, Patricia W. "The Legacy of Caleb Starr." *Chronicles of Oklahoma* 61 (Fall 1983): 288–307.

Lopinot, Neal H., and Jack H. Ray, "Brief Summary of Ozarks Prehistory." *OzarksWatch* 11 (Fall 1998): 5–7.

Love, Robertus. "Making Niagaras in the Ozarks." *Technical World Magazine* 20 (September 1913): 139–40.

"Mace's Show in Thirtieth Year." *Sun Scenes: The Lake's Entertainer* 6 (May 20, 1983): 14.

McGinnis, A. C. "Pearl Search Began in 1897." *The Independence County Chronicles* 9 (July 1968): 25–29.

Maury, Dabney H. "Recollections of the Elkhorn Campaign." *Southern Historical Society Paper* 2 (1876): 81–83.

"Meramec Iron Ore Project Starts Production at Pea Ridge." *Engineering and Mining Journal* 165 (April 1964): 93–108.

Miller, E. Joan Wilson. "Ozark Cultural Region as Revealed by Traditional Materials." *Annals of the Association of American Geographers* 58 (March 1968): 51–77.

Missouri Game and Fish News (April 1926): 8, 14–15.

Missouri's Environment 3 (March 1977): 4.

Moffatt, Walter. "Transportation in Arkansas, 1819–1840." *Arkansas Historical Quarterly* 15 (Autumn 1956): 180–97.

Moke, Irene A. "Canning in Northwestern Arkansas: Springdale, Arkansas." *Economic Geography* 28 (April 1952): 151–59.

Morrow, Lynn. "Trader William Gilliss and Delaware Migration in Southern Missouri." *Missouri Historical Review* 75 (January 1981): 147–67.

———. "Louis Miller: Master Craftsman and Folk Artisan of Southeast Missouri." *Gateway Heritage* 4 (Summer 1983): 26–37.

———. "Joseph Washington McClurg: Entrepreneur, Politician, Citizen." *Missouri Historical Review* 78 (January 1984): 168–201.

———. "Ozark/Ozarks: Establishing a Regional Term." *White River Valley Historical Quarterly* (Fall 1996): 4–11.

———. "Estate Builders in the Missouri Ozarks: Establishing a St. Louis Tradition." *Gateway Heritage* 2 (Winter 1981–1982): 42–48.

———. "The St. Louis Game Park: Experiments in Conservation and Recreation." *White River Valley Historical Quarterly* (Spring 1997): 7–19.

———. "The Arlington Hearth: St. Louisans, Perry Andres, and Commercial Tourism." *Newsletter of the Phelps County Historical Society* 18 (October 1998): 3–18.

———. "What's in a Name, like Johnboat?" *White River Valley Historical Quarterly* 37 (Winter 1998): 9–24.

———. "New Madrid and Its Hinterland: 1783–1826." *Missouri Historical Society Bulletin* 36 (July 1980): 241–50.

———. "Rose Cliff Hotel: A Missouri Forum for Environmental Policy." *Gateway Heritage* 3 (1982): 38–48.

———, and Dan Saults. "The Yocum Silver Dollar: Sorting Out the Strands of an Ozarks Frontier Legend." *Gateway Heritage* 5 (Winter 1984–1985): 8–15.

———. "Fighting Flat, Carriage Paint, and Toilets in the Brush." *White River Valley Historical Quarterly* (Winter 1988): 3–4. Condensed and edited by Lynn Morrow from "Conditions of Schools in Ozark County," *St. Louis Star* (January 22, 1925).

Newton, John P. "Paleo-Indians in the Arkansas Ozarks: A Preliminary Statement." *Arkansas Archaeologist* 16–18 (1975–77): 85–92.

Olmstead, Clarence W. "American Orchard and Vineyard Regions." *Economic Geography* 32 (July 1956): 189–236.

Otto, John S. "Slavery in the Mountains." *Arkansas Historical Quarterly* 39 (1980): 35–52.

———. "Reconsidering the Southern 'Hillbilly': Appalachia and the Ozarks." *Appalachian Journal* 12 (Summer 1985): 324–31.

"The Ozark Water Mill Trail." *Ozarks Mountaineer* 16 (June 1968): 21.

Palmer, Bruce. "Back from the Ashes." *Missouri Conservationist* 61 (September 2000): 8–12.

Penprase, Mike. "Borer Beetle Could Harm Local Forests." *Springfield News-Leader,* July 1, 2001, 1A, 13A.

Piston, William G. "'Springfield Is a Vast Hospital': Dead and Wounded at the Battle of Wilson's Creek." *Missouri Historical Review* 93 (July 1999): 345–66.

Pitcaithley, Dwight. "Zinc and Lead Mining along the Buffalo River." *Arkansas Historical Quarterly* 37 (Winter 1978): 293–305.

Poeschel, Michael. "The Vineyards of Hermann, Missouri." *Western* 3 (October 1849): 53–55.

Price, Cynthia R. "Patterns of Cultural Behavior and Intra-Site Distributions of Faunal Remains at the Widow Harris Site." *Historical Archaeology* 19 (1985): 40–56.

Price, Edward T. "The Melungeons: A Mixed-Blood Strain of the Southern Appalachians." *Geographical Review* 41 (1951): 256–71.

———. "The Central Courthouse Square in the American County Seat." *Geographical Review* 58 (1968): 29–60.

Quick, David, and Lynn Morrow. "The Slab Rock Dwellings of Thayer, Missouri." *Proceedings of the Pioneer America Society* 13 (1990): 35–43.

Rafferty, Milton D. "Agricultural Change in the Western Ozarks." *Missouri Historical Review* 69 (April 1965): 299–322.

———. "Missouri's Black Walnut Kernel Industry." *Missouri Historical Review* 63 (January 1969): 214–26.

———. "Population and Settlement Changes in Two Ozark Localities." *Rural Sociology* 38 (Spring 1973): 46–56.

———, and Dennis Hrebec. "Logan Creek: A Missouri Ozark Valley Revisited. " *Journal of Geography* 72 (October 1973): 7–17.

———. "Ozark House Types: A Regional Approach." *Proceedings of the Pioneer American Society* 2 (1973): 93–106.

———. "The Golden Age of Mass Transit in Springfield, Parts I and II." *Springfield Magazine* 3, Pt. I (March 1982): 13–16; Pt. II (April 1982): 39–48.

———. "Curtis F. Marbut: Geographer." *Soil Survey Horizons* 26 (Spring 1985): 13–15.

———. "Crowley's Ridge: An Ozarks Outlier?" *Ozarks Mountaineer* (4 parts) (March–April, June–July, August–September, October–November 1989).

———. "Edward Frink Returns to Boyhood Home after 69-Year Absence." *Kanhistique* 24 (January 1999): 8–10.

Riggs, Margaret. "Valley Contrasts in the Missouri Ozarks Region." *Journal of Geography* 35 (December 1936): 351–59.

Roberts, Clarence N. "History of the Structural Brick Industry of Missouri." *Missouri Historical Review* 47 (July 1953): 318–28.

Rollinson, Paul A., and Suzanne Goldsmith-Hirsch. "Reason for Hope: A Framework for Resolving Conflict between Homeless Shelters and Their Neighbors." *Dig* 2 (Fall 1999): 1–14.

Rothrock, Thomas. "A King That Was." *Arkansas Historical Quarterly* 33 (Winter 1974): 324–33.

Salberg, Gloria. "The New Madrid Land Claims in Howard County, Missouri." *Missouri Mineral Industry News* 7 (May 1967): 69–79.

Sauer, Carl O. "Status and Change in the Rural Midwest—A Retrospect." In *Mitteilungen der Österreichischen Geographischen Gesellschaft* 105 (1963): 357–65.

Scarpino, Phillip V. "Slavery in Callaway County, Missouri: 1845–1855." Pt. 2. *Missouri Historical Review* 71 (April 1977): 266–83.

Schroeder, L. E. "The Battle of Wilson's Creek and Its Effect upon Missouri." *Missouri Historical Review* 71 (January 1977): 156–77.

Schroeder, Walter A. "Spread of Settlement in Howard County, Missouri, 1810–1839." *Missouri Historical Review* 63 (1968): 1–37.

Self, Nancy H. "The Building of the Railroads in the Cherokee Nation." *Chronicles of Oklahoma* 49 (Summer 1971): 180–205.

Shea, William L. "A Semi-Savage State: The Image of Arkansas in the Civil War." *Arkansas Historical Quarterly* 48 (Winter 1989): 309–28.

Shipley, Ellen C. "The Pleasures of Prosperity, Bella Vista, Arkansas, 1917–1929." *Arkansas Historical Quarterly* (Summer 1978): 99–129.

Spier, William D. "A Social History of Manganese Mining in the Batesville District of Independence County." *Arkansas Historical Quarterly* 36 (Summer 1977): 130–57.

"Stepping Stones over 75 Years of Service." *Midwest Motorist* 48 (February 1977): 12–13.

Still, Mary. "Leo Drey: Land Magnate of the Ozarks." *Missouri Resource Review* 2 (Winter 1983–84): 24–26.

Stroud, H. B. "Problems Associated with the Regulation of Recreational Land Development in Arkansas." *Arkansas Journal of Geography* 1 (1985): 12–25.

Trewartha, Glenn T. "Types of Rural Settlement in Colonial America." *Geographical Review* (1946): 568–96.

———. "The Unincorporated Hamlet: One Element of the American Settlement Fabric." *Annals of the Association of American Geographers* 33 (1943): 32–81.

Trieman, Thomas. "The State of Missouri's Forests: Tracking the Well-Being of Our Trees." *Missouri Conservationist* 61 (September 2000): 4–7.

"Vollenweider Pioneer Grower Makes Seymour Apple Capital of the Ozarks," *Ozarks Mountaineer* (October 1955): 5.

"What Orval Hath Wrought," *Time Magazine* (September 23, 1957).

Wiehe, Mark. "Abandon 700 Miles of Missouri Rails?" *Today's Farmer* 71 (November 1979): 6- 7.

Wood, James, and Milton D. Rafferty. "Mentor, Missouri: Forty Years Later." *Missouri Geographer* (Fall 1976): 21–26.

Wooster, Ralph. "The Arkansas Secessionist Convention." *Arkansas Historical Quarterly* 13 (1954): 183–84.

Wright, Gary A. "Ohio Hopewell Trade." *Missouri Archaeological Society Newsletter* 269 (1973).

"The Yoachum Dollar of 1822." *World Exonumia* (September 4, 1984): 453.

REPORTS AND TECHNICAL PAPERS

Amonker, Ravindra G., and Russel L. Gerlach. *The Changing Population of Missouri: Trends and Patterns*. Springfield, Mo.: Center for Social Research, Southwest Missouri State University, 1988.

Austin, Morris E. "Land Resource Regions and Major Land Resource Areas of the United States." *Agricultural Handbook No. 296*. Soil Conservation Service, U.S. Department of Agriculture, Washington, D.C., 1965.

Baver, Leonard D. "Soil Erosion in Missouri." *University of Missouri Agricultural Experiment Station Research Bulletin no. 349, 1935*.

"The Beauties of Ha-Ha-Tonka." *Forty-third Annual Report of the Missouri State Board of Agriculture: A Record of the Work for the Year 1910*. Jefferson City, Mo.: Hugh Stephens Printing Co., 1911.

Bennitt, Rudolph, and Werner O. Nagel. "A Survey of Resident Game and Furbearers of Missouri." *University of Missouri Studies* 13 (April 1937).

Biennial Report of the Public Service Commission, 1943–1944. Jefferson City: Missouri Public Service Commission, 1944.

Biennial Report of the Public Service Commission, 1953–1954. Jefferson City: Missouri Public Service Commission, 1954.

Bretz, Harlan J. *Geomorphic History of the Ozarks of Missouri*. Missouri Geological Survey and Water Resources, 2d Series, 41, Rolla, Mo. 1965.

Brugger, Brenda, compiler. *Guide to the Historical Records of the Frisco: St. Louis-San Francisco Railway Company and its Predecessor, Subsidiary and Constituent Companies*. Rolla: University of Missouri Western Historical Manuscript Collection, 1989.

Buckley, Ernest, and H. A. Buehler. "The Geology of the Granby Area." *Missouri Bureau of Geology and Mines*, 2d Series, 4, Rolla, Mo., 1905.

Buehler, H. A. *The Lime and Cement Resources of Missouri*. Missouri Bureau of Geology and Mines, Vol. 6, 2d Series. Jefferson City, Mo.: Hugh Stephens Printing Co., 1907.

Citizens Recommendations Regarding Formulation of Area Development Program. Republic: Southwest Missouri Local Government Advisory Council, 1977.

Comprehensive Report on Missouri Schools, 1967. Jefferson City: Missouri Department of Education, 1967.

Dake, Charles L. *The Sand and Gravel Resources of Missouri*. Missouri Bureau of Geology and Mines, Vol. 15, 2d Series, 1918.

Drake, J. A., and A. T. Strahorn. *Soil Survey of Webster County, Missouri*. Washington, D.C.: U.S. Department of Agriculture, Bureau of Soils, 1904.

Employment Record. Jefferson City: Missouri Department of Labor and Industrial Relations, August 19, 1997.

Ganser, David A. *Timber Resources of Missouri's Southwestern Ozarks*. Bulletin B845. Columbia: University of Missouri, January 1966.

Howe, Wallace B., coordinator, and John W. Koenig, ed. *The Stratigraphic Succession in Missouri*. Missouri Geological Survey and Water Resources, Vol. 40, 2d Series, Rolla, Mo., 1961.

Krusekopf, H. H., and F. Z. Hutton. *Soil Survey of Greene County, Missouri*. Washington, D.C.: U.S. Department of Agriculture, Bureau of Soils, 1915.

Lane, W. L., and T. R. Yanske. "Pillar Extraction and Rock Mechanics at the Doe Run Company in Missouri." *Proceedings of the Thirty-seventh U.S. Rock Mechanics Symposium* (Vail, Colo., June 6–9, 1999): 285–92.

Late Quaternary Faulting and Earthquake Liquefaction Features in Southeast Missouri: The Identification of New Earthquake Hazards. Prepared for the Forty-third Annual Meeting and Field Trip of the Association of Missouri Geologists, Missouri Department of Natural Resources, Division of Geology and Land Survey, Gape Girardeau, Mo.: September 21–22, 1996.

Local Climatological Data, Annual Summary: Springfield, Missouri, 1999. Asheville, N.C.: National Climatic Data Center, 1999.

Lopinot, Neal H., Jack H. Ray, and Michael Conner. *The 1997 Excavations at the Big Eddy Site (23CE426) in Southwest Missouri*. Springfield: Southwest Missouri State University Center for Archaeological Research, Special Publication No. 2, 1998.

McKeown, F. A., and L. C. Pakiser, et al. *Investigations of the New Madrid, Missouri Earthquake Region*. Washington, D.C.: U.S. Geological Survey, Professional Paper 1236, 1982.

Marbut, Curtis F. *Soils of the Ozark Region: A Preliminary Report on the General Character of the Soils and Agriculture of the Missouri Ozarks*. Research Bulletin No. 3, University of Missouri College of Agriculture, Agricultural Experiment Station, Columbia, Missouri, 1910.

———. *Soil Reconnaissance of the Ozark Region of Missouri and Arkansas*. Field Operations of the Bureau of Soils, 1911. Washington, D.C.: Bureau of Soils, U.S. Department of Agriculture, 1914.

Missouri Iron Company: An Act to Charter the Missouri Iron Company. Jefferson City: John Jamison, Speaker of the House of Representatives; Franklin Cannon, President of the Senate, 1837. Photocopy in the State Historical Society of Missouri archives.

Morgan, Gordon D., Dean Cagle, and Linda Harned. "Black Hillbillies of the Arkansas Ozarks." A report of the Department of Sociology, University of Arkansas, Fayetteville, 1973.

Morrow, Lynn. "A Preliminary Survey of Richwoods Township, Miller County, Missouri, 1870." Fiscal Year 1980–81 Historic Preservation Program, Center for Ozarks Studies, Southwest Missouri State University, Springfield, Missouri, 1981.

———, and Robert Flanders. "An Overview of Seven Ozark Counties." West Plains: South Central Ozarks Council of Governments, 1989.

Moser, David, John S. Shonkwiler, Richard G. Boehm, Michael W. Woolverton, and William C. Bailey. *Missouri's Transportation System: Condition, Capacity, and Impediments to Efficiency.* Jefferson City, Mo.: Office of Administration, Division of Budget and Planning, 1976.

Offield, T. W., and H. A. Pohn. *Geology of the Decaturville Structure, Missouri.* U.S. Geological Survey Professional Paper 1042. Washington, D.C.: U.S. Government Printing Office, 1979.

Osgood, Otis T. "Farm Planning in the Eastern Ozarks," *Arkansas Agricultural Experiment Station Bulletin, no. 435.* Fayetteville: University of Arkansas College of Agriculture, 1943.

"Plan for Managing National Forest in Missouri." Mark Twain National Forest. Rolla, Mo.: 1976.

Schweitzer, Paul. *A Report on the Mineral Waters of Missouri.* Geological Survey of Missouri, First Series, No. 3, 1892.

Shepard, Edward M. "A Report on Greene County." *Geological Survey of Missouri,* 12, Part I, Sheet Report no. 5. Jefferson City: Tribune Printing Co., 1898.

Snyder, Frank G., et al. *Cryptoexplosive Structures in Missouri.* Missouri Geological Survey and Water Resources Report of Investigations No. 30. Rolla, Mo.: 1965.

Sweet, A. T., and Howard V. Jordan. *Soil Survey of Lawrence County, Missouri.* Washington, D.C.: U.S. Department of Agriculture, Bureau of Soils, 1928.

Turnbo, S. C. "A Long Time Ago." Turnbo Manuscript Collection. Springfield-Greene County Public Library, Springfield, Missouri. Document 615, vol. 21, 19. (Transcribed by library staff and indexed by James F. Keefe and Lynn Morrow.)

Wharton, Hayward M., et al. *Missouri Minerals: Resources, Production, and Forecasts.* Missouri Geological Survey and Water Resources, Special Publication No. 1. Rolla: 1969.

Wilson, W. T., and J. W. Reid, "Livestock and Forestry Enterprises on Farms in the Ozark Region." *Arkansas Agricultural Experiment Station Bulletin No. 419.* Fayetteville: University of Arkansas College of Agriculture, 1942.

Yanske, Thomas, and W. L. Lane. "Pillar Extraction and Rock Mechanics at the Doe Run Company in Missouri." *Proceedings of the Thirty-seventh U.S. Rock Mechanics Symposium* (Vail, Colo., June 6–9, 1999): 285–92.

MAPS AND ATLASES

Batesville Quadrangle. 7.5-minute series. Denver, Colo.: U.S. Geological Survey, 1943. Photorevised 1981.

Carter County, Mo. Plat Book. Rockford, Ill.: W.W. Hixson and Co., *circa* 1920.

Copeland, Curtis, and City of Branson, Missouri, Engineering and GIS Division. *Digital Geographic Information Systems (GIS)Files.* Branson: City of Branson Press, 2000.

Fredericktown, Mo., Quadrangle. 7.5-minute series. Washington, D.C.: U.S. Geological Survey, 1980.

General Highway Map: Shannon County. Scale 1/2 inch equals 1 mile. Jefferson City: Missouri Highway and Transportation Department, Division of Planning, 1988.

Gladden, Mo., Quadrangle. 7.5-minute series. Denver, Colo.: U.S. Geological Survey, 1967.

Harrison, Ark.-Mo. 1: 250,000 Series. Denver, Colo.: U.S. Geological Survey, 1985.

Jasper, Ark., Quadrangle. 7.5-minute series. Denver, Colo.: U.S. Geological Survey, 1967.

Johnson, Brent. *Railroad Map of the Ozarks.* Department of Geography, Geology, and Planning, Southwest Missouri State University, Springfield, 1999.

Lobeck, A. K. *Physiographic Diagram of the U.S. 1:3,000,000.* Madison: University of Wisconsin, 1954.

Missouri Rail Freight Carriers. Jefferson City, Mo.: Jefferson City Department of Transportation, 1999.

Official Kansas State Railroad Map. Topeka, Kans.: Department of Transportation, 1998.

Oklahoma Railroad Map. Oklahoma City: Department of Transportation, 1998.

Parthenon Quadrangle. 7.5-minute series. Denver, Colo.: U.S. Geological Survey, 1980.

"Plats and Field Notes." U.S. Department of the Interior, General Land Office, 1893. A true and liberal exemplification of the official plats surveyed between 1835 and 1840. Available in the Greene County Surveyor's Office, Springfield, Missouri.

Rafferty, Milton D. *Historical Atlas of Missouri.* Norman: University of Oklahoma Press, 1982.

Railroad Map of Arkansas. Little Rock, Ark.: Department of Transportation, 1999.

Russellville, Ark. 1:250,000 Series. U.S. Geological Survey Map. Denver, Colo.: U.S. Geological Survey, 1985.

Rand McNally 1999 Commercial Atlas and Marketing Guide. 130th edition. Chicago: Rand McNally and Co., 1999.

Weaver, Bill, and Mike Fonner. *Digital Geographic Information Systems (GIS) Files.* Springfield: City of Springfield, Missouri, 2000.

THESES AND DISSERTATIONS

Belser, Thomas A. "Military Operations in Missouri and Arkansas, 1861–1865." Parts 1 and 2. Ph.D. dissertation, Vanderbilt University, 1958.

Blevins, Brooks R. "Fallow Are the Hills: A Century of Rural Modernization in the Arkansas Ozarks." Master's thesis, Auburn University, 1994.

———. "A Social History of the Arkansas Ozarks." Ph.D. dissertation, Auburn University, 1999.

Brownlee, Richard L., II, "Guerrilla Warfare in Missouri, 1861–1865." Ph.D. dissertation, University of Missouri, 1955.

Cathey, C. W. "Slavery in Arkansas." Fayetteville: Master's thesis, University of Arkansas, 1936.

Clendenen, Harbert L. "Settlement Morphology of the Southern Courtois Hills, Missouri, 1820–1860." Ph.D. dissertation, Louisiana State University, 1973.

Cralle, Waldo Odro. "Social Change and Isolation in the Ozark Mountain Region of Missouri." Ph.D. dissertation, University of Minnesota, 1934.

Fritz, Gayle J. "Prehistoric Ozark Agriculture: The University of Arkansas Rockshelter Collections." Ph.D. dissertation, University of North Carolina, 1986.

Gilmore, Robert K. "Theatrical Elements in Folk Entertainment in the Missouri Ozarks, 1886–1910." Ph.D. dissertation, University of Minnesota, 1961.

Hale, Ruth F. "A Map of the Vernacular Regions of the United States." Ph.D. dissertation, University of Minnesota, 1971.

Handley, Lawrence R. "A Geography of the Missouri and North Arkansas Railroad." Master's thesis, University of Arkansas, 1973.

Henderson, John R. "The Cultural Landscape of French Settlement in the American Bottom." Master's thesis, Illinois State University, 1966.

Herlinger, Elizabeth. "Historical, Cultural, and Organizational Analysis of Ozark Ethnic Identity." Ph.D. dissertation, University of Chicago, 1972.

Hill, Leslie G. "History of the Missouri Lumber and Mining Company, 1880–1990." Ph.D. dissertation, University of Missouri, 1949.

Hogg, Virginia. "Urban Pattern of Springfield, Missouri." Master's thesis, Washington University, 1934.

Holliday, Donald R. "Autobiography of an American Family." Ph.D. dissertation, University of Minnesota, 1974.

Johnson, Hugh N. "Sequent Occupance of the St. Francois Mining Region." Ph.D. dissertation, University of Missouri, 1950.

Kostbade, J. Trenton. "Geography and Politics in Missouri." Ph.D. dissertation, University of Michigan, 1957.

Loberg, David L. "The Mapping of Arkansas: 1541–1900." Master's thesis, University of Arkansas, 1976.

McFarlane, Larry A. "The Missouri Land and Livestock Company, Limited, of Scotland: Foreign Investment on the Missouri Farming Frontier, 1882–1908." Ph.D. dissertation, University of Missouri, 1963.

McKinney, Edgar. "Images, Realities, and Cultural Transformation in the Missouri Ozarks, 1920–1960." Ph.D. dissertation, University of Missouri, 1990.

McMahon, David F. "Tradition and Change in an Ozark Mining Community." Master's thesis, St. Louis University, 1958.

Makris, George A. "A Survey of Transportation in the State of Arkansas." Master's thesis, University of Arkansas, 1933.

Megee, Mary. "The Geography of the Mining of Lead and Zinc in the Tri-State Mining District." Master's thesis, University of Arkansas, 1950.

Morrison, Kathleen. "Poverty of Place: A Comparative Study of Five Rural Counties in the Missouri Ozarks." Ph.D. dissertaton, Memphis State University, 1999.

Poletti, Peter J. "An Interdisciplinary Study of the Missouri Grape and Wine Industry: 1650–1989." Ph.D. dissertation, St. Louis University, 1989.

Rafferty, Milton D. "Persistence Versus Change in Land Use and Landscape in the Springfield, Missouri, Vicinity of the Ozarks." Ph.D. dissertation, University of Nebraska, 1970.

Roome, Charles C. "Selected Aspects of the Southeast Missouri Mining Region." Master's thesis, University of Missouri, 1962.

Rowe, Ruth. "The Geographic Saga of an Ozark Family." Master's thesis, Washington University, 1939.

Schiefer, Carl L., Jr. "Washington County, Arkansas: A Geography of Population Change, 1840–1970." Master's thesis, University of Arkansas, 1976.

Schrock, Wally. "Varying Fortunes of Small Towns: Case Studies in Rich Hill, Sarcoxie, and Nixa, Missouri." Master's thesis, Southwest Missouri State University, 2000.

Seffker, Angela R. "Understanding a Planner's Role: A Case Study of the Amish Community in Webster County, Missouri." Master's thesis, Southwest Missouri State University, 1992.

Slechta, Don B. "Dr. John R. Brinkley: A Kansas Phenomenon." Master's thesis, Fort Hays State College, 1952.

Smith, Stuart A. "Houston, Missouri: An Example of a Changing Cultural Landscape in the Rural Missouri Ozarks." Master's thesis, University of Missouri, 1991.

Sovine, Melanie Lou. "The Mysterious Melungeons: A Critique of the Mythical Images." Ph.D. dissertation, University of Kentucky, 1982.

Spier, William D. "Farming and Mining Experience: Independence County, Arkansas, 1900–1925." Ph.D. dissertation, Washington University, 1974.

Stepp, Peggy. "Jonathan Fairbanks: 'Mr. Springfield Public Schools.'" Master's seminar paper, Department of History, Southwest Missouri State University, 1972.

Tadros, Helmi R. "Return Migration to Selected Communities in the Ozarks: A Predominantly Rural, Economically Depressed Region." Ph.D. dissertation, University of Missouri, 1968.

Taussig, Mary Boland. "Factors Influencing School Attendance in the Missouri Barytes Fields." Master's thesis, Washington University, 1938.

Walz, Robert B. "Migration into Arkansas, 1834–1880." Ph.D. dissertation, University of Texas, 1958.

White, Jason W. "Spatial Assessment of Nonpoint Phosphorus Sources Using Streambed Sediment Monitoring in the

Kings River Basin, NW Arkansas." Master's thesis, Southwest Missouri State University, 2001.

MISCELLANEOUS

Aerie Acres Advertisement Leaflet. Ava, Mo.: Aerie Acres, circa 1973.

Blunk, J. R. "History of Missouri and the Yoachum Silver Dollar, 1822." Typescript manuscript. Springfield, Mo., 1985. Copy in possession of the author.

Boesch, Mark J. "History of Mark Twain National Forest." Typescript manuscript. Rolla, Mo.: Mark Twain National Forest, 1968. Copy in possession of the author.

Branson-Tri-Lakes Telephone Directory. St. Louis, Mo.: GTE Midwest, Inc., May 1999.

Burton, W. J. "History of the Missouri Pacific Railroad." Typescript, St. Louis, Mo., Union Pacific Railroad, July 1, 1956.

"Cedar Farm Lodge." Typescript copy of the recollections of Professor Donald H. McInnis, Springfield, Missouri, August 28, 2000. A copy is in possession of the author.

Claxton, O. C. Area Community Development Agent, Ava, Missouri. Personal correspondence with the author, July 18, 1969.

Company Profile, World Cooperage Company. Napa, Calif.: World Cooperage Company, 2000.

Cook, Delbert. "Abandoned Railroads in Missouri." Research Paper. Department of Geography and Geology, Southwest Missouri State University, 1977.

1998 Environmental Briefing Book: A Guide for the Missouri State Legislature. St. Louis: Missouri Coalition for the Environment, 1998.

Figg, Dennis. "Is Every Grassland a Prairie?" Presentation, Missouri Natural Resources 2000 Conference, Tan-Tar-A Resort, Lake of the Ozarks, February 2–4, 2000.

Flanders, Robert. "Shannon County of the Ozarks." Developmental Grant proposal, Southwest Missouri State University, Springfield, 1977.

Frazer, Timothy C. "American Dialect Acquisition in Foreign Settlement Areas." Paper presented in American Dialect Society meeting, November 1976, Western Illinois University, Macomb.

Jefferson City Telephone Directory. Shawnee Mission, Kans.: Sprint, June 1999.

Kelso, Margaret Gilmore. "Memoirs." Manuscript, n.d. In possession of Martha Gilmore, Springfield, Missouri.

Martin, James W., and Jerry J. Presley. "Ozark Land and Lumber Company: Organization and Operations." Unpublished manuscript, School of Forestry, University of Missouri-Columbia, January 31, 1985.

Merchants and Manufacturers Record of Springfield, Missouri. Springfield, Mo.: A. Owen Jennings, 1906.

Rafferty, Milton D. "Central Places in Southwest Missouri." A research paper summarizing the fieldwork of the Geography of Missouri class, Spring 1970. Springfield: Department of Geography, Geology, and Planning, Southwest Missouri State University, 1970.

———. Ozark House Types. Springfield, Mo.: Aux-Arc Book Company, 1979.

———. "Field Reconnaissance of Settlement Patterns in Linn Township, Christian County, Missouri, 1992." Unpublished research paper. Department of Geography, Geology, and Planning, Southwest Missouri State University, December 1992.

Russell, Bonnie Eagans. "Life in Booger County." Springfield, Mo.: Unpublished manuscript, 1999.

Sacklet, Norbert. "Trackage Abandonment, 1948–1974." Unpublished notes in the archives of the Missouri Public Service Commission, Jefferson City, 1974.

Seeger, Cheryl M. "Ozark-Ouachita Highlands Assessment." Unpublished report, Missouri Department of Natural Resources, Division of Geology and Land Survey, Rolla, Mo., 1999.

Silver Mines Self-Guided Trail. Brochure. Fredericktown, Mo.: District Ranger, Mark Twain National Forest, n.d.

Southwestern Bell Springfield-Branson Telephone Directory, 2000/2001. St. Louis, Mo.: Southwestern Bell, May 2000.

"Springfield Manufacturers' Survey, 1968." Department of Geography, Geology, and Planning, Southwest Missouri State University, Springfield, Mo., 1968. A report based on a telephone survey by the urban geography class.

To Get to the Other Side. Tyson Foods 1999 Annual Report. Springdale, Ark.: Tyson Foods, 1999.

Tornadoes—Greene County. Typewritten record of tornadoes abstracted by the author from the Springfield Weather Station records, March 2000. The record is in the possession of the author.

Velikonja, Joseph. "The Italian Contribution to the Geographic Character of Tontitown, Arkansas, and Rosati, Missouri." Translated by Don Fisher, Southwest Missouri State College, Springfield, 1971. Manuscript in Meyer Library, Southwest Missouri State University, Springfield.

Williamson, Hugh P. *Restrictions and Rights of the Missouri Sportsman.* Jefferson City: Missouri Department of Conservation, n.d.

Yanske, Thomas R. "Missouri Lead Mining Information." Typescript document. Doe Run Company. Viburnum, Mo., November 22, 1999.

NEWSPAPER ARTICLES AND BROADCASTS

"Arkansas Ice Storm." KY-3 television, Springfield, 10:00 P.M. news report, January 16, 2000.

Barnett, Jennifer. "Wanted: Ideas Built to Last." *Springfield News-Leader,* February 28, 2000.

Buckstaff, Cathryn. "Ride the Monorail to the Land of Never-Was Ideas." *Springfield News-Leader,* February 28, 2000.

———. "Time-Share Packages Increasing in Popularity." *Springfield News-Leader,* February 28, 2000.

"Burlington Northern-Santa Fe to Cut 1,400 Jobs." *Springfield News-Leader,* May 25, 1999.

"Classified Advertisements." Real-Estate section. *Springfield News-Leader,* September 10, 2000.

Culp, Karen E. "Industrial Park's Impact Praised." *Springfield News-Leader,* June 27, 2000.

———. "College Street Banks on Business Revival." *Springfield News-Leader,* July 6, 2000.

———. "Hagale Losing to the World." *Springfield News-Leader,* August 23, 2000.

Dale, Michal. "Katy Trail Runs between Sedalia and St. Charles." *Springfield News-Leader,* July 27, 1998.

"Death of Monte Ne." *Springfield Leader-Press,* December 10, 1961.

Dunlap, J. E. "Harrison Survives '100 Year Flood' Damage." *Harrison Daily Times,* Sesquicentennial edition, July 4, 1986.

"Engineer's Report Traces Crooked Creek Floods." *Harrison Daily Times,* Sesquicentennial edition, July 4, 1986.

Farmer, Frank "Ozarks on Skids: Ice Paralysis Stuns Wide Area." *Springfield News-Leader,* December, 12, 1972.

"First There Was Nashville . . . Then Came Branson." *Atlanta Journal-Constitution,* July 4, 1993.

"Gerald L. K. Smith Helped Cultivate Racism's Deep Roots." *Springfield News-Leader,* June 26, 1966.

Groves, Johnathan, and Angela Wilson. "Sewage Rushes into Creek." *Springfield News-Leader,* July 30, 2000.

Heierman, Kelly. "Victim Left Behind Thirteen Children." *Springfield News-Leader,* January 16, 2000.

———. "Winrod Trial Moves Rapidly." *Springfield News-Leader,* January 31, 2001.

"Herschend Brothers Run Business by Complimentary Efforts." *Springfield News-Leader,* March 1, 1981.

"Hundreds Watched Hanging in 1938." *Springfield News-Leader,* January 26, 2000.

"Jewish Renewal Growing in Joplin." *Springfield News-Leader,* October 15, 2000.

Johnson, Doug. "Chip Mills Investigated." *Springfield News-Leader,* April 18, 2000.

———. "Hillbilly Jokes Start Opinion War in Ozarks." *Springfield News-Leader,* January 14, 2001.

Keyes, Robert. "Council Sees Four Plans for Glenstone." *Springfield News-Leader,* June 21, 2000.

———. "City Focuses on Buying Land." *Springfield News-Leader,* August 31, 2000.

Leicht, Linda. "Nazi Symbols Painted on Gravestones." *Springfield News-Leader,* Feburary 7, 2001.

McDonald, Jennifer. "Plant Closings Change Ozarks." *Springfield News-Leader,* January 9, 2000.

"Man Dies in Buggy Accident: Was Nephew of Woman Killed in a Similar Accident." *Springfield News-Leader,* August 27, 2000.

Menner, Laura B. "Missouri Town Worried, Intrigued." *Springfield News-Leader,* December 31, 1999.

———. "Police Scour Rural Fields for Carjacking Suspect." *Springfield News-Leader,* December 31, 1999.

———. "Fugitive Linked to Second Death; Manhunt Continues." *Springfield News-Leader,* January 2, 2000.

"Missouri's War against Texas Herds." *Springfield Leader and Press,* January 30, 1977.

"Mobile Meth Lab Found in SUV." *Springfield News-Leader,* January 13, 2001.

"Move over Nashville." *St. Louis Post-Dispatch,* September 11, 1988.

"Now That's What You Call a Rain." *Springfield News-Leader,* July 2, 1973.

O'Brien, Mike. "Storm Rips County, Kills One." *Springfield News-Leader,* December 15, 1971.

O'Dell, Kathy. "Refugees." *Springfield News-Leader,* August 12, 2000.

Ott, Diane. "Vietnamese Celebration Descends on Carthage: Tens of Thousands Join in the City for the Annual Religious, Cultural Event." *Springfield News-Leader,* August 27, 2000.

Overstreet, Sarah. "Determined Women Played Role in Lady Bears' Success." *Springfield News-Leader,* February 11, 2001.

"Ozark Greenways Going for the Gold: Group to Start Fund Campaign to Finish Off the Frisco Trail." *Springfield News-Leader,* April 27, 2000.

Penprase, Mike. "Threat to Water Sinking In." *Springfield News-Leader,* July 30, 2000.

———. "Recent Rains Helped Open Sinkholes." *Springfield News-Leader,* August 5, 2000.

———. "Fires Storm through Ozarks." *Springfield News-Leader,* March 9, 2000.

Poneleit, Sandy Z. "Dairy Industry in Danger." *Springfield News-Leader,* February 6, 2000.

Portman, Jennifer, and Traci Bauer. "Forest Land Burns by Buffalo River." *Springfield News-Leader,* November 19, 1999.

Rafferty, Milton D. "The Marbut Place: A Touch of New England in the Ozarks." *Springfield News-Leader,* July 22, 1973.

"Renaissance of Monte Ne." *Springfield News-Leader,* February 27, 1977.

Riley, Claudette. "Ozark Schools Get List of Attire No-Nos." *Springfield News-Leader,* July 28, 2000, 1A.

"Silver Dollar City Bonanza in the Ozarks." *Springfield Leader Press,* June 25, 1961.

"Sports Talk," a radio talk show broadcast on KWTO, 560 AM, from Springfield, Missouri, January 20, 2001.

Strait, Jefferson. "An Incredible Appetite." *Springfield News-Leader,* August 13, 2000.

———, and Claudette Riley. "Ozarks Buried." *Springfield News-Leader,* December 14, 2000.

Stark, Harlan. "Killer Tornado Leaves Three Dead in Neosho." *Neosho Daily News,* April 25, 1975.

Special Storm Edition. *Neosho Sunday News,* April 27, 1975.

Sutherland, Bill. "Holiday Storm Darkens Ozarks." *Springfield News-Leader,* December 26, 1987.

"Three Negroes Lynched by Mad Mob." *Springfield Republican,* April 15, 1906.

"Towns, Entrepreneurs Breathe New Life into Old Schools." *Springfield News-Leader,* September 28, 2000.

"Two-Year-Old Girl Drowns after Truck Swept Away." *Springfield News-Leader,* February 28, 1997.

"250,000 Visitors Expected This Year." *Springfield Leader-Press,* June 25, 1961.

"Ward's Weather: Heavenly." *Springfield Leader and Press,* December 11, 1977.

Wilson, Angela. "Workers Start Repairing Pipe." *Springfield News-Leader,* August 7, 2000.

Winn, Robert G. "Coal in the Ozarks." *Washington County Observer,* April 21, 1977.

Woods, Willard. "Is Springfield Ready for Yet Another Cashew-Chicken Restaurant." *Springfield News-Leader,* June 17, 1990.

Zimmerman, David. "Country Stars Light the Way to Branson." *USA Today,* June 17, 1992.

CENSUS MATERIALS

U.S. Bureau of the Census. *Thirteenth Census of the United States: 1910, Agriculture,* 6. Washington, D.C.: U.S. Government Printing Office, 1913.

U.S. Bureau of the Census. *Thirteenth Census of the United States: 1910, Population,* 2. Washington, D.C.: U.S. Government Printing Office, 1913.

U.S. Bureau of the Census. *Fourteenth Census of the United States: 1920, Agriculture,* 4, part 1. Washington, D.C.: U.S. Government Printing Office, 1922.

U.S. Bureau of the Census. *Fourteenth Census of the United States: 1920, Population,* 3. Washington, D.C.: U.S. Government Printing Office, 1922.

U.S. Bureau of the Census. *Fifteenth Census of the United States: 1930, Agriculture,* 2, part 1. Washington, D.C.: U.S. Government Printing Office, 1932.

U.S. Bureau of the Census. *Fifteenth Census of the United States: 1930, Population,* 3, part 1. Washington, D.C.: U.S. Government Printing Office, 1932.

U.S. Bureau of the Census. *Sixteenth Census of the United States: 1940, Agriculture,* 1, part 2. Washington, D.C.: U.S. Government Printing Office, 1942.

U.S. Bureau of the Census. *Sixteenth Census of the United States: 1940, Census of Business Retail Trade: 1939.* 1, part 3. Washington, D.C.: U.S. Government Printing Office, 1942.

U.S. Bureau of the Census. *Sixteenth Census of the United States: 1940. Population,* 2, part 4. Washington, D.C.: U.S. Government Printing Office, 1943.

U.S. Bureau of the Census. *United States Census of Agriculture: 1950. Counties and State Economic Areas, Missouri,* 1, part 10. Washington, D.C.: U.S. Government Printing Office, 1952.

U.S. Bureau of the Census. *United States Census of Population: 1950. Missouri,* 2, part 25. Washington, D.C.: U.S. Government Printing Office, 1952.

U.S. Bureau of the Census. *United States Census of Business: 1954. Retail Trade-Area Statistics,* 2, part 2. Washington, D.C.: U.S. Government Printing Office, 1956.

U.S. Bureau of the Census. *United States Census of Population: 1954. Counties and State Economic Areas, Missouri,* 1, part 10. Washington, D.C.: U.S. Government Printing Office, 1956.

U.S. Bureau of the Census. *United States Census of Population: 1960. General Population Characteristics, Kansas,* final report PC1–18B. Washington, D.C.: U.S. Government Printing Office, 1961.

U.S. Bureau of the Census. *United States Census of Population: 1960. General Social and Economic Characteristics, Kansas,* final report PC1–18C. Washington, D.C.: U.S. Government Printing Office, 1961.

U.S. Bureau of the Census. *United States Census of Population: 1960. Characteristics of Population, Arkansas,* 1. Washington, D.C.: U.S. Government Printing Office, 1963.

U.S. Bureau of the Census. *United States Census of Population: 1960. Characteristics of the Population, Oklahoma,* 1, part 38. Washington, D.C.: U.S. Government Printing Office, 1963.

U.S. Bureau of the Census. *United States Census of Population: 1960. Missouri,* 1, part 27. Washington, D.C.: U.S. Government Printing Office, 1963.

U.S. Bureau of the Census. *United States Census of Agriculture: 1964, Statistics for the State and Counties, Missouri,* 1, part 17. Washington, D.C.: U.S. Government Printing Office, 1967.

U.S. Bureau of the Census. *Census of Population: 1970. Number of Inhabitants, United States Summary.* Washington, D.C.: U.S. Government Printing Office, 1971.

U.S. Bureau of the Census. *United States Census of Population: 1970. Characteristics of the Population, Arkansas,* 1, part 5. Washington, D.C.: U.S. Government Printing Office, 1973.

U.S. Bureau of the Census. *United States Census of Population: 1970. Characteristics of the Population, Kansas,* 1, part 18. Washington, D.C.: U.S. Government Printing Office, 1973.

U.S. Bureau of the Census. *United States Census of Population: 1970. Characteristics of the Population, Missouri,* 1, part 27. Washington, D.C.: U.S. Government Printing Office, 1973.

U.S. Bureau of the Census. *United States Census of Population: 1970. Characteristics of the Population, Oklahoma,* 1, part 38. Washington, D.C.: U.S. Government Printing Office, 1973.

U.S. Bureau of the Census. *United States Census of Population: 1980. General Population Characteristics, Arkansas,* 1, chap. B. Washington, D.C.: U.S. Government Printing Office, 1982.

U.S. Bureau of the Census. *United States Census of Population: 1980. General Population Characteristics, Kansas,* 1, chap. B. Washington, D.C.: U.S. Government Printing Office, 1982.

U.S. Bureau of the Census. *United States Census of Population: 1980. General Social and Economic Characteristics, Arkansas,* 1, chap. C. Washington, D.C.: U.S. Government Printing Office, 1982.

U.S. Bureau of the Census. *United States Census of Population: 1980. General Social and Economic Characteristics, Kansas,* 1, chap. C. Washington, D.C.: U.S. Government Printing Office, 1983.

U.S. Bureau of the Census. *United States Census of Population: 1980. General Population Characteristics, Missouri,* 1, chap. B. Washington, D.C.: U.S. Government Printing Office, 1982.

U.S. Bureau of the Census. *United States Census of Population: 1980. General Social and Economic Characteristics, Missouri,* 1, chap. C. Washington, D.C.: U.S. Government Printing Office, 1983.

U.S. Bureau of the Census. *United States Census of Population: 1980. General Population Characteristics, Oklahoma,* 1, chap. B. Washington, D.C.: U.S. Government Printing Office, 1982.

U.S. Bureau of the Census. *United States Census of Population: 1980. General Social and Economic Characteristics, Oklahoma,* 1, chap. C. Washington, D.C.: U.S. Government Printing Office, 1983.

U.S. Bureau of the Census. *United States Census of Population: 1990. General Population Characteristics, Arkansas,* 1, chap. B. Washington, D.C.: U.S. Government Printing Office, 1992.

U.S. Bureau of the Census. *United States Census of Population: 1990. General Social and Economic Characteristics, Arkansas,* 1, chap. C. Washington, D.C.: U.S. Government Printing Office, 1993.

U.S. Bureau of the Census. *United States Census of Population: 1990. General Population Characteristics, Kansas,* 1, chap. B. Washington, D.C.: U.S. Government Printing Office, 1992.

U.S. Bureau of the Census. *United States Census of Population: 1990. General Social and Economic Characteristics, Kansas,* 1, chap. C. Washington, D.C.: U.S. Government Printing Office, 1993.

U.S. Bureau of the Census. *United States Census of Population: 1990. General Population Characteristics, Missouri,* 1, chap. B. Washington, D.C.: U.S. Government Printing Office, 1992.

U.S. Bureau of the Census. *United States Census of Population: 1990. General Social and Economic Characteristics, Missouri,* 1, chap. C. Washington, D.C.: U.S. Government Printing Office, 1993.

U.S. Bureau of the Census. *United States Census of Population: 1990. General Population Characteristics, Oklahoma,* 1, chap. B. Washington, D.C.: U.S. Government Printing Office, 1992.

U.S. Bureau of the Census. *United States Census of Population: 1990. General Social and Economic Characteristics, Oklahoma,* 1, chap. C. Washington, D.C.: U.S. Government Printing Office, 1993.

U.S. Bureau of the Census. *County Business Patterns: Missouri, 1997.* Washington, D.C.: U.S. Government Printing Office, 1999.

U.S. Bureau of the Census. *Census of Agriculture: Historical Highlights, 1987,* 1, Part 51. Washington, D. C.: U.S. Government Printing Office, 1988.

U.S. Bureau of the Census. *Census of Agriculture, 1997: Missouri, State and County Data,* 1, Geographic Area Series, Part 25. Washington, D.C.: U.S. Department of Agriculture, 1999.

U.S. Department of Agriculture. *1997 Census of Agriculture.* Washington, D.C.: U.S. Government Printing Office, 1987.

U.S. Department of Interior, Census Office. *Seventh Census of the United States: 1850.* Washington, D.C.: Robert Armstrong, Public Printer, 1853.

U.S. Department of the Interior, Census Office. *Eighth Census of the United States, 1860: Census of Population,* I, table 2. Washington, D.C.: U.S. Government Printing Office, 1862.

U.S. Department of Interior, Census Office. *Ninth Census of the United States: 1870: Census of Population,* 1, table 2, Washington, D.C.: U.S. Government Printing Office, 1872.

U.S. Department of Interior, Census Office. *Ninth Census of the United States: 1870. The Statistics of the Wealth and Industry of the United States,* 3. Washington, D.C.: U.S. Government Printing Office, 1872.

U.S. Department of Interior, Census Office. *Tenth Census of the United States: 1880. Population of the United States.* Washington, D.C.: U.S. Government Printing Office, 1883.

U.S. Department of Interior, Census Office. *Tenth Census of the United States: 1880, Products of Agriculture.* Washington, D.C.: U.S. Government Printing Office, 1883.

U.S. Department of Interior, Census Office. *Tenth Census of the United States: 1880, Census of Population,* 1, table 5. Washington, D.C.: U.S. Government Printing Office, 1882.

U.S. Department of Interior, Census Office. *Compendium of the Tenth Census: 1860–1880.* Washington, D.C.: U.S. Government Printing Office, 1883.

U.S. Department of Interior, Census Office. *Report on the Statistics of Agriculture in the United States at the Eleventh Census: 1890.* Washington, D.C.: Government Printing Office, 1895.

U.S. Department of Interior, Census Office. *Eleventh Census of the United States: 1890, Population of the United States.* Washington, D.C.: U.S. Government Printing Office, 1895.

U.S. Department of Interior, Census Office. *Twelfth Census of* the United States: 1900, Agriculture, 6, part 2. Washington, D.C.: U.S. Government Printing Office, 1902.

U.S. Department of Interior, Census Office. *Twelfth Census of the United States: 1900, Population,* 1, part 1. Washington, D.C.: U.S. Government Printing Office, 1901.

INTERNET SOURCES

"About Us: Ameren Corporation." Ameren Corporation. http://www.ameren/abut/ AU_amcorp.htm (August 3, 2000).

"Batesville, Independence County, Arkansas." Development Information Network of Arkansas. http://batesville.dina.org/industry/majemp.html (July 10, 2000).

Bergland, Robert. "Deregulation." Ozarks Electric Co-op Connection. http://www.ozarkssecc.com/Newsletter3.html (August 3, 2000).

"Black population, 1998." http://www.census.gov/population/www/estimates (June 8, 2000).

"City of Cape Girardeau, Missouri." http://www.showme.net/capecity/welcome/indes.htm (July 10, 2000).

"Counties Ranked by Hispanic Population, July 1, 1998." Washington D.C.: Population Estimates Program, Population Division, U.S. Census Bureau, 1999. http://www.census.gov/population/estimates/county/rank/hisp-a.txt

"County Population Estimates, 1998: Missouri." Population Estimates Program, Population Division, U.S. Census Bureau. http://www.census.gov/population/estimates/county/co-99–1/99_29.txt (May 15, 2000).

"Fayetteville, Arkansas, Economic Data." Fayetteville Chamber of Commerce, Fayetteville, Arkansas. http://www.fayettevillear.com/data.htm (July 13, 2000).

"Federal Information Processing Standards Publication 8–6." Announcing the Standards for Metropolitan Areas, March 1995. http://www.itl.nist.gov/fipspubs/fip8–6–0.htm (August 6, 2000).

"Forest Inventory and Analysis Data Base Retrieval System." U.S. Department of Agriculture, Forest Service, Starksville, Miss.: SRSFLA, 1999, http://www.srsfia.usfs.msstate.edu/scripts.ew.html (April 17, 2000).

Forsythe, Roger W. "City of Park Hills History: A New Union for Progress." http://www.pacific-pages.com/parkhill/history.htm (August 20, 2000).

"General Information for Tahlequah." Oklahoma Department of Community Development, Data and Statistics. http://www.odoc.state.ok.us/oknet/co (July 10, 2000).

"Jefferson City Chamber of Commerce, Jefferson City, Missouri." http://www.jcchamber.org (July 10, 2000).

"Jimmie Driftwood." Bill Slater Webpage. http://billslater.com/driftwood.htm (September 12, 2000).

"Metropolitan Area Population Estimates for July 1, 1998." Population Estimates Program, Population Division, U.S. Census Bureau, Washington, D.C. http://www.census.gov/population /estimates/metro-city/ma98–01.txt (June 2, 2000).

"Metropolitan Areas." U.S. Census Bureau, Washington, D.C. http://www.itl.nist.gov/fipspubs/ fip8–6–0.htm.

"Midwest Regional Rail System: A Transportation System for the Twenty-first Century." Missouri Department of Transportation, Jefferson City. http://www.modot/state.mo.us./trans/ mwrailsum.pdf (August 23, 2000).

"2000 Missouri School District Computing Census." http//www.dese.state.mo.us/ computingcensus/2000/ (June 10, 2000).

"National Population Estimates." U.S. Department of Commerce, U.S. Census Bureau, Washington, D.C.: Laura K. Yax and the Population Division, 2000. http://www.census.gov/ population/www/estimates/popest.html (April 15, 2000).

"National Streams Database." USGS Publications, 1995. U.S. Department of the Interior, U.S. Geological Survey, Rolla, Mo. http://www.usgs.gov (January 25, 2000).

"Population Estimates for Places: Annual Time Series, July 1, 1990 to July 1, 1998, Missouri." Washington, D.C.: Population Estimates Program, Population Division, U.S. Census Bureau, 1999. http://www.census.gov/population/estimates/metro-city/sets/SC98T_MO-DR.txt (May 15, 2000).

"Population Estimates for Places, Arkansas, Block 1 of 2. Annual Time Series, July 1, 1990, to July 1, 1998." Washington, D.C.: Population Division, U.S. Census Bureau, 1999. http://www.census.gov/population/estimates/metro-city/sets/SC98T_MO-DR.txt (May 15, 2000).

Population Estimates for Places, Missouri, Block 1 of 2. Annual Time Series, July 1, 1990, to July 1, 1998." Washington, D.C.: Population Division, U.S. Census Bureau, 1999. (http://www.census.gov/population/estimates/metro-city/sets/SC98T_MO-DR.txt) (May 15, 2000).

"Population Estimates for Places: Oklahoma." Annual Time Series, July 1, 1990 to July 1, 1998. Population Estimates Program, Population Division, U.S. Census Bureau, Washington, D.C., 1999. http://www.census.gov/population/estimates/metro-city/sets/SC98T_MO-DR.txt. (May 15, 2000).

Storm Data Base. National Oceanic and Atmospheric Administration, National Climatic Data Center, Asheville, N.C. December 1999. http://www4.ncdc.noaa.gov/cgi-win/wwcgi.dll?wwEvent~Storms (May 8, 2000).

"Unimin Corporation." http://www.cisa.org/members/unimin.htm (August 21, 2000).

"University of Arkansas Stats." University of Arkansas, Fayetteville. http://www.uark.edu/admin/urelinfo/info/briefing-book/stats.html (August 5, 2000).

"Welcome to Harrison, Arkansas." Development Information Network of Arkansas. http://harrison.dina.org/ (July 8, 2000.).

"Welcome to Independent Stave Company." Independent Stave Company, Lebanon, Missouri. http://www.cooper-age.com/welcome.html (July 12, 2000).

"Wood Chip Mills Invade Missouri." 1998–99 Environmental Briefing Book, Nonsustainable Forestry, Missouri Coalition for the Environment. http://www.moenviorn.org/chmill.htm (August 20, 2000).

INTERVIEWS AND CORRESPONDENCE

Bridges, C. O. Stock farmer. Ozark, Missouri. Personal interview with the author, August 24, 1968.

Bridges, Percy. Retired Teacher. Ozark, Missouri. Personal interview with the author, April 30, 1968.

Carver, Finus. Fruit Farmer. Marionville, Missouri. Personal interview with the author, August 1, 1968.

Cavender, C. C. Manager of Hammons Products Company in Stockton, Missouri. Personal interview with author, November 20, 1967.

Casteel, Larry W. Mining executive, St. Joe Lead Company. Personal interview with the author, June 11, 1978.

Claxton, O. C. Area Community Development Agent, Ava, Missouri. Personal correspondence with the author, July 18, 1969.

Gibbons, Robert. Founder and first president of the Bonniebrook Historical Society. Springfield, Missouri. Telephone interview with the author, August 17, 2000.

Gilmore, Martha. Videotaped interview for "Just That Much Hillbilly in Me." Video produced by Mark Biggs, associate professor of Media, Southwest Missouri State University, Springfield, Missouri, 1999.

Hatch, Roger. Mark Twain National Forest Fire Control Officer. Personal interview with the author, March 5, 1969.

Hermann, Miss Ladonna. Associate of the Rural Parish Workers of Christ the King, St. Louis Catholic Diocese, Fertile (Washington County), Missouri. Personal interview with the author, March 29, 2001.

Information office, Greene County Highway Department, Springfield, Missouri. Telephone interview with the author, August 17, 2000.

Jones, James. Director of Research, Hammons Products Company. Orientation and field trip at the Hammons Products Experimental Farm, July 1995, for administrators in the College of Natural and Applied Sciences, Southwest Missouri State University. Attended by the author.

Kremer, Gary. Professor of History, William Woods University. E-mail correspondence, January 29, 2001.

Kurtz, Vincent. Professor of Geology, Southwest Missouri State University. Personal interview with the author, April 15, 1978.

Marchi, Robert. Park Manager, H. S. Truman Dam and Reservoir. Telephone conversation with the author, September 13, 2000.

Morris, James (a.k.a. Jimmie Driftwood). Folk musician and songwriter. Personal interview with the author, Timbo, Arkansas, July 23, 1977.

Ozark Wood Fiber. Goodman, Missouri. Personal interview by the author with mill personnel, October 4, 2000.

Rainey, Leo. Area development agent, Batesville, Arkansas. Personal interview with the author, June 16, 1977.

Registrars' Offices, Southwest Missouri State University, Drury University, Evangel University, Ozark Technical Community College, Baptist Bible College, and Central Bible College. Telephone interviews by the author with registrars' office personel, July 5, 2000.

Schaeffer, Fred. Judge (Commissioner). Greene County Court (Commission). Personal interview with the author, September 6, 1968.

Springfield-Branson Regional Airport, Marketing Department. Telephone interview with the author, June 30, 2000.

Story, A. L. Owner of Wolf Island Farms. Wolf Island, Missouri. Personal interview with the author, May 15, 1994.

Sutton, Deborah S. Director of Instructional Technology, Missouri Department of Elementary and Secondary Education. E-mail correspondence with the author, September 19, 2000.

Swartz, Samuel C. Amish spokesperson. Rural Webster County. Personal interview with the author, August 31, 1968.

Vanderheide, Harry. Retired machinist, Route 1, Ozark, Missouri. Personal interview with the author, August 10, 1968.

St. Louis-San Francisco Railroad (Frisco), 70, 103, 105, 129, 160, 177, 203, 206, 256
St. Louis World's Fair of 1904 (Louisiana Exposition): the Japanese pavilion, 227; the Maine building, 197
St. Mary's, 47
St. Michael's. *See* Fredericktown, Mo.
Stockton, Mo., 231
Stockton Dam, 33
Stockton-Pomme de Terre tourism area, 231
Stone, Gov. William J., 197
Stone and Webster Engineering Corporation, 212
Stone Hill Winery, 164
storms, 24–25
Story, A. L., 101
Stout's Shut-ins, 132
St. Paul, Ark., 107
St. Peter sandstone, 21, 141
Strafford, Mo., 69
Straight, M. J., 203
strawberries, 185. *See also* agriculture, truck farming
Stringtown, Mo., 139
the Strip. *See* highways, by name
suburban and lake subdivisions, 77
Sugar Creek Valley, 217, 219
Sugar Loaf Mountain, 201
Sugar Loaf Nature Trail, 232
Sugar Loaf Springs. *See* Heber Springs
Sugar Mountain, 18
Sulphur Spring (Jefferson County, Mo.), 204
Sulphur Springs, Ark., 202
Summit Railway, 128
Sunbelt, 73
Sunklands, 15
Sunnyland Stages, 115
Sunset Hotel (Bella Vista, Ark.), 218
Sutherland, Daniel, 90
Swan, William T., 154
Swanson (foods), 170
swastika, 68
Swedes, 65
Swift and Company, 170
Swiss colony (in Mo.), 63

Table Rock Dam, 95, 211, 229
Tahlequah, Okla., 18, 54, 76, 87; economy and manufacturing in, 267; as the Nursery Capital of the Midwest, 267; population of, 267; strawberry shipping point at, 163; as a tourist destination, 234
Tahlonteskee (Cherokee Old Settlers capital), 54
Talbert's Ferry, 144
Talontuskee, Chief, 37
Taneycomo Hotel, 211
Tan-Tar-A (resort), 225–26
Taos, Mo., 63
Taum Sauk Mountain, 7, 12; as a tourist attraction, 195, 226
Teamsters, 142, 177
Tebo and Neosho Railroad, 103
telephone, 117–18; exchanges, 117; multi-party lines, 117
television broadcasting, 119–20
temperatures, 25–26; ranges of, 26; extremes of, 26
Temple Israel (Springfield, Mo.), 67
Temple Shalom (Fayetteville, Ark.), 67

Tennessee, 82
Tennis, Zed, 118
Terry, T. S., 218
Tertiary Period, 21
Texas (Spanish) fever, 171
Thayer, Mo., 274
theatrical productions, 244
Theodore Lead Company, 70, 129
Theodosia, Mo., 8
Thickety Creek bloomery, 138
Thompson, J. C., 182
Thompson, Maj. William G., 5
Thomson, William H., 272
Thornton, C. Calhoun "Coon," 89
Thorntonsburg, Mo., 49
Thrailkill, John, 89
Tia Juana, Okla., 77
tie hackers, 177, 185
tie rafts. *See* crossties, rafts and rafting on
tidewater settlements, 57
Tidioute, Pa., 180
Tidioute Savings Bank, 180
tiff. *See* tripoli; barite
Tiff Belt (District), 20, 121, 130
Tillis, Mel, 223
Tillman, Sen. Ben "Pitchfork," 216
timber resources. *See* lumber industry
time distance, 251
Tipton, Mo., 105
Tipton Upland, 12
Title 9 legislation, 243
tobacco. *See* farm crops
Todd, George, 89
Tolerton, Jesse, 197
Tolliver Pond, 181, 183
toll roads, 111
tomato farming. *See* agriculture, truck farming
Tomball, Tex., 217
Tonight Show, 5
Tontitown, Ark., 62, 65, 228; Italian immigrants in, 164; vineyards in, 165
Topaz Mill, 281
tornadoes, 24–25
touring, 197–99; automobile, 198; bicycle, 197–98; bus, 199; creating demand for improved roads, 198; modern routes of, 199. *See also* "shunpiking"
tourism and recreation, 193–250; advertising for, 215; for elites, 195, 207; landmark developments in, 215–24; origins of Ozark, 194–95; resources for, 194; traditional recreation, 193. *See also* tourism-recreation regions
tourism-recreation regions of the Ozarks: Big Springs, 227–28; Lake of the Ozarks, 224–27; Ozark Playground, 228–31; the Ridge Road, 226; River Hills, 232–34; St. Francois, 226–27; White River Folk Culture, 231–32
Towell, William, 187
towns: characteristic range of population and services in, 252; economic health of small, 252; form and appearance of, 253; population trends in, 252; small-town growth, 76
trade hinterlands, 253
traders, 36; fur trade, 44–45
traditional lifestyle, 246–50
Trail of Tears, 39, 41, 53–54, 108

trails and traces, 108–110. *See also* roads
tram lines, 178, 183
transportation, 97–123
TransWorld Airlines, 115
Travis, Randy, 224
Treaty of Edwardsville, 36
Treaty of Fort Harrison, 36
Treaty of Fort Osage (originally Fort Clark), 37, 51
Treaty of Hopewell, 35
Treaty party. *See* Ridge party
Trimble family, Dr. Bruce, 221; Mary, 221; Mark, 221. *See* Shepherd of the Hills Homestead
tripoli (tiff), 141
Tri-State Mining (Lead-Zinc) District, 4, 21, 67, 103–5, 124, 132–36, 166, 210, 262; landscape of, 135; mining camps and towns in, 134; the most productive mines of, 134
truck farming. *See* agriculture, truck farming
Tsa-La-Gi village, 267
Tulsa World-Tribune, 116
tungsten, 147
Turkey Creek mines, 133
Turner, Gen. John W., 272
Turner, John, 59
Turner, John B., 272
Turner, Kathleen, 290
Twin Lakes area, 231
Tyrell, Dr. Abijah, 146
Tyrell, Frank, 146
Tyson family: Donald "Don," 169; John, 169, 290
Tyson Feed and Hatchery, 169–70
Tyson Foods, 67, 169–70

Ulster (Ireland), 57
Ulstermen, 55
Ulster Plantation, 55
unconformity, 20
Underhill, Dillon, 121
Unimin Corporation, 141
Union, Mo., 35, 110
Union Army, 69, 83–92, 99, 144
Union Electric and Power Company, 121, 135, 211. *See also* AmerenUE
Union Gap Experiment Station, 191
Union garrison towns, 80
Union League, 93
Union sympathizers, 83, 94, 144
Uniontown, Mo., 233
United States Army, 53, 66
United States Army Corps of Engineers, 33, 41, 77, 100, 122, 250; at Mountain Home, Ark., 214
United States Department of Agriculture, 168
United States Forest Service, 131, 185–86, 188; forest management practices of, 188; game management and hunting regulations of, 209; and reforestation, 188
United States Hotel, 193
United States House of Representatives, 95
United States Land Survey system, 38; base lines surveyed by, 301n
United States National Park Service, 188; Operation Outdoors, 194
United States of America, 73
United States Post Office Department, 112

United States Senate, 70
University of Arkansas, 67, 70, 164, 228
University of Missouri, 51, 171, 186, 226
University Plaza Hotel and Convention Center, 256
uplift (geologic), 21
Upper Great Lakes region, 73
Upper South, 62
Upton, Dell, 272

Valley Home estate, 272
values: attachment to the land, 247; heritage and family ties, 246–47; individualism, 247; rural living, 246; self-reliance, 247
Van Buren, Ark., 88, 163, 253; strawberry center in, 162
Van Buren, Mo., 206
Vanderbilt, Commodore Cornelius, 102
Van Dorn, Gen. Earl, 87; biographical sketch of, 307n
Van Ravensway, Charles, 269
vernacular houses, 276
vernacular regions, 4
Verona, Mo., 65
Versailles, Mo., 105
vertical integration: in the poultry industry, 170
Vial, Pedro, 110
Viburnum, Mo., 138; and religious sectarianism, 245
Viburnum Mine, 130, 137
Viburnum Trend. *See* New Lead Belt
Vichy, Mo., 204
Victorian houses, 271
Vietnamese immigrants, 71–73
Vietnam War, 41
vigilance committees (groups), 93–95
Village Hall (Bella Vista), 218
villages: characteristics of, 252
Vinton, Bobby, 223
Virginia, 45, 82
Voigt, David, 242
Vollenweider and Sons Orchards, 161
volcanic ash, 23
voyagers, 44

Wagoner, Porter, 118–19, 290
Wakely, Jimmy, 120
Waldenses, 65
Walkingstick Mountain, 18
Waller, Charles, 242
Wal-Mart Stores, Inc, 67, 253, 258; founding of, 265. *See also* Walton, Sam
Walnut Ridge, 67
Walnut Street Historic District, 230
Walnut Valley, 9
Walton, Sam, 265, 290
Walton Arts Center, 291
Ward, John, 29
War Eagle Mill, 281
War Eagle Valley, 169
Warneke, Lon, 242
Warner, Capt. Will T., 100
Warner, Edwin T. B., 99
War of 1812, 36, 50, 51, 146
War of the Rebellion, 88
Warren Oil Company, 180
Warrenton, Mo., 289
Warsaw, Mo., 88, 98, 105; river port in, 171, 251
Warsaw formation, 21
Washburn, Rev. Cephas, 170